POLITICS IN THE
AMERICAN WEST

POLITICS IN THE AMERICAN WEST

Edited by Frank H. Jonas

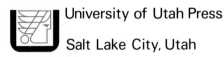

University of Utah Press

Salt Lake City, Utah

To Frederick C. Irion

In Memoriam

PREFACE

In 1961, a volume titled *Western Politics* was published by the University of Utah Press. The present book, *Politics in the American West*, although concerned with the same basic theme, is a new volume. It recognizes the growing importance of the West in American politics and supplements the previous study in the light of changes these past seven years.

In *Western Politics* (1961) emphasis was placed on the period 1940 to 1960, but since the book appeared so short a time after the elections of 1960 the results were treated only briefly in that work. Analyses of these elections in all the western states are included in the present volume, which concentrates on the period 1958 to 1968. Despite this emphasis on a specified time span, contributors were not limited to a consideration of just those years. Thoroughgoing analysis of a state's politics obviously requires historical perspective, and the authors wholeheartedly accepted the editor's invitation to provide such perspective wherever necessary. Each is well-qualified in his field: many have become actively and practically involved in the politics of their respective states. While each writer is responsible for the factual accuracy and adequacy of his own contribution, the editor assumes full responsibility for the general quality of the volume.

The pressure of time that precluded analysis in *Western Politics* of the 1960 elections operates again to exclude from the present volume a consideration of the crucial 1968 elections. In a continuation of its series of election articles dating back to 1948, however, the *Western Political Quarterly* will feature analyses of the 1968 elections in all thirteen western states in its June 1969 issue. Many of the *Western Political Quarterly*'s articles were prepared by contributors to this present volume, five of whom have edited the series during the past twenty years. Thirteen of the sixteen contributors are members of the Standing Committee on Western Politics of the Western Political Science Association, including the chairman, Frank Jonas, and the vice-chairman, Totton J. Anderson. To a large extent, then, this book is the product of this Committee.

As editor, I want to express my appreciation to all contributors for their cooperation in the preparation of this volume. Working from their own resources, without promise of royalties or remuneration for their expense, they have been patient and cooperative in supplying updated data as several deadlines have come and gone, often because of the usual—but sometimes because of the unusual—circumstances attending an endeavor of this kind. Brief biographical sketches are included in the back pages of this volume.

Regretfully, one of the contributors to *Western Politics*, and a scheduled contributor to *Politics in the American West*, passed away while the book was in preparation. It is to this man, Frederick C. Irion, that this book is respectfully and affectionately dedicated. Irion wrote the election-analysis articles on New Mexico for the *Western Political Quarterly* in 1956, 1958, 1960, and 1962. In his zeal for research he assembled a basement full of files on New Mexico politics, and to the day of his death he remained a generous, untiring advocate of the importance of making the data he gathered available to students, teachers, and readers generally.

Much of the successful reception of *Western Politics*, which went out of print soon after publication, can be attributed to the dedicated and inexhaustible efforts of Mrs. W. Harold Dalgliesh, who served as copy editor and prepared the manuscript for the press. Copy editor of the *Western Political Quarterly* for many years, she has once again demonstrated the meticulous care and judgment that are all important in achieving a balanced result from the work of numerous hands.

I wish also to thank:

The University of Utah Research Committee for a substantial grant-in-aid toward the production of my own chapter on Utah politics;

The University of Utah Publications Advisory Committee for its approval of this manuscript for publication;

Neal A. Maxwell, University of Utah Executive Vice-president and member of the Political Science Department, who was especially helpful in seeing this book through. In addition to his encouragement of the over-all project, his own chapter marks an important contribution in the field of western politics;

Professor Ellsworth Weaver, director of the Institute of Government, University of Utah, for his encouragement of the efforts to complete this volume;

My wife and family for their intense interest and patient cooperation. My own activity in local politics and in writing about it for thirty years have entailed sacrifices on their part which only they—and most other families, probably, who are saddled with husbands and fathers who write—can understand;

My students for their help in ferreting out pertinent details from government sources;

The staff of the University of Utah Press for their interest and efforts in publishing this volume;

Mark Hafey for his careful workmanship on the map of each state showing county boundaries and the revised congressional districts;

Mrs. LaVon West and Mrs. Violet Holfeltz for their cooperative and efficient typing services.

Also, for permission to use quotations and materials from the book, *Rocky Mountain Politics*, and from the *Utah Historical Quarterly* and the *Western Political Quarterly*, I wish to thank the director of the University of New Mexico University Press and the editors of the two periodicals.

As editor, and in behalf of all contributors, I wish to thank the many politicians, public officials, interest and pressure group representatives, and their aides and staffs for assistance rendered unselfishly and understandingly in our quest for the best and most complete information available.

For myself, as author of several of the chapters, I am especially grateful to Utah state, county, and city public officeholders, practicing politicians, and newspaper political editors who have shared with me so generously their valuable time and their hard won knowledge of national as well as Utah politics.

Frank H. Jonas
Editor

Salt Lake City, Utah, 1968

CONTENTS

MAPS

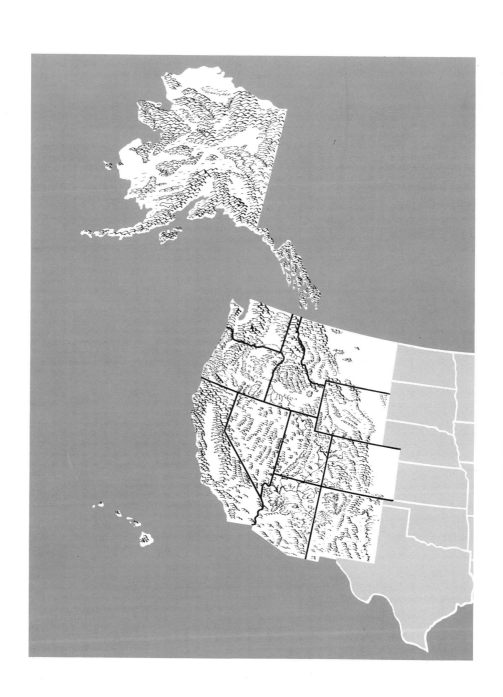

Frank H. Jonas

THE WESTERN SCENE

To the eye of a stranger the West can appear desolate and bleak, and to the tourist from the East who had driven over dirt roads from Zion National Park in Utah to Fredonia in Arizona enroute to the North Rim of the Grand Canyon National Park during prohibition days, it was very, very dry. Tunnels through mountains, asphalt roads through valleys, and modern automotive vehicles with air conditioning have made desert travel faster and more comfortable, but they have not altered the scenic beauty of the cactus land and of the brilliantly colored handiwork of nature, nor have they changed what a closer inspection would reveal, a land rich in great deposits of useful, precious, critical and strategic metals.

Gradually the wilderness yielded to the trappers, the trader, the missionary, the soldier, and finally the settler. Then came cattle raising on the open range, the prairie, and the grasslands of the Rockies; wool and wheat raising; orange growers in the southwest and apple growers in the northwest; lumbering, and finally the health rush and the tourist trade.

What do we mean when we speak of the West? What area does it encompass? Is it a distinct entity? There are various interpretations. One author, writing some thirty years ago, speaks of the West as follows: "The Mountain States—a familiar geographic expression, conjuring up a picture of a vast area which tourists delight to explore and which must be crossed to reach the Pacific Coast! It is also a convenient expression for census purposes, since these eight states form a block of the right shape for map-making and the right size for statistical tables. But do they form an economic region with common interests which distinguish it from other regions, or a political section with a well-developed character of its own in national politics?"[1]

Another writer, the editor of *Rocky Mountain Politics*, voiced a doubt that the eight intermountain states constituted either a region or the West. He recognized that Montana and Idaho were bracketed sometimes with Oregon and Washington and designated the Northwest, and that Arizona and New Mexico were grouped sometimes with Texas and Oklahoma and called the Southwest. His interest at the time did not extend to the three Pacific Coast states which by virtue of their contiguity to the sea have common interests although the hinterlands of Seattle, Portland, San Francisco, and Los Angeles soon take on the typical topography of the West.[2] Bernard de Voto, a native Utahn, maintained that only Utah,

---

1. A. N. Holcombe in the Foreword to *Rocky Mountain Politics*, ed. Thomas C. Donnelly (Albuquerque: University of New Mexico Press, 1940), p. v. This volume is probably the pioneer work in political science which deals with an entire region or group of contiguous states.

2. Donnelly, *op. cit.*

Idaho, Montana, Wyoming, and Colorado by virtue of common physiographic features and economic interests could properly be called the West.[3] Indeed, the range of mountains beginning in southern Idaho, cutting Utah in half from north to south, and ending only a few miles from the Arizona border could be considered a region. Life in this area, with its "Mormon Village,"[4] was more like that in early New England than life in the surrounding livestock country which produced the ranch, the gun-toting cowboy and the "wild, wild West," and which became the image of the West in the rest of the nation and abroad.[5]

Recently, however, the tendency among some historians and politicians has been to consider the legitimate West that area beyond a halfway point on the road to the Pacific, the West of the Plains and Rockies, the Great Basin and the Pacific Coast, with Alaska and Hawaii thrown in for good measure. Indeed, John W. Caughey, the historian, and his counterpart in politics, President Lyndon Johnson, when he was a senator, added the two Dakotas, Nebraska, Kansas, Oklahoma, and Texas. United States senators from these six states would tie this whole tier to the West through their concern with reclamation. "Although the notion that there is, or should be, something distinctive about the politics of the eleven western states, thirteen with Alaska and Hawaii, has long had considerable appeal, proof of the point remains elusive. To designate these states as the 'West' may be a useful kind of shorthand, but it does not establish them as a political entity—how can there be a West without Texas? Oklahoma? the Dakotas?—nor does it establish or identify any common basis for regional politics."[6] Perhaps the line should be drawn, as Caughey has suggested, from north to south somewhere near the middle of these states.[7] In truth, as one travels west across Texas, he senses a difference as he leaves Dallas and Fort Worth, and as he drives across Nebraska, he is reminded by many historical markers, the Overland Trail, the Pony Express, and Buffalo Bill, that "This Is Where the West Begins." He is in the West when he can smell sagebrush.

Actually, however, the purpose of this book is neither to argue nor to settle the claims of any combination of states for regional recognition or for designation as the West, but to bring the politics of the thirteen most western states to the attention of students of political parties. Nevertheless, it would seem that the eleven traditional states, with Alaska and Hawaii, today are a more than well-defined party area, and that they can be viewed as a region with an underlying unity in physiographic features, economic impulses, and political objectives.

This is a land where environment has to be taken into account. It may be lavish in resources, but unlike a South Sea Island with its coconuts and breadfruit, it does not automatically flourish. The mark of the land is strong on its history, and the facts of geography are these:

3. Bernard de Voto, "Footnote on the West," *Harpers Monthly Magazine*, 155 (November 1927), 302-12.

4. See Lowry Nelson, *The Mormon Village: A Study in Social Origins*, reprint from the *Proceedings* of the Utah Academy of Sciences, Arts and Letters, VII (1930), 11-37.

5. For an article debunking this image of the West, see Peter Lyons, "Wild, Wild West," *American Heritage*, XI (August 1960), 32-48.

6. Edgar Lane, "The Western Stance in Congress: Notes Toward a Sectional Theory," paper presented before the Western Political Science Association, San Diego, March 22, 1960.

7. John W. Caughey, "Toward an Understanding of the West," *Utah Historical Quarterly*, XXVIII (January 1959), 8-24.

First, it is a big country, a land of distances, of remoteness. The problem of transportation has always been uppermost for those who wanted to use or develop the West.

Second, it is a rugged land, a land of sharp uplifts, canyons, and gorges, a region complex in topography and with a great deal of exposed geology. The multiplicity of land forms—the alternation of plains, mountains, basins, mesas, valleys—complicates the transportation problems.

It also sets up a broad diversity of climates. The isothermal lines climb the mountains more rapidly than they do the degrees of latitude. Zones of climate ranging from sub-tropical to arctic may be only a few miles apart, and the precipitation on one side of a mountain range often is much greater than on the other side.[8]

The political implications of this terrain have been revealed in efforts to equalize competition with the other states through public policy. The great problem of the West has been and still is transportation. The West as a region, particularly the Rocky Mountain area, has been economically disadvantaged by discriminatory railroad freight rates, and although some gains have been made to make them more fair, high rates still constitute a problem to entrepreneurs and politicians of this area. The Pacific Coast does not feel this economic pinch because it is served by ocean shipping.

Historically, this area has sought high tariff rates on the importation from foreign lands of beef, metals, sugar, and wool. Indeed, it has been in a cold war, and still is to a great extent, with the rest of the nation in an attempt to break the bonds of colonialism which are obscured from view by high freight rates, hidden charges, indirect taxation, and stock dividends. Although the subjects of absentee ownership and economic colonialism have been pretty well beaten by other writers, they still apply strongly to most states in the West, particularly in the intermountain area.

If there is one single common interest among the states of the West, with the exception of Hawaii and Alaska, it is water, or rather the scarcity of water. But the need for water, and therefore water politics, has not united all the western states into either a region or a political bloc for voting purposes in Congress. Indeed, the scarcity of water and each state's struggle for what it calls its share have been divisive influences which have split the West into combinations of states or small voting blocs in which each state is struggling for advantage and for survival in terms of any future development of its resources and its growth in population, and in opportunities for its people, especially the youthful employment market.

Even among the combinations of states which for a single purpose form a temporary political alliance there are several divisions based on geographic and economic grounds. For example, Oregon, Washington, Idaho, and Montana have combined to resist the request of Colorado River Basin states for a share of the Columbia River water. Washington is split between its west and east sections, with Seattle and Spokane as the principal trade centers. Oregon is split in the same manner, except that the eastern part of Oregon has no "capital" of its own; in this sense it looks either to Spokane or Boise, Idaho. Montana, too, is split, with mining and forestry interests in the west and wheat farming in the east. Idaho is split even more; indeed, for very good reasons it is called the sectional state. It is commonly said that it has two "capitals," Salt Lake City and Spokane! But this concept of Idaho may be undergoing a significant change. Modern transportation and communication facilities, which ignore state boundaries, are overcoming regional physical barriers.

8. *Ibid.*

Wyoming is split between east and west, and so is Colorado. The eastern part of New Mexico has been called Little Texas. Nevada is split four ways, with Las Vegas and Reno as the main trade centers. Natural interest would have attached Las Vegas to either Arizona or Utah. Instead, human activities—principally gambling and recreation and real estate dealings and the supplying of electrical power by Hoover Dam to southern California—have brought transportation facilities which have tied southern Nevada to California. Mining in the eastern part of the state has attached it to Utah. Only Utah, southern Idaho, eastern Nevada, and southwestern Wyoming form a region without any split in the central state, Utah. No part of this area has a trade center to compete with Salt Lake City.

The creation of the states in the Rocky Mountain and southwest areas was almost entirely political. State boundaries were politically conceived and arbitrarily imposed on the states in the West, and tended to promote and perpetuate disunity. Nor was there much logic to the order of admission to the Union. Nevada, with the least reason for statehood, was first to be admitted; it was needed by the Republican party—so that the Thirteenth Amendment might be passed in Congress before the presidential election in 1865. The Republican party, "frustrated in its effort to perpetuate its ascendancy at Washington, by Freedmen's votes in the South,"[9] secured the admission of Montana, Idaho, and Wyoming. The Republicans also were frustrated by an uncompromising demand for free silver and the rise of the Populists. Utah, with more people than several of the Mountain states already admitted, was kept out of the Union because its politics were suspect.

New Mexico and Arizona, the last states to be admitted before Alaska and Hawaii, were not thought to have sufficient prospects for future growth to justify their formation into more than one state. Several states did not have enough people to make up one full-sized congressional district, and in 1940 two of them still did not possess such a population. Today the only three states which have only one representative each in Congress are Wyoming, Nevada, and Alaska. Three decades ago political scientists and politicians were quick to point out the disparity in congressional representation between Nevada with 90,000 people and New York with 12,000,000, but each state with two United States senators. Today, though still far behind most other states in population, Nevada is the fastest growing in the nation, and the growth in Arizona and New Mexico since the war has been phenomenal.

The principal economic role of the West has been to supply raw materials. At first it supplied furs, then sandalwood from Hawaii and cowhide from California. Later it was gold and silver, wheat and beef, salmon from the West Coast and Alaska, sugar from Hawaii, Utah, and Colorado, lumber, wool, wine, fruit, vegetables, oil and gas—and uranium.

The lifeline, the prime source from which the land derived value, was the railroad. From 1890—when the era of the gold and silver rushes, the pony express, the stage line, the Indian wars, and the railroad builders came to a close—until 1920, the West lived by the railroad. No single feature such as the railroad, with its political implications in government regulation, freight rates, and tariffs, so dominated the scene after 1920. The age of the automobile, the airplane, and the engineer, supplementing but more and more often supplanting the railroad, brought industrial capacity to the West. The war was responsible for the steel industry and for such names as Geneva, Fontana, Hanford, and Los Alamos.

9. Holcombe, *op. cit.*, p. vi.

Probably the most significant economic change in the West during the past three decades has been the shift which has placed agriculture second and mining third to manufacturing as the chief sources of income and employment. But important as manufacturing and processing are to the region, the basic output is still in raw products. Surpassing manufacturing in total employment in most states is government and public administration.

What has characterized the West is the great increase in the defense industry, which has sought inland security, a more stable and traditional labor market, and, in the case of aircraft and ordnance, the needed space and uninhabited areas for testing purposes. Also, the fact that the places where American troops have been deployed for actual and sustained conflict, Korea and Vietnam, have been in the Pacific area has also influenced the locating of aircraft repair, seafaring crafts of all kinds, and supply depots in western states. Although some of these locations have been abandoned, others have increased their facilities. Examples would be the abandoned Clearfield Naval Supply Depot in Utah which employed 6,000 personnel and Hill Air Force Base which increased its workers by approximately the same number and which now employs a total of 18,500 persons.[10]

The story of the West in this decade is the urbanization of its population. Only in Wyoming and Montana are there no large populated centers. In these states and in Idaho, Arizona, New Mexico, and Nevada there are still the long distances between towns which have characterized the West in the past. Distances, however, principally between populated areas in neighboring states, have been reduced considerably by shorter routes, improved roads, highways, and automotive transportation, and have been almost obliterated by the airplane. Distances between towns in a single state have been reduced greatly by the same factors, although to a lesser extent. Indeed, politicians and state public officeholders in the West have made increasing use of the airplane to reach their constituents in outlying areas. In some states politicians have used personally piloted planes for campaigning purposes.

Only two decades ago, if a person residing in Salt Lake City or farther north wanted to travel to Albuquerque, he journeyed by train or bus by way of Denver; if he wanted to go to Phoenix, he journeyed by way of Los Angeles. The opening up of north and south transportation between key cities—such as Salt Lake City, Phoenix, and Albuquerque and localities in between such as Cedar City in Utah; Page, Grand Canyon, and Flagstaff in Arizona; and Farmington in New Mexico—by plane, automobile, bus, and truck, has brought many a remote corner, its people and its resources, closer to the nation's economic beltlines and the region's centers of political activity.

Probably what has happened in some corners of the West would illustrate its changing, yet still fundamental character. Thirty years ago a *Saturday Evening Post* editorial writer found that sections of Utah were among "the most arid and broken up in the nation," and that in the southeast corner of Utah may be found "the last frontier, of which it has been said that the Mormons have explored it all and rejected most of it, and where the Mormon cannot reclaim the desert, the gentile is advised not to try."[11] Actually this is the Four Corners area where the

10. In June 1950, just before the involvement of American troops in Korea, employment at Hill Air Force Base had reached a postwar low of 3,500. Indeed, on the very eve of United States entry into Korean hostilities 200 dismissals were in the mail only to be recalled the next day. Since then this facility has steadily and greatly expanded both its military and civilian personnel.

11. December 24, 1938. The area was almost inaccessible to the early settlers on the

boundaries of Colorado, Utah, Arizona, and New Mexico touch. What the Mormons failed to do, modern engineering is now doing. Located in Arizona, but backing up the waters of the Colorado River more than one hundred and seventy-five miles into Utah to form Lake Powell, the huge Glen Canyon Dam has changed the meaning of the geography in this area. Natural features may not change, but human hands and human ingenuity change their significance. This fact characterizes the West today.

Formerly almost inaccessible, the region is now being opened up by good roads to tourists and recreationists. Most of the recreationists are motorboaters and fishermen from Arizona and Utah. Additional roads will bring Coloradoans and New Mexicans into the region and assist in developing the areas they open up both economically and recreationally. Even the primitive Navajo in Utah, Arizona, and New Mexico has become modern; he is administering a park—Monument Valley—for tourists. Opening up the area still further will aid the Indian in many ways.

Politics—public policy—has been employed to enhance and speed up this development. The Four Corners area, comprising 92 counties in Arizona, Colorado, New Mexico, and Utah, was the fourth region established under the 1965 Public Works and Economic Development Act, which authorized the U.S. Department of Commerce to aid areas with lagging economies. Papers establishing the area were signed in 1966 by former governors Samuel P. Goddard (D-Arizona) and Jack M. Campbell (D-New Mexico), and governors John A. Love (R-Colorado) and Calvin L. Rampton (D-Utah). Planning and development of the region is being guided by a five-man commission made up of the governor of each state, and a federal chairman appointed by the President with confirmation by the Senate.[12] The Four Corners is eligible for federal aid under the 1968 Public Works and Economic Development Act by virtue of the fact that the average family income in the region is below the national median for 80 percent of the nation.

Although government and private enterprise have tended to cooperate in furthering the basic economic development of the West, the facts suggest that its main political consideration is its dependence on the federal government. This is the only source capable of meeting its financial needs for the full utilization of all its great natural resources. The government serves also as an equalizer of opportunities for its citizens by redistributing to the area its fair share of the returns for its efforts in supplying the nation with raw materials.

Other sections of the country, through their representatives in Congress, are reluctant to help the West—by financial appropriations and governmental organizations—to realize fully its industrial potential beyond the point of the tools and

west side of the Colorado River. A dramatic and almost impossible feat was accomplished by pioneers in south central Utah who tried to find a passage to a Colorado River crossing. They literally constructed a road through a rocky crevice too narrow for a wagon. See David E. Miller, *Hole-in-the-Rock: An Epic in the Colonization of the Great American West* (Salt Lake City: University of Utah Press, 1959). See also David Lavender, *One Man's West* (Garden City: Doubleday and Company, 1956), for a description of life in the dry desert area.

12. Political overtones were not lacking. An Arizonan, Orren Beatty, was appointed director, with headquarters in Washington, D.C. He was formerly an aide to Secretary of the Interior Stewart L. Udall. A Utahn, Alan Howe, former president of the National Young Democratic Club and an aide to Senator Frank E. Moss (D-Utah) and to Governor Calvin L. Rampton (D-Utah), was appointed the western or the on-the-ground director. His headquarters was established in Farmington, New Mexico. In a recent action, the Golden Circle Committee, composed of highway officials of Arizona, Utah, New Mexico, and Colorado submitted to the Four Corners Regional Commission a $127,589,000 four-state road-building program. The development of roads is high on the Commission's priority list.

power needed to extract raw materials from the soil and to convert these into forms for shipping to eastern processing and finishing plants. In 1939 all eight Rocky Mountain states received more in subsidies from the federal government than their residents paid in taxes. Amounts received for each tax-dollar paid ranged from $15.00 for Idaho to $2.00 for Colorado.[13] In 1958, in eight of the eleven western states, the "Federal expenditures by state of recipient or activity" were higher than the "Federal tax revenue by state of origin." Only in Idaho, Nevada, and Oregon were the federal expenditures less than the tax revenue.[14] In 1966, among the thirteen western states, only Californians paid more in taxes to the federal government than their state received in aid.[15]

Every computation made for a single state and published, however, carries the same result, that federal aid to all but one of the thirteen western states has exceeded the taxes paid by the people of each state. The message to the West, particularly to the intermountain states, is that it would do well to receive all the money it can get from the federal government. Federal distribution of funds is an effective method for the equalization of shares in economic goods and, therefore, in social opportunities. At least some portion of the money which western states receive from the federal government is from the taxes paid by corporations based in the East from the net proceeds they realize from western mining operations. In this situation, perhaps western states need not be too concerned about the earth's resources which, when once extracted, can never be replaced.

Is there a political West? Perhaps there is on the basis of the appeals made to the federal government for technical and financial assistance in the development of the area's tremendous natural resources. The particular reference at this point is the use made of water to generate electrical power to be used in industry. Water is the West's greatest problem, both the need for a greater supply and the exploitation of its river sources for multiple uses. The earliest use of water was for culinary and irrigation purposes. Water for domestic use is increasing in importance because of increasing populations, and, as a result, for expanded industrial use as well.

The completion in the last few years of such projects as the Glen Canyon Dam in Arizona, Flaming Gorge Dam in Utah, and the John Day Dam in Oregon, projects which hold vast potential for the development of surrounding states, has increased the available electric power, but it has not increased the water supply. Private enterprise has aided in the increased availability of hydroelectric power. After two decades of national controversy and high speed construction, the Idaho Power Company completed in May 1968 its 250 million dollar, three-dam development in Hells Canyon of the Snake River. But the need and demand for water and reclamation projects to harness its flow and distribution have increased faster than people and government have been able to supply them.

At the present time power from the Glen Canyon Dam, dedicated in 1964, is being transmitted principally south into Arizona. In the Four Corners area a thermoelectric plant—the first phase of a project that was considered impossible a

13. Donnelly, *op. cit.*, pp. 3-4.

14. The conclusions stated here were derived from "Federal Taxation and Expenditures in the Several States," *Legislative Reference Service* (Washington: Library of Congress, July 29, 1959).

15. U.S. Secretary of the Treasury, *Annual Report of the Secretary of the Treasury of the State of the Finances, 1966*, p. 846. Also, Tax Foundation Incorporated, *Facts and Figures on Government Finance, 1964-65*, p. 113. Every analysis of this situation is modified by the statement that it is difficult to make such computations.

decade previously–was dedicated in 1966 by Secretary of Interior Stewart L. Udall.[16] It will serve nine states, California, Wyoming, Idaho, Nevada, Texas, and the Four Corners states. The plant when completed is expected to produce a new type of cooperation between all segments, public and private, of the power industry. The project, established by the Western Energy Transmission and Supply Association (WEST), is adjacent to one now operated in Arizona by the Arizona Public Service Co., one of six companies participating in the project.[17]

It is not intended here to detail the story of the water crisis and of water resource development or of water politics. This cannot be done even briefly for the West, let alone for the nation. Emphasis is given here to the Rocky Mountain and Colorado River Basin areas because they represent, in terms of modern development, the disappearance of the last frontier in America. Recent developments in conserving, distributing, and utilizing the waters from the underground streamlets and the surface streams and rivers and lakes in the West will be mentioned in order to indicate the progress which has been made in this decade and to delineate the problems in future developments.[18] Herein lie the seeds of disunity and conflict, as well as those of unification, since rivers are not confined by state boundaries.

Those elements in the water crisis in the West which are involved in water politics will be reviewed here. The basic factor in both crisis and politics is the scarcity of water. There just is not enough water in the Colorado River to give to the basin states, Wyoming, Utah, Colorado, New Mexico, Arizona, Nevada, and California, the water which was allocated to them in the division made in 1922, let alone to fill their present needs. As a result there are numerous rivalries between states and between combinations of states, between the upper and the lower basin areas. Apparently, there is not only a definite and limited amount of water to be distributed, but there is also a limit to the money available each year to be spent for reclamation projects which make such distributions possible. In other words, politics exists in the sense, although a somewhat narrow one, of Lasswell's famous definition–politics is who gets what, when, and how, and the study of politics is a study of influence and the influential. Actually the West has not fared badly on Capitol Hill. Astute western politicians have made good bargains with their fellow congressmen; and some states have been sufficiently politically minded to allow their elected senators and representatives to remain in Congress long enough to gain the necessary seniority for their appointment to important committee memberships and as chairmen. Such states have been Arizona, New Mexico, Washington, and Colorado. California has fared well from another standpoint. With sufficient funds this state began making use of her share of water under the original allocation. The other states have lagged behind in the development of their resources and shares of Colorado River water. Probably the worst state in this category has been Utah, a state that has demonstrated a distrust for the federal government, and has sent to Washington representatives who had special interests in other areas than water resource development.[19]

16. Peter M. Kelly, "Power Plant Dedicated for Nine States," UPI dispatch, Salt Lake *Tribune*, October 12, 1966.

17. *State Government News*, the Council of State Governments, February 1967, p. 7.

18. The water problem has been well reviewed by Senator Frank E. Moss (D-Utah) in *The Water Crisis* (New York: Praeger, 1967).

19. In the days prior to the New Deal, key Utah politicians who showed great concern for water resource development were considered radical, especially if they advocated that the federal government assume a greater role in this development.

Washington has probably been the greatest beneficiary of the Columbia River Basin development. For years this state has sent Democratic senators to the nation's capitol, although its record is not quite so consistent for representatives. In any event, the response of this state to revolutionary rumblings came early in the thirties with the construction late in that decade of the Grand Coulee Dam. The Columbia Basin has ample water, and along with the Tennessee Valley is one of the two most developed water resource areas in the nation. Pollution is now the problem in the Northwest, not scarcity. The plentiful supply, with an excess flowing into the Pacific Ocean, has engendered another political division: the Colorado River Basin states would like to divert some of the Columbia River water to alleviate their own acute shortage. It is readily apparent that in some instances the western states have cooperated in developing their water resources, but in many other cases they have been in conflict over water use. These conflicts appear to have overshadowed the cooperative endeavors to the extent that water resource development has been the cause of more divisiveness than unity—the one common factor which might have brought about political solidarity and welded the western states into a voting bloc in Congress has instead been the cause of disunity.

At the end of the fiscal year, June 30, 1965, four storage units had been authorized for construction—Flaming Gorge in Utah, Glen Canyon in Arizona, Curecanti in Colorado, and Navajo in New Mexico.[20] In addition, sixteen participating projects were authorized, and several others have been added to the list since 1965.

In Nevada is one of the oldest and largest dams and lakes in the United States. The only controversy connected with this dam has been over its name. Originally christened Boulder, which Democratic administrations preferred, it is now called the Hoover Dam. Recently a project involving several million dollars to develop Lake Mead as an outstanding boating and recreational area has been launched. Together with Howard Hughes's and Governor Laxalt's far-sighted planning for the Las Vegas area, this driest of dry spots may become one of America's greatest playgrounds.

Dams have been constructed on the Colorado River in lower California. The objective here is more water for the famous desert gardens of Imperial Valley and more electrical power for Los Angeles and environs which already draw heavily on Hoover Dam's production of power.

Three participating units in Utah are the Central Utah project which will bring the waters of the high Uintahs through aqueducts to Utah's Wasatch Front, Dixie in the south, and the Ute Indian project in the east. The chief characteristic of the projects cited here as an example of what is happening to other states is that they have waited a long time for money and for starts. The delays, in the instances cited, have been attributed to the ineptitude of Utah's delegations in Congress. However, party politics and political ineptitude have not been the chief causes for delay.[21] Priority has been acknowledged by Utah's delegations of both parties for

20. See Ninth Annual Report to the Congress of the United States, Colorado River Storage Project and Participating Projects, United States Department of the Interior, Bureau of Reclamation. Both storage units and participating figures are accumulative since 1956, the year of the Colorado River Storage Project and Participating Projects Act of April 11, 1956 (70 Stat. 105).

21. When the question about party politics was put to Senator Frank E. Moss, he replied, "I don't think there has been anything political in the schedule set up for developing Central Utah. It is a big, complex problem... it required detailed studies and planning. Also,

the construction of Glen Canyon and Flaming Gorge dams, and generally of other storage facilities.

In the northeast corner of Utah, on the Green River, which has its headwaters in Wyoming, the Flaming Gorge Dam has now been completed.[22] This dam will connect with Glen Canyon power lines to send electric power to surrounding industrial centers. Formerly a refuge for outlaws fleeing from pursuing posses, this remote corner of three states will provide water for metropolitan and agricultural areas, electricity for industry, and recreation for inhabitants and tourists. The population of the small county which contains the dam increased from 364 to 1,159 or 218.4 percent during the decade from 1950 to 1960—not large in number but symbolic of what is happening in the West. The presence of this dam has also caused the Uintah Basin in eastern Utah to grow in population and as a trade and scenic center, encompassing the Dinosaur National Monument, which extends into Colorado. A feeder water resource development is scheduled here in the near future. What is needed in this area, as in similar areas in the West, is considerable road work.[23]

Western delegations have had to struggle and then make deals with congressional delegations from New England and eastern states which want federal aid for the improvement of harbors, and from other eastern delegations, most notably from New York, which became alarmed recently over the long drought in their own areas. Complacent about water problems, not only pollution but supply as well, eastern delegations thought about water only as something that, if one wanted it, he had only to go out and get it from rivers and lakes. When drought hit their own states they looked closer at appropriations for water resource development in the West. Also, mideastern, eastern, and southern delegations have not wanted another great industrial area to compete with those in their own states.

Many states are trying to bring new industry into their areas. The availability of water is the basic consideration in the location of almost every industrial development.[24] Almost all industrial plants use enormous quantities of water, in one

the decision was made to go ahead with the storage dams such as Flaming Gorge and Glen Canyon, first, and to follow along with other projects later, and this makes sense. I don't see any signs that Central Utah was delayed because Utah did not always send Democrats to Congress. The Upper Colorado River Storage Act was passed in 1956, and since 1958 Utah has always had at least one Democrat in Washington, and for one session we had three. We have had two for two other sessions. Nevada has done better on Democrats and so have Montana, Washington, New Mexico and one or two other reclamation states. But others have not done nearly so well. Reclamation funds have been cut by the demands of the Vietnam War—as have most other development programs—and any delay has been caused more by a lack of funds than by politics. We did a good job on Reclamation under Kennedy, and would have done better under Johnson, I am sure, if the War had not intervened." Letter to the writer, dated June 5, 1967.

22. For the political significance of its dedication by Mrs. Lyndon B. Johnson, see Frank H. Jonas, "President Lyndon Johnson, the Mormon Church, and the 1964 Political Campaign," *Proceedings*, Utah Academy of Sciences, Arts and Letters, 44 (Part I, 1967), 79-82.

23. See [Senator Wallace F.] "Bennett Urges Priorities on Gorge Road Work," Salt Lake *Tribune*, September 20, 1966. The senator said, "The people of Utah and the West are becoming increasingly impatient over the fact that brilliant new recreation and industrial areas are opened up in the form of Flaming Gorge Reservoir, yet the access roads are still little more than dreams or in the talking stages." See also Carl E. Hayden, "Flaming Gorge," Salt Lake *Tribune, Home Magazine*, July 10, 1966, pp. 19-22.

24. For example, in 1965 a multi-million dollar mine-mouth coal-burning power plant was projected by three southwestern private utility corporations. These planned to use coal from the Kaiparowitz Plateau in south-central Utah and new long-line transmission techniques to generate and transport electricity to load centers in Arizona and southern California. The first step was to sign a contract by which they would receive 102,000 acre feet of Utah's share of Colorado River water each year for fifty years.

way or another. In addition, an explosive population increase in the West and urbanization, spawned by a rising standard of living, have cut the water supply even as affluence has increased demand. The real reason for the water crisis has been the failure to husband resources. Although everyone, general public and leaders alike, has known how rapidly the population has been increasing and has known that a higher standard of living requires more water, political and social action, as usual, has lagged behind technological change. "Science can solve our water problems, given the opportunity, insofar as the solutions can be purely scientific. We have long known how to get salt out of water. In limited instances we have made rain. We regularly purify waste water. Recirculation systems have been built, cutting drastically the amount of water needed to make a ton of product. But science cannot solve the political and legal problems that often must be dealt with first."[25]

Massive investments in dams, hydroelectric plants, treatment installations and sewers, reservoirs, and irrigation works, plus the advantages that regions and industries have gained from the use of water, have generated giant political pressures involving cities, states, the federal agencies, trade and service associations, big business, conservationists, farmers, and the Congress.

The Water Quality Act in 1965 aroused business executives who attacked the federal government; they favored local standards and controls. They sought to intimidate Congress and the new Water Pollution Control Administration. They also used the familiar argument that better results would emanate from voluntary and cooperative efforts of industry, municipalities, and state governments to conserve and redeem water resources than from programs handled by Washington's many agencies. As usual the federal government has stepped in when the private or state government efforts to correct a situation or to keep one from developing have either failed or have not been made in the first place.

With a federal investment of $50 billion in water projects, it would be naïve to expect that the federal government would abandon its interests to the very private groups and state agencies which failed to prevent the conditions which now have to be corrected. Payrolls and business profits depend as much upon congressional authorizations and appropriations as flood control, hydroelectric power, and regional economic growth. As long as private business and the states cannot find enough money, particularly in the Rocky Mountain states, to finance even their own educational needs, the federal government remains not only the sole resource for providing the necessary money but also the only agency to settle the conflicts between states and regions over the uses of water and to enforce standards.

In 1949 a powerful combination defeated the Columbia Valley Authority, which never got past the hearing stage.[26] In this combination were the following: National Association of Electric Companies (private utilities), National Rivers and Harbors Congress, National Association of Manufacturers, U.S. Chamber of Commerce, the National Wildlife Federation, Republican governors of northwestern states, Pacific Northwest Development Association.

California and Arizona once locked horns in a desperate struggle over sharing lower Colorado waters. The litigation which ensued dragged on for years. *Arizona*

---

25. Moss, *op. cit.*, p. 5.

26. Proposed by President Harry S. Truman. A CVA meant an independent agency with broad powers for river valley development. It meant the elimination of the Corps of Engineers from future developments; it meant above all public power on a massive scale in the Northwest. Moss, *op. cit.*, p. 24.

v. California has the distinction of providing the longest oral argument made before the U.S. Supreme Court in this century. In an average case the court hears about an hour of oral argument. The offshore oil cases involving Louisiana and Texas were allotted 16 hours; *Arizona v. California* was allotted 22 hours. Two Special Masters were appointed successively. Their work took eight years, hearing 340 witnesses, reviewing 25,000 pages of testimony, and reporting the finding in a 433-page volume. Arizona won the case in 1964, obtaining the right to 2.8 million acre-feet of water from the Colorado River. *Arizona v. California* has symbolized the increasing struggle to get water for competing uses and rival regions. However, these two states soon drew together in their determination to transfer waters from surplus areas. A new information service was formed, "Water for the West," with a Washington office in the National Press Building, where the lobbyist for the Colorado River Association is also housed. The new organization was called a joint cooperative effort of the Central Arizona Project Association and the Colorado River Association, recently two rivals. This combination opposed private associations which were resisting western resource development.

The Colorado River Association is committed to bringing more water to southern California. Its most important member is the Metropolitan Water Board of Southern California. The Central Arizona Project Association is dedicated to divert water of the Colorado River for a last proposed massive lower basin irrigation project. Both organizations have joined hands to push for Bridge Canyon and Marble Canyon dams.

Two supporting dams in the Central Arizona Project were those of Marble Canyon and Hualapai, the former on the east of the Grand Canyon National Park, and the latter on the west. Both dams were suggested to supply the power necessary to pump water from the Colorado River to aqueducts that would then carry the water to Maricopa County. Both were opposed by the Sierra Club on the grounds that they would destroy the scenic beauty of the practically inaccessible area. The comments of Sierra Club spokesmen were indicative of the opposition from private groups to Colorado River development. One East Coast official of the Sierra Club reported that "the typical Eastern reaction to the Hualapai project was 'a mixture of disbelief, outrage and anger' at the proposition that 'one or two, or even seven, states think they have a special right to spoil one of the greatest national and scenic resources of the nation and indeed the world.' "[27] Representative Craig Hosmer retorted that "The Sierra Club's agitation against Hualapai and Marble is the most outrageous demagoguery to hit town since Barnum left. Not only will Grand Canyon not be ruined but a beautiful new lake stretch, miles up from Hoover Dam's Lake Mead, will be created, accessible for the enjoyment of all Americans, just not a few hardier and wealthier Sierra Club types."[28]

In any event, opposition to these two dams was strong enough to see them both eliminated from the plans for the Central Arizona Project. It would seem that private facilities will now produce the necessary power to pump the water from the Colorado River to the plateau for transportation to centers in the state. If necessary, Arizona would go it alone in constructing and developing the facilities to bring its share of the Colorado River to its populated and needful areas, such is the pressure for more water in that semi-arid state.

Governmental agencies have also served to divert or withhold funds for water resource development and in so doing have extended their functions to policy

27. *Ibid.*, p. 16.
28. Salt Lake *Tribune*, August 10, 1966.

making—in brief, politics. These have been the Soil Conservation Service and especially the Bureau of the Budget. Other pressure groups have been concerned with water, the National Parks Association, the Wilderness Society, the Izaac Walton League, the Sports Fishing Institute, the Trustees for Conservation, the National Audubon Society, and the Citizens Committee for Natural Resources. Public power groups as well as private power companies have been successful lobbyists, for example, the National Rural Electric Cooperative Association and the American Public Power Association. Organized labor, industrial unions, the National Grange, and the Farmers Union have supported multi-purpose developments. Even the Auto Workers and the Farm Bureau Federation, though on opposite sides, have been interested in pollution, conservation, and power. The League of Women Voters has supported beneficial legislation from the standpoint of national interest.

One should not leave the subject of water and politics without a comment about the conflicting attitude of one of Arizona's leading citizens, Barry Goldwater. In the 1964 presidential campaign not only did some observers research Goldwater's mistakes, but they also revealed the hypocrisy of his position by pointing to the involvement of the federal government in the development of the resources in Arizona. As one looks out from his hilltop house in an easterly direction in Maricopa County, one can see the green fields of that area and the beautiful homes in almost every direction which depend almost exclusively on the development of the Salt River Valley water project in which the federal government has played a significant and conspicuous role.[29] In Arizona, water is politics.

Water resource exploitation and hydroelectric power production and distribution have been both divisive and unifying factors in the development of the West. Never have the thirteen western states, nor even the eleven or twelve (Alaska added) continental states, voted in concert on a bill in Congress directly affecting the economic welfare of the area. As many as 12 out of 69 members of the House of Representatives have either voted "no" or have been absent on roll calls. More interesting have been five states who in recent votes have split their delegations in the Senate. These splits have been along party lines and on the grounds of ideology with reference to the division between private and public power development. Many private power companies, many corporate big-business interests, have aided financially the election of senators and representatives. In many instances these representatives have voted favorably for measures directly favoring their own states and including the involvement of private utilities in a project. Also, federal hydroelectric projects have received a more general support in Congress from western delegations if the distribution of power has been left for private utility companies. Power produced by governmentally operated plants has been instrumental in forcing private utility companies to meet the demands of private enterprise for lower rates. Huge enterprises involving water resource exploitation and hydroelectric development have also forced private enterprise to act and become involved. There have been three such developments in the West in very recent years.

One is called "Intertie." This is Secretary of Interior Stewart L. Udall's idea of a power system link-up of the Pacific Northwest and the Pacific Southwest.

29. See Frank H. Jonas, "The Spirit of Contemporary Politics in the American West," *Western Political Quarterly*, XVIII (September 1954), 10. "Goldwater alienated tens of thousands of voters by proposing to sell TVA to private industry, even though, back home in Arizona, the Senator fought actively for every possible federal dollar for the proposed Central Arizona Project." Moss, *op. cit.*, p. 24.

The Intertie is the projected construction of four principal lines that will connect major federal, public, and private electrical systems in eleven western states, and provide adequate low cost power.

According to Department of Interior spokesmen, "WEST" will tie in with Intertie to form this power grid complex. WEST (Western Energy Supply and Transmission Program) is a nine-state, non-federally financed, $10.5-billion power complex, which, when completed in twenty years, will create an electrical brotherhood between the Pacific Northwest, Pacific Southwest, the Rocky Mountains, and Northern Texas. It will become the major power system in the western states, capable of producing 36 million kilowatt hours of electricity. This is equal to 18 Grand Coulee Dams or three times the capacity of the Tennessee Valley Authority (TVA).

This system is expected to provide avenues of relief for excess electrical capacities from one state to another. States in need of electrical power boosts during peak usage periods will be able to get them. For example, Utah's summertime electrical production can be diverted to Arizona to aid that state in running its air conditioners, which place a heavy demand on its power plants.

This high voltage combine is headed by officials of major private power organizations in the West. The organization held its first formal meeting in January 1964. Headquarters for WEST are in Albuquerque, New Mexico. The Utah Power and Light Company is the hub for this electrical grid with Glen Canyon of the Colorado River Storage Project serving as the tie-in point between the Pacific Northwest and the Pacific Southwest.[30]

Construction of thermonuclear generating plants is contemplated by the WEST organization. WEST officials indicate these plants could also be used for desalinization programs. When WEST is completed, this system is expected to have created an additional 6,000 jobs.

Two other schemes were added to the Interior Department's program. One is a 500-kv a-c line of 1,000 mw capacity from John Day Dam on the Columbia River to the Vincent Substation near Los Angeles, California. This line is scheduled for completion by the Bonneville Power Administration, Pacific Power and Light Company, and the California Power Pool (Pacific Gas and Electric Company, Southern Edison Company, and the San Diego Gas and Electric Company). The second project is a 500-kv a-c line from John Day Dam to Table Mountain in Central California. It will connect with a 500-kv line to be built by the California Power Pool. Completion was set for 1968 for both of these projects.

Also included in the Intertie package is an assurance of Canadian treaty power for California's Water Project of 1968-83, assuming the treaty is implemented. Also, there was assurance that the Interior Department could supply 4,000,000 kilowatts for California Central Valley preference customers. Cost of Intertie has been estimated at $697 million. Private investment would be about $417 million. The remainder of the funds will come from the federal government. The Interior

30. Present company members of WEST are: Utah Power and Light, El Paso Electric, Nevada Power, Public Service of Colorado, Public Service of New Mexico, San Diego Gas and Electric, Sierra Pacific Power, Southern California Edison, and Tucson Gas and Electric. The Los Angeles Department of Power and Water, Burbank Public Service Company, Glendale Public Service Department, Pasadena Municipal Light and Power Company, and the Imperial Irrigation District were invited to join the organization. Other private power systems could also join. But federally backed power agencies, because they are not locally owned, are not eligible for membership.

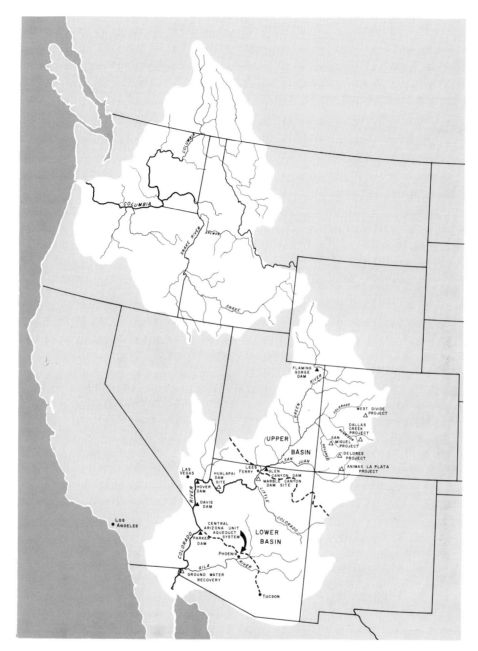

COLORADO RIVER BASIN PROJECT

Department in its news releases stated that the eleven participating states will reap $2.6 billion over a fifty-year period. Other expected benefits are technological improvements, conservation of water resources, reduction of generation reserves, and improved national defense capabilities.

Some $280 million is the federal government's part of the Intertie cost. Some money—$8.5 million—was allocated for this project in the 1964 Public Works Bill. Shortly thereafter bill S1007 was introduced in the Senate by Senator

Henry Jackson (D-Washington), which prevented the use of these funds without first assuring the Pacific Northwest preference for power generated in that area, defined as Oregon, Washington, Montana (west of the Continental Divide), and portions of Idaho and Wyoming in the Columbia River Drainage basin as well as Utah. This bill was passed and became law on August 31, 1964. The 1965 Public Works Bill provided an additional $45.5 million for Intertie.

These two giant power complexes, Intertie and WEST, are not connected to the same compatible power pole, and their cross currents are blowing fuses all over the West. According to the Assistant Secretary of the Interior, Intertie and WEST will eventually become connected into one huge system with dual management. Private power interests object to this plan, believing that Intertie is another move to encroach upon them, that Intertie facilities are not needed yet, and that the Interior Department is creating an unnecessary expense.[31] However, several private power companies are members of both the WEST and Intertie systems. These dual-member companies are in California and Arizona. California will benefit most from Intertie activity. Arizona comes in a close second: small municipal companies are not able to provide the type of power strength required by this fast-growing state.

WEST is going on its way towards completion of its twenty-year goal—and Intertie is not included in plans along the way. One major accomplishment of WEST was the completion of a $12 million, 230,000 volt transmission line from Salt Lake City to the Arizona border on October 20, 1964.

At the present time, the Pacific Northwest appears to have an overabundance of hydroelectric power. It appears that an added overabundance will be created in Alaska. A speculative venture, which would result in the construction of the North American Water and Power Alliance (NAWPA), a huge dam on the Yukon River, has been gaining momentum. More than $1.4 billion in federal funds would be expected to flow into the Alaskan economy. If such a venture becomes a reality, the system will need customers. These customers will be the western states. Canada could be a customer, but that country has no power problems in its western frontiers, nor too many customers. Such a system, tied in with WEST and Intertie, would surely bring enough cheap hydroelectric power to the western states for all their needs.[32]

Thermonuclear generating plants are also another aspect to consider. These plants will make most hydroelectric power obsolete, at least over long-distance transmission lines. The fact that WEST considers such plants for the future could be this organization's stopper for federal power spending.

From the record on legislation for Intertie, it is apparent that western congressmen are in favor of federal funds for these projects, with the possible exception of Utah which appears to be split over acceptance. Strife between federal and private interests is age-old, but factionalism is not conducive to progress for the benefit of all concerned. WEST was created after the push for Intertie and is a clear case of creating competition for Intertie. On the other hand, Intertie bound-

31. The purpose of this writing is not to become involved in the controversy between private and public power. Interesting sidelights may be found in "BPA Still Attempting to Invade Area," Salt Lake *Tribune*, May 16, 1965. "Federal vs. Private Power: S. Idaho Fight Flares," *ibid*., May 2, 1965. In the Salt Lake *Tribune* and Utah Power and Light Company central files there are no anti-WEST articles, nor anti-Intertie news. There are no pro-Intertie articles either, but there are plenty of pro-WEST and anti-BPA in both files. The *Tribune* has a very large circulation in southern Idaho.

32. See Moss, *op. cit*., pp. 242-54 for the story to date of NAWPA.

ary designations are not designed to foster friendly relations with powerful western private utilities. A pattern of cooperation has already been established in several areas of the country, but not in the western states. There needs to be an overall program for the expansion of hydroelectric power in the West which should include Alaska. Such a program would require unity of purpose on the part of all western power factions. If federal funds should become available for such a program, the West would perhaps do well to accept them. According to a power survey by the U.S. Department of Interior, 75 to 80 percent of the national power industry is privately owned, so there does not appear to be a take-over by the federal government.

It has been suggested that the establishment of these power complexes in the West will not create a position of regional strength, since there are other power complexes around the country, perhaps not so big, but with more congressional manpower backing them. Yet these power complexes will strengthen the West's position with respect to other reclamation projects. With all western states tied in to the same fuse box, there would exist a reason for regional unity.

Another economic area in which government and private enterprise come into conflict is in the development of oil resources. Oil in Wyoming was exploited early, with pipelines running to local refineries as well as those in the Salt Lake City and Denver areas. Only twenty years ago the oil deposits in Utah, Colorado, and New Mexico lay too deep to be fully exploited. Today, with improved technology, these states have greatly increased production. For example, in twenty years Utah's production increased from about 500 barrels of crude oil annually to nearly 40 million barrels (1939-59). In this state, oil has dethroned copper as the most valuable resource. This example is symbolic of recent developments in oil production throughout the Rocky Mountains. Oil and natural gas production is concentrated in areas beginning in southern Montana, covering nearly all of Wyoming, and continuing in northeastern Arizona and northwestern New Mexico. Some of the most valuable oil and natural gas resources have existed in California for decades. In Wyoming, oil has been the dominant economic factor since 1912.

In 1964 in the heat of the presidential campaign, news about oil shale deposits in Wyoming, Utah, and Colorado broke anew and with superlatives about their vastness and richness. It was averred that exploitation of oil shale could wipe out the billion dollar national debt overnight. Estimates of the Green River shale deposits of Utah, Colorado, and Wyoming place their potential at 1.4 trillion barrels of oil in Colorado alone, 100 billion in Utah, and 10 billion in Wyoming. Full-scale oil shale development could attract a million persons to the Colorado River Valley in Glenwood Springs and the Rifle-Grand Junction area and create a vast new urban center within a decade.[33]

The presence of this oil shale in these three states has been known for fifty years. Indeed, there has been some small-scale development.[34] Thousands of claims had been filed. Many lapsed. These lapsed claims have become a major legal headache, and a vast amount of legal underbrush must be cleared before real development can get underway.

33. Dr. Charles Prien of the Denver Research Institute has estimated that the oil shale industry in the Rocky Mountains could produce 1.5 million barrels of petroleum a day by 1975.

34. One plant at Rifle, Colorado, was constructed in the 1940's and pursued shale research for several years until it was closed down in 1956. Representative Wayne N. Aspinall (D-Colorado) in 1964 announced a governmental lease agreement between the Interior

Much of the land in which the shale lies is federally owned. In question is the relationship between the states and the federal government, as well as the relationship between private industry and the federal government. Who will mine the oil? No one wants to experience another Teapot Dome scandal. As usual private enterprise is chaffing at the bit, and states are anxious to receive royalties from the lands. However, there is no immediate need for the oil, although nearly all fuel needs for producing energy are supplied by oil and gas. This huge deposit has strategic value for military as well as civilian use.

In the Rocky Mountain area, mainly between Utah and Colorado, are practically all the known uranium deposits in the nation. In the 1950's there was a flurry in uranium prospecting reminiscent of the gold rushes. Over-night fortunes were made, and some persons became legendary. Recently activity has increased in this field. Beryllium has been found in Utah and Idaho. Dawsonite, a sodium aluminum carbonate, and nahcolite, a sodium carbonate, have been found in the oil shale area. Phosphates, potash, and sulphur are being mined in commercial quantities. Natural gas pipelines connect El Paso and Seattle, and branch off to southern California cities. Coal deposits in the mountain states will last the nation for hundreds of years at the present rate of production. Largely replaced by gas and oil for heating and electric generating purposes, coal went into an eclipse, but it is now back in industrial plans for power plants.[35]

With its abundance of natural resources now largely undeveloped, the West, almost one-half the area of the nation, will not experience a shortage in energy for centuries to come. The West offers nine-tenths of the whole nation's hydroelectric potential. Neither the Columbia River basin, which begins in Wyoming and takes in most of Idaho, western Montana, Oregon, and Washington, nor the Colorado River basin, of vital interest to the rest of the continental western states except Alaska, has been fully developed. This development will constitute a major interest in western politics for many years to come; it may yet translate a regional and party area into a political bloc for voting purposes on common objectives in Congress and in national councils, in spite of the many divisive influences in the many energy-producing enterprises.

Neither politics nor economic development may bring about regional unity in the West, but reliance on the federal government may do so. But more than this is the great stake the federal government has developed in the West. The amounts of money it spends in the region, coupled with its ownership of approximately 50 percent of the land area in the West, and its over one-half million employees, constitutes a tremendous power base, with a commensurate interest in politics.

THE FUTURE OF THE WEST

Has the West been recognized in national politics as a political entity? Is there a *political* West? Can it use its regional status as an effective instrument to

Department and the Colorado School of Mines Research Foundation to reopen the plant. Shortly after the 1964 elections the President appointed six members to the Federal Oil Shale Advisory Board. There was disagreement among them: one urged immediate extraction; another hinted at possible scandals if oil shale development were accelerated, advocated an indefinite delay in leasing oil shale lands, and suggested strong federal controls. The chairman, Dr. Joseph L. Fisher, estimated oil reserves to be as high as 2,500 billion barrels—more than one thousand times the annual production of oil in the United States.

35. The Secretary of the Interior has announced an agreement with members of WEST for development of a massive coal-fired steam and electric generating and transmission complex in the Southwest. Plants are projected for Mohave and the Four Corners, and the Kaiparowitz Plateau. Hanford now uses coal for its generating plants.

improve its position? Before Alaska and Hawaii came into the Union, the eleven western states had become a geographic area for business and governmental administration units and for voluntary social, business, and political associations. Since World War II, Congress has devoted more attention to the West, and eastern newspapers and national periodicals have given increased news and feature play to some of its election campaigns, and its political issues and personalities.

In national nominating conventions, westerners have played an increasingly active role. At the 1960 Republican convention, Oregon's Mark Hatfield nominated a native Californian, Richard M. Nixon, for the presidency. Arizona's Barry Goldwater came to the convention as the chairman of the Republican Senatorial Campaign Committee and as a vice presidential aspirant; he left as the leader of the nation's Republican conservatives, and won the presidential nomination four years later. In the Democratic convention, Senator Frank Church from Idaho gave the keynote address. Senator Lyndon B. Johnson, the Texan who had identified himself with the West, was chosen as the vice presidential nominee, while Washington state's vice presidential aspirant, Senator Henry Jackson, became the party's national chairman.

The picture for the West, from the standpoint of recognition by those who control the party apparatus, seemed quite bright, at least until the 1964 national conventions. But in the most important places, in both party conventions on the platform committees, the West as a bloc has had little influence. Even in the separate party regional conventions very little attention has been paid to the problems of the West. The regional meetings have dealt mainly with party problems and how to snare votes. From 1964 to the present (1968) the regional party meetings, although apparently well-organized, have not been well attended either by national party officials and representatives or by state party leaders. Many key persons have been conspicuous by their absence.

In 1960 an executive committee was appointed by the Democratic party after its regional meeting, and largely through its efforts many planks particularly beneficial to the the thirteen western states were written into the national platform, dealing largely with water resource development and reclamation. For a very short time after the election of a Democratic administration and Congress, the expectation of legislation to implement these promised benefits seemed on the way to fulfillment. It was not long, however, before this expectation gave way to the administration's concern with the Vietnam war. There appeared to be a slight upsurge of western interest between 1960 and 1964, but what was happening was mainly the fanfare by the party in power over the finishing of a few large projects, which its predecessor had begun. No significant starts were made in the various individual states.

The West has not received the economic and political consideration to which it was entitled after the 1960 and 1964 elections, and will not do so for many years to come. It simply does not have the base for exercising the necessary power. In a democracy, the vote is dictator. He who can get the vote, either of the electorate or of its representatives in the legislature, is in the position to exercise political power. The West simply does not have the vote to determine its own destiny. It has 26 percent of the Senate and 16.8 percent of the House membership. In the decade from 1943 to 1953, the West had 49 representatives in Congress. This number rose to 59 in the next decade, and after the 1960 census the number was increased to 69. Much increase in House membership after the 1970 census is unlikely. The electoral vote now stands at 95. The numbers by themselves are not significant. They can become meaningful in case of a close party division, but bloc voting by the West has not developed in the Congress.

The West has not acted as a region either in Congress or in party conventions in seeking favorable recognition of its problems and objectives. There are some common attitudes among western Democrats and western Republicans, particularly in the field of resource development, but there are also many points of disagreement in this field between and within the parties. Senator Gale McGee states that "there can be immense differences of opinion between western senators about water. For example, I have long been opposed to Senator Hayden's Central Arizona Project because it would deplete Wyoming's water resources. Oftentimes, too, western senators are at variance about agriculture programs. Senator Dominick's [R-Colorado] views on agriculture are quite different from mine. Perhaps one conclusion I would draw is that party considerations are more dominant than geographical considerations when it comes to en bloc voting." He continues, "Oftentimes western senators band together in regard to legislation that they feel will be beneficial to their area. A case in point might be extractive minerals legislation or water legislation."[36] On the other hand there has been disagreement over oil depletion allowances and over federal electric power disposal policies.[37]

Senator Mike Mansfield had no statement to make "relative to the possible designation of the thirteen states (West) as a region, or a political area, or even as a voting bloc in Congress." However, he did say that "there are some things on which most of us, regardless of party, agree, but there are many differences as well, perhaps, because of party."[38]

Another United States Senator, Thomas H. Kuchel, has stated, "During my more than fifteen years in the Senate, there has been no bloc effort I can recall to exert political strength on behalf of western states in the direction of influencing distribution of federal monetary aid. I have co-operated on occasions with California colleagues, of course, to see that equity is done and to prevent any discrimination against legitimate interests and needs of our state and its people. Similarly I have joined Senate colleagues from other western states from time to time in pressing legislation we felt was of major significance to the area, such as in regard to water problems, maritime matters, mining and other nature resources development or activity, and the like."[39]

Political power finds its base not only in economics and industrial plants and production but also in population-potential. The western bloc has enjoyed the highest rate of growth in this category of any region in the nation. In 1959 the total estimated population of 26,299,000 represented an increase of approximately six million persons during the first nine years of that decade. The estimated resident population in 1966 was 30,747,300; in 1967 the projected estimate was 33,045,000. Although the rate from 1960 to 1968 has decreased somewhat over that in the previous decade, it is still higher than in any other region in the United States. In net in-migration it is more than twice that of all other regions combined.[40]

36. Letter to the writer from U.S. Senator Gale McGee (D-Wyoming), dated April 2, 1968.

37. Letter to the writer from Senator Henry Jackson (D-Washington), dated August 18, 1960.

38. Letter to the writer from Senator Mike Mansfield (D-Montana), dated April 3, 1968.

39. Letter to the writer from Thomas H. Kuchel (R-California), dated April 2, 1968.

40. *Current Population Reports*, Population Estimates, U.S. Department of Commerce, Bureau of the Census, November 24, 1967.

There is no strong sociological challenge comparable to the problem of Negro segregation in the South. Lacking in the West is the high degree of industrialization with attendant economic problems which has provided a common cause for political action by eastern states.

The great diversity of agriculture acts as an impediment to the promotion of political sectionalism. Political partisanship is not so well established in the West as in other areas of the nation. And California overwhelms all other western states combined in both population growth and economic activity, which may possibly be the greatest single obstacle to politicizing the West as a region.

With about half the electoral college votes in the West and the decision of California parties to play big state politics, it is not likely that the other twelve states would relish playing the role of satellites to California. It is precisely at this point, when sectionalism has become discredited, that the stirring of political self-consciousness is clearly discernible in the regional West.[41]

The West seems to be gaining as a regional entity. One of the most important external pressures contributing to this development is the relationship between the thirteen states and the federal government. In land size, the West lacks only 42,981 square miles of representing half of the area of the United States. The national government owns roughly one-third of this total, exclusive of Hawaii and Alaska. With these states, especially Alaska, the fraction rises to about one-half.

In addition, Washington, D.C., has acquired vested interests from both the billions of dollars in loans, grants-in-aid, and subsidies expended on the economy in the West and the over one-half million civil servants residing and working in the region. This figure represents approximately one-fourth of the federal employees in the fifty states who reside outside the area of the national capital. Again, California has led the way with the largest number of employees in this category and with one-half the number in the western area. It is very doubtful, however, if any advantage accrues to the party in power as a result of the association of such a vast army of employees with administration. Civil servants generally are neither party- nor administration-minded when it comes to elections.

In 1959 the thirteen states and their local governments received about $1,236,689,000 in grants from the federal government. This expenditure represented one-fifth of the total $6,313,134,000 spent in the nation that year. In 1966 the total aid expenditures in the area came to $3,571,000,000, which still represents one-fifth of the total $17,210,000,000 allocated or spent by the federal government in the nation.

The large portion of its budget the federal government spends, the army of civil servants it maintains, produce pressure groups which are nurtured by these factors. The reciprocal reactions of the federal and state governments to this kind of power situation may well supply the basis for a sectional unity.

Not too much can be achieved as a result of state or local government action. Even California will hardly achieve its aims by virtue of its own efforts alone. Other states are still simply too small to do much. Both the historian and the politician probably would agree that the regional approach has far more to recommend it than the alternatives of state or nation on which the West has been depending.

The western states should and will lead this nation into [a] new age, but in order to do so we must develop a regional consciousness to match our fortunate position and potential.

41. These divisive influences are pointed out by Totton J. Anderson in "The Political West in 1960," *Western Political Quarterly*, XIV (June 1961), 287-99.

We must learn that that which divides us is less important than that which joins us together. . . . We must convince the West that regional consciousness is neither new nor improper in the history of our county. The South has been—and is—articulately and powerfully represented as a region, as is the industrial Northeast and the productive Middle West. The "New West" is . . . a region blessed by plentiful resources, a region free from crippling class and caste systems, a spacious and hospitable region where people can live and grow and enjoy life.[42]

The West has come far in economic development, population increase, and even in political influence. "Today by every test modern civilization makes, by population, productivity, climate, raw materials and power potential, the West has earned the right to individual commercial and cultural equality."[43] Perhaps this is true; but earning something and receiving it, if others are in a position of power and do not wish to grant it, are two different things.

Much will depend on the West itself. Its best chance is to make the most of the water supply that is available, to attain peak efficiency in hydroelectric power development and distribution, to achieve a maximum reclamation program, and to eliminate discriminatory freight rates. To give western industry a chance, it must challenge on the broad front of a regional approach. To do so the West must rise above provincialism, cultivate its essential unity, and strive for at least a measure of solidarity. There are divisive and unifying factors in the West. There is no indication as to which are the more pervasive, but the sheer presence of divisive factors offers hope. The unifying pressures in the West may come either from its great reliance on the federal government for aid in developing its resources, or they may come from the Gargantuan stake the federal government has in the region.

What strikes the student quite forcibly is the realization that the whole area, even excluding Hawaii and Alaska, has not acted nor reacted in concert on a single proposed policy. A paragraph from Wallace Stegner's description of the West as "more than one thing" is worth reproducing in order to review the diversity that is reflected in the differences—and the conflicts—of congressional delegations and of governors.

It is the highest land in the United States, also the lowest; the driest, also the wettest; the newest, also the oldest. It is shortgrass plains, mountains, forests, lava beds and scablands, sand and sagebrush, alkali flats, red stone, ocean shore. It is lonely ranches, industrialized, super farms, cities, slums. It is at least six regions and as many different histories, one of them eighty years older than Plymouth Rock, and others nearly encompassable within the memories of living men. It is two major folk figures, the mountain man and the cowboy, and several lesser ones; and for each of these there is a vast literature and a developed mythology that continues to shape the present. It is ways of life as different as San Francisco's North Beach joints and Salt Lake City's sedate ward houses. It is likewise a series of notions, all of which have the intention or effect of turning this multiplicity back into unity: the notion of the frontier as a mystically-shared experience, the notion of a western character shaped by that frontier, the notion of a western literature exploiting this most native experience and this large and essentially heroic character.[44]

The threads of unity and diversity are inextricably intertwined. Yet as one contemplates such huge accomplishments as the completion of the John Day Dam, the biggest, most powerful, most costly dam ever built by the Army Corps

42. Caughey, *op. cit.*, p. 24.

43. Letter from Calvin Rawlins to Alex Miller, Democratic National Committeeman from Alaska, dated July 20, 1960.

44. Wallace Stegner, "Commentary," *American West Review*, I (March 15, 1967), 12.

of Engineers, which will ultimately generate three million kilowatts of power for the benefit not only of the entire Columbia River Basin but also of all the Mountain West, and as one reads of concerted plans of the eight-state Rocky Mountain Federation to effect a water distribution system from Canada to the Gulf of Mexico, one feels that the difficulties of achieving political unity seem petty. Political party differences seem puerile and insignificant. Parties will neither advance nor impede the developing unity. Social forces and not personal forces ultimately will bring about an accumulation of accomplishments which in turn will demand the political unity necessary for the task of maintaining and distributing the shares in the total achievement. What Frederick Paxson has called "the relentless frontier" is neither gone nor dead.

ALASKA:

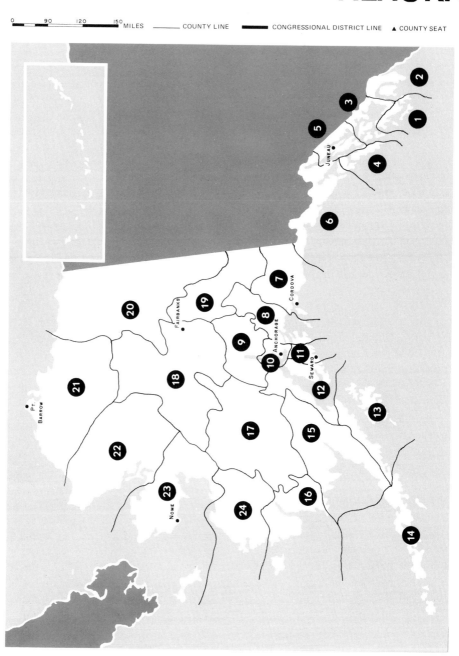

Herman E. Slotnick

Empire of the North

With the acquisition of statehood in 1959 the long quest of Alaskans to secure self-government was over. Almost from the date of the purchase of Alaska in
1867 from Russia, Alaskans had complained about their neglect by and inferior
position in the American union. No civil government existed in the first seventeen
years of American rule. The territory was merely a possession of the United
States, administered first by the Army and then by the Navy. When Congress finally acted, it seemed to do so in haste. The first Organic Act, passed in 1884, gave
only the semblance of government to Alaska: The laws of Oregon, then the nearest state, were extended to the territory, at least insofar as they were applicable.
Alaskans were forbidden to have a legislature of their own or to send a delegate to
Congress. A governor was to be appointed by the President, but he was an official
in name only. Alaska became a full-fledged territory in 1912, but many of its
inhabitants still remained dissatisfied. They claimed that their legislature had
been delegated little authority, and complained that the real control over the resources and economy of the territory was in the hands of a Congress and federal
agencies which seemingly knew little and cared less about Alaska. Supporters of
the statehood movement, which became increasingly stronger after World War II,
insisted that federal control and federal ownership of over 99 percent of its land
had retarded the development of Alaska. They argued vigorously that its growth
and development could be achieved only when the destinies of the territory were
placed in the hands of men and women familiar with Alaskan conditions and
problems.[1]

Statehood has not brought the millennium to Alaska. Prices are much higher
than elsewhere in the nation. The economy is very heavily dependent upon the
activity of the federal government, and the state's resources are still waiting to be
developed. Although Alaska is the largest state of the Union in territory, it has the
smallest population. Its native peoples—Aleuts, Eskimos, and Indians—do not enjoy the same standard of living as the white man.

Statehood is no longer an issue in Alaskan politics. A petition to restore the
state to territorial status received little support. Yet the Democratic domination
of the state government and Alaskan politics in general has been a very live issue.
Republicans have attributed all the ills which have beset the young state to the
Democratic control of the government, while the Democrats naturally like to take
credit for all that has been achieved in Alaska since 1959. Republicans deplore the
Democratic administration's squandering of the funds received from the federal
government to help Alaska make the transition to state government; the prolifera-

1. See arguments in *Statehood for Alaska: A Report on Four Years of Achievement*
(Juneau: Alaska Statehood Committee, 1953), p. 19.

tion of the state's bureaucracy; the roads that have not been built; and the new debts which have been accumulated by the state. Democrats boast of the steady growth of the population since statehood; of the increasing prosperity of Alaskans in the past seven years; of improved educational facilities and other services; and of the great strides made by the fishing, oil, gas, and coal industries.

GEOGRAPHY AND RESOURCES

One need not be a geographical determinist to appreciate how the settlement of Alaska has been affected by its size, geographical location, and physical features. From the viewpoint of the white man, Alaska is new; the Northwest Pacific, of which it is part, was the last major area of the world to be explored and settled. Alaska has an area equal to one-fifth of the United States; it is more than twice the size of Texas, the next largest state; its coast line is double that of all the other states combined; and it extends into four time belts. The myth of "Seward's Ice Box" still persists, although the state has not one but several climates. Only a fourth of its territory lies north of the Arctic Circle, and much of its coastal area is milder than many parts of the United States. Southeastern Alaska has an annual rainfall from 60 to more than 150 inches a year. Sitka and Ketchikan, two of its larger cities, have only one or two days a year when the temperature drops below zero. Ketchikan's growing season is 165 days a year, that of Point Barrow on the Arctic, 17, while in the interior, where temperatures have been recorded of 70° below zero in the winter and over 100° in summer, there are from 54 to 90 days a year without frost.[2]

Much of the Alaskan terrain is mountainous. To the south along the coast lies the St. Elias Range, and the Chugach, Wrangell, and Kenai mountians. North America's highest peak, Mt. McKinley, is part of the Alaska range of the interior; and far to the north just below the Arctic Ocean rises the rugged Brooks Range.

Very little of the state is suitable for agriculture, probably one million acres at most, although much submarginal land could be put into production if the need for food in the United States were ever to become critical. Much of the soil is either "too thin, too steep, too cold, or too wet for economical production. . . ."[3] This, plus the higher costs of operation in general, makes it exceedingly difficult for Alaskan farmers to compete even in the local markets with food imported from elsewhere. Alaska does have large stands of virgin timber which are now being commercially exploited.

When the Russians came to Alaska their efforts were confined almost exclusively to the fur trade: few became permanent settlers. As the profits from furs dwindled, the colony, which was looked upon as a military liability in the event of war with a great power, became more and more expendable. Although the Russians knew of the existence of rich deposits of gold, Alaska was sold to the United States. Mining and fishing supported a small population in the early years of American rule. The great change in the economy came with the outbreak of World War II when millions of dollars were spent in the construction of military bases and other activities related to the war effort. Even today, more than twenty years after the surrender of Germany and Japan, the Alaskan economy is heavily dependent upon federal spending. More than a third of the population is employed

2. George W. Rogers, *The Future of Alaska: Economic Consequences of Statehood* (Baltimore: Johns Hopkins Press, 1962), pp. 25-30.

3. *Ibid.*, p. 41.

directly by the government of the United States in either a military or a civilian capacity.[4] Any threatened cutback is sufficient to arouse the congressional delegation. Several years ago political and business leaders protested that the closing of Ladd Air Force Base near Fairbanks would seriously weaken the defenses of Alaska, and they might have added, the economy of Fairbanks. Their feelings were somewhat mollified when the Army took over the base from the Air Force. Elmendorf Air Base near Anchorage continues to use coal as a fuel, because of the effect that a changeover to gas might have upon the Alaskan coal industry.[5]

The inhabitants are acutely aware of the precarious nature of the state's economy. Many believe that the solution for Alaska's problems lies in the development of its great resources which would provide steady employment for many as well as revenues for the state government. The constitution of Alaska, adopted in 1956, instructs the legislature "to make proper laws and regulations for the utilization, development and conservation of all natural resources belonging to the State, including lands and waters, for the maximum benefit of the people." Both political parties have pledged their support to efforts that will attract capital from the outside, which will be used to help develop the state's resources.

A great deal of controversy has arisen over the question of how resources are to be used. Decisions will have to be made as to what is to be done with the more than 103,000,000 acres of land which the state will eventually receive from the federal government under the terms of the Statehood Act. Some Alaskans believe that the land should be transferred gradually to small owners, while others desire immediate exploitation or sale even if this were to mean that private speculators would profit the most. It undoubtedly would be somewhat of an exaggeration to say that Alaska is locked in a battle between conservationists and developers, but the two groups hold widely divergent views concerning which direction Alaska should take. Senator Ernest Gruening, who described himself as a sensible conservationist, has carried on a long struggle to liberalize restrictions on the use of Alaskan lands. He attributes the failure of coal mining to become a prosperous local industry to unwise regulations drafted by Theodore Roosevelt and his successors. He warns that similar action today hinders and could prevent the oil industry from developing in Alaska. He has sought unsuccessfully to induce the federal government to increase the amount of land oil prospecting companies might lease. Gruening believes that the conservation laws are generally not applicable to Alaskan conditions, but were drafted to husband rapidly dwindling resources in other states. However, with the exception of the fisheries, in which he admits overexploitation has taken place, the resources of Alaska have hardly been touched. Conservation measures thus have the effect of "locking up the resources" of Alaska and putting them, so to speak, in a "deep freeze" for the benefit of posterity.[6]

Conservationists are in a minority, and by no means united in their opposition to the developers. Some feel that "development" will completely alter the Alaska they love, while others fear that the developers, in their haste to industrialize the state, would readily dispose of its resources without benefiting the people. Conservationists have sponsored a water code which the state legislature recently

4. Much of the material is taken from George W. Rogers and Richard A. Cooley, "Alaska's Population and Economy: Regional Growth, Development and Future Outlook," *Report to Division of State Planning, Office of the Governor* (Juneau, 1962), Vols. I and II. I am much indebted to both Dr. Rogers and Dr. Cooley for a good deal of information which I received from them in the course of various conversations.

5. Rogers, *op. cit.*, pp. 228-33, 250.

6. Ernest Gruening, *The State of Alaska* (New York: Random House, 1954), pp. 129-31.

adopted. They enthusiastically supported an administrative order of President Eisenhower's, establishing a vast stretch of land in northwest Alaska as a game preserve, which the state's two senators and the representatives of the mineral industries just as vigorously opposed. Developers and conservationists are currently debating the merits of constructing a gigantic dam on the Yukon River, which would cost over a billion dollars to build and would take over thirty years to complete. When finished its area would be larger than the state of New Jersey. Proponents of the dam argue that its construction is essential to produce the low-cost power needed for the establishment of new industries in the state.[7] Conservationists are just as firmly convinced that the whole idea of such a dam is simply a make-work project, that no real benefit would accrue from the building of it, and that it would destroy more than it would create.[8] Their claim that the construction of the dam would be most harmful to the fish and wildlife of the area has brought about the retort that conservationists are more interested in ducks than the people of the area (whom the dam presumably would benefit).[9]

POPULATION

Alaska has been one of the fastest growing states for more than two decades. The population has more than tripled in the past quarter of a century. This increase appears somewhat less than spectacular if one keeps in mind that there were only slightly over 72,000 people living in the territory in 1940, and that Alaska is still one of the least densely populated regions of the earth. World War II furnished the impetus for growth. Thousands of men flocked north to take part in the building of air bases and military installations. At one time there were more than 152,000 men stationed in the territory. With the cessation of hostilities many of the troops were withdrawn, but as a result of the growing antagonism between the United States and the Soviet Union, the various services began to add to their forces and construction boomed again as a result of military demand. In 1950, the Bureau of the Census reported that 127,117 people were living in the territory, of whom 20,000 were serving in the armed forces. By 1960, the population had increased 74 percent to 226,117. Of these, 47,000 were military men, many of whom had brought dependents. In general, Alaska's population is highly mobile. In the past decade almost as many people have left the state as have entered it each year, and today the single most important factor in the growth of the population is the natural increase among Alaskans themselves.

The southwestern and interior regions benefited most from the military boom. Anchorage, which in 1939 had about 3,000 inhabitants, is today the leading city with a population of over 50,000. Fairbanks, the second city, has close to 20,000. More than half the residents of the state live in the Anchorage and Fairbanks areas, which means that the population is basically urban. Southeastern Alaska, the oldest section of the state, lost its primary position largely because of the burgeoning pulp and lumbering industries. With the revival of the fisheries, it is now undergoing a new growth. Even the northern and western areas, the least developed regions of the state, have been experiencing something of a population

7. Ernest Gruening, "The Plot to Strangle Alaska," *Atlantic Monthly*, 216 (July 1965), 53-59.

8. Paul Brooks, "The Plot to Drown Alaska," *Atlantic Monthly*, 215 (May 1965), 53-59.

9. Gruening, "The Plot to Strangle Alaska," p. 58.

explosion. Here recent improvements in sanitation and medical facilities have sharply reduced infant mortality and have increased the life expectancy of the people who are mainly of indigenous stock.[10]

Alaska's native peoples, as the Indians, Eskimos, and Aleuts are generally called, now number about 45,000 to 50,000. They constitute the only true ethnic minority, since there are no blocs of nationals of European origin clustered together in any part of the state. In the past discrimination against the natives was widespread. Under the prodding of Governor Gruening, laws were enacted by the territorial legislature forbidding public places such as restaurants and hotels to refuse service to the natives, and prohibiting discrimination against them in employment. The natives have a much lower standard of living than the Caucasians. The depletion of the fisheries added to their woes and they are unable to adapt to the white man's economy. A high percentage is on relief, and the incidence of tuberculosis among them is much higher than among the whites. The natives are especially interested in improved educational facilities for their children, and better housing for themselves. Several of their leaders have been elected to the legislature. An Indian, Frank Peratrovich, has been the president of the Senate. He is a Democrat, but natives have supported both parties in the past.[11]

EDUCATIONAL POLITICS

Alaska has been most generous in support of its schools. A very substantial proportion of the state's budget goes for education. The teachers have organized an effective lobby and have been successful in obtaining pay raises and fringe benefits. They favor an amendment to the state constitution which would make the commissioner of education directly responsible to a nonpartisan board rather than to the governor.

Alaska actually has two systems of education. Schools in the rural areas and on military bases are operated directly by the state Department of Education. Those in the more populous places are controlled by independent school districts. While the state contributes to the latter, it pays the total cost of the rural schools and is reimbursed by the federal government for the expenses of the on-base schools. City dwellers, who pay both local and state taxes for schools, believe that they are in effect being charged unduly for the support of education in the state. To remedy this inequity they would have rural residents pay local taxes for the support of schools in their own communities.

Alaskans are in general agreement that much needs to be done in improving the educational system for the native peoples, but are by no means in agreement as to how this is to be achieved. Although schools have been established on the primary level in native communities, the problem of secondary education is more complex. Very few of the native communities are large enough to support a high school. The federal government now operates a secondary school for natives, Mt. Edgecumbe, which is located just outside Sitka in the southeastern part of the state. Mt. Edgecumbe is overcrowded and unable to take care of all the children who desire admission. Even if it were adequate, there are many parents, especially those living in the far north, who are reluctant to send their children to a school which is over a thousand miles away. Some would like to have the state build

10. See Rogers and Cooley, *op. cit.*, I, 61-63.

11. Philip Drucker, *The Native Brotherhoods: Modern Intertribal Organizations on the Northwest Coast*, Smithsonian Institution Bureau of Ethnology Bulletin 100 (Washington: Government Printing Office, 1958), pp. 49-50.

secondary schools in or near their own communities. Objections have been raised that this would merely continue a segregated system of education which does little to prepare the child for the competitive life of the white man's world or for ultimate success at the University. As an alternative, it has been suggested that children be sent to high school in one of the larger cities where they would live in dormitories or, it is hoped, in private homes. Plans are being made for the state to take over the educational system of the Bureau of Indian Affairs, but this is dependent upon financial arrangements which will have to be worked out in cooperation with the federal government.[12]

A good deal of controversy is brewing in the field of higher education. Any chosen site for the state university would be inconvenient for many students. Parents frequently choose to send their children outside the state because of the distance to College, a suburb of Fairbanks, where the university is now located, and because of the rigors of the cold winters of interior Alaska. The towns of southeastern Alaska—Ketchikan, Juneau, and Sitka especially, and even Anchorage—have been asking for greater support for their community colleges, which are affiliated with the university, and presumably, less support for the university itself.

The situation in Anchorage is somewhat complicated by the presence there of Alaska Methodist University, a private college established in 1960. Its president, Fred McGinnis, looks upon the expansion of the community college in Anchorage as a threat to his institution. He has made allegations on several occasions that the University of Alaska is seeking to establish a branch in Anchorage that would draw students away from his institution, and is endeavoring to secure for itself a monopoly of higher education in Alaska, a charge which William R. Wood, the state university's president, has denied. Anchorage itself is split on the issue. The *Anchorage Daily Times* and some Anchorage politicians have supported Dr. McGinnis, while others have attempted to secure for the community college more and better facilities.[13]

NEWS MEDIA AND PUBLIC OPINION

Alaska, which until 1966 was overwhelmingly Democratic, has a Republican press. The half-dozen daily newspapers in the state—the *Anchorage Daily Times*, the *Anchorage Daily News*, the *Sitka Sentinel*, the *Ketchikan Daily News*, the *Fairbanks Daily News Miner* and the *Daily Alaska Empire* of Juneau—usually support Republican candidates, but there are signs of change. The *Daily News Miner*, which was most vitriolic in the campaign of 1958 against the election of Ernest Gruening to the Senate, was a model of nonpartisanship in its news coverage four years later when the Senator was a candidate for re-election. The *Anchorage Daily Times*, whose owner, Bob Atwood, has been a leading figure in the Republican party as well as a candidate for political office, supported President Johnson in the campaign of 1964, because Barry Goldwater favored "things Alaskans don't want" and was against "things Alaskans needed most."[14]

12. I am indebted to Dr. Chester W. Youngblood, Head of the Department of Education, University of Alaska, for much of the information concerning current problems in public education in Alaska.

13. Compare *Anchorage Daily Times*, March 9, 1963, p. 1; February 22, 1963, pp. 1 and 4; *Anchorage Daily News*, February 20, 1963, p. 1; March 9, 1963, p. 1; *Fairbanks Daily News Miner*, March 13, 1963, p. 6.

14. *Anchorage Daily Times*, September 18, 1964, p. 4.

The *Times* has the best national and international news coverage of any newspaper in the state. Its influence, which is considerable, is mainly in the Anchorage and Cook Inlet districts, where almost half the population of the state lives. Both the *Times* and the *Anchorage Daily News*, its competitor, have arranged for daily deliveries in other cities such as Fairbanks. But neither the *Times* nor any other newspaper can readily serve a state as large and as sparsely settled as Alaska where transportation facilities are not too good. In Fairbanks, which is 400 miles from Anchorage, the *Daily News Miner* is not very much troubled by the competition of the Anchorage press. With the exception of a few weeklies it has almost a monopoly in interior Alaska. A small newspaper, such as the *Nome Nugget*, can exercise an authority out of all proportion to its size. The *Nome Nugget* is the only newspaper published in the vast area of northwest Alaska.

Candidates for political office are making increasingly greater use of the radio and television facilities within the state. There are presently about a dozen radio and seven television stations, located mainly in the larger cities of Anchorage, Fairbanks, Ketchikan, Juneau, and Sitka. There is no live TV in Alaska from the other states, and the radio stations seldom receive programs directly.

Personal contact counts for a great deal in Alaska politics—probably more here than in most of the more settled states, for many Alaskans believe they are living in the land of the "last frontier." Although the state is large, the smallness of the population means that a candidate is able actually to meet a relatively high percentage of the voters. Generally no candidate or officeholder is so busy that he will refuse to address a high school audience—even though high school students do not vote—or come into a freshman class in government at the university to tell the students of his experiences in the legislature or in Congress. Personal appearances influence votes. For example, Ernest Gruening effectively overcame the hostility which the press showed him in 1958 through a vigorous campaign of personally visiting not only the larger cities but also the native villages. Again, in 1966, personal contact with the voters won the congressional seat for Howard Pollock, who traveled throughout the state while the Democratic incumbent, Ralph Rivers, remained in Washington.

NOMINATIONS AND ELECTIONS

There are only two positions in the executive branch of the government in Alaska which are filled by election, those of the governor and the secretary of state. Nominations for each are made separately, but in the general election the nominees of the various parties for each position run together as a team and cannot be considered separately. Since statehood there have not been any hard-fought party contests in the primary with the exception of state legislative positions. Nineteen-year-olds may vote in Alaska. It is believed that Richard Nixon, who was very popular among younger people, received sufficient support from this group to achieve his victory in the 1960 presidential contest in the state. Although the Alaska constitution states that voters must be able to read or speak English, the courts have recently held that this provision has not been applied in such a way as to violate the antidiscrimination clauses of the recently passed national election law.

Alaska has an open primary. Voters may, but do not have to, state their party preference prior to voting. They are given a single ballot and are limited to choosing from among candidates listed in the column of one party. The legislature did away with a previous system allowing a person to cross-vote and to select nominees for each position without regard to their party affiliation. This change was supported mainly by Democrats who claimed that Republicans, with fewer people competing in the primary, frequently attempted to influence the proceedings by voting for the Democrat who was considered easier to defeat in the general election. Recently the legislature passed a bill, which was signed by the governor, to restore the old method because many Alaskans believe that their freedom of choice is being unduly restricted if they have to vote for candidates of a single party in the primary.

Both parties have attempted to influence the primaries. Caucuses have been held beforehand for the purpose of endorsing candidates, and occasionally a district central committee gives its blessing to one of the political hopefuls. A party may also nominate a candidate by filing a petition stating that it desires and intends to support him in the general elections. The names of 50 people must be secured in behalf of a person running for a district office, and at least 1,000 for a statewide or national position.

Alaska election procedures and laws appear bewildering and extremely casual to newcomers. A refugee instructor at the University of Alaska was very much taken aback the first time he voted in the state. When he entered the grocery store where the polls were located, he was simply asked to sign his name before receiving his ballot, which he marked while using a shelf as a writing table. "How do they know who I am?" he asked. "Something like this could never happen in Vienna, only Alaska." A pre-registration bill has been introduced in several legislative sessions without results. Opponents claim that the enactment of such a measure would work a great hardship upon people living far from any community and those, such as fishermen, whose occupation prevents them from being readily available for registration.[15]

PARTY ORGANIZATION AND PARTY LEADERS

Strong political organizations have made little headway in Alaska. The Alaskan voter, although he usually has supported Democratic candidates, likes to think of himself as an "independent." A prominent Democratic legislator from northern Alaska recently announced his support for the re-establishment of the old system of cross-voting, claiming that both parties were "hollow," and that neither had a popular following or many active party workers.[16]

Political parties in Alaska face many formidable obstacles. Undoubtedly the vastness of the state, the great distances between the cities, and the isolation of many communities make it extremely difficult for any group to enforce the authority needed to create a political machine. Party chairmen and members of the central committee have but a small voice in party matters. The ineffectiveness is further limited because only a few can afford to attend party meetings, the costs of which they must bear themselves. Under the Democratic administration before 1966 the control of state appointments was retained almost exclusively by Governor Egan. He usually picked his own men and allowed the central committee to record their approval or disapproval. Prospective candidates for federal positions were screened by the Democratic national committeeman. Republicans were shut out entirely from appointments, and no federal positions were available to them.

15. In the 1968 primary the people of Alaska will be voting on a referendum to accept or reject a measure passed by the 1968 legislature to establish pre-registration.

16. *Anchorage Daily Times*, March 28, 1966, p. 1.

This picture changed drastically when the 1966 elections spelled the end of one-party domination in the state.

Although the Democrats have been much more successful in winning elections they have not been able to work well together. Egan versus anti-Egan groups, liberals versus conservatives, complaints by the northern and western party members that they are given too little voice in party affairs indicate some of the divisions which existed among them. Several years ago, the state chairman, John S. Hellenthal, was stripped of much of his power at the behest of the "liberals" who were angered by his stand on unemployment compensation. A five-man committee, which included the state chairman, was elected and was given authority to speak for the party when the central committee is not in session.[17]

Mike Stepovich, the last appointed governor of Alaska, has been the leading figure, though not necessarily the dominant personality, in Republican politics since statehood. He was his party's unsuccessful candidate against Ernest Gruening for the United States Senate in 1958, and was beaten for the governorship four years later by William A. Egan. He was again unsuccessful in gaining his party's nomination for the gubernatorial post in 1966. Egan, who had been active in territorial politics for years and who was the president of the Alaska constitutional convention, was the first elected governor of Alaska. He won overwhelmingly in 1958 but barely beat out Mike Stepovich in 1962. Although the governor is limited by the state constitution to two terms, Egan's supporters claimed that he was eligible for re-election in 1966, because his first administration was several weeks shy of a full four-year term. His opponents argued that the Governor was nevertheless violating the spirit, if not the letter, of the constitution.[18]

The Republicans had three contenders for the office. Walter J. Hickel, an Anchorage hotel man and contractor, achieved his hope to be the "new face" which he said the party needed to break the Democratic monopoly. He won the gubernatorial nomination in the most exciting primary since statehood from Stepovich and Bruce Kendall, another Anchorage hotel man and former speaker of the House of Representatives, and went on to defeat incumbent Governor Egan by a very narrow margin, thus breaking the stranglehold which the Democrats have had on all the state and national positions of Alaska since statehood.

With the re-election of Senator E. L. "Bob" Bartlett the U.S. Senate still remains a Democratic sacred preserve. Bartlett was first elected as a delegate to Congress in 1944. He is extremely popular and led the ticket in 1958 and again in 1960 when he ran for the Senate. His three-to-one majority in 1966 attests to his continuing personal popularity. His junior colleague, through the flip of a coin, Ernest Gruening, served as governor of Alaska longer than any man.[19] He was first appointed in 1939 by President Franklin D. Roosevelt and remained in the position until the advent of the Eisenhower administration in 1953. Gruening, who was born in 1887, has been a controversial political figure. As governor he antagonized many people by his aggressive policies in support of legislation he favored. In the election of 1958 he was denounced as a "carpetbagger" and was considered the most vulnerable candidate on the Democratic side. Four years later he received the greatest number of votes of any candidate in the election and probably pulled several Democrats through.

17. *Ibid.*, March 29, 1960, p. 9; April 5, 1960, p. 1.

18. Letter of Jeff Barry to Wendell Kay, *Jessen's Weekly* (Fairbanks), June 15, 1966.

19. E. L. "Bob" Bartlett won on the toss of a coin and was declared to be the "senior" senator. He drew the two-year term, and Ernest Gruening drew a four-year term.

Ralph Rivers, a former territorial attorney general, held the state's one seat in the national House of Representatives until 1966, when he was defeated by a Republican state senator, Howard Pollock. Pollock received the endorsement of the native groups in the northwest by promising to support their land claims, which Rivers had refused to do.

Both Republican candidates capitalized on the vulnerability of the Democrats in 1966—who could readily be blamed for anything and everything wrong in the state, since theirs had been the exclusive control since the beginning of state government in Alaska. Concern about the economy persisted; unemployment was still high; no ready solution to the problems affecting the native peoples had been found; and the costs of the growing bureaucracy had been increasing year by year. So the governorship and the congressional seat went to the Republicans.

PRESSURE GROUPS

Under the Alaska law, all lobbyists must register, declare the name of the organization which they represent, and then file a statement at the end of the session as to how much they spent in their attempts to influence special items of legislation. From 1913 to 1949, the representatives and agents of the Alaska Salmon Industry, Incorporated, and the Alaska Miners Association were called "The Alaska Lobby." Both industries were engaged in exploiting natural resources under control of the federal government. Their interests insofar as legislation was concerned were almost identical. They had nothing positive to ask of the territory; they sought only to keep the legislature from passing bills which might tend to increase the costs of government, and hence their taxes. To achieve its aims, "The Lobby" needed the support of 8 of the 16 members of the Senate who could prevent any bill from being enacted into law. Representatives of "The Lobby" did not disguise their contempt for the "yokel" legislators.[20]

The Alaska legislature today has much greater influence upon the economy than it did in the territorial era, and presumably has a good deal more to offer. When the legislature is in session Juneau is virtually besieged by representatives of various groups and interests asking for the support or defeat of measures of concern to them. Legislators are no longer treated with contempt, at least not openly. The cocktail lounge of the Baranof Hotel allegedly is the "third house" of the legislature where the important decisions are made by legislators and lobbyists. Lobbyists do serve a very useful purpose in the legislative process in Alaska as they do elsewhere. Frequently they supply the senators and representatives with a good deal of useful information which cannot otherwise be obtained.

The requests of the lobbyists are as varied as their interests. Today the Alaska Miners Association does have positive demands to make upon the state, such as a road to a mining area, or assurances that legislation restricting the activities of the Miners will not pass. The Miners have been particularly disturbed by repeated requests of sportsmen's associations and conservation groups to set up game preserves and to ban the use of the streams for waste from the mines. An organization called Yukon Power for America has obtained financial support from the state to publish material stressing the desirability of building a dam at Rampart. Travel agents and airline representatives believe that the legislature should appropriate more money for promoting the tourist industry. A representative of the Alaska

20. George W. Rogers, *Alaska in Transition: The Southeast Region* (Baltimore: Johns Hopkins Press, 1960), pp. 163-67.

Educational Association permanently resides in Juneau and is very active in seeking legislation benefiting the teachers. Both Indians and Eskimos now have their spokesmen in the Capital City. The Alaska Native Brotherhood is an old society and is much stronger among Indians than Eskimos. It has fought for equality with the whites, better educational facilities, and aid for building up the economy of the natives. An Eskimo group, the Arctic Slope Native Association, has recently been formed. It challenges the title of the state's claim to many lands which it says belong to the Eskimos and has given notice to a number of Alaska politicians that they must do much more for the natives if they expect to continue having their votes.[21] The State Chamber of Commerce seeks to keep an eye on state expenditures. It wants the legislature to reduce appropriations and has vigorously fought any increase of unemployment compensation benefits. Members of the Chamber are afraid that if Alaska becomes known as a "labor state" it will become increasingly difficult to attract the private investment needed to develop its resources. Representatives of the contractors' associations, construction unions, and the liquor interests probably constitute the dominant lobby groups in the state.

Labor's political organization, COPE, has been very active at the legislature and in endorsing candidates. Although it usually supports Democrats for office, it has not hesitated to "purge" Democrats who have bolted the labor party-line, especially on the issue of unemployment compensation benefits, and has endorsed Republicans whose views have been more satisfactory.[22]

LEGISLATIVE POLITICS

When the Alaskan constitution was adopted in 1956, few restrictions were placed upon the legislature. Acting upon the advice of the Public Administration Service, the framers of the constitution gave it the power to act. Meetings of the legislature are held annually, and there is no time limit on the length of the ordinary session, although special sessions must be concluded within thirty days after they are convened. The section of the constitution dealing with the enactment of special or local legislation is taken almost verbatim from the Model State Constitution.[23] Despite internal wranglings the Alaska state legislature in its short history has performed creditably and enacted much worthwhile legislation.

Few who sat in the first meeting of the state legislature in 1959 are still members. Defeat, retirement, and death have contributed to the change of personnel. Many senators and representatives, among them some of the most able, simply believe they cannot afford to leave their businesses and occupations three months of the year to attend legislative sessions in Juneau. In 1966 the House and Senate voted to raise salaries to $6,000 a year in the hope of attracting and keeping good people, but how many people will be influenced to remain, or go into, a profession as hazardous as politics is problematical. This turnover affects the composition of committees. Few legislators have been members of the same committee for any length of time. But even more important is the role played by the speaker of the House and the president of the Senate in handing out assignments. In 1965 veteran Democratic legislators in the House were by-passed and all committee

21. *Tundra Times* (Fairbanks), May 13, 1966, p. 1.

22. See *Anchorage Daily Times*, March 25, 1960, p. 11; April 5, 1960, p. 1.

23. Compare *Constitutional Studies*, prepared on behalf of the Alaska Statehood Committee for the Alaska Constitutional Convention by the Public Administration Service (Juneau, 1955), II, 10, with Article II, Section 19 of the Alaska State Constitution.

chairmanships were given to freshman representatives.[24] Further changes were effected by reason of former Governor Egan's reapportionment of the Senate by executive order, which meant that there were no holdovers in 1967.

The legislature is aided in its work by the Legislative Council and the Legislative Audit Committee, both of which are authorized by the state constitution, although the Council was actually established by the territorial government in 1953. Professional staff members of the Council have been most helpful to senators and representatives in drafting legislation, preparing reports, undertaking research, and holding public meetings. Five senators and five representatives, including the speaker of the House and the president of the Senate, who alternately act as head of the Council, comprise its membership.

Committees of both houses cooperate with each other. They sometimes meet together to listen to the testimony of witnesses. Prior to the 1965 legislative session a joint finance committee was in operation. The Alaska legislature has certain features which John Doyle, the executive secretary of the Legislative Council, describes as unicameral. Both houses sit as a single body to vote their approval or disapproval of gubernatorial appointments and to consider overriding vetoes.

Alaskan legislators are engaged in a variety of ways of making their living. Many are businessmen and professional people. There is usually a doctor or two among them, and several educators. Unlike many of the states, Alaska has few lawyers in her legislature. In the 1963-64 session, a dentist, Dr. E. I. Baggen, headed the judiciary committee of the House because of the lack of Republican lawyers in that body.[25] Some of the legislators are skilled laborers and trade union officials. Invariably the fishing industry is well represented, which is not surprising, since the legislature does not meet during the fishing season.

Democrats have usually controlled the legislature, sometimes by lopsided margins. Since statehood the Republicans first came close to success when they achieved a tie in the House of Representatives in 1963, when each party obtained twenty seats. With the aid of some dissident Democrats the Republicans were able to organize the House, elect the speaker, and pose as the majority party. Factionalism frequently has vitiated the Democratic strength. At no time was this more apparent than in the legislative session of 1966 when the three Republican senators practically held the balance of power because seventeen Democrats could not work together. Real Republican control was finally achieved in the 1966 election, when the party won the majority of seats in both the House and the Senate.

Republican legislators have concentrated their attack upon the alleged Democratic mismanagement of the state government and have in the past advocated amending the constitution to strip the governor of some of the vast powers he possesses. They would add several state positions to the elective list (which now includes only the governorship and the secretary of state's office), particularly that of the attorney general. They would place the responsibility for naming the heads of the departments of Education and Fish and Game in a commission independent of the governor. They generally portray the Democrats as the party of spenders and pose as the defenders of prudent fiscal management.

Actually there are few ideological differences between the two parties. The Democrats are not as liberal as they claim to be, nor are the Republicans as conservative. Democrats have been as vocal as Republicans in calling for economy in

24. *Anchorage Daily Times*, January 31, 1966, p. 1.

25. Terry C. Eakin, "Who Makes Our Laws: The Alaska Scene," unpublished manuscript presented to the Alaska Science Conference, Anchorage, Alaska, August 1963.

government. Republicans see no inconsistency in asking federal assistance to build a dam at Rampart while declaiming against the encroachments of a federal bureaucracy. Republican argument with the Democrats, with the exception of the ultra-conservative wing which has little voice in the party, boils down to a claim that they can do what the Democrats have done, only better. The 1966 election has given them an opportunity to make good their claims.

Sectional issues more than party differences divide legislators. The "Ice Bloc" is composed of the representatives from the North who have been loud in their protests that their section, which is the poorest and least populated area of the state, has been short-changed. They not only want more and better schools, and aid for their economy, but they also advocate the building of a road from Nome to Fairbanks which would serve only a handful of people. They in turn see little reason to support the state-owned ferry system which serves as a marine highway for the towns of southeastern Alaska which are shut off from the rest of the state and each other by mountains and water. Republican legislators from south central and interior Alaska, where the bulk of workers engaged in the seasonal construction trades live, have joined with Democrats to raise payments for unemployment compensation. There is an abiding fear that Anchorage will become increasingly more powerful in state affairs. The new reapportionment scheme, recently promulgated, increased the already large representation of Anchorage in the legislature. In 1960 and 1962 the voters turned down an initiative measure which would have moved the state capital from Juneau in the southeast to a place "closer to the center of population" in the Anchorage area.

VOTING HABITS

Alaska is too young a state and the majority of the population is too new for any definite patterns of voting to have developed. Most of the people with the exception of the natives were not born in the state. Whatever voting habits they might have, they probably brought with them. One woman has attributed the large Democratic vote in Alaska to the many Southerners living in the state, but Alaskan Democrats do not generally reflect the traditional Southern attitudes. In general the Democrats find their greatest strength in the outlying areas rather than in the urban centers. It was the vote from the "bush" which saved Representative Rivers from defeat in 1964 after he had lost his home town, Fairbanks, and Anchorage, the state's two largest cities. But it defeated him in 1966. Anchorage, which was formerly looked upon as a Democratic stronghold, seems to swing alternately from one party to the other. Southeastern Alaska, which was most opposed to statehood and was regarded as probably the most conservative section of the state, is changing as a result of the increasing development of the pulp and lumber industries. It now leans Democratic. Although Alaska has been very much a Democratic state in the past, the Democrats have learned that they cannot afford to dismiss the Republicans lightly. Democratic successes in the past are partly due to their better known and more experienced candidates at the top levels. Democrats were rudely shaken when Richard Nixon defeated John Kennedy in the presidential election of 1960 in Alaska, and again two years later when the Republicans won the same number of seats in the House of Representatives as they. But they were really jolted out of their complacency in 1966.

Although Alaska Republicans may well rejoice over the outcome of the 1966 election, they should remain cautious in evaluating its significance. Two years after a defeat that seemed to doom them to a decade of opposition they have become the majority party, no longer subject to the taunts of being a mere faction or splinter group. They were able to work together much better than in years past, and were far less divided among themselves than were the Democrats. Their campaign had a more professional look. They were able to make inroads upon the Arctic natives and labor groups who did not support the Democrats as strongly as in the past. They brought new faces into politics which may have helped in winning the 1966 election and in building up their image for the future. They succeeded in recovering a very strong segment of the press support which they had lost in 1964. But in a state where Democratic registration is still in a majority of more than two to one, the Republican roots are shallow and must continue to be cultivated.[26]

IMPACT OF NATIONAL POLITICS AND TRENDS

National issues play only a small role in Alaskan politics unless they directly affect the interests of the state. Alaska's dependence upon the federal government has been repeatedly mentioned, and the need for federal support to develop its resources is great. In 1964 the percentage of the population voting for President Johnson was greater in Alaska than in the country as a whole. This was not so much in support of the President as a vote against Goldwater whose policies Alaskans believed would, if carried out, be harmful to the state. The reaction against the Republican candidate was so great that it undoubtedly helped to carry a good many Democrats to victory.[27] Republicans, who had gained much in the 1960 and 1962 elections, suffered a humiliating defeat and were reduced to a handful in the Senate and only slightly more in the House, only to win outstanding victories in the nonpresidential year of 1966.

Alaska, which borders on the Pacific, is very much concerned about American relations with the Soviet Union and Japan. Resentment against the Russians is strong in many areas because of the encroachment of their fishermen in waters Alaskans regard as their own. Repeated requests have been made to the State Department for strong action against these interlopers. The attitude toward Japan is quite ambivalent. Alaskan officials have protested to the State Department, as in the case of the Russians, about Japanese fishing in the Alaskan area. But Alaska also looks to Japan as an even greater market for its raw materials and its representatives support the liberalization of trade relations between the Japanese and the American governments.

Senator Gruening has taken the unpopular side of the debate in the Vietnam war. He condemns American involvement as being illegal as well as immoral. He has been a critic of the American aid program, and believes that the money which is being spent, sometimes in behalf of countries whose friendship toward the United States is dubious, might be much better used in helping the poor of America, and in helping to develop Alaska. The Senator's personal popularity still appears to be strong in the state.

---

26. See Herman E. Slotnick, "The 1966 Election in Alaska," *Western Political Quarterly*, XX (June 1967, Part 2), 524-28.

27. See Slotnick, "The 1964 Election in Alaska," *Western Political Quarterly*, XVIII (June 1965, Part 2), 439-42.

ARIZONA:

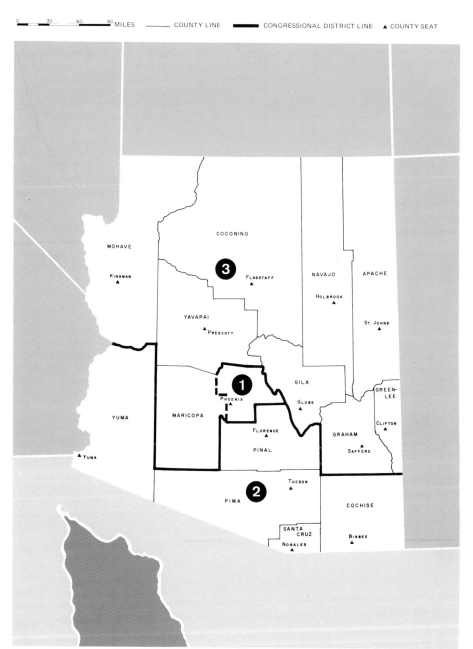

MOHAVE

KINGMAN ▲

COCONINO

③ FLAGSTAFF ▲

NAVAJO

HOLBROOK ▲

APACHE

ST. JOHNS ▲

YAVAPAI

PRESCOTT ▲

YUMA

MARICOPA

① PHOENIX ▲

GILA

GLOBE ▲

GREEN-LEE

CLIFTON ▲

FLORENCE ▲

PINAL

GRAHAM

SAFFORD ▲

▲ YUMA

PIMA

② TUCSON ▲

COCHISE

SANTA CRUZ

NOGALES ▲

BISBEE ▲

Ross R. Rice

Politics in Transition

Lusty, young Arizona was recognized as "liberal," "progressive," "radical" at its time of statehood (1912). Yet most of the state's subsequent political history has been one of conservative hue under the label of the Democratic party, which is only now seeing a moderately liberal wing emerge. Since World War II the Republicans, centered in metropolitan areas and in part even more conservative than Arizona's early Democrats, have made inroads into state politics. Arizona's political future may be at least moderately conservative, although the years to come may bring about a working two-party system with perhaps some shifts among the groups wielding effective economic and political power.

Significant factors helping to explain Arizona's political present include political myths perpetuated from a brief past, vast distances, sparse but booming oasis population, limited water sources, mineral and other natural resource development, influence of the press, rural-mining overrepresentation in the state Senate, a skewed tax structure, near one-party domination in past elections, and volatile interests thrust forward by the state's newcomers.

GEOGRAPHY AND RESOURCES

Arizona covers 113,909 square miles, placing it sixth in land area nationally. Topographically, there are three zones. To the northeast is a vast expanse of the Colorado Plateau, 5,000 to 7,000 feet above sea level, with scant precipitation and sparse population, consisting largely of Indian reservations (the Hopi and Navajo). A second, narrower, rugged, timbered mountain zone traverses the state diagonally, southeast to northwest. Here precipitation is higher, but population is still scattered. The third zone which covers the southwest quadrant is semiarid, referred to inaptly as "desert," where population is concentrated in two "oasis" areas. Here the annual precipitation sinks to a mere 7.20 inches at Phoenix and to an even scantier 3.03 inches on the Colorado River at Yuma. The range of elevation in the state extends over 10,000 feet.

Land, minerals, and forests exist in variety and abundance. A fourth natural resource, water, has been in continuing scarcity, conditioning economic development and the growth of population. The first wave of white men entered the territory following the Civil War, many engaging in mining gold, silver, and copper. Vast areas were available for cattle grazing. Copper and cattle were the big "C's" of the economy to the days of statehood in 1912. Arizona has led the mining states in copper production continuously since 1910; and more recently lead, zinc, uranium, manganese, and sand and gravel used in building construction have been of increasing importance. The decade of the 1950's saw the state's first gas and oil wells in the Indian country of the "four corners" area of the northeast.

The forests of Arizona cover mountainous areas from the White Mountains along the New Mexico border northwestward to the Grand Canyon. Hardwoods are scarce, the mainstay being the relatively soft ponderosa pine.

Facing a deficit of precipitation in the fertile valleys of central and southern Arizona, man early sought ways to provide dependable supplies of supplemental water. Virtually every body of surface water within the state has been impounded behind stone, concrete, and earthen dams. Roosevelt Dam on the Salt River was dedicated in 1911 as the pioneer project of the newly created United States Bureau of Reclamation.

Along the Colorado are Glen Canyon, Hoover, Davis, and Parker dams. These and others supply water for hydroelectric power, flood control, and recreation, plus water for the Yuma and Imperial valleys and the Metropolitan Water District of Los Angeles. During and since World War II underground water was "mined" by electric pumps in the Salt and Casa Grande valleys chiefly for cotton production. A falling water table prompted the state legislature to place a moratorium on the drilling of further wells for agricultural purposes.[1]

For nearly half a century mining led the brief list of Arizona industries on a dollar basis. The copper-mining counties of Cochise, Gila, Greenlee, Pima, Pinal, and Yavapai count such corporate giants as Phelps-Dodge and Kennecott. The long reign of copper was brought to a halt by the rise of agriculture, particularly crop agriculture led by cotton, during World War II. The leading cotton counties have been Maricopa and Pinal. Through the 1950's agriculture continued to surpass mining in dollar production, except for a brief period in the middle of the decade. Tourism has experienced a rise throughout the past two decades. Central and southern Arizona are popular meccas where "winter visitors" from colder regions of the nation headquarter from early December into April, while the higher elevations of the northern part of the state lure the residents of the southern desert during the hot summer months. During the last half of the 1950's manufacturing grew to occupy the first position among Arizona industries. Refrigeration equipment, aluminum, aircraft, and aircraft components have appeared in the past two decades, and, more recently, transistors and computers. The most recent important industry is electronics, which has risen rapidly, due partially to the decision of the U.S. Army Signal Corps to locate its electronic proving ground at Fort Huachuca in 1954. Motorola is the largest industrial employer in the state. Those manufacturing industries which have experienced particular growth have been those whose products are in the high-value-low-weight classification.

The construction industry has prospered steadily in both residential and commercial categories. Middlewestern and eastern capital has been attracted in quantity in recent times, and speculation in raw desert acreage has been common practice. The pattern of land ownership in the state contributes more than a little to the recent speculative surge. Of Arizona's land area, 71 percent is either federally owned or held in federal trust, 14 percent is state owned, and 15 percent is privately owned. The pressure on both federal and state land management agencies to make more land available to private development is mounting.

The per capita income for the state was $2,528 in 1966, below the national average. Partly accounting for this is the high Arizona percentage of low-paying jobs in trades and services, plus the fact that many of the state's Indians still live on job-scarce reservations. The climatic attractions and advantages to health-

1. Arizona water problems, politics, and administration are covered in Dean E. Mann, *The Politics of Water in Arizona* (Tucson: University of Arizona Press, 1963).

seekers result in depressed wage and salary scales due to competition for available jobs. With more than two-thirds of the state's land area in such forms as Indian reservations, national forests, national parks and monuments, and military installations, the impact of federal spending is considerable.

POPULATION FACTORS

White men entered Arizona from Old Mexico as early as 1539, but substantial peopling of the area has been relatively recent. At the time of the Civil War an estimated five hundred whites lived in the territory. The United States acquired Arizona by the Treaty of Guadalupe-Hidalgo ending the Mexican War in 1848, and by the Gadsden Purchase five years later. Arizona was part of a joint territory with New Mexico until 1863, when Congress separated the two. The end of the Indian wars, the railroads, further exploration, limited economic exploitation, and population growth by the end of the century made statehood possible in 1912.

By that time Arizona could claim 204,354 inhabitants. Subsequent population increase was modest yet steady, but the impact of immigration did not hit until the war years of the early 1940's. During this decade the percentage of population increase was second only to that of California, and fourth nationally during the 1950's. In this twenty-year period the population rocketed from half a million to 1,302,161 in 1960. An estimate of July 1, 1967, placed the state's inhabitants at 1,660,000.[2]

Recent growth has been concentrated principally within two counties of the south-central region. The most populous county, Maricopa, about doubled between 1940 and 1950, when a total of 331,770 was reached. In the next decade it doubled again, reaching 663,510. By July 1967 it had climbed to an estimated 890,000, coinciding with reports of a somewhat slackened economy. The same pattern was true in Pima County—from 72,838 in 1940 to an estimated 328,000 in July 1967. Maricopa County (Phoenix) has just over 50 percent and Pima County (Tucson) over 20 percent of the total state inhabitants, but these combined had only four votes in the state Senate before reapportionment in 1966. Further, the four smallest counties total only approximately 4 percent of the population, but together had eight votes in the upper house.

Although births outnumber deaths in Arizona, the chief cause of the great population jump has been immigration from other states. Many ex-servicemen, who spent the war years at military installations in Arizona, were attracted as permanent residents. In the decade before World War II, migration was largely from the Democratic states of Oklahoma and Texas, but the war years saw the balance swing to the Middlewest and East. Today nearly two-thirds of the state's residents were born elsewhere. Since 1960 the five states supplying the largest number of new Arizonans were as follows: California, Illinois, New York, Ohio, and Texas. Net migration population gain slackened after 1960, reaching its lowest valley in 1964, followed by a peaking period once again.

The fastest growing age brackets in the past two decades have been for those under 15 and over 65 years. The socioeconomic characteristics are being further modified by the addition of many married couples over fifty years of age, many of whom come to the state to escape the rigors of northern winters. They are often well situated financially, perhaps able to open a small business. But Arizona has a

2. *Arizona Statistical Review* (Phoenix: Valley National Bank, 1967).

young population: there are more persons under five years of age than over sixty-five.

Churches of most denominations abound in the state. Among those perhaps better represented in Arizona than in numbers nationally are Roman Catholics, Mormons (Church of Jesus Christ of Latter-day Saints), Seventh Day Adventists, and Southern Baptists. Various Pentecostal groups are active, frequently sponsoring tent revivals.

The 1960 census figures placed the ratio of Caucasians to Indians at fourteen to one with Negroes numbering less than 4 percent of the state's population. In all, Arizona's nonwhite population in 1960 was just over 10 percent, and thus not far from the national percentage. But Arizona has fewer Negroes and many more Indians than is true nationally. A concentration of Negroes lies in a strip along the south side of Phoenix, near the Southern Pacific railroad yards adjacent to an area largely inhabited by persons of Spanish-American extraction. There have been one or two Negroes from South Phoenix legislative districts in the state House of Representatives over the past decade and a half, and one Negro was elected to the Senate in 1966.

Arizona's 83,000 Indians (1960 census) are largely living on reservations, and include Apaches, Navajos, Hopis, Papagos, and Pimas. The Navajo, once one of the poorer tribes, is currently experiencing new wealth as a result of uranium, oil, gas and coal development in the northeastern part of the state. Because of the vastness of the Navajo reservation and the difficulty in accounting for Indians living off reservations, it is impossible to secure reliable census data. A recent estimate of the Bureau of Indian Affairs would place the present number at about 91,500 on reservations alone—evidence of a current increase of the state's Indian population.

Approximately 194,000 residents are of Mexican extraction and have Spanish surnames; to hear Spanish spoken on the streets and in the stores of many Arizona communities is commonplace. These persons may experience some difficulty in finding employment, but less than that encountered by Negroes. The political influence of the Mexican-Americans has never been great, in contrast to the situation in neighboring New Mexico. Both minority groups, Negroes and Mexican-Americans, are making attempts to learn and practice the political skills and organization of whites and "Anglos." Arizona is, therefore, a composite of several cultures: Indian, Spanish (and later Mexican), the South, and the West of the United States. Arizona has a rapidly changing urban population and this is a factor that underlies its political change.

EDUCATIONAL POLITICS

Arizona makes a considerable effort to give financial support to education particularly at the elementary and secondary school levels. High teacher certification standards have been established, and considering its limited economic resources, the state endeavors to meet the rising costs of education largely by increases in state and county aid.

Currently Arizona is one of the five states requiring five years of preparation for elementary school teachers, and one of eight requiring five years for secondary school teachers. While the state's per capita income is about one-third of the distance from the bottom of the scale, teachers' salaries have stood consistently among those of the top ten states nationally until recently.

Schools are financed primarily by the property tax levied at the school district level, by state support, by county support (established by state legislative action), and by federal funds, in that order. Over 300 school districts exist in the state, but no real effort has been made toward their consolidation.

In the area of higher education, the organizational and financial aspects are less impressive. A single Board of Regents is responsible for policy development for the university and college system. There are only three state institutions beyond the junior college level. Considerable sectional jealousy has been evident in the development of the University of Arizona (Tucson), Arizona State University (Tempe), and Arizona State College (Flagstaff), the last-named institution becoming Northern Arizona University in 1966. The establishment of the first medical school in the state illustrated the sectional rivalry between the Phoenix and Tucson areas. In August 1961, the Board of Regents gave the nod to the University of Arizona as the location of the proposed new medical school, rejecting a site in the Phoenix area and affiliation with Arizona State University. The University of Arizona is the land-grant institution, having a variety of professional schools. Arizona State University and Northern Arizona University were, at one time, teacher colleges, but a number of professional programs have been established in the past decade in both institutions.

In 1960 the Arizona legislature passed a junior college law creating a state junior college board and authorizing the establishment of junior college districts in counties that met certain minimum criteria. Junior colleges are in operation in Yuma, Graham, and Cochise counties, and three branches exist in Maricopa County (with two more coming). There is a junior college planned for Pima County, the home of the University of Arizona. Similar colleges are slated for Pinal and Yavapai counties.

The development of private colleges within the state has been slow. The only four-year private institutions are Grand Canyon College (Phoenix), founded by the Southern Baptists, and Prescott College under the auspices of the United Church (Congregational). The Latter-day Saints church (Mormon) acquired property for a university site in Phoenix, but no development has commenced. There is no Catholic-supported college as yet. The unique American Institute of Foreign Trade (near Glendale) trains young men in area studies for business and industrial positions abroad.

THE PRESS AND PUBLIC OPINION

Thirteen daily and some fifty weekly newspapers operate within the state. Residents of Tucson have, in the past, had the opportunity of choosing between competitive dailies, the morning *Arizona Daily Star*, published by William R. Matthews, and the evening *Tucson Daily Citizen*. The *Star* generally has favored Democratic candidates, while the *Citizen*, published by William A. Small, has endorsed Republican candidates. Both dailies have been printed by the same physical facilities for a number of years. In January 1965 the *Citizen* purchased the *Star*, leading to the filing of an anti-trust action against the *Citizen*.

Residents of the Phoenix metropolitan area may read either of two large metropolitan dailies published by Eugene C. Pulliam. The morning *Arizona Republic* and the evening *Phoenix Gazette* employ separate editorial staffs, and infrequently differ on minor local issues. Pulliam, who also owns Indiana newspapers, came to Arizona in the late 1940's and dedicated himself to utilizing his two Phoenix newspapers to make Arizona a two-party state. For over a decade the Pulliam newspapers in Phoenix served as a significant force in raising Republican fortunes to a more competitive position with those of the Democrats. These Phoenix newspapers lent editorial endorsement, in many instances, to Republican candidates. The existence of the *Arizona Republic's* conservative stance is illustrated by its editorial support of the John Birch Society in late 1960. Several years later, the *Republic* disavowed the Society's leader, Robert Welch. Early in 1964, both Pulliam newspapers added new opinion pages, which feature a selection of columnists identifiable as liberal writers, in varying degree. In 1962, the Phoenix dailies supported the re-election bid of United States Senator Carl Hayden (Democrat) against the Republican nominee Evan Mecham. The realization that Arizona was approaching a level of two-party competition was perhaps reflected in the Phoenix newspapers' editorial support of Samuel P. Goddard, Democrat, in his contest for the governorship in 1964. Admiring the conservatism of Arizona's presidential candidate Barry Goldwater in 1964, the Pulliam newspapers refrained from sharp attacks against the publisher's long-time acquaintance, Lyndon B. Johnson, and only in the closing days of the campaign did the Phoenix dailies give lukewarm public support to Goldwater.

Two efforts in recent years to commence opposition newspapers, one on the Democratic-liberal side and the other of ultra-conservative Republican hue, have proved to be unsuccessful thus far.[3]

There are in the state eleven television channels: four in Phoenix (one educational TV), three in Tucson (one educational), and two in Yuma. The unusually large number of twenty-four radio stations operate in the Phoenix area, but their programing in many cases is limited to nonpolitical canned music.

Phoenix area radio station KRUX intersperses a steady diet of teen-age rock and roll music with conservative-line editorials, one frequent target being the stands and activities of the PTA. Phoenix radio station KOOL does some labeled editorializing, but the approach is cautious.

Outdoor advertising is a big business in the state with campaigners utilizing this mass medium. Some Republican campaigners have in the past "overlooked" including the Republican label in billboard advertising, concentrating upon an appeal directed to Democratic and independent voters to vote for "the man." More recently, because of an increase in the number of Republican primary contests and the political heat they engender, the name "Republican" has become more politically respectable and of more widespread campaign use.

Arizona has had no "Campaigns, Inc.," but public relations firms have regularly played leading roles in planning and managing recent campaigns. Recently the pharmaceutical manufacturing business of Stephen Shadegg has been the location of much Republican strategy development, particularly for past campaigns of Barry Goldwater. In his campaigns for governor, Sam Goddard used opinion surveys by a California-based firm. Barry Goldwater, who had been managed in 1958 by Stephen Shadegg (Shadegg a doubter of polling), turned to campaign management by an Arizona-based opinion survey firm in anticipation of his U.S. Senate race in 1968.

Newspaper editorial opinion cannot wholly be equated with public opinion in Arizona, of course. Editorials more frequently coincide with election results

3. Other dailies are the *Bisbee Daily Review*, *Douglas Daily Dispatch*, *Arizona Daily Sun* (Flagstaff), *Mesa Tribune*, *Nogales Daily Herald*, *Prescott Evening Courier*, *Tempe Daily News*, *Yuma Sun* and *Sentinel*, and the *Scottsdale Progress*.

for initiative and referendum measures than with election results for candidates. The very complexity of the propositions on the ballot throws the less-informed voter onto the editorial advice of the newspaper he reads. The electorate will also have the opportunity to assess political candidates at home via television and radio broadcasts but much campaigning across the state by automobile persists. An increasing number of campaigners have taken to airplane travel to fulfill speaking engagements, Barry Goldwater being noted for piloting his own aircraft while enroute to political gatherings.

NOMINATIONS AND ELECTIONS

The electoral system in Arizona encompasses the permanent registration system, low registration of voting eligibles, nominations by closed primaries without pre-primary endorsements, nomination by plurality, and use of the party-column ballot form.

Voters who participate in either the primary or general elections (or both) every two years remain registered under the state's system of permanent voter registration. Of 919,000 estimated eligibles, only 584,284 were registered in 1966, constituting an unimpressive 62.8 percent of eligible voters actually registered. The usual voter qualifications of U.S. citizenship, minimum age of 21 years, and state (one year) and county (30 days) residency apply. Effective in 1964 the residency requirement was lowered to six months for voting for presidential electors only. Arizona has a literacy requirement of the ability to read the U.S. Constitution in English and to sign one's name, but seldom is this requirement posed as a test for a person seeking to register. The Federal Voting Rights Law of 1965 seemed to abolish the literacy requirement, and several Arizona counties (led by Apache) appeared at first as possibilities for the use of federal voter registrars, but the final outcome was in the negative. Voter disqualifications eliminate from balloting the usual groups such as the insane, the mentally deficient, those deprived of civil rights for conviction of felonies, and those under guardianship. The last of these excluded reservation Indians from use of the franchise until a 1948 state Supreme Court decision held that court-appointed guardianship, not that of "Uncle Sam," was the meaning of the constitutional restriction. This decision affected several counties, in particular Navajo and Apache which contain large numbers of Hopi and Apache Indians; but other factors of illiteracy, distance, semi-poverty, and lack of motivation have contributed to keep many reservation-dwellers from the polls.

An underlying factor in the rise of the Arizona Republican party over the past two decades has been a striking rise in Republican registrations in that period. From a 7-1 Democratic margin in 1934, the ratio dropped to 4.5-1 by 1950. The postwar influx of Republicans into the state continued to narrow the margin to 2.5-1 by 1954. Democrats still outregister Republicans in all counties, but statewide the Democrats lost 2 percent in registrations between 1964 and 1966.

Table I makes county comparisons of voter registration by parties, the percentage of registered voters actually voting, and percentages of the total statewide vote in the general election of 1966. It should be noted that 1966 was a victory year for Republicans in Arizona and that voter participation was below normal. Voter registrations now stand at 3-2 favoring the Democrats.

Although narrowing margins in some counties such as Maricopa, Pima, and Yavapai (Prescott) still cast the Republican party in those counties in the under-

TABLE I
ARIZONA VOTING STATISTICS
1966 GENERAL ELECTION

County	Democratic % of Registered Voters of Two Major Parties	% of Registered Voters Participating	County % of Statewide Vote
Apache	74.7	56.4	1.0
Cochise	79.2	69.7	3.3
Coconino	64.5	60.6	2.3
Gila	88.5	72.6	2.2
Graham	78.1	68.3	1.1
Greenlee	93.6	74.8	.8
Maricopa	56.8	67.7	55.5
Mohave	72.9	63.4	1.0
Navajo	71.1	65.7	2.0
Pima	61.4	66.3	20.6
Pinal	80.6	68.0	3.6
Santa Cruz	83.0	71.6	.7
Yavapai	59.0	71.7	2.9
Yuma	74.6	63.7	3.0
Total for state			100.0
State average	62.2	67.3	

Source: Secretary of State, *General Election Registration*, October 24, 1966.

dog role, a glint of electoral success in the party precinct organizations can bring out the Republican registrants in the face of Democratic lethargy and more appealing Republican nominees. An Arizona political tradition antedating World War II had new residents of Republican persuasion registering as Democrats in their newly adopted state because of Democratic political preponderance, but the trend since 1945 has been toward registration in the Republican party for newcomers whose politics had previously been of that stripe. As in the case with other postwar growth areas (e.g., California and Florida), party registration is not synonymous with party loyalty on general election days.

Third parties have been included in Arizona primaries, but none were listed recently until the Socialist-Labor party appeared in 1960 and 1964. Statutes provide that a party keeps its place in the primaries by receiving 5 percent of the total vote cast in the last election for governor, or a new party may gain recognition by petitions showing signatures amounting to 2 percent of the total vote cast in at least five counties in the preceding election. Despite these modest requirements the state was without third parties on the ballot for a dozen years, a situation which coincides with the national eclipse of minor parties during the same period. A legislative act of 1961 (passed at a peak of anti-Communist fervor and led by the John Birch Society), establishing a loyalty oath for state and local government employees, also declared that the Communist party "shall not be entitled to be recognized or certified as a political party under the laws of the state of Arizona." The oath has since been invalidated by the U.S. Supreme Court.

Nominations for federal, state, and county offices are made by closed party primary elections held eight weeks preceding the general elections (this makes the primaries fall about the middle of September) every even-numbered year. This late primary date, one of the last in the nation, leaves little time to a party for licking wounds inflicted in the primary contests, for organizing the precinct, county, and state committee machinery, and for mapping campaign strategy and tactics aimed at the rapidly approaching general election date. Because of lack of contested primaries, Arizona Republicans have not until recently suffered much intra-party damage. The party has actually had uncontested primaries (or has lacked candidates completely) for certain statewide offices, some legislative seats, and many county offices.

Some recent successful Republican nominees, such as Howard Pyle, Barry Goldwater, and Paul Fannin, were recruited through party machinery, but from outside state party politics. Pyle, for the governorship in 1950, came from radio broadcasting; Goldwater, for the U.S. Senate in 1952, was drawn from business and the nonpartisan Phoenix City Council; and Paul Fannin, for the governorship in 1958, came from a successful business venture, which had made the name "Fannin Gas" known throughout the state. These "drafted" candidates had the benefit of escaping the rigors of primary campaigns.

The Arizona Republican party experienced a three-way gubernatorial primary in 1956, but this lacked the bitterness of some Democratic primary fights, and of Republican primaries to come in the decade of the 1960's. A particularly hard fought intra-party battle in 1962 aided in producing a decisive victory for the Democratic veteran senator, Carl Hayden. In a successful attempt to create party harmony, Harry Rosenzweig of Phoenix, a long-time political associate of Barry Goldwater's, who assumed the state party chairmanship in May 1965, invited six known-to-be-willing gubernatorial candidates to a meeting of precinct committeemen in the fall of that year, letting each candidate speak, and hoping to extract a pledge from each not to become an active candidate if the working precinct committeemen could reach a consensus to support but one hopeful in the 1966 primary. At least two additional candidates made their interest known after Rosenzweig's meeting, which had deferred its attempt at agreement until early in 1966. In the end, three moderates made the race, and followed the theme of California's "Parkinson's eleventh commandment," refraining from attacking each other, but joining in the attack on the incumbent Democratic governor.

Arizona Democrats have engaged in wide-open party primaries over the state's history. The state's election code provides for nomination by plurality (no run-offs), and the Democrats, for example, gave the nomination for the governorship in 1950 to a woman candidate, Mrs. Ana Frohmiller, who had a winning 29 percent in a field with five male opponents. Incumbent officeholders of both parties may use their patronage to develop personal vote-getting organizations designed to assist them through future primaries. In the absence of any method of pre-primary endorsements by party machinery, the recently formed Arizona Democratic Council (patterned after the successful California club movement) met in the summer of 1964 and again in 1966 to hear and endorse candidates for major statewide offices. A number of ranking Democratic leaders have expressed concern over their party's tendency toward wide-open primaries and sometimes wounded feelings that result, and have looked with some interest at pre-primary endorsements by auxiliary party organizations. Most of such interest has come from the party's liberal wing, and included then U.S. Representative Stewart Udall (now Interior Department Secretary) following Democratic losses in the general election in 1958.

The failure of Republican candidates to bring out a sizable primary vote is not surprising in view of the lack of races. But a small vote does not necessarily augur a candidate's defeat in the general election. For example, Barry Goldwater received only 38,025 votes in the 1958 no-contest primary, but eight weeks later he was elected with a total vote of 164,593. Ernest McFarland picked up only 17,601 votes in the general election over his primary vote, while Goldwater was reaping 126,568 additional votes over his September amount. In 1966 Jack Williams, whose primary showing was only 37,409, won the governorship with 203,438 votes—53.8 percent of the statewide total.

A number of bills was introduced in the state legislature throughout the 1950's to move the Arizona primaries to an earlier date, one in June being most commonly suggested. Precinct committeemen are elected in the primaries, one committeeman to be chosen for each multiple of 125 votes cast for the party's nominee for governor in the last election. County and state committees, for which officers will be elected, are required by law to meet in conventions before the end of September. Both parties could benefit from a longer period in which to perfect their party organization and plan campaign strategy, but up to the present the Democrats would have received greater advantage from an extension of time to heal intra-party wounds remaining from their bitter primary contests. Although little opposition has been voiced toward moving the date, action, which would benefit both parties, has not materialized.

The Arizona election code calls for the use of the Indiana party-column ballot. Despite the ease thus created for straight-ticket voting, split ballots have been increasing over the past two decades. Electrical voting machines are now in use in the larger precincts of Maricopa and Pima counties; paper ballots are still used in smaller precincts and in outlying counties. Grouped at the top of the November general election ballot are the offices of judges of the supreme court, the courts of appeals and superior courts, and tax commissioner, under the heading "Judicial Offices." These are presumably nonpartisan because no party label is attached, but nominations are made for these offices eight weeks earlier in the party primaries. Following this group the party columns begin and a straight ticket can be voted for the balance of the ballot.

On the extreme right hand of the ballot or machine (Shoup machines are more common) appear any propositions to be voted on, which may include initiative and referendum measures either to amend the constitution or to add to the statutes. This placement is a contributing factor to their smaller vote than that cast for the prominent offices placed on the left side of the ballot. All offices and propositions appear on a single ballot, but the ballot is long. The 1964 general election ballot in Maricopa County contained sixty-four offices and six propositions; the 1966 off-year ballot carried thirty-one offices and but one proposition.

The only use of party conventions in Arizona to make nominations (other than to choose a substitute in the case of a nominee who dies after the primary) is to name delegates to the national nominating convention every presidential election year. No presidential primary exists in Arizona. The state committee which is chosen late in September of an off-year election meets in Phoenix in the spring of the next presidential election year to name national convention delegates. In 1964 Arizona had sixteen votes in the Republican convention, nineteen in the Democratic gathering. As in the past, the Democratic state convention in 1964 named twice as many delegates as there were votes—each delegate casting one-half vote—(plus the national committeemen with full votes) and voted to bind the Arizona delegation to abide by the unit rule.

The Democratic state convention of April 1960, after considerable uproar, resulted in control of the national delegation going to the liberal group, the losing conservative strength being chiefly from Maricopa County. U.S. Representative Stewart Udall, whose personal choice for the nomination was John F. Kennedy, was later elected chairman of the delegation. Governor Nelson Rockefeller never had real support in Arizona Republican circles, the nod going to Richard Nixon until the Goldwater boomlet started in the late spring which resulted in the designation of the Arizona senator as a favorite-son candidate.

The style of campaigning in the state has undergone change in the period since World War II. Public rallies, picnics, and barbecues have lost their popularity to television and other forms of diversion. Public relations firms are increasingly employed to package whole campaigns. Despite the potentialities of reaching the multitudes through the media of modern mass communications the personal touch in campaigning is still valued. Howard Pyle's campaign manager for the governorship in 1950, Barry Goldwater, flew the candidate into even out-of-the-way communities of the large state. Many candidates still depend upon footleather, a smile, and a handshake up and down dusty small-town streets, with visits into stores and shops to greet patrons and proprietors alike. Caravans of candidates have traversed the state by auto. Morning coffees involving a single candidate and a small, intimate group of ladies in a home have gained popularity in the state. U.S. Representative John J. Rhodes has used this technique considerably.

The Arizona statutes are certainly not overrestrictive in placing bounds on campaign spending. Statutory limitations on spending apply only to the primaries: $3,500 for U.S. senator, $2,500 for member of Congress or governor, with other offices scaled lower. The statutes do not limit spending by the various party and citizen committees, although these groups are required to file reports. Furthermore, the categories of expenditures made exempt by the statutes are more costly than the categories which fall under the restriction. Exempted are costs of television, radio, motion pictures, printing and advertisements in newspapers, outdoor advertising signs, stationery, postage, and personal traveling and subsistence. The few classifications of expenditure which are limited are of minor importance and have no actual restrictive effect.

A candidate for the U.S. Senate running from this state of a million and a half inhabitants must be able to tap sources yielding in the neighborhood of $200,000 if he is to keep up with his competition. Prior to 1966 Republican candidates have had an advantage in being able to concentrate their spending on the general election campaign, whereas Democratic nominees may have used up sizable portions of their budgets in capturing the primary party nominations.

The statutes clearly specify that names and addresses of donors must be reported, but an examination of the filed reports will disclose anonymous contributions and others where first names or addresses have been omitted. The secretary of state has neither staff nor funds to assure that the reports are properly filed. Once received, they go into a folder only to be disinterred by an occasional enterprising newspaper reporter or researcher. In 1967 the state Republican party organization was endeavoring to establish a statewide fund-raising program, with such funds then to be centrally channeled to nominees. The effort seemed to be aimed at persuading donors to give to the party rather than to individual personalities. Arizona Democrats have the same problem of funds going to individual candidates and not to the party organization for dispersal.

Campaign funds are derived from a number of sources. Besides "fatcats," the "kitty" or "flower fund" may still be in operation in some offices headed by elective officials, many of whom must seek re-election every two years. Such funds are presumably voluntary, but the political employee has had no civil service protection if he fails to do what is expected of him. Fund-raising dinners supply additional monies. Senator Goldwater's contributors have included oilmen, and the roster of donors listed in his expense report filed in 1958 looked like a "Who's Who" of American business. COPE has made contributions in a number of instances. Founder Robert Welch of the John Birch Society reported a donation to Senator Goldwater's re-election campaign in 1958.

PARTY ORGANIZATION AND PARTY LEADERS

Formal party organization in Arizona resembles the pyramidal structure found in other states. There are precinct committees, perhaps informal area committees (as in Maricopa County), and county and state committees. One element lacking is ward and city organization. Most municipal elections are conducted along nonpartisan lines, the principal exception being the city of Tucson.

Candidates for the party office of precinct committeeman qualify to have their names appear on the primary ballot by submitting nomination papers with a sufficient number of signatures. A party is entitled to one committeeman per precinct for every 125 votes cast in the precinct for the party's candidate for governor in the last general election. Prior to 1967, when a Republican was serving as governor, as in 1951-55 and 1959-65, the minority Republican party was in the anomalous position of being entitled to more precinct committeemen than the Democratic party—the party which had 3-2 voter registrations and held most statewide elective offices.

The state statutes specify the membership, officers, and meeting time for organization of the county committees. The precinct committeemen elected in the September party primary attend or send written proxies to a county convention. State committees consist of the chairman from each county plus one delegate for each 400 votes cast in the county for the party's candidate for governor in the last election.

The day following the state conventions, the statutes require "party councils" consisting of the nominees, the national committeemen, and members of the state executive committee, to meet at the capitol to formulate party platforms. In 1958 the Republican party council took the approach that a brief statement of principles would be more realistic than a platform and accordingly drafted only a 400-word declaration. Since that time Republicans have continued to produce abbreviated platforms.

Due to the cumbersome size of the state committee a smaller executive committee is provided by law. It consists of a member of the state committee and one representative from each county for each 3,000 votes for the party's nominee for governor in the last general election. Its functions are the usual ones of fund raising, campaign planning and management, and consultation on patronage matters.

Job patronage has contributed to the lifeblood of Arizona politics, but usually taking the form of contributing to personal political machines of elective politicians and not to the major parties per se. Several administrative departments, whose activities depend largely upon federal funds, had joined to establish a merit system. Otherwise, the patronage system prevailed. The legislature did not enact a merit system by law until 1968.

In the early years of statehood Arizona's seven-term governor, George W. P. Hunt, built up a political machine entrenched through patronage particularly in the state Highway Department. Sidney P. Osborn, who won four consecutive gubernatorial elections in the 1940's, gained control of most boards and commissions through his appointive power. In a moment of frustration at some of these plural bodies he is said to have conceived the idea of asking new appointees to sign undated letters of resignation at the time of appointment. These letters could then conveniently be pulled from the governor's file at a future time for dating and press release if the governor and a board member fell into disagreement.[4]

In more recent years two governors, Howard Pyle (Republican, 1951-55) and Ernest McFarland (Democratic, 1955-59) earned the displeasure of their party leadership by exercising a degree of independence from the party machinery in making appointments. An Arizona governor has little opportunity to perform the spectacular,[5] but McFarland's administration hit a low mark, perhaps, in 1958 when he called a special session of the legislature to consider a five-point program—only to see it adjourn after fourteen days without enacting a single item. One of McFarland's special interests was the preparation of the state's case in the Arizona-California suit over Colorado River water, evidence being presented in San Francisco to a special master of the U.S. Supreme Court. Stepping from the governor's office in 1958 McFarland tried to oust Barry Goldwater from his former Senate seat, only to have Goldwater handily win the off-year election. McFarland was elected to the Arizona Supreme Court in 1964.

The significant political plums to fall into the hands of the Republicans at the state level have stemmed from the election of Republican governors in six of the nine latest contests for that office. Because of the plethora of boards and commissions having long terms and overlapping memberships, Republican control leading to important appointments has been delayed. Patronage, however, is more a matter of individual than party political machines.

4. For statistical data on races for more important offices see Bruce B. Mason, *Arizona General Election Results, 1911-1960*, Research Study No. 3 (Tempe: Bureau of Government Research, Arizona State University, 1961).

5. On the powers of Arizona governors as chief legislators see Roy D. Morey, *Politics and Legislation: The Office of Governor in Arizona*, Arizona Government Studies No. 3 (Tucson: Institute of Government Research, University of Arizona Press, 1965). Former Governors McFarland and Fannin comment on their gubernatorial experiences in *The Office of Governor in Arizona*, Public Affairs Series No. 7 (Tempe: Bureau of Government Research, Arizona State University, 1964).

The election of Republican governors in a Democratic state is one of the peculiar phenomena of Arizona politics. In 1958, with the backing of the Pulliam press, Paul Fannin of Phoenix was elected to fill the governor's chair, aided in no small measure by a successful and affluent business background and an unblemished political record. In 1960 he was re-elected, and took a third consecutive term two years later by defeating Sam Goddard, a Tucson lawyer who had acquired a liberal Democratic label. Fannin's political star continued to ascend when he stepped into the Senate seat vacated by Barry Goldwater in 1964.

With Paul Fannin out of the race for governor, the Arizona Republican party was the scene of a very significant intra-party battle for the gubernatorial nomination. While the Democrats were having one of their regular multiple primary fights (four candidates), the Republicans had a two-way race between Richard Kleindienst, a Goldwater confidant, former state party chairman, and a leader in the Republican "establishment," and Evan Mecham, who was identified with the more right-wing Republican elements. These had gained confidence in their strength starting in early 1961 when the Phoenix area became a center of John Birchist activity. To the Mecham wing of the party Barry Goldwater's dedication to conservatism was suspect, and Goldwater himself had had to enter into a state party struggle earlier in an effort to cut Mecham off as a candidate for chairman of the state party organization. Kleindienst defeated Mecham by 3-2 in the September primary, but the subsequent embitterment of the Mecham supporters with Kleindienst and the regular Republican organization contributed to a win by Democrat Goddard in the November general election. Goddard had no primary opposition (a rarity in Arizona Democratic politics), and his endorsement by the Pulliam newspapers in Phoenix signaled his new coloration of political moderation in place of his liberal complexion of two years earlier.

Governor Goddard incurred some political reverses during his term of office, which contributed to his defeat in his second-term attempt in 1966, the only renominated incumbent governor ever to be defeated for a second term in Arizona history. His primary nomination was by a narrow margin after a three-man intra-party fight which left him labeled as a weak leader. In the general election he was defeated by Jack Williams, radio executive and former nonpartisan mayor of Phoenix, and now identified as a moderate Republican. Much of the Williams vote was anti-Goddard; but Williams had for his campaign the services of Stephen Shadegg, who had managed former Goldwater campaigns (and who has since experienced a break with the ex-senator).

The only other statewide office to be captured by the Republicans in the decade of the fifties was that of attorney general in 1951. It was won back by the Democrats two years later, but again fell into Republican hands in 1960, where it has since remained. Republicans made a clean sweep of all state partisan offices which they contested in 1966, capturing in addition to the governor's and attorney general's posts the offices of treasurer, mine inspector, and superintendent of public instruction. In addition, they gained control of both houses of the state legislature—de jure control of the House, where formerly it had been only de facto by virtue of controlling a majority coalition, and actual control of the Senate for the first time in history. Furthermore, they won two of the three congressional seats.

The national voting trend, combined with a low voter turnout, effects of congressional redistricting and legislative reapportionment, absence of the usual biennial county elections from the ballot, the hangover effects of a bitter Democratic intra-party contest for the gubernatorial nomination, and inclement weather, proved too much for Arizona Democrats who went down to ignominious defeat in this once near one-party (Democratic) state.[6]

Anyone who even glances at Arizona's history of representation in the Congress of the United States is immediately struck by the arresting record of Carl Hayden. A native of Tempe, Hayden first went to Washington in 1912 as Arizona's lone representative in the lower house. There he remained until his election to the Senate in 1926. In 1962 Hayden was re-elected to his seventh consecutive Senate term, and in 1967 reached his ninetieth birthday, having served longer in Congress than any person in history. Hayden's seniority has given him the chairmanship of the Senate Appropriations Committee, a key committee for a state where federal expenditures are so important. Hayden rarely makes a speech on the Senate floor, but has a reputation among his colleagues for his quiet effectiveness in the committee room and in the informality of the cloak room. He likes to describe himself as a "work horse" rather than a "show horse." His voting record has tended toward the liberal side. Republican election opposition to Hayden in recent years has been less than nominal—even the Phoenix newspapers pull their punches when it comes to Hayden. His last re-election campaign witnessed some developments with far-reaching significance for the state's politics. Since he had only token primary opposition in his own party, the two Phoenix newspapers endorsed him. The Republican primary nomination had been won by Evan Mecham, the spokesman for right-wing party elements more conservatively oriented than Barry Goldwater. Goldwater avoided any primary endorsement despite the fact that Mecham's opposition was Stephen Shadegg, reputed ghostwriter of Goldwater's *Conscience of a Conservative*. With a split developing within Republican ranks in the primary that subsequently failed to heal, Hayden easily bested Mecham.

Henry Fountain Ashurst, as literate and flowery an orator as the U.S. Senate has had in the present century, lost his seat in 1940 to McFarland. Most observers ascribed Ashurst's defeat to neglect of his relationships with his Arizona constituents. McFarland was swept aside after two terms by the personable Barry Goldwater in 1952.

Barry Goldwater's attractiveness as a candidate in statewide politics has twice been demonstrated.[7] In 1952 he carried the state by only 7,000 votes, trailing Eisenhower so badly that Goldwater conceded his indebtedness to the General's coattails. In 1958's off-year election the Senator bettered his 1952 margin without the President's help. Not much was heard from Goldwater during his first term in Washington, but as a member of the Senate Labor and Education Committee (and representing a right-to-work state) he acquired a reputation for attacking the role of Walter Reuther in labor-management relations. A syndicated newspaper column and a series of books soon gave him recognition as the spokesman for domestic conservatism and for total victory over communism in external relations. He became widely sought as a public speaker and fund-raiser on a national scale; he also served as chairman of the Republican Senatorial Campaign Committee. The Arizona delegation to the Republican national convention of 1960 put up Goldwater's name for the presidential nomination, but he withdrew from the

6. For a full discussion of the 1966 election see Ross R. Rice, "The 1966 Election in Arizona," *Western Political Quarterly*, XX (June 1967, Part 2), 529-34.

7. Barry Goldwater's rise in politics is told by Edwin McDowell, an editorial writer for the *Arizona Republic*, in his *Barry Goldwater: Portrait of an Arizonian* (Chicago: Regnery, 1964). See also the books by Stephen Shadegg.

nomination fight. Following the Nixon defeat of 1960, a national effort to support a conservative presidential candidate in 1964 was set in motion and soon turned to Goldwater as its choice. In January 1964 he announced that he would be a candidate for the presidential nomination and offer "a choice, not an echo." His term of office was to expire in 1964, and he chose to give up another try for a Senate seat in favor of a race for the White House.

Paul Fannin won an uncontested nomination for the vacant Senate seat, and successfully bested Roy Elson, the winner in a six-man Democratic primary. Elson, who was administrative assistant to Senator Carl Hayden, waged a well-financed campaign. Fannin, as senator, continued in the Goldwater vein early in his Washington service by active leadership in the successful Senate fight to keep Section 14B of the Taft-Hartley Law.

Arizona's population increase did not produce a second seat in the U.S. House of Representatives until after the 1940 census. In 1947 the legislature divided the state into two congressional districts, Maricopa County as District 1 and the balance of the state as District 2. In the Eisenhower year of 1952 a young Republican Mesa attorney, John J. Rhodes, won the First District away from a Democratic incumbent and has successfully held on to his seat since that time. Rhodes has not acquired the strongly conservative reputation of Barry Goldwater, and made a record for himself as a leader of the younger Republican element in the House which was dissatisfied with the leadership of Joseph Martin and Charles Halleck. Rhodes' hold on his seat was definitely assured by his re-election in 1966.

In the Second District Stewart Udall (D) of Tucson, a youthful attorney, first won the district seat in 1954 and held it through the 1960 election. His early support of John F. Kennedy's bid for the presidential nomination in 1960 placed him in line for his subsequent appointment as Secretary of the Department of the Interior in the new cabinet. His vacated House seat was won in a special election by his brother Morris Udall, who retained the seat in the 1962, 1964, and 1966 elections. The Second District was divided after the 1960 census when population growth warranted a third congressional seat for the state. The First District remained all of Maricopa County (half the state's inhabitants), while the eight southern counties (with about 35 percent of the population, including the city of Tucson) became a new Second District. The eight sparsely populated counties of northern Arizona became a new Third District (with only 15 percent of the state's residents). A Globe attorney and former member of the state Corporation Commission, George F. "Duke" Senner, Jr. (D), was the first victor in this new district, repeating his win in 1964. He was defeated in 1966 by Sam Steiger, Republican rancher, TV personality, and war correspondent.

Despite a Federal Court warning to redistrict, the state legislature failed to accomplish the task in 1965. In February 1966 a three-member Federal Court panel ordered both congressional redistricting and legislative reapportionment according to the court's own scheme. Some 200,000 western Maricopa residents were shifted from District 1 to District 3, and District 2 was left intact. The effect was to strengthen the re-election chances of the three incumbent congressmen, but District 3 belied the prediction and elected a Republican. In the newly redrawn First District, the Democratic registration percentage dropped from 57.68 to 54.7 percent, which, coupled with the practice of many nominal Democratic registrants to vote Republican for the top offices on the ballot, gave Representative Rhodes a safe district, and probably will continue to do so for as long as he cares to keep his present post.

As of early 1967, state chairmen for the two parties are Tucson attorney Richard Duffield of the Democrats and Phoenix jeweler Harry Rosenzweig of the Republicans.

Women's and young people's groups have been active in both parties. Women workers have been of particular assistance to the Republicans. The Young Republican organization took credit for the "draft" of Howard Pyle in 1950, and the Young Democratic organization was the springboard for the election of a group of youthful attorneys to the only liberal-controlled House of Representatives in the state's history, 1955-56.

Arizona's colorful political history has been the stage for bosses and leaders, machines, and organizations. One looks in vain, however, for a single "state boss."

PRESSURE GROUPS

Interest groups realize their objectives in the Arizona legislature through two principal avenues. First, some groups have built-in access through overlapping memberships in the legislature and, second, some engage in lobbying.[8] Two economic interests in particular have profited from built-in access: the mining corporations and the cattle ranchers. For years certain legislators, especially senators, admitted wearing "copper collars." Appropriation committee meetings were at times held in a downtown Phoenix hotel where copper-county lawmakers frequently lodged during legislative sessions.

The Senate president and the speaker of the House of Representatives have frequently come from mining counties. Legislative apportionment has, from statehood to the 1966 reapportionment, favored the mining (essentially rural) counties.

While copper has been the strongest single economic interest in politics throughout the state's history, the utilities have come to play an increasing role in the politics of pressure. The Arizona Public Service Company may support legislative candidates, and the Salt River Project (both operate in Maricopa County) is beginning to display more interest in legislative matters. In southern Arizona, the principal utility is the Tucson Gas and Electric Company. The Arizona Railroad Association, consisting of the Santa Fe and Southern Pacific companies, has competent legislative representation. Likewise, Mountain States Telephone and Telegraph Company has a representative on hand during legislative sessions.

The state's agricultural interests are led by the Cattle Grower's Association and the American Farm Bureau. These interests have benefited from built-in access and have had less need to lobby openly.

Over three-fourths of the state's population lives in municipalities, whose governments are represented by the League of Arizona Cities and Towns. These city officials have reported in recent legislative sessions more support in the state Senate (rurally dominated) for urban-sponsored bills, and surprisingly less support in the urban-dominated House of Representatives.

Taxpayer associations are active. A number of the state's largest economic interests, such as the banks and utilities, support the activities of the Arizona Taxpayers' Association, and the Maricopa County Taxpayers' Association is particularly active at budget time in sending its representatives to public bodies about to fix their new property tax rates.

8. Despite a constitutional mandate that the legislature was to adopt legislation to regulate the practice of lobbying, no such laws have been adopted and in consequence no systematic effort is made to require registration of lobbyists.

Of growing but immeasurable influence is the activity of the Arizona Academy. This organization, having some business orientation, holds semiannual Town Halls to which some seventy-five prominent leaders from throughout the state and representative of many social, economic, and political groups come together to study intensively some broad problem of the state for a three-day period. The advance research studies and the recommendations adopted by the participants at the conclusion of each Town Hall are brought to bear on legislators and public via the press and a speaker's bureau.

Of growing political muscle is the "school lobby." The frequent alliance of such organizations as the Arizona Education Association, the Arizona School Board Association, and the Arizona Congress of Parents and Teachers may produce impressive victories, as was the case in 1964 when they spearheaded a change in the financing of state aid to local school districts. The 15,000 elementary and high school teachers in the state affiliated with the Arizona Education Association have the potential of greater political weight if the members of the teaching profession tend to greater participation in politics. The American Federation of Teachers, a union, is becoming active in a few districts.

Illustrative of the successful aligning of groups interested in public education was the PTA-sponsored Proposition 103 in 1964, designed to make funds available to school districts on grounds of need rather than average daily school attendance. After the PTA took the initiative, the Arizona Education Association and the School Board Association secured the necessary number of signatures on petitions to qualify for the ballot, and waged a successful pre-election campaign. Following the November victory of Proposition 103, the same forces kept the issue alive before the legislative session of 1965, until the legislature finally took action to find the sources of revenue which were necessary to underwrite the new school aid program.

Organized labor is not, by admission of its own leaders, a driving force in Arizona politics. Its enemies tend to overstress the importance of labor in order to create a "straw man" in election campaigns. Arizona was one of the first states to adopt a "right-to-work" constitutional amendment after World War II, and no really strong effort has been made for its repeal. Former Senator Barry Goldwater, and his successor, Paul Fannin, have both staunchly called for the retention of Section 14B of the Taft-Hartley Act which permits state adoption of right-to-work legislation. The AFL-CIO through its political arm, COPE, has made periodic candidate endorsements and, as in most other states, more Democrats than Republicans receive favorable support. The nature of the Arizona economy has not produced large, militant unions aiming at liberal legislative reforms. Rather, among the strongest Arizona unions have been those in the construction industry, unions not nationally identified with liberal causes. Organized labor has been identified with the liberally oriented Democratic minority in the state House of Representatives and has greater impact in blocking hostile legislation than in initiating legislation favored by that faction.

Minority groups, such as Mexican-Americans and Negroes, give indication of greater political involvement in the future and may refrain from permanent alliances with any major political party (although the Democratic party has generally been looked upon as the most natural ally for the political goals of these minorities). For the first time, a Negro was elected to the 1967 state Senate. The Arizona Indian population wields little political weight, although numerically it has a future political potential in Apache County.

Extremist political activity is more noticeable on the political right than on the political left. The John Birch Society and its sympathizers had an early start in 1960-61 in the Phoenix metropolitan area but achieved only marginal successes. Evan Mecham, a newspaper publisher and auto dealer, is recognized as a political spokesman of the ultra-conservatives. Loyalty oaths for public employees and the "Liberty Amendment" have been among legislative objectives. Two early figures in the Birch movement in Arizona were the late M. T. Phelps, a one-time Supreme Court judge, and Frank Cullen Brophy, retired banker and inveterate letter writer. Both were registered Democrats at the time of the rise of the Birch movement.

LEGISLATIVE POLITICS

To discover "Who runs Arizona government?" one has had to look not at the governor's office but at the men and women serving in the legislature and the leadership of the majorities in each house.

Legislative politics has had a distinctly conservative character, a consequence of influence of the mines, railroads, utilities, and the cattle-raising industry. But the recent rate of growth has outstripped any past era of expansion, and manufacturing has surged to the fore. The extent to which political power necessarily follows shifts in economic power has yet to be determined.

Until a constitutional amendment in 1953 gave each Arizona county two seats, the method of apportionment had given four mining counties eight Senate seats out of a total of nineteen. These counties (Pima, Cochise, Yavapai, and Gila) could also count on the one vote each of Pinal and Greenlee, the latter almost wholly a copper county economically. As in other western mining states the mining corporations have concentrated on holding down state appropriations and the property tax rate. They also oppose shifting any greater incidence of taxation upon mines. Logrolling between copper and cattle interests has thwarted both a severance tax and increases in grazing fees on state lands.

In 1953 a package constitutional amendment to change the basis of representation in both houses was successfully referred by the legislature to the people.[9] Opposed by publisher William R. Matthews of the *Arizona Daily Star*, the amendment lost in Pima County. But the Phoenix dailies editorialized in favor of the change, and the favorable margin in Maricopa County put the amendment across in the statewide totals. The approved amendment increased the Senate membership to twenty-eight, two from each county, and "froze" the House of Representatives at eighty, allocated on a variable number of votes cast in each county for the office of governor in the last election. Of the eighty seats Maricopa had thirty-seven and Pima sixteen. No other county had more than four, and three counties were entitled to only one seat each.

Arizona experienced the frustrations of numerous other states generated by the U.S. Supreme Court's decisions in the early 1960's calling for legislative reapportionment based on the "one man, one vote" principle in both houses. On the heels of these decisions a young University of Arizona law student filed suit in April 1964 in Federal Court. A blue-ribbon committee appointed by Governor Paul Fannin produced recommendations, and a study made for a legislative committee presented alternative plans to the legislature upon which it might act. In a

9. This effort at reapportionment is analyzed in David A. Bingham, "Legislative Apportionment: The Arizona Experience," *Arizona Review*, Bureau of Business and Public Research, University of Arizona, Vol. 11, No. 10 (October 1962).

special session in late 1964 the legislature, unexpectedly to some, voted to increase the Senate size from twenty-eight to thirty-one by combining counties in such a way as to give some weight to population. The legislature failed at the time to change congressional districting or to modify representation in the state House of Representatives.

February 2, 1966, will be remembered in Arizona history as the day a three-man Federal District Court panel (by a 2-1 vote) ordered sweeping changes in both houses of the legislature and in congressional districting.[10] The legislature, for the 1966 election at least, was to consist of a slightly larger Senate (thirty instead of twenty-eight) and a considerably smaller House (sixty instead of eighty). Future legislative elections were to be based upon eight new electoral districts as shown in Table II. The legislature could reapportion for elections after 1966, using the "one man, one vote" principle.

TABLE II
ARIZONA'S REAPPORTIONED LEGISLATURE
(Federal court-ordered: 1966)

District	Counties	Number of Legislators	
		Senate	House
1	Mohave Yavapai	1	2
2	Cochise Graham Santa Cruz	2	4
3	Apache Greenlee Navajo	2	4
4	Coconino	1	2
5	Gila Pinal	2	4
6	Yuma	1	2
7	Pima	6	12
8	Maricopa	15	30
	TOTAL SEATS	30	60

One effect of reapportionment was to give Maricopa County half the state Senate seats, instead of only two seats out of twenty-eight as in the past. Pima County got 20 percent of the Senate seats. Republican prospects appeared to be bettered in the Senate, where only two Republicans were serving at the time of

10. *Gary Peter Klahr v. Samuel P. Goddard, Governor and Wesley Bolin, Secretary of State*, Civil Action 5112, Phoenix, Federal District Court.

the Court's decision. Reapportionment was certainly expected to produce sizable Republican Senate gains, but few Republicans in their moments of greatest optimism expected to win numerical superiority in both houses as they did in 1966. One effect of reapportionment has been to create several very large districts to campaign in, the new District 3 stretching more than 320 miles in length. As far as legislative voting behavior is concerned, future legislatures may give closer scrutiny to smog control legislation, sales tax distribution to the counties, apportionment of state aid for schools and establishment of kindergartens, county building codes, and make-up of county supervisory districts and state Highway Commission districts.

The Federal Court reapportionment order asked opposing attorneys to get together and submit redistricting plans for populous Maricopa and Pima counties. For the 1966 elections no individual electoral districts were established within the six new smaller districts, but the Court approved districting plans for the two large districts (the two largest counties). Within these, however, in 1966 candidates for the House ran at large in the fifteen new Maricopa County districts and the six new Pima County districts. The Maricopa districts average 21,501 voter registrations each.

In Maricopa County Republican nominees for the legislature have demonstrated their ability to win in districts having up to as high as a 3-2 Democratic registration advantage. Initial reaction to the newly approved districts found Republican county leaders laying claim to up to ten of the fifteen districts, while Democratic officials were branding seven districts as Democratic and one even. In the 28th Legislature (1967-68), Republicans possessed thirty-three out of sixty House seats, while in the Senate the score was sixteen to fourteen.

In the 1967 regular legislative session there were abortive efforts by the Republican majorities at redistricting by legislative action in anticipation of the 1968 election year. Success at getting sufficient Republican support behind a single proposal was not possible until the governor called a special session in late Spring.

The Republican-approved redistricting plan adopted increased Senate size from thirty to thirty-two seats, and House size from sixty to sixty-four. Representation was to be based upon voter registration, rather than population. Democratic critics charged that use of voter registration figures would give no weight to minors and to Arizona's sizable non-voting adult Indian population. Democrats also pointed to a number of newly carved districts and charged "gerrymandering" by the Republicans in order to preserve future Republican control. In an effort to block the new redistricting act, Democrats considered both judicial action and possible resort to the referendum process. As of the Fall of 1967 the Democrats had filed referendum petitions blocking use of the new plan for the 1968 election, while also hoping that the Federal Court panel might not give its approval to the new redistricting plan arranged by the controlling Republicans. The Democrats' strategy was to favor the court-ordered status quo over the "gerrymandering" voted by the Republicans in the special session.

The Democratic party enjoyed numerical superiority in both houses of the legislature from statehood in 1912 to 1966, giving Arizona the designation of a state where one party is dominant. Table III shows Arizona election results from 1944 through 1966 for seats in the state legislature and for federal and statewide offices. Republicans have held the governorship at several points in history, thus the state is not classified as a one-party state. During the period since World War II

TABLE III

ELECTION RESULTS BY OFFICE AND PARTY: 1946-66

Office	1946	1948	1950	1952	1954	1956	1958	1960	1962	1964	1966
President		D		R		R		R		R	
U.S. Senator			D			D			D		
	D			R			R			R	
U.S. Representative											
District 1	D	D	D	R	R	R	R	R	R	R	R
District 2	D	D	D	D	D	D	D	D	D	D	D
District 3									D	D	R
State Legislature											
Senate											
Democratic	28	28	28	24	26	26	27	24	24	26	14
Republican	0	0	0	4	2	2	1	4	4	2	16
House											
Democratic	53	52	61	50	60	58	55	52	48	45	27
Republican	5	6	11	30	20	22	25	28	32	35	33
Governor	D	D	R	R	D	D	R	R	R	D	R
Attorney General	D	D	D	R	D	D	D	R	R	R	R
Secretary of State	D	D	D	D	D	D	D	D	D	D	D
Superintendent of Public Instruction	D	D	D	D	D	D	D	D	D	R	R
Auditor	D	D	D	D	D	D	D	D	D	D	D
Treasurer	D	D	D	D	D	D	D	D	D	D	R
Mine Inspector	D	D	D	D	D	D	D	D	D	D	R

Source: Secretary of State, *Official Canvasses.*

all the remaining western states have approached closer in varying degrees to real two-party electoral competition than has Arizona.

Insofar as the Senate is concerned, the rapid changes taking place in Arizona's economic, social, and political structure were being felt only to a minor degree in that body prior to reapportionment. The durability of Senate leadership was typified by the president of the Senate, who served six consecutive two-year terms. Mining and cattle interests continue the dominant role in affairs of the Senate that they have enjoyed since statehood in 1912, joined more recently by the Arizona Public Service Company. The general approach to the legislative process in the Senate has been to keep new legislation to a minimum, hold down appropriations, and adjourn. Between the 1958 and 1966 elections the twenty-eight member Senate had never numbered more than four Republicans at a time. No sizable minority, therefore, really existed, little factionalism appeared; at most a few mavericks strayed from the herd from time to time. Few legislative measures reached the floor without previous caucus approval, and inasmuch as there was no real minority, floor debate was perfunctory and dispirited. The House leadership found difficulty in bargaining with Senate leaders in efforts to prod Senate action on House-approved bills because of the basic disinterest in the Senate for new legislation.

In the period since the 1958 elections the Republicans moved up from 31 percent of the House seats to over 43 percent and then jumped to 55 percent in 1966. These Republican gains occurred in the two big urban counties where in Maricopa, for example, over 80 percent of the county representation in the House is Republican (1967-68). The key to effective control in the House is the election of a new speaker every two years. From that crucial showdown flows assignment of the individual legislator to the most committees, the more powerful committees, committee chairmanships, and the opportunity to have pet measures given some chance of consideration and passage. In committee assignments and in chairmanships no seniority principle obtains, and the proportion of majority bloc members on key committees is characteristically larger than the proportion of majority bloc membership in the entire House.

In 1959-60 in the Arizona House a majority coalition of most Democrats and all Republicans controlled the House. Two years later defectors from Democratic ranks in the majority were added to the liberal Democrats of the past minority to give the Democrats control without Republican aid. In 1963-64 the thirty-two-member Republican minority cooperated with sixteen conservative Democrats to create a new majority coalition. In the 27th Legislature (1965-66) the speaker was elected by the cooperation of the thirty-five Republicans and eighteen conservative, largely outstate Democrats. The Republicans in the 1967-68 House were in a clear majority. The conservative coalition was ended, and the Republicans elected one of their own to the speakership.

The "majority coalition" which dominated the House of Representatives from 1953-66 (except for a two-year interval) was a conservative coalition consisting of "Pinto Democrats" and conservative Republicans.[11] These joined, following elections, to choose a Pinto Democrat as House speaker, then continued to caucus regularly and produce a calendar of bills to be given priority consideration. Majority caucus approval of a bill usually assured its approval on the floor. Republican lawmakers have come principally (80-95 percent over the period) from the two urbanized counties—Maricopa and Pima. From 61 to 73 percent of Regular Democrats (liberal in the main) have resided in these two urban counties; whereas, from 54 to 82 percent of the Pinto Democratic faction came from outlying counties (where copper and cattle have been dominant).

Since 1951 there have been annual general legislative sessions instead of biennial, and the frequency of special sessions has been reduced. Several factors other than the "built-in" influence of mining and cattle interests exist to impede legislative action. One is the fact that there is no provision for the carry-over of bills from the first session to the second of a given legislature. Another factor contributing to the "bottling" of bills is the committee system, which calls for multilateral reference of bills to as many as three or four committees in each house. Dean Mann has concluded:

11. "Pintos" are horses of more than one color. The relative strengths of Pinto Democrats, Regular Democrats, and Republicans in electing a House speaker and in developing and pushing a legislative program are found in Roderick A. Jacobsen, "Election of the Speaker in the Arizona House of Representatives During the Era of Coalition" (master's thesis, Arizona State University, 1967).

The multilateral reference practice *appears* to provide increased opportunities for minorities to block legislation, since all committees must report a bill before it can be considered on the floor; but the control that the majority bloc exercises in each committee assures that few bills not wanted by the majority will be reported. The committees have become the most important devices in the Arizona legislature for preventing action on the chamber floor in either house.[12]

Direct (popular) legislation is possible in Arizona through the use of the initiative and referendum. The requisite number of signatures on a petition to initiate an amendment is 15 percent of the total votes cast for the office of governor in the last election. For a new law 10 percent of that total is required. The measure is then submitted to the electorate where the requirement is approval by a majority of votes cast on the proposition itself. Neither a gubernatorial veto nor legislative repeal is applicable to an initiative measure approved by a majority of eligible voters.

The referendum process requires mandatory referral of constitutional amendments originating in the legislature. The legislature has the optional power to refer bills to the electorate, an action rarely taken. An act, not including an emergency clause, has a waiting period of ninety days after the close of the session in which it was enacted. If petitions bearing 5 percent of the total number of votes cast for the office of governor are submitted before the expiration of this period, the act is placed upon the next election ballot. Most bills introduced contain an emergency clause, however, and most bills enacted carry by more than the necessary two-thirds vote to declare an emergency to exist. In practice the initiative and referendum processes have been used with restraint, quite in contrast with use in neighboring California. The average vote on propositions has been in the vicinity of 60 percent of the vote for governor. Less than 23 percent turned out in the crucial special election of 1953 which resulted in changing the basis of representation in both houses of the legislature.

Arizona's constitution of 1910 makes it one of twelve states in the nation having the recall process. Through the collection of petitions bearing signatures totaling 25 percent of the vote cast for the office in the last election, a special recall election can be forced. The incumbent officeholder is automatically a candidate, and opponents may have their names printed on the ballot by filing nominating papers in the usual fashion. It was the application of the recall provision to judgeships that caused President William Howard Taft to object to the proposed constitution for Arizona, forcing its voters to act to exempt elective judges. With the constitution thus modified, Arizona statehood was granted (proclaimed February 14, 1912). One of the first post-statehood acts, however, was voter approval of an amendment to make judges once again subject to the recall process—a provision of the constitution standing to the present. The recall has seldom been used, and where it has been used it has frequently failed to oust the incumbent. A successful attempt to remove a judge (superior court) occurred in Pinal County in 1924. No holder of a high state office has ever been removed, most attempts occurring at the county, municipal, or school district level. One reason for its limited use is the cost involved, but recalls are only one illustration of the expense of campaigning.

State government finances as approved by the legislature reflect the pattern of political power in the state. Rarely has a member of the liberal Democratic

---

12. Dean E. Mann, "The Legislative Committee System in Arizona," *Western Political Quarterly*, XIV (December 1961), 941.

minority received an appointment to an appropriations committee. Appropriations committee sessions may at times be closed, and in earlier days it was the
practice for some to be held at a downtown hotel instead of at the capitol. An
executive budget system was not instituted by the legislature until 1966.[13] During Ernest McFarland's gubernatorial tenure a sum was provided his office by the
legislature for the employment of a budget officer, but the provision was permitted to lapse later. Governor Paul Fannin included in his 1960 legislative program
an unfulfilled request for a budget officer, and Governor Sam Goddard made his
number one legislative objective in 1966 the creation of a state finance office,
with a budget officer responsible to the governor. Following legislative approval,
Goddard named the state's first budget director.

Approximately half of the state's funds in recent years has gone for education. Nearly two-thirds of that amount is aid to the school districts and about
one-third goes for higher education. Highways, welfare and correction, general
government, and other lesser categories of spending follow. Large taxpayers, e.g.,
mines, utilities, and railroads, have established a record in holding down the lid.

The five largest sources of state taxes occur in the following order: property
taxes, income, education excise, motor fuel, and sales taxes. But federal aid to the
state eclipses any of the top five revenue sources listed above. A statewide property revaluation program extending over several years before it was finished has
been completed and may result in removing a variety of property tax inequities.
The legislature in 1965 referred a $100 million bonding authorization to the elec-
torate, ending in overwhelming defeat (leaving the state on pay-as-you-go financing for capital improvements). A foremost quandary for future legislatures will be
to locate nonborrowing (or modified bonding) sources of revenues, largely required for new construction at the state's three universities.

In 1967 fiscal problems included implementation of the property revaluation program which was to set "full cash values." With home owners in a rebel-
lious mood (largely over local property tax rates for schools), the legislature faced
the sticky problem of fixing percentages of full cash values for seventeen different
classes of property. Some answers offered included ending veterans' exemptions,
lower rates on owner-occupied homes, an increased income tax, and a single statewide district for raising school funds from property taxes. If percentages of "full
cash value" were to be identical on all classes of property, home-owners would
not get a hoped-for tax reduction, farmers and ranchers would pay more, and
railroads and mines less. The state has no severance tax on minerals.

Arizona has had but one constitution, that drafted in 1910, which provided
for an executive branch with a decentralized system of elective offices, boards,
and commissions. The state has never seen a successful movement aimed at administrative reorganization, although a 1949 study by Griffenhagen and Associates
offered proposals for consolidation of the more than one hundred agencies of
state government that had accumulated over the years.[14] One trained observer,
commenting on the subsequent failure of the legislature to implement these proposals, concluded: "The most recent and most nearly successful attempts to secure administrative reorganization were caught up in a whirlpool of opposition

13. On budget-making in Arizona see Paul Kelso, *State Budget Preparation in Arizona*,
Arizona Government Studies No. 1 (Tucson: Institute of Government Research, University
of Arizona Press, 1964).

14. "Report on General State Organization," Supplement to Arizona, *State Journal*,
Nineteenth Legislature, First Special Session, 1950.

generated by unfortunate factional conflicts, political partisanship, obstruction of groups of job and office holders, and the push of special interests who feared the loss of favored positions under the status quo."[15] A package of administrative reorganization amendments was to go before the electorate in 1968—the somewhat partisan product of the Republican-controlled legislature.

VOTING PATTERNS

The present-day voting habits of Arizonans at the polls confirm the statement that Arizona today has shifted to the category of a one and one-half party state, and in some aspects to a two-party state. Voter registrations have narrowed to the point where in 1966, 60.8 percent of the registrants listed themselves as Democrats, and 37.0 percent as Republican. Greatest concentrations of Republican registrants are in Maricopa, Pima, Yavapai (Prescott), and Coconino (Flagstaff) counties. Figure I shows the discrepancy between the higher vote for the Republican nominees for governor and state representatives, and the lower Republican share of party registration over the past twenty years. Only five years ago the voter registration ratio stood at 2.5-1, but since has dropped to under 3-2, and is even closer in the two most populous counties. Particular Republican concentrations are found in north Phoenix precincts plus the retirement community of Sun City. Scottsdale, south Tempe precincts, and Mesa are Republican centers. Higher income precincts in the east Tucson area are inhabited more densely by Republicans.

PERCENT OF REPUBLICAN VOTER REGISTRATION, REPUBLICAN
VOTE FOR GOVERNOR, AND REPUBLICAN SEATS IN HOUSE (1946-66)

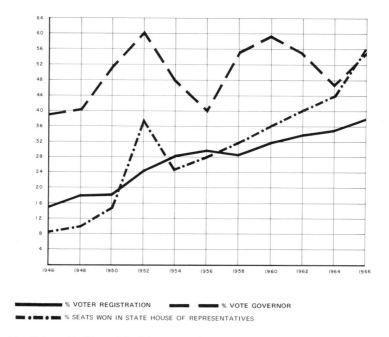

15. Robert E. Riggs, *The Movement for Administrative Reorganization in Arizona*, Arizona Government Studies No. 4 (Tucson: Institute of Government Research, University of Arizona Press, 1964), p. 64.

But a closer approximation of Arizona politics is to view the Democratic party as two parties or factions: one (the older) conservative and largely rural, and the other (the younger) liberal and more urban. Many registered Democrats (sometimes called "pintos") in the older, conservative, rural party have tended over the past decade and a half to vote Republican when an avowed conservative seeks statewide elective office. Thus Barry Goldwater carried ten counties in his 1958 re-election bid. Liberal Democrats tend to be located in urban-suburban areas where they survive in the politically hostile environment of conservative Republicans. Republican victories in statewide races are fashioned out of the strategy of getting up to 90 percent of their registered party members to the polls while (hopefully) the Democrats are doing no better than getting 70 to 75 percent of their registrants to the voting places. Republicans, therefore, have benefited from the following elements of political advantage:

1. A higher proportion of Republicans than Democrats go to the polls.

2. The ratio of registered voters between the parties has narrowed because of Republican migration from normally Republican strongholds in other states.

3. The economy attracts higher-paid professional and technical workers, plus retired persons, while minority-group, lower-paid, union workers find less promise.

4. There have been many attractive candidates who escaped the rigors of intra-party primary battles.

5. There is superior party motivation of workers who seemingly thrive in their role of laboring for a minority party.

6. National attention was focused for a decade upon the charismatic Barry Goldwater.

But not all transformations in the state's voting habits may be said to be benefiting the Republican side. Republican politics increasingly is the battleground of the "Establishment" versus the more rightist wing of the party. The Establishment leaders are former Senator Goldwater, Senator Fannin, Representative Rhodes, and the present state party chairman, Rosenzweig. The more right-wing elements include Birchists in positions within the party apparatus and who politically are identified with Evan Mecham or with state Senator John B. Conlan, Jr., of Scottsdale. A former county party chairman has charged that the Maricopa County Republican organization has been taken over by Birchists, and Frank Cullen Brophy of Phoenix (a national Birch Society councillor) has placed Arizona membership at about 2,000 formed into some 100 chapters.[16] This Republican split, evident in the 1962 U.S. Senate primary and the 1964 gubernatorial primary, augurs problems of maintaining party unity, despite the seemingly solid front presented in 1966. With Barry Goldwater out of office (but engaging actively in state politics starting early in 1966), his base of power is weakened. Goldwater's rise in the 1950's as spokesman for Republican conservatives nationally, has denied whatever liberal element there is within the party any effective leadership in the state.

Arizona was one of two states in the nation to buck the Democratic tide in 1958 (the other was New York) as the state continued its economic prosperity at a time of national recession. A downturn in its rate of economic growth in the mid-1960's (led by a cutback in the construction industry), may politically be

16. Bernie Wynn, a political writer for the *Arizona Republic*, wrote a seven-part series on the Birch Society and the Republican party of Arizona (December 12-18, 1965).

ascribed by Democratic politicians to the recent Republican and conservative image of the state. Doubt remains that articulate, young Democratic candidates will appear to take advantage of such opportunity. Liberal Democrats appear to be more active in the Tucson than in the Phoenix area, attributable perhaps to the politically competitive newspaper situation in Tucson and the liberalizing influence of the University of Arizona. In the greater Phoenix area the center of party activism today may be with liberals, but voting habits of Democrats still tend to be conservative.

The pattern of voting in the state, then, does not correspond to the percentages of voter registration and is the reverse of that found in many of the older northeastern states where Democratic majorities are rolled up in the big cities. In Arizona Republican nominees for statewide offices look hopefully on election night for commanding leads in the early returns from the voting machine precincts in the Phoenix and Tucson areas, in order to stand off Democratic challenges coming in later from outlying counties where paper ballots are still in use. Republican victors over the past decade and a half—Pyle, Goldwater, Fannin—have had to draw from Democratic defectors to win in November, and at a Republican victory dinner in Phoenix in early December 1966, Governor-elect Williams personally thanked those Democrats whose votes had elected Republicans. Ticket-splitting is an accepted Arizona voting habit.

It is conceivable, given the proportions of Arizona voting behavior, that population increases in Maricopa County may continue to give the Republicans some chances at sweeping national and statewide offices whenever a strong national trend toward the party is present. In 1963 Conrad Joyner suggested that it is "possible for the Republicans to gain a monopoly of statewide and national offices during the next decade."[17] Two years later, John P. White differed as follows: "But if by a 'monopoly' we mean a stable situation, persisting over several elections, in which Republicans win all or almost all statewide contests, such a phenomenon seems highly unlikely unless there is some sharp change in established trends."[18] White also questioned the future influence of the senior-citizen vote, referring to census figures which point out that Arizona has a youthful population. Neither of these analysts envisioned the Republican sweep which occurred in 1966.

For nearly its first half-century Arizona enjoyed the reputation of being a bellwether state in American presidential elections, a standing blemished by voting deviations in 1960 for Nixon and 1964 for Goldwater. Thus, in seven out of fourteen presidential contests Arizona has given its slender electoral vote to Republican nominees. In contrast to such Republican successes for high office, the Republican party has been shut out almost consistently from elective offices in the outlying, rural counties, commonly not even presenting any opposition to Democratic nominees for these local posts.

Both parties are faction-ridden, but the 1966 results may have cleared out some of the Democratic party "deadwood." Republicans face a problem with their far-right wing, and outgoing Governor Goddard emits sounds of running again in 1968. With U.S. Senator Carl Hayden at ninety years (and subjected to recent illnesses), Barry Goldwater is on the sidelines along with an array of Demo-

17. Conrad Joyner, "The 1962 Election in Arizona," *Western Political Quarterly*, XVI (June 1963), 391.

18. John P. White, "The 1964 Election in Arizona," *Western Political Quarterly*, XVIII (June 1965, Part 2), 448, 450.

cratic prospects. The Democrats lack new names at the grass-roots level to assist in rebuilding party fortunes.

The elections of 1968 will test the Goldwater popularity, the Republicans as the majority party controlling the governorship and both houses, Republican ability to submerge factionalism and to maintain the better-organized party machinery, and the Democrats' capability of rebuilding a shattered party organization.

NATIONAL POLITICS

The state, developed to a great extent by federal largess and aid, is approaching a stage of lessened dependence on national treasury.[19] New capital is being attracted, in part from eastern industrialists who were at one time winter visitors. Yet water remains a critical factor for Arizona's future growth, and the state turns to the federal government as a realistic first source for the needed funds to bring additional water into the state's population and agricultural centers.

The pioneer project of the U.S. Bureau of Reclamation was Roosevelt Dam on Arizona's Salt River. Arizona's unwillingness to sign the Santa Fe Compact kept the Boulder Canyon project uppermost in state politics even long after the completion of Hoover Dam. The Arizona Power Authority expresses the state's interest in obtaining and marketing hydroelectric power. Since World War II the issue of transporting supplemental Colorado River water to central Arizona has been kept alive. The U.S. Senate, under the urging of Senator Hayden, passed a proposed Central Arizona Project bill early in the 1950's, only to be blocked by the much larger California delegation in the House of Representatives. Then followed a protracted legal battle before the U.S. Supreme Court over the division of lower basin water with California. A favorable decision to Arizona in the early 1960's restored the struggle to the political realm once again.

This time Secretary of the Interior Stewart Udall supported a Southwest Water Plan and California and Arizona interests were finally able to settle their differences and agree to back a regional plan which encompassed the Central Arizona Project. Principal features of the revised project called for guaranteeing California 4.4 million acre feet of mainstream Colorado River water, a system of aqueducts and pumping stations to carry water into central Arizona, and construction of Bridge and Marble Canyon Dams, which along with Hoover Dam power revenues, would finance the water delivery system. The regional Colorado River Basin Project bill included projects estimated at $1.5 billion, which were sought by both upper and lower river basins. It appeared to be headed for a hearing before the House Interior and Insular Affairs Committee in 1966. Passage there would be followed by action in the Senate. The picture for passage in 1966 became increasingly murkier as the question of importation of water into the Colorado River Basin from outside sources entered the scene, along with possible suits involving Indian lands along the river in Arizona and conservationist interests opposing construction of Bridge and Marble Canyon Dams which might affect the adjacent Grand Canyon. In 1967 the Senate approved a Central Arizona project bill, but

19. Arizona's senior senator, Carl Hayden, was an originator of the modern grant-in-aid concept in his successful co-sponsorship of the Hayden-Cartright Act making federal funds available to the states in the 1920's for building the interstate highway system. Both Hayden and Representative John Rhodes have valued positions on their respective congressional appropriation committees. Arizona's continuing participation in federal aid programs is described in two studies by Louis S. Meyer. See "Federal Aid and Its Impact on the State of Arizona" (master's thesis, Arizona State University, 1962), and "Federal Grants-in-Aid and States' Rights in Arizona" (Ph.D. dissertation, University of Arizona, 1964).

deleted both dams on the Colorado River. Chairman Wayne Aspinall (Colorado) held up the legislation in his House Interior Committee.

With a large Indian reservation population, the Washington delegation and the state legislature concern themselves with moves to transfer certain problems of the Indians from federal to state government. A close watch is also kept on federal legislation concerning public lands, wilderness areas, grazing and lease legislation, and mineral exploration. Members of the Arizona congressional delegation, regardless of party or ideological differences, have usually been found together in support of maintaining copper tariffs and peacetime stock-piling of strategic minerals such as manganese. Agricultural legislation is significant because of the importance of cotton in the Arizona economy and the large numbers of migrant farm laborers in the state.

The myth of Arizona as a last bastion of American conservatism, of two-fisted rugged individualism, has of course been embellished by the recent national attention focused on former Senator Barry Goldwater and his philosophy of states' rights and rejection of federal assistance. The rise of Goldwater to national political prominence undoubtedly suggested that Goldwater's home state must necessarily be the heartland of his philosophy, but there may be validity to the argument that Goldwater's most pristine support is actually in Orange County, California, where he fared better in the 1964 presidential election than he did in his home county, Maricopa, Arizona. The 1964 election results did prove something in Arizona; the decided trend since that time has been for school boards and municipal governments (even in Goldwater's immediate backyard) to vote to accept federal aid programs.

CONCLUSION

In transition at present, it is realistic to view Arizona politics as a series of observations rather than as conclusions. Therefore, we may observe that at the time of statehood in 1912 Arizona fitted into the progressive era of American politics with the adoption of a liberal constitution. Subsequent politics have tended toward conservatism, first under the Democratic label and today under both major party labels. Republican conservatism in Arizona is suburban in strength, but a more vocal Democratic liberal strain is beginning to appear in urban centers. The state has become highly urbanized, but its economic growth has not moved in directions favoring the Democratic party. Republicans are at a nearly 3-2 voter registration disadvantage, but benefit from greater activism among workers and more effective party organization. Democratic candidates have frequently cannibalized one another in party primaries, but Republicans have only commenced to have intra-party nomination fights. The powerful state legislature has been dominated by copper and cattle interests in the past, but more recently urban interests have gained strength, and legislative reapportionment will hasten change in directions still to be determined fully. Split-ticket voting for Republican candidates seeking high office exemplifies the lack of party regularity among nominal Democratic voters.

CALIFORNIA:

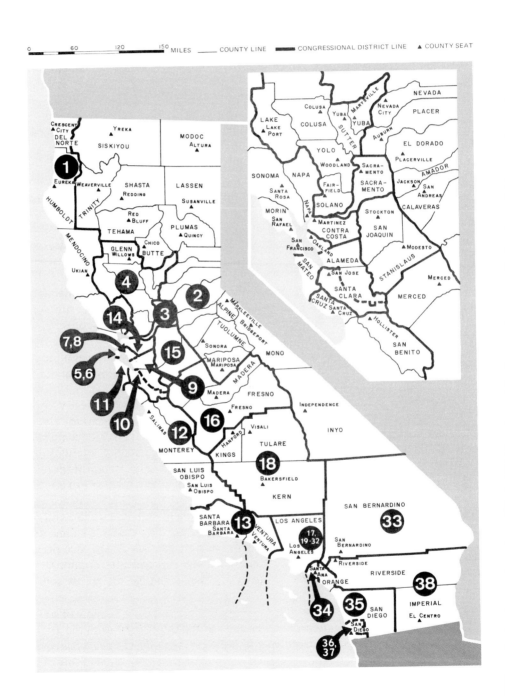

0   60   120   150 MILES ___ COUNTY LINE ▬▬ CONGRESSIONAL DISTRICT LINE ▲ COUNTY SEAT

Totton J. Anderson

Enigmatic Eldorado of National Politics

California politics, to paraphrase a key Churchillian remark, is an enigma inside a riddle, wrapped up in a mystery. Informed analysts constantly invoke such terms as "unique," "atypical," "unorthodox," and "nonconformist," in an attempt to portray the intricate pattern which seemingly violates the accepted canons of American state politics. The symptoms of confusion are readily ascertainable in the polemics utilized by authoritative commentators in classifying California as a one-party state, a two-party state, or simply "a state of mind"!

Without denying the efficacy of the stereotype of unconventionality, Californians are apt to seek its origin in the western heritage of rugged individualism which prompted a dynamic and imaginative citizenry to seek pragmatic solutions to indigenous political problems. The inherent vitality of California politics is exemplified in a wide range of political experimentation, from the sophisticated practice of cross-filing to the frenetic espousal of "loony" panaceas for redistribution of wealth.

The resultant free-wheeling, political milieu is marked by many singular and seemingly incongruous rules, circumstances, and modes of behavior, running counter to accepted norms. Guided by the solicitous ministrations of professional publicists, for instance, the voters have developed a penchant for participating actively in the legislative process through use of the initiative and referendum. The powerful political leverage of patronage has been sacrificed upon the altar of an expanded, virtually all-inclusive civil service system.

Where else in the United States has there been such a heavy traffic in voters crossing party lines at election time under the banner of "nonpartisanship"? Not the least of these political vagaries has been the formulation of a fluid coalition between conservatives in both major parties to protect the economic status quo, come what may! In attempting to follow the vacillating and opportunistic political leadership in his state, where candidates are exceedingly reluctant to admit publicly their party affiliation, the voter has developed a certain ambivalence toward his party loyalties. His consequent behavior sometimes borders upon a rather bizarre political neutralism and provides some of the distinguishing hallmarks of the California mores. On the other hand, the state has failed only once since 1912 either to follow or to produce the national trend in presidential elections. In 1960, Nixon managed to defeat Kennedy by the incredible margin of some 35,713 absentee ballots.

Since the abolition of cross-filing in 1954, the Republican monopoly of state politics yielded to the temporary ascendancy of the Democrats, until the 1966 election when there was a resurgence of Republican strength. The result has been the establishment of an effective two-party system for the first time in this century. With an electorate recruited from the nation as a whole, it is not surprising to find the California political pattern moving from the atypical, toward a more conventional mold.

California was spared the usual probationary period in official territorial status. The leaders of the American colony, newly acquired from Mexico, formulated a state constitution and gained ratification from the electorate November 13, 1849. The territory was admitted into the Union as a free state September 9, 1850. Its institutional framework was patterned after that of the other American states. Little of the influence of several centuries of Spanish and Mexican rule remains, with the exception of laws relating to riparian rights, community property rights, land grant titles, and certain aspects of commission government. However, much of the romantic charm of Old Spain is reflected in the way of life, particularly of southern Californians.

For the first hundred and ten years of its existence, from the election of Democrat Peter H. Burnett as governor on November 13, 1849, until the inauguration of Edmund G. Brown in January 1959, the predominant party political influence in California was Republican. Of thirty-two governors (four acting) during this period, seventeen were Republicans, thirteen were Democrats and two belonged to "hyphenated" parties.[1] One more Republican was added to the list in 1966 with the election of Ronald Reagan. Since the turn of this century, the Democrats have been able to win only three gubernatorial elections, Culbert Olson in 1938 and "Pat" Brown in 1958 and 1962. During the past two decades the Democratic registrants, an overwhelming majority in the electorate, have been unable or unwilling to control the political machinery in the state. After they finally elected Governor Olson in 1938, they promptly lost the gubernatorial office for the next twenty years: the most logical explanation, attributed to former Democratic Attorney General Robert Kennedy, was that Olson believed he had a mandate to "create the millennium in the biennium."

Republican dominance of the state Senate has been even more impressive, extending from 1891 to 1956. In 1956 each party shared the forty-member body equally, but two Republicans deserted to the opposition and the Democrats organized the upper house for the first time in over sixty-five years. The membership of the first state Assembly, meeting from 1849 to 1850, was nonpartisan. For the succeeding forty years the major parties alternated control for periods extending from two to six years. Beginning in 1894 the Republicans established a virtual monopoly of the lower house until the New Deal era of 1937-40, after which they again controlled the electorate until the Democratic landslide of 1958. Although Republican gains in 1966 were impressive, the Democrats managed to retain a narrow margin in the Senate, the Assembly, and the congressional delegation.

Republicans also maintained a predominant position in national politics. Of the twenty-nine presidential elections in which California has participated since its first one in 1852, the Republicans have been successful eighteen times and the Democrats, eleven.[2] The people of California have been directly electing their United States senators only since 1914. The Republicans have had a complete monopoly of one seat and have shared the other with the Democrats roughly 50 percent of the time. The importance of partisan control of the governor's office

1. The American ("Know-Nothing") party in 1855 and the Union (Republican) party in 1863. Both major parties splintered into factions from time to time: the Lecompton Democrats (southern, pro-slavery) held the governorship for a short period (1859-61) and the Progressives or liberal Republican wing elected Hiram Johnson twice, in 1910 and 1914.

2. A Whig (1860) and a Progressive (1912) are included in Republican victories.

was dramatically demonstrated by Earl Warren, who held the Senate seats firmly with the Republican party by power of appointment: Knowland (1945) and Kuchel (1952). The Republicans also dominated the state's congressional delegation from 1900 to 1932 and again from 1946 to 1958.

California politics cannot be described accurately, however, in terms of nominal party control over policy, or the machinery by which policy is made. During certain periods of the state's history, interest groups completely dominated state government, splinter groups captured the traditional party organizations, and nonpartisanship became a standard mode of political action despite party labels. Throughout the 1870's and into the early 1890's, for instance, the Southern Pacific machine manned by the "Big Four," Collis P. Huntington, Mark Hopkins, Charles Crocker, and Leland Stanford, manipulated state politics. Even under the aegis of a new constitution drafted in 1879, and with the platforms of the Republican, Democratic, Independent, Workingmen's, and Temperance parties denouncing monopoly, unequal taxation, and the great land barons, the machine virtually was the government. In 1916 the old-line Republicans lost control of their party to Progressives. Under the leadership of Hiram Johnson and the reformers of the Lincoln-Roosevelt League the insurgents became the dominant wing of the Republican party from 1910 to 1914.[3]

In 1934, Socialist party leader Upton Sinclair changed his registration to Democrat, seized the leadership of that party and was nominated as the Democratic candidate for governor. Governor Warren (1943-53) was ostensibly Republican, but his support was bipartisan and his administrative policy was markedly nonpartisan in character. So was that of his successor, Governor Goodwin J. Knight (1953-59). In order to maintain nominal control over California politics in recent years, at least, the Republican party has been forced to make substantial compromises in both party principles and public policies. The failure of the blatantly partisan campaigns of conservatives William F. Knowland for governor in 1958, and Barry Goldwater for president in 1964, represent two recent attempts to abandon the middle of the political road in contemporary California politics. Richard Nixon's 1962 gubernatorial campaign as a moderate was waged against an incumbent Democrat in the Warren tradition. Reagan, in his successful gubernatorial bid in 1966, moved steadily from right to center of the ideological spectrum.

GEOGRAPHY, RESOURCES AND ECONOMY

California's terrain offers dramatic contrasts in natural phenomena. Its land area of 156,573 square miles places it third in size and its 18,234,000 population now exceeds that of New York. Principal topographic features include the Coastal Range facing the Pacific Ocean and extending the entire length of the state, while the Sierra Nevadas lie on the eastern border. The mountains host vast timber resources of fir, pine, and redwood, offer watershed protection for agricultural crop land, and provide valuable grazing for a flourishing cattle industry. The northern counties of Napa and Sonoma grow the grapes for the wine industry, while Santa Clara produces fruit, nuts, berries, and cattle. Cradled between the two mountain ranges is the Great Central Valley, one of the most fertile agricultural areas in the world. The variety of crops produced is astonishing: tomatoes, asparagus, alfalfa, sugar beets, fruit, barley, walnuts, celery, hops, and wheat, to mention only a few.

3. See Robert C. Cleland and Glenn S. Dumke, *From Wilderness to Empire* (rev. ed.; New York: Knopf, 1959), pp. 190, 251.

On the west coast, Salinas in Monterey County is rightly called "the salad bowl" of the nation.

The Tehachapi Mountains constitute the southern boundary of the Great Valley, creating a natural geographic, economic, and political barrier, dividing the state in two. The forty-four counties in the north surround the vital trade area of metropolitan San Francisco, while the fourteen counties in the south are oriented toward the giant, sprawling metropolis of Los Angeles, constituting the second primary trading area of the state.[4] Below the Tehachapis and to the east are the Mojave and Colorado deserts; to the south and west southern California is ribbed by smaller transverse mountain ranges. Here thrive the lucrative cotton growers of Kern County, the walnut and lima bean farmers of Ventura, the lemon, orange and grapefruit orchards of Los Angeles, Orange, and Riverside counties, and the productive truck farms of San Bernardino, San Diego, and the Imperial Valley. Throughout this area may also be found some of the most valuable oil and natural gas resources in the United States.

Only about one-fourth of the 100,206,720 acres constituting the land area of the state is level, the remainder being rolling hills and rugged mountains. Nearly half of the land is publicly owned. The federal government controls 44,996,000 acres or roughly 44.9 percent of the total. Much of this is in national forests, monuments, parks, recreation areas, and installations of the Air Force, Army, and Navy.

The equable climate is one of the most important facts in the political life of the state. It is a tourist attraction augmenting the economy; it is one cause of the incredible "population explosion" which has catapulted the state into first place in the Union; but most importantly, the distribution of rainfall is one of the causes of the politically significant north versus south and urban versus rural influences in state politics. The average annual rainfall in the northeastern corner is one hundred and ten inches; in the southeast it is two inches. Efforts to redistribute the available water supply and to tap new resources have brought the allegation that California "is just one big reclamation project." The equitable distribution of water throughout the state through federal, state, or private agencies, the respective claims of the counties of origin in the north and those of greatest need in the south, and the stark implications of limited future expansion for the state as a whole because of inadequate water constitute one of the greatest single complexes of issues of public policy facing the electorate today. State planners estimate that in the next several decades over 10 billion dollars will be required to anticipate the demands of industrial expansion and the increase in population. The completion of such a water project might well become the most significant undertaking of any state government in the present generation.

About 255,828 of the more than two million rural inhabitants, or less than 2 percent of the population, work the 99,000 farms in the state. Although Californians led the nation in 1963 with a $3,430,400,000 income derived from agriculture, only about 9 percent of the land area is under cultivation.[5] With the exception of tobacco, every major commercial crop in the United States is grown in

4. The U.S. Census Bureau groups the fifty-eight counties into ten statistical areas: North Coast, Sacramento Valley, Sierra, San Francisco Bay, South Central Coast, San Joaquin Valley, South Coast, Los Angeles Metropolitan, San Diego, and Southeast. This serves as a useful basis for analyzing election returns and for assembling other political data.

5. The average size of the California farm has grown from 250 acres in 1920 to 372 in 1964, and the number of farms over 1,000 acres in size from 4,906 to 6,013 during the same period. Roughly 16.6 million acres are designated as actual and potential cropland, but

California. Cotton, the state's most important cash crop, is heavily subsidized by the federal government and is a prime example of "big business" in agriculture. Over 666,319 bales or roughly 40 percent of the total 1958 crop was "forfeited" for federal subsidy loans.[6] Most of the nation's supply of lemons, grapes, almonds, apricots, plums, prunes, walnuts, olives, dates, and figs are California grown. Three counties lead the country in specific agricultural accomplishments: Fresno claims the greatest value in total agricultural products sold; Los Angeles is the top producer of dairy products; and Monterey is foremost in the value of vegetables harvested for sale.

Important changes affecting agriculture on a national scale are apparent in the state. The rapid growth of industrial phases of farming—processing, canning, and freezing—is converting agricultural economics from small farm to large corporate enterprises. A by-product of this development is the progressive depletion of the farm population and the origin of a farm factory-labor problem.[7] The influx of over 1,500 new residents every day, most of whom settle initially in the cities, has caused the pre-emption of choice farmland for housing developments, especially in Los Angeles and Orange counties. One of the most perplexing agricultural problems, fraught with international political overtones, arises from the nature of the truck and fruit farming enterprises which demand seasonal labor correlated with crop harvesting time. Farmers have met the periodic seasonal labor demand from local, residential labor sources, migrant labor supply, and contract labor, primarily of Mexican nationals imported for the purpose.

The initial impetus to the state's industrial economy came with the discovery of gold at Sutter's Mill near Coloma in 1848: four years later California was credited with more than 60 percent ($81,000,000) of the world's gold production. The first oil boom developed in the early 1860's, and output reached four million barrels annually by the turn of the century, to be followed by commercial exploitation of natural gas in the late 1920's. In 1963, the output was 300 million barrels of petroleum, 26 million barrels of natural gas liquids, 646 billion cubic feet of natural gas—together worth 1.0 billion dollars. Other valuable products include cement, sand, gravel, stone, boron minerals, clays, gold, and lime. During these decades the motion picture industry and tourist trade grew, and the second world war triggered expansion in the aviation, automobile, and electronics industries. Since 1940 the economic structure of the state has altered from a predominantly basic-industries economy, producing agricultural, mining, forestry, and fishing products, to a manufacturing economy.

The Chamber of Commerce in an economic survey lists the following reasons for the rapid expansion of industry in California: population growth in the West providing a market of over 28,000,000 persons; increases in transcontinental freight rates which have forced major business enterprises into a program of plant decentralization; expanded western regional sources of supply for basic raw materials and semifinished components for fabrication or assembly; enlargement of

only 12 million can be utilized without an artificial water supply. Total net income per farm in 1958 averaged $7,556 (about three times the national average).

6. *Los Angeles Mirror News*, November 4, 1959; twelve farmers or farm corporations received over $100,000, the range being $128,488 for 709 bales to $707,970 for 3,900 bales. Grain storage payments in fiscal 1959 totaled $8,144,000. Total government subsidy to agriculture in 1963 was $32,200,000.

7. Farmer cooperatives were organized many years ago to process, store, and market crops such as walnuts (Walnut Growers' Exchange), citrus (Citrus Growers' Exchange), and raisins, prunes, and apricots. Other farm interest groups include the Wool and Cattlemen's associations.

the labor supply and attractive living conditions; the expansion of power, fuel, and water supplies; and finally, the market potential of the Pacific Basin.[8]

The total labor force in California reached an all-time high of 6,852,000 in 1963, representing a net increase of 211,000 over the preceding year. Civilian labor increased by 189,000 in 1962-63, to a new high of 6,441,000. During the past decade the growth of California's labor force has been more than twice that of the nation; 35.4 percent compared with 14.4 percent. Membership in organized unions totaled 1,824,100 in 1965. As a rule, California's ratio of employed to unemployed approximates the national average, while the per capita income of $2,974 in 1963 was 21.4 percent above the national average.

POPULATION

A most significant political fact in the life of Californians of the present generation is the post-World War II "population explosion" and its consequences. Each succeeding decennial census has seen the progression of the center of population across the United States from a starting point near Baltimore, Maryland, circa 1790, to a temporary resting place six and one-half miles north and west of Centralia, Illinois, in 1960. The direction of the movement is unmistakably toward the Pacific Coast and California, where the population has doubled each twenty years since statehood. Since World War II, California's population has increased 130 percent, from 8.3 to 19.3 million. In the last decade the civilian population has been augmented by approximately 572,000 persons a year or somewhat more than 1,500 new residents each day. The 5,220,000 new inhabitants represent an increase of 48.5 percent compared to 18.5 percent increase for the nation as a whole. Nor is the common shibboleth that the state is a retirement haven for "oldsters" true: it has less than the national average of persons over sixty-five years of age. Emergency production demands of the federal government's national defense policy during and following World War II was probably the most important single factor in the population growth of the state.[9] Manufacturing claims the largest segment of the non-agricultural working force, 1,458,000; trade is a close second with 1,346,000; followed in order by service workers, 1,181,000; government employees, 1,005,000; construction workers,

8. *California Bluebook*, 1958 (Sacramento: State Printing Office, 1958), pp. 826-27. For this entire section, see the essay entitled "Economic Survey of California" prepared by the Research Department of the California State Chamber of Commerce.

9. Unless otherwise credited, statistics relating to population and the economy are from: *California Statistical Abstract*, 1964, and the U.S. Bureau of the Census, *Statistical Abstract*, 1964.

Year	Per Cent Increase	California in National Ranking	Total Population
1900-10	60.1	21	2,377,549
1910-20	44.1	12	3,426,861
1920-30	65.7	8	5,677,251
1930-40	21.7	6	6,907,387
1940-50	53.3	5	10,586,223
1950-60	49.5	2	15,717,204

Census Bureau projections indicate that the present population of 18,234,000 will expand to a possible total of 22,000,000 by the year 1970, at which time California will contain 11 percent of the nation's inhabitants. In 1963 California surpassed New York to become the most populous state in the nation.

386,000; transportation, utilities and communication, 381,000; agriculture, forestry, fisheries, 335,000; and finance, insurance and real estate employees, 318,000.

The political implications of the invasion of migrants also includes national origins, characteristics, deployment throughout the state, and mode of livelihood. The 1960 census reveals the national origins of the major groups of foreign-born white migrants to be (in descending numerical order): Mexico, Canada, United Kingdom, Italy, Germany, Asia, U.S.S.R., Sweden; the entire category constitutes a total of 2,837,557. This pattern reflects the impact of the federal immigration laws. The non-white segment of the state's population represented 8 percent of the total in 1960. Approximately 883,861 were Negroes, who constitute 5.6 percent of the population. Other non-white groups of foreign descent include 157,317 Japanese; 95,600 Chinese; 39,014 Indians; 65,459 Filipinos; and 20,723 miscellaneous. The non-whites have settled in the major urban areas where they are increasing more rapidly than the Caucasians. Minority racial or national groups having significance in the tactics of political campaigning are the Mexicans, Negroes, Japanese, and Chinese.

Migration has been the major source of population growth from the days of the gold rush. Eighteen different states have each contributed over 100,000 inhabitants to California, lending credence to the allegation that "natives" are scarce! In 1940, for instance, one person in eight had come from another state within the preceding five years. By 1960, over 52 percent of the population had migrated to California from other states. Also, California has a high degree of urbanization and one of the highest percentages of intra-state migration in the United States.

The political implications of the incredible burgeoning of the state's population are not yet altogether discernible. Republicans have dominated state politics during the present century in spite of the presence of a latent Democratic majority in the electorate since New Deal days. The pattern was held virtually intact through the 1956 election, regardless of the impact of over several million migrants on the resident population during the preceding eight years. The Democratic victory on the state and congressional levels in 1958 may have marked a turning point in state politics; but observers are aware that the split within the Republican party, coupled with two controversial issues on the ballot, may have been more important than any awakening in the Democratic party as an explanation of the Republican defeat.

An interesting thesis has been posited and contested, that the majority of the post-World War II migrants came from the South, and are conservative Democrats. Upon viewing the Republican state party platform, they identify themselves with its candidates in state elections, but respond to traditional partisan leanings in the national election and vote the Democratic ticket. Registration figures show that the Republicans enjoyed a substantial majority running as high as 75 percent until 1934, when the Democrats forged ahead with a total of 52 percent, a lead that the party has not yet relinquished. The change in registration advantage from one party to the other has yet to alter the basic patterns of state and national politics in California.

The extreme mobility of the population in terms of intra-state migration may be an important factor influencing party identification. Precinct and party ties are undoubtedly made and broken frequently. This factor and the hypothesis that Democrats moving from metropolitan areas join the resident Republican majority in suburbia are well worth further investigation. Some evidence of this development is apparent in the ring of Republican assembly districts surrounding the largely Democratic central city of Los Angeles. Another problem relates to the geographic disposition of in-migrants belonging to minority groups. The assumptions are yet to be tested as to whether they join existing colonies in the metropolitan areas, or strike out for new locations; and in the latter instance, how they identify themselves politically. One vital fact relating the problem of migration to politics is that 60 percent of the population is located in the ten southern counties known as southern California, while the remaining 40 percent is scattered over the forty-eight northern counties. This circumstance is at the heart of the entire problem of reapportionment, since the balance of political power is firmly implanted in the "southern state" of California!

EDUCATION

Population pressure and the enthusiastic response of the electorate in supplying funds for the establishment, ensures that education will remain among the major issues of public policy in the state for the foreseeable future. California maintains the largest system of tuition-free higher education in the world. There are 368,000 students enrolled in eighty-two junior colleges, 133,000 in fifteen state colleges (two more are planned) and 65,000 on the six general campuses of the University of California (two more are planned). Meanwhile, the private institutions charging tuition are training 33 percent of all students attending four-year colleges. On the secondary level, state and local school districts are paying approximately $3.0 billion a year to maintain the elementary and high school systems, which require the addition of 10,000 classrooms annually.[10]

Since funds for this vast system of public education must be provided by the state government, the education committees of the legislature, the speaker of the Assembly, the governor and the elected state superintendent of public instruction become focal points for political activity. Professional leadership in public education on both the administrative and teacher level has become highly politicized and all echelons of the system lobby the legislature.

The University of California, backed by a large and powerful alumni association, wages a continuous battle with the state college system over the allocation of funds to higher education. Using its privileged legal sanctuary as a corporation with constitutional status, the University obtains over $150 million a year (projected to $300 million in the next decade or so), roughly one-third more than the total appropriations for all of the state colleges. Behind the struggle for funds is the question of the respective roles these institutions are to play in the field of higher education; such matters as the prerogative of granting higher academic degrees, which in turn affects student admission policies, salary scales for recruitment of professional talent, and adequate library facilities are involved. The position of the state colleges has been strengthened recently by the attainment of a large measure of administrative autonomy under a separate Board of Trustees. The creation of a consultative and planning agency known as the Coordinating Council for Higher Education representing the University and state college systems, the public junior colleges, and the private colleges and universities, has alleviated the rivalry to some extent.

10. The $1.0 billion annual appropriation for education represents 40 percent of the state budget.

The office of superintendent of public instruction is considered to be "non-partisan," but both parties view statewide elected officials as potential gubernatorial candidates and become active in their campaigns. In recent years conservative groups, with a Republican bent, have maintained a continuing attack upon the curriculum, teaching methods, and textbooks of the public school system. In the 1962 election they found a champion in Dr. Max Rafferty, former teacher and (very briefly) school superintendent, who was pitted against a liberal, UCLA English Professor, Democrat, and one-time president of the Los Angeles Board of Education, Dr. Ralph Richardson. Richardson was actively aided by Democrats and endorsed by union-labor and professional-educator groups of teachers and administrators, including the outgoing state superintendent and all but one member of the state Board of Education and by Governor Brown. Rafferty was supported by Republican business interests and conservative groups, generally, including the state American Legion. He felt compelled to disavow official membership in the John Birch Society.

The key emotional issue of the campaign, developed in a seemingly endless series of debates between the two candidates, centered upon the dichotomous proposition of "Dewey Progressivism" versus the "Three R's," with Richardson accusing Rafferty of having the "finest mind of the twelfth century" and Rafferty charging his opponent with "sympathy for left-leaning liberalism." Rafferty won in a close election, 2,681,651 to 2,461,801, and since then has been the center of controversy in education policy-making circles because of his conservative views, forcefully expressed. In the Spring of 1968, he won an astonishing victory in the Republican primary over the incumbent United States senator, Thomas H. Kuchel.

Solutions to the problems of a rapidly expanding state system of higher education have been difficult to achieve in an atmosphere of urgency created by the impact of sheer numbers upon existing facilities. Student unrest has been evidenced by demonstrations over "alienation"; "the loyalty oath"; "free speech" and "dirty speech" controversies, along with other activist incidents in respect to the Vietnam War. The Reagan administration faced these "happenings" with stern disapproval reflected in severe budgetary cuts for both the University and State Colleges in the name of economy. The net effect has been to compromise the public image of one of the largest and most progressive systems of higher education in the nation and to "politicize" the issue in terms of partisanship.

THE PRESS: FROM CRUSADING LIBERALISM TO CONSERVATIVE REPUBLICANISM

The *Californian* was the first newspaper published in the area. Its initial edition of August 15, 1846, carried a feature story of the declaration of war by the United States against Mexico. California journalism has a proud tradition created by able and public-spirited editors, who fought the corruption of vested interests which were making a shambles of democratic government in San Francisco, Sacramento, and Los Angeles during the latter half of the nineteenth century.

One of the first successful dailies, the *Alta Californian*, had Bret Harte as an editor and Mark Twain as a contributor. James King of the *Daily Evening Bulletin* crusaded in San Francisco in the 1850's, at the time when James McClatchy in the *Sacramento Bee* championed the embattled Sacramento Valley farmers in their fight against land monopoly. Fremont Older of the *Bulletin* along with his fellow

Californian, Lincoln Steffens, exposed the all-powerful Southern Pacific Railroad Company which dominated the state government at the turn of the century. [11] Unfortunately, the tradition is dead, or at least dormant. Newspaper publishing has itself become a multi-vested interest, penetrating every important segment of the economy and exercising vast influence over public opinion. The press is conservative, business-oriented, and Republican. With the gradual elimination of Democratic papers California is now virtually a one-party press state.

The size and competence of the press corps assigned to the "capitol beat" in Sacramento today testifies to the importance of California as a national news source. The Associated Press has thirteen men in its bureau, the UPI has eight: altogether, fifty-five accredited correspondents covered the 1965 session of the state legislature. Each major daily has at least one correspondent in Sacramento, or is associated with a special news service. Fourteen correspondents provided the radio and television coverage for each major network and for the independents.

Three leading Republican dailies have exerted the greatest political influence in the state. The *Los Angeles Times* is published by the Chandler family, irreconcilable foe of union labor and vigorous ally of the Merchants and Manufacturer's Association in the promotion of the economic future of southern California. The *San Francisco Chronicle* has had an important voice in shaping the political and economic destiny of its metropolitan area. The *Oakland Tribune*, published by former United States Senator William F. Knowland, has exerted varying degrees of influence in the affairs of people living in the East Bay region and in Oakland, third largest city in the state.

The Hearst press, comprising the *San Francisco Examiner*, the *Los Angeles Herald Express*, and *San Francisco News-Call Bulletin*, sought a new policy under the direction of William R. Hearst, Jr. Editorially the papers expressed more moderate political views, but economic pressures among other considerations caused the Hearst interests to seek opportunities to merge their papers, dividing the morning and afternoon markets with principal competitors. The morning *San Francisco Examiner* was merged with the afternoon *News-Call Bulletin*, leaving the morning field to the *Chronicle* for a six-day week; the two papers join in publishing a Sunday edition. The *Los Angeles Examiner* was unable to meet the competition of the *Times* and Hearst merged it with his afternoon *Herald-Express*. Chandler then discontinued publishing the afternoon *Mirror-News*. Thus two papers disappeared from the Los Angeles scene, leaving the morning field to the *Times* while the *Herald-Examiner* had the afternoon market. Both papers are Republican in editorial policy. The only Democratic daily in Los Angeles, the tabloid *Daily News*, succumbed some years ago to the competition of the afternoon Republican *Mirror*. The Democrats do not have a major metropolitan paper sympathetic to their party anywhere in the state.

The smaller newspaper chains include: the three independent McClatchy papers, the *Bee* of Sacramento, of Fresno, and of Modesto; the Democratic-independent John P. Scripps papers in Tulare, Redding, and Ventura, anchored by the *Ventura Star-Free Press*; the arch-Republican Copley press, the *San Diego Union* and *San Diego Tribune*, and the Ridder papers in San Jose, Pasadena, Long Beach, and Orange County. There are several fine, locally run papers such as the *Oroville Mercury*, the *San Jose Mercury-News* and the *Woodland Democrat*. The Negro press in California consists of about half-a-dozen papers. One of the oldest, the

11. Federal Writer's Project, *California: A Guide to the Golden State* (New York: Hastings House, 1939), pp. 109-16.

California Eagle, has been published since 1879. Others reporting their circulation figures to *Editor and Publisher* include: the *Los Angeles Eagle*, 27,500; the *Los Angeles Sentinel*, 30,735; *Oakland Voice*, 12,500; *San Diego Voice*, 10,500; *San Francisco Reporter*, 8,762; and a "throw-away" merchandising paper, the *Herald Dispatch*, claiming about 21,000 which is published in southern California. The combined press leaves a great deal to be desired in the matter of a constructive representation of the Negro's interest; none of the papers, for instance, can be classed with the *Chicago Defender* or the *Pittsburgh Courier*. Foreign-language newspapers service the various nationality and linguistic groups in the state. Those with the largest circulations include the following: Chinese, Japanese, Italian, French, Spanish, Russian, German, and Greek.

The preponderantly significant press influence in state and local politics has been the triumvirate of the *Los Angeles Times*, the *San Francisco Examiner*, and the *Oakland Tribune*, known as the "journalistic axis" when acting in concert. Formation of this alliance in 1922 in support of conservative Republicanism is credited to Kyle Palmer, long-time political editor of the *Times*.[12] The axis often joins in support of conservatives as opposed to liberals within the Republican party and opposes virtually all Democratic candidates as a matter of principle. The various publishers exert great influence at city hall. A persistent legend harbored by political sophisticates is that the city of Oakland is run from "the Tribune Tower" and Los Angeles, from the "foot of Spring Street" (i.e., the location of the *Times* Building).

This axis suffered a spell of political deviationism after the 1958 primary election. The *Chronicle* withdrew its support from Knowland in the gubernatorial race on the grounds that "we have been unfavorably impressed with his subsequent campaign."[13] The *Los Angeles Times* has moved away from its often blatant Republican partisanship in recent elections. In the 1962 gubernatorial contest between Richard M. Nixon and Edmund G. "Pat" Brown, the paper was cited by both parties for thoroughness and professional objectivity in reporting. The paper supported Nelson Rockefeller in the 1964 presidential primary, but was trapped into shifting to Barry Goldwater in the general election by a prior announcement that it would "endorse the Republican nominee." Unfortunately for the journalistic climate of the state, the western edition of the *New York Times* was short lived.

There is ample evidence to support the contention that the press is overwhelmingly Republican.[14] *Editor and Publisher*, for instance, found that of ninety-five newspapers reporting the 1960 presidential election, sixty-five with a circulation of 3,797,660 supported Nixon and twenty with a circulation of 471,871 endorsed Kennedy; ten papers with a circulation of 172,986 remained independent. The Goldwater candidacy temporarily broke the Republican-support pattern in 1964. The division favored Johnson. He received support from thirty-six papers including the *San Francisco Chronicle*, the *San Francisco Examiner*, and the *Los Angeles Herald-Examiner*. He was endorsed by papers having a total circulation of

12. The issue was the election in 1922 of Friend W. Richardson, a conservative gubernatorial candidate favored by the *Times*. The liberal incumbent, Republican William D. Stephens, was defeated by the axis at the urgent behest of the *Times* publisher. See Richard V. Hyer, "California," in Robert A. Allen (ed.), *Our Sovereign State* (New York: Vanguard Press, 1949), p. 382.

13. Editorial, October 30, 1958.

14. Note: *Editor and Publisher* for October and November 1960 and 1964; also 45th Annual *Yearbook*.

2,300,991 while the Goldwater figure was 1,502,958. Thirteen papers with a circulation of 217,769 remained independent.

Analyses of such criteria as editorial policy, party space assignments, placement of partisan news, number and position of photographs printed, slanting of headlines, editorializing in news-columns, suppressing unfavorable news, and even propagandizing in the society section indicate that several of the most influential Republican papers in California are vulnerable to charges of "manipulating" political news.

The situation would be competitive if a strong Democratic daily existed in each of the four major metropolitan areas. The independent-Democratic press, such as the *Bee* chain in the Valley, and relatively isolated papers such as the *Woodland Democrat* or the *Ventura Star-Free Press*, although influential in their areas, scarcely provide a countervailing influence to the relatively violent Republican partisanship in the rest of the press of the state.

In the last several years the conservative press has encountered problems in adjusting to ultra-rightist groups. The California Newspaper Publisher's Association launched a counteroffensive against extremist groups intent upon intimidating individual newspapers in order to dictate editorial policy. A committee of the Association reported in the first week of November 1964 that "members of the John Birch Society and other extreme right wing groups have joined the long list of left wing extremist groups which . . . have vigorously and viciously attacked the integrity of the reporting in the press. . . ." The Association proposed to set up machinery for investigating, weighing, and recommending action in specific cases of organized pressure brought to its attention.[15]

The *Los Angeles Times* received a barrage of letters from irate subscribers when it accepted and printed, as paid advertising matter, a brochure on the controversial John Birch Society. In a statement of his paper's policy, Editor Nick B. Williams replied:

We think that we must accept paid political advertising even from those with whom we strongly disagree. For advertising, we believe, is subject to the same general concept of the free press that governs editorial discussion and reporting. I ought also to make it clear that our Advertising Department does have the authority to reject advertising matter, and it has done this. It rejects material that clearly violates the laws of libel, it rejects material of incontrovertibly bad taste, it rejects material that it believes is an incitation to violence, and it rejects material from any group that appears on the official governmental list of subversive organizations. The John Birch Society is not so listed, although the Ku Klux Klan and the Communist Party are indeed so listed.[16]

NOMINATIONS AND ELECTIONS

Nominations to elective office in California are conducted through a series of primary elections. The nonpartisan primary is used to select judges, school officials, and county and municipal officers. The direct partisan primary has been employed since 1909 to designate candidates for Congress and for state offices, with the exception of the nonpartisan position of state superintendent of public

15. The author has drawn upon articles covering the 1962, 1964 and 1966 elections co-authored for the *Western Political Quarterly* with Eugene C. Lee of the University of California. Acknowledgment is also made of the aid rendered by Faith Windsor, Teaching Assistant at the University of Southern California, in gathering data for this revision.

16. *Los Angeles Times*, October 4, 1964.

instruction. The presidential primary serves to designate delegates to the national party conventions.[17]

Abandonment of the corrupt convention system and adoption of nomination by primary election was part of the Progressive reform movement of 1900-1920. To loosen further the control of lobbies over the party system, the state legislature passed a statute in 1911 permitting popular election of United States senators. In 1913 cross-filing was introduced, sanctioning the attempt of a candidate to obtain the nomination of one or more parties other than his own.[18]

During the forty-six years it was in use (1913-59), cross-filing was frequently cited as a primary cause for the general weakness of the party system in California. Some of the consequences of the practice were: reduction of a partisan primary to virtually a nonpartisan election, with voters in both major parties often receiving identical ballots listing candidates without party identification; reduction of the number of candidates presented to the electorate in the primary because of the rise of extra-party, pre-primary, endorsing auxiliaries; occasional election of minority candidates; perpetuation of "incumbent empires," partly because of the automatic placement of the incumbent's name at the head of the candidate list; and loss of partisan identification with issues of public policy, since candidates campaigned under a "middle-of-the-road" banner, often refusing to identify themselves publicly with any party.[19]

The effect of cross-filing in California politics was mitigated by adoption in 1952 of an amendment to the election law requiring the identification of the candidate's party, by printing "Rep." or "Dem." on the ballot after his name. (The candidate must now have been a registered member of his party for a minimum of three months and have remained unaffiliated with any other party for the year preceding the filing of his nominating petition.) The results were spectacular: in

17. Principal national elective officers: 2 United States senators, 38 representatives, 86 to 163 delegates to each national convention and 40 presidential electors. State officers: (every four years) governor, lieutenant governor, treasurer, controller, secretary of state, attorney general, 4 members of the Board of Equalization, superintendent of public instruction (nonpartisan), 40 senators (one-half every two years for a four-year term), and 80 assemblymen (80, every two years).

18. A candidate might enter his name on the primary ballot of any party, no test of party affiliation being required. The voter received a ballot listing the candidates without any party identification (until 1954); however, he received only the ballot of the party in which he was registered since all candidates did not cross-file. A "decline to state" registrant was not permitted to participate. To win a "double nomination" the candidate had to obtain a plurality of votes in his own and the opposition party; he was disqualified if he won only the nomination of the opposition party. If he won both, his name appeared on the November ballot carrying both party labels, his own appearing first. Cross-filing was not permitted for either nonpartisan or strictly party offices. See Bernard L. Hyink, Seyom Brown, and Ernest W. Thacker, *Politics and Government in California* (3rd ed.; New York: Crowell, 1963), pp. 33-48. For the topics in this section see: Henry A. Turner and John A. Vieg, *The Government and Politics of California* (3rd ed.; New York: McGraw-Hill, 1967), chaps. 3, 4.

19. Between 1914 and 1950, the offices of attorney general, secretary of state, and controller were won in the primary in seven out of ten elections; in 1932 only 8.9 percent of the candidates seeking congressional nominations cross-filed, while in 1952 the number reached 85.2 percent; in 1944, admittedly a high point in the history of the cross-filing system, more state Senate seats were uncontested than contested; of 20 seats, 12 went by default, 6 were determined in the primary, and only 2 were decided in the general election. In the same election 22 state Assembly seats went by default and of the 58 remaining, 39 were determined in the primary, leaving only 19 to be contested in the general election. Charles G. Bell, "A Study of Four Selected Factors which Contributed to the Inability of the Democratic Party to Mobilize Successfully Its Latent Majority" (Master's thesis, University of Southern California, 1958), pp. 115-50.

the 1952 congressional race with no party label, 14 seats out of 30 were won in the primary by cross-filed or unopposed candidates; in 1954 the number fell to two and rose to three in 1956. Only 18 of the 80 state Assembly seats were contested in the general election of 1952, but there were 58 contests in 1954 and 62 in 1956. The results in the state Senate were similar, if not quite so spectacular.[20]

The precipitous decline in the number of contests settled in the primary, coupled with the rising cost of running two campaigns and the fact that Governor Brown campaigned on the issue to end cross-filing, prompted the state legislature to repeal that section of the law in 1959. There is some doubt whether cross-filing prevented the reappearance of political machines in California politics, as supporters of the practice maintained, or merely caused a shift in control of public policy to a group of well organized lobbies, aided by influential elements of the powerful and conservative press. It is generally believed that incumbents were aided by the system, regardless of party affiliation. Clearly, however, the positive identification of the candidate's party has stimulated genuine partisan interest in the state politics within the electorate. This development may yet be found to be a primary cause of the resurgence of Democratic party strength in the elections held between 1956 and 1964—and certainly active partisan interest was evident in the impressive regrouping of Republican forces in 1966.

It is probably too soon to assess the effect of the 1961 apportionment upon the status of incumbency. For the 138 legislative posts open in 1964 in the House of Representatives, the state Senate and Assembly, 132 officeholders stood for re-election; only two were defeated. When compared to the 44 open seats in 1962, or even the 14 in 1960, this represented a near record in incumbent success in re-election. Nevertheless, the status of incumbency was not too secure in light of the rising factionalism in both parties; conservatives among Republicans and liberals among Democrats are both carrying increasingly bitter battles into primary campaigns, thus testing party discipline to the utmost.

As a result of reapportionment and GOP gains, the turnover in the California legislature following the 1966 elections was one of the greatest in the state's history. In the Assembly, only 46 incumbents returned to Sacramento at the start of the 1967 session. The pattern in the state Senate was more complicated and more interesting. While 18 incumbents were returned to office in the 40-man chamber, 14 ex-assemblymen were also elected. Significantly, there were more Democrats among this number (9) than there were Democratic incumbent senators. And the 8 Democratic incumbents were also outnumbered by 10 returning Republican senators. As the 1967 legislature commenced, it seemed likely that normal patterns of organization and leadership in the tradition-bound upper house might become unstrung as the various groups and factions—including the new assemblymen—vied for power.

California also employs the direct partisan primary for the election of delegates to national political conventions. Adherents of a presidential aspirant may circulate a petition containing the names of those who would constitute the delegation pledged to the candidate. In order to qualify, the slate must receive at least one-half of 1 percent (and not more than 2 percent) of the votes cast by the party in the last gubernatorial election. If the required number of names is obtained (along with the candidate's personal endorsement), his name, but not the names of the delegates, will be presented to the voters of his party in the June primary of

20. Totton J. Anderson, "The 1956 Election in California," *Western Political Quarterly*, X (March 1957), 105-7. The 1964 primary represented a continuation of trends starting in 1958 with the modification and final elimination of cross-filing.

a presidential election year. The candidate receiving a plurality of votes from partisan supporters may assume that his slate of instructed delegates will support him at least in the initial ballot of the national convention of his party. A recent change in the law now permits the selection of an unpledged delegation. Presidential primary politics in California reveals the power centers in the major parties, the dominant personalities, any factionalism which may be present, and the ideological and economic compromises which exist in support of coalitions negotiated within the party.

Certain restrictions hamper the parties in performing their normal function of sponsoring qualified candidates for the presidency, and should be added to the long list of causes for the weakness of the state's party system. The state central committee may neither select nor support a slate of delegates for the national convention; county committees may not render pre-primary endorsements or participate in the primary election. Although a candidate for delegate must file a statement of preference for a presidential candidate (except for an unpledged delegation), the question is essentially unresolved as to whether the pledge to support him must be carried beyond the first convention ballot.

These restrictions are so confining that the parties have sought ways and means to circumvent them. One of the most important is the creation of auxiliary groups such as the Republican Assembly and the Democratic Council, to which party leaders may belong. Doffing the party hat in favor of that of a private citizen, they may then render pre-primary endorsements, raise and spend money, campaign, and form slates of convention delegates.

Many other unwritten rules and customs govern the formation of a convention slate. Since the Republicans have dominated the governorship, the incumbent traditionally has led the delegation as a "favorite son" and has used the bargaining power of the large California vote to support one of the presidential aspirants. The Democrats, devoid of strategically placed favorite sons, until recently have supported a bona fide presidential aspirant. Slates of both parties contain a liberal representation of party leaders from both northern and southern California. It is also an unwritten rule that factions within the party be mollified, if possible, by including their leaders in the semi-official group of delegates.[21]

Presidential nomination politics in California invariably reveals the deep fissures in party ranks. Due to the lack of party discipline and leadership, the state is plagued by "personality factions," consisting of ambitious individuals backed by organized elements in both parties. Their support is quite frequently based upon belief in the future destiny of a particular candidate, although ideological orientation may offer powerful motivation.

Representative James Roosevelt, leader for a time of the liberal Democrats, attempted to stampede the Truman delegation to Eisenhower (before his commitment to the Republicans) in anticipation of the 1948 Democratic convention. In 1952 he jumped the Brown "free choice slate" to support Kefauver. His own candidacy for governor (1950) alienated the conservative wing of the Democratic party. Brown lost to Kefauver 485,578 to 1,155,839, but Roosevelt failed to establish his influence in the party which he had served as state chairman.

In 1956 Paul Ziffren, Democratic national committeeman, was taxed to establish a coalition between the Kefauver and Stevenson factions after a Donnybrook primary battle won by the latter. His device was ingenious: he persuaded

21. See Thomas S. Barclay, David G. Farrelly and Charles L. Clapp, "California" in Paul T. David *et al.* (eds.), *Presidential Nominating Politics in 1952: The West* (Baltimore: Johns Hopkins Press, 1954), pp. 217-51.

the National Committee to double the California delegation (from 68 to 136), permitting each delegate to cast half a vote. All factions of the party in California were given an opportunity for representation in the delegation and the party made its best showing at the polls in two decades.

The hand-picked Nixon delegation in 1960 was termed a "composite of organizational and regional elements of the party, with a strong representation of prominent financial backers." Legislators complained that they had been overlooked since only 5 of 44 Republican assemblymen and state senators were on the slate, with 4 alternates. The Democratic delegation in the same year was broadly representative of the statewide party leadership including 40 of the 72 state legislators and 15 of the 16 Democratic congressmen, with 15 legislators selected as alternates. So effective was the selection process that all of the presidential candidates, including Senator Kennedy, stayed out of the primary.[22]

The Barry Goldwater delegation in 1964, for instance, was very carefully screened to eliminate liberals and moderates as either delegates or alternates, by what amounted to a loyalty test to the candidate. Such ideological commitment was apparently the answer to the dissident sentiment among both Republican professionals, such as the county chairmen, and the Republican voters at large.

Campaigning in California presents several novel features. The party organization is forced to divide its efforts north and south of the Tehachapis as if it were campaigning in two separate states. Office staffs are duplicated under northern and southern managers, with San Francisco and Los Angeles headquarters; money is raised and spent in each locality; local candidates are supported along with those seeking statewide offices; and a spate of regional committees for veterans, women, labor, Republicans-for-Democrats, and vice versa, are established.

The political geography of California, which conditions the strategy and tactics of campaigning, consists of urban, suburban, rural-non-farm, rural-farm, and peripheral areas. The centers of population harboring the most significant voting blocs of union labor, Negroes, Jews, Mexican-Americans, Japanese-Americans, Chinese-Americans, and Catholics are the six counties of the San Francisco-Oakland Metropolitan Area, the Los Angeles Metropolitan Area (Los Angeles and Orange counties) and San Diego County. The rural-non-farm and rural-farm vote is centered in the agricultural heartland of the state comprising the eight counties in the Sacramento Valley, eight others in the San Joaquin Valley, and three in the southeast region. The north coast, mountain, and south coast counties constitute the more sparsely settled, economically mixed, peripheral areas as far as campaigning is concerned.

Candidate itineraries concentrate upon San Francisco and Los Angeles, with side trips to their metropolitan satellites, Oakland and San Diego. Occasional tours in the farm belt begin in the oil and cotton community of Bakersfield and progress through Fresno, and possibly Merced, to the state capitol at Sacramento.

Employing county differences from the statewide percent of the two-party vote for president and governor from 1936 to 1960, Eugene C. Lee has made a definitive study of the geographic distribution of party strength in California.

... Republican strength was concentrated in the southern California counties outside of Los Angeles, in the coastal counties in both northern and southern California, in the desert-mountain counties of the eastern slope of the Sierra, in a few suburban counties in the San Francisco Bay region, and in a few small agricultural counties in the northern half of the

22. For a discussion of delegation politics see Eugene C. Lee and William Buchanan, "The 1960 Election in California," *Western Political Quarterly*, XIV (March 1961), 311-13.

Sacramento Valley. (Los Angeles and Orange counties in southern California remain the heartland of right-wing Republicanism.) Relative Democratic strength, on the other hand, was to be found in three large San Francisco Bay area counties, throughout most of the San Joaquin and Sacramento Valley[s] , in Los Angeles and adjoining Ventura counties, and in most of the small Sierra and Mother Lode counties of northern and central California.

. . . these data . . . reveal important facets concerning the state's politics which in the early 1960's stood in marked contrast to several large Eastern and Midwestern states. The traditional urban-rural, Democratic-Republican split was absent in California. Both parties had a base in several of the state's large metropolitan areas, and this strength included both central cities and suburbs. Both parties had strength in agricultural areas. Both parties . . . had been able on occasion to win in each county of the state. And, as the 1960 figures suggest, both parties remained strong enough in almost every county of the state that none could be completely taken for granted.[23]

If there is a residue in the political mores from the days of the "wild west," it is probably the rugged nature of political campaigning in California, politely characterized as "vigorous," but occasionally more accurately described as "dirty." The campaign against Upton Sinclair in 1934 was a classic exhibition of political vilification. The tensions which develop between the ideological wings of each party and between the two major parties are invariably reflected in unfair, unethical, and illegal campaign practices. Among the many explanations of this phenomenon, several have at least the semblance of plausibility. The weaknesses of the party system deny the candidates normal leadership, financial support, and discipline. Thus candidates are often largely "on their own" and their behavior often reaches the lowest common denominator of the least ethical contestants in the campaign, whose credo is "win at any price." Successful candidates build "incumbent empires" and declare their independence of any party control. Moreover, candidates for all major offices usually hire professional, political campaign-management firms, whose fees and longevity in the business are contingent upon a reputation for winning an election. Finally, the conservative Republican control of state politics was severely challenged during the days of the New Deal at a time (1934) when Democratic voters first became the majority party within the electorate.

An added complication to normal campaigning was cross-filing, which tended to blur party lines. Since Republican victories were often contingent upon winning conservative Democratic support, the Republican press attempted to equate Republicanism with "nonpartisanship" in the eyes of the electorate, thus placing Democratic candidates beyond the pale of political respectability. As recently as the 1962 campaign, former Vice President Nixon was pleading with the citizens to "vote the man, not the party" and the recommended candidates, to the last man, were Republicans!

During the 1958 campaign, Charles P. Taft, chairman of the Fair Campaign Practices Committee, stated that his file on campaign smear tactics contained more material from California than all of the other states combined. Since the depression years, supporters of Republican candidates have played variations on the theme of communism in attacking the Democratic party and many of its candidates. Allegations have varied from outright name-calling, through the limbo of guilt-by-association, to the 1958 formula of "radicalism" employed by Eisenhower when he campaigned in the state.[24]

23. Eugene C. Lee, *California Votes: 1928-1960* (Berkeley: Institute of Governmental Studies, University of California, 1963), p. 76.

24. For examples see Totton J. Anderson, "The 1958 Election in California," *Western Political Quarterly*, XII (March 1959), 292-98.

In the 1962 gubernatorial campaign Governor Brown repeatedly demanded a "full explanation" of a Nixon family loan made by the Hughes Tool Company with the inference that the Republican candidate was personally responsible for using his influence to promote a questionable financial transaction. During the 1964 campaign Democratic National Committeeman Eugene Wyman insisted that Republican U.S. senatorial candidate George Murphy's headquarters was distributing "paranoic junk" authored by the John Birch Society. The Fair Campaign Practices Committee claimed that no evidence had been presented to connect either Murphy or his organization with the tracts. Even in the primaries smear tactics have appeared, as in 1966 when George Christopher and Ronald Reagan were vying for the Republican gubernatorial nomination.

Syndicated columnist Drew Pearson printed information about supposed altercations that Christopher had had with government authorities regarding his dairy business in Marin County more than 26 years ago. Among the charges was a misdemeanor conviction. These disclosures contributed to the reversal of the trend of Christopher's steady advance in the public opinion polls, giving Reagan a comfortable 17 percent lead days before the election. Christopher initially charged the Reagan organization with trying to "destroy" him. Later he alleged that the Democratic hierarchy had conspired to release the politically damaging information to Pearson after having reached the decision that Reagan would be the easier candidate to defeat. Christopher and Pearson exchanged lawsuits in the millions of dollars.

As a possible significant aftermath of such roughhouse tactics Democratic National Committeeman Eugene L. Wyman disclosed his intent to request a congressional investigation of the role of television and radio in election campaigns. California has 33 television channels and 322 radio stations. Television "editorials" endorsing candidates and propositions have become commonplace; radio "talk shows" where persons call a station and engage in discussion with commentators either supporting or attacking a candidate are thriving; prediction of the outcome of an election before the polls close is standard practice on the major networks and "newscasts" occasionally come perilously close to outright endorsement of a candidate. Wyman's contention is "that as licensees of the federal government, radio and television stations should not be allowed to use the public airwaves to endorse a candidate for public office."

Many of the excesses in campaigning revolve around the "hate themes" inspired by groups supporting or defending ballot propositions. Proposition 16 in 1958, for instance, advocating the return of parochial school property to the public tax rolls, instigated a veritable flood of religious and racial campaign tracts. The "right-to-work" measure (Proposition 18) in the same election was the source of employer-employee, class warfare propaganda.

Occasionally, California presents the ludicrous picture of party civil wars which place lethal campaign propaganda in the hands of the enemy. Thus in the 1950 Democratic senatorial primary election, newspaper publisher Manchester Boddy's attack on incumbent Helen Douglas handed Nixon supporters a neatly packaged smear campaign which they deftly embroidered and used successfully in the general election.[25] In 1958 when the incumbent Republican governor, Goodwin Knight, was forced out of the gubernatorial election and into the senatorial

25. For a discussion of the pros and cons of the "linkage with communism" technique employed by Richard Nixon against Jerry Voorhis in 1946 and Helen Douglas in 1950, see Earl Mazo, *Richard Nixon* (New York: Harper, 1959).

race to make way for William Knowland, his indignant protestations produced an indictment of his fellow Republican which the Democrats adroitly exploited in the general election.

Candidates and interest groups have utilized professional political campaign firms more fully in California than in any other state. The first and most successful of these was originally the husband-and-wife team, Clem Whitaker and Leone Baxter, operating Campaigns Incorporated, which has successfully handled both candidate and issue campaigns since 1933.[26]

Speculation on why such a phenomenon should have flourished in California centers upon the size of the state; the difficulty of capturing the attention of a politically heterogeneous, and to some degree migratory electorate lacking in political tradition; the very high and continuingly increasing cost of commandeering the mass media; and, most significantly, the absence of a strong party system which has forced both candidates and interest groups to resort to other channels to reach the electorate.

Although not uniformly successful, campaign management firms have compiled an impressive list of victories. Whitaker and Baxter claim seventy successes in California campaigns against only five defeats between 1933 and 1955. They guided Earl Warren to the governor's mansion in his first attempt in 1942 and elected Goodwin Knight lieutenant governor in 1946. They defeated the private utilities in a Central Valley Project referendum in 1933, defeated Socialist-turned-Democrat Upton Sinclair in the 1934 gubernatorial race, won the San Francisco mayoralty campaign for Elmer E. Robinson twice, and defeated the recall of Mayor Roger Lapham. The firm compiled a remarkable record for defeating attempts at direct legislation by the electorate, including proposals for increasing state aid to public schools in 1946, 1948, and 1952; legislative reapportionment and the railroad "full crew" laws in 1948; and several pension proposals, including the colorful "ham and eggs" issue. The health insurance plans of both President Truman and Governor Warren were defeated by this formidable combination.[27]

A Los Angeles-based firm, Baus and Ross Company, served as the state agency for the 1964 Goldwater primary and Herbert M. Baus served as state campaign manager, winning a crucial victory against the Rockefeller forces. The organization has specialized in ballot propositions for twenty years, claiming to have won 90 percent of the campaigns undertaken. Their recent successes were the passage of Proposition 15, an initiative measure preventing "Pay-TV" and the defeat of Proposition 16, a measure authorizing a state lottery. The partners maintain that

26. For citations to this and similar firms, see Totton J. Anderson, "Bibliography on California Politics," *Western Political Quarterly*, XI (December 1958), 48-50. For campaign management see Robert J. Pitchell, "The Influence of Professional Campaign Management Firms in Partisan Elections in California," *ibid.*, XI (June 1958), 278-300, and Charles G. Mayo, "Professional Campaign Management Firms in California Politics" (Master's thesis, University of Southern California, 1960). Clem Whitaker, Jr., now operates the firm, Campaigns Incorporated. See also Walt Anderson, "Spencer-Roberts: Dynamic Duo of California Politics," *Los Angeles Times West Magazine*, December 11, 1966; and Jack Langguth, "Political Fun and Games in California," *New York Times Magazine*, October 16, 1966.

27. In a single campaign in 1948, Whitaker and Baxter used "10,000,000 pamphlets and leaflets, 4,500,000 postal cards, 50,000 letters to key individuals, 70,000 inches of newspaper display advertising in 700 papers, 3,000 radio spots and 12 fifteen-minute network radio programs, 1,000 twenty-four sheet billboards and 18,000-20,000 smaller posters, theater slides and trailers in 160 theaters," as well as a three-months' publicity campaign in all of the newspapers and thousands of speeches delivered in every community in the state. Pitchell, *op. cit.*, p. 291.

press endorsements are far more effective in determining the outcome of proposi-tions than are candidates.[28] Professional campaign management has become vir-tually a necessity in California gubernatorial elections and many observers believe that the skillful guidance of Spencer-Roberts and Associates contributed greatly to Reagan's success. The firm participated in all aspects of the 1966 campaign with the exception of fund-raising and controlled the organization, schedule, itin-erary, and the selection and timing of issues.

No definitive evaluation of the impact of professionally hired campaigning upon the democratic process has yet been made. Proponents of the practice urge that since most firms suffer an occasional defeat, other forces counterbalance technical proficiency in campaigning. Detractors belittle the "box score ap-proach" to measuring the amoral, professional manipulation of the public interest for a substantial monetary consideration, ranging from $25,000 to perhaps $100,000 or more.

The cost of campaigning in California is increasing with each election due to the steady growth of the electorate, the tendency of candidates to employ profes-sional campaign concerns, and the progressively inflated costs of the communica-tion media.[29] Each of the principal gubernatorial candidates in 1962 acknowl-edged approximately half a million dollars spent on his behalf in the primary: Brown, $449,000; Nixon, $454,000; and Shell, $532,617. First official reports for the general election alone found Nixon's statewide organization acknowledg-ing receipts of $1,456,473 with expenditures of $1,421,653. The comparable Brown organization, consolidated with reports of various support groups, ac-knowledged receipts of $1,380,711 and expenditures of $1,482,206.

It is difficult to equate presumably comparable costs in campaign-expense reports. However, providing some impression of the magnitudes involved, items found under the same categories in both the Brown and the Nixon statements include (Brown figures first): radio and television, $513,520 and $315,696; sala-ries and wages, $158,299 and $341,972; newspaper advertising, $52,288 and $130,248; billboards and signs and posters, $75,700 and $144,141; travel, $33,383 and $108,971; distribution of printed literature, $51,961 and $92,665; and a unique entry on the Nixon ledger, $214,786 for "repayment of loans."

It is doubtful that sources of campaign funds in California differ significant-ly from those categories common to the other forty-nine states. Laws requiring candidates to file statements of receipts and expenditures are ambiguous and lax-ly enforced. Public records are incomplete, unpublished, and represent only to-ken manifestations of vast but indeterminable sums of money spent in primary and general elections. Estimates of campaign expenditures vary with circum-stances, such as the amount of volunteer help available, the size and population of the district, the degree of previous "political exposure" of the candidate, whether

28. Baus and Ross, *Private Line*, September and November 1964.

29. An experienced political campaign manager, pleading anonymity, recommended the following "realistic budgets" for the various elective offices: for the state Assembly, $12,000-$15,000 in the primary and $15,000-$30,000 in the general election; for Congress, $20,000-$30,000 in the primary and $30,000-$40,000 in the general election; and for a statewide office, up to $500,000 in the primary, with a probable maximum of $1,000,000 in the general election. The last estimate compares favorably with the acknowledged expendi-tures of the 1958 gubernatorial candidates: Brown spent $402,391.56 in the primary and $789,864.57 in the general election, while the totals for Knowland were $546,170.87 and $915,999.26, respectively. The largest listed sum in the general election for Congress was $30,931.75. See also Alan Cranston, "A Million Dollar Loser Looks at Campaigning," *Fortune*, November 1964.

the district majority is in the candidate's party, and whether or not his opponent is an incumbent.[30] In the 1966 gubernatorial election, preliminary and incomplete reports indicated that Reagan's organization spent over $2.6 million and Brown's over $2.0 million. This may well have been by far the most expensive election in the state's history.

PARTY ORGANIZATION AND PARTY LEADERS

The formal party organization in California is prescribed in great detail by statutory law. The party structure rests on a geographical base of 31,500 precincts, 80 assembly districts, 58 counties, 38 congressional districts, and the state serving as a single district. Ideally, party organization would consist of a captain in each precinct, assembly district committees, county central committees, congressional district committees, a state convention, the state central committee, an executive committee, the state officers, and a national committeeman and national committeewoman. But the party machinery is rarely, if ever, manned in full; the personnel who do serve emanate from two sources. County central committeemen, numbering from a minimum of 21 to possibly 30, are elected every two years at the direct primary election. They serve with incumbents and party nominees of the state legislature residing in the county who are ex-officio members of the committee.[31]

Counties harboring urban populations usually maintain permanent offices, and a full complement of committeemen with an active and capable chairman. Here the functions of fund-raising, patronage appointments, registration drives, precinct organization, and campaigning are effectively performed. Most county committees are inactive between elections, however, and in recent years over half of the posts for committeeman have been uncontested. The attempt of Republican conservatives to capture the party apparatus in 1963 and factionalism within Democratic ranks have renewed the intra-party competition for these seats. The effect of cross-filing in blurring party lines and the ruling of the state attorney general enjoining county committees from participating in pre-primary endorsement of candidates tended to render the county organization ineffective. Candidates rely upon party auxiliaries and their own campaign organizations for support usually supplied by the party. It is possible that with the abolition of cross-filing and the influx of hundreds of thousands of new voters party responsibility and county organization activity may be regenerated.

The state convention and central committee constitute the higher echelon of party organization. Contrary to general practice, the convention is a small body of only 170 persons, including the party's incumbents and nominees for partisan office, meeting biennially to formulate the party platform. The central committee is composed of the members of the convention, three other members appointed by each nominee (one of the same and two of the opposite sex), and each county committee chairman in the state. Members of a party with over 3,200,000

30. See Leonard Rowe and William Buchanan, "Campaign Funds in California: What the Records Reveal," California Historical Society *Quarterly*, XLI (September 1962), 195-310. The authors list sources for legislative office as: self and family, party (and auxiliaries), labor unions and lobbies. See also John R. Owens, *Money and Politics in California: Democratic Senatorial Primary, 1964* (Princeton: Citizens' Research Foundation, 1966).

31. Los Angeles elects 263 members to the county committee every four years. Assembly or supervisorial districts provide the constituencies for county committeemen. *California Elections Code*, Sections 8401-8405.

registrants (only the Democrats qualify) are given a bonus of two additional appointees without regard to sex, and members of a party under the registrant quota (only the Republicans qualify) are given a bonus of five appointees. The latter modification of the law was made on June 17, 1964, in time to prevent Goldwater supporters from gaining control over the Republican state central committee. The approximately 1,000 members meet every two years to elect the state officers and to constitute the executive committee of the party.[32]

The executive committee, acting for the central committee, varies in number from 174 for the Democratic party to 75 for the Republican party. The party chairman and vice-chairman are elected for two-year terms and the officers must be selected alternately from northern and southern California. Finally, the national committeeman and committeewoman are elected by the delegates to the national convention. As a generalization, party organization in California suffers from lack of coordination between its various elements. The state organization has little control over the county apparatus. County officials often have no control over candidates' organizations while the delegates to the national convention have very tenuous relationships with the party.

The complexities of organizing a statewide campaign in California, coupled with the inability of the party system to function normally, has given rise to the creation of a plethora of volunteer political groups. These range from *ad hoc* committees which sponsor an issue or a candidate during a single election, to state representation of established national associations such as the youth and women's groups, to orthodox auxiliaries, virtually integrated with the two major parties through overlapping personnel in key positions.

In the wake of the overwhelming defeat suffered in 1932, the more liberal element among the Republicans began a "grass roots" club movement to revive the party and to wrest leadership from the reactionaries who had lost to the New Deal forces.[33] Under the leadership of Edward Shattuck and Earl Warren, this embryonic movement of 1933-34 was incorporated into the California Republican Assembly in July 1935. A state Board of Directors with representation from regional associations in each of the thirty-eight congressional districts is empowered to charter county, assembly district, and local Republican Assembly units. State conventions of approximately 450 delegates are now held four times a year, representing a statewide C.R.A. strength of 15,000 members.[34]

Through the process of performing specific services which are denied to the party by the state primary law, the Republican Assembly became integrated with the party organization. The amalgamation extended to sharing office space with the various Republican central committees and having key officials in the party hold key positions in the Assembly. This effective, ambidextrous approach to state politics served to circumvent the one prohibition in the law which most critically crippled the parties' activities, namely, the nomination of primary candidates. Through the medium of candidate and fact-finding committees on the congressional district level, possible nominees for national and statewide offices are

32. The state convention consists of the nominees and incumbents for state and federal offices meeting alone to draft a state party platform and nominate candidates to serve as presidential electors. The 170 delegates of the Democratic party meet annually while the Republicans meet biannually. *California Elections Code*, Sections 8002, 8003. The personnel of the convention constitute the nucleus of the state central committee.

33. Markell C. Baer and Robert H. Power, *The Story of the Republican Assembly* (rev. ed.; Vacaville, California: Reporter Co., 1955).

34. Assemblies usually exist in all 58 counties. The Los Angeles County Assembly is empowered to issue sub-charters to the many units under its jurisdiction, some with memberships in the thousands.

recruited, investigated, and screened with recommendations for endorsement reported to the state convention of the C.R.A. Committees in the appropriate legislative districts endorse candidates for those districts, with the result that for over two decades the Republican party has been remarkably successful in mobilizing its minority in the electorate in support of a single, carefully selected candidate for each partisan office in the primary election.

Since Earl Warren became Republican state party chairman one year after the incorporation of the Assembly and received its endorsement for governor in 1942, 1946, and 1950, the organization was unofficially termed his "personal political machine." However, virtually every nationally known Republican political figure from California and scores of state senators and assemblymen have received C.R.A. support, ranging from pre-primary endorsement to finances and campaign services.[35]

In addition to preventing bitter intra-party rivalry between two or more candidates in the primary election the Republican Assembly often attempts to serve as the "voice" of the party between elections. At a convention held in Coronado in March 1959, for instance, resolutions were passed in support of the loyalty oath for public servants, for continuation of the Un-American Activities Committee, in approval of the admission of Hawaii as a state, and in admiration of the "stimulating leadership" of such prominent Republican leaders as Nixon, Dulles, and Eisenhower. Occasionally, the C.R.A. is the center of power struggles within the Republican party, usually resulting from forays by two or more party factions to capture control of the machinery. Thus, although Warren "willed" the Assembly to Knowland when he accepted the Supreme Court appointment in 1953, Governor Knight's supporters manned the controls; with the defeat of Knight in his 1958 race for the U.S. Senate, Nixon forces are reputed to have dominated the C.R.A. The ideological factionalism between reactionaries and the "middle-of-the-roaders," and the rivalries between candidates for control of the party machinery are also apparent in the activities of the Assembly.[36]

The supporters of Barry Goldwater captured the C.R.A. and the Young Republicans and a new auxiliary, the United Republicans of California, during the 1964 campaign. The disarray within the party ranks caused by the candidate's campaign produced several other organizations reflecting varying shades of party doctrine such as the California Republican League, the Republican Alliance, and the Republican Council of California, all attempting to emulate the functions performed so effectively by the C.R.A. The Republican hierarchy performed a minor political miracle under the leadership of State Chairman Gaylord G. Parkinson, who mediated between the warring factions and united the auxiliaries behind the Reagan candidacy in 1966.

35. Candidates without Assembly support often did not fare well: incumbent Attorney General Frederick N. Howser was defeated for re-election in 1950; incumbent Congressman Patrick J. Hillings running for attorney general in 1958 lost, even with Nixon's support; however, Harold J. Powers was elected lieutenant governor in 1954 without Assembly endorsement.

36. One rather disgruntled party official told the author that the Assembly "didn't amount to a hill of beans" in Republican party politics, and it is true that none of Warren's successors used the organization as effectively as he did. In the 1958 election, for instance, the Nixon-Knowland-Knight rivalry practically immobilized it. The divisiveness within the Republican ranks before the 1964 election is illustrated by an Associated Press poll of 56 chairmen: Goldwater was the personal choice of 17 leaders, 9 preferred Nixon, 6 Rockefeller, 4 Lodge, 3 Scranton, one Nixon or Scranton, one Lodge or Nixon, one Scranton or Lodge, while 9 had no opinion and 5 no preference. A Louis Harris poll indicated that five days before the election 50 percent of the Republican voters did not support either Rockefeller or Goldwater.

Plagued by a generally hostile press, lack of proper financing, poor leadership, and a bemused electorate trying to cope with the vagaries of cross-filing, the faction-ridden Democrats watched with dismay while the Republicans often captured their own and the Democratic nominations in the primary.[37] Rationalizations for successive defeats extended from citations of skillfully gerrymandered legislative districts to tacit agreement with a Republican boast that their candidates were better qualified. Over a twenty-year period of uninterrupted Republican Assembly successes, the Democratic party became demoralized. Prominent conservative Democrats virtually made a political career of defecting to the enemy, while Democratic candidates for public office frequently mounted their campaigns without reference to the official party organization.

Although sporadic attempts were made to form local auxiliary clubs and county councils before 1952, the candidacy of Adlai Stevenson in that campaign is credited with providing the impetus for a statewide, amateur "club movement."[38] The California Democratic Council was formed as the result of a state convention of over 500 club representatives held in Fresno in November 1953. The Council represents a federation of about 40,000 members grouped in 500 local clubs, coordinated by assembly and congressional district councils and headed by a State Board of Directors. Local clubs are chartered by the official Democratic County Central committees, but assembly and congressional district councils are chartered by the state C.D.C. Thus there is an important link between the county organization and the grass-roots club movement. One member of the Board of Directors is selected from each of the thirty-eight congressional districts.

Two specific purposes of the C.D.C. are to "promote . . . pre-Primary Assembly, County and Congressional District conventions, for the purpose of selection of Democratic candidates for nomination to public office" and "to make pre-Primary endorsements . . . for statewide partisan public office."[39] Thus by February 1954, when parties were identified on the ballot for the first time in a generation, the Democrats had finally developed an auxiliary which might compete effectively with the Republican Assembly.

The C.D.C. differs from the C.R.A. in several respects. It does not operate through fact-finding committees, and endorsements to major posts are won or lost in open convention battles. Moreover, its very existence as well as its program has been frequently challenged by vested party interests (including heavy donors to the party organization), the party leadership, and firmly entrenched incumbent legislators. It must contend with factionalism within its ranks, although the membership is largely liberal, and with the powerful labor unions that usually pursue a policy different from, but often parallel to, the Democratic party line.

Nevertheless, the initial venture of the C.D.C. in endorsing candidates was spectacularly successful; the party had a complete ballot for statewide offices for the first time in recent years as a result of the 1954 state convention. In both 1956 and 1958, candidates who were refused endorsements–Congressman Samuel W.

37. In 1950, for instance, the Republican party took four of six Democratic nominations for statewide office in the primaries. Bell, *op. cit.*, pp. 63, 65.

38. State Senators George Miller, Jr., of the San Francisco Bay area, Richard Richards of Los Angeles, and State Controller Alan Cranston of Los Altos (an early club leader) are credited with major roles in revitalizing the Democratic party, along with Democratic National Committeeman Paul Ziffren, an attorney. A comprehensive description of the club movement may be found in Francis Carney, *The Rise of the Democratic Clubs in California* (New York: Holt, 1958).

39. Constitution and By-Laws of the California Democratic Council, 1958.

Yorty for the U.S. Senate and State Senator Robert I. McCarthy for attorney general—lost the Democratic nominations to C.D.C.-backed candidates.

In addition to its function of candidate endorsement, the C.D.C. attempted, with limited success, to become the voice of the Democratic party in the interim between election campaigns. In a series of resolutions passed at its convention held in Fresno in March 1959 the organization demanded "a major voice in the affairs of the Democratic party"; repeal of the state loyalty oath; abolition of the House Committee on Un-American Activities; passage of a California FEPC law; abolition of cross-filing; abolition of capital punishment; increase of aid to the needy, blind and senior citizens; creation of a State Economic Development Agency; extension of unemployment insurance benefits; comprehensive state and federal support for education; public development of public power; and disarmament.[40]

The insistent espousal of these and similar issues has been an embarrassment to many Democratic candidates. A major feature of Nixon's unsuccessful gubernatorial campaign in 1962 was to charge Brown with responsibility for embracing the C.D.C. positions. Brown felt compelled to disassociate himself from the more extreme recommendations. As an aftermath of the feud between Brown and Assembly Speaker Jesse Unruh, both with gubernatorial aspirations in 1966, the latter organized a substantial portion of the southern California C.D.C. into his own support auxiliary called the Democratic Volunteers Committee.

These partisan auxiliaries have served to stimulate party activity and loyalties. With the abolition of cross-filing, however, and with reasonable assurance that each party will capture nominations for its own members, their future is in doubt. Moreover, the proliferation of such groups, their bent toward party factionalism, their ideological orientation, and their specific candidate preference, have compromised their original mission. They are now little less than machine organizations for individual candidates.

The ranking California Republican in public office in 1968 was the fourteenth Chief Justice of the United States Supreme Court (1953), Earl Warren. Warren's deliberate climb up the political status ladder began as district attorney of Alameda County (1925) and progressed to the state attorney generalship (1938). Three successive gubernatorial victories followed (1942, 1946, 1950), punctuated by an unsuccessful attempt for the vice presidency on the Dewey ticket (1948), but capped by the signal honor of the Eisenhower appointment to the highest judicial post in the land.

Adopting the spirit of the Hiram Johnson Progressives, Warren ignored the extreme wings of his party to establish a "middle-of-the-road," nonpartisan program with broad appeal in both political parties. He dominated the party during his regime as governor with his own brand of "new Republicanism," and sponsored legislation in the fields of public education, health insurance, state institutional reform, and the general welfare.

Richard M. Nixon, the thirty-sixth Vice President of the United States (1952), left public office in 1960. He entered politics in 1946 as a conservative, war-veteran candidate for the Twelfth Congressional District seat, then occupied by Jerry Voorhis, a popular, liberal Democrat. In 1950 he defeated another liberal, Democratic incumbent congresswoman, Helen Gahagan Douglas, in a race for the United States Senate. Two years later Nixon was elected Vice President of the

40. California Democratic Council, "Report of the Resolutions Committee" (mimeographed), Fresno, March 14, 1959.

United States on the Eisenhower ticket. He was re-elected in 1956 and became the Republican presidential nominee in 1960.

Since Nixon had not held a state office and others of his party have dominated California politics, his reputation with the electorate was based primarily upon his campaign behavior and views in respect to national politics. Utilization of the "linkage with communism" campaign tactic made him a controversial figure among most Democrats in the state and with a sizable number of liberal Republicans as well.[41] The nature of the Nixon support in the state indicated that conservative Republicans were willing to tolerate his essentially internationalist views on foreign policy in return for a basically conservative attitude toward domestic issues. And it was the absentee vote, probably of many of these same conservative Republicans, that gave him his thin California margin over Kennedy. Nixon made an unsuccessful bid for the governorship in 1962, losing to incumbent Democrat Brown. He remained in contention for high office by virtue of his position as the Republican presidential nominee in the summer of 1968.

Two other prominent California Republicans, former United States Senator William F. Knowland and former Governor Goodwin J. Knight, may be placed respectively in the right and left wings of their party. In contrast with Nixon, Knowland has held many key positions of his party in both the state and the nation.[42] He served a term in the state Assembly (1933-35) and one term in the state Senate (1935-39). Returning from a tour of duty with the Army (1942-45), he was appointed to the United States Senate (1945) by Governor Warren to complete the unexpired term of Hiram Johnson. Knowland was elected in the primary to the same post in 1946 and won again in the general election of 1952. He left a distinguished career in the Senate to contest the gubernatorial election of 1958 with Edmund Brown, presumably as a step toward the Republican presidential nomination. His defeat occurred in a bitter campaign, marked by personal rivalry with Knight and Nixon and confusion caused by two controversial ballot issues, "the right-to-work" proposal and taxation of parochial school property. Knowland, a genuine conservative in the Hoover-Taft tradition, won the loyal support of the right wing of his party in the state, managed the state Goldwater campaign in 1964 and headed the Republican delegation to the national convention in San Francisco.

Goodwin Knight launched his public career through an appointment to the superior court in 1935, was elected in 1936 to that position and re-elected in 1942. He ran successfully for lieutenant governor in 1946 and was re-elected in 1950. He succeeded to the governorship in October 1953, with the elevation of Governor Warren to the Supreme Court, and was re-elected in 1954. In 1958 he became a candidate for the Senate seat vacated by Knowland, losing to Democrat Clair Engle in the general election. During his career Knight held many of the key positions in the Republican state organization.

Knight adopted and exploited the Warren tradition of nonpartisanship. His political eclipse may be attributed to alienation of conservative Republican politi-

41. In the fall of 1959, Rockefeller organizers in California admitted to the writer that anti-Nixon Republicans formed a substantial element among their adherents. The planned move to create a "new image" of a so-called "mature" presidential candidate was at least partially vindicated by the Nixon victory over Brown in the 1960 primary "popularity contest," and completely so when Nixon carried the state in November.

42. Among others: California national committeeman, 1938-42; chairman of the Executive Committee of the Republican National Committee, 1941; chairman of the Senate Republican Policy Committee and minority leader of the 83rd Congress.

cal support through overly enthusiastic solicitation of labor sponsorship, and personal feuding with Nixon in 1956 and with Knowland in 1958. The combined forces of his opponents staged the "squeeze play" which proved his undoing, forcing him out of the gubernatorial race and into the unsolicited and unwanted senatorial contest.

United States Senator Thomas H. Kuchel had miraculously steered past the political shoals created by the ambitions of his fellow Republican leaders. He served in the Assembly (1936 and 1938), the state Senate (1940 and 1944) and after a tour of duty with the Navy, was appointed state controller in February 1946. He was elected to the latter post in November 1946 and again in 1950. In December 1952, Governor Warren appointed Kuchel to fill Nixon's unexpired term in the Senate; he won the election in 1954 and was re-elected in 1956 and 1962. In the Senate he served on the Interior and Insular Affairs and Appropriations committees, on the Republican Policy Committee, and as Republican party whip until his defeat in the 1968 primary by ultra-conservative Max Rafferty, State Superintendent of Public Education.

Latest comer to the California stage is Governor Ronald Reagan, who had virtually no political experience prior to having been recruited by the Republican State Committee in 1966, when an attractive candidate was needed to defeat Brown. Reagan had held no political office, was a former president of the Screen Actors' Guild, a registered Democrat until 1962, and state co-chairman for the California Committee for Goldwater-Miller in 1964. The party placed him under the skilled management of one of the most successful public relations firms in the nation, which created an image of a political moderate acceptable to all. Reagan swept the 1966 primary with a 63 percent victory, dominated by 80 percent margins in southern California, leaving few grounds for intra-party dissension. He won a vote of confidence from every major Republican auxiliary organization. His 58 percent general election vote carried all but three California counties. Not since Earl Warren's 65 percent vote in the 1950 victory has a Republican candidate for governor demonstrated such strength. Reagan's position as leader of one of the two most populous states in the union marks him as a potential presidential nominee in 1968. Despite his political inexperience, he has a pronounced appeal for the conservatives within the Republican party.

Prominent among Democrats in California politics circa 1966 was Edmund G. "Pat" Brown, the second member of his party to win the governorship in over half a century. He failed in his first attempt at elective office when he ran for the state Assembly in 1927 as a Republican. He was elected district attorney of San Francisco as a Democrat in 1943 and was re-elected in 1947. In 1950 and again in 1954 he campaigned successfully for the state attorney generalship. He defeated Knowland by nearly 1,000,000 votes in the 1958 gubernatorial race and won handily over Richard Nixon in 1962. Brown may be characterized as a moderate Democrat. In the Warren-Knight tradition, he minimized partisanship during his campaigns, disassociated himself from several C.D.C. positions in 1962, and accepted substantial financial aid from Republican sources. A nonpartisan evaluation of his administration would acknowledge an era of unusual economic and social progress during the greatest period of expansion and prosperity in the history of the state. Despite the failure of his third-term bid for office, he retains a position of leadership.

Jesse M. Unruh, who has been speaker of the state Assembly since 1961, is widely regarded as one of the most influential members of the Democratic party.

He began his public career by unseating a sixteen-year Republican incumbent in 1954, and became an expert in fiscal policy serving as chairman of the Ways and Means Committee in his third term. As speaker, he was deeply involved in much of the Governor's successful legislative program. Another signal success was the reapportionment of the legislative districts after the 1960 decennial census. Unruh managed the southern California gubernatorial campaign for Governor Brown in 1958, and served in the same capacity for John F. Kennedy in the 1960 presidential campaign. During the Kennedy years, he was considered the President's Democratic party liaison official for the state of California. Unruh has often been mentioned as a potential gubernatorial candidate.

Donald Bradley has become somewhat of a legend in the Democratic party as one of the most accomplished professional politicians in the state. As a youthful member of the Marine Cooks and Stewards Union, he worked in the successful Culbert L. Olson gubernatorial campaign in 1938. In 1952 and again in 1956 he managed the Adlai Stevenson campaign in California and helped launch the Democratic Club movement. He ran the unsuccessful Richard Graves gubernatorial campaign in 1954 and the successful Clair Engle senatorial campaign in 1958. In the interim he won several special elections to both the state Senate and Assembly. He is credited with the successful role of field-general in marshaling the financial and personnel resources of the Democratic party during the period of its renaissance in state politics from 1952 to 1958, as a "coordinator" for the state central committee. He has said that he does not aspire to public office.

James Roosevelt, son of the late Franklin D. Roosevelt, is probably the best-known Democrat serving recently in the House of Representatives, partly because he was known nationally before he came to California and because of the unsuccessful gubernatorial campaign he waged against Earl Warren in 1950. Roosevelt was elected to Congress in 1954 and won his 1964 election handily. Negro and labor interests were unusually strong in his district. He has served as chairman of the California Democratic state central committee and is a liberal by conviction. In August 1965 he accepted an appointment as United States representative to the United Nations for UNESCO.

Other prominent party personalities among the Republicans are: Lieutenant Governor Robert H. Finch, successful Inglewood attorney and middle-of-the-road Republican who outdrew Reagan by 92,000 votes in 1966, managed Nixon's campaign in 1960, and although a loser in two congressional elections, has so comported himself in Sacramento as to become a promising gubernatorial candidate; former motion picture actor, businessman and state party chairman (1953-54), George Murphy, who defeated Pierre Salinger for the U.S. Senate seat of recently deceased Clair Engle; Joseph Shell, businessman and former minority leader (1959-62) in the Assembly who contested Richard Nixon in the 1962 gubernatorial primary; George Christopher, former mayor of San Francisco, who lost out in the 1966 gubernatorial primary; and finally, Robert Monagan, dynamic minority leader in the Assembly who has instilled new life in the partisan contests in the legislature.

Additional Democratic leaders include Roger Kent, twice state chairman and twice northern California vice-chairman of the party, a capable professional politician and adept money-raiser, in no small measure responsible for the upswing in Democratic fortunes prior to 1966; former State Controller Alan Cranston, a founder of C.D.C., the 1964 primary foe of Pierre Salinger for the United States Senate and winner of the 1968 Democratic primary for the seat vacated by

Senator Kuchel; state Senator Hugh Burns, his party's indisputable leader in that body; Eugene Wyman, state chairman of his party, and Mayor Samuel Yorty of Los Angeles, renegade Democrat, former congressman and loser to Brown in the gubernatorial primary of 1966.

INTEREST GROUPS AND LOBBYING

Lobbying has been an integral part of legislative politics in California since the first legislature, meeting in 1850, earned a dubious reputation as "the legislature of a thousand drinks."[43] Steeped in the mores of the gold rush days it is not surprising that ethical and moral standards of political behavior reflected indulgence in bossism with its attendant evils of bribery, blackmail, and intimidation. Between the 1860's and the second decade of the twentieth century, the railroad interests—particularly the Central (later Southern) Pacific—emerged as the dominant influence in the legislature.

The reform movement beginning in 1910 modified some of the worst aspects of machine politics by introducing an era of competition between numerous interest groups representing various segments of the economy. By the middle 1930's the semblance of bossism was again brought to the attention of the public in the machinations of a super-lobbyist named Arthur H. Samish, representing at various times liquor, beer, motor transport, and horse-racing interests. Although well known to the legislators, many of whom had been his beneficiaries at one time or another, Samish was unknown to the public until the publication of the now notorious "Philbrick Report" in 1938. The corruption revealed in this compendium was uncovered by a Sacramento County Grand Jury, with the aid of a firm of private investigators at the request of a legislative subcommittee. The document was entered in the *Senate Daily Journal*, but stricken the following day, partly because its damaging revelations affected legislators as well as lobbyists!

As the specific target of alleged bossism, Samish remained unscathed. Attempts in 1941 and 1945 to move against the scandalous situation in the legislature, where Samish purportedly controlled thirty of the eighty votes in the Assembly, were quashed. Finally, in 1949, a two-article exposé by Lester Velie, published in *Collier's* and given added nationwide circulation by the *Reader's Digest*, focused attention on Samish to the acute embarrassment of members of the legislature. Richard V. Hyer wrote that "the third House owes allegiance to no party; it flies no flag but the beautiful green banner of the United States currency." After a titanic struggle in the legislature, in which Governor Earl Warren used his influence to the utmost, a legislative lobby control act was passed in the same year. This legislation as amended in 1950 and 1955, and augmented by Section 35, Article IV, of the state constitution, represents the basic law on the subject.[44]

State regulations on lobbying are patterned closely on federal legislation. A lobbyist, called a legislative advocate, is designated as any person hired to influence the passage or the defeat of legislation. He must register his own and his

---

43. See "Regulation of Lobbying in California," in David Farrelly and Ivan Hinderaker, *The Politics of California* (New York: Ronald Press, 1951), pp. 197-200.

44. See State of California, Senate and Assembly Committees on Legislative Representation, "Analysis of Law Relating to Influencing or Attempting to Influence Legislation" (Sacramento: State Printing Office, 1956). For comment see Frank C. Newman, "Legal Aspects of Representation," in *Legislator's Orientation Conference: 1957, op. cit.*, pp. 131-36; Lester Velie, "The Secret Boss of California," *Collier's*, August 13 and 20, 1949; Hyer, *op. cit.*, p. 375.

employer's name and address, as well as the purpose, duration, and compensation of employment. He is required to file monthly reports on the sources, purposes, and amounts of all receipts and give details on all transactions involving expenditures over $25. He must report the hiring either by himself or his employer of a legislator to act as counsel. All split-fee recipients must be identified. He must also account for any publications for which he has been responsible.

Lobbying by offering a bribe or employing intimidation is declared a felony and carries a sentence of one to ten years in prison, while receipt of a bribe may bring a penalty of one to fourteen years. Introduction of a "cinch bill" and solicitation of funds to prevent its passage is punishable by a fine of $5,000 or a prison term, or both. In recognition of flagrant "vote buying" in the past, the legislature enjoined transportation companies from offering free passes to legislators. Finally, the lobbyist is admonished to live by a standard of conduct suggested by the legislature.

It is impossible to categorize effectively the myriad groups involved in lobbying at Sacramento, but a few illustrations may suffice. Business groups include public utilities, the petroleum industry, the alcoholic beverage industry, insurance and banking, aviation and electronics, shipping, advertising, fishing and canneries, building trades, retailers, grocers, real estate, race tracks, and employers and business associations.[45] Besides the commodity organizations such as the Sunkist Orange and Diamond Walnut groups, agriculture is represented by the California Farm Bureau Federation, Grange, Associated Farmers, and Agricultural Council. In addition to the California Labor Federation, AFL-CIO, many of the individual unions such as the Teamsters Legislative Council and the railway brotherhoods are also represented. Government and public employee lobbies of considerable influence include the League of California Cities, the County Supervisors Association, the cities of Los Angeles and San Francisco, and the State Employees and Highway Patrolmen's associations. Effective professional groups are the California Teachers' Association, the Medical, Bar and Dental associations, the University of California, and the State College Association. Finally, there are many reform, religious, and patriotic organizations such as the League of Women Voters, the Council of Churches, the Friends Committee, various temperance societies, the American Legion, and the Veterans of Foreign Wars.

The California Teachers' Association with a membership of 142,000 is the most powerful teachers' group in the state. Its lobby in Sacramento is invariably rated among the ten most successful in obtaining its legislative objectives. The folklore of the capitol provides an interesting rule-of-thumb evaluation of the

45. Typical examples in this category represented either directly or indirectly are: Pacific Gas and Electric Co., Standard Oil of California, Bank of America, Lockheed Aircraft, Transamerica, Kern County Land Co., Bankers Association of California, California Real Estate Association, California Growers Association, Matson Lines, Los Angeles Turf Club, Foster and Kleiser (outdoor advertising), California Retailers Association, California Motor Transport Association, Merchants and Manufacturers Association, California Taxpayers Association, and the California State Chamber of Commerce. See, for a complete listing: *List of Legislative Advocates and Organizations*, annual (Sacramento: State Printing Office). A select list appears in Joseph P. Harris and Leonard Rowe, *California Politics* (2nd ed.; Stanford: Stanford University Press, 1959), p. 22. Identification of the "most powerful" interest groups has been a preoccupation of journalists and scholars alike. In 1947, John Gunther presented such a list in *Inside America* (rev. ed.; New York: Harper, 1951), pp. 37-41, adding the Associated Farmers, the American Legion, and CIO. In 1949 Hyer, *op. cit.*, pp. 375-413, dwelt almost exclusively on Artie Samish. In 1954, Cresap, *op. cit.*, p. 102, reproduced Gunther's list and added representatives of the petroleum "independents," the railroads, the California Teachers' Association, and George H. McLain, old age pension promoter.

CTA grass-roots strength: each teacher is worth a minimum of five votes, there-fore, CTA can commandeer 710,000 troops for any issue it considers vital! The University of California has its own legislative advocates as have the state colleges. Their lobbying activities have already been discussed in the section entitled Edu-cational Politics.

The strength of interest groups in California politics results from a combina-tion of factors. On the lobbyists' side may be listed unusually capable leadership, occasionally provided by former members of the legislature; an intelligently vig-orous advocacy of self-interest programs, involving research in depth on adopted issues; provision of extensive services for legislators, including prepared bills and speeches; and finally, adherence to policies not wholly exclusive of the public interest. On the legislative side of the ledger has been the lack of leadership, organ-ization, discipline, and funds in a chronically weak party system.

Interest groups have frequently usurped normal party functions such as the selection of key officers and committee chairmen in the legislature itself, and the dictation of the selection of candidates for public office and administrative ap-pointment. No one interest group has controlled the legislature in the past decade or so, but particular groups, in coalition, have certainly made public policy in their respective fields.

Interest groups in California tend to intervene in the legislative process when certain specific areas of public policy are considered. They resist taxation, both as applied to their respective enterprises and when increased revenue is to be em-ployed for purposes they choose to designate as "socially undesirable." They be-come highly energized with any attempt at government regulation of their activi-ties. They will fight bitterly to utilize public policy in gaining a competitive advan-tage over some segment of their own industry and finally, they will often attempt to obtain legal protection or financial subsidy through legislative action.

Acting in concert, interest groups have effectively prevented vitally neces-sary constitutional reform in California. Five times since 1879 the electorate has had the opportunity to vote on the question of calling a convention for constitu-tional revision. The proposition was rejected four times, winning in 1934 by the close margin of 37,837 votes. Strong interest-group pressure prevented legislative action, however, and no convention was called. Successive interim committees on constitutional revision have held hearings to no avail. In 1948 a Joint Senate and Assembly Interim Committee of twenty legislators and a widely representative Citizen's Advisory Committee with members from labor, industry, trade, voca-tional and professional associations, auto clubs, state and public employees, tax-payers, church, fraternal, local government and women's groups, could not agree on any positive program, other than the proposal to eliminate certain obsolete sections of the constitution. Interest groups do not wish to replace, modify, or in any manner disturb the channels of access so carefully constructed into the cen-ters of power in state government.[46]

Examples of major issues which stimulated concerted interest-group activity during the first year of the Brown administration included the Fair Employment Practices Act, which found business groups arrayed against successful labor spon-sorship; a 90-cent-an-hour minimum wage bill for farm labor, supported by the unions but defeated by farm groups; and the entire issue of conservation, flood

46. California Legislature, Joint Interim Committee on Legislative Constitutional Re-vision, "Report," *Journal of the Senate* (Regular Session, 1949), pp. 804 ff. Another of the innumerable interim committees scheduled hearings on constitutional revision in the spring of 1960.

control, and power production. Private electric utilities, municipally owned systems, urban vs. rural and north vs. south protagonists took positions on the Eisenhower "partnership plan," as opposed to state power development. Governor Brown offered a compromise plan for a bond issue to be voted on in 1960 which instigated vigorous interest-group controversy. Finally, the oil lobby mobilized to defeat a 2 percent oil severance tax, which was an important part of the Governor's policy for meeting an anticipated deficit in fiscal 1960-61.

Interest-group strategy is executed in at least three different theaters of operations: lobbying in the legislature, supporting or defeating a candidate in his home district, and appealing to the public at large, primarily on an "issue campaign." Lobbyists used to be permitted on the floor of both houses of the state legislature; later, they were confined to visitors' galleries. Lobbyists spend money generously in the campaigns of favored candidates, but reporting procedures are so completely lax that no realistic picture of influence exerted in this manner is ascertainable.[47] It may reasonably be conjectured, however, that it is far from minimal.

Lobbying is more respectable than in the days when Artie Samish was quoted by Lester Viele as knowing when "a man wants a baked potato, a girl, or money." Representation of the legitimate programs of interest groups is now accepted as not only tolerable, but a necessary adjunct to the democratic process. The first session of the 1959 legislature found five lobbyists in Sacramento for each legislator. Their stock in trade was still free meals and libations, and a goodly measure of "socializing," coupled with generous and grimly purposeful dispensation of campaign contributions.[48]

The effect of the apparently stringent state law on lobbying has been at least to minimize, if not completely to eliminate felonious bribery, blackmail, and intimidation per se. Despite the appointment of committees on legislative representation in both houses to assist in implementing the regulations, a recent report stated that "there has been almost no enforcement of the law and little attempt to publicize it." Attorney General (later Governor) Brown reported only two "apparent infractions" in eight years, neither of which was prosecuted.[49]

47. A cursory examination of the official records of 50 assemblymen who chose to file financial reports on the 1958 campaign shows that 24 acknowledged receiving sums ranging from $50 to $100 from the Pharmaceutical Institute; 18 acknowledged $100 to $350 from the Teamsters Union; and 14 mentioned $200 to $800 from James D. Garibaldi, lobbyist for the race tracks and liquor industry. The candidate of the Sixth Assembly District listed $2,761.33 of a total expenditure of $7,360.33 as "anonymous cash contributions"; candidates in districts 3, 7, 8, 12, 30, and 31 were elected in the primary, so filed no statement on campaign expenses. A candidate in the Fifth District reported the smallest sum, $92, which he contributed himself; the largest acknowledged amount in this sample was $13,462.44, received by a candidate in the Fiftieth District.

48. Much of the bitterness of the lobby fraternity against Samish was based upon jealousy rather than any widespread moral indignation over his tactics.

49. State of California, Assembly Committee on Legislative Representation, *Lobbying* (Sacramento: Assembly Interim Committee, 1955-57), Vol. II, No. 1. An interesting and significant series of studies on legislative behavior supported by grants from the Political Behavior Committee of the Social Science Research Council is that authored by Professors Heinz Eulau, William Buchanan, Leroy Ferguson, and John C. Wahlke. Data represent intensive investigations of the state legislatures of California, New Jersey, Ohio, and Tennessee. Two typical citations: "The Political Socialization of American State Legislators," *Midwest Journal of Political Science*, Vol. III (May 1959), and "The Role of the Representative: Some Empirical Observations on the Theory of Edmund Burke," *American Political Science Review*, Vol. LIII (September 1959).

LEGISLATIVE POLITICS

The state legislature has experienced several minor internal revolutions with political connotations during the past decade.[50] The powerful and conservative rural-district bloc which dominated the Senate until the mid-1950's was gradually liquidated by normal political attrition. This group of wealthy and astute politicians, who maneuvered to sidetrack or moderate much of the liberal legislation advanced by the Assembly, had no immediate heirs. Their successors, elected from the farm belt, were primarily young Democrats who had the conventional obligations to their political party and appeared to be more amenable to party regularity in their voting behavior.

The Assembly concurrently felt the impact of an internal reform movement, when in 1951 a bipartisan group of insurgents made a move to "de-Cannonize" the speaker by depriving him of the power to appoint committees and assign bills. The primary goal was not achieved, but the insurgents were successful in establishing a Rules Committee which some thought might serve as an instrument for curbing the power of the speaker, a reform adopted two decades ago by the Senate.[51]

As presently constituted, the Committee on Rules serves as the "housekeeping" committee of the Assembly. The chairman is appointed by the speaker while six other members, three from each party, are nominated by party caucus and elected by the membership of the Assembly. The speaker pro tempore and the majority floor leader are ex-officio members of the committee. A committee member is not permitted to serve as chairman of any standing committee. The Rules Committee serves as an interim committee during recess of the legislature.

The speaker is a power in controlling the machinery of the Assembly, although in recent years this authority has been used in moderation. He appoints the majority floor leader, who serves as his personal representative on the floor of the Assembly, and the personnel of the twenty-seven standing committees. This function is the responsibility of the Rules Committee in the Senate. Finally, the speaker manages the legislative program through the prerogative of referral of bills to committees. Nearly 400 bills have been introduced in a single day in the Assembly and the average for a session is 5,000. It was estimated that in the 1965 session the legislature approved 2,243 of 5,020 bills introduced; the Governor signed 2,070 into law and vetoed 173.

From the instigation of the reform movement of the Progressive era to the rise of the Democratic Club movement in the mid-1950's, the enervating tenet of nonpartisanship has prevailed to greater or less degree in California politics. The legislature was Republican-dominated, but incumbency was often more significant than party identification in electioneering for office. The speaker of the Assembly has nearly always been elected by a bipartisan coalition reflecting sectional and interest-group influences which carried over into committee appointments.

50. For topics in this section see the following sources: Mary Ellen Leary, "The Legislature," in *California State Government* (Stanford: The American Assembly, 1956), pp. 21-30; Arthur A. Ohnimus, "Organization and Procedure of the Assembly," in *Legislator's Orientation Conference: 1957* (Sacramento: State Printing Office, 1957), pp. 91-111; Winston W. Crouch, John C. Bollens, Dean E. McHenry and Stanley Scott, *California Government and Politics* (3rd ed.; Englewood Cliffs: Prentice-Hall, 1964), chap. 6, pp. 115-41; Dean R. Cresap, *Party Politics in the Golden State* (Los Angeles: Haynes Foundation, 1954), pp. 52-63; Dick Meister, "With all Deliberate Speed," *Frontier*, X (April 1950), 16-17, and "End of the Beginning," *ibid.* (July 1959), 10-12; Gladwin Hill, "That Dark Horse Named Brown," *New York Times Magazine*, December 6, 1959, pp. 38, 90, 95.

51. Leary, *op. cit.*, p. 22. The Senate Committee on Rules consists of the president pro tem. who serves as chairman and four members elected by the Senate membership.

In the Senate, the president pro tempore representing the majority party is in the key position on the Rules Committee to control all other committee appointments. The traditional control device of the caucus has existed in some form in the Assembly (but not until recently in the Senate) since about 1935. It has been employed, however, principally for discussion and persuasion purposes; legislators have enjoyed a great measure of freedom in voting inasmuch as party discipline is lacking. Their obligations to interest groups are more important and often prove decisive in terms of voting behavior.

A recent study of voting alignments in the legislature presents an interesting analysis of the status of partisanship as reflected in key roll-call votes of the members.[52] Partisanship has definitely increased since 1957, the year before the Democratic landslide, but is still minimal compared to other northern, urban states. Particularly sensitive issues which stirred interparty debate were reapportionment, and labor and welfare bills. As the majority party, the Democrats have improved their coefficient of party cohesion vis-à-vis the Republican party in both houses, but there were fewer votes registering party disharmony in the state Senate. Nevertheless, there is a discernible increase in partisanship with the continuance of Democratic control through the middle sixties; the legislators and the public, who for over a generation were forced to choose sides from among the various alternatives of Republican policy, now have a genuine opposition party position with which to identify.

In considering the politics of the legislature, two of the most persistent assumptions over the years were the split voting over urban-rural and north-south interests. Whatever the past history of such conflicts might have been, the assumption that rural interests in the Senate coalesce politically to defeat urban interests per se is no longer correct, except upon a few specific issues such as the distribution of the state's water supply. Even in this exception, it is difficult to distinguish such an alignment from a division of north-south interests or possibly a split of intra-urban interests. The north-south dichotomy in legislative voting behavior is actually minimal when examined in terms of roll-call votes, no matter how strong the feelings of the legislator when conditioned by sectional loyalty. Moreover, an equitable solution to the water problem would leave the north-south split a mere reflection of the traditional rivalry between San Francisco and Los Angeles.

The 1959 session of the legislature had some historic significance. *New York Times* reporter Gladwin Hill recalls the skepticism directed at the Brown administration in its infancy inherent in predictions that it might be so "indecisive and ineffectual as to unravel the achievements of Californians right back to the Gold Rush."[53] Brown enthusiasts, on the other hand, drew an analogy between his first few months in office and "the first 100 days of the New Deal."

The theme of the Governor's program was "responsible liberalism," and of the forty major legislative bills he sponsored during the session, only five failed of passage. Each of these was "lobby-ridden" to oblivion, aided by bipartisan political cooperation. New legislation included: raising $200 million in new revenue to meet an impending fiscal deficit, a legacy of the previous administration; a fair employment practices act; a comprehensive water plan for the state involving a

52. Charles M. Price, "Voting Alignments in the California Legislature: A Roll Call Analysis of the 1957-1959-1961 Sessions" (doctoral dissertation, University of Southern California, 1965). See also: William Buchanan, *Legislative Partisanship: The Deviant Case of California* (Berkeley: University of California Press, 1963).

53. Hill, *op. cit.*, p. 38.

$1.75 billion bond issue subsequently approved in the 1960 election; a state economic development commission; a consumer's council; abolition of cross-filing; and initiation of many other projects such as a significant Master Plan Survey of the state's vast and complicated system of higher education. The temporary setback in Republican party effectiveness may be attributed to: a generation of political dominance during which demands for organizational control were minimal and conflicts were often sectional rather than partisan; involvement of personalities in a struggle for power within a party unaccustomed to the political dynamics of minority opposition; and significant ideological differences between ultra-conservatives and "middle-of-the-roaders," sharpened by the bitter factionalism engendered during the 1958 campaign. The installation of the office of party whip in 1959 has increased the effectiveness of the caucus system in both parties.

A succession of five Democratic victories resulting in substantial majorities in both houses has given Speaker Jesse Unruh and President pro tem Hugh Burns the opportunity to gain a firm grasp upon the machinery of the legislature. Unruh particularly, has assembled a group of young, able, and loyal lieutenants to chair the key committees in the Assembly.

Contrary to past years when committee chairmanships were shared by both parties, in 1965 twenty-four of the twenty-five were chaired by Democrats and nine Republicans were given vice-chairmanships. Unruh also introduced the party caucus method of electing the speaker, thus abandoning the traditional party coalition method of sponsoring nominees. The team of Unruh-Burns was largely responsible for the considerable success of Governor Brown's legislative program, a circumstance which has caused some friction from time to time.

During the 1965 session, the Republican party in the Assembly abandoned the moderate leadership of Charles J. Conrad in favor of the more partisan voice of Assemblyman Robert T. Monagan. Since the Democratic majorities in both houses fell short of the two-thirds required to pass the budget, Monagan was able to instill a considerable degree of partisanship during the legislative session. He also was able to mount an attack upon Governor Brown's announced intention to run for a third term.

REAPPORTIONMENT

Democratic control of the legislature for the first time in this century as a consequence of the 1958 elections coupled with the constitutional requirement for mandatory redistricting following the 1960 census made reapportionment a central issue of legislative politics in 1965. The background of the controversy stemmed from the constitution of 1879, which provided that the members of the Senate and the Assembly be elected according to population, with due respect for county lines. It was not long before the broad diversification of economic interests in the state, reflected in the commitments of both legislators and lobbyists, erupted in violent controversy over matters of public policy. Pressure groups and sectional interests sought to strengthen their positions by changing the basis of legislative representation.

The basic cleavages pitted north against south and urban against rural areas. The political coalition of northern and rural interests centering in San Francisco finally cracked under the strain of the pressures caused by the growth of southern California and the concentration of population in the urban centers of the state. As a consequence of the bitter fight for legislative representation after the 1910 census, a stalemate of factional interests was reached causing the postponement of reapportionment until passage of a constitutional amendment in 1926 sponsored by farm interest groups. The resultant "federal plan" favored the rural areas by providing for geographic representation in the Senate based upon the county as an electoral district, considered either singly or in combination.

California suffers both from a form of the "silent gerrymander" as a consequence of certain constitutional limitations governing apportionment, and from a political gerrymander imposed by the party controlling the legislature. By law, no county may have more than one senator and not more than three counties may be combined to form a senatorial district. Assembly districts must be equal in population, contiguous, composed of whole counties, or completely contained within a county. Congressional districts must be contiguous, and composed of whole assembly districts within a county and whole counties if two or more are incorporated into a single congressional district.[54]

In light of these strictures, the Republican party is credited with performing one of the most proficient, technical gerrymanders in the state's history in the reapportionment of 1951.[55] Using 15 percent as the maximum permissible deviation from the ideal population norm of 132,328 inhabitants per district, one-half of the eighty assembly districts were gerrymandered: eight were underpopulated and therefore overrepresented, while twelve were overpopulated and underrepresented. Half of the thirty congressional districts deviated from the ideal average of 352,874 inhabitants: eight were under and seven over the norm. Moreover, the geographic configuration of many of the districts proved conclusively the skill with which Democratic votes had been immobilized while well-scattered Republican votes provided narrow margins of victory.[56]

Conceding the established practice of protecting incumbents in any reapportionment plan, Greenfield et al. found that "seven of the eight congressional districts that were overrepresented in the 1951 redistricting voted Republican . . . in 1952 and with one exception . . . continued to vote Republican in 1954, 1956 and 1958. . . . Of the seven significantly underrepresented . . . districts, only two were Republican in 1952."[57]

54. In a consultant's report to the Assembly, the opinion is expressed that provisions which would inevitably create unequal electoral districts are now invalid. California Assembly, Committee on Elections and Reapportionment, *Reapportionment in California: Consultant's Report to the Assembly*, Vol. 7, No. 9, April 1965 (Sacramento: State Printing Office, 1965). The legislature, in fact, violated these restrictions in complying with the court order to reapportion.

55. California Assembly, Interim Committee on Elections and Reapportionment, *Reports* (Sacramento: State Printing Office, 1951, 1955 and 1957); Margaret Greenfield, Pamela Ford, and Donald R. Emery, *Legislative Reapportionment: California in National Perspective* (Berkeley: Bureau of Public Administration, University of California, 1959); Ivan Hinderaker, "Responsiveness to the Will of the People," in *California State Government*, pp. 39-42; and *California State Constitution*, Art. IV, secs. 6 and 27.

56. In Los Angeles County, four congressional districts (the 17th, 19th, 23rd, and 26th) represented by Democrats all had over 400,000 inhabitants: only one Republican district, the 15th, was in this category. Five Republican districts (the 16th, 18th, 20th, 22nd, and 24th) all had less than 275,000. The Seventeenth District (Democratic) with 409,334 inhabitants was contiguous to the Eighteenth (Republican) with 270,185. For an able defense of the gerrymander by the chairman of the committee which prepared the 1951 reapportionment legislation and a political scientist who served as one of his advisers, see Ivan Hinderaker and Laughlin E. Waters, "A Case Study in Reapportionment—California, 1951," *Law and Contemporary Problems*, XVII (Spring 1952), 440-69. See also Hinderaker, "Responsiveness to the Will of the People," *loc. cit.*

57. Greenfield, Ford, and Emery, *op. cit.*, pp. 57-61. All of the underrepresented districts continued to vote the same congressional ticket in the succeeding three elections. Much the same situation prevailed in the 31 Assembly districts of Los Angeles County; al-

Since the Democrats are the majority party in the state, their control over the legislature and the congressional delegation may extend over the foreseeable future. But the flood of new registrants, coupled with accelerated intra-state migration, changes the political complexion of a district so rapidly that any presumption that a gerrymander will render permanent control for either party is fallacious.[58]

The 1962 election proved that the Democrats were the equal of the Republicans in the art of gerrymandering.[59] Ideally a congressional district should have had 413,610 residents. Nine of the thirty-eight districts showed deviations of over 15 percent; six were over and three under. Twenty-four of the assembly districts deviated from the norm of 196,465.

The figures however do not reveal the consummate skill with which Democratic and cooperative Republican incumbents were allowed to survive, while recalcitrant Republicans were jettisoned. Of the eight new congressional districts, the Democrats won six and the Republicans two, delivering the congressional delegation to the majority party by 24-14, in place of the previously narrow margin of 16-14. The Democratic plurality in the Assembly was increased by eight and the Republican membership reduced by six, leaving the final division 52 to 28.

The critical problem of reapportionment in California, as elsewhere, is the application of the "one man, one vote" principle to the state Senate. Prior to 1926, both houses were popularly elected. Conservative interests such as the California Farm Bureau Federation, the California State Grange, the Farmer's Union, the Agriculture Legislative Committee and the several Chambers of Commerce and other interested groups in the San Francisco Bay region sponsored the "Federal Plan" making the county, as a representative geographic unit (singly or in combination), the basis of senatorial representation.

Agitation to return the Senate to the practice of election on the basis of population began early in the 1940's. Previous attempts to accomplish this objective were defeated by referendum in 1928, and by initiative constitutional amendment in 1948, 1960 and 1962.[60] Business interests played an important role in defeating the most recent attempt. Typical were the corporations acknowledging contributions of over $5,000 to fight the ballot measure: Southern Pacific Railroad, Standard Oil of California, and Pacific Gas and Electric. It seemed a reasonable assumption that the addition of a dozen or more urban senators would upset

though the Democrats had one-third more registrants during 1952-56 than the Republicans, the latter won 68 percent of the county's Assembly seats in 1952, 55 percent in 1954 and 52 percent in 1956. California has a Reapportionment Commission, empowered to act when the legislature fails to redistrict, composed of the lieutenant governor, attorney general, secretary of state, controller, and superintendent of public instruction.

58. The results of the 1960 census released during the summer of 1961 gave the state 5,130,981 new inhabitants, changing the average size of the congressional districts from 352,874 to 413,611 and entitling California to 8 new congressmen or a total of 38. The new reapportionment legislation sponsored by the Democratic party became law on July 8, 1961. The state Senate was not affected by the reapportionment legislation.

59. For the 1961 reapportionment and especially for a comparison of the 1951 and 1961 results see: California Assembly, Interim Committee on Elections and Reapportionment, *Reports: 1959-1961*, Vol. 7, No. 5 (Sacramento: State Printing Office, 1961).

60. The popular votes on the issue were: 1948–2,250,937 to 1,069,899; 1960–3,408,090 to 1,876,185; 1962–2,495,440 to 2,181,758. Whenever abandonment of the Federal Plan is advocated, counter-proposals are advanced to split California into two states at the Tehachapi Mountain Range. Republican state Senator Richard J. Dolwig introduced such a bill in the January 1965 session of the legislature which received short shrift from his colleagues.

the delicately coordinated channels to political power currently enjoyed by the conservative business community.

The many discrepancies in popular representation in the Senate were ludicrous indeed. The six million people in Los Angeles County, for instance, had a single senator as did the 15,000 citizens of Alpine, Inyo and Mono counties, which together constituted a senatorial district. One wag calculated the worth of the Los Angeles senator's vote as 1/450th of that of the senator from the 28th (Northern Sierra) district! Thirty-seven of the forty senatorial districts deviated from the norm of 392,930 by more than 15 percent, making the California Senate one of the lowest in representativeness in the nation.

The inequity may be illustrated by the fact that half of the state's population is centered in four southern California counties which had less than 10 percent of the representation in the Senate. Thus largely rural counties with only a fraction of the popular vote could and did veto both legislation and constitutional amendment proposals, usually of liberal hue.

Concerted court action to enforce reapportionment of the Senate on a population basis following *Baker v. Carr*, began early in 1964. The drive culminated in a favorable 2-1 decision by an especially constituted Federal District Court on December 3, 1964, ordering reapportionment by July 1, 1965, under penalty of court assumption of the task (*Silver v. Johnson*). In an appeal to the U.S. Supreme Court, the ruling was upheld on June 1, 1965.

The representation of Los Angeles County was the crux of the difference between the Senate and Assembly bills for reapportionment; both failed of passage in the waning days of the 1965 session of the legislature. The county was entitled to 15 1/2 senators on the population basis: the Senate bill recommended 12 seats and the Assembly the full 15 1/2. Behind the bare figures is a fascinating political intrigue. Democrats were pitted against Democrats and the Assembly against the Senate in competition for the newly created Senate seats. The Assembly modified the Senate bill assuring that 14 assemblymen would have gerrymandered districts from which to ascend to the Senate; it split 25 city boundaries between two districts to accomplish this end, tampering with 23 of the 40 senatorial districts. When the Senate rejected these revisions, the Assembly produced its own version, granting 15 1/2 seats to Los Angeles County, a solution entirely unacceptable to the upper house, but a maneuver which gave the court an alternate plan and placed the Assembly in a position to participate in any eventual solution to the problem. It is obvious that neither house made a genuine effort toward a solution and both desired the courts to take over.

The stalemate was resolved by an order of the state Supreme Court in mid-1965 calling for reapportionment of the two houses. The legislature met in special session in the fall, finally approving a plan which was signed into law by Governor Brown on October 27, 1965. Ratified by the state Supreme Court in December, the plan returned the state Senate to the strict population basis which had been in effect from 1850 to 1930, reducing the number of senators representing the 50 northern counties from 31 to 18 while increasing southern California representation from 9 to 22. Senate representation for Los Angeles County, hitherto the most underrepresented district in the nation, was increased from 1 to 14 1/5. Minor adjustments were made in the Assembly, with the main change a reduction in San Francisco's representation from 5 to 4 seats.

For the first time since becoming a state the balance of political power in the legislature has been relocated from northern to southern California. The eight southern counties from Santa Barbara to San Diego now control more Senate and Assembly seats than the fifty remaining counties in the state. Since most of the historic issues which have divided the state geographically have been resolved, the evaluation of the full significance of this change must await future developments.

INITIATIVE AND REFERENDUM POLITICS

Citizens of the state of California have been empowered to participate in direct legislation since the adoption of the constitution of 1849, which required that all amendments be submitted to popular vote by the legislature. It was not until the culmination of the reform movement in the election of 1911, however, that statewide initiative, referendum, and recall became an integral part of the constitution.[61]

California employs several types of initiative and several categories of referenda. A petition carrying the valid signatures of 8 percent of the vote cast for governor in the preceding general election will qualify a constitutional amendment, and 5 percent a direct initiative for statutory legislation. The categories of referenda are: compulsory, applying to bond issues and constitutional amendments; a petition-referendum, supported by 5 percent of the preceding gubernatorial vote, which causes the suspension of a newly enacted statute until its acceptance by the electorate at the next general election; and, finally, referenda involving a decision on whether or not to call a constitutional convention.

The procedure of direct legislation is certainly not unique to California, since the practice exists in more than a fourth of the states. But Californians have utilized it with a high rate of frequency.[62]

Evaluation of the substantive aspects of direct legislation indicates some interesting trends. The first decade of the reform movement found many proposals dealing with moral and economic problems, such as prohibition, antivivisection, prize fighting, compulsory vaccination, reading of the Bible in public schools, usury, and the eight-hour day. Interest in the 1920's turned to public education where a series of successful attempts was instituted to shift a greater share of its cost to the state. Efforts to improve state administrative practices resulted in the adoption of the executive budget, often cited as among the signal achievements of direct legislation in the state's history.

61. Winston W. Crouch, *The Initiative and Referendum in California* (Los Angeles: The Haynes Foundation, 1950); Wallace H. Best, "Initiative and Referendum Politics in California, 1912-1952" (doctoral dissertation, University of Southern California, 1955). Crouch's basic statistical research was updated through 1952 by Best and data cited below are from this latter source.

62. Between 1912 and 1952 there were 568 distinct attempts on the part of the interested public to seek official petition titles for potential legislation. By numerical count alone, these attempts have enjoyed only moderate success, statutory initiatives having been rejected by a ratio of better than 3-1 and constitutional initiatives by a ratio of 2.5-1. Constitutional decisions sponsored by the state legislature enjoyed greater acceptance, 183 having been adopted and 121 rejected from a total of 304 submissions between the years 1912 and 1952.

Of these, 163 survived for submission to the popular vote: 75 as constitutional and 49 as direct initiatives, 35 as optional referenda, and 4 in the form of indirect initiatives. Submissions originating with the state legislature exceeded those of the electorate by a ratio of 2-1. Of the 326 in this category, there were 288 constitutional referenda (required by law), 24 bond issues, 9 measures and 5 convention calls.

Vieg and Turner, *op. cit.*, report that the number of statewide proposals between 1911 and 1964 reached a total of 591, that of these 420 were constitutional amendments and other proposals submitted by the legislature, while 171 were initiatives and referenda.

The mid-1930's were marked by numerous attempts to promote social and economic reform, principally through various pension plans. One such panacea known as "Ham and Eggs" appeared five times between 1938 and 1948. The more widely known Townsend Plan, or "Sixty Dollars at Sixty," qualified for the ballot but lost in the election of 1944. The one successful venture in this field, a proposal of George McLain of Los Angeles to reorganize and staff the department of social welfare, as well as modify the qualifications for old age pensions, won in the 1948 general election, but was repealed in a special election the following year.

On the whole, the electorate has shown rather nice discernment in moderation, when approving or rejecting direct legislative proposals. All of the more extreme pension plans have failed. Significant statutory initiatives served to provide for the University of California Building Bond Act (1914), the Usury Law (1918) and the permanent registration of voters (1930). Constitutional initiatives brought such reforms as repeal of the poll tax (1914), the executive budget (1922), and the "federal plan" of reapportionment (1926).

The proposition that direct legislation is the ideal legal handmaiden of representative democracy is open to debate. The entire process has become thoroughly politicized and access to the procedure by minority groups has been made extremely difficult, if not practically impossible, due to the increase in the size of the electorate, the consequent change in campaign techniques, and the exorbitant cost.

Political manipulation begins with the attorney general, who may refuse to issue a petition title, or issue two separate titles to pre-empt the subject field. In 1942, for instance, one Marshall E. Leahy, a San Francisco attorney, was given the titles, "Limiting Retail Sales Tax" and "Repeal of Sales Tax." Another tactic involved identical ballot titles termed "Aged and Blind Aid" for two different propositions, one granting such assistance (1948) and one repealing the previous measure (1949), thus causing great confusion in the ranks of the pensioners. In a more recent instance, Edmund G. Brown, then attorney general, changed the title of Proposition 18 (1958) from "Right-to-Work" to "Employer and Employee Relations," thus rendering ineffective the battle cry of conservative Republicans.

Confusion over titles is only a beginning to political manipulation and is followed by comparable treatment of circulation procedures, signature verification and certification, assignment of ballot position, the "pro" and "con" arguments appearing in the official literature which accompanies the sample ballot for the voter, and finally, the rulings of the attorney general, the secretary of state, and the various county registrars of voters during the entire period of activity.

A second hazard to the implementation of theoretical democracy through the direct legislative process rests more upon the circumstances of life in the twentieth century than political partisanship or the vagaries of the personal economic and social philosophies of government officials. In 1914, an initiative petition could be qualified with 74,136 names at an approximate cost of $5,930, or five cents per name. Eight percent of the 5,255,777 popular votes cast for governor in 1958 would represent 420,462 names, or the total required to qualify a petition between 1959 and 1962. The cost for professional petition circulators had reached forty cents per name in 1952, exclusive of any aid given in the campaign to gain a favorable vote from the electorate.[63] A conservative estimate for profes-

63. The breakdown: fifteen cents for the individual solicitor, three cents for the precincting contractor, thirteen cents for overhead and nine cents profit. Unforeseen difficulties, last-minute circulations, or a sizable margin of signatures over the minimum required

sional petition qualification alone would be $175,000 and campaign costs might range from $25,000 to $2,000,000, or much more. The alternative to possession of adequate financing for professional guidance of an initiative measure through both the petition qualification and campaign stages would be a competently led, statewide organization with substantial membership on the grass-roots level. The two requirements for success, money and organizational strength, narrow the opportunities for participation in direct legislation to major interest groups.

The California Teachers' Association has scored a succession of notable victories in the utilization of the initiative. Even with the prerequisites of an efficient organization and adequate funds, and the added psychological advantage of identifying its cause with the emotional overtones of the "welfare-of-youth" argument, the group felt obliged to retain the professional campaign management firm of Whitaker and Baxter to guide the destinies of its propositions in 1944, 1946, and 1952.

The oil industry has mounted campaigns on the battlefield of initiative politics on a truly colossal scale. In a battle over oil conservation, the antagonists on Proposition 4 (1956), christened the "millionaire versus the billionaire" corporations, spent an estimated $5,000,000. Business interests sponsoring Proposition 18 on "right-to-work" in 1958, reported expenditures of $954,389, and organized labor countered with $2,556,037 to defeat the measure. In the same election the sponsors of Proposition 16 to tax under-collegiate, parochial school property spent $471,631, and their opponents acknowledged $1,340,817, while the professional campaign firm of Baus and Ross reported a fee of $25,946 to handle the negative side.

The significance of the change of venue of "the trial of public policy by political influence" from the lobby-ridden halls of Sacramento to the electorate at large, where initiative politics are played, has yet to be evaluated. It is undoubtedly significant that the American Legion is so uniformly successful in gaining desired legislation through action by the state legislature that utilization of initiative measures is rarely, if ever, necessary, and that Whitaker and Baxter can point to a phenomenal record of eighteen successes of twenty attempts in initiative campaigning. Republican party sympathizers virtually defeated the move of their Democratic opponents to abolish cross-filing in 1952 (Proposition 13) by placing a competing proposition on the ballot (Proposition 7), calling for identification of candidate party labels. More recently, a proposition to enjoin the state from denying, limiting or abridging the right of the individual to sell, lease or rent his property to anyone he chooses evoked widespread controversy because of its accentuation of racial problems centering about discrimination in housing. The proposition passed in 1966, but was subsequently invalidated by the United States Supreme Court.

The California voter in the decade of the 1950's frequently faced twenty or more propositions of various types on his ballot. Even when highly motivated, his knowledge of the importance of these issues of public policy is largely received through the mass media channels available for hire to the best financed interest groups. The question may at least be posed whether or not the initiative will continue to be utilized in the interests of democracy and whether its use should be re-examined in terms of the goals of representative government.

might add $10,000 to the total bill. Best, *op. cit.*, p. 196. A referendum required 262,789 signatures between 1959-62.

THE BUDGET

Politics in state finance has been played with new rules following the establishment of the executive budget by constitutional initiative in 1922. The governor now submits the budget, an appropriation bill, and a budget message to the legislature within the first thirty days of the budget session held in even-numbered years. Moreover, he enjoys the power of item veto over appropriation bills; he may reduce or reject, but not increase, individual items. He directs his fiscal policy through the most powerful member of his cabinet, the director of finance, and must work with two other officials elected on a statewide basis, the treasurer and the controller.

Between 1941 and 1955, the legislature developed a formidable system of committees and semi-administrative advisory personnel to assist in the formulation of its fiscal policy. To the traditional Senate Finance and Assembly Ways and Means committees have been added a Joint Legislative Budget Committee, with a legislative auditor (now known as the legislative analyst) as secretary, and a Joint Legislative Audit Committee, with an auditor general serving as consultant.

The Joint Legislative Budget Committee is composed of seven senators: the president pro tempore and six others appointed by the Rules Committee; and seven assemblymen appointed by the speaker. Members usually belong to the fiscal committees of their respective houses. With the assistance of the legislative analyst, this committee deals with budgetary analysis and reviews and makes recommendations for fiscal efficiency in government. Members of the committee may disagree on the floor of the legislature with particular recommendations made by their own legislative analyst.

In order to run its own check against expenditures, the legislature created a Joint Legislative Audit Committee composed of three members of each house empowered to employ an auditor general with authority to examine the records of any state agency. The legislature is thus in a position to receive an independent and complete post-audit report as the basis for its annual review of the budget.

In spite of this elaborate machinery, the budget bill which the governor presents to the appropriations committees represents only a portion of the total expenditures of the state for the current year. In California roughly two-thirds of the expenditure requirements are fixed either by provisions of the constitution or by statute and require supplementary appropriations legislation.[64]

The increasing and rapid expansion of population in California has had a tremendous impact on fiscal policies. A comfortable budgetary surplus in the 1940's disappeared, along with a "rainy day" or deficiency reserve fund, during the last days of the Goodwin Knight administration, a circumstance which became an issue in the 1958 gubernatorial election.

Former Governor Brown's budgetary requests doubled in seven years, progressing from $2.19 billion in the fiscal year 1959-60 to $4.02 billion in 1965-66.

64. The legislature exercises limited control over approximately 70 percent of the total expenditures due to such mandatory requirements as salaries of state legislators, interest and redemption payments on bonds, public school appropriations, and payments toward the salaries of superior court judges. These requirements can be changed only by direct popular legislation. More than 1/3 of the budgetary requirements of the state have been "built in" by statute, without provision for annual review, including state highway construction and maintenance, old age and security payments, aid to the needy, State Employees' Retirement costs and the sharing of certain state-collected revenues with local governments. These latter requirements may be changed by legislative statute, but rarely are. See Malcolm M. Davisson, "Financing State Government," *California State Government, op. cit.*, pp. 48-55.

In the latter year, education claimed 46.0 percent of the budget dollar, health and welfare 21.5, and highway transportation 12.8 percent. Other categories included resources, 3.9; corrections, 3.3; fiscal affairs, 1.7; business and commerce 1.1; public safety 0.8 and all other, 8.9, including sums returned to local governments.

The state sales tax provides the largest single share of the income dollar (29.1), followed by taxes on highway users (20.7), banks and corporations (12.0), personal income (11.2), tobacco tax (6.0), motor vehicle license fees (5.1), inheritance and gift taxes (3.2), insurance tax (3.0), liquor taxes and fees (2.4), horse racing fees (1.4), and all other (5.8).[65]

In recognition of the pressures exerted by interest groups in budget hearings of the Senate Finance and the Assembly Ways and Means committees, the budget session of the legislature has been succinctly characterized by political sophisticates as "the biggest floating crap game in the world."

CONSTITUTIONAL REVISION

California's 70,000-word constitution is notorious as second in length only to that of Louisiana and as the most frequently amended fundamental law of the 50 states. In responding to changing times by amendment rather than revision, the people and their representatives have created a document characterized as: too long; containing subject matter more appropriately belonging in statutes; freighted with much obsolete, repetitive and contradictory material; difficult to amend; and both poorly drafted and out of date.

The present version of the constitution was adopted in 1879, and had been amended 325 times by 1960. Of the 565 proposed amendments during that period, 490 originated in the legislature (304 adopted) and 75 were generated through the initiative process (21 adopted). The most important single motivating force toward amendment has been the persistent demands of interest groups to seek the protection of constitutional law.[66]

Only four proposals sponsored by the legislature since 1900, each calling for a referendum on the question of a constitutional convention, received the necessary two-thirds majority and were submitted to the people (1913, 1919, 1929, 1933). The first three were rejected by the voters and although the fourth proposition passed, creating a popular mandate for calling a constitutional convention, the legislature subsequently failed to pass the necessary enabling legislation. The legislature has acted unilaterally to authorize studies of the need for revision. No action was taken on a proposal submitted by a fifteen-member commission appointed by the Governor under appropriate legislation in 1929. A Joint Interim Committee on Constitutional Revision, supported by a widely representative Advisory Committee in 1947, succeeded in having eight proposed amendments eliminating 14,500 words from the constitution passed by the legislature in 1949.

65. State of California, Governor's Office, *Budget for the Fiscal Year, July, 1965-June, 1966.*

66. On the topic of constitutional revision: Ernest A. Englebert and John G. Gunnell, "State Constitutional Revision in California" (pamphlet), (Los Angeles: Bureau of Governmental Research, University of California at Los Angeles, April 1961); Bernard L. Hyink, "The California Legislature Looks at the Constitution," *Western Political Quarterly*, XV (March 1962), 157-69; John A. Busterud, "Politics of Constitutional Revision," in Eugene P. Dvorin and Arthur J. Misner (eds.), *California Politics and Policies* (Palo Alto: Addison Wesley, 1966), pp. 106-29; and the staff studies of the California State Constitutional Revision Commission, 1965-68.

The most recent attempt to effect revision began with a constitutional amendment in 1962 authorizing the legislature to propose and submit for popular ratification, an amendment or amendments, for the revision of the constitution in whole or in part. Subsequently, under the strong leadership of Assembly Speaker Jesse Unruh, the Joint Committee on Legislative Organization was authorized to appoint and work with a Constitutional Revision Commission (upon which its members served ex-officio). The Commission included three additional senators appointed by the Senate's Committee on Rules and three assemblymen appointed by the speaker. The Commission membership "shall be broadly representative of the various political, economic and social groupings within the state" and consist of not less than 25 and not more than 50 citizens.

As constituted, the citizens' "Blue Ribbon" Commission included 43 lay members representing the "third house" of business, labor and agriculture, women's organizations, prestigious members of the bar, present and former officers of major corporations, and a number of academicians, principally political scientists and several university presidents. The political complexion of the Commission was bipartisan.

The Commission held its first meeting on February 20, 1964, and within two years prepared articles dealing with the executive, legislative, judiciary, and civil service for submission to the legislature (Articles III, IV, V, VI and XXIV, constituting roughly one-third of the constitution). These proposals (with the exception of Article XXIV), as modified by the Assembly and Senate were submitted to the electorate in 1966 as Proposition I-A. Receiving strong bipartisan support in the legislature from Speaker Unruh and Minority Leader Robert T. Monagan and including the endorsement on television of both Democratic Governor Brown and Republican gubernatorial candidate Ronald Reagan, the proposition was overwhelmingly approved by the citizenry, 4,132,997 to 1,477,109.

Encouraged by this initial success, the Commission submitted its second "package" of six articles covering education, public institutions, local government, corporations and public utilities, civil service, state lands, and constitutional amendment on February 15, 1968 (Articles IX, X, XI, XII, XVIII and XXII).

The initial revision contained a few substantive and procedural changes including: annual general sessions for the legislature; permission for the legislators to set their own salaries (they immediately raised their yearly stipend from $6,000 to $16,000); a mandate to the legislature to pass a conflict-of-interest law; elimination of the indirect initiative and reduction of the requirement for signatures for an initiative statute petition from 8 percent to 5 percent of the gubernatorial votes cast in the last election; authorization of the Supreme Court to determine executive disability; regularization of the procedure for gubernatorial succession; and authorization for the legislature to allow the governor to reorganize the executive branch of the government.

The political dynamics of constitutional revision in California has yielded a rather modest increment of reform. In no state in the Union are interest group prerogatives more thoroughly impacted in the fundamental law, to a large extent through hundreds of constitutional amendments. The interest groups served notice early during the Commission's deliberations that they would not permit the relegation of the "legal freight of special privilege" to ordinary statute law. A novel solution to this dilemma was proposed, which might have effected far-reaching constitutional reform. However, the Commissioners were unable to agree to it.

The proposal was the creation of an intermediate body of law to be known as an "Organic Law Code" or a "Fundamental Law" to provide interest groups with a legal sanctuary somewhere between sub-constitutional and supra-statutory status. Such a code would require an extraordinary vote to repeal or amend, thus protecting special interests from predatory attacks mounted through ordinary statutory legislation, and at the same time, free the constitution for a simple statement of the basic principles of government.

The Commission has eliminated or compressed verbiage, cutting the document by between one-third to one-fourth of its former content. The tortuous mid-nineteenth century phrasing has been restated in lucid contemporary prose. Finally, the subject matter has been given a logical frame of reference, no small accomplishment considering the fact, for instance, that topics on finance alone scattered in seventy different sections in seven separate articles are to be drawn together into a heretofore nonexistent article on finance! The possibility remains that more substantial substantive changes may be effected in the second and third "packages" which the Commission was readying for the legislature in mid-1968.

VOTING BEHAVIOR

The political hallmark of the decade 1954-64 was the administrative and spiritual renascence of the Democratic party with the resultant reinstitution of the two-party system in the state. Upon his election in 1962 Governor "Pat" Brown joined Hiram Johnson and Earl Warren as the only governors to be elected more than once since the four-year term was adopted in 1862; and Brown was the first Democrat to be re-elected since 1853. For the first time in this century the Democrats won control of the legislature for longer than a four-year period—and continued to hold it, albeit with a narrowing margin, through the 1966 election, despite the loss of the governor's chair.

Three salient aspects of the California electorate during the past generation are: that its numbers have doubled; that a solid Republican majority has yielded (1934) to a 60-40 Democratic majority; and that the Republican party has dominated state politics for most of the last half-century.

The number of registrants jumped from 1,532,384 in 1922 to 3,140,114 in 1934 and reached 8,340,868, the largest in history, by 1966. During 1960 an incredible 1.6 million registrants were added to the rolls bringing the total to 80 percent of the number of persons over 21 years of age in the state; these were joined by 1.75 million more between January and September of 1964, and by another 150,000 in the next biennium.

A significant corollary development found the traditional Republican majority descending from 63.2 percent in 1922 to 45.6 in 1934 and reaching 41.5 in 1966, while the Democratic minority percentage of 20.8 in 1922 rose to a plurality of 49.6 in 1934 and reached 58.5 in 1966. The Democrats have not relinquished their position of ascendancy in registrants since achieving it in 1934.

The partisan complexion of the electorate at the time of the 1966 election was: Democrats, 4,720,597 (58.5 percent); Republicans, 3,350,990 (38.3 percent); declined-to-state, 223,677 (2.7 percent) and miscellaneous 41,308 (0.5 percent). The Prohibitionist party, which had been a part of the political scene since 1875, failed to qualify as a result of the 1962 election.

The results of the 1960 and 1962 primary elections tested the hypothesis that cross-filing had inhibited intra-party contests and created sinecures of "nonpartisan incumbency." In the cross-filed primaries of 1956 and 1958 there had been 57 and 54 contests, respectively, for the congressional and state legislative seats. In the first primary after the formal abolition of cross-filing (1960) there were 81 intra-party races. In 1962, after the redistricting of legislative seats, the voters faced more candidates, more seats to be filled (8 new congressional districts), and more intra-party contests (146), than in the state's recent history. It is too early to stipulate that a definite trend has been established because the number of intra-party contests fell to 40 percent in 1964 from 53 percent in 1963; because of intra-party and interparty ideological battles; and because of the sweeping reapportionment of the state Senate. Nevertheless it would appear that the proponents of the abolition of cross-filing were correct; the closed primary has increased the opportunities for intra-party competition.

On the other hand, the status of the incumbent remained relatively secure. The great majority of the primary elections did not involve contests. In 1960 there were 166 seats held by incumbents; only 19 were challenged and one defeated. In 1962 (the first election after reapportionment when many incumbents chose to run for a higher office, or were gerrymandered out of their districts) there were 94 incumbents and 61 did not face opposition. In 1964 there were 132 officeholders who stood for re-election; only two were defeated. The basic change represented an increase of Democratic rather than Republican incumbents due to the 1962 apportionment by a Democratic legislature. The court-ordered reapportionment in 1965 required that all 40 Senate seats be contested in 1966, double the usual number. Of 20 seats, mostly in the new districts in the southern half of the state, there were no incumbents seeking election. In contrast, in five districts in the north a total of 12 incumbents thrown together by reapportionment competed for their party's nomination. An additional 11 senators found it advantageous to retire from office entirely. Of the 27 Senate incumbents choosing to run, only 3 faced opposition in the primary from other than fellow senators. However, attracted by the large number of "open" seats, a record number of 211 candidates competed in the senatorial primary, nearly four times the usual figure. Included among their number were 19 assemblymen, lured from the lower house by the prospect of a four-year term (assemblymen serve only two years), the added prestige of a "senator," and highly advantageous partisan districting in which they had participated only a few months before. That the "case of the ambitious assemblymen" was a success is suggested by the fact that 16 of the 19 won their primary contests and 14 went on to win Senate seats in the general elections.

As a consequence of the attempted move of assemblymen to the Senate and the retirement of several others, a total of 29 Assembly seats were without an incumbent in the primary. Here, too, the lure of "open" seats attracted a record number of 385 candidates. In contrast, relatively few incumbents faced opposition from within their own party primary. This pattern was equally true in the congressional primaries in which 37 out of 38 incumbents ran for re-election; less than half of the incumbents faced opposition from within their own primary and the number of congressional candidates was markedly fewer than in recent years.

In sum, the key variable in legislative races in terms of both numbers of candidates and contested primaries was the number of incumbents contesting the election. That a decline would occur in intra-party competition in 1968 and 1970 as the "new" incumbents established themselves seemed likely. And that incumbents would rarely be defeated within their own primary seemed equally true. In 1966, the only primary losses suffered by incumbents were in senatorial races contested by other incumbent senators or, in one case, by an assemblyman seeking a senatorial seat. It is quite possible, even probable, that in California elections, at least at the legislative level, incumbency outweighs party loyalty in the mind of the voter.

Three developments in the voting behavior of the California electorate during the 1960's are particularly noteworthy: the Republican party has been able to command a greater degree of loyalty from its adherents than have the Democrats; the voter responds differently to statewide elections and those contested in legislative districts; and there is some evidence to indicate that there are sectional differences in the preference of voters in each party.

In spite of the relative stability (since 1936) of the ratio of party strength at 60-40, favoring the Democrats, the Republicans register a greater proportion of their party members, turn them out at the polls in larger numbers, and obtain more consistent partisan support in votes cast. Republicans outvoted Democrats by a 7 percent margin in 1960, enjoyed a differential of 82 percent to 78 percent in 1962, and a 89.1 to 88.0 percent margin in 1964. The narrowing advantage may well be due to recent measures taken by the Democrats such as paying a "bounty" to deputy registrars for Democratic registrants in 1960, and expending $150,000 in selected precincts of Los Angeles County to get out the vote in 1962. But in 1966, in terms of partisan distribution, the GOP once again demonstrated its superior ability to mobilize its registrants, of whom 84 percent voted compared to 77 percent of the Democrats. Coloring all of the statistics, however, was the fact that more than three million California adults were unregistered, a commentary both on citizen apathy and the need for registration reform.

There appear to be three separate elective arenas in California: statewide races for gubernatorial, senatorial, and presidential offices, primary contests in congressional and assembly districts, and the as yet undefined level of state senatorial district competition.[67] Although the Democrats with a larger registration have the advantage in gubernatorial and United States senatorial races, the voter shows a propensity for splitting his ticket in this arena. A large share of the three-quarters of a million vote margin won by Republican senatorial candidate Thomas H. Kuchel in 1962, for instance, was provided by middle and upper income Democrats and Democrats from the Negro and Jewish communities. In the 1960 presidential and 1962 gubernatorial races, according to the *California Poll*, Richard Nixon won only 17 percent of the registered Democrats, and 12 percent of the Republican vote went to the Democratic candidates. He won the state by a narrow margin in the presidential race and lost the gubernatorial contest. In 1964 George Murphy won the U.S. senatorial election with the help of one-fourth of the Democratic vote, while Pierre Salinger could only muster 14 percent of the Republicans. In 1966, the polling data conclusively demonstrate Reagan's inroads into Democratic ranks, the key, of course, to Republican victory. While in 1962 Brown had commanded the allegiance of 82 percent of decided Democratic voters in the last pre-election poll, the comparable figure in 1966 was 73 percent. Republican strength, on the other hand, remained as strongly for Reagan as it had for Nixon in 1962. Undecided voters were substantially higher than in 1962, and of these 72 percent were Democrats, many of whom apparently voted for the Republican candidate.

67. For the "arena" concept and sectional differences in voting see Eugene C. Lee, "The Two Arenas and the Two Worlds of California Politics," in Eugene C. Lee (ed.), *The California Governmental Process* (Boston: Little, Brown, 1966), pp. 46-53.

The same situation is not true on the second competitive level; the congressional and state legislative districts are gerrymandered, and frequently are one-party districts. The consequences favor incumbency and place the competitive emphasis upon the closed party primary. Once he wins the majority party primary, the candidate in a safe district is virtually assured of victory. Experience has indicated that Democrats tend to run 5 percent behind their party's registered strength; if the margin increases to 10 percent, the candidate is usually in trouble (as Kennedy discovered in 1960). Republicans consider any Democratic legislative district, if lost by only 55 percent, a possible prize in the succeeding election. Most Democrats do not consider a district safe that is won by less than 65 percent of the vote. The noncompetitive nature of these second-level contests in the 1960's is indicated by the 1964 election, wherein only 5 of the 38 congressional seats and 11 of the 80 Assembly contests were won by margins of less than 55 percent.

The nature of the competition in the third arena of state politics, the senatorial districts, will become clear as the results of the 1965 reapportionment are evaluated. It is evident, however, that with the Senate restored to a strict population basis, it will be dominated by voters from the southern part of the state.

A tentative hypothesis which will stand further examination is that there are significant sectional differences in the voting pattern of the electorate. In 1964, for instance, southern Californians in both parties supported George Murphy to a greater extent than did the voters in the north. Twice as many northern Republicans as southern ones favored his rival, Pierre Salinger, while Democrats in the north supported the former press secretary by 80 percent compared to 72 percent in the south. In another example, Lyndon Johnson received twice the support in the north that he obtained in the south, although the predominant voting strength is in the latter region. In response to ballot Proposition 14, prohibiting state interference in the free choice for disposal of privately owned residential property, twice as many northern Republicans of upper-and-middle income status were opposed to the initiative as were southern Republicans.

Perhaps most noteworthy in the Reagan victory was the blurring of the north-south split which featured the 1964 presidential race. In that year, 10 percentage points separated the vote above and below the Tehachapis. In 1966, the margin was reduced to 5 percent. Democrat Brown was able to run a close race only in the San Francisco Bay Area, but even there trailed the GOP challenger. The remaining northern counties, which had provided him with a 64 and 55 percent vote in 1958 and 1964, respectively, voted 43 percent Democratic in 1966.

Whether the north-south dichotomy is undergoing change will require continued and detailed analysis. Perhaps the main example of the split in 1966 was in the vote on the so-called anti-obscenity amendment, Proposition 16. Supported by Reagan and an expensive campaign, the initiative proposition was attacked by other leaders in both parties as unconstitutional and unworkable. The marked regional difference in the resulting vote, 53 percent "no" in the south and 62 percent "no" in the north, suggests that differences in political culture within the state are very much alive.

Many reasons have been advanced to explain Republican domination of a state with a majority of Democratic registrants: press support, greater financial resources, better and more experienced candidates, less factionalism, utilization of pre-primary nomination machinery, gerrymandering of assembly and congressional districts, and the practice of cross-filing which deprived the parties of both the right to nominate their own candidates and the right to normal partisan support at the polls.[68]

To the degree that the factors cited explain the ascendancy of the Republican party, they may also support the thesis that Republicans have been better equipped to capture a larger share of this swing vote. Another important consideration is the fact that there is a long-established trend in California politics indicating the voters prefer incumbents, regardless of party. Candidate incumbency has definitely favored the Republicans during recent years.

Only one thing appeared certain in 1967—a fundamental and permanent shift of political power to southern California. Predictions that there would never again be a governor or U.S. senator from above the Tehachapis were no doubt premature. But that the future of California would increasingly be dominated by the decisions of Los Angeles and Orange county voters was the key political fact of life in the Golden State.

IMPACT OF NATIONAL POLITICS AND TRENDS

California has contributed perhaps a half-dozen prominent personalities in national politics during the past generation, but there has been a signal lack of influence and strength commensurate with its economic and social importance in the life of the nation. National attention was focused on California's presidential politics several times during the first decades of the present century. The electorate abandoned its traditional Republicanism to support Progressive Theodore Roosevelt and his California running mate, Governor Hiram Johnson, thus aiding in the defeat of William H. Taft and the election of Woodrow Wilson in 1912. It was California's vote that gave Wilson his narrow margin of victory in 1916. By 1928, California had produced its own first successful presidential candidate, albeit not a native son, in Republican Herbert Hoover. But by 1968, only seven Californians had achieved cabinet rank. During the first hundred years of congressional representation only eight held major committee chairmanships in the House and eight in the Senate.[69]

Several explanations may be offered for the state's delayed rise to national political prominence, including late entry into the Union, geographical remoteness from the power centers of the eastern seaboard, and the gradualness of economic integration. Undoubtedly a primary cause has been the weak party system which has proven chronically incapable of providing elected officials with the necessary length of service, and the resulting seniority, vital to the establishment of claims to national power. Furthermore, the congressional delegation has reflected the schisms which dominate state politics.

The post-World War II era has evidenced symptoms of a change in the destinies of the state in national politics, and reflects the integration and accelerated growth and development of the economy, begun under forced draft by the demands of war. California is deeply involved in a representative cross-section of the

68. Harris and Row, *op. cit.*, pp. 13-15, and Bell, *op. cit.*, pp. 281-82, *passim.*

69. See David Farrelly and Maurice A. Hall, "Californians in Congress," in Farrelly and Hinderaker, *op. cit.*, pp. 228-37. California's "doubtful state" status in national politics would tend to belie such a paucity of national recognition: the presidential elections of 1880, 1892, and 1912 were each won by a margin of less than 300 votes, and in 1873, 1896, and 1916 the margin was less than 5,000. The change of a single vote in each of the state's precincts would theoretically have provided Dewey with victory in 1948. See also Ivan Hinderaker, "Politics of Reapportionment," in Dvorin and Misner, *op. cit.*, pp. 134-36.

major issues of national policy such as agricultural subsidy; highway and school construction; health, welfare and old age assistance; public housing; conservation; water and hydroelectric power development; unemployment compensation; civil defense; veterans' affairs; unionism; racial and religious minority problems; tariff and trade policy; and foreign policy. In fiscal 1966 the Federal Bureau of Internal Revenue collected almost 10 billion dollars ($1,967.1 million) from the state while federal aid payments to state and local governments totaled over $1,616.2 million.

Under the impetus of in-migration the burgeoning population, now approximately one-tenth of the nation's total, is providing the raw material for political power. The abolition of cross-filing and the resounding Democratic victories of 1958, 1962, and 1964 seemed to presage the beginning of a genuine two-party system, which was not denied by the Republican resurgence in 1968.

Added to the possibilities inherent in an internal political rejuvenation of the party system in California is the assumption by leaders in both parties of leading roles in the regional associations of the thirteen western states. The Far West is tied together by shared economic interests of great importance in national policy. Both major parties are attempting to transpose this natural affinity for joint economic action into the realm of national politics. Whereas all thirteen states will undoubtedly share in such plans, none will benefit more than California. The state led the nation with nearly 6.0 billion dollars of federal contract awards in 1963 and 1964.

The recent manifestations of the state's political power-potential are impressive. San Francisco provided the site for the Republican conventions of 1956 and 1964, and Los Angeles similarly served the Democrats in 1960. California has provided the Republican candidates for the vice presidency during three recent elections: Earl Warren in 1948 and Richard Nixon in 1952 and 1956. Governor Warren was appointed Chief Justice of the Supreme Court in 1953. William F. Knowland enjoyed a distinguished career (1945-58) as Republican minority leader and policy chairman in the United States Senate. These events, coupled with the appointment of Senator Thomas Kuchel to the position of Republican party whip, testify to the capability of the traditionally dominant party in the state to project its influence into the national political scene. The nomination of Vice President Nixon as the Republican candidate for the presidency in 1960 was further evidence of the state's enhanced importance. The presidential aspirations of both Nixon and Governor Reagan command serious attention and speculation in 1968. In the politics of both the national conventions and the electoral college "doubtful" California will soon assume the role of *primus inter pares* among the fifty states.

Finally, the influence of California in the Congress is growing steadily, particularly within the Republican party. The state surpassed all others in number of Republican representatives (15) in the 89th Congress and replaced New York as the only populous state in which Republicans held both Senate seats. With 23 Democratic representatives, the state tied Texas, after New York, in the size of that party's delegation in Congress. Two House committee chairmanships were held by Californians, both Democrats: Chet Holifield of the Joint Committee on Atomic Energy and George Miller, Science and Astronautics. Republicans who held top-ranking committee positions were Representatives William S. Mailliard on the Merchant Marine Committee, Craig Hosmer, senior Republican in the Joint

Atomic Energy Committee, and H. Allen Smith, ranking minority member of the House Rules Committee.

By 1966, representation also included Appropriations, Armed Services, Banking and Currency, Education and Labor, Foreign Affairs, Government Operations, Interstate and Foreign Commerce, Judiciary, Veterans' Affairs, and Ways and Means committees. With the probable increment of six additional congressmen by 1970, the state should be thoroughly entrenched in the congressional committee system.

No matter how devious the political path Californians have trod historically, the state seems destined to become the national axis of the two major parties. The increment of eight electoral votes following the 1960 decennial census makes California's total of forty a prize in the presidential race second only to New York's forty-two.[70] Political leaders look forward with confidence to assuming first place after 1970. The national leadership of both parties has shown keen interest in the rocketing importance of the Golden State on the political horizon. It undoubtedly faces a brilliant political destiny in the future of the nation.

70. Electoral votes:

	1941		1951		1961		1971 (Est.)	
	No.	Place	No.	Place	No.	Place	No.	Place
California	25	5	32	3	40	2	(44)	(1)
New York	47	1	45	1	42	1	(41)	(2)

COLORADO:

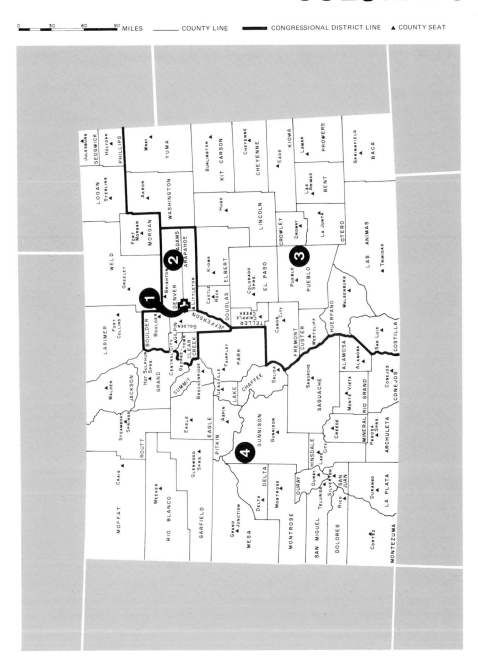

0 30 60 90 MILES   ——— COUNTY LINE   ▬▬▬ CONGRESSIONAL DISTRICT LINE   ▲ COUNTY SEAT

JULESBURG
SEDGWICK
HOLYOAK
PHILLIPS
WRAY
YUMA
BURLINGTON
KIT CARSON
CHEYENNE
CHEYENNE
EADS
KIOWA
LAMAR
PROWERS
SPRINGFIELD
BACA

LOGAN
STERLING
AKRON
WASHINGTON
HUGO
LINCOLN
LAS ANIMAS
BENT
OTERO
LAS ANIMAS

FORT MORGAN
MORGAN
BRIGHTON
ADAMS
ARAPAHOE
KIOWA
ELBERT
CROWLEY
ORDWAY
LA JUNTA

WELD
GREELEY
DENVER
LITTLETON
CASTLE ROCK
COLORADO SPRS.
EL PASO
PUEBLO
PUEBLO
TRINIDAD

LARIMER
FORT COLLINS
BOULDER
BOULDER
GOLDEN
JEFFERSON
DOUGLAS
CRIPPLE CREEK
TELLER
CANON CITY
FREMONT
CUSTER
WESTCLIFF
HUERFANO
WALSENBURG

HOT SULPHUR SPRS.
GRAND
CENTRAL CITY
GILPIN
GEORGETOWN
CLEAR CREEK
FAIRPLAY
PARK
SALIDA
SAGUACHE
SAGUACHE
ALAMOSA
ALAMOSA
SAN LUIS
COSTILLA

JACKSON
WALDEN
SUMMIT
BRECKENRIDGE
LEADVILLE
LAKE
CHAFFEE
MONTE VISTA
RIO GRANDE
CONEJOS
CONEJOS

STEAMBOAT SPRINGS
EAGLE
EAGLE
ASPIN
PITKIN
GUNNISON
GUNNISON
CREEDE
MINERAL
PAGOSA SPRS.
ARCHULETA

ROUTT
GLENWOOD SPRS.
HINSDALE
LAKE CITY

MOFFAT
CRAIG
MEEKER
RIO BLANCO
GARFIELD
GRAND JUNCTION
MESA
DELTA
DELTA
MONTROSE
MONTROSE
OURAY
OURAY
TELLURIDE
SAN MIGUEL
SILVERTON
SAN JUAN
RICO
DOLORES
DURANGO
LA PLATA
CORTEZ
MONTEZUMA

GUNNISON

Rudolf Gomez

The Colorful State

Colorado was admitted into the Union in 1876. Her politics since that time can be divided into three clearly discernible periods: ". . . a period of Republican dominance from 1876 to 1909; one of Democratic dominance from 1910 to 1919; and a period since 1920 of nearly equal competition."[1] From time to time, Colorado has also experienced third-party movements which have enjoyed varied electoral successes. They serve to confuse the student of Colorado politics for they suggest a maverick element which cannot be ignored, but about which not much can be said. Third-party movements attracting significant electoral support in Colorado have included the Populist, Socialist, Bull Moose, Silver Republican, National Silver, and others.[2]

The membership of the Colorado General Assembly at the turn of the century gives some indication of the strength of third-party movements. In the 1902 Senate there were 20 Democrats in contrast to 13 members for all four other parties. The Republicans shared honors with the Single-tax party, each having only one senator. In the House, 32 of the 57 members were Democrats, 6 were Republicans, and the rest Populists and Silver Republicans.[3] These data suggest an unstable element in Colorado politics over a long period of time. It is currently manifested in the legislature by variable voting behavior and in the electorate by a similar variability. This lack of consistency appears to be the distinguishing characteristic in much of Colorado's political behavior.

GEOGRAPHY AND RESOURCES

The eastern half of Colorado, stretching from the mountains which bisect the state to its borders, has flat alluvial high plains and broad prairies. The unifying feature of this area is its arid or semi-arid character (arid, 0-15 inches annual rainfall; semi-arid, 10-20 inches). It produces a diversity of agricultural products and livestock, and subsurface resources including oil, gas, and coal. The state's western half is a land of high mountains, mountain and river valleys, high plateaus, rugged canyons, and some of the most magnificent scenery in the nation. Much of this region is heavily timbered and underlaid with oil, coal, the largest oil shale reserves and molybdenum supply in the country, and numerous other minerals. The importance of these geographical details cannot be overemphasized for they constitute some of the prizes over which many of the political struggles in the state are waged.

1. Curtis Martin, *Colorado Politics* (Denver: Big Mountain Press, 1960), p. 10.
2. Colorado State Planning Commission, *Colorado Yearbook*, 1959-1961 (Denver, 1962), p. 185.
3. Colorado, *Senate Journal* (1902), p. 2771, and *House Journal* (1902), p. 205.

Colorado ranks first in the United States as a producer of minerals such as molybdenum, vanadium, tin, oil shale reserves, and beryllium. It ranks high in the production of uranium, coal, tungsten, pyrite, lead, silver, zinc, pumice, gold, copper, natural gas, pig iron, crude petroleum, and gem stones.

Agriculturally, it is second ranking in sugar beet production, and third through tenth in such commodities as spinach, sheep and lambs, sorghum, green peas, onions, dry edible beans, potatoes, wheat, cattle and calves, wild hay, and barley. A great part of the economic life of the state is tied to the production of minerals and agricultural commodities and these factors play an important role in Colorado politics through interest group activities.

POPULATION

The single most noticeable feature of the state's politics in recent years has been the demands made upon it by the large numbers of people who have moved into the state since 1950. A few statistics will illustrate this population growth. An 8 percent increase took place between April 1, 1960, and January 1, 1963, bringing the total number of inhabitants to 1,753,947. About half of this increase (27,000 annually) was due to migration. The bulk of this population (roughly 581,700) has settled in the suburban "ring" around Denver, where most of the new industry is concentrated.[4] There is a close relationship between population influx and these new industries.[5] The concentration of people in the metropolitan areas is significant for two reasons: first, it means that the old, established rural centers of political power have been challenged by these new population centers; and, secondly, that until July 1964 these new population centers were underrepresented in the state legislature. The struggles between these groups have formed the nucleus about which legislative politics has raged in Colorado since the early 1950's. Evidence of this struggle can be seen in the conflict over legislative reapportionment and redistricting in the 1960's, which will be discussed below.[6] However, before considering specific political issues, it is necessary to identify and discuss briefly some of the actors and factors which affect the conduct of Colorado politics.

EDUCATIONAL POLITICS

Educators in Colorado have played an important role in the formulation of public school finance policy. Since 1952 the General Assembly has attempted to finance public education in the state according to the so-called equalization principle. The idea underlying this principle is that the state seeks to guarantee each of

4. The Bureau of Business Research at the University of Colorado published a study which nicely illustrates this point. See *Colorado Basic Data Report No. 5: Manufacturing* (Boulder: University of Colorado, 1958), p. 3.

5. In January 1961 former Governor Stephen L. R. McNichols cited the following figures: "The Directory of Manufacturers published by the University of Colorado shows a tremendous increase in new plants in both 1959 and 1960. For 1959 this report showed a total of 2,364 plants—an increase of 143 over 1958. For 1960, the number of plants jumped to 3,079. It is safe to say that half the increase, 355 or so, represents new plants." See his "Colorado—A Mile High and Still Growing," address to Denver Chamber of Commerce, January 13, 1961, p. 3.

6. See Curtis Martin and Rudolph Gomez, *Colorado Government and Politics* (Boulder: Pruett Press, 1964), pp. 181-85; Governor's Reapportionment Commission, *Report of Executive Committee*, 6 vols. (Denver, 1957); and League of Women Voters of Colorado, *Representative Government in Colorado: The Challenge of Reapportionment* (Denver, September 1961).

its school-age children the same quality of education regardless of the location or affluence of each school district. Since this principle was made the base for the appropriation of state funds for public education, legislative conflicts over the distribution of these funds have developed annually. Generally, the legislature has resolved the problem by distributing funds collected from the state's wealthier counties to those with less wealth.[7] This method of distribution has undermined the political efficacy of educational interest groups in the state for it has stimulated those who are advantaged by it to support it, while those who are disadvantaged attempt to bring pressure on the General Assembly to distribute the funds more equitably (so they can be advantaged).

State aid to education has long provided a rallying point for partisanship in politics in Colorado.[8] Generally, the Republican party favors the allocation of funds for public education from the state's wealthier (usually urban) counties to the state's poorer (usually rural) counties. The Democrats, on the other hand, appear to be split over the issue; the Denver Democratic delegation would like to see more of the state's money for public education remain in the counties in which it was raised; non-Denver Democrats appear to favor the position taken by Denver's delegation when it is financially beneficial for them and at other times appear to favor the position taken by the Republicans—also when it appears to benefit them financially.

The question of higher education in Colorado has become the focal point about which much controversy has raged between both major political parties. The controversy is carried on at two levels: First, there is the more or less enduring controversy generated at the University of Colorado relating to academic freedom, and promotion and tenure of faculty members. The University of Colorado is governed by popularly elected, partisan regents who often become involved in the administrative problems previously mentioned. The partisan composition of the Board of Regents currently (Spring 1968) is four Republicans and two Democrats.[9] The latest incident to provoke a conflict on the Board of Regents with regard to promotion and tenure involved an assistant professor of Political Science, Clark Bouton, who was granted tenure only after University President Joseph Smiley voted to break a tie on the Board. Contributing to the incident were factors alluding to the pacifism of Professor Bouton, his opposition to the war in Vietnam, and, finally, departmental dissension.

A second type of controversy concerns the allocation of the state's revenues to higher education. The point at issue is whether the state ought to support the

7. For a brief description of this system in operation see Rudolph Gomez, "Legislative Voting Behavior in Colorado," *Western Political Quarterly*, XVII (September 1964, supp.), 71.

8. Rudolph Gomez, "Voting Behavior in the Colorado General Assembly on Selected Issues: 1958-1963," paper delivered at the Western Political Science Association's Annual Convention, Salt Lake City, Utah, March 20, 1964. For abstract of paper, see note 7, above.

9. The University of Colorado, *Alumni Magazine*, Fall 1967.

Regent	Party	Term Expires
Harry Carlson	Republican	1972
Joseph Coors	Republican	1972
Dale Atkins	Republican	1968
Charles Bromley	Republican	1968
Fred M. Betz	Democrat	1970
Daniel F. Lynch	Democrat	1970

creation of a "great" university at the Boulder campus of the University of Colorado or whether the revenues should be spent to create a statewide network of four-year colleges. If the number of colleges now in existence can be used to adduce a conclusion to the problem, it would seem that the advocates of a network of four-year colleges are winning the conflict. Table I makes the point clear.

TABLE I

STATE INSTITUTIONS OF HIGHER LEARNING

IN COLORADO, 1968

State Colleges and Universities

Name	Location
The University of Colorado	Boulder
The University of Colorado	Denver Campus
The University of Colorado	Colorado Springs Campus
Colorado State University	Fort Collins
Colorado State College (Education)	Greeley
Colorado School of Mines	Golden
Western State College	Gunnison
Southern Colorado State College	Pueblo
Adams State College	Alamosa
Fort Lewis College	Durango
Metropolitan State College	Denver

State Junior Colleges

Name	Location
Rangely Junior College	Rangely
Mesa Junior College	Grand Junction
Northeastern Junior College	Sterling
Lamar Junior College	Lamar
Otero Junior College	La Junta
Trinidad Junior College	Trinidad

In 1963 Governor Love organized a Committee on Higher Education whose major responsibility was to suggest a system of higher education which would make maximum use of the state's revenue while at the same time making it possible for each major area in the state to have access to higher education either in the form of a four-year college or at least a junior college. The Committee has issued several reports but nothing substantive has come of them—and the higher educational system of colleges and junior colleges continues to have the appearance of proliferating even further.

NEWS MEDIA AND PUBLIC OPINION

Bernard Berelson has argued that political democracy is possible only when there is sustained interest on the part of a minority, and a willingness on the part of the majority to take part in critical political situations.[10] How is this interest created and maintained in Colorado? The answer to this question is simple—by the various communications media. It is more difficult to answer the more meaningful question about the efficacy of these media in influencing political behavior in the state.

In the mid-1960's, people in Colorado enjoyed the services of 24 daily newspapers; 130 weeklies; unenumerated trade or interest papers (for example, the *Cattle Guard* of the Colorado Cattlemen's Association); 10 television stations; and 72 radio stations.[11] Political information and reporting is disseminated as a matter of course by these media. Each of the television and radio stations regularly schedules public service programs which are, in large measure, concerned in some way with politics. During election contests of every kind—primary, general, bond issue, school board, and local—radio and television stations devote a significant measure of their advertising time to the merits of candidates, programs, and issues.

At least 14 stations in Colorado are reported to be assigning a specific number of hours weekly, varying from one-half hour to 70 hours, to special programs in languages other than English, including Spanish, Italian, German, and Polish. During the 1964 general election campaign radio stations in southern Colorado regularly extolled the merits of candidates of both political parties in Spanish.[12] Only the most impressionistic conclusions about the influence of this type of broadcasting upon political behavior in the state can be made here. It appears that both parties allocate funds for broadcasting the merits of their candidates in a form which will attract the various ethnic groups in the state; and that some return on the investment has materialized, for the radio and television stations continue to carry such political advertising in election campaigns.[13]

Each section of the state has access to some local daily newspaper in addition to the widely circulated *Rocky Mountain News* and *Denver Post*. For the most part, the politics of these papers appears to range along a conservative-moderate continuum.[14] The pattern for most of the dailies in the state appears to follow that set by the *Denver Post* which has displayed considerable political independence by supporting the presidential candidacies of Dwight Eisenhower, John Kennedy, and Lyndon Johnson. In the 1964 general election it endorsed the candidacies of two Republicans and two Democrats for the four seats Colorado is entitled to in the U.S. House of Representatives.[15]

There is one major daily newspaper which does not fall into the conservative-moderate political continuum of most of the other Colorado dailies—the Col-

10. Bernard Berelson, "Democratic Theory and Public Opinion," in Heinz Eulau, Samuel J. Eldersveld, and Morris Janowitz (eds.), *Political Behavior: A Reader in Theory and Research* (Glencoe: Free Press, 1956), p. 108.

11. These data abstracted from *Colorado Yearbook*; 1959-1961, pp. 584-90, and *ibid.*, 1962-1964, p. 665.

12. The author heard the Spanish language programs. No study exists which examines the impact of this type of broadcasting on its clientele or on political behavior in Colorado.

13. These inferences might easily be invalidated by research. One of the serious shortcomings in examining mass political behavior in Colorado is that no research on it has been done.

14. Inferred from reading the editorial stand taken by most of these dailies on the reapportionment issue in Colorado as reported by the Governor's Reapportionment Commission, *op. cit.*, p. 7, and *passim.*

15. *Denver Post*, November 2, 1964.

orado Springs *Gazette Telegraph*. This paper is owned and published by Raymond Cyrus Hoiles whose political philosophy has been described by his enemies as being to the "right of Herod. . . . he has attacked Herbert Hoover and the National Association of Manufacturers as too left-wing, called all taxes 'the theft of wages,' argued that fire departments, public libraries, highways, and even the armed forces ought to be maintained strictly by voluntary contributions."[16] There is no evidence to suggest that the political arguments put forth in the *Gazette Telegraph* have convinced great numbers of people in the state of the evils of government.

There is very little reliable information as to whether people vote as their favorite newspapers recommend. It is alleged that the *Denver Post* does swing some political weight. The *Post* crusades with great persistence and usually achieves its objectives. It devotes an unusually large percentage of its space to local political news. Its editorial policy probably does influence the outcome of elections,[17] but the evidence that this is so is not overwhelming. Probably the most that can safely be said about the influence of the press on political behavior in Colorado is that suggested by other students of American politics: that it reinforces political predispositions, that it informs and encourages, but that it does not make wholesale conversions for particular candidates or for a particular editorial point of view.[18]

PARTY ORGANIZATION AND PARTY LEADERS

Formal party organization in Colorado is similar to that of many other states in that state statutes create its boundaries, outline its functions, and outline its methods of procedure.[19] The formal party hierarchy is organized from the precinct caucus at the base, through the county central committee to the state central committee at the apex. Theoretically, the streams of communication flow in clearly outlined channels from the rank and file membership at the bottom of the hierarchy to the leadership at the top while the lines of authority reach from the top of the hierarchy, the state central committee, through the chain of command down to the rank and file. Speaking practically, party organization in Colorado is characterized by the importance of personality, personal contact among party regulars, and informality in inter-organizational relations. It is almost nonsensical to speak of a general party organization in Colorado. We speak of party organizations, and add a prefix to identify the one of which we speak. Both parties are faced with the same types of problems and they attempt to solve these problems in roughly the same manner—by creating more organization. Party organizations in the state can be classified as strong and moderate. The criterion for this classification is the amount of influence they exert over the nominating process. If an

16. *Time*, April 19, 1963, p. 94. For further samples of Hoiles' political philosophy see any editorial in the *Gazette Telegraph*. For example, for arguments against the United Nations see editorial for March 6, 1964; against American relations with South America, January 17, 1964.

17. See Martin and Gomez, *op. cit.*, pp. 174-75.

18. V. O. Key, Jr., *Politics, Parties, and Pressure Groups* (5th ed.; New York: Crowell, 1964), pp. 478-79; and Nelson W. Polsby and Aaron B. Wildavsky, *Presidential Elections: Strategies of American Electoral Politics* (New York: Scribner's, 1964), p. 45.

19. For a detailed description of formal party organization in Colorado see Martin and Gomez, *op. cit.*, pp. 133-44.

organization is able to "name" the candidate with a minimum of conflict and without alienating too many organization "regulars" (used in this sense, regulars are members who devote all their free time in nonelection years to keeping the organization viable), it is considered to be strong.[20] A moderate organization is one which is not able to so "name" the candidate—and one that relies upon persuasion to influence the nominating process.

The selection of nonincumbent Democratic gubernatorial and senatorial candidates is characterized by a negotiating process occurring over a relatively long period of time. The chairman and regular[21] members of the various levels of party organization get together on an informal basis at designated times weekly, monthly, or both, and try to reach a consensus of *one* candidate for the office. This consensus, if indeed it emerges, is arrived at slowly, informally, and seemingly without direction by anyone. Once arrived at, the party organizations throughout the state unite behind the person selected.

If a consensus cannot be achieved informally, then the nominating process shifts to the designating assembly.[22] Efforts are made at the assembly to designate as few candidates as possible in order to keep the organizations from splitting and diluting their strength in intra-party fights. If it is still impossible to unite behind one candidate in the designating assembly, then the candidate is selected in the primary election. While the primary, in this instance, could be used to confirm V. O. Key, Jr.'s, suggestion that direct primaries have a tendency to undermine the strength of party organizations,[23] it could also be interpreted to mean that the

20. A random sampling of state, county and district party chairmen of both parties was taken for this study. Open-ended interviews comprised the information-gathering method. Most of those interviewed thought the party organization that most nearly fitted the "strong" classification is the Denver County Democratic party which Irwin has described as follows: "... the normal presumption of Democratic success in Denver elections for the state legislature has put a high premium on party nomination, not unlike that in one-party areas of the United States. Despite the fact that Colorado has a direct primary system, the Denver County Democratic leadership has been able, with few exceptions, to control nominations through extensive use of a preprimary convention designation system which is as old in Colorado as the primary itself.... Because it is difficult for each of twenty-one candidates of the same party, running at large in the same constituency for identical office, to finance his own campaign, campaign funds are normally raised and expended on behalf of all the candidates by the party's Central Committee." William P. Irwin, "Colorado: A Matter of Balance," in Malcolm E. Jewell (ed.), *The Politics of Reapportionment* (New York: Atherton Press, 1962), p. 73. The influence wielded by the Democratic organization in Denver is not a dominant factor in the nominating process for other state or national offices. Other "strong" organizations named by the chairmen interviewed were the Pueblo Democratic, the El Paso County Republican, and the Weld County Republican organizations.

21. The party regulars are those who attend the regularly scheduled meetings of the state organization, those who do the homework for the organization between elections, and those who have maintained contact with their counterparts in other parts of the state. The selection of regulars is a highly informal process—one characterized by selection by default. If a regular ceases to attend the scheduled meetings he no longer is privy to the activities, to the negotiations, to the inside jokes that transpire; in short he is no longer "in the know." He ceases to be a regular—although all he has to do to regain his status is to become active once again.

22. Candidates receiving 20 percent of the votes at a designating assembly earn the right to have their names placed on the primary ballot. Candidates are ranked on the ballot in accordance with the percentage of votes received. Thus A, with 45 percent, would be placed in first position; B, with 30 percent, second; etc.

23. V. O. Key, Jr., "The Direct Primary and Party Structure: A Study of State Legislative Nomination," *American Political Science Review*, XLVIII (March 1954), 13.

nominating process was merely shifted to another arena of party organization for the sake of preserving some modicum of party unity.[24]

The informal nominating process just described has been relatively successful in selecting candidates for major offices. Between 1950 and 1962, for example, there were only four primary elections to select candidates for governor and U.S. senator. This suggests that party organization is more influential in choosing candidates for major offices than for lesser ones. How can we account for this? The stakes are so high at that level that the party organizations cannot risk losing in the general election by engaging in intra-party fights in the primaries. Therefore every effort is made during the long informal negotiating process described earlier to select a candidate by consensus. Party regulars believe that this process enhances their party's chance of winning the general election since the party remains relatively cohesive and united.

Why, then, are there so many primaries at the congressional and state legislative levels? Here the answer does not come so easily, for there is considerable difference of opinion. The following hypotheses have been suggested to explain the presence of the primaries: (1) these offices are relatively minor and not worth the effort of engaging in the long negotiating process used for nominating candidates for the U.S. Senate and for the governor's office; (2) these offices are considered prizes to be fought over by party regulars as rewards for past services; (3) the primary is considered a place to test the attractiveness of alternative candidates.

Whichever of these hypotheses is the most valid is difficult to say. If the probability of victory is high in a particular district for one party then the chances are that there will be a primary election for the office in that party. Similarly, if chances for victory are high for both parties it appears that both will hold primary elections.[25]

Moderate party organizations in both parties in Colorado are characterized by their reliance upon persuasion as their *modus operandi* in the nomination of nonincumbent candidates for major offices. Into this classification fall most of the party organizations in the state.

The strength of both types varies over time and with their leadership. For example, it was suggested that the late "Tiger" Muhick of Pueblo carried the strength of the Pueblo County organization to the grave with him.[26] Muhick had discovered a method for keeping his brawling organization together with a minimum of friction. He assigned his critics to the county executive committee and tested their talents in the crucible of competition. If they survived and delivered they identified with the leadership (Muhick); if they did not they were considered political dilettantes and not worth worrying about. This example illustrates the fact that organizational strength is variable at all levels in the state. The single most important factor in ensuring strong organization is to ensure the succession of strong leadership.

---

24. This interpretation was suggested by a county party chairman who regarded the direct primary as a court of ultimate decision in the selection of candidates for certain offices.

25. This conclusion supports V. O. Key's statement that "the extent to which a party's nominations are contested in the primary by two or more aspirants apparently depends in large measure on the prospects for victory for the nominee in the general election." "The Direct Primary and Party Structure: A Study of State Legislative Nominations," *loc. cit.,* p. 4.

26. Interview.

Largely, this leadership is self-recruited. Individuals willing to donate their time and talents to the organization are repaid in a number of ways—with vicarious election victories, with the satisfaction of knowing they help "make" or "break" governors, and most important of all, they are repaid with the coin of leadership. They are the caretakers of the organization, the ones who keep open the lines of communication to all levels of the party between elections, and they are the ones in the "know"; in short, they are the party leaders *because they choose to lead.* Since they are willing to pay the price of giving their non-livelihood life to the party they expect to lead the party in election years, in the nominating process, and occasionally in the formulation of program.

Discipline is relatively unknown in most party organizations in Colorado. It is true that Democratic state legislators from Denver can be disciplined by the organization but this is the exception and not the rule, even in the Denver organization.[27] It is also true that the state Democratic chairman, in accord with party rules, may drop members from the state central committee for various reasons. This remedy is seldom used, for a member so treated may regain his seat on the central committee if his own county organization re-elects him to the post.[28] The difficulty in making party discipline "stick" and in enlisting workers for the party, generally, has created a live-and-let-live attitude among active organization members. The regulars of each party are more concerned with the recruitment of more regulars than with the problem of discipline. Besides, a sort of party discipline emerges from the informal communications process mentioned earlier—organization regulars know what sorts of actions are permissible, what the limits of party behavior are, and they usually find it relatively simple to live within this framework.[29]

Patronage is not available in large enough quantities nor in high enough quality for either party to use as an inducement for discipline. Each party can expect a few jobs "in the post office" when its party is in power nationally but patronage is considered to be a "pain in the neck" since it is difficult to award without alienating "somebody."[30] When a party is in power in the state a "few" positions at the race track and in the state house are available, but they are not attractive enough to serve as inducements to reward "good" organization people. The patronage that is available is minimal and is distributed in such a way as to support Sorauf's observation that

. . . the poor pay and generally dismal future prospects that attend most patronage jobs discourage many potential jobholders. Especially in a period of full employment, qualified men and women can find more attractive career possibilities than those which patronage systems offer. More educational levels on which the parties increasingly rely for leadership will find

27. The last time Denver Democratic legislators were disciplined occurred in the 1962 general election when the names of Lela Gilbert and Bert Gallegos were placed at the bottom of the ballot. Thereby, they claimed, they lost the election. Mrs. Gilbert subsequently registered as a Republican.

28. Dr. John Farley (M.D.) was so removed in 1962 for supporting the candidacy of Peter Dominick (a Republican) for the U.S. Senate. He was re-elected to his old post on the central committee by the Pueblo Democratic party.

29. This idea was expressed in an interview by one regular who actively supported Frank Evans (D), who won his 1964 campaign for the U.S. House of Representatives from Colorado's Third Congressional District: "Frank knows that most everything he will do in the House is okay with me—but he knows he can't fool around on civil rights [vote against civil rights legislation] and still expect help from me."

30. Interview.

little to tempt them in patronage as it exists in most states today. As a result most patronage jobs fall to the lower skill groups who also lack the political skills the parties need.[31]

Curiously enough, this lack of patronage is regarded as a mixed blessing by the organization people interviewed. They believe that patronage might be used to weld together stronger organizations if it were available in larger quantity and higher quality; but since it is not, most believe that lack of it is "good" because those who become active in the organization do so for intrinsic reasons. The quality of such people, it is argued, is higher than that of those joining the organization solely for material rewards.

Party organizations for both parties in Colorado are interested first in winning office and then in program. This is not to suggest that program is unimportant in campaigning for office, but it comes later, after a candidate has been located and agreed upon. Tom Gavin, political writer for the *Denver Post*, described an informal nominating process in this manner:

> Nowhere. That's where Bob Maytag, state Democratic chairman, got at a recent quiet meeting of the party's Executive Committee with a suggestion for making the 1966 candidate selection process more orderly. . . . Prompting Maytag's suggestion is the swelling probability that Democrats will be wrenched every which way in '66 by a multiplicity of competing candidates. Maytag sees at least four potential competitors for both top nominations. They are: For governor: Lt. Gov. Bob Knous (a certainty), former Gov. Steve McNichols (a probability), House Speaker Allen Dines (a question mark) and state senator Roy Romer (a young man with talent and ambition itch).
>
> For senator: McNichols again (this is the race many Democrats think he should make), former Sen. John Carroll (restive in retirement), Bill Grant (another who itches), and Romer.[32]

Gavin did not mention program as being a consideration at this stage of the process. After the candidate has been agreed upon, after the party heals itself, then program becomes important and comes to the fore.

The program is formulated in a manner similar to that outlined for the selection of candidates—informally, within the party organization. All levels of party organization are involved in the formulation of program. In some parts of the state the Young Republicans and Young Democrats are able to swing considerable influence, in other parts, other levels of party organization. It is at this stage that interest groups become active in the camps of both parties, and apparently they pay off after the election to the victorious one.[33]

Money for political activities in Colorado is raised by party organizations at all levels. During campaigns numerous committees are in the business of raising funds for party and candidate. The money so raised is allocated differently by each. For example, committees primarily interested in the election of one candidate will use the funds they raised solely for his benefit. County organizations, on the other hand, allocate one-third of the funds they raise to the state organization and retain two-thirds for their own use. The state organization contributes to the national organization and spends for the entire party ticket. Some party organizations in Colorado currently are attempting to raise funds by securing annual

31. Frank J. Sorauf, "Patronage and Party," *Readings in Political Parties and Pressure Groups*, Frank Munger and Douglas Price, eds. (New York: Crowell, 1964), p. 210.

32. Tom Gavin, "Dem Poll Plan Hits Snag," *Denver Post*, December 30, 1964, p. 13.

33. It was revealed in an interview that Holly Sugar Company regularly pledges a campaign contribution to the Democratic party in one of the congressional districts. The only time it fulfills its pledge is when the Democrats win the congressional race in the district.

pledges which can be paid in four quarterly installments. The attempt to raise funds in this fashion is relatively untried but its supporters are sanguine about its income-producing possibilities. Estimates of the cost of conducting campaigns in Colorado are admittedly vague and perhaps unrealistic. Table II lists the probable figures for nonincumbents seeking state and national offices.[34]

TABLE II
ESTIMATED COSTS OF CONDUCTING CAMPAIGNS
FOR NON-INCUMBENTS IN COLORADO

OFFICE	COST
Governor	$200,000 to $300,000
U.S. Senator	200,000 to 300,000
U.S. Congressman	30,000 minimum
State Official (Attorney General)	No estimate
State Legislator	2,000 to 3,000
County Commissioners	3,000 to 5,000
Local Officials	300 to 500

There is no reliable index to establish the cost of waging campaigns for incumbent officials in the state. Alexander Heard has stated that "types of expenditures and levels of costs vary with the office sought, the locale, the candidate, the character of the competition, local financing habits, and other factors. . . ."[35] He stated that "headquarters expenditures for statewide races in most of the country run between 10 and 25 cents for every vote cast. . . . Other candidates have spent both more and less . . . but these sums are representative under typical conditions."[36] Using Heard's figures we can compute, roughly, the campaign costs of electing a Colorado governor. In the 1962 gubernatorial election about 612,000 votes were cast.[37] At ten cents a vote, $61,200 was spent; $91,800 at fifteen cents; and $153,000 at twenty-five cents.

The bulk of expenditures in any campaign in the state is for publicity. Costs are shared between regular party organizations and *ad hoc* election committees— the regular organization maintains campaign headquarters and assumes the responsibility for financing the publicity for the party's entire ticket; the *ad hoc*

34. This table formulated from information garnered in interviews, and its figures are admittedly estimates.

35. Alexander Heard, *The Costs of Democracy* (Chapel Hill: University of North Carolina Press, 1960), p. 424.

36. *Ibid.* The figures were arrived at from information contained in Table 56, p. 425.

37. There was an actual total of 612,232 votes cast in this election. See Martin and Gomez, *op. cit.*, p. 131.

election committees bear the burden of financing the individual candidates.[38] Apparently one reason for the relatively independent status of the majority of public officials in Colorado is that their financial ties to the party organization are, at best, quite tenuous.

Party organization in Colorado is characterized by the informality of its operation, by its emphasis on personality as the grease which smooths the wheels of operations, and by its lack of effective discipline. It has not suffered the dry rot which Key suggests is induced by the direct primary system.[39] It appears that the informal consensual process described earlier is instrumental in the selection of candidates for major office as well as in the formulation of program. We may therefore conclude that party organizations in Colorado are the moving force in major candidate selection and that the direct primary system has not undermined party organizational strength—indeed, it is regarded by some organization regulars in Colorado as a sort of supreme court where disputes over the selection of candidates are resolved. The supposed merit of this arrangement is that it settles the controversy with a minimum of intra-organizational bloodletting, which in turn facilitates post-primary organizational reunification.

All this suggests that party organization, weak though it may be by other standards (e.g., party discipline), is the major controlling factor in the selection of candidates in Colorado. While the primary and pre-primary systems currently employed play a part in the nominating process, it is subordinate to that played by party organizations.

To attempt to identify major party leaders is a tricky business, since leadership is not coincident to elected office—at least not in the opinion of certain of the organization chieftains interviewed for this study. Nevertheless, elected officers do provide an index of leadership in both major parties since it is assumed that they, in order to win electoral office, had to persuade the organization chieftains to support them. In this sense then, it is reasonably safe to equate party leadership with elected officials who have been able to put together winning coalitions of organization chieftains. Using elected officials, then, as the basic index to describe party leadership in Colorado, a list of Republican party leaders must include Governor John A. Love, U.S. Senators Gordon Allott and Peter Dominick, and U.S. Representative Don Brotzman. Each of these, save only Governor Love, were "organization chieftains" before becoming elected officials. Their service in the state legislature and in other state offices testifies to their leadership ability. Senator Allott served as district attorney for the Fifteenth Judicial District in 1946. In 1950 he was elected lieutenant-governor and was re-elected in 1952. In 1954 he was elected to the U.S. Senate, where he is now in his third term. Senator Dominick served two terms in the Colorado General Assembly before being elected to the U.S. House of Representatives in 1960. He went to the U.S. Senate in 1962. Representative Brotzman also served in the Colorado General Assembly, and was an unsuccessful candidate for governor before winning his first election to the U.S. House of Representatives in 1962. He lost his seat in the Goldwater defeat of 1964, but won re-election in 1966 over his Democratic opponent Roy McVicker.

Governor John Love was not an organization chieftain in the sense the others were. The only race he engaged in prior to winning the governorship was a

38. For details of campaign expenditures see Tom Gavin, "Dems, GOP Nearly Equal in Campaign Spending," *Denver Post*, January 1, 1965, p. 34.

39. "The Direct Primary and Party Structure: A Study of State Legislative Nominations," *loc. cit.*, p. 14.

losing one in El Paso County where he was defeated by Colorado Springs attorney Weldon Tartar for the post of Republican County Chairman.

The leadership of these men has been revealed in a formal sense during the various nominating conventions held throughout the state during election years. Some, or all in the case of nominating conventions for major offices, are present during the conventions to unify the party, cheer the faithful, and express confidence in the Republican Way of Life, and, of course, in the successful outcome of the general election. More informally, their leadership is apparent in discussions with organization chieftains, who refer to them as sources of party authority and doctrine.

Since the Democrats do not at the present time occupy major electoral offices to the extent that the Republicans do it is more difficult to name their leaders. However, the Democrats do have three incumbent congressmen: Byron Rogers (First Congressional District); Frank Evans (Third Congressional District); and Wayne Aspinall (Fourth Congressional District). Further listing is based impressionistically upon newspaper reports, conversations with organization chieftains, and Democratic elected officials. The names most frequently mentioned as leaders of the Democratic party include: former Governor Stephen McNichols, currently campaigning for his party's nomination as a senatorial candidate; Lieutenant-Governor Mark Hogan, mentioned by organization chieftains as their choice for candidate for governor at the next election for that office; State Senator Allan Dines, currently an unannounced candidate for the U.S. Senate seat held by Republican Peter Dominick. Finally, there is a group of Democrats serving in the legislature who are sometimes mentioned by the organizational people as "possibles" for major political office. They include George Brown, state senator from Denver; Kenneth Monfort, state senator from Weld County, who is also seeking his party's nomination for the U.S. Senate race in 1968; Clarence Decker, state senator from Denver; and Jefferson County's District Attorney Martin Miller.

One is forced to conclude by the data that there is no clearly established "leadership" for either of the two major parties in Colorado. The only time it can be said to exist in a demonstrable way is probably during election years and then only for the duration of the campaign—when the unity forced upon each by its partisan counterpart acts as the binding agent upon the rank-and-file party membership—binding them to accept, briefly, certain individuals as more or less undisputed leaders of the party.

PRESSURE GROUPS

In 1963 there were approximately two hundred lobbyists registered with each house of the General Assembly. Many of these were duplicates, the same lobbyists registering with each house. "They represented interests all the way from architecture to onions."[40] No effort will be made here to catalogue the number and activities of the interest groups which exist in Colorado today. Rather, an attempt will be made to describe selected interest group activity in the state. Interest groups selected for inclusion here are typical ones associated with agriculture, labor, education, veterans, business, and public.

The Colorado Cattlemen's Association, one of the many organizations associated with agriculture, was founded in Denver on November 30, 1867.[41] That it

40. Martin and Gomez, op. cit., p. 165.

41. Harry P. Stumpf and Associates, "The Colorado Cattlemen's Association," the Rocky Mountain Center for Education in Politics, Colorado State University, Fort Collins,

has become the champion of free enterprise is illustrated by the type of resolutions passed by its membership since its inception. It has steadfastly opposed "New Deal" policies, and recommended greater restrictions for labor unions, state control of water regulation, economy in government, etc. The CCA feels that its members have had to struggle desperately to attain their present economic status, and credits their success to individual initiative. It views government aid as undesirable paternalism. The Association maintains a publication, the *Cattle Guard*, which is used to convey official positions of the organization to its members. Since the publication was founded in 1955 it has had two editors, Richard Goff and Thomas Lawrie, both of whom have taken editorial positions favoring such legislation as the "Right to Work" Amendment. The organization has not restricted its activities solely to the state scene; Editor Goff summarized the political aims of the CCA vis-à-vis the national government for 1964 as follows: "(1) to gain lower quotas on Australian and Argentinian beef imports and (2) to gain better regulation of railroad freight rates."[42]

The *Cattle Guard* expresses the sentiments of the local branches of the CCA; these agree that the state organization well represents their interests most of the time.[43] The legislative influence of the organization has been most effective since it enjoys access to legislators, many of whom come from rural districts, and since it maintains a permanent committee charged with the responsibility of examining all bills introduced into each house during each legislative session. The CCA also employs a skillful lobbyist.[44] One example, which resulted from the struggle over reapportionment, will illustrate the flexibility and tenacity with which the CCA attempts to fulfill its political objectives in Colorado.

The Colorado General Assembly was reapportioned and redistricted in a special session of the legislature early in 1964 on the basis of population, the latest step in the struggle between rural and urban interests over political representation. Agricultural groups supporting "federal" reapportionment suffered a major defeat. But they have hit upon a tactic which tends to cushion the impact of the new reapportionment act upon their interests: namely, the transfer of their political power from the state capitol building to the county courthouse. F. R. Carpenter of Hayden, Colorado, called for county home rule at the annual mid-winter convention of the Colorado Cattlemen's Association held in Colorado Springs in December 1964, stating: "The state legislature as a whole is unable to solve a local problem as well as the local people can solve it."[45] The Colorado Cattlemen's Association is spearheading efforts to construct another bastion of rural political power in the county courthouse.

Veterans' organizations in Colorado are at present a somewhat dormant force in state politics. The membership of the Veterans of Foreign Wars and the

Colorado, 1964, p. 9. This paper was prepared for the regional meeting of the RMCEP held in Denver in May 1964.

42. *Ibid.*, p. 20.

43. Questionnaires were mailed to 70 local Cattlemen's organizations; 30 responded, and of these, 26 agreed that the policy of this publication reflected their own ideas and thoughts. *Ibid.*, p. 28.

44. To discover legislative opinion on the efficacy of Dave Rice as a spokesman for the CCA the research team sampled opinion from 30 legislators, most of whom commented favorably on his skill and effectiveness. For information about research methods see *ibid.*, pp. 30-44.

45. *Gazette Telegraph*, December 4, 1964, p. 1.

American Legion combined totals roughly 30,000. Both organizations function on the local level and both watch over the state legislative process.[46]

The major benefit accruing to Colorado veterans came in 1944 and in actuality did not result from direct state legislative action. In response to the national Serviceman's Act of 1944, better known as the G.I. Bill of Rights, an amendment to the state Civil Service Act of 1918 was proposed by initiative petition, and adopted by a majority of Coloradoans and the wartime state legislature.[47]

The major task facing veterans' organizations in Colorado today is that of preserving the fruits of wartime legislation.[48] To ensure that these fruits are preserved both veterans' organizations work through the state Senate Committee on Military and Veterans' Affairs, which they have used as an avenue to introduce legislation calling for the teaching of Americanism in the public schools.

Both the VFW and the American Legion emphasize the importance of numbers for political action. Bulletins are issued urging post members to let their presence be known to legislators who are concerned with legislation of interest to veterans. According to a former chairman of the state Senate Committee on Military and Veterans' Affairs, Roy H. McVicker (D-Jefferson), the legislative influence of these two organizations does not derive from their periodic letter-writing campaigns, but from the fact that the public feels obligated to continue the programs benefiting the veterans for the services they rendered during World War II and the Korean War. Senator McVicker also indicated that pressure from veterans' groups upon his committee had never been intense and that in fact they had been rather quiescent during his tenure in the Senate.

From 1896 to 1956, the American Federation of Labor dominated the labor scene in Colorado.[49] Late in the nineteenth and early twentieth century Colorado experienced a period of violent labor-management conflicts which literally forced labor in the state to organize. Since then, labor's political activity in Colorado has been considerable.[50]

Labor originally pursued its political goals under the leadership of the legislative committee of the state AFL, which sponsored the legislative program endorsed by the annual convention of the State Federation of Labor, and lobbied to prevent unfavorable legislation from being adopted. State Labor Political Conventions were introduced in 1920 to discuss and endorse candidates for state and national offices. In 1947 the Colorado Labor League for Political Education was created. It was replaced in the late 1950's by the Colorado Committee on Political

46. The VFW through an individual, Elmer Hagar, and the American Legion through a three-man legislative committee. See Diane Cox, Bradley Scharf, and Herman Whiton, "Colorado Veterans' Groups: Their Role in the Legislative Process in Colorado," pp. 2-3; paper given at the regional meeting of the Rocky Mountain Center for Education in Politics, Denver, May 1964. Two other small veterans' groups are the Disabled American Veterans and the G.I. Forum (Spanish-American veterans).

47. This amendment provided for a five-point addition to examination grades of all veterans seeking state civil service employment, and a ten-point addition for disabled veterans. Special provisions for vocational retraining and rehabilitation for disabled veterans and for the creation of a nursing and rest home at Homelake, Colorado, were also included.

48. Interview with Leland Day, Department Adjutant Quartermaster, Colorado American Legion. See Cox, Scharf and Whiton, *op. cit.*, p. 8.

49. Much of the information for this section came from George Bardwell and Harry Seligson, *Organized Labor and Political Action in Colorado: 1900-1960* (Denver: College of Business Administration, University of Denver, 1959).

50. For a brief account of this struggle see: Herrick S. Roth, "A Story of Colorado's Organized Labor Movement," *Western Business Review*, 3 (February 1959), 20-21.

Education. When the national AFL and CIO merged in 1956 the Colorado State Labor Council was established.[51]

The period from 1900 to 1939 was, in the long run, a fruitful one for labor. During that time the major components of present-day state labor policy were instituted. Labor's legislative program from 1939 to 1959 was characterized by attempts to amend existing laws rather than to formulate new legislation. Legislative opposition to labor-sponsored legislation underwent significant changes during this period, which can be inferred from the following figures: from 1939 to 1949, 29 percent of all labor bills considered on third reading in the General Assembly were "opposed" to labor, while in the following decade less than 2 percent fell into this category.[52] This decrease suggests a general lessening of legislative hostility toward labor.

The major threat to labor in Colorado in the past ten years came from a "right-to-work" amendment to the constitution proposed in 1958. Labor organizations united and succeeded in beating down the proposed amendment in the general election by a 118,000 vote margin.[53]

Large-scale apathy characterizes the labor movement in Colorado at the present time. Herrick S. Roth, president of the Colorado Labor Council, said in May 1964 that "up to thirty percent of union members disqualify themselves from voting by not registering."[54] The significance of this is that the credibility of labor as a potent political force wanes as its voting power decreases and, as a result, it is forced to reassert its political potency by aggressive tactics. This, in turn, has created internal struggles among the leadership. Colorado labor has attempted to reassert its political strength by suggesting to members of both parties that it is no longer informally allied with the Democratic party and that it is returning to the old Gomperian position of rewarding its friends and punishing its enemies.[55]

Programs presently advocated by organized labor in Colorado include the usual bread-and-butter ones: higher minimum wages, shorter working hours, and improved working conditions. In addition to these, labor has attempted to secure for its members longer benefit periods and moderated qualification requirements under the State Unemployment Compensation Program.

Generally, labor has not succeeded in attaining these goals. Five pro-labor bills were defeated in the legislature in 1962, one in 1963, and the benefit period and qualification requirements of the Unemployment Compensation Program were generally "stiffened," also in 1963.[56] It appears that organized labor is presently undergoing a period of retrenchment and consolidation and playing a waiting game. The Democratic party's capture of the House of Representatives in the 1964 general election did not provide any more fertile ground for labor's proposals than it has provided in the past session, and hopes for the future dimmed with the Republican victories (38 of 65 seats) in 1966.

51. Bardwell and Seligson, *op. cit.*

52. Harry Seligson and George Bardwell, *Labor-Management Relations in Colorado* (Denver: Sage Books, 1961), Table 3, p. 320.

53. The voting on the amendment was 318,480 against and 200,319 for. See State of Colorado, *Abstract of Votes Cast*, 1958.

54. Richard Carroll *et al., Labor and Legislation in Colorado*, paper given at meeting of Rocky Mountain Center for Education in Politics (Denver, May 1964), p. 4.

55. See Morton L. Margolin, "State Labor Leaders Ponder 'Friendly Divorce Dems,' " *Rocky Mountain News*, n.d., September 1962.

56. Carroll, *op. cit.*, p. 5.

The political efficacy of educational interest groups was evaluated as follows in 1964: "Although there are a multiplicity of groups interested in educational legislation they did not seem to be respected [by members of the state legislature] or effective. Most of the groups lobbied for broadening the tax base and increasing state aid [for education]....they were rebuffed in the 44th General Assembly....state support of schools . . . was reduced in 1964 from 24 percent to 23.3 percent. This is to be compared to 85 percent in New Mexico and [to] about 35 percent as a national average."[57]

The groups representing business and public interest in Colorado are many and varied. Those most often associated with the "business outlook" are the state and local chambers of commerce and the various functional associations. Generally, they support policies calling for economy in government; reduction of state inventory tax laws; application of regulation provisions of industries and trade to labor unions; reapportionment of the state legislature on a "federal" principle; and, support for policies calling for an end to federal regulation of business.[58] Business groups in Colorado have often suffered reversals at the hands of labor and agriculture because they have failed to use the General Assembly as skillfully as they might.[59]

Since 1958, however, local chambers of commerce throughout the state have been conducting seminars in practical politics that have been well attended. While the success of this operation has not been investigated it appears likely that business groups have been better represented in the state legislature since 1958, as witnessed by the passage of such legislation as that tightening the terms and qualifications of the Unemployment Compensation Program.

The public interest groups in Colorado have never been completely enumerated. They vary from purely local organizations, such as the Colorado Springs Charter Association, to national organizations composed of state and local affiliates. Perhaps the most widely known is the League of Women Voters, whose work has centered about the reform of state and county government. Indeed, the impetus for county government reform in Colorado may have been provided by the League when it published a two-part study outlining the shortcomings of county government and suggesting alternatives to it.[60] The League is a prestigious organization among legislators; the six volumes of the Governor's Reapportionment Commission Report contain many comments praising the work of the League in the state.[61]

When examined closely the interest group phenomenon in Colorado appears very like that manifested in other states—with some few major differences. For

57. Nik Brietwieser *et al.*, "Educational Pressure Groups and the 44th General Assembly," Rocky Mountain Center for Education in Politics, May 1964, p. 6. (Paper delivered to regional meeting in Denver, May 1964.) Groups included in this study are: Colorado Association of School Administrators, Colorado Association of School Boards, Colorado Council on Educational Legislation, Colorado Education Association, Colorado Parent-Teacher Association, Colorado Federation of Teachers, the Denver Classroom Teachers Association, the Denver Federation of Teachers, and the Committee on Educational Endeavor.

58. For examples of some of these attitudes see Governor's Reapportionment Commission, *Report*, Vol. I, Exhibit B; Vol. III, Exhibit F; and Vol. VI, *passim*.

59. Martin, *op. cit.*, p. 67.

60. League of Women Voters of Colorado, *Cooperation or Confusion: Local Government in Colorado* (Denver, April 1960); and *The State's Role in Solution of Problems of Local Government in Colorado* (Denver, July 1962).

61. For example see *Report*, Vol. VI, Part I, *op. cit.*, p. 21 and *passim*.

example, Duane Lockard[62] suggests an interest activity pattern for Connecticut which somewhat resembles that for Colorado in two respects: that groups devote little effort to building up majorities for their legislation by direct contact with legislators and that there is a deep commitment between certain pressure groups and one party, which makes it difficult to make contacts with the opposition party leaders. Yet, after the similarities have been noted, the differences that remain suggest further inquiry to discover if a Colorado interest activity pattern can be isolated and identified. Certainly most of the groups aligned themselves unequivocally on the highly controversial issues of reapportionment and redistricting, which pointed up their connection with and influence on the politics of the legislature.

LEGISLATIVE. POLITICS

The Colorado General Assembly has been characterized by its two-party composition,[63] its relatively low party-voting cohesion, and its demonstrable rural bias. The evidence to support this evaluation is impressive. Since 1928 the General Assembly has been captured eight times by the Republicans and six times by the Democrats, and has been divided for seven regular sessions.

Malcolm Jewell has sampled roll-call votes to measure party legislative voting cohesion and has found that such cohesion is low for both political parties in the state,[64] and Curtis Martin and others have found that there is evidence to suggest that rural members of the General Assembly have translated their preponderant position into helpful legislation.[65]

Yet, when one examines more carefully, a different, a more varied and complex picture emerges, one in which the relatively simple urban-rural dichotomy becomes a trichotomy featuring urban-rural, rural-rural, and rural-suburban legislative voting conflicts; one in which party voting takes on a more partisan hue than those suggested but still one in which the relatively simple partisan lines are bent out of "true" by involuted voting patterns which reveal fratricide among parties and urban and rural groupings. Generally, these fratricidal tendencies emerge when there is a difference of opinion among members of the same party or the same functional grouping (urban or rural or professional) about the same public policy. Two instances will illustrate the point. The first indicates how a division occurred among rural legislators and the second illustrates the same point in a split between members of the same political party.

Funds for the construction and maintenance of state highways are allocated to each county on the basis of "adjusted mileage" within each and in accord with the percentage of the state's rural vehicles that are registered in each. Adjusted mileage is computed using a formula designed to distinguish equitably between the relative difficulties of building and maintaining mountain and plains roads. In 1953 when a bill providing for the distribution of state funds to the counties was

62. *New England State Politics* (Princeton: Princeton University Press, 1959), pp. 288-89.

63. Belle Zeller (ed.), *American State Legislatures* (New York: Crowell, 1954), p. 200.

64. Malcolm E. Jewell, "Party Voting in American State Legislatures," in John C. Wahlke and Heinz Eulau, *Legislative Behavior: A Reader in Theory and Research* (Glencoe: Free Press, 1959), p. 126.

65. Martin, *op. cit.*, pp. 12-13, and Rudolph Gomez, "Urban and Rural Voting in the Colorado General Assembly: 1902-1960," (Ph.D. dissertation, University of Colorado, 1963), pp. 170-76.

pending, a sharp fight occurred between rural legislators over the question of allocating such funds.[66] This rural versus rural legislative dispute suggests that there is no single rural interest in the state—nor is it easily identified.

Party voting cohesion in the Colorado General Assembly was measured by Malcolm Jewell for the 1941 and 1947 regular sessions. He found that the cohesion was rather low: the parties were on opposite sides of roll-call votes for 36 and 38 percent of the votes in the Senate and House respectively.[67] Stated conversely, *both parties voted on the same side* 64 percent of the time on roll-calls in the Senate and 62 percent in the House. Jewell's measurement was based on random samples of roll-call votes—non-selected legislation—taken during two entire regular sessions of the Assembly, on non-controversial as well as on controversial bills.

A somewhat different picture of party voting behavior emerges when the unit of measurement is shifted from non-selected to selected samples. When experience shows that both parties have taken different positions on a fundamental state policy in successive sessions, it behooves us to measure such voting in order to perceive the party differences which do exist. The assumption underlying this method is that both parties assume a partisan stance only when a major public policy is in the offing and when clear differences exist between them. In other words, partisan conflict can be hidden if legislative voting behavior were examined in the aggregate. Yet, this type of conflict is important to locate and measure for it may be the only indicator of deep-seated differences. One instance of such voting behavior was analyzed for this study, involving public school funds.

The partisan voting pattern which emerges after examining twenty-three roll-call votes, taken from 1958 through 1963 on bills allocating funds for public education, indicates that while 89.6 percent of the Republicans voted together on all twenty-three roll-calls, only 70.8 percent of the Democrats voted together.[68] The reason for the split in Democratic voting has already been alluded to: Denver Democrats find it difficult to get out-of-city Democratic support for their proposals.

These findings suggest that on some issues—the more substantive ones, affecting state expenditures and state income—there is a significant degree of difference between the two major parties in Colorado. The data supporting this conclusion are as yet scanty, but they do suggest that both parties attempt to enact such differences[69] into law when they control the state legislature.

That legislative politics is influenced by outside pressures was very clearly demonstrated in the 1960's in the protracted struggle over reapportionment. Each of the interest groups described earlier was involved for years in the conflict over legislative reapportionment and redistricting. The position they took, the actions taken by the General Assembly vis-à-vis reapportionment and redistricting, and the action taken by the electorate on the problem provide the outlines from which emerge a picture of the support the various interests in the state command, and the part they play in the partisan politics of the legislature.

Prior to the court-induced[70] reapportionment and redistricting acts of 1964 it was theoretically possible for 29.8 percent of the electorate in Colorado to elect

66. *Ibid.*, p. 76.

67. *Op. cit.*, p. 127, Table 8.

68. Gomez, "Voting Behavior . . . ," p. 8.

69. Gomez, "Urban and Rural Voting . . . ," chap. VI, pp. 70-75.

70. *Lucas et al. v. Forty-Fourth General Assembly of Colorado et al.*, 377 U.S. 713 (1964).

a majority to the upper house and for 32.1 percent to elect a majority to the lower.[71] This condition patently favored the state rural areas and conservative interests generally. Interest groups took diametrically opposed positions on the reapportionment problem. Agriculture, business, and veterans' organizations supported federal plans of reapportionment whereas labor and the League of Women Voters favored population-based reapportionment. The latter was extremely active in suggesting solutions to the problem which would take into account all interests in the state but which "should largely be based upon population as a controlling factor."[72]

After the legislature adjourned in the spring of 1962 without reapportioning itself, two initiated amendments to the constitution were proposed by two clusterings of groups. The campaign to place the two alternative amendments on the 1962 general election ballot was unsuccessful. The one incorporating the so-called "federal" plan was specifically supported by the Chamber of Commerce, the Colorado Cattlemen's Association, and the Republican party organization. Legislative apportionment on the basis of population was supported by the AFL-CIO, Colorado Education Association, and the League of Women Voters.

Generally, both parties campaigned against this latter amendment, with the exception of the Democratic organizations in Denver and Pueblo. The obvious reason for this alignment is that the amendment based on population would benefit the urban interests of both parties in a heavily weighted rural legislature. The amendment was defeated in every county in the state.[73]

The amendment that was adopted "provided for House representation based strictly on population and [fixed] Senate representation in permanent districts weighted heavily in favor of low population areas."[74] The voters by an almost two-to-one vote chose *not* to put representation in their Senate on a strict population basis.

Congressional redistricting was the next problem to be solved. An extraordinary session of the General Assembly was called to deal with it and passed an act on April 29, 1964, which redistricted the state to the decided advantage of the Republicans. Both the legislature and the electorate bestowed their confidence, in the forms of votes, upon the GOP-agricultural-business coalition.

"But on June 16, 1964, the U.S. Supreme Court virtually dropped a bomb on the General Assembly. In the case of *Lucas v. the Forty-fourth General Assembly of Colorado* . . . the constitutional amendment adopted in 1962 and its supporting apportionment statute were declared not to be 'sufficiently grounded on population to be constitutionally sustainable under the Equal Protection Clause.' The case was remanded to the U.S. District Court of Colorado for further disposition."[75]

71. Advisory Commission on Intergovernmental Relations, *Apportionment of State Legislatures* (Washington: Government Printing Office, December 1962), Appendix B, p. A-7.

72. For the League's position on reapportionment in Colorado, see *Report*, Exhibits H through H-9. Also, League of Women Voters of Colorado, *Representative Government in Colorado: The Challenge of Reapportionment.*

73. For a very good account of the later stages of the reapportionment struggle see Malcolm E. Jewell (ed.), *The Politics of Reapportionment* (New York: Atherton Press, 1962), pp. 68-71, and Glendon Schubert (ed.), *Reapportionment* (New York: Scribner's, 1964), p. 158.

74. Conrad L. McBride, "The 1964 Election in Colorado," *Western Political Quarterly*, XVIII (June 1965, Part 2), 476.

75. *Ibid.*, p. 477.

A second extraordinary legislative session was thereupon called by Governor Love, which, in a very brief time, filed an apportionment proposal with the District Court which provided for single member districts for both House and Senate. This was approved.

It is still too early to predict the ultimate results of reapportionment in terms of party control of Colorado's legislative politics. In 1966 Republicans captured a healthy majority of seats in the House, while in the Senate their 20 to 15 majority remained unchanged.

Of more than passing interest in the General Assembly elections was the fact that all elections in populous counties, with more than one seat at stake, were conducted on an at-large basis for the last time. Colorado may well be the first state to conform completely to the directives of the U.S. Supreme Court in *Reynolds v. Simms*. In any event, the opportunity to design the election districts, and the consequent partisan advantages potentially derivable therefrom, rests with a strong Republican majority in both houses of the General Assembly. Democrats are understandably apprehensive.

The image of the legislature that emerges from this brief analysis is not as sharp as that suggested by Jewell, Martin, or Gomez a few years ago. In place of the earlier, relatively simple, picture the later one emerges as a collage, one in which the gray color of nonpartisan voting is enlivened with the crimson of sharp interparty voting and one in which sharp angular abstractions of rural-urban conflicts are softened by dilution brought about by intra-group conflicts.

VOTING HABITS

V. O. Key, Jr., pointed out in his monumental *Southern Politics* that most of the one-party states in the South have pockets of sustained partisan opposition.[76] When we examine popular voting behavior in Colorado along the lines suggested by Key, two patterns emerge, one suggesting that the Democratic party is supported by inhabitants of the more heavily industrialized, urbanized, and the more ethnically variegated areas, and the other suggesting that the Republican party finds most of its supporters among the more ethnically homogeneous, from among the less industrialized, and from among the more suburban and rural areas. These patterns emerge from an examination of the data found in Table III.

Popular support for each party in the state appears to vary with the type of election. The Republican party enjoys more stable electoral support in both presidential and gubernatorial elections than does the Democratic. The *implication* is that the Republicans enjoy an edge in electing their candidates to the chief executive's post on both the state and national level. Such does not prove to be the case, however. The statistical advantage enjoyed by the Republicans appears to hold only for presidential elections: it does not extend to gubernatorial elections.

The gap between counties usually supporting Democratic presidential and gubernatorial candidates is not as fundamental and lasting as it appears. Dwight D. Eisenhower was the Republican nominee for president for two of the four presidential elections studied here. He obtained significant amounts of "friends and neighbors"[77] support since he was regarded by many Coloradoans as a "native son" by virtue of his marriage. Mrs. Eisenhower was reared in Denver, and her

76. V. O. Key, Jr., *Southern Politics* (New York: Vintage edition, n.d.), pp. 75-81, for one example of such activity.

77. For discussion of the "friends and neighbors" idea, see *ibid.*, pp. 37-41 and *passim*.

widowed mother lived there when his administration began. Of the state's 63 counties, 59 supported his candidacy in 1952, and 61 in 1956.

If the suggestion about the relationship between popular voting and Eisenhower's candidacy is valid, it then appears that the index representing durable popular partisan commitments in Colorado should be based on data compiled from gubernatorial elections for they reflect more "normal" voting behavior. These elections reveal that nineteen counties usually support Republican platforms and candidates, and eighteen counties, those from the Democratic party. The remaining twenty-six can be classed as two-party since they split their vote in the four elections studied here.

The nature of the committed counties can be inferred by examining their major economic activity, their ethnic composition, and their population. Those usually supporting the Republican party are rural, suburban, Anglo-Saxon, and agricultural. Those usually supporting the Democratic party are urban, industrialized, mining-rural, and ethnically variegated. Both parties, then, in the normal course of events, can expect to share control, more or less equally, of the state

TABLE III
COUNTY PARTISAN SUPPORT IN PRESIDENTIAL AND
GUBERNATORIAL ELECTIONS, 1952-1964◇

Traditional Republican□ Both elections		Traditional Democratic□ Presidential	Gubernatorial	Two-Party△
Boulder	Lincoln	Costilla	Adams	Eagle	The remaining
Douglas	Logan	Huerfano	Alamosa	Gilpin	counties
Elbert	Morgan	Las Animas	Archuleta	Huerfano	(There are 63
El Paso	Otero	Pueblo	Bent	Lake	counties in
Grand	Phillips		Clear Creek	Las Animas	Colorado)
Hinsdale	Pitkin		Conejos	Montezuma	
Jackson	Washington		Costilla	Montrose	
Jefferson	Weld		Denver	Pueblo	
Kit Carson	Yuma		Dolores	San Miguel	
Larimer					

◇A careful comparison of voting behavior by counties for the years 1952-64 in both presidential and gubernatorial elections resulted in the data summarized here.
□Counties were classed as Republican or Democratic if a majority in each county supported candidates of one party for president in three out of the four elections selected for analysis here.
△These counties split their vote equally between parties for the four elections examined.

government. They both have "staying power"—they can sustain major defeats without endangering the existence of the party. One can speculate that the independent character of legislative voting behavior noted earlier is but a relection of, and partially attributable to, similar popular voting behavior. Finally, the fact that popular electoral support in Colorado frequently oscillates suggests that the ideological content of each party is perceived to be different by the electorate who expects that difference to be translated into public policy.

The 1966 elections amply illustrate this tendency to oscillate. Republican Senator Gordon Allott won re-election for a third time, while three Democratic congressmen (Byron Rogers, Frank E. Evans, and Wayne Aspinall) were also re-elected. At the same time, former Congressman Donald G. Brotzman won back his old seat which he had lost to a Democratic opponent in 1964. In that year, Republicans had held a 20-15 majority in the state Senate, while Democrats had a 42-23 edge in the House. Two years later, although the Senate ratio remained unchanged, the House altered radically, Republicans winning 38 of its 65 seats. The Republicans also maintained their hold on the executive department by virtue of the re-election of incumbent John A. Love. He won his race with the Democratic candidate, then Lieutenant-Governor Robert Knous, by a 356,730 to 287,132 margin.[78]

Since 1928 the Democratic party has won the governor's office ten times, control of the legislature six times, and captured the presidential electoral vote four times. The Republican party, on the other hand, has won the governor's race eight times, control of the legislature nine times, and captured the presidential vote six times. Control of the legislature has been divided between both major parties a total of five times.[79] The Republicans' resurgence from their 1964 electoral defeat is in keeping with the shifting, fundamentally two-party pattern of alternating control of government that characterizes state elections in Colorado.

NATIONAL TRENDS

During the 1962 gubernatorial campaign the question about the proper relationship between national and state governments was raised by the Republican party. The Republican gubernatorial nominee, John A. Love, repeatedly suggested that the national government get out of state government and politics and the "government in Colorado be returned to the people." After winning the election, Governor Love created a citizens' committee to study the roles of national and state government in order to recommend proposals for returning government to the people. While no wholesale suggestions have been forthcoming the point is worth mentioning for it indicates that there is a demand among some elements of the Colorado populace for an examination of nation-state relationships.

Perhaps the most reliable index we can use to estimate Colorado's influence on national policies is to examine her national legislative delegation and see if it wields any formal influence over any significant area of national policies. We can infer such formal influence for Colorado by virtue of the chairmanship held by Representative Wayne N. Aspinall (D-Fourth Congressional District), of the Committee on Interior and Insular Affairs.[80] This committee is an important one from the standpoint of Western interests for it is concerned, among other things, with the utilization of water resources, an area of public policy which is of paramount importance for such semi-arid states as Colorado, New Mexico, Wyoming, Nevada, California, and Arizona. No research has been done to determine if Representative Aspinall has been able to translate the power potential of his chairmanship into legislation helpful to Colorado. (It has been rumored that had not Aspi-

78. See Conrad L. McBride, "The 1966 Election in Colorado," *Western Political Quarterly*, XX (June 1967, Part 2), 555-60.

79. These data are abstracted from Curtis Martin and Rudolph Gomez, *Colorado Government and Politics* (2nd ed.; Boulder: Pruett Press, 1967), pp. 146, 147, 152, and 153.

80. This committee is one of four House standing committees which may bring certain bills to the floor without having to go through the Rules Committee. See Daniel M. Berman, *In Congress Assembled* (New York: Macmillan, 1964), p. 204.

nall been chairman of this particular committee the Fryingpan-Arkansas Water Diversion Project in southern Colorado would never have become public policy.) We can conclude, nonetheless, that Colorado wields some influence in Congress by virtue of Aspinall's seniority in the House of Representatives.

Nicholas A. Masters has devised a legislator classificatory system which can be adapted to assay the relative strength of state congressional delegations by examining committee assignments of freshman representatives.[81] Masters' scheme can be adapted to non-freshmen as well as to freshman legislators. By so doing we find that the entire Colorado House delegation belongs to the non- and semi-exclusive committees.[82] Although the Colorado House delegation does not serve on nationally "prestigeful committees," it is not politically impotent, considering the importance of conservation and natural resource policy to Colorado. Indeed, Colorado's political influence in the national Congress is disproportionately great in view of her population and her small congressional delegation.

Conclusions about the political potency of the Colorado senatorial delegation may be drawn in like manner from their committee assignments.[83] Donald Matthews has formulated an index on the relative desirability of certain assignments in the U.S. Senate by noting member movement from less desirable committees to more desirable ones. He found that eight committees—Foreign Relations, Appropriations, Finance, Armed Services, Agriculture, Judiciary, Commerce, and Banking and Currency—recorded net gains while the seven remaining committees—Interior, Public Works, Labor and Public Welfare, Government Operations, Rules and Administration, Post Office and Civil Service, and District of Columbia—suffered a net loss of membership. When we match the membership of the Colorado senatorial delegation with this index we find that both senators from Colorado—Gordon Allott (R) and Peter Dominick (R)—enjoy assignments on "desirable committees." Allott, Colorado's third-term senator, is a member of the second most desirable, Appropriations, while Dominick is a member of the eighth most desirable, Banking and Currency. The differences in committee assignments can be explained by one word—seniority. Allott has been a senator since 1954 and Dominick since 1962. Both senators' second assignment is the Interior and Insular Affairs Committee. This assignment is not one ordinarily desired by most senators. Yet, Matthews observes that "the tendency for senators to be attracted by committees of special importance to their constituents is well known. The postwar Committee on Interior and Insular Affairs, for example, was overwhelmingly made up of senators from the public land states: there were about three times more members from the Rocky Mountain and Pacific states

81. Nicholas A. Masters, "Committee Assignments," *New Perspectives on the House of Representatives,* eds. Robert L. Peabody and Nelson W. Polsby (Chicago: Rand McNally, 1963), Table III, p. 48. House committees are classed as exclusive, semi-exclusive, or non-exclusive depending upon whether members may hold one or more committee assignments. For example, a legislator serving on Appropriations or Ways and Means may serve on no other committee so we consider his committee assignment exclusive: members serving on two or more committees are classed as serving on semi-exclusive or non-exclusive committees. See *ibid.,* p. 44.

82. Representatives and their committee assignments: Rogers (D-1st Congressional District), Judiciary; Brotzman (R-2nd District), Interstate and Foreign Commerce; Evans (D-3rd District), Armed Services; Aspinall (D-4th District), Interior and Insular Affairs and Joint Committee on Atomic Energy. Source: *Congressional Directory,* 88th Cong., 2nd sess., January 1964.

83. This assumption is the basis for some of the work done by Donald R. Matthews in *U.S. Senators and Their World* (New York: Vintage edition, 1960). See especially pp. 148-52.

than one would expect on the basis of chance."[84] We can therefore infer Colorado is amply represented in the national government, and is able to wield some minimal influence[85] on public policy by virtue of the *formal* positions occupied by its two senators.

The *informal* influence of Colorado's entire congressional delegation cannot be assessed for lack of information. Committee members, both majority and minority, learn "role expectations and institutional norms within informal groups,"[86] and must attempt to live up to them if they entertain hopes of ever achieving their own expectations.

A second rough index illustrating the relationship to the national government is provided by the number and type of federal expenditures in Colorado. First, the national government listed expenditures of $136,435,535 in Colorado for 1960.[87] Second, the national government allocated $76,929,933 to the state treasury in 1960 for grant-in-aid programs of various sorts, and it allocated $3,035,287 for employment security programs, $163,937 for other programs (e.g., Clarke-McNary Forestry); and finally, it allocated $4,175,982 to the counties in Colorado for a variety of programs (Forest Reserve Funds, Taylor Grazing Act, etc.).[88] The grand total of federal funds allocated to the state treasury for 1960 was $84,305,139.

The sums mentioned in the preceding paragraph total $220,740,674, roughly.[89] However, they comprise but a small portion of money spent by the federal government in Colorado. Any rough estimate must take into account the fact that in 1960 the federal government maintained 154 major installations (Air Force Academy, Fort Carson, *et al.*) and activities (National Bureau of Standards in Boulder, *et al.*) in the state. In addition to this type of federal expenditure is the type associated with the letting of contracts for national defense. Martin Missile Company near Denver is the state's largest single employer and is dependent upon defense contracts for its existence. Ball Space Laboratories in Boulder have received sizable federal contracts for astronautical research and development. When items such as these are included in the estimate, it becomes obvious that suggestions about federal expenditures in Colorado totaling over a billion dollars annually since 1960[90] have some basis in fact. To paraphrase one part of Lyndon Johnson's 1965 State of the Union Address, "today the state of Colorado depends, in large measure, upon the state of the Union."[91]

84. *Ibid.*, pp. 153-54.

85. The influence wielded is minimal since both senators are members of the minority party on Capitol Hill.

86. Alan Fiellin, "The Functions of Informal Groups: A State Delegation," in *New Perspectives on the House of Representatives*, p. 76.

87. *Colorado Yearbook*: 1959-1961, p. 212.

88. *Ibid.*, p. 218.

89. According to the Colorado State Planning Commission (*Colorado Yearbook*: 1962-1964, p. 261), the sums spent by the national government in Colorado for 1963 total $163,916,050. The reason for the disparity between the figures given for 1960 and 1963 is that the State Planning Commission does not include in its 1963 total the sums allocated by the national government for the programs listed above—for grant-in-aid programs relating to employment security, Clarke-McNary Forestry Act, Taylor Grazing Act, and so on.

90. Federal expenditures in both the 1962 gubernatorial and the 1964 presidential elections. The Republican party argued that the federal government was spending too much, etc., whereas the Democratic party suggested that Colorado's economy was dependent upon such expenditures for its health.

91. As reported in the *Free Press* (Colorado Springs), January 5, 1965, p. 2.

There are a number of indications that the electorate in Colorado perceives and understands this local-state-national governmental relationship. One will help to make the point. The Colorado Cattlemen's Association has advocated federal controls on beef imports for years. Its position is similar to that voiced by the California Cattlemen's Association which called for a reduction of foreign beef imports late in 1963.[92] George L. Mehren, U.S. Assistant Secretary of Agriculture, reminded the Cattlemen's Association that "although it abhors controls of any sort it . . . gets plenty of help from Uncle Sam. . . ."[93] Secretary Mehren stated that "some $3 billion of public money" has gone into financing soil and water conservation practices on livestock farms and ranches.[94] Even those groups in Colorado who argue against federal programs and activities in their state are beneficiaries of the system they are criticizing.[95]

There are virtually no indicators of the relationships between party in Colorado and national party politics. Only the most impressionistic conclusions can be drawn. After the 1964 general election[96] which resulted in a Democratic landslide, the state Republican party appears to have undergone an abrupt transformation. The impact of this election was felt immediately by most members of the state GOP Central Committee who divided on whether the party image of 1964 should be scrapped "by divesting itself of ultra-conservative leadership."[97] The chairman of the Colorado Republicans, Paul Wolf, who won his position early in 1964 largely because of his support for Senator Goldwater, stated that the party must now stand for a moderate approach.[98] The lead was taken by Governor John Love at the Republican National Nomination Convention where he made the first seconding speech for the presidential candidacy of Governor William Scranton of Pennsylvania. It is by virtue of this speech and by the support generally tendered Scranton and other GOP moderates by Love that the now-moderate Colorado GOP may be able to generate some influence for itself in national party politics. Certainly the party made an impressive come-back in the 1966 elections.

The state Democratic party is now without substantial influence in national party politics. The three present Democratic congressmen are too pedestrian or too new to swing much weight in high councils of the party. Frank E. Evans was elected for the first time in 1964. Byron Rogers, congressman from Denver, has been in office since 1950 and in that time has managed to steer clear of partisan entangling alliances—on any level. (His chief claim to fame is that he manages to get re-elected every two years without unduly taxing himself in any fashion.)[99] Representative Aspinall, congressman from the Fourth District, appears to minimize his partisan affiliation when campaigning in order to cash in on the

92. "Rugged Cattlemen Reminded of Help," *Denver Post*, December 16, 1963, p. 13.

93. *Ibid.*

94. Aid included building 207,000 wells for livestock water on farms and ranches at a cost of $76 million, and 49 million feet of pipe for livestock water, costing $13 million. Also spent were $50 million for rangeland cover and $7 million for range tillage. *Ibid.*

95. For other examples see "Bracero Wage Floor for Colorado Decried," *Denver Post*, December 20, 1964, p. 1; and entire February 1959 issue of *Western Business Review*, Vol. 3, No. 1.

96. See the *Denver Post*, November 4, 1964, for complete election coverage.

97. Tom Gavin, "State GOP Bubbling with Battle Rumors," *Denver Post*, November 6, 1964, p. 44.

98. *Free Press*, Colorado Springs, Colorado, November 5, 1964.

99. See the *Denver Post*, November 4, 1964.

built-in rural conservatism of his district, and apparently has chosen to continue on this course at all other levels of party organization. The old guard, the ones who have had access to party politics at levels other than district and state, have chosen to ignore party associations and activities at such levels, and as a result the voice of the Colorado Democratic party does not appear to sound in national party politics.

The older members of the state Democratic party have no base from which to operate, and hence, from which to influence national party politics. Former governor Steve McNichols is now a national committeeman. He has been relatively quiet since losing the 1962 gubernatorial election. Former U.S. Senator John Carroll has been inactive politically since his defeat by Peter Dominick in 1962. It has been suggested that his political influence has not been entirely debased by his defeat since he still retains "contacts" among nationally active Democrats; but there appears to be an attitude on the part of organization regulars in the state that he has become shopworn and that a new face is needed to revive the chances for a Democratic senatorial victory, and hence for increasing the Democratic party's influence nationally.

Both parties in Colorado are hampered when attempting to affect national party politics by an insufficient power base. Colorado's six electoral votes are simply not sufficient to permit state party leaders to bargain, or even to negotiate, about national party matters with heads of more powerful state party organizations. It appears that Colorado's major opportunity to have an effect on national party politics is through the *personalities* of its party leaders. At the present time it appears that Governor John A. Love, Chairman of the Republican Governors' Conference, stands the best chance of any of the state's politicians of having such an effect. The state Democratic party will have to wait for the emergence of such a personality before it can count on having any impact on national Democratic politics.

HAWAII:

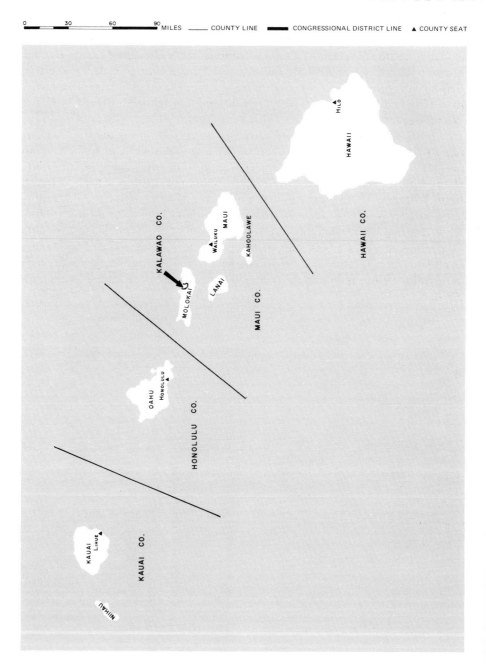

0   30   60   90 MILES   —— COUNTY LINE   ▬▬ CONGRESSIONAL DISTRICT LINE   ▲ COUNTY SEAT

HILO

HAWAII

HAWAII CO.

KALAWAO CO.

MAUI
WAILUKU
KAHOOLAWE

LANAI

MAUI CO.

MOLOKAI

OAHU
HONOLULU

HONOLULU CO.

KAUAI
LIHUE

KAUAI CO.

NIIHAU

Norman Meller
Daniel W. Tuttle, Jr.

The Aloha State

Within the span of a century, Hawaii moved from the isolated, Stone Age culture discovered by Captain Cook to a nation whose sovereign sought to take his place among the world powers by extending his rule from the Hawaiian archipelago through the South Sea Islands. During the same period, absolute rule evolved into constitutional monarchy. Then, while awaiting annexation by the United States after the overthrow of the monarchy, Hawaii enjoyed an interregnum republic. Upon annexation in 1898, and adoption by Congress of the Hawaiian Organic Act in 1900, the Islands embarked upon their half-century of territorial tutelage. On August 21, 1959, Hawaii was admitted by presidential proclamation as the fiftieth state in the Union.

Many of the factors which contributed to these changes in governmental form continue to influence Hawaii's political and administrative processes as the newest state in the Union. However, during the most recent decade, older forces tending toward "standpattism" have given way to factors more recently introduced and their tendency toward innovation. New political leaders are in office, and most segments of the population now share actively in the political process.

GEOGRAPHY AND RESOURCES

The Hawaiian Islands are more distant from a continental land mass than any other large island group in the world. This isolation in the North Pacific has afforded a sense of unity sufficient to compensate for the internal separation of the various island units. Rough as the ocean channels sometimes become, they have proved no barrier to ready communication, which facilitated the centralizing of Hawaii's administrative system. Paradoxically, physical separation by water has permitted each island's people to conceive of themselves as an entity and has contributed to intra-state cleavages which loom largest in the separation of Oahu from the Outer Islands, or as the latter prefer to be called, the "Neighbor Islands."

The seven major inhabited islands are strung along a span of about 350 miles. Approximately 64 miles of ocean separate the northernmost inhabited islands of Kauai and Niihau from Oahu. Some 22 miles to the south of Oahu, Molokai forms a cluster with Lanai and Maui.[1] Each cluster has long been grouped for local government, and, in the first decade of territorial status, they became, respectively, the counties of Kauai and Maui. The largest and most southerly of the islands in the state is Hawaii, 26 miles distant from Maui. This island constitutes the county of the same name, and alone represents almost two-thirds of the total land acreage of the chain. In none of these three counties are there organized cities, so that

1. A fourth island, Kahoolawe, was always named with the group, but is now uninhabited.

their urban areas—such as Hilo, on Hawaii, with its 29,000 people—along with their rural population are all included within the jurisdiction of the county. Similarly, the boundaries of the City and County of Honolulu are coterminous with the whole island of Oahu and also encompass some of the minor outlying islets not within the other counties.[2]

The political designation "City and County of Honolulu" is somewhat misleading, since it carries overtones of a mainland metropolitan area. While it is true that the urban coastal strip on the leeward of Oahu, stretching from about Pearl Harbor to the easterly tip of the island, has been designated the "city" for certain administrative purposes and is fully metropolitan, Oahu contains more rural than urban acreage and produces a sizable share of the state's major products of the soil. Hawaii does not present the picture of a predominantly rural upstate New York or a downstate Illinois aligned against an almost exclusively urban metropolis. Nor is the City and County of Honolulu like the "heart" city and county of San Francisco with its dormitory suburbs in adjoining counties. Business and industrial centers, residential areas, plantations, and farms fall within the jurisdiction of this one local governing unit. Notwithstanding this uniqueness of Honolulu, the old battle of the county districts vis-à-vis the power of the big city is as evident in Hawaii as in many mainland areas.

Lacking minerals—not even the bauxite and titanium deposits recently found are of commercial quality—exploitation of Hawaii's resources has depended upon intensive cultivation of the soil and has capitalized on the year-round growing season possible in the tropics. The monopolistic pattern of land ownership, the lack of adequate markets other than for crops taking up to two years to mature, and the expense of farm development all contributed to the growth of the large-scale sugar plantation, whose economic feudalism replaced that of old Hawaii which disappeared with the absolute power of Hawaiian royalty. The plantation also satisfied much of the need for local government. Until recently, from over a quarter to a third of Hawaii's total civilian population and from at least 30 to as much as 50 percent of the people dwelling outside urban Honolulu and Hilo have lived on sugar plantations.

Hawaiian economic institutions are today undergoing rapid transformation as overseas capital flows into the Islands and asserts management prerogatives, while Hawaiian-founded firms diversify their holdings with mainland and foreign investments. Anti-trust legislation enacted by the state legislature in 1961 has both hastened the integration of subsidiaries with their parent companies and encouraged the severance of interlocking ties between diverse commercial organizations. The old oligopoly which was Hawaii has been broken, and with it there has been accompanying political change.

Initially Hawaii depended upon the sandalwood trade; then whaling became its major source of external income; and finally the economic institutions of modern Hawaii rose around its sugar plantations. The large wholesale and retail houses in Honolulu, locally known as "factors," diverted their capital to sugar growing. Just as in the case of the plantations, the number of the factors shrank as they grew in size, until five remained to dominate the field. Today, the Big Five by contract, stock control, or by outright ownership direct the conduct of all but one of the remaining twenty-five sugar plantations. A second institution, the Hawaiian Sugar Planters' Association, developed out of the mutual problems of the

2. The Hansen's Disease settlement on a Molokai peninsula is declared to be a fifth county, Kalawao; actually, it is administered by the state Department of Health.

plantations: through it, a united stand toward the rest of the community could be taken. A third illustration of the centripetal forces within the sugar industry is found in its marketing cooperative which operates the largest sugar refinery in the world at Crockett, California. As sugar for long was the dominant economic interest of the Islands, so it was consequently the dominant political interest. A commentator as late as 1935 noted that "the governors, legislators and government officials since 1900 [territorial status] have been to a large degree determined by and considerate of the sugar leaders."[3]

Raising and canning pineapple was long the Islands' second largest industry, unimportant until 1910, when a history of rapid but sporadic expansion began. It, too, relied upon the plantation system. This industry knows a competition and mainland participation different from that of sugar. Notwithstanding, profiting from the example of the sugar industry, it has displayed a united front with respect to common problems, joining with sugar in creating a favorable climate for centralized government. Even though the factor system has not taken deep root, the same individuals who set the policy for sugar have been able to exert their influence over a majority of the pineapple companies.

Mechanization of the plantations, with a marked reduction in their labor force and a demand for skilled labor, brought dramatic change by the end of World War II. Concomitantly, the rise of militant unionism to challenge the private government of the plantation introduced a disturbing power element into the Islands' economic oligopoly. Ultimately, the International Longshoremen's and Warehousemen's Union came to encompass practically all of Hawaii's sugar workers, pineapple workers, and longshoremen. There has been gradual assumption by public agencies of many of the local services formerly borne by the plantation areas, and their vote has now generally shifted to the Democratic party, so that plantations are no longer regarded as Republican strongholds.

Hawaii's strategic position in the Pacific has brought an ever-increasing volume of federal defense money to its shores. Today, income from federal expenditures ($751 million, of which $517 million was for armed forces expenditures) far exceeds that from sugar and pineapple ($305 million).[4] While once plantation crops were considered to be the mainstay of the economy, present hopes are pinned on the growth of the tourist industry, which now represents the Islands' second largest single source of income, and may soon become its major industry. In 1967, tourism provided roughly $400 million from purchases of goods and services, and it is estimated that one million tourists visited Hawaii during the course of the year.[5]

The hundreds of millions of dollars which poured into the Islands during World War II resulted in sizable capital accretions, particularly by non-*haoles*.[6] In the peak year of 1944 alone, the federal government paid out $625 million to persons in Hawaii. The billion dollar total personal income of Hawaii in that year contrasts markedly with the $218 million income for prewar 1939.[7] Today annual personal income reaches the two billion dollar mark. The small entrepreneurial,

3. Frank E. Midkiff, "The Economic Determinants of Education in Hawaii" (Ph.D. dissertation, Yale University, 1935), p. 132.

4. Bank of Hawaii, "Economy of Hawaii: 1967" (Honolulu: 1967 Annual Economic Report), p. 8.

5. Preliminary estimates.

6. *Haole*, a Hawaiian word, primarily refers to Caucasians of North European stock.

7. U.S. Department of Commerce, Office of Business Economics, *Income of Hawaii* (Washington: Government Printing Office, 1953), pp. 15, 18.

home owning, middle class has rapidly grown in importance. New wholesale outlets have developed and mainland-type retail merchandising, such as the supermarket, has sprung up, independent of the Big Five. Fortunes have been made and reinvested in extensive subdivisions; agricultural fields, dairy lots, and pig pens on Oahu are grudgingly giving way to suburban rooftops. Waikiki hotels and Neighbor Island tourist destination areas sprout like cement toadstools almost overnight. Mainland chains now operate retail stores, hotels, commercial services, and communication media. The prominent position of the Big Five in the Island economy has been eclipsed, and the political balance of power has shifted from the small group in control of Hawaii's sugar, pineapple, and allied activities to larger and more diverse publics.

Most of this change has added to Oahu's stature, and the schism between the City and the County of Honolulu and the Neighbor Islands has widened. The new state constitution attempted to preserve control of the Senate by the Neighbor Islands, but court-mandated reapportionment has changed this. While still a territory, it had become the fashion to assure representation of each outside county on major territorial boards and commissions within the executive branch. This trend has been reinforced by statehood, and the pattern incorporated in state reorganization legislation generally provides Oahu with but a bare majority on executive boards. As the wealth and population of Honolulu grow, the other counties seek collectively to make joint cause in order to achieve their common goals.

POPULATION

The introduction of western civilization with its attendant diseases and the debilitating results which flowed from cultural contact rapidly decimated the native Hawaiian population. From around 300,000 at the time of Captain Cook's discovery, the population decreased to less than 20 percent of that figure. This trend was reversed in the 1870's, and by the mid-1920's the 300,000 figure was passed. Today, the resident population numbers around 790,000, of which about 50,000 is accounted for by resident military personnel and their dependents stationed in the Islands. As early as the census of 1900, Oahu had far outnumbered all other islands. Here four-fifths of Hawaii's people now live. Despite the expansion of the state's population, at each census over the last few decades, there have been fewer people in the Neighbor Island counties as residents moved to Oahu or the mainland, and only recently has a reverse trend appeared.

The tenfold expansion of Hawaii's population in less than a century was largely achieved through combing the labor markets of the world for plantation workers. In all, some 400,000 foreign-born laborers, including their wives, children, and relatives, came to the Islands in the last century. Many of the immigrants subsequently either continued on to the mainland United States or returned to their homeland, but enough settled in Hawaii to reshape completely the demographic landscape. The population is unique by virtue of the diversity of its ethnic strains and their combination through intermarriage. Today, Hawaii is the only state of the Union in which Orientals comprise a majority. All seven of the major ethnic groups imported—in order of their introduction, Chinese, Japanese, Portuguese, Puerto Rican, Korean, Spanish, and Filipino—have become integral parts of the Island community, along with the Hawaiians and the *haoles* who early joined with them in governing the Islands. Of all groups, the children born of intermarriage—the cosmopolitan group—appear to be experiencing the fastest growth rate.

Over the years, the latest immigrant group to arrive has tended to occupy the place of lowest esteem and subsequently has risen in stature as it left the plantation or came to fill plantation positions of status.[8] Not all movement up the ladder of success has followed exactly the same course, or occurred in an equal time span, for in the past, top management positions remained closed to Orientals. Today representatives of each ethnic group are beginning to be found in all but the highest levels of Big Five management, and even here the portent of coming events is casting its shadow. The mechanization of the plantations has assured that the Filipinos will be the last ethnic group in the Islands to start as plantation laborers.

Peoples from all ethnic stocks in Hawaii actively engage in formulating public policy, externally through pressure groups and the electoral process and internally as officeholders and government employees. This has been a gradual development which has taken half-a-century to manifest itself: Oriental participation markedly increased only after World War II. Due to federal limitations on naturalization, many of the aliens were ineligible for formal political roles; it was not until about 1950 that citizens of Oriental extraction comprised over half of the adult population and probably a similar proportion of the registered voters. By 1955, Orientals also accounted for a little over half of the elected officials and a comparable percentage of territorial government employees. Among the ranks of the public school teachers, they probably enjoyed a larger share. Only in the class of appointed officials was the Oriental lag still evident,[9] but new appointments in the last few years have brought their component in this area beyond the midpoint.

Almost contemporaneous with their advent in the Islands, *haoles* began exerting a formative influence over government. From the Mission days, the *haoles* carried over the concept of the natives as a people who must be carefully guided into following the proper course of public policy and adopting only approved methods for effectuating it.[10] Later, through a number of legal stratagems, the *haoles* achieved protection against the numerical superiority of the Hawaiians and immigrant labor imports. With the Organic Act of 1900, the Congress of the United States would accept none of the former restrictive political practices, and for a short time thereafter, the enlarged and predominantly Hawaiian electorate captured the legislature, but the executive and judicial branches remained safely in *haole* hands through appointments from Washington. However, after the first turbulent years of the Hawaiian's Home Rule party, the *haoles* again assumed positions of political leadership. Until recently, most of the Islands' *haoles*, "as members of the favored economic and social strata in Hawaii," have been Republicans.[11] The Democratic party has had greater appeal to large segments of the laboring peoples. To an extent this also had ethnic overtones, but both major parties, alarmed by the ill-fated attempt of the short-lived Home Rule party to make a racial bloc of the Hawaiian vote, early adopted the policy of appealing to all races.

8. See Andrew W. Lind, *An Island Community* (Chicago: University of Chicago Press, 1938).

9. See George K. Yamamoto, "Political Participation Among Orientals in Hawaii," *Sociology and Social Research*, XLIII (May-June 1959), 359; and Norman Meller, "Centralization in Hawaii: Retrospect and Prospect," *American Political Science Review*, LII (March 1958), 98.

10. See Norman Meller, "Missionaries to Hawaii: Shapers of the Islands' Destiny," *Western Political Quarterly*, XI (December 1958), 788.

11. Andrew W. Lind, "Hawaii at the Polls," *Asian*, XXXVI (October 1936), 644. See also Robert M. C. Littler, *The Governance of Hawaii* (Stanford: Stanford University Press, 1929), p. 72; Stephen B. Jones, "Geography and Politics in the Hawaiian Islands," *Geographical Review*, XXXVIII (April 1938), 211.

The last several decades have witnessed the entry into politics of citizens of ethnic groups not dependent upon *haole* economic and political leadership for their livelihood or advancement. Politically, their opportunity lay in the perennially disorganized Democratic party. From World War II the hegemony of the *haole*, transliterated in political terms of ties with the Republican party control, has been challenged. As might be expected, one of its manifestations has been the burgeoning of the Democratic party in the Islands and the overturning of the near monopoly which the Republicans long enjoyed. A new power element has been introduced into the political scene, one which is fully understandable only through a knowledge of Hawaii's ethnic past. Lest these new developments too readily be interpreted as just an ethnic drive, particularly a move by the Oriental majority, organized through the Democratic party against the *haole* minority, it need only be pointed out that in the first statehood general elections held in Hawaii, the Republicans ran as candidates but one *haole* for the five top federal and state posts to be filled, while the Democrats ran three. Similarly, when in 1962, Democrats for the first time elected both governor and lieutenant governor, *haoles* and Hawaiians, respectively, vied for these posts. As on the mainland, ethnic factors within the Islands' population enter into politics, but are hardly sufficient in themselves to determine the outcome.

EDUCATIONAL POLITICS

A good part of the explanation for the upward mobility of Hawaii's ethnic groups lies in the Islands' educational system. Relatively early in the history of the monarchy, an Islands-wide, centralized public school system was established. Despite certain past discouragement of high school education for the laboring groups, which carried with it ethnic overtones, students were not expressly barred because of their race. Paralleling the public schools is a private educational structure, many of its schools with parochial ties. Some of the latter were founded for the express purpose of educating non-*haoles*, and even the most exclusive, whose student bodies are primarily *haole*, admit students of other races.[12] Publicly supported collegiate education dates back to the founding in 1907 of what is now the University of Hawaii, supplemented recently by small, private, denominational colleges. It is this system which has equipped Hawaii's polyglot population with the understanding, ideals, and skills necessary to participate in political affairs, and prepared the children of the immigrant plantation laborers to enter Island business and professional life and play their part in Hawaii's peculiar game of ethnic musical chairs.

Considerable dissatisfaction has been voiced over the central board of education's alleged lack of concern for grass-roots opinion. The state constitution originally provided for a state board appointed from nominees named by local advisory boards. At the special session in 1959 which followed statehood, an amendment to require election of the state board of education was pushed through the Democrat-controlled House of Representatives. However, the Republican majority in the Senate killed the proposal, and it was not until 1964 that the Democratic majorities in both houses of the legislature placed the issue of an elected board on the ballot. Meanwhile, provision for popular election of the local advisory boards

12. There is an exception—Kamehameha Schools, which were established for the education of Hawaiians.

dissipated some of the pressure demanding grass-roots participation. Neverthe-less, with the PTA militantly advocating an elected school board, the constitu-tional amendment passed by a ratio of 7 to 3. The success of the amendment only opened a whole series of new problems to be resolved, among them the state board's membership, the method of electing its members, and the state board's relationship to the local advisory boards. For the 1966 elections, the state legisla-ture specified that eight members were to be elected from school board districts and three at large from the City and County of Honolulu. It also made provision for both partisan and nonpartisan candidates, and run-offs at the general election. Since the Republican party offered no candidates, as to be expected the Demo-crats captured ten of the eleven board seats. However, with the formal problems met, many other difficulties remain to be solved as the new board prepares to establish its place in the Hawaiian polity.

Island sentiment has long favored the establishment of public institutions of higher learning. In addition to the main campus of the University, a branch in Hilo offers a junior college curriculum, and pressure on the University regents to set up similar institutions in other Neighbor Islands has been heavy. The spread of Hono-lulu's population also favors the provision of comparable education on Oahu at sites removed from the main campus of the University. In an attempt to place all higher education in the hands of the regents, post-secondary technical schools have been transferred from the jurisdiction of the state Department of Education, and the regents are establishing a statewide system of two-track community col-leges as well as continuing to operate the University of Hawaii.

NEWS MEDIA AND PUBLIC OPINION

Hawaii's press, like most other Island activity, is concentrated in Honolulu. Nineteen newspapers are published regularly in the state. However, only one of the seven which are issued daily, the *Hilo Tribune-Herald* is published outside Honolulu. The weekly *Garden Island* serves Kauai, and the *Maui News* appears twice-weekly on Maui. All others, whatever their frequency of publication, ema-nate from Honolulu.[13]

When circulation is considered, the pattern of concentration is even more evident. Readership of more than 15,000 can be claimed by only two newspapers (excluding the suburban advertising media), the morning *Honolulu Advertiser* and the evening *Honolulu Star-Bulletin*, both of which fly daily editions to the Neighbor Islands. Average daily sales of the *Star-Bulletin* now exceed 112,000, approximately 67 percent more than those of the *Advertiser*. The *Sunday Star-Bulletin and Advertiser*, produced by the *Advertiser*, enjoys a current circulation of approximately 160,000 copies.

The *Star-Bulletin* is a member of the Associated Press, houses the local office of this association, and maintains a Washington Bureau. The *Advertiser* is serviced by United Press International and accommodates its Hawaii office. Together these newspapers share a modern production, advertising, and circulation facility, and the majority stock of both is locally owned, thereby freeing them from any controlling "chain" attachments. In format, size, coverage, and features these dai-lies compare favorably with those published in metropolitan areas with compara-ble population. National and international events are given special attention in

13. N. W. Ayers and Sons, *Directory Newspapers and Periodicals*, 1965 (Philadelphia, 1965).

weekly inserts. Whereas in the recent past each news organization was commercially allied with a radio-television outlet, both have sold their television and radio interests.

All newspapers in Hawaii maintain either a "Republican" or an "Independent" editorial policy. Insofar as press political policy may be viewed as an asset, the Republicans have enjoyed a distinct statewide advantage, most keenly felt in Democratic circles. Notwithstanding, the Democrats have mounted no sustained attacks on Hawaii's press coverage; rather, most party leaders appear to have believed that greater advantage could be gained by exploiting the competitive position of the two major dailies. Such informal strategy has, in recent years, resulted in considerable dividends for Democrats, including the fact, however coincidental, that the two long-time Republican statewide dailies now officially list themselves as "Independent."

The *Honolulu Star-Bulletin*, owned and published by a group of Honolulu businessmen who in 1961-62 bought it from the one-time politically prominent Farrington family, has recently abandoned its traditional official listing of "Independent Republican" for that of "Independent," while the *Advertiser* has moved during the past decade from an extremely conservative Republican position to an "Independent" policy as of the period 1958-59. The *Advertiser*'s policy is perhaps best illustrated by its open endorsement of Democrat Daniel K. Inouye for the U.S. House of Representatives in the 1959 statehood general election, by equally firm support for Republican Governor William Quinn at the same election, by its support in 1962 of Inouye for a U.S. Senate seat against Republican Benjamin F. Dillingham whose family was a prominent stockholder, and by the 1964 endorsement of Lyndon B. Johnson for President of the United States. Such an election-time policy not only underscores a departure from the straight Republican-line stand formerly taken by the *Advertiser*, but also serves to assure the Island public of a contrast to the policy positions of the *Star-Bulletin*.

Since 1953, radio and television broadcasting in Hawaii has expanded rapidly, so that the state now has 24 radio stations (17 on Oahu), 5 television stations, and more than 15 television satellite outlets. All of which means that competition has been keen and that the consuming statewide public has not lacked for a choice, at least within the limits defined by such competition. Such development also means that candidates for public office have come to rely heavily upon these media and to allocate large portions of their budgets for this purpose. During the period 1955-62 in particular, Democrats found them a very useful alternative to other outlets. The plethora of stations has provided ample opportunity for experimentation with many call-in type shows and for the presentation of several public service political series involving considerable production effort. Several radio stations and two television outlets have, from time to time, aired a management editorial policy. Until 1964, all television stations (three allied with national networks) were locally owned, but none now fully retains this status. What, if any, effect this significant commercial change will have upon local public service programming or times available for political broadcasting by, or in behalf of, candidates cannot as yet be evaluated.[14]

Other than opinion which has emerged from the vote of a statewide public at election time and impressionistic, partial glimpses obtained from letters-to-the-

14. An educational television station under the supervision of the University of Hawaii began operations in 1967.

editor columns and interest-group publications, very little is known about state-wide public opinion in Hawaii on a continuing basis. Because the territorial delegate lacked a vote and his role relegated him to a position of less influence in Washington than that enjoyed by the appointed governor through the secretary of the interior, popular interest in the delegate race never coalesced. Except at brief moments when all Hawaii has appeared united, as in the ground-swell support for the appointment of Samuel Wilder King as governor, little occasion for universal expression of opinion presented itself until 1959, when five statewide positions were filled at the first state election.

In 1948 and again in 1955, fairly comprehensive surveys of political opinion were conducted by the Hawaiian Economic Service. These and other indicia showed little change over the years in the pattern of personal identification with political parties until 1959. In 1955, most islanders (52 percent) appeared to consider themselves "Independents"; about 20 percent claimed Republican and 28 percent Democratic identification. The 1955 survey also gave some depth insight into issues, showing that Hawaii's citizens were most concerned about job opportunities, schools, taxes, housing or sewerage, roads, streets, and the high cost of living and that many (36-42 percent) voters who held opinions felt that neither major political party was "being run" by a "special group." Some 28 percent identified the Republican party with business groups and 1 percent with labor groups, while 17 percent tied Democrats with labor and 2 percent with business.[15]

Other surveys conducted in 1959, 1961, and 1963 have provided some further insight concerning Island attitudes toward political issues. A majority (53 percent) of the persons interviewed by a Democratic-sponsored poll in 1959 cited some "economic" matter as being the Islands' biggest problem—the need for new industry, for more jobs, for land reform. Thirty-three percent mentioned educational problems. Next in line of concern were taxes (22 percent) and roads (13 percent). Six percent were fearful of future strikes. In addition, this poll reported that 39 percent considered themselves "Independent"; 36 percent, Republican; and 25 percent Democratic.[16] A 1961 poll conducted by a University of Hawaii group revealed that when pushed to voice a preference for apparent future party programs, 57 percent selected the Democratic party and only 29 percent, the Republican party.[17] Subsequently, in 1963, a poll conducted by the State Department of Transportation showed public interest in issue-image areas to fall in the following order: better public schools, inter-island transportation, land reform, county projects, and a foreign trade center.[18] The program of the Democratic party during the past decade has stressed most of these issues, and the findings of these recent surveys have been largely confirmed by subsequent election results.

Publics identified with a particular island have long been evident in Hawaii. They have actively expressed themselves at county and legislative elections, with attention usually focused more upon personalities than upon issues. With enlargement of the legislature and its reapportionment shortly before statehood, these diverse cultural, economic, and religious publics were given additional opportunity for expression and, through their representatives, figured prominently in the

15. *Honolulu Advertiser*, November 17, 1955, p. D-1.
16. Louis Harris and Associates, Inc., "A Study of Voter Preferences and Attitudes in the Hawaiian Islands," May 1959, p. 15.
17. *Sunday Advertiser*, November 26, 1961, pp. 1-1A.
18. State of Hawaii, Department of Transportation, *Inter-Island Ferry System: Public Opinion Poll–1963* (Honolulu, 1964).

continuing 1964-65 struggle to reapportion the state Senate. Generally, however, the content and contrast of their collective attitudes and the extent of their influence have yet to be analyzed fully.

NOMINATIONS AND ELECTIONS

All adult citizens, twenty years or over, may register and vote in Hawaii excepting those who are unpardoned felons, mentally incompetent, or illiterate. State citizenship is achieved only after a year's residence. By express provision of the constitution, illiteracy is defined as inability "to speak, read and write the English or Hawaiian languages."[19] The Hawaiian component of the Islands' population has long been able to meet an English test, so attention to the enforcement of a comparable literacy provision in the Organic Act was unnecessary. However, with the recent relaxation of the federal naturalization laws, permitting a number of aged Oriental residents to achieve citizenship after passing examinations in their ancestral tongues, this limitation has again assumed temporary importance. In view of the youth of Hawaii's population, the reduction of the voting age to twenty in 1959 has greater import than would be true for a similar change on the mainland. The impact of this new voting group on Island politics has yet to be evaluated.

Hawaii has a system of permanent registration. Once an elector registers, as long as he continues to vote at the primary and general elections his name remains on the official rolls. Periodically the rolls are purged. Hawaii prides itself on its consistently high turnout of voters at the polls. Lest it be assumed that the phenomenal 93 percent vote of the 183,000 registered voters at the July 1959 general election can be explained solely in terms of enthusiasm for statehood, it need merely be pointed out that in the 1958 election, 88 percent of the 175,000 registrants appeared at the polls, that 90 percent turned out in both 1962 and 1964, and 87 percent of the 253,000 registrants in 1966. Even if these percentages were to be discounted by computing into the base the unregistered citizens otherwise qualified to vote, Hawaii's election participation would yet remain high when measured by mainland standards.[20]

Officers are elected to federal, state, and county posts at the general election after having first succeeded in obtaining nomination at a primary election. By amendment added in 1967, nonpartisan candidates will have to run at the primary; and for their names to appear on the general election ballot, they must have received at least 10 percent of the total vote cast at the primary. In view of the refusal to apply a narrow construction to the definition of "political party," it may be easier to run as a candidate of a splinter group, which need merely declare itself in token fashion to be a party, as did the "Commonwealth party" which ran candidates in 1958 and 1959.[21]

Neither the new state constitution nor subsequent legislation has modifed election dates or most other long-standing electoral procedures. The people of

19. A constitutional amendment to eliminate the literacy qualification for voting was defeated in 1964 by 72,529 to 79,211 (with 62,954 voters not voting on the question).

20. An estimated 84.4 percent of the population eligible to vote under the state's constitution actually voted in 1964; despite the claim of large abstentions from registering, it is estimated that as much as 80 percent of the eligible population participated in the 1966 election.

21. Several candidates seeking office under a "nonpartisan" label were, by court order, placed on the 1964 general election ballot.

Hawaii still choose their legislators from multi-membered tickets, inasmuch as the century-old practice of multi-membered districts remains unchanged.[22] Hawaii continues to hold its primary elections on the first Saturday of October in each even-numbered year and, approximately one month later, on the Tuesday after the first Monday in November, its general elections.

For the last quarter-century territorial and county elections have been consolidated, and statehood has not disturbed the dominant part played by the central government in their conduct. Joint elections continue to be held at the same time, place, and with one set of election officers. The governor and lieutenant governor determine the number and size of precincts, locate the polling places, and appoint the election officials. Automatic data processing of ballots cast on punch-cards was instituted in 1968 for about 85 percent of the electorate. State instructions guide the election officials, and state appropriations cover the salaries of poll officers at both primary and general elections as well as the expenses of setting up the polls. Ballot and supply expenses are shared between the state and the several counties. Only on rare occasions will a county be called upon to meet the full cost of an election, as in 1958 when Honolulu voted at a special election on the adoption of a proposed charter.

Since 1949, Hawaii's primary law may be best classified as "open." In that year, legislation (promptly signed by the governor in order to prevent quick recall) deprived the voter of his earlier privilege of cross-voting. However, pursuant to a law passed in 1963 (after years of aborted platform pledges made by both major parties), the state is now moving toward a fully "closed" partisan primary in 1970. Under this legislation, registrars in 1968 will record the party preferences of all primary voters and each will receive only the ballot of his party in the 1970 primary unless at least three months prior to the primary he registers a change of party affiliation. New voters in the 1970 and subsequent primaries will be free without restriction to make an initial selection of a party ballot, and, prior to 1970, all primary voters will be similarly free of such restrictions, save that no one shall receive the ballot (now consolidated) of more than one political party. Although voter reaction to the new primary law is difficult to appraise, some voter objection to the initial stage, namely, loss of the choice of a party ballot inside the voting booth, and to the consolidated party ballot was apparent in the 1964 and 1966 primaries. However, since participation dropped only slightly, appeals for prompt repeal by a few state lawmakers failed to result in serious consideration of such action. It is also well known that Governor John A. Burns is a continuing advocate of the "closed" primary system.

To prevent the subversion of the election process, Hawaii's election laws expressly declare it to be a crime to bribe voters or to seek to influence them through threat or promise of reward. Similarly, interruption of the orderly process of the holding of an election is made criminal. Harkening back to the days of election *luaus* (feasts), the furnishing of food or entertainment on election day to affect the vote is proscribed by law. As an added precaution, candidates and parties may not locate their headquarters on premises licensed to sell alcoholic beverages nor may campaigning take place within 1,000 feet of polling places.

Within twenty days following an election, both candidates and agents or committees acting on their behalf are required to file sworn itemized statements

22. An observation subject to change due to this being one of the major issues before the constitutional convention which is to meet in July of 1968.

of expenditures. Although permissible expenditures are detailed in the law—printing and advertising, stationery and postage, rent and supplies, salaries of clerks and messengers, poll watchers, and a candidate's personal expenses—no maximum amount is stipulated. The Democrats publicly acknowledge that at the 1959 state primary and general elections the equivalent of more than $600,000 was spent "by or on behalf of the Democratic party,"[23] and the lavish campaigns on the part of some Republican aspirants that year suggest that GOP expenditures materially exceeded that amount. In subsequent campaigns, although party expenditures do not appear to have greatly increased, spending on behalf of most candidates has grown by as much as 25 percent. Post-campaign statements of many candidates uniformly fail to reflect comprehensive accounting, and committees, as has been most customary, do not even bother to file. A 1954 test of the validity of Hawaii's corrupt practices law found Hawaii's Supreme Court holding the filing of the reports by candidates to be mandatory, but silent on the inadequacy of the law's administration.[24] In the absence of effective policing, this portion of Hawaii's corrupt practices law has become virtually meaningless.

PARTY ORGANIZATION AND PARTY LEADERS

Beyond defining a political party and directing each organization to file a list of its officers before the primary election, Hawaii's statutes leave virtually all other party matters to be resolved by the parties themselves. As a result, both the Republicans and Democrats operate under rules established by their respective state conventions. Although legally free to experiment, both have generally followed mainland precedents and have constructed organizations which are remarkably alike.

Because Hawaii has yet to experience a genuine closed primary law, the parties have been forced not only to develop organizational structures and procedures, but also to define and record membership.[25] Each limits participation to those who have registered with the party and who carry properly authenticated "party cards." Any elector or person eligible to become one at the next state general election may, without fee, join. The Republicans will, in addition, accept persons as young as sixteen.

The organizational hierarchy is essentially the same for both parties. It includes precinct clubs (246), district committees (18, corresponding to the state House of Representatives districts), county committees (4), and the state committee. Both parties hold state conventions, the Republicans meeting annually and the Democrats, biennially. In order to minimize the adverse effects of factionalism, for the past ten years Republicans have chosen their officers in off-election years and reserved pre-election conventions mainly for platform drafting. Since 1958, Democrats have provided for county conventions which must meet at least semiannually.

As a territory, Hawaii did not participate in presidential elections. Notwithstanding, since 1900 Hawaii's parties have sent voting delegates to national conventions and have enjoyed representation on the national committees equal to that accorded each of the several states. Both parties continue to utilize the state

23. *Honolulu Advertiser*, August 16, 1959, p. A-23.
24. *Territory v. Fasi* (1954) 40 Haw. 478.
25. Since 1963, county clerks are required to maintain party membership lists deposited with them as a public record.

convention for choosing national delegates and committee members. Normally, there is some preconvention maneuvering, but delegates customarily go to the national conventions uncommitted to presidential aspirants and unbound by any unit rule. Despite the deterrent of distance, Hawaii is usually well represented at major national party meetings today, including those sponsored by youth and women's organizations.[26]

Enrolled party members in Hawaii probably do not exceed 15 percent of the electorate, and only a fraction of these are active in organizational work. Membership bookkeeping has been poor and contests over membership status have plagued more than a few precinct clubs, particularly at times when territorial or state convention delegates were being chosen. Even today, neither party can give a precise membership total. The county clerks are now directed to receive membership lists from the county committees of political parties and maintain a filing system. Republicans have been able for some years to maintain a fairly permanent secretariat, but Democrats have been able to do so only in very recent years.

Many precinct clubs are inactive in both parties save at biennial club election meetings, and some fail to function even then. The district committees (newly created since reapportionment in 1958) and county committees tend to be more efficiently handled. During the territorial period, central committees were never very active because only the delegate contest occurred on a territory-wide basis and there was little business to transact. Most activity at this level centered around the territorial chairman. With statehood, candidates now seek six statewide elective offices, and minor revitalization of the central committees has been noted.

State conventions, like their national counterparts, are large, unwieldy assemblies, usually numbering around 1,400 delegates in the Republican and about 1,000 in the Democratic organization. Proxy systems (modified in more recent years) prevail in both parties to augment delegates in actual attendance.[27] All but a few of the delegates attend as a result of their selection at the precinct level. Platforms, usually drafted with great care, have been less well publicized in recent years than in the decade of the fifties.

Rules of both parties provide for revocation of membership, but seldom is any attempt made to enforce them. Although active support of candidates running under the aegis of the opposite party is cause for dismissal, such practice customarily goes unpunished. Censure at the polls has appeared to be equally difficult.

Hawaii's party organizations today are in most respects similar to those in other states. Membership-wise, they are probably more aware of their weak foundations than parties in jurisdictions where affiliations are registered publicly for primary election participation. Lack of sufficient organization workers, reliance upon part-time volunteer leadership, poorly equipped secretariats, unwieldy basic policy bodies, factional quarrels, and lack of funds combine to insure that only those tasks which somehow must be accomplished are actually undertaken.

Interparty competition has developed rapidly since 1954, but personality politics remains a dominant tendency. Prior to 1954, this approach seemed to be the only way whereby Democrats could secure even isolated offices. The Republicans, too, had many a "lone wolf," although, in the main, Republican candidates

26. See David, Paul T., Malcolm Moos, and Ralph M. Goldman, (eds.), *Presidential Nominating Politics in 1952: The West* (Baltimore: Johns Hopkins Press, 1954), V, 268-84.

27. Republicans held the first Neighbor Islands state convention in 1962, with a significant decline in attendance.

were apparently able to sweep into office on the basis of their party's support by the dominant economic groups and the feebleness of the Democratic opposition. There has been no sustained effort in either party to encourage the development of leadership separate from the successful or perennially aspiring candidates. The lesser economic groups in Hawaii, later to constitute core strength for the Democratic party, had neither the time, resources, nor educational background to support many who could be termed party leaders as opposed to candidate personalities. The dominant economic (and usually well-educated) groups, content with their possession of political influence through the Republican party, had little reason to build a strong professional party leadership which might substantially differ with them. Lack of a hierarchy of elective offices in the past may have been a major deterrent not only to many persons who might otherwise have risked the uncertainties of political careers, but also to others who would have been attracted to leadership positions within the party if there had been greater scope for their political talents. Today's viable two-party system and the newly created federal and state elective offices augur well for the appearance of a more strongly institutionalized party leadership, but, as was apparent in the 1966 primary, noticeable progress in the Democratic party is contradicted by grave leadership identification problems evident within the opposition group.

Current leadership patterns in both of Hawaii's parties largely reflect the dynamics of interparty competition which led to the spectacular Democratic successes of 1962, 1964, and 1966, and to the conversion of the state from a Republican to an apparent Democratic stronghold. The intensified efforts within each party to institutionalize leadership through party organization have not been able to overcome these dynamic external factors. Intra-party conflicts have also militated against strong cohesion.

In perspective, this situation reveals a remarkable case study concerning the power of reform or innovation politics over a politics of orthodoxy. As of the period 1959-60, the ascending hopes of Democrats for a first-time sweep of state (or territorial) government were stymied by the shambles of their 1959 statehood election effort. Then (1959), unwilling to assign a high priority to the matter of statewide leadership, they failed to build up five years of pre-statehood legislative-level electoral success and, due to overt factionalism, lost the gubernatorial contest as well as control of the state Senate. Contrariwise, many disheartened Republicans felt that the election of a governor would resolve their problems of leadership which had been mounting since 1952. However, in 1962, two remarkable developments occurred. Democrats, after a stormy state convention early in the year, cast aside factionalism and found surprising unity in the gubernatorial candidacy of former delegate John A. Burns and the congressional candidacy of Thomas P. Gill, both of whom had been leaders of major factional groups. In addition, as these partisans placed their party "reform" program above and beyond factionalism, theretofore divided Island labor groups established a "unified front," meaning that the usual warring International Longshoremen's and Warehousemen's Union, the AFL-CIO, and the Teamsters "buried the hatchet" to help Democrats tout their unity theme. Second, liberal Republican Governor William F. Quinn soon found himself opposed by his own, more orthodox partisans in the state Senate. Unable to obtain majority Republican senators to work with him, he ended up fighting for his political life in a 1962 primary with his lieutenant governor, James K. Kealoha—a bitter contest that undoubtedly contributed to his defeat later that year.

Today, Democratic leadership fans out, with uncommon precision (for this party), in a series of concentric circles which on the state and local levels revolve about Governor John A. Burns, Lieutenant Governor Thomas P. Gill, House Speaker Tadao Beppu, Senate President John Hulten, Honolulu Councilman Matsuo Takabuki and Maui Chairman Elmer Kravalho. This core is supplemented on the national level by Senator Daniel K. Inouye and Congressmen Spark M. Matsunaga and Patsy Takemoto Mink. Of these on the day-to-day front, the influence of Burns, Kravalho, and Takabuki appears to be pre-eminent, and a corps of officers generally agreeable to their definitions of party program and procedures stand at the helm of both the state and Honolulu party committees. This is not to imply that areas of tenuousness are not present to disturb the pattern. Although Hawaii's presidential form of executive government tends to rule out excessive factionalism in the sphere of administration, legislative and organizational dissent are not infrequent. On numerous occasions in recent legislative sessions, the Democratic majority in the state Senate was split, and the leadership was forced to rely upon Republican cross-over support. Also, dissappointed with the Governor's seeming lack of interest in the organizational party, dissident voices occasionally complain and threaten revolt. A bitter intra-party fight in the 1966 Democratic primary threatened loss of the governorship, which was avoided only by strenuous work to patch up differences and heal wounds. Notwithstanding, Governor Burns's party leadership position appears to be as real as the title suggests.

Republican leadership problems, resharpened by the Kealoha-Quinn rift which materially contributed to the latter's defeat for a second elective term in 1962, continue to plague this party. Although the re-election of Republican U.S. Senator Hiram L. Fong and Honolulu Mayor Neal S. Blaisdell in 1964 halted further depression in Republican ranks, neither officeholder is widely viewed as one around whom much long-range party rebuilding will rally. Senator Fong's lines of communication to the Islands are obviously long; Mayor Blaisdell has consistently depended upon background campaign assistance from Democrats, and neither gentleman, by age, is well equipped to attract and mobilize young talent to the Republican cause. Yet both are recognized as able leaders. Beyond such factors, state organizational rebuilding under the new leadership of former territorial secretary Edward E. Johnston is in large part devoted to the identification and encouragement of new young leaders who can assume key statewide roles by 1970. These include state senators D. G. "Andy" Anderson, Percy Mirkitani, Fred Rohlfing, and Wadsworth Yee. Other party stalwarts can be expected to assist materially in party rebuilding, with emphasis upon the location of young recruits and attractive new platform planks. Recognizing the hindrance of long-standing ideological rifts, which were heightened by 1964 pro- and anti-Goldwater differences, state chairman Johnston apparently seeks to build a GOP which will minimize all labels other than that of the party itself.

PRESSURE GROUPS

There are at least 250 interest organizations in a position to influence the course of governmental policy in Hawaii. All attempts to enact a lobby registration law have failed, so any catalog of groups which such a law might afford is lacking. In the absence of provision for popularly initiated legislation, these groups exert pressure on government mainly through lobbying in the legislative and executive branches.

Lobbying on an organized basis characterizes post-World War II Hawaii to a far greater extent than in the prewar years, when large businesses and business groups could mainly direct their appeal locally to the "organizational man" of the Republican party. The art of influence was confined largely to the use of highly direct and personal techniques by sugar, pineapple, shipping, and mercantile interests. With ownership and management interlocked in an intricate pattern, these groups were able with little apparent difficulty to block legislation inimical to their basic interests. Even the fact that the vicissitudes of national presidential elections might see the appointment of an unfriendly governor did little to threaten such a situation. Whenever necessary, these groups could and did forward to Washington, without much fear of contradiction, information favorable to their interests, sufficient to satisfy national leaders who had little reason to become concerned about problems of the mid-Pacific.

Apart from sporadic labor movements with an ethnic character, labor unions were slow to develop in Hawaii. The American Federation of Labor primarily concerned itself with organizing urban occupations and missed the opportunity to unionize the plantations. By 1946, the International Longshoremen's and Warehousemen's Union had not only organized the dockhands but could also claim most plantation workers as members. AFL activity had also borne results in greatly expanded representation. Labor contracts in force jumped from a mid-war figure of 12 to 167 in 1946. By mid-century labor groups had been sufficiently successful in their immediate economic objectives to exert growing political influence. The CIO Committee on Political Action became active in 1944, and COPE, which came into being in the early 1950's, has given evidence of growing effectiveness since the first state election.

Contemporaneously, rapid organization was also taking place on professional, civic, and broad social fronts. Businessmen intensified their efforts to organize. Today, pressure groups cover virtually the entire spectrum of human endeavor in the Islands. Not all attempt direct legislative lobbying, but those which do have found a fertile field in Hawaii's environment of rapid political change.

The larger pressure groups employ full-time executive secretaries, professional lobbyists, or both. Those which do not, usually retain, on a part-time basis, attorneys or others skilled in public presentations, including former legislators. Most evident in legislative corridors are the representatives of the chambers of commerce (organized along both geographic and ethnic lines), the ILWU, the Hawaii Government Employees Association, the United Public Workers, the AFL-CIO, the Hawaii Education Association, Tax Foundation, Visitors Bureau, Hotel Association, and Small Business Association. Individual concerns, such as a number of airlines and shippers, and the several counties all have their own representation in direct attendance during the legislative sessions. Although during the decade of the fifties most major pressure groups utilized mass media in an effort directly to influence public opinion and, thereby, public policy formulation, these groups have recently abandoned such efforts.

Official and covert endorsements of candidates for public office have been made by a growing number of organizations during the past 10 years. Thus, major unions in Hawaii customarily make public endorsements for most elective offices. Public employee and teacher groups have become increasingly aggressive in this regard. Business groups have, on the whole, been more restrained in their public pronouncements, but a number remain heavily involved behind the scenes and today, unlike the past, may support Democratic as well as Republican candidates.

Although the tendency toward selective endorsements may be cited as the general rule, when labor unity has been realized, as in 1962, it has contributed markedly to the success of the Democratic party.

Most controversial of all pressure groups is the International Longshoremen's and Warehousemen's Union, largely because of its solidarity, aggressiveness, and the alleged past Communist associations of its leadership. It shares control with shipping companies over Hawaii's vital surface transportation link with the mainland. Moreover, its participation in the rapid development of the Democratic party after World War II early caused division in party ranks and remains, today, as a background problem.

The ILWU is recognized as a major factor in most county, district, and state races. Candidates of both parties from all but districts of high socio-economic rank customarily hope for union neutrality or seek union support. Neighbor Island politics is far more responsive to union wishes than that on Oahu. Estimates suggest that the union currently influences 10,000 to 20,000 votes on a statewide basis, but only 3,000 to 6,000 votes on Oahu. Well known in political circles is the rule-of-thumb appraisal which past election results support: the ILWU, except in its strongholds of Kauai and Maui, may not be able to elect you, but in any island and some statewide elections, it can most certainly defeat you, barring extraordinary personal popularity and campaign effort.

Since 1956, the ILWU has sought to pitch its political pronouncements to a lower key. It has been less active on radio and has now abandoned public circulation of a much-discussed press organ. Notwithstanding, the group's political effectiveness was recently well illustrated when in 1964 it played a significant role in the re-election of U.S. Senator Hiram Fong over Congressman Thomas P. Gill who enjoyed the support of most other segments of Hawaii labor.

Since 1960, with the establishment of more harmonious labor-management relations, the public political role of the ILWU has been muted, and few political leaders have been inclined openly to fan old flames or to publicize a general breakup of the "labor unity" observable in 1962. Whereas the political role of the ILWU was much discussed in the gubernatorial contest of 1959, its efforts concerning the same race (between identical finalists) in 1962 were seldom singled out for debate. Explanations for this may be found in a complex series of developments, not the least of which is the rapid emergence of a more diverse economy and an overriding desire on the part of business for labor peace in a period of unparalleled Island affluence. Nevertheless, the administrative and legislative influence of the ILWU has developed apace, stands now at its highest level, and enjoys formal representation (previously denied) in governmental circles. Further expansion of its present prominent role is, however, problematical, due to continued economic change, shifts in basic internal characteristics of the union, and the probable effects of state legislative reapportionment on Hawaii vote patterns.

LEGISLATIVE POLITICS

In the past, the legislature has been the keystone of party politics in Hawaii, playing a role in policy-making that was relatively greater than that of most counterparts on the mainland because of the Islands' extremely centralized administrative system. Legislators have not been adverse to fishing in local governmental waters, passing special legislation for particular counties, sometimes to the chagrin of the county officials. The simplicity of Hawaii's system of local government and the absence of "home rule" powers which would label areas of municipal jurisdiction as *kapu* (protected, sacrosanct) have facilitated such legislative interference. Hawaii's new constitution authorizes local self-government charters, but the first attempt to draft them suffered a setback in 1964 when the voters in all three of the Neighbor Islands rejected the charters proposed by locally appointed commissions.[28] It was not until 1968 that all the counties finally succeeded in obtaining self-government. The constitution also contemplates the conferring of powers upon local units by general laws only. As legislators are now becoming familiar with the technique of classifying counties, it is questionable whether this restriction will mark any significant change in past practice.

No person is eligible to serve in Hawaii's twenty-five member Senate unless he has attained the age of thirty. Delegates to the fifty-one membered House of Representatives must be at least twenty-five. Residence in Hawaii for three years and status as a qualified voter of the district from which the candidate seeks to be elected are also required. Most states fix lower minimum age and shorter residence requirements: nevertheless, legislators in Hawaii tend to be relatively young, and the three-year span of residence may well carry little importance, as nearly all legislators are *kamaainas* (native-born), or long-time residents. In the 1965 state legislature, for example, more than four-fifths of the members were born in the Islands, and the non-*kamaainas* for the most part had long Island residence. The median age of the senators was fifty, their seniority contrasting with the forty-two year median age of the representatives. Admitting incomplete data for previous sessions, it would appear that until recently the average age of legislators had been gradually declining during the last three decades. The introduction of young blood into political activity since World War II clearly showed its impact in this manner; however, by 1965 this trend apparently had been slowed if not reversed.

For many years, lawyers comprised the largest single occupational group in the legislature, but their number slipped from a majority in 1959 to about three-eighths in the 1965 legislature. The election of labor leaders as representatives has lost all novelty. Each session a few women are elected, but in the main, their role has been minor, with their influence greatest in the areas of education and welfare. For the decade immediately prior to the augmentation in size of the 1959 legislature, between 50 and 60 percent of the members were returned to office at least once, while turnover statistics for previous comparable periods indicate that only 40-50 percent came back to the legislative halls. After the expansion of the legislature, this longevity was accelerated, and by 1965 about seven-eighths of the legislators serving were veterans of some previous session. The over-all impact of these changes has been to emphasize the role of the professional legislator.

Legislators in Hawaii do not mirror well the characteristics of the population which elected them. Distributively, the ethnic composition of the legislature has tended to reflect that of Hawaii's adult citizen population,[29] with the Japanese component currently a little exaggerated. Members' religious affiliations are atypical, Protestants exceeding the combined number of Roman Catholics and Buddhists. Legislators are better educated; non-*haoles* display greater virtuosity in their ancestral tongues;[30] more of them are married; and, on the average, all enjoy a higher socio-economic status than is true of the adult population of Hawaii. All

28. The Honolulu self-government charter was adopted prior to statehood in 1958.

29. See Meller, "Centralization in Hawaii," p. 103.

30. See Norman Meller, "Bilingualism in Island Legislatures of the Pacific as an Index of Acculturation—A Hypothesis," *Sociology and Social Research*, XLIII (July-August 1959), 408.

this lends credence to the conclusion that the Islanders seek qualified men for their legislative halls, rather than merely choosing at random among their own ranks.

Republican strength in Hawaii has best been illustrated by the number of party members elected to the legislature. After the "Lady Dog Legislature" of 1901 in which the Home Rulers captured a majority of seats, the Republicans organized[31] every subsequent one until 1955. The success of the Democrats in electing half the members of the House of Representatives in 1946 carried the portent of events to come, even though one Democrat ultimately joined with the Republicans in the 1947 session to permit them to organize the House. Finally, in 1955 the Democrats succeeded in obtaining a majority in each house, a feat they duplicated in 1957 and 1959. With the statehood elections in 1959, the Democratic tide superficially appeared abated when the Republicans again captured control of the Senate. However, the collapse of the Republican party occurred in 1963 when the Democrats swept both houses of the legislature (as well as secured the gubernatorial post) and remained evident as the Democrats continued to hold fifty-five seats to the Republicans' twenty-one in 1965 and lost only one of these legislative posts to the Republicans in 1967.

The party profiles in the legislature markedly contrast the differences consistently appearing over the last decade despite the enlargement by nearly two-thirds of each house, reapportionment, statehood, and now the transfer of majority control. On the average, the Democratic legislator is younger, more highly educated, and more apt to be Island-born than his Republican counterpart. Ethnically, Hawaiians and *haoles* account for larger components of the Republican while Orientals and other Caucasians make up the bulk of the Democratic delegation. More Democrats than Republicans give their occupations as lawyers, while the number of members who are self-employed or managerial employees has consistently loomed larger in Republican than Democratic ranks. Incomplete evidence would indicate comparable differences in religious affiliation (Republicans with more Protestant) and party participation (Republican legislators with a greater proportion of long-time party members as well as experience in party posts). Despite the introduction of new blood through the inclusion of "first termers" and the return of former members, sometimes after long absences, these same party profile differences appear in the statistics of the last few legislatures.

Republican legislative victories in the past were so complete that up to World War II, in only one session (1914) could a Democratic governor rely upon a large enough legislative minority of his own party to sustain his veto. Not until Governor Stainback's (Democrat) first term in 1945, did the Democrats finally obtain in each session more than a third of the membership in one of the legislative houses. With such a dominant position in the legislature until the end of World War II, the Republicans, when united, could force their program through for the whole of the Islands, irrespective of the political affiliation of the governor. When the Democrats commenced organizing the legislature in 1955, they found themselves in a power position in relation to the Republican-appointed governors that was comparable to the Republican position since 1945. It took them three sessions (1955, 1957, and the special session of 1957) to enlist the aid of a few sympathetic Republicans in order to pass a Democratic tax reform bill over a gubernatorial veto.

31. However, the majority of the 1903 House of Representatives, although nominally Republican, chose a Home Ruler as speaker and battled with a Republican governor. Today, the Democrats hold safe majorities in the House of Representatives (39-12) and Senate (15-10).

PARTY PROFILES IN RECENT HAWAIIAN LEGISLATURES

Background	Democrats					Republicans				
	1957 (30)	1959 (49)	1959◊ (44)	1963 (55)	1965 (55)	1965 (21)	1963 (21)	1959◊ (32)	1959 (27)	1957 (15)
Median Age (years)	43½	38	37	40	43	51	50	44	47	51
Ethnicity (%)□										
Hawaiian	13.3	10.2	9.1	12.7	10.9	23.8	28.6	21.9	25.9	6.7
Haole	13.3	16.3	9.1	7.3	9.1	42.9	38.1	43.7	37.0	53.3
Other Caucasian	13.3	6.1	9.1	9.1	9.1	4.8	4.8	6.2	3.7	
Japanese	53.3	57.1	63.6	58.2	56.4	28.6	28.6	25.0	25.9	40.0
Other Oriental	6.7	10.2	9.1	12.7	14.5			3.1	7.4	
	100.0	100.0	100.0	100.0	100.0	100.0	100.0	100.0	100.0	100.0
Education (%)										
At least 12th grade	96.7	95.9	97.7	96.4	96.4	80.9	80.9	93.7	88.9	86.7
At least college graduation	63.3	65.3	61.4	63.6	61.8	52.4	52.4	50.0	48.1	46.7
Advanced college degree	56.7	57.1	54.5	49.1	38.2	42.9	38.1	40.6	29.6	20.0
Place Born (%)□										
Same island as elected	53.3	57.1	75.0	70.9	63.6	57.1	52.4	50.0	51.8	46.7
Different island	30.0	24.5	13.6	16.4	21.8	19.0	19.0	21.9	22.3	20.0
Outside of Hawaii	16.7	18.4	11.4	12.7	14.5	23.8	28.6	28.1	25.9	33.3
	100.0	100.0	100.0	100.0	100.0	100.0	100.0	100.0	100.0	100.0
Occupation (%)□										
Lawyers△	56.7	55.1	59.1	49.1	38.2	33.3	38.1	40.6	33.3	26.7
Mgrs., employees, self-employed	23.3	20.4	11.3	20.0	30.9	47.6	42.9	43.8	40.8	60.0
Others	20.0	24.5	29.6	30.9	30.9	19.0	19.0	15.6	25.9	13.3
	100.0	100.0	100.0	100.0	100.0	100.0	100.0	100.0	100.0	100.0

◊The first legislative session in 1959 was territorial; the second, state.
□May not round off to 100%.
△Includes district court practitioner.

During the first year of statehood, continued Republican control of the governor's office and, once again, of the Senate assured that party a share in lawmaking somewhat reminiscent of its earlier role. It was not until the 1963 session of the state legislature that capture of both the legislature and the governor's post fixed unequivocal responsibility upon the Democrats for implementation of their party's program.

Both the Democratic platform and predispositions of the Democratic legislators are reflected in the actions taken by recent legislatures. Hawaii under the Republicans had been characterized by a high degree of economic centralization as well as government concentration in Honolulu. It is not surprising, then, that the Democrats have enacted property tax revision in various guises, all motivated by the desire to tax large land-holdings more adequately and encourage their maximum use; anti-trust legislation designed to introduce greater competition; and labor legislation taking such forms as a "little Norris-LaGuardia Act" and expanded unemployment compensation and workmen's compensation benefits. In the area of political decentralization, the Democrats initially transferred a number of functions from state to local government, authorized the counties to draft their Home Rule charters, and sought enlarged citizen participation by providing for the State Board of Education to be elective. Due to limited local resources, the 1965 Democratic legislature had seemingly to reverse its position on decentralization of government, and transferred to the state government practically full responsibility over education, health, and a miscellany of minor functions, the administration of which had previously been shared with the counties.[32]

Statewide land classification and green belt legislation comprise one possible example of where the Democratic delegation enabled the consideration of more complicated problems and the evaluation of more sophisticated solutions. The "home town boy" nature of the Democrats probably found expression in loan aid to small businessmen, economic development of the Neighbor Islands, and the initial drive for the strengthening of local government. Attempts to encourage home ownership, revision of the public land laws, and other comparable action may also be similarly attributed. But above all, concentrated attention upon the many facets of education, including expansion of programs and the major increase of public appropriations therefor, best marks the congruence of party program and pre-conditioning of Democratic legislators: for many of them, personal advancement from humble beginnings may be directly traced to opportunities opened by public schooling.

Various forms of non-party factionalism have long distinguished Island politics. The schism between Oahu and the Neighbor Islands assures that geographical lines may have greater impact upon certain issues than party labels. The position of any majority in the House of Representatives is particularly vulnerable inasmuch as Neighbor Island members until 1967 constituted a majority in the Senate. Party leaders were therefore obliged to compromise. Mandatory requirements for Neighbor Island membership on state boards and commissions and disproportionate (population-wise) allocation of state revenues have been the price of intra-party harmony.

Another deterrent to tighter party discipline in the legislature is the range of ideologies represented within each party, and powerful legislative figures have not hesitated to utilize this to their own advantage. The organization of the House of Representatives in 1953 by a Republican minority faction which joined with Democrats, and a comparable coalition of a Democratic minority which enlisted the aid of Republicans in 1959, both illustrate the leverage afforded to groups attendant on strong legislative figures. Democratic factionalism also emerged in 1967 in the state Senate, but in this instance the GOP exercised new-found organizational forbearance and avoided interparty coalition.

A final line of cleavage, which dramatically came to the fore at the state legislature's first special session of 1959, is that separating the two houses. Occasionally, chamber loyalty transcends all other factors. This was well evidenced

32. Democrats had not, however, at any time advocated giving responsibility for education to the counties. Public health has been almost wholly centrally administered, so the importance of the 1965 health amendments lies mainly in their symbolism.

when all fifty-one members of the House of Representatives, Democrats and Republicans, voted for adjournment because they considered the honor of the House had been impugned by Senate conferees allegedly reneging on a free conference agreement. In view of all of this, the growth of party polarization within the legislature will fall short of full realization unless it meets the challenge of countervailing pulls of geographical, ideological, and charismatic factionalism.

Forewarned by the inability of the territorial legislature to reapportion itself for half a century, the constitutional convention of 1950 provided for automatic gubernatorial apportionment of the lower house every decade. Should the governor fail to act, any registered voter may apply to the Supreme Court for a writ of mandamus to compel him to perform his duty. Errors made in reapportionment may similarly be corrected through court action. Even before the state constitution became effective, these provisions were engrafted into the Organic Act by Congress, moving to forestall judicial reapportionment as the result of a suit brought by a citizen resident of Honolulu claiming denial of equal protection and due process of law.[33]

The 1956 amendments to the Organic Act increased the size of the House of Representatives to fifty-one. The eighteen multi-membered House districts are grouped by counties, and under no circumstances can a county fail to have at least one representative. Beyond this minimum, a county's share is determined by the number of registered voters. The actual apportionment is accomplished by applying the mathematical formula of equal proportions. Should a representative district drop below roughly 1 percent of all registered voters in the state, the county will be redistricted, so that the county's share of representatives will be spread among a smaller number of districts.[34]

Statehood did not mark an end to Hawaii's reapportionment problems. In view of the previous amendments to the Organic Act, the governor would have been required to reapportion the territorial House of Representatives after the 1959 regular session. However, the statehood enabling legislation passed by Congress called for the special election of the first state legislature to be conducted in accordance with the provisions of the constitution drafted in 1950. The schedule of districts in the constitution did not reflect the population shift which had taken place during the ensuing decade, so the districts which stood to gain by reapportionment pressed the governor for action, while those whose delegations would be reduced insisted upon strict observance of the enabling legislation. Adding to the emotional content of the dispute, the Neighbor Islands stood to lose three seats to Honolulu. The Attorney General sided with the strict constructionalists, the Governor followed his advice, and a test suit heard by the territorial Supreme Court gave a decision to the advocates of reapportionment.[35] Thus it was that the state legislature which convened in special session on August 31, 1959, represented the first application of Hawaii's automatic reapportionment provisions.

The "one man one vote" rule enunciated by the U.S. Supreme Court in the line of cases following *Baker v. Carr* cut directly across the web of representation embodied in the Hawaii constitution. The composition of the Senate, with the Neighbor Islands controlling three-fifths of the seats, clearly conflicted with the

33. *Dyer v. Abe et al.* (1956) 138 F. Supp. 220.

34. See Kenneth K. Lau, *Reapportionment of the Territorial Legislature*, Legislative Reference Bureau Report No. 2, 1958 (Honolulu: University of Hawaii, 1958).

35. *Davis et al. v. Quinn et al.* (1959) 43 Haw. 261.

federal courts' reapportionment adjudications; the fact that this proportion of the state constitution could not be amended without the consent of the Neighbor Islands hardly added to its legal viability. But the federal decisions also carried the threat of overturning the apportionment in the House, for Hawaii apportions representation by registered voters rather than population, and large blocs of military personnel and their dependents who fail to meet the technical requirements for registration never show in the apportionment computations. And finally, legislators are elected to both chambers from multi-membered districts, and in the first flush of the federal reapportionment cases this practice seemed challenged. Not alone were incumbent legislators faced with the assurance that Oahu was going to capture the Senate if reapportionment were ordered, but they also faced the prospect of redrawing the boundaries of all districts as well as the possibility of a drastic realignment within the Oahu delegation in both houses of the legislature.

What transpired yet remains unfinished: governor, legislators, state and federal courts all sought to resolve the problem while the politics of the situation offered no ready solution. First the governor called a special session in the summer of 1964, proposing reapportionment before the courts ordered it. The governor's recommendation for single member districts fell on deaf legislative ears, but the two houses were no more successful in arriving at a compromise for reapportioning the Senate. Test suits were then brought before the state Supreme Court and a special three-man federal court. The results found the composition of the House of Representatives sustained against attack, the 1964 election of senators permitted; but the 1965 legislature was ordered to provide for the reapportioning of the Senate through constitutional means before enacting any other legislation. After petition, the federal court modified its direction to permit the state legislature to enact a law detailing reapportionment of the Senate, and for a short period the prohibition against enactment of other legislation by the 1965 legislature was raised. Relatively few bills were enacted before the federal three-man court found the new Senate reapportionment act invalid and again prohibited enactment of any state law until after the 1965 legislature took the necessary steps to bring the question of a constitutional convention before the voters. The legislature adamantly refused, and the federal court decision was appealed to the U.S. Supreme Court. Meanwhile the governor continued the life of the legislature by granting extensions, the legislature marked time in recess, and before the 30-day maximum on extensions had expired, the prohibition on further legislative action was lifted by Associate Justice Douglas. Quickly finishing up its business, including the enactment of the state's budget, the legislature adjourned.

The U.S. Supreme Court on April 25, 1966,[36] decided that large multi-member districts for Hawaii's state senators did not run counter to the 14th Amendment and refused to sustain the three-man federal court's criticism of alleged arbitrariness in temporarily drawing the Senate district boundaries. Continued use of registered voters as the basis for apportionment was countenanced. However, the lower court was directed to retain jurisdiction to see that Hawaii's permanent reapportionment conformed to constitutional requirements. The election of senators at the 1966 election thus constituted but an interim arrangement, and final reapportionment now awaits the action of the constitutional convention called for the summer of 1968.

The Islands have been governed under six constitutions and an Organic Act. However, only the last constitution, that of the state of Hawaii, was ever submit-

36. *Burns v. Richardson* (1966) 384 U.S. 73, 86 S.Ct. 1286, 166 L. Ed. 2d 376.

ted to the people. It alone has made provision for popular ratification of amendments and for a vote at least every decade on the question of calling a convention
for constitutional revision. No mention of either initiative or referendum is contained in the state constitution, and the attitude prevails among many Islanders
that such devices are suspect as being somewhat radical: consequently, they have
consistently voted against their adoption.

The Democratic party advocated both the initiative and the referendum in
its 1956, 1958, and 1960 platforms. The Democratic legislative majority made
the initiative part of its program, but failed to pass a bill putting it into effect. Use
of either form of direct legislation on the territorial level was legally questionable,
due to the terminology of the Organic Act, and is equally doubtful now under the
state constitution. However, the 1958 charter for the City and County of Honolulu expressly permits popularly initiated charter amendments, and it can be anticipated that the issue will again come to the fore when the state constitution is
subjected to scrutiny in 1968.

A degree of direct popular participation in government may, however, be
noted by review of the years since the turn of the century. In 1910, the people in a
plebiscite voted against prohibition more than three to one, and residents of the
City and County of Honolulu on two occasions since approved local bond issues
at the polls. In 1958, at a special election called for the purpose, the charter for
the City and County of Honolulu was ratified, the voters defeating a number of
alternative proposals. Even more recently (1964) the voters in each of the Neighbor Island counties defeated proposed home rule charters, but undaunted, their
commissions returned to the task and all three charters as re-drafted eventually
succeeded of adoption. More than two decades ago (1940), in an Islands-wide
plebiscite, statehood was approved. Again, after the passage of enabling legislation by Congress, voters approved statehood and also agreed to certain modifica-
tions in the proposed constitution and to special provisions on public land as set
forth in the enabling legislation. An Islands-wide vote in 1962 adopted the legisla-
ture-proposed constitutional amendment making the state Board of Education
elective; and again in 1966, the calling of a constitutional convention was overwhelmingly voted by the electorate. It is only a matter of time before the state
becomes accustomed to considering the latter question each decade.

VOTING HABITS

Prior to 1954, the general pattern of party support by voters in Hawaii was
clearly Republican. Until then, Republicans on the legislative level maintained
majorities which, except for the period 1945-54, were customarily sufficient to
override the vetoes of Democratic governors, and Democrats were able to elect
only three delegates to Congress whose combined tenure totaled only six years.
However, beginning in 1954, Democrats have increasingly been able to enjoy a
reversal of this voting pattern, the new trend culminating in their 1962 sweep of
state government and current 3 to 1 control of the state's delegation in Congress.
Although recent Democratic pre-eminence in the minds of voters has been more
subject to major "personality breakthroughs" by its opposition than characterized the half-century long Republican era, Democratic percentage strength among
the statewide electorate today rivals that of previous best years for Republicans.

Explanation for the now historic reversal of party dominance rests upon a
number of factors. Attractiveness of Democratic slates since 1954 undeniably

captured the imagination of Island voters. Their reform proposals not only congealed favorable sentiment in plantation areas on all islands and in lower economic areas on Oahu, but also proved satisfying to middle-income groups. The latter conclusion is borne out by the fact that only high-income areas remained Republican in 1962, 1964, and 1966, and isolated Republican victories involved intensive appeals to definable publics within now normally Democratic areas. Democratic accent upon youth and ethnically balanced slates has also materially contributed to this party's success.

In spite of noticeable trends toward greater voter interest in parties as agencies capable of advancing and implementing campaign program-promises, there is considerable evidence that "ballot-scratching" or "split ticket" voting remains traditional for most Hawaii voters. A sample of ballots cast on Oahu in 1948 indicated that only about 26 percent voted along straight party lines for territorial senators and representatives,[37] and a similar sample cast for executive and legislative officials in Honolulu's 1954 city-county election revealed even more extensive cross-party voting, showing that only about 12 percent had solely supported candidates of one or the other major party. This pattern was further illustrated in 1959, when Democratic congressional candidate Daniel K. Inouye polled 111,-727 votes while Republican lieutenant governor aspirant James K. Kealoha in his race was able to amass 90,652. In 1964, Republican U.S. Senator Hiram L. Fong won with 53 percent of the vote in spite of Democratic President Lyndon B. Johnson's landslide margin in Hawaii of 79 percent. (According to research conducted by the Library of Congress, Senator Fong ran further ahead of his party's national ticket than any other senatorial candidate in American political history.) The most recent illustration of Island voter independence occurred at the 1966 election, when the Democrats handily retained their two congressional seats and control of both houses of the state legislature, but barely succeeded in electing a Democratic governor.

On the basis of admittedly inconclusive information, women apparently vote more heavily for Republican candidates than do men. This has been apparent in opinion studies conducted during recent years among students at the University of Hawaii,[38] and by a series of community polls conducted by University students prior to the 1959 state election, which indicated that women may well have been a determining factor in electing the state's first governor, Republican William Quinn.[39] However, evidencing the tentativeness of the generalization, their support for Democrat Inouye as U.S. Representative was somewhat more pronounced than among men, a finding confirmed by a 1959 pre-election poll conducted by Robert S. Craig Associates which utilized completely different sampling techniques.[40]

In ethnically diverse Hawaii, the question of the extent of ethnic bloc voting has inevitably arisen. Findings are contradictory and inconclusive. A survey conducted by a Joint Faculty Committee and student teams in 1948 at the University of Hawaii reported little tendency to vote solidly for all Japanese, all Caucasian,

37. Joint Faculty Committee, University of Hawaii, "Voting Behavior in the Territory. . . ," May 1949, unpublished.

38. Daniel W. Tuttle, "A Quantitative Analysis of Public Opinion at the University of Hawaii, 1957-58," *Proceedings of the Hawaiian Academy of Science*, XXXIII (1958), 30-31.

39. Daniel W. Tuttle and William McIntire, "The 'University of Hawaii Poll'—An Experience Report," *Proceedings of the Hawaiian Academy of Science*, XXXVII (1963), 25.

40. *Pali Press* (Kailua, Oahu), August 13, 1959, p. 2.

or all "other" candidates.[41] Later, in 1954, two University researchers applied the technique of multiple factorial analysis to the precinct vote recorded at the combined territorial and city-county election on Oahu and to a sample of ballots cast on the city-county level. Two major factors emerged: party affiliation and ethnic affiliation. "Of the two factors, party affiliation appeared to be somewhat stronger."[42] The results of a pre-election poll conducted by Robert S. Craig Associates pointed clearly to heavy bloc voting along ethnic lines at the 1959 general election.[43] Pending further research results, it may be tentatively hypothesized that generalized ethnic cohesion rather than unmitigated ethnic bloc voting characterizes the Island voting public.[44]

It would be naïve to discount completely the influence of ethnic considerations on political events in Hawaii. Strategists of both parties give rather careful consideration to devising slates which are balanced to reflect the various major groups present in the population.[45] Lacking specific knowledge, just as on the mainland, voters appear to identify with candidates of their own ethnic group. This probably characterizes, in particular, the groups only recently introduced to fuller participation in Hawaii's politics. Nevertheless, mainland stereotypes are hardly applicable. Let a candidate play too hard upon the theme of race, correlatively demeaning that of an opponent, and he may well find he has alienated rather than garnered votes. The same may apply on a broad front with respect to a political party that appears to overlook a major group in the presentation of its slate of candidates.

IMPACT OF NATIONAL POLITICS AND TRENDS

Hawaii has participated only in the presidential elections of 1960 and 1964. As a result, depth public interest in national politics is still a-building. Under territorial status, apart from changes in the governorship and judiciary which reflected presidential shifts, national campaigns and election results were little more than a matter of passing interest to the man-in-the-street and had little apparent influence on trends in the Islands. Although during this period several Island residents did occupy positions of prominence in national party work, these appeared to be of only minor importance to Hawaii's citizenry.

Due to size and geographic location, even after statehood Hawaii has remained largely on the fringe of presidential campaigns. Only one of the eight major presidential and vice presidential aspirants visited the state as a candidate in the first two campaigns. Senator John F. Kennedy was expected to match Vice President Richard Nixon's early campaign swing through the state in 1960, but he did not make the trip, and in 1964, none of the four national ticket contenders came to the Islands.

Lack of campaign visits and the excitement which they can generate in a small compact state should not, however, overshadow the rapid development of interest in nation-state politics. Public interest in the close 1960 Nixon-Kennedy

41. Joint Faculty Committee, *op. cit.*

42. John M. Digman and Daniel W. Tuttle, "Statistical Analysis of 1954 General Election: Patterns Emerging From the Vote as Reported by Precincts," *Proceedings of the Hawaiian Academy of Science*, XXXI (1956), 10.

43. *Pali Press, loc. cit.*

44. Comprehensive studies of Hawaii voting behavior are currently in progress.

45. One of the recent recognized weaknesses of the Hawaii Republican party has been its seeming inability to attract strong Japanese candidates to its partisan banner.

race was prolonged as all of Hawaii's votes were recounted by volunteers under court supervision, a process which ultimately gave the state's first electoral votes to President Kennedy. In 1964, although electioneering was less intense than four years earlier, Goldwater forces campaigned strenuously and stirred up a degree of public interest in spite of overwhelming odds which were lengthened due to Senator Goldwater's negative vote on the Civil Rights Act of 1964. Yet, concern with national political developments in the Islands goes well beyond concern with presidential politics. Congressional races have uniformly been spirited, and the state's delegation in Washington, D.C., works overtime through the various news media to keep its public abreast of Hawaii's role and stake in national affairs. The nature of this public involvement extends from an unusually large number (for the size of the state) of personal visits by constituents to the Nation's Capital, through the complex of full utilization of federal funds, to implementation of Hawaii's expressed desire to lend its talents to national development in the Pacific and to increased international understanding. Indeed, this spectrum of relationships has been quickened and sometimes dramatized by close personal ties existing between Democratic Governor Burns and President Lyndon Johnson. Substantive topics of nation-state importance, such as astro-space tracking and research, oceanographic study, and East-West Center educational activity, are frequent subjects of public discussion and promise to recur again and again, well into the future. In fine, the suggestion at the time of statehood that the impact of developments in Hawaii might be felt in national political circles to an extent beyond that denoted by the area's size and distant location is demonstrably in process of being borne out.

IDAHO:

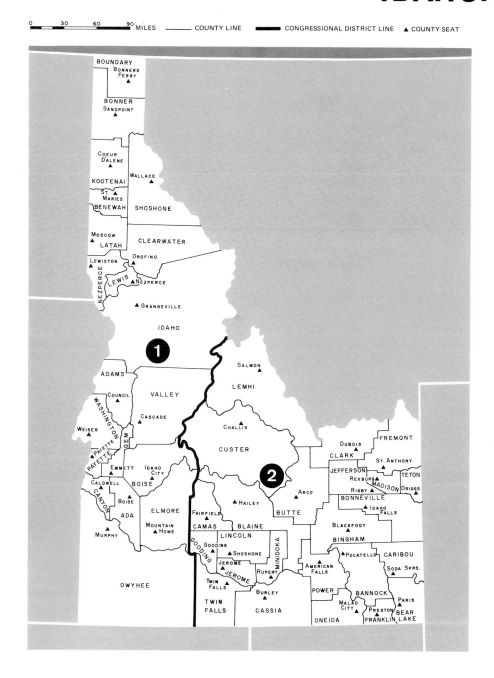

0 30 60 90 MILES   ——— COUNTY LINE   ▬▬ CONGRESSIONAL DISTRICT LINE   ▲ COUNTY SEAT

BOUNDARY
Bonners Ferry ▲

BONNER
Sandpoint ▲

Coeur D'Alene ▲

KOOTENAI
Wallace ▲

St. Maries ▲
BENEWAH
SHOSHONE

Moscow ▲
LATAH
CLEARWATER

Lewiston ▲
NEZPERCE
Orofino ▲

LEWIS
Nezperce ▲

▲ Grangeville

IDAHO

1

ADAMS
Salmon ▲

LEMHI

Council ▲
VALLEY

Cascade ▲

WASHINGTON
Challis ▲

Weiser ▲
CUSTER

GEM
PAYETTE

Payette ▲

Emmett ▲
Idaho City ▲
2

Caldwell ▲
BOISE
Arco ▲

CANYON
Boise ▲
Hailey ▲
BONNEVILLE

ADA
ELMORE
BUTTE
Idaho Falls ▲

Murphy ▲
Fairfield ▲
Blackfoot ▲

Mountain Home ▲
CAMAS
BLAINE
BINGHAM

LINCOLN
Pocatello ▲
CARIBOU

GOODING
Gooding ▲
Shoshone ▲
MINIDOKA
American Falls ▲
Soda Sprs. ▲

Jerome ▲
JEROME
Rupert ▲

Twin Falls ▲
POWER
BANNOCK
Paris ▲

TWIN FALLS
Burley ▲
CASSIA
Malad City ▲
Preston ▲
BEAR LAKE

OWYHEE
ONEIDA
FRANKLIN

Dubois ▲
CLARK
FREMONT
St. Anthony ▲

JEFFERSON
Rexburg ▲
MADISON
Rigby ▲
TETON
Driggs ▲

Boyd A. Martin

The Sectional State

Idaho, "geologically young," with her rivers, mountains, and plains probably formed within the last sixty million years, is also historically young. Prior to 1805 little is known of the state's history. It was in that year that Captain Meriwether Lewis and Captain William Clark, generally recognized as the first white men to see Idaho, led their expedition of thirty men into the territory near Salmon City. As the party moved north from Salmon City over Lo Lo Pass they met both Lemhi and Nez Percé Indians who apparently had never before had contact with white men.

Following the Lewis and Clark expedition, knowledge of Idaho spread among people of strong hearts and pioneer spirits. Fur traders were soon looking for both adventure and fortune in the fabulous mountains and plains of the new country. In September 1809, just three years after Lewis and Clark left the Nez Percés in the Kamiah Valley for their return home, David Thompson, an English explorer, traveled into Idaho from the north to erect a trading post (known as Kullyspell House) at Hope on the northeast side of Pend d'Oreille Lake. Fur trading became increasingly important and competitive. Hudson's Bay Company, operating out of Fort Vancouver, Washington, and the Northwest Company, with headquarters at Fort Williams on Lake Superior, were major competitors until their merger in 1821.

Idaho's fur-trading days were filled with examples of heroism, tough competition, disappointment, and riches. Donald McKenzie was the first to visit the Boise Valley. John Jacob Astor organized the Pacific Fur Company in 1809 and sent traders to Fort Astoria in 1810. By 1811 Wilson Price Hunt and his party were gliding down the Snake River in canoes. By 1825 Peter Skene Ogden was exploring, trading, and being harassed by Indian problems in the Snake River country. Between 1820 and 1830 Idaho passed through her most rewarding and dramatic fur-trading period.

The missionaries followed the fur traders in their efforts to Christianize the Indians. The Nez Percés, the most religious of all the tribes, sent a small delegation in 1831 to St. Louis to seek help from Captain William Clark in learning about the white man's religion. Henry H. Spalding and Marcus Whitman came to the new Oregon country in the summer of 1836 where the former immediately founded the Spalding Mission on the Clearwater River. He was followed by numerous other missionaries, among them Father Peter DeSmet who made frequent trips to Idaho and the Northwest. DeSmet Mission, south of Coeur d'Alene, was named for him. Many Protestant missionaries carried their work into the new mining camps. The first wagon train of Mormons (Church of Jesus Christ of Latter-day Saints) moved into Lemhi Valley in 1855, to found one of the first settlements in southern Idaho. This event proved to be one of the most significant in the state's history as the "Mormon" question became a burning political and economic issue for decades to follow.

While the early missionaries were spreading the word of God, miners began to seek yellow dust in the streams and mountains. Many found their way west on the trails made by the fur traders, missionaries, and explorers. Numerous immigrants moved across the territory to Oregon and California and then returned to Idaho. The miners often followed a similar course. The discovery of gold in Orofino Creek by Captain E. P. Pierce started the great gold stampede and led to the establishment of Idaho Territory in 1863. At this time also, the Republican North was looking for new states to offset the future readmission of southern states following the Civil War. One discovery led to another until Idaho became one of the chief mining states in the Union. Miners were followed by wholesale and retail firms which served the mines, and gradually settlers filled the ranks as the mining stampede declined. Agriculture slowly acquired the dominant position in the state's economy and has retained it to the present day.

Unlike many western states, Idaho's economic growth has been stable but slow. At first more immigrants passed over the plains area of southern Idaho—on the Oregon Trail—than settled. Later, with the gradual introduction of irrigation in the arid southern area and the discovery of the rich non-irrigated farming and mining areas in the north, settlers moved in on a slow but steady schedule.

In the beginning of Idaho's territorial days three factors largely determined the political complexion of the state: first, religious strife growing out of the Mormon question; second, sectionalism which started from the first; and third, a strong pioneer democracy where great emphasis was placed upon the equality and the significance of the individual, free from class lines. These three characteristics still play an important role in the background of Idaho's political behavior.[1]

GEOGRAPHY AND RESOURCES

Geography has been a major determinant of sectionalism in Idaho politics. The shape, the topography, and the climate of the state has much to do with its politics. With 83,557 square miles, Idaho is thirteenth in size in the nation, but still is larger than Maryland, Delaware, and the New England states combined. Nevertheless, the total population of approximately 713,000 persons is fewer than the city and county of San Francisco claim. Both distance and topography make Idaho one of the most fantastic states in the Union. It is in excess of 500 miles by highway from Bonners Ferry south to the State Capitol in Boise; and yet the state is less than 50 miles wide at the Canadian border. The direct distance from Idaho's southern to her northern boundary (480 miles) is, on the same line, the total distance for Washington and Oregon combined.

More important than distance is the unique topography. Agriculture and community life follow the Snake River from its upper valley across southern Idaho, then north to Lewiston, where this river, the longest to flow in any one state, enters Washington and joins the Columbia. Central Idaho, America's largest primitive area, divides the state so completely that no railroad runs from Boise to Lewiston, let alone Coeur d'Alene, Sandpoint, or Bonners Ferry. There is neither highway nor railroad from Idaho Falls running northwest to Lewiston. Consequently,

1. Histories of Idaho include: Cornelius J. Brosnan, *History of the State of Idaho* (rev. ed.; New York: Scribner's, 1948), an eighth-grade text, still one of the best; and Merrill D. Beal and Merle Wells, *History of Idaho* (Lewis Historical Publishing Co., 1960), the most complete.

with the exception of traffic carried on highway U.S. 95, most north- and south-bound traffic is diverted through either Oregon or Montana. Culturally, economically, and especially religiously, southeastern Idaho is more closely linked to Utah than to its own state. Southwestern Idaho is closely allied with adjacent Oregon, and the northern part of the state has very close relationships with the Spokane area in Washington. In like manner geographically and politically, the state is divided into three sections—southeastern and southwestern, with the dividing line near Twin Falls, and northern Idaho, with the dividing line at the Salmon River.

Southern Idaho is a rich agricultural area comprised of irrigated and grazing lands. The north is rich in farming, lumbering, mining, and livestock raising. With the exception of a small part of the southeast, the entire state lies in the basin of the Columbia River. Lewiston, Idaho's only port, stands at the head of navigation some 480 miles from the Pacific. The completion of dams on the Snake will bring slack water to Lewiston making it a promising port for major water transportation.

Contrary to common belief, Idaho lies wholly west of the Continental Divide. The northern part of the state averages lower in elevation than much of the central and southern portions. The lowest point, at Lewiston (738 feet), is lower than the towers of the Golden Gate Bridge, while the highest is Mount Borah (12,655) in Custer County. Idaho has neither a continental nor a coastal climate. However, the influence of the Pacific Ocean is noticeable in the northern part, while a continental climate prevails in the southeastern section.

The average annual temperature is a product of both geography and topography. The highest averages are found in the lower elevation of the Clearwater and Little Salmon River basins and in the Snake River Basin from Bliss to Lewiston. The highest mean is 54.8 degrees at Swan Falls and the lowest, at Obsidian, is 35.7 degrees. Monthly mean temperatures of 32 degrees prevail in the Snake River area between Idaho Falls and Twin Falls from December through February. The areas in and around Riggins and Lewiston have no monthly means below freezing.

Precipitation varies greatly. The Clearwater, Payette, and Boise River basins receive an average of 40 to 50 inches of rainfall per year. Challis has an average of 7 inches, while upper Snake River plains and the southwestern valleys receive less than 10 inches. The major mountain ranges accumulate heavy snow during the winter months. In the Snake River Basin above Weiser, the melting snows furnish irrigation water for approximately two million acres. Hurricanes are practically unknown in the state, although windstorms are common over most of the region. Destructive storms, as compared to those in the central part of the United States, are few and mild. Floods occur most often during April and May when the mountain snowpacks start to melt. Principal flood areas are in the Kootenai River Valley near Bonners Ferry and the Upper Snake River Valley above Idaho Falls. Flood control dams have been generally successful.[2]

Idaho is predominantly agricultural. Of the total land area, 10.3 percent is cropland farms and 43 percent is pasture and range land. Of the three chief sources of personal income derived from basic industries, agriculture accounts for approximately 25 percent, forestry for 12 and mining for 10 percent.[3] The largest

2. The author is indebted to David G. Stevlingson, who wrote *Climate of the States, Idaho*, U.S. Department of Commerce, Weather Bureau, Climatography of the United States, No. 60-10.

3. Much of the information concerning agriculture was furnished by Dr. James Kraus, dean of the College of Agriculture, director of the Agricultural Experiment Station,

source of agricultural income is field crops (e.g., wheat, potatoes, sugar beets, hay, edible beans, barley) which produce about 53 percent of the total. Although Idaho is the nation's largest producer of small seeds, such as seed corn, the total income from this is negligible compared to other field crops. The rest of the farm income is derived from livestock and livestock products, of which the cattle business produces 21 percent, dairy products produce 14, and sheep and lambs, 5.5.

The above figures do not indicate the extent of agriculture in the state. The variety of crops, livestock, and general farming activities is broad and highly specialized in different areas. Idaho ranks third in the United States in the production of potatoes. Ninety percent of these are grown on 110,000 acres of irrigated land on the Snake River Plains. Seventy percent of Idaho's potato crop is processed in the state while the remainder goes into a premium market. Another 100,000 acres of irrigated land in Gooding and Minidoka counties are devoted to the raising of dry edible beans of which the state is the third largest producer, as it is of sugar beets to which another 50,000 acres are devoted. It ranks first in the nation in the production of clover seed and wheatgrass, second in pears and prunes, and fourth in sheep and lambs.[4]

The significance of agriculture is vividly portrayed by the fact that Idaho's farm population of 20 percent, as compared to 12 percent for the nation, has the fifth highest ratio in the United States of gross farm income to total consumer spendable income. Its gross farm income is in excess of $500,000,000.[5] A significant trend is the growth of larger size farms in rural counties. In counties with populations above 40,000 (Ada, Canyon, Bannock, Bonneville, and Twin Falls, with a total population in 1960 of 289,212, representing 43.3 percent of the state's population) the average size farm is 230 acres, an increase of 28 percent in the decade 1950-60. For counties varying from 20,000 to 40,000 (Kootenai, Bingham, Nez Perce, Latah, and Shoshone, with a total population of 128,886) the average size is 445 acres, representing an increase of 56 percent. Those counties varying from 10,000 to 20,000 (Elmore, Cassia, Bonner, Minidoka, Idaho, Payette, Jerome and Jefferson with a total of 112,110 souls) average 445 acres per farm, an increase of 58 percent. Counties ranging from 5,000 to 10,000 (Gooding, Madison, Gem, Fremont, Clearwater, Franklin, Washington, Bear Lake, Owyhee, Benewah, Caribou, Lemhi, and Boundary, totaling 99,310 persons) average 852 acres, an increase of 48 percent. A number of counties with fewer than 5,000 people (Blaine, Lewis, Power, Lincoln, Valley, Oneida, Butte, Custer, Adams, Teton, Boise, Camas, and Clark, totaling 39,673 persons) average 852 acres per farm, an increase of 28 percent between 1950 and 1960.[6] In addition, the total number of farms has decreased by 25 percent and the proportion of land in farms has increased by 54 percent in the last 25 years.[7]

and of the Agricultural Extension Service, University of Idaho. The above figures were furnished by Dr. William Folz, head of the Department of Agricultural Economics.

4. Of Idaho's total land area of 52,972,000 acres, 22,659,000 is in pasture and range lands, 5,476,000 in crop lands, and 1,855,000 in irrigated crop lands. It is estimated that at least 4,400,000 additional acres could be put under irrigation.

5. See *Idaho's Major Mass Market*, an advertising brochure published by the *Idaho Farmer*, 1959. See also *Idaho Will Grow*, a research bulletin, University of Idaho, 1967.

6. See Harry C. Harmsworth, *Population Trends in Idaho*, 1950-1960, Department of Social Science, University of Idaho, 1964, pp. 20-21, 34.

7. See *Idaho Economic Report*, Idaho Department of Commerce and Development, 1963 and the *Idaho Almanac*, Territorial Centennial Edition, 1863-1963, Idaho Department of Commerce and Development, pp. 365-95.

Idaho's agriculture and forests are closely related, especially in the cut-over timber lands, mountains, meadows, and valleys. Twenty-seven percent of the state's total area is in forest lands,[8] of which ten million acres lie north of the Salmon River. The state has 3.2 percent of the country's total forests and 2.9 percent of its commercial forest lands. Various agencies of the national government own 72 percent of the total land area; 22 percent is privately owned; and 6 percent belongs to various Idaho governmental agencies. Currently, approximately 6 percent of the nation's live sawtimber is located in Idaho; the major portion of this is softwood. There is an estimated sustained yield potential of three billion board feet per year. Forty percent (13.4 million acres) of the forested land produces timber of commercial value. The major species of trees are the western white pine, ponderosa pine, western red cedar, western hemlock, western larch, Engelmann spruce, lodgepole pine, and the Douglas fir. The nation's largest stand of white pine is in northern Idaho.[9]

The mountains, the streams, and the rivers constitute resources beyond measurement. Eighty-one mountain ranges are located within the state. Major ranges include the Clearwater Mountains, Salmon River Mountains, Sawtooth Mountain Range, Yellowjacket Mountains, and the Bitterroot Mountain Range. Mountain lakes and streams have made possible the development of tourism and recreation to the point that they constitute the third largest industry.

Idaho's greatest resource, except her youth, is water. Five great river systems serve the state, with an annual flow of 71,490,000 acre feet. Equally important to the development of agriculture are the almost untapped underground water resources. Rathdrum Prairie, in the north, and the Upper Snake River Basin are two of the greatest underground water flows in the United States. Few states, if any, are so well situated in terms of water development.[10]

Many Americans associate the mining industry in Idaho with the stampede following the discovery of gold in 1860. Gold is now largely a by-product of mining for other minerals, especially for silver, lead, and zinc in Shoshone County.[11] As the significance of gold declined other metals rapidly took its place in

8. The author is indebted for much of the data here presented on agriculture, forestry, and mining to R. A. Postweiler, formerly of the College of Business Administration, University of Idaho, and to an address of his entitled "A Survey of Idaho's Natural and Human Resources." See also his article, "Idaho," University of Washington *Business Review*, College of Business Administration, Vol. XIX, No. 3. Robert H. Seale, Associate Dean, College of Forestry, University of Idaho, furnished considerable data on forestry and the timber products industry. Also his address presented to the Latah Chamber of Commerce in 1958 on "The Significance of Forest Resources and Forest-Based Industry in the Economy of Northern Idaho" was very useful.

9. E. Malcolm Hause, "Idaho," *American*, XIV, 650-60.

10. *Idaho Economic Report*, *op. cit.*, p. 30.

11. For data concerning mining the author is especially indebted to Dr. E. F. Cook, former dean of the College of Mines and director of the Idaho Bureau of Mines and Geology, and two of his addresses entitled "The Future of Idaho's Mineral Industry" and "The Idaho Mining Industry in a Year of Decision." Also see the chapter by Kenneth D. Bober, Frank B. Fulkesson, and Norman S. Peterson, "The Mineral Industry of Idaho," *Minerals Yearbook*, 1958, Vol. III, Area Reports, Bureau Minerals Industry Surveys, Bureau of Mines, Department of the Interior; *The Mineral Industry of Idaho in 1959*, Area Report B-74, Minerals Industry Surveys, Bureau of Mines, Department of Interior. The author has drawn heavily on the very complete report, *Mineral and Water Resources of Idaho*, Special Report No. 1, 1964, compiled by the U.S. Geological Survey in cooperation with the Idaho Bureau of Mines and Geology, Idaho Department of Highways and Idaho Department of Reclamation. In addition see 64th annual Report of the Mining Industry of Idaho for 1963-64.

major production. In the one hundred and two years since records have been kept, Idaho has produced approximately 2.6 billion dollars in mineral wealth, and 90 percent of this has come from lead, zinc, silver, copper, and gold. But today gold accounts for less than 1 percent of the mineral production. More than half the value of all the minerals has come from those mined since 1938. Currently Idaho produces 40 different mineral products, leading the nation in zinc, silver, columbium and tantalum, and being second in the production of lead. The significance of the major metals has been declining in relation to the growing importance of strategic materials such as phosphate and construction minerals. These now represent 30 percent of the state's total. The value of the mineral output has fluctuated from $22 million in 1935 to $84 million in 1951. This variation demonstrates the critical position of the mining industry. A large percentage of its production is of metals very sensitive to business cycles, to national defense needs, and to foreign competition. Nonmetallic minerals are in a much more favorable position pricewise.

Metals are currently mined in twenty of the forty-four counties. This has resulted in the industry having more political influence, especially in the Capital, than its relative position in the production of wealth or in the number of people employed might warrant. This situation is changing, however. Gradually the industry has been developing and expanding in a few centers. The principal production comes from Washington, Bannock, Caribou, Lemhi, Bonneville, Custer, and Shoshone counties: Shoshone produces 65 percent of the total value. The following metals are mined: antimony, beryllium, cadmium, cobalt, columbium-tantalum, copper, gold, iron ore (new), lead, mercury, nickel, silver, titanium, tungsten, uranium, zinc, and zirconium. A number of nonmetals—including barite, cement, clay, garnet, gypsum, mica, phosphate rock, pumice, volcanic cinder, sand and gravel, stone, sulfuric acid—are either mined or produced. The importance of the production of phosphate rock, gypsum, and mica in recent years has been beyond expectations. Idaho now produces 43 percent of the world's output. Florida and Tennessee are the only states producing more. Nonmetallic minerals now account for approximately 37 percent of the value of all minerals produced.

POPULATION

In population,[12] Idaho is forty-third nationally and sixth among the Rocky Mountain states. Only five, New Mexico, Montana, Wyoming, Nevada, and Alaska, have a lower population density than Idaho's 8.1 persons per square mile. Jumping from 14,999 in 1870 to 667,191 in 1960 represents an amazing growth in ninety years, which is still continuing: it had reached 713,000 by January 1964. Over 60 percent of the people live in nine counties—Ada, Bannock, Bonneville, Canyon, Twin Falls, Bingham, Nez Perce, Kootenai, and Latah. Population figures for twenty counties have declined since 1920 or before. Agriculture and geography have been the major factors in determining the distribution. Irrigated

12. The author has relied heavily upon two recent publications by Harry C. Harmsworth, *Sixty Years of Population Growth in Idaho*, 1890-1950, General Research Project No. G-8, Department of Social Sciences, University of Idaho, 1952, and *Population Trends in Idaho*, 1950-1960, Special Research Fund Project in the preparation of this subject. He is also indebted to the 1960 reports of the United States Bureau of the Census; Morris E. Garnsey, *America's New Frontier, the Mountain West* (New York: Knopf, 1950); Donald J. Bogue and Calvin L. Beale, *Economic Areas of the United States* (New York: Free Press, 1961); and the *Basic Economic Projections, United States Population, 1965-1980*, Stanford Research Institute.

farming results in a denser population than non-irrigated farming. The period of greatest growth was from 1900 to 1910. From 1920 to 1930 the increase was only 3 percent, but since then the rate has remained constant. However, Idaho ranked at the bottom of the Rocky Mountain states in terms of percentage increase between 1950 and 1960, and was thirteenth in the nation.

Six counties in southwestern Idaho (Washington, Payette, Gem, Canyon, Ada, and Owyhee) and twelve in southeastern Idaho (Fremont, Jefferson, Madison, Teton, Bonneville, Bingham, Caribou, Power, Bannock, Bear Lake, Franklin, and Oneida) gained 17 percent from 1950 to 1960 while the state gained only 13.4 percent. The southern central section, consisting of six counties (Gooding, Lincoln, Jerome, Minidoka, Cassia, and Twin Falls) containing 15 percent of the state's population, increased by 4.8 percent. These three areas now include 70.6 percent of Idaho's people. The central mountain area (thirteen counties—Shoshone, Clearwater, Idaho, Adams, Valley, Lemhi, Boise, Custer, Clark, Bonner, Boundary, Elmore, Blain, Camas, and Butte) has 16.2 percent, and the Lewiston-Moscow-Pend d'Oreille area (five counties—Kootenai, Benewah, Latah, Nez Perce, and Lewis), 13.2 percent. When politicians speak of northern Idaho they are referring to the ten northern counties, at lower elevations north of the Salmon River, where 22.8 percent of the people live. Counties making the largest percentages of growth are those which already enjoyed the largest populations. For example, only Jerome and Shoshone, in excess of 10,000, declined in numbers.

Of thirteen counties with fewer than 5,000 persons, nine lost residents. Typical of the national trend, Idaho's counties with the highest degree of industrialization made the greatest percentage of increase. Approximately 52.5 percent of Idaho's people are urban although in 1960 only three cities were above 30,000: Boise with 51,977, Idaho Falls with 33,161, and Pocatello with 38,594. Eleven cities have over 10,000. The Stanford Research Institute estimates Idaho's population for the future as 746,400 by 1970, 800,300 by 1975 and 859,000 by 1980.[13]

In the early mining days, conflicts were common between the natives and the Chinese who migrated into the mining camps. Since then, Idaho has had a very homogeneous population, if not the most homogeneous in the nation. Since the first settlement the state has been predominantly white, with the exception of the indigenous Indians. The Caucasian population has never dropped below 90 percent: in 1960, the percentage was 98.5 Most of the Negroes and Chinese live in cities while most of the Indians and Japanese live in the rural areas. The number of Negroes has never exceeded 920: the total non-white population is less than 5,000. Politically, the state has no race problems. Approximately 20 percent of the people are of foreign stock as compared to 26 percent for the nation. With the exception of those from Canada, most of the foreign stock derive from Europe, particularly Germany, England, Norway, Sweden, and Denmark. The birth rate has always been slightly above the national rate and the mortality rate one of the lowest in the nation.

Migration, both external and internal, has had relatively little influence upon the politics of the state. Native-born residents will probably continue to constitute an increasing percentage of the population. Most of the migrants traveled long distances to come to Idaho. Most of the internal migration has been from

13. *Op. cit.*, p. 14 of the document (no printed page nos.). According to *Current Population Reports, Population Estimates*, Bureau of the Census, U.S. Department of Commerce, Series P-25, No. 301, February 26, 1965, pp. 4-7, the figures are 738,000 by 1970; 797,000 by 1975; and 865,000 by 1980.

dry-land farming areas to irrigated land and to the city. This trend is gradually changing the political picture. The urban labor vote is becoming much more important, especially in statewide elections where the impact of its numbers counts most.

EDUCATION

Idaho has had difficulty in meeting all of its educational needs. The University of Idaho, created by the territorial legislature in 1889, discovered it was necessary to start a preparatory school. Young men and women of college age had been unable to attend high schools—which were then few and far between. However, the people of the state have long believed that every child is entitled to whatever level of education he is capable of achieving, without the payment of tuition or institutional fees.

For years Idaho passed through the stage of creating hundreds of independent school districts, with local boards of control, subject to a minimum of state regulation and supervision. Many of these maintained one-room schools with one teacher for the eight elementary grades. Almost every village had a local high school regardless of its population or assessed valuation. The state has completed an enormous consolidation program which has greatly reduced the number of schools and districts. Probably the most common sight on the highways in the early morning and late afternoon hours is the hundreds of school busses carrying thousands of children, in some cases great distances, to and from consolidated schools.

Idaho is more fortunate than many states in that the educational duties of the legislature are clearly defined in the constitution. A constitutional amendment passed in 1912 places control over all public education in the State Board of Education, which is also the Board of Regents for the University of Idaho as well as the State Board for Vocational Education. Thus, a single board is the chief policy-forming body and the chief executive body, with the exception of the state superintendent of instruction, over all schools. In spite of this fact, in recent years there has been a growing need for a higher degree of coordination. Historically the one lay board arrangement has been satisfactory, but the need for professional advice, coordination, and statewide direction has become increasingly apparent. Consequently, the legislature in 1965 passed House Bill No. 307 which increased the membership of the State Board of Education from five to seven members, but left the membership of the Board of Regents of the University of Idaho at five, and created a new executive director. This act, passed to correct a recognized need, may lead to confusion. The executive director (appointed by the State Board of Education, not by the Regents) according to the law is to supervise all public institutions of higher learning above the twelfth grade. He is also an ex officio member of the Board of Regents of the University of Idaho and serves as executive director of both boards. The state superintendent of public instruction, who was formerly executive officer of both boards, is now an ex officio member of the State Board of Education and its executive officer for all schools and institutions under its control except institutions of higher learning.

The major educational problem has been inadequate finance. Local districts, with great differences in assessed valuation, depended largely upon the property tax. This proved inadequate to support the schools and resulted in great variation in the quality of education. Consequently, the legislature has been appropriating state monies on an equalization basis. For several decades Idaho avoided a realistic solution of the financial needs of public education. Finally, the legislature in 1965, with the passage of a sales tax and a modification of the property tax rates and income tax rates, raised the state appropriation for public school equalization from $40,000,000 for the 1963-65 biennium, to $57,300,000 for 1965-67. Thus, the first major step was achieved towards solving this most critical problem.

The state has long been proud of her institutions of higher learning. The University at Moscow consists of ten colleges and is the land-grant institution. Its experiment stations and programs of agricultural extension cover the state. It has a commendable record of high-level teaching and research, offering degrees through the doctorate. Lewiston State Normal, originally created in 1893, became Northern Idaho College of Education in 1947. It was closed four years later and reopened in 1955 with a two-year program, and renamed Lewis-Clark Normal. In 1963 the legislature provided that it was to become a degree-granting, liberal arts institution. Idaho State University at Pocatello was created in 1901 as the Academy of Idaho, a two-year institution, and became Idaho Technical Institute in 1915. It was given two major roles—to provide a junior college and a Vocational Trade School. From 1927 to 1947 it served as the Southern Branch of the University of Idaho. Then it was made a four-year institution, independent of the University, and was named Idaho State College. By legislative act it became Idaho State University in 1963. It has colleges of Liberal Arts, Education, Pharmacy, and Business Administration, and a school of Trade and Technical Education. It has become especially recognized for its College of Pharmacy. It offers bachelor's and master's degrees in the various academic fields.

Junior colleges have earned a secure place in Idaho's public educational pattern. Boise Junior College and North Idaho Junior College at Coeur d'Alene have both academic and non-academic programs. They serve the needs of the local communities and give sound training for those who wish to transfer to senior colleges and universities.[14] A new junior college at Twin Falls, Southern Central College, opened in September 1965. That year the legislature provided that junior colleges in districts with an assessed value of $70,000,000 and a population of 90,000 may establish upper division curricula for third and fourth year programs in liberal arts, business, and education. The upper division is to be kept separate from the junior college. Boise College, on the Boise Junior College grounds, has now been created. It is to become a part of the state system of higher education in 1969.

There are also several excellent private schools. The College of Idaho, at Caldwell (Presbyterian) is an old liberal arts institution. Ricks College at Rexburg (a junior college) is part of the L.D.S. program of higher education centered at Brigham Young University in Utah. Northwest Nazarene College at Nampa has a program in education and liberal arts. Two new schools are the Magic Valley Christian College at Albion and St. Gertrude's Academy at Cottonwood. The latter is just starting junior training. Magic Valley has launched a four-year program.

A weakness of the educational program from the viewpoint of state solidarity results from the fact that a large percentage of the population in southeastern Idaho, members of the L.D.S. church, have strong religious and cultural ties to institutions in Utah. The headquarters of their church is in Salt Lake City; and

14. Although out-of-date, the best description of Idaho's schools is *Public Education in Idaho*, a Report of the Idaho Education Survey Commission, George Peabody College for Teachers, Nashville, Tennessee, n.d. See also, *Long Range Planning for Higher Education in Idaho*, Stanford Research Institute, S.R.I. Project No. II-3973, Menlo Park, California, 1963.

three major educational institutions—the University of Utah, Utah State University, and the church's Brigham Young University—are all in close proximity. It is natural that thousands of Mormon boys and girls raised in southeastern Idaho would migrate to Utah to go to college.

NEWS MEDIA AND PUBLIC OPINION

The rural character of the state is demonstrated by the fact that there are seventy-three weekly newspapers with a total circulation of 100,000 but with an average circulation of only 1,356. The smallest has a circulation of 200 and the largest, 3,606. There are thirteen daily papers, forty radio stations covering the state, and six television stations. Twelve of the daily papers have registered as being politically independent, but this means they are basically Republican. Of the weekly papers, only a few are Democratic.

Idaho is influenced by several important out-of-state papers. Those published in Salt Lake City have special editions with wide circulation in southern Idaho, especially in the southeastern section. The Spokane papers cover most of the area north of the Salmon River. Papers from Portland, Oregon, have relatively wide circulation within the western border. The major political influence of these out-of-state papers is Republican.

Public opinion is rather conservative. On questions of public finance the Democrats are often just as conservative as the Republicans. On questions of morality, gambling, Sunday closing laws, and the like, the people are quite conservative. Church groups, including the Mormons, Methodists, Presbyterians, and numerous smaller Protestant sects have had considerable influence. The state is predominantly Protestant.

While conservative in morals and public finance, the voters, especially in the north, do not hesitate to vote for candidates advocating a high Hell's Canyon Dam and various economic and social reforms. They are usually quite liberal on questions of human rights, and have elected many liberal candidates. The attitudes toward Mormons and Orientals are exceptions to these liberal trends. In this regard the state cannot be proud of its record.

Although the people of Idaho have seldom taken the lead in governmental reforms or major social legislation, there has been a basic acceptance of certain fundamental concepts of neighborhood democracy. The legislature passed a good civil rights act before the civil rights issue became so acute in 1964-65. The people as a whole, except in some of the larger cities, have resisted the hardening of class lines. Intermarriage among people of different economic levels is common, and intermarriage among persons of different religions, although strongly opposed by several churches, is becoming more common. There is great faith in the opportunity for a free education and the ability of the individual to succeed, regardless of his cultural heritage, in politics, business, farming, or whatever occupation he may choose. The people of Idaho believe in and practice democracy.

NOMINATIONS AND ELECTIONS

The pattern of elections and the process of nominating in Idaho are not unique. But Idaho has had more experience with a greater number of varieties of the direct primary than almost any other state. Before the passage of the direct primary law in 1909, various forms of committees and nominating conventions were used. Since then almost all types of nominating procedures, except the closed primary and the blanket primary, have been tried.

Election administration in Idaho is typical of other states. The secretary of state is the chief election officer. Most of his duties are ministerial and involve little or no discretion. He sets the machinery in motion for the preparation of the election ballots, and candidates for congressional or statewide office file with him. The county clerk is the chief local election officer. The county commissioners select election officers on a bipartisan basis; these are paid by the county. Third parties are not represented on any of the boards, agencies, or offices conducting any part of the election process. Election officers are chosen entirely on a partisan basis or a basis of who is available and willing to serve. Elderly retired women or housewives most commonly serve in these posts.

To qualify for suffrage one must be twenty-one years of age, a citizen of the United States, and a resident of Idaho for six months and of the county for thirty days. The normal disqualifications provided by law include insanity, treason, felony, embezzlement of public funds, selling votes, and prostitution. Voting participation is above the national average. The primary vote seldom runs below 50 percent of the eligible and commonly runs to 70 percent. Participation in the general election is normally higher; for instance, in the 1960 and 1964 elections 83.3 and 81 percent, respectively, voted.[15]

Idaho's corrupt practices laws are not only inadequate to accomplish their objectives but are easily evaded. No effort is made to control the sources of funds. Persons, corporations, labor unions, interest groups, farmers, and others wishing to give to a party or candidate need not report such gifts to a state official. Parties and party committees are virtually beyond the law in this regard. The major effort is to control personal expenses. This provision limits what a candidate may spend in behalf of his own primary election. Idaho has not worked out a planned policy for corrupt practices legislation. There has been little public demand for such a program. The cost of conducting a campaign often eliminates candidates of great potential.

Nominations for practically all public offices, with some minor exceptions, are made by direct primary. New parties or parties which have not been able to poll 10 percent of the vote in the previous election may make nominations by convention. The only recent example of this was the action of the Progressive party in 1948.

Under the direct primary law candidates file with the secretary of state if seeking a national or state office and with the county auditor if seeking a county office. The declaration of candidacy involves a statement that the candidate is a member of the party and represents its principles. For the office of governor or United States senator, the declaration must be supported by a petition signed by 1,000 party voters and not more than 50 signers may be from any one county. This has already proved to be a barrier to some hopefuls. The preparation of the ballots is directed by the secretary of state and the county auditor. All costs of conducting the primary election are borne by the county and the state. After a brief trial with a run-off direct primary and also with a semi-closed direct primary, the legislature in 1963 provided a pre-primary convention method of party endorsement. Candidates who wish party endorsement to run for nomination in the direct primary nominating election, both for county and state office, file their

15. See *Biennial Reports* of the Secretary of State.

declaration of candidacy the first week of May. County assemblies (really conventions) consisting of members of the respective party central county committees meet the third Friday of May to designate candidates for county offices and to select delegates to the state assemblies. The respective state party assemblies meet on the second Friday and Saturday of June to endorse candidates for state and national offices. State assemblies may endorse for each office two candidates who have filed declarations of candidacy. All candidates who receive at least 20 percent of the ballots cast, when at least two receive more than 20 percent, are officially endorsed. Unendorsed candidates, those receiving less than 20 percent but at least 10 percent of the votes at the assembly, may file a second declaration and run as unendorsed party candidates.

In spite of sporadic complaints, Idaho's experience with the direct primary has been favorable. The direct primary did overcome most of the abuses of the convention method of nomination, and it has encouraged wide participation in politics. Oddly, one of the current complaints against the direct primary is the increased number of candidates. The pre-primary convention was introduced to correct this alleged weakness. Other dissatisfactions center around the number of minority nominations and party raiding. The run-off election, introduced to overcome the problem of minority nominations, failed to win combined legislative approval because of the small voter participation which, according to the opinion of some, altered the outcome.[16] The problem of party raiding has not been widespread. Ada County Republicans and Latah County Democrats have been the major offenders. In the former case, the desire to weaken the leadership of the opposition party has been the motivating factor, and in the latter, dissatisfaction with their own party's candidates prompted their raiding.

Thus, Idaho, still remembering her experience with the nominating convention, still unwilling to adopt a closed primary because many voters are fearful of revealing their party affiliation, and still failing to recognize that all nominating systems face the necessity of eliminating candidates, seeks the advantages of the nominating convention by using the technique of the pre-primary convention, and seeks the advantages of the open primary by providing a method of certifying candidates not endorsed by the pre-primary convention.[17]

PARTY ORGANIZATION AND PARTY LEADERS

Formal party organization in Idaho is determined by the direct primary law. The county central committee of each party consists of the precinct committeemen who are chosen by the party voters at the primary election. The county central committee elects a chairman, a state central committeewoman and committeeman, a secretary, and a vice-chairman. The chairman, the committeewoman and the committeeman are delegates to their party's state assembly, which is held prior to the primary election. This assembly is called by the state chairman. The

16. For example, in the 1960 primary election five Democratic candidates entered the senatorial race. No one received 40 percent of the vote; consequently, the two receiving the highest number of votes participated in the run-off election. R. F. McLoughlin, running second in the primary with a plurality of 179, as compared to Gregg Potvin, who ran first with a plurality of 1,830, won the run-off election with a majority of 943. Many blamed the run-off primary for the result, not realizing that the voters were exercising a first, second, and third choice and that the result without doubt represented the actual choice of the voters.

17. See Boyd A. Martin, *The Direct Primary in Idaho* (Stanford: Stanford University Press, 1945).

assembly elects its own chairman and such other officers as it desires and adopts its own rules of procedure. It adopts a platform, elects the state chairman, vice-chairman, delegates to the national conventions, a national committeeman and committeewoman, and presidential electors, and endorses candidates for national and state offices.

The 1963 statute made it impossible for candidates to be delegates to the state assemblies. Formerly, candidates and party officers attended a special platform convention. Since the new state assemblies consisting exclusively of county party officers draft the platform and elect officers who are supposedly a state central committee, this results in increasing the power of county party officers and greatly reducing the power of candidates. For years many party officers had opposed permitting candidates to participate in platform conventions on the grounds that candidates who could not have won nomination from a state convention, and who could win in a direct primary, should not influence the adoption of a platform and party policy. The old question of who should control the party—the party hierarchy or the party voters—is still an area of disagreement.

Geographical diversity and distance make political campaigns both difficult and costly. The Republicans traditionally have a better financed campaign and a tighter party organization. Both parties find it difficult to maintain continuous working arrangements with county committees. Both parties are plagued by candidates who establish their own campaign headquarters and attempt to separate themselves from the party. This is prompted, in part at least, by the independent nature of the Idaho voter. The major financial support to both parties comes in the form of indirect help from interested groups engaging in campaigns independently of the parties. For example, organized labor usually has national representatives in the state promoting the interests of labor. Their activities tend to aid the Democratic party. In recent years the Grange, the Farm Bureau, and the Idaho Allied Civic Forces have lent support to Republican candidates.

Party leadership in Idaho is difficult to define and to locate. The major leadership may lie with a United States senator, a congressman, a governor, a state chairman, or with some person working entirely behind the scenes. For example, the late Senator William E. Borah (R), although generally considered to be larger than his party, never gained control of it. Senator Glen Taylor (D) won over the opposition of both his own party organization and the Republicans, but seldom gained control of the state central committee. Recently the major leadership of the Democratic party has been shared by the senior senator and the state chairman. On occasion major decisions have been made by a banker, a real estate broker, or a person of great influence, unknown in the state as a party leader.

Idaho has had some great and colorful leaders. George L. Shoup, the last territorial governor, left his mark indelibly on the state. Fred T. Dubois, a champion of statehood and Idaho's anti-Mormon crusader, gained control of the Republican party. William J. McConnell, the late Senator Borah's father-in-law, served as United States senator and Idaho's third governor, for two terms. Governor Frank Steunenberg, who also served two terms, lost his life at the hands of an assassin over the northern mine labor troubles. Frank R. Gooding served as governor twice and as United States senator. Few leaders have had greater influence than Senator Weldon B. Heyburn. He fought Borah in his efforts to secure the adoption of the direct primary. Governor and author James H. Hawley won when Democrats weren't supposed to win and won because he stood on a definite program of progressive leadership. Governor David W. Davis put through Idaho's first and only administrative reorganization bill. Other distinguished leaders would include

Burton L. French, congressman-at-large and later for the First District, for twenty-six years, and Senator William E. Borah who served for a third of a century. C. Ben Ross, three times governor, was one of the most colorful leaders in the state's history. He definitely gained control of his party. Robert E. Smylie, Republican, who served longer than any previous incumbent, and who at the time of his defeat in 1966 had had a longer term than any incumbent Republican governor in America, had the peculiar role of serving as a "captive governor" while the Democrats controlled the legislature part of the time and all other elective state offices.

Leadership in Idaho politics has not been difficult to achieve. The candidates who have stood for definite and sound principles and who have been articulate in expounding these principles have risen to the top. The harmony candidates who had few ideas, let alone the courage of their convictions, have found it difficult to gain real statewide recognition.

PRESSURE GROUPS

Not all interest groups engage in pressure activities and not all pressure groups represent legitimate interests. Idaho has had her share of experience with all kinds. The major interest groups are farmers of various types, the forest interests, the mining people, the utilities, the railroads, and small manufacturers. There are dozens of less well-known groups. The farmers can control the state when and if they wish to do so. They are less articulate than most groups unless their problems are more acute. There are many specialized farm groups, such as the Idaho Wool Growers Association or the Idaho Cattlemen's Association. There is no single pressure group which represents all farmers. The public school teachers have become very powerful as they have an organization in every school. At times the liquor interests, especially the beer people, become vocal and powerful. The activities of these groups depend largely upon the issues up for consideration. For instance, a few years ago a bill was introduced regulating drugstores. Almost overnight the drug people were converging on Boise to stop the legislation. A number of small groups have far more influence than their numbers or income would justify. Over the years the utilities have probably been the most consistent in their efforts to influence policy formulation. Several times one individual, usually highly placed in some business, has been able to defeat or get approval for legislation against the activities of several groups.

Contrary to common belief, lobbying groups in Idaho seldom rent a floor of a Boise hotel. More often they work alone and buttonhole legislators and members of the executive branch in the hotel lobbies, the corridors of the legislature, and at the city's principal bars. Most lobbying is done in a quiet way, sometimes using false information, subtle propaganda, and occasionally outright distortion. Some lobbyists serve a real function in that they furnish the legislators with much needed information. Most interest groups have been honest and fair in pressing for their needs. Often it is impossible to know who or what group is supporting a lobbyist. There has been little real public demand for lobby regulation or registration. Not even the legislature itself seems to be concerned.

LEGISLATIVE POLITICS

Few voters in the nation are as independent as are those of Idaho. Scratching a ballot is commonplace. The voter thinks nothing of sending a member of each party to the United States Senate and to the House of Representatives, splitting up the elective offices in the executive branch of the state government, and doing the same for the state legislature. Idaho voters are extremely discriminating. This is especially true in elections for the legislature. On a county level the voters are often personally acquainted with all the candidates. Local and county problems, as well as neighborhood friendship, may have more to do with voting patterns than party labels.

For many years it was common practice for the village lawyer to go to the legislature. He was often employed by some of the principal interest groups and was, therefore, on the alert for their interests in the legislature. This pattern has changed greatly; some recent sessions have had few lawyers. For example, in the two houses of the 1957 legislature, farmers and ranchers totaled 44 members out of a possible 103, while business had 23, lumbering 7, law 13 (a high number for recent years), service businesses 11, all others 5. Legislative inexperience is quite common. In 1957, 29 members had not served before.

The Republicans have controlled the legislature more often than have the Democrats. During the period 1920 to 1930 they had a firm command. The tidal wave of 1932 swept the Democrats into power which they held until after 1936. Currently, the Republicans are in control of both houses.

Historically, sectionalism has been a dominant factor in Idaho politics, but now other issues common to all sections are becoming increasingly important. Robert J. Huckshorn's study of the legislature indicates how modern problems of a statewide character have influenced the thinking and attitudes of legislators.[18] Seventy-two members of the legislature believed questions of public finance to be the most important facing them. Thirty believed that financing education is the major problem, and twenty-one held labor legislation to be the most important. A majority of the members of the Thirty-Fifth Session believed the major dividing issues to be "spenders vs. hold-the-liners," "labor vs. labor opposition," "liberals vs. conservatives," "governor's supporters vs. governor's opponents," and "Republicans vs. Democrats."

Until the United States Supreme Court ruled in *Baker v. Carr* (1962) and *Gray v. Sanders* (1963) that "the conception of political equality from the Declaration of Independence, to Lincoln's Gettysburg Address, to the Fifteenth, Seventeenth and Nineteenth Amendments can mean only one thing—one person, one vote," Idaho had not been seriously concerned about legislative reapportionment. There has been, from time to time, discussion about redistributing the two congressional districts. The Second in recent years has had approximately 153,000 more people than the First. The proposal to gerrymander by adding Republican Ada County with 93,460 people to the First District has been made numerous times. This was not accomplished until 1965. However, until recent years, because of the rural character of the state, the pressure to recognize the increasing problem of population growth of cities versus rural areas has been nominal.

In 1965 the First Extraordinary Session of the Thirty-Eighth Session of the state legislature was forced to act. Suits were pending in both state and federal courts. To carry out the mandate of the United States Supreme Court in *Gray v. Sanders* and the requirements of the Idaho constitution would have resulted in a

18. From materials in Robert J. Huckshorn's unpublished memorandum based upon results of a project conducted in 1958-59 under a grant from the Committee on Political Behavior of the Social Science Research Council.

legislature of 667 members in each chamber.[19] The Extraordinary Session responded by passing reapportionment acts for the houses and redistricting the congressional districts. All were in dire need of change. For both houses of the legislature a system of combining counties into districts was adopted. The United States District Court invalidated the Senate reapportionment because the senate districts, consisting of combinations of counties, provided for nominating senators from each county within the district. Consequently, a third Extraordinary Session was called in February 1966 to attempt to meet the legal requirements of apportionment. The plan provided for 35 legislative districts, each electing one senator and two representatives. In some instances counties are divided into different election districts. The degree of distortion from perfect representation has been approved by the Court. The senator representing the smallest population comes from a district of 16,121 people while the senator from the largest represents 22,678. The smallest district for the House contains 8,061 and the largest, 12,587; the average population per representative is 9,531. Congressional redistricting was accomplished by moving Owyhee, Elmore, and Ada counties (119,554) to the First District and Custer and Lemhi (8,812) from the First into the Second.

The 1966 election showed that reapportionment does not necessarily change the party composition in the legislature. Republicans increased their majorities by four seats in the Idaho legislature, about what might be expected in a Republican year. They gained majorities of 22-13 in the Senate and 38-32 in the House.

Although Idaho has had the recall, initiative, and referendum since 1933—one of the first states to adopt such legislation—only slight use has been made of these legal provisions. The author knows of no case where a major state official has been displaced by a recall election. The initiative has been used seven times. Three of these really constituted one action known as the anti-gambling acts.

Three major pieces of legislation have been approved by initiative elections. The Idaho State Fish and Game Commission Act was approved in 1938. The Senior Citizens Grant Act was approved by a large plurality of 39,746 votes in 1942 only to be repealed by the next legislature, which action was sustained by the State Supreme Court. The Dredge Mining Law was enacted in 1954. In 1946 three separate propositions, the Anti-Gambling Act, the Sobriety Act, and the Local Option Act, commonly referred to as the anti-gambling acts, were easily defeated. In 1958 the so-called "Right-to-Work Bill" lost by 3,072 votes. Idaho's referendum provisions were used only once before 1966, but with resounding results that time. In 1936 the sales tax was repealed by 75,468 to 68,728 votes. Because of this action the legislature was unable to enact another sales tax until 1965—twenty-nine years later, and in this period most candidates standing for such a tax were defeated either in the direct primary or in the general election.

In 1966 the tax was again an issue in the gubernatorial campaign. A referendum petition against the tax gained sufficient signatures to place the issue on the November 1966 general election ballot, where it was defeated, 61 percent of the votes being in favor of retaining the tax. Donald W. Samuelson, who had voted against the tax, succeeded in defeating incumbent Governor Robert E. Smylie in the Republican primary, carrying all but seven of Idaho's forty-four counties. He

19. See the excellent report to the Idaho Legislative Council entitled *Reapportionment of the Idaho Legislature*, Idaho Legislative Council, Research Publication No. 2 (1964), p. 1.

went on to win the general election by 41 percent in a four-man race, two candidates having been put on the ballot by petition—Perry Swisher, a pro-sales tax
state senator, and Phillip Jungert, pro-gambling, both of whom ran as independents—in addition to the Democratic candidate, Cecil Andrus, who voted for the
sales tax. "The sales tax may have contributed to Samuelson's victory in two
ways. Although the tax passed with 61 percent of the vote, there were many voters who were neutral or opposed to the tax who voted for Samuelson. Moreover,
Don Samuelson may have received many votes from persons who favored the tax
because of educational needs but preferred a conservative state fiscal policy in
non-educational programs."[20]

VOTING HABITS

In most presidential elections Idaho could serve as a barometer for the nation. However, certain exceptions stand out. In 1892 the Populists carried the
state, as did William Jennings Bryan in 1896 and 1900. In 1952 Idaho gave General Eisenhower 65.4 percent of its vote, comparable to the Republican vote in
Maine. In 1960, for the first time in sixty years the state failed to give its vote to
the country's choice for President. Minor and third parties have played a profound part at certain periods. From 1895 to 1900, the Silver Republicans, the
Progressives, and the Fusion party all won one or more seats in the legislature. In
1918 the Non-Partisan League stole the Democratic party by filing in the Democratic direct primary. The Progressive Republicans caused grave concern for the
Republican party for many years, especially from approximately 1915 to 1924.
This splinter consisted of liberals who were opposed to the conservative position
of the Grand Old Party. The GOP conservative position was demonstrated by the
actions of a number of the regular party members on more than one occasion in
their efforts to prevent Senator William E. Borah's renomination. Also the struggles over the enactment of direct primary legislation have been largely within the
ranks of the Republicans. The Progressive Republicans voted with the Democrats
in favor of such legislation. Such informal coalitions were common from 1915 to
1924.

Two major early-day issues, anti-Mormonism and demands for the annexation of northern Idaho to Washington, left deep imprints on the sectional character of Idaho politics. Since most of the Mormons migrating into Idaho from 1860
to 1872 settled in the southeast, it was natural that the Mormon question should
become a sectional problem. Sectionalism is still a dominant characteristic of the
state's politics and is reinforced by topography. Although southeastern Idaho has
no mountains separating it from the southwestern part of the state, it is culturally
and religiously tied to Utah and especially to Salt Lake City, the headquarters for
the L.D.S. church. For years many of these Idaho Mormons considered themselves to be citizens of Utah. Numerous communities were at least 95 percent
Mormon. Local anti-Mormonism spread across the state and especially into southwestern Idaho, the opposition developing for both religious and economic reasons. The issue was carried so far that Mormons were denied the privilege of holding office in 1884. Vigorous attempts to deny them the privilege of suffrage at the
constitutional convention were narrowly defeated. The controversial role of the
L.D.S. church in Idaho's politics has continued through the years. The Mormons

20. Herbert S. Duncombe and Boyd A. Martin, "The 1966 Election in Idaho," *Western Political Quarterly*, XX (June 1967, Part 2), 568-75.

have failed to elect a governor or a United States senator from among their ranks although both parties will give them congressmen, superintendents of public instruction, secretaries of state or other comparable offices to balance a ticket. Anti-Mormon feeling has declined rapidly in recent years, although the church was again charged in 1956 with telling its members how to vote. It is obvious that most anti-Mormons have developed a more tolerant attitude in recent years.

Because the Mormons constitute almost one-fourth of the state's population and because of their religious, economic, and social solidarity, they have been accused of voting as a bloc, especially Republican. Elmer R. Rusco's study, *Voting Behavior in Idaho*, indicates "that the Mormon population is both southern and agricultural, the two factors associated in Idaho with Republican voting."[21] There does not seem to be reliable evidence to prove that there is now a solid Mormon vote.

The other major issue of sectionalism arose over a demand for uniting northern Idaho, eastern Washington, and western Montana to form a new state, to be called Columbia or Lafayette. Cut off by the Salmon River Mountains, people from northern Idaho strongly felt closer ties with these areas than with southwestern Idaho and especially southeastern Idaho. Many times the southwest, especially the Boise area, has been able to maintain a balance of power by playing northern and southeastern Idaho off against one another. This sectional conflict has made it virtually impossible for the northern part of the state to elect a governor or a United States senator. The latter has been achieved (with only two exceptions) when Boise Republicans have taken the initiative in promoting a northern candidate in an effort to balance the ticket. The sectional position of Boise is strong because it is the center for about 30 percent of the state's population. One of the wonders of Idaho politics has been the reluctance of the northern and southeastern sections to form a coalition against Boise. This reluctance is probably due to sectional rivalries and to the fact that each section has stronger ties to other areas outside the state.

Idaho's sectionalism has an economic basis as well as geographical and social foundations. Northern counties invariably cast the smallest percentage of Republican votes and southern counties the largest. The dominant position of mining and lumbering in the north and of agriculture in the south contribute to creating a Democratic majority in the former and a Republican majority in the latter area.[22] Herman Lujan's study indicates that in many instances unless another dominant prevailing factor is present, Idaho's liberal and Democratic vote is rural and the conservative Republican vote is urban. For instance, Latah County, which was strongly Republican for many years, casts its strongest Democratic vote in rural areas and villages and its strongest Republican vote in Moscow.[23]

Idaho's voters, like those of the nation, have been changing slowly.[24] A majority of the early settlers came from below the Mason-Dixon Line. Consequently, politics in the early days was compromised by southern attitudes. But gradually

21. Reno: Bureau of Governmental Research, University of Nevada, 1966, pp. 20-28.

22. See excellent study of Elmer Rusco cited above and the one by Herbert Sydney Duncombe and Katherine D. Pell, *Idaho Election Statistics 1960-1964*, Research Memorandum No. 4 (Moscow: Bureau of Public Affairs Research, University of Idaho, 1966).

23. Herman D. Lujan, "Voting Behavior in Idaho 1950-1962: A Study of Party Predisposition at the Precinct Level" (Ph.D. dissertation, University of Idaho, 1964).

24. See Quentin H. Whybark, "The Dynamics of Idaho Politics, 1890-1920" (Master's thesis, University of Idaho, 1950), and Garrett O. Forbes, "Dynamics of Idaho's Politics 1920-32" (Master's thesis, University of Idaho, 1955).

the influence of the Republican Homestead Acts was felt. Although Idaho became a protest state from 1892 to 1900 and partially from 1914 to 1918, the gradually increasing power of the Republicans was apparent. Republican supremacy, firmly entrenched during the decade 1920 to 1930, was broken in 1932. The state voted consistently for Roosevelt and Truman. But Republican strength, on a local level, was on the mend during New Deal and Fair Deal supremacy, and the Republicans were soon winning back some of the major state offices. Republican strength has always been greater for offices in the legislature and state government than for United States senators and presidents. In off-presidential elections, Idaho has voted Republican 70 percent of the time; half of the time it has also voted against the party controlling the White House. In presidential elections, Idaho has voted Democratic 60 percent of the time since becoming a state.

The farm and labor vote is becoming increasingly significant. Although farm and ranch voters tend to be Republican during prosperous times, they do not hesitate to go Democratic when prices drop. A new force in Idaho politics is the labor vote. Approximately 160,000 laborers are located in fifteen of the most industrialized counties. These voters are difficult to contact. If they are not immediately concerned they may not vote; if they are concerned they have been able to throw the election. For example, in 1950 at least 34 percent of them stayed away from the polls; that year the Republicans carried ten of these fifteen counties; in 1948 they carried two.

Idaho has long had a sizable liberal vote. This vote seldom reaches a majority but when combined with a party's normal dependable support it spells success. This is illustrated by the election of Senators William E. Borah, Glen H. Taylor, and Frank Church. Borah combined the liberal protest vote with the regular Republican vote to win. Taylor, until he decided to run for Vice President on the Progressive party ticket in 1948, won by combining the liberal protest vote with the regular Democratic vote. Church succeeded with the same combination.[25]

Currently, Idaho votes Republican by 51.9 percent. Lujan found that fourteen counties which are normally Democratic comprise only 31.9 percent of the state's population; five, which are the strongest Republican counties, comprise 40.1 percent; and twenty-two counties, which normally vote Republican, comprise 68.1 percent. Consequently, a Republican can be elected by holding normal Republican counties, while a Democratic candidate, to be elected, must carry normal Democratic rural counties and make inroads on the more populated counties with large numbers of middle-class voters.

Idaho Republicans made impressive gains in 1966. Senator Len B. Jordan and Congressman George V. Hansen were re-elected by increased margins over Democratic opponents. In Idaho's First Congressional District, state Senator James A. McClure upset incumbent Democratic Congressman Compton I. White. Republicans retained the governorship with Donald W. Samuelson defeating incumbent Governor Robert E. Smylie in the primary and winning the general election. The Republican majorities increased from six to nine in the Idaho Senate and from five to six in the State House of Representatives. Republicans now hold all national and statewide elective offices in Idaho except the Senate seat held by Frank Church and the offices of auditor, treasurer, and superintendent of public instruction.[26]

25. See the articles on elections in Idaho in the *Western Political Quarterly*, March of 1949, 1951, 1953, 1957, 1959, and 1961, December of 1954, and June of 1963, 1965, and 1967.

26. Duncombe and Martin, *op. cit.*, p. 568.

IMPACT OF NATIONAL POLITICS AND TRENDS

The statement "such a proposal is a violation of states' rights" is still good for considerable emotional response, but the citizens of Idaho have been quick to look upon the national government as their government also. Had it not been for federal grants-in-aid, Idaho farmers would still be in the mud. Although Idaho is more isolated than some states, the people take an active interest and participate directly in many national events. Most appeals to the slogan of states' rights are used by those opposed to a proposed activity rather than by those with any real conviction on the matter of states' rights. This does not mean that Idahoans will not defend the traditional state activities, but it does mean they will not hesitate to cooperate with the national government on such activities as the Social Security Act, federal highways, airports, the National Defense Education Act, etc. Idaho, like all states, is taxing her citizens heavily to meet her obligations. She, too, looks to other sources of income—even from Washington.

Idaho is a part of the developing national culture. Most Americans read the same weekly journals and syndicated press columns as well as watch the same television programs. They read the same plays, books, and headlines. Consequently, local provincialism is declining. The substitute may not be better, but it is different. With modern transportation, San Francisco, Seattle, or Washington, D.C., are almost as close for large segments of the state's population as is Boise. Idahoans read, see, and hear of more events from Washington, Moscow, London, or Tokyo than they do from Boise. This does not indicate a decline in interest concerning problems of the state, but it does indicate a new level of national and international sophistication. These new interests do not, however, detract from the significance of local and state issues. They simply mean Idaho's people are carrying more responsibilities than ever before.

MONTANA:

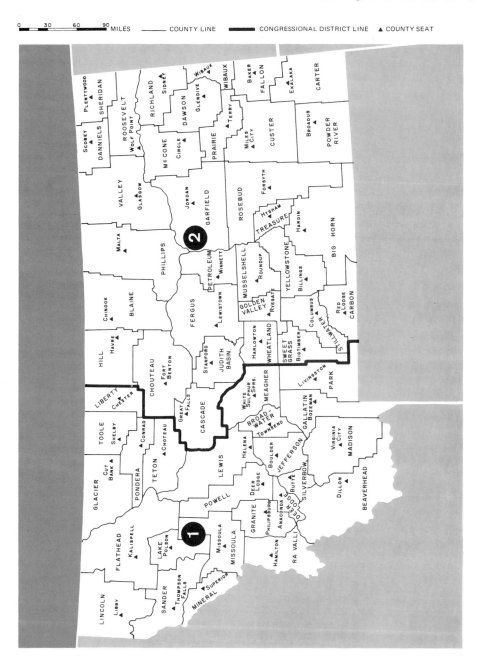

0 30 60 90 MILES ——— COUNTY LINE ■■■■ CONGRESSIONAL DISTRICT LINE ▲ COUNTY SEAT

Thomas Payne

Politics Under the Copper Dome

Montana is a land of arresting and unforgettable contrasts in its terrain, its weather, and its politics. To the east the land stretches away to the horizon in seemingly endless level plains, cut here and there by rivers and their accompanying gorges or "breaks," the view sometimes obstructed by the pattern of buttes and jutting limestone formations which checker the landscape. This is the Montana of high plains country, vast cattle ranches, and strip farming. As the observer steeped in this land moves westward he meets abruptly with the Rockies and finds himself in a markedly different terrain of mountain streams, green, forested, mountain slopes, and lush, irrigated valleys. The weather, too, can change abruptly. Variations of 75 degrees in temperature readings have occurred within a twenty-four hour period, although these are exceptional.

If Montana's political pendulum sometimes swings as widely and unpredictably as the sudden changes in terrain and weather, it is indicative both of the highly personal character of its politics and the essentially "unstructured" nature of its political system. Geography produces the inevitable rivalry between eastern and western Montana. Some enduring economic interests have emerged. But the state has vast distances, with a sparse and mobile population not yet anchored in any discernible pattern of traditional behavior either in mores or politics. Communication in an environment such as this is often inadequate. Volatile and unpredictable in political behavior, Montana appears unwilling to settle down into a more conventional (and predictable) political order.

A search for clues to the volatile pattern of political behavior must start with a survey of the history of this colorful state.[1] From its organization as a separate territory in 1865 (following discovery of gold at Bannack, Alder Gulch, and Last Chance Gulch) to the present, the Treasure State has known in kaleidoscopic intensity the experiences in economic development and politics which elsewhere occurred over greater periods of time. If benefit was derived from the political and governmental experience of older commonwealths, it is not often apparent from reading either the history of Montana or its constitution.

Contemporary political developments have their origin, to some extent at least, in the nature of the economy which evolved after settlement. Early settlers were attracted by a treasure-house of rich resources—vast copper reserves, gold,

1. The best recent works which deal extensively with Montana's past are: Joseph K. Howard, *Montana: High, Wide, and Handsome* (rev. ed.; New Haven: Yale University Press, 1959); and K. Ross Toole, *Montana: An Uncommon Land* (Norman: University of Oklahoma Press, 1959). Of less general interest but containing much valuable detail are: Merrill Burlingame and K. Ross Toole (eds.), *History of Montana* (3 vols.; New York: Lewis Historical Pub. Co., 1957); and John W. Smurr and K. Ross Toole (eds.), *Historical Essays on Montana and the Northwest* (Helena, Montana: Western Press, 1957).

silver, abundant stands of virgin timber, and a fabulous sea of grass which earlier had sustained enormous herds of buffalo. Few then spoke for conservation and they were rarely heard. Most were concerned with the business at hand: to exploit the rich resources which seemingly were theirs for the taking. Hillsides were denuded, grasslands overgrazed, and sod never intended for cultivation plowed. An "extractive economy"[2] developed quickly, in which the prime objective was to get all that could be gotten and then clear out. A background such as this was not conducive to the development of a stable political tradition.

The most colorful and, perhaps, significant heritage out of Montana's political past is derived from the titanic struggle for economic and political supremacy carried on for a dozen years before the turn of the century between the "copper kings,"[3] William A. Clark and Marcus Daly. In brief, Clark, having built a huge fortune from mining and banking, aspired to a seat in the United States Senate while his equally affluent adversary Daly, the founder of the Anaconda Copper empire, determinedly opposed these aspirations. Enormous sums of money were expended on both sides, augmented by the employment on an intensely personal and flamboyant basis of the newspapers owned by the two dynasties. Charges of large-scale bribery—some merely alleged, others proved—were fairly common. Indeed, in a later struggle with Amalgamated Copper the colorful F. Augustus Heinze was accused of bribing the judiciary of Butte!

It is possible under these circumstances to understand (if not to justify) the determination of the powerful Anaconda Company, once it attained economic hegemony in the state, to maintain a tight control of the press and politics. Clark, Daly, Heinze, and others had demonstrated that control of newspapers could be a powerful weapon in public affairs. Henceforth, Anaconda would own outright most of the major newspapers of the state[4] and, through a web of pecuniary relationships, would use its enormous power to block changes which it deemed detrimental to its interests. The press became and, on the whole, has remained neutral and politically sterile.

Although the political heritage of Montana reveals a tarnished past, signs on the contemporary horizon point hopefully toward better days to come. There is some evidence to indicate that the days of her extractive economic practice and philosophy are past. The major mining and timber interests have been converted to conservation. Moreover, an economic structure long noted for its monolithic character is moving toward diversification. Inevitably, this has brought in its train a healthier competition among the emerging interests. Among the dominant corporate interests there are indications of a growing sense of community responsibility and of political and social maturity. As the trend toward urbanization continues, a rustic politics which has emphasized political personalities will give ground to an urban politics which has greater interest in political issues.

GEOGRAPHY AND RESOURCES

The politics of the Treasure State is profoundly affected by factors of geography and resources. Its geographical location (and relative isolation) destined it to be a raw materials producing state rather than an industrial one. The existence

2. A term employed by Toole in *Montana: An Uncommon Land.*

3. A popular but useful treatment is found in Carl B. Glasscock, *The War of the Copper Kings* (New York: Grosset & Dunlap, 1935).

4. Until June 1959, when the "Company" papers were sold to the Lee Syndicate.

of substantial deposits of precious metals precipitated the initial development of mining activity. Limited rainfall determined the kind of agriculture that could flourish—cattle ranching, strip farming for grain, and irrigated valley farming in some areas. Much, if not all, of the economic development has been conditioned by these factors—rainfall, distance, and resources. This development, in turn, has shaped the political context to an appreciable degree. Thus we can speak of a politics of copper, a politics of wheat, a politics of cattle, and so on.

Montana's allegiance is divided, as a result of geography, between the Great Plains and the Pacific Northwest. It is bounded by Canada, the Dakotas, Wyoming, and Idaho. Its total area of 147,138 square miles is exceeded only by that of Alaska, Texas, and California. A land of great distances, it is 560 miles from the most westerly point to the eastern boundary, and nearly 320 miles from the Canadian border to the southernmost limit.[5]

Montana owes its name to the mountainous terrain which dominates the western one-third of its landscape. Traversing the state from north to south is the main range of the Rockies, which forms the Continental Divide. Here the headwaters of both the Missouri and Columbia River drainage systems originate. Major mountain chains other than the Rockies include the Bitterroot Range which forms part of the western boundary with Idaho, the Mission Range, the Belt Mountains, the Crazy Mountains, and the northern portion of the Absaroka Range. Although Montana has the lowest mean elevation (3,400 feet) of the Rocky Mountain states, four peaks rise above 12,000 feet: the lowest elevation is 1,800 feet at the point where the Kootenai River leaves the state in the northwest.

The eastern two-thirds, while not completely devoid of mountains, is predominantly a region of high level plains sloping gradually toward the eastern boundary. Through this generally treeless section course two of the state's principal rivers, the Missouri and the Yellowstone, both augmented by numerous tributaries. The principal river systems of western Montana are the Clark Fork and the Kootenai.

The Continental Divide separates the state into two climate regions: that to the west receives its weather pattern largely from the Pacific Ocean, while to the east of the mountains weather is more typical of the northern plains and of Canada's prairie provinces. The mean temperature is 43 degrees, but extreme fluctuations may occur. Montana must be classified as semi-arid with average annual rainfall ranging from about 18 inches in the western portion to as little as 13 inches in the east. It is not surprising that the development of water resources has remained an enduring issue in the state's politics.

The principal resources, soil, water, minerals, and forests, determine the principal types of economic activity. The soil is quite fertile, requiring, however, more moisture than is commonly available through rainfall. Consequently, there are three principal kinds of agriculture—strip farming, irrigated farming, and grazing livestock. Agriculture is, and has been for many years, the principal single source of personal income. Agricultural production normally is divided about equally between crops and livestock. The principal cash crop is wheat, in which the state ranks third in the nation. It has consistently ranked among top livestock producing states both in cattle and in sheep and wool. Other major agricultural products include hay, barley, and sugar beets.

5. Much of the factual data in this section is taken from *The Montana Almanac* (Missoula: Montana State University Press, 1958), *passim*, and from Roland R. Renne, *The Government and Administration of Montana* (New York: Crowell, 1958), pp. 1-10.

Farms and ranches are considerably larger than those found in the Midwest and South. In the past decade the more than 34,000 farms and ranches averaged 886 acres, with an average value of $43,000. As in the nation as a whole, the trend in the state has been toward larger farm and ranch units, with a consequent reduction of the number who are directly engaged in agriculture. At the same time agriculture is becoming more diversified with less reliance on wheat and livestock.

The vital importance of water resources has been recognized since territorial days. Speaking before the Montana Constitutional Convention in 1889 John Wesley Powell, the noted conservationist, remarked that "all the great values of this territory have ultimately to be measured to you in acre feet." Montana long has been interested in the development of reservoirs on major streams. Major multipurpose dams have been completed at Fort Peck and Canyon Ferry on the Missouri River, at Hungry Horse on the South Fork of the Flathead River, and at Yellowtail on the Big Horn River. These dams provide storage for irrigation and flood control, and also generate large quantities of hydroelectric power. Their existence, and the question of constructing other similar projects, makes public power a perennial and lively issue in politics. A less controversial multi-purpose dam is under construction at Libby on the Kootenai River in the northwestern part of the state. Greatest controversy in the 1950's and early 1960's centered around a proposal of the Corps of Engineers to build a dam either at Paradise on the Clark Fork or at Knowles on the Flathead (above the confluence of the two streams). Well-organized groups both of proponents and opponents quickly developed, with the liberal Democratic Senator Lee Metcalf leading the fight for the dam, and the Montana Power Company providing substantial leadership for its opponents. With the completion of the Columbia River Treaty with Canada, which gave a green light of construction at Libby, the Paradise-Knowles project appears to be shelved for the moment, but is certain to be revived later.

Proposals for development of the Columbia and Missouri River Basins often elicit cries of "Montana water for Montanans!" Such slogans may become more prevalent in the future. Each year sees more proposals from the water-poor Southwest for transferring some of the surplus water of the Northwest southward. In 1965 no less than 38 bills instructing the Secretary of the Interior to begin studies of the feasibility of diverting water from the Northwest to the Southwest were pending before Congress. Congressman Tunney of California, for example, has suggested that as much as 15,000,000 acre feet might be taken from the Northwest and placed in the Colorado River. Geography, as well as water resources, indicates the strong likelihood that Montana water will be considered for such a transfer. The outcome of such a scheme is uncertain, but the political repercussions are bound to be heard.[6]

Montana aptly has been called the "Treasure State" because of its vast storehouse of mineral deposits. Copper has been the most important mineral product to date, although rising petroleum production may alter its status in the future. More than 2 billion dollars' worth of copper, one-fourth of all copper produced in the United States, has been taken out of Butte, earning it the title, "richest hill on earth." The giant firm born in Butte, the Anaconda Company, has become the world's largest producer, smelter, and fabricator of copper. Other important metallic minerals include silver, gold, lead, manganese, and chromium. Among non-

6. *Daily Missoulian*, August 3, 1965.

metallic minerals, coal, petroleum, and natural gas exist in enormous quantities. Known reserves of sub-bituminous coal would be sufficient, if converted to gasoline, to supply the needs of the United States for four hundred years at present rates of consumption.

Petroleum production in the state began in 1915 in the Montana section of the Elk Basin field near the Wyoming boundary and continued to develop at modest proportions until 1951, with major discoveries in the Williston Basin. By the 1960's total crude oil production exceeded 30,000,000 barrels which, while only a small portion of the nation's total output, was triple the state's production only ten years earlier. As a result of this growing production and prospects for the future, major oil companies have established refineries in the state chiefly in the Billings area, causing the rapid growth of that city since 1950. Natural gas, a by-product of petroleum production, is also produced, with reserves in 1962 estimated to be in excess of 600 billion cubic feet.

The development of the petroleum industry has helped alter the political complexion of the state. For one thing it has created a substantial new interest, which is not necessarily allied with the existing power structure. The emergence almost simultaneously of a major lumber industry in the state, with the consequent articulation of the lumber interests has, together with the petroleum interest, given a somewhat pluralistic cast to a political pattern which had been dominated by the monolithic copper mining industry for at least a generation. A major issue in the mid-1950's, when the petroleum industry was expanding rapidly, was the question of policy with respect to leasing state-owned school lands which were believed to contain substantial petroleum reserves. Republican Governor Hugo Aronson took a position generally favorable to the oil industry, while his Democratic adversary on the state land board, Arnold Olsen, favored more stringent leasing terms. The issue came to a climax in the 1956 gubernatorial campaign, when the two men were opposing candidates and Aronson won.

One-fourth of Montana's land area is in forests, the bulk of which is concentrated in the eleven national forests. Much of the forest acreage is suited for commercial timber production, and this, now managed largely on a sustained yield basis, provides the raw material for the flourishing and expanding lumber and timber products industry. The principal species used in lumber production—all softwoods—are ponderosa pine, western larch, Douglas fir, and Engelmann spruce.

Montana's recreational resources have become an increasingly important part of her economy through the tourist trade. They have also precipitated the development of powerful recreational groups, whose influence in politics continues to grow. Sportsmen's groups do not hesitate to take stands on questions of construction of dams, stream diversion for road construction, and the establishment and preservation of wilderness areas. On the borders of Montana are two major national parks. Within the state are some of the largest wilderness areas in the entire country. Hunting, fishing, dude ranching, and pack trips have assumed considerable importance with the constant pressure from urban areas for recreational opportunities. National forest recreation areas in the state are being expanded. The rapid development of ski areas and other winter sports facilities suggests that recreation will continue to loom large in the future. The political implications of this remain somewhat unclear, but such interests are likely to enter the political arena.

POPULATION

Montana is blessed with an abundance of space, but relatively few people, ranking 48th in population density nationally.[7] For 1960, the Census Bureau reported a population of 674,767, an average of 4.6 persons per square mile, compared with the national figure of 50.5. Such abundance of space and scant population has long affected the state in many ways. It is, for example, a "high cost" area with respect to transportation and distribution charges. Montanans have consistently made a substantial effort, on a per capita basis, to support education, only to have this effort blunted by the dearth of population and the area to be served. While definitive studies have not been made, it may safely be assumed that the costs of maintaining governmental services are somewhat higher, too. The maintenance of a network of highways is a case in point.

Montana's population growth rate has been lower than the national rate and considerably less than that of some of her neighbors. Among the eleven contiguous western states, Montana ranked ninth in rate of population growth from 1950 to 1960, with an increase for the period of 14.2 percent, compared with the national increase of 18.5 percent. Between 1930 and 1950, the rate of increase was only 9.9 percent. Since 1960 about the same pace has been maintained, with a total increase of 4.5 percent estimated from 1960 to 1964. The population was officially estimated by the Census Bureau to be 705,000 on July 1, 1964.

The 1960 census revealed that for the first time, a majority of Montana's people live in urban areas (50.2 percent of the total, up from the 1950 figure of 42.8). The rural population was divided as follows: rural non-farm, 34.2 percent, and rural-farm, 15.6 percent. Past trends indicate a continuing drop in rural and rise in urban population as farm size increases and industry expands in urban centers.

There are but few major cities, the larger ones being Billings, Great Falls, Butte, Missoula, and Helena. Only fourteen cities have populations in excess of 5,000 and there are only thirty urban centers altogether, including all incorporated places of more than 2,500. All told, approximately half the inhabitants are concentrated in eight counties. Of the fifty-six counties in the state, only twenty-one have more than 10,000 people, highlighting the rural character of most of Montana.

Persons of the white race account for 96.4 percent of the total population. Indians constitute the largest non-white group: they numbered 21,181 in 1960. The foreign-born come chiefly from Canada, the British Isles, and the Scandinavian countries. The population as a whole is largely Anglo-Saxon, Irish, Germanic, and Scandinavian in origin. The Irish have long been a dominant group in Butte, while Scandinavians have been an important ethnic bloc along the High-Line section between the Missouri River and the Canadian border.

About one-half of Montana's people are affiliated with some organized religious group. Slightly more than half of those who are church members are of the Roman Catholic faith, the rest being Protestants. Among the latter, the leading

7. The principal source for population data is: U.S. Department of Commerce, Bureau of the Census, *Census of Population: 1960, I, Characteristics of the Population*, Part 28, "Montana" (Washington: Government Printing Office, 1963), *Census of Population: 1960, I, Characteristics of the Population,* Part I, "United States Summary" (Washington: Government Printing Office, 1964). See also W. Gordon Browder and Harold J. Hoflich, *Population and Income in Montana* (Missoula: Bureau of Business and Economic Research, Montana State University, 1953).

denominations are Lutheran, Methodist, Presbyterian, Episcopal, and Congregational, in that order. The Mormon church, a powerful force in parts of the intermountain West, has a small membership in Montana but has been proselytizing
and expanding vigorously in the past few years.

Religion has not played a large role in Montana politics. Protestants and
Catholics are so evenly balanced that religion appears to have been neutralized as a
factor in the political equation. Undercurrents of strong, if indeterminate, reli-
gious identification with issues in politics may be detected occasionally, however.
To what extent, for example, Butte's persistently strong identification with the
Democratic party is due to the heavy population of Irish Catholics in that city is
unknown. On the whole a greater degree of religious tolerance probably exists in
Montana than in the East or South, and the political system benefits accordingly.

EDUCATIONAL POLITICS

Education always has been valued highly by most Montanans who, in turn,
have contributed more to its support than to that of any other function in the
state. A school system was established by the first territorial legislature in 1865
and a state-supported university system was created by the 1893 legislature. In
1960 the median years of schooling completed by those over twenty-five was
11.6, compared with a national median of 10.6, a ranking of eleventh among the
50 states. Eight western states ranked higher than Montana in this category, however. Montana has consistently had one of the lowest incidences of rejection in the
military draft for mental disability of any state in the Union.

The six publicly supported institutions of higher learning are known collectively as the Montana University System. Control is vested in an eleven-member
Board of Education which consists of three ex-officio members (the governor,
attorney general, and superintendent of public instruction) and eight appointive
members selected by the governor equally from the two major political parties for
eight-year overlapping terms.

Elementary and secondary schools are administered through school districts, of which there were 819 in 1963, most of them operating small one- and
two-teacher elementary schools.[8] Only California among the thirteen western
states has more school districts. This excessive number results in inefficient utilization of funds. Montana's $493 per pupil expenditure for education in 1964
compares favorably with the national average of $455 and the state ranks 13th
nationally in this regard. Yet, in part because of her archaic pattern of school
district organization, Montana ranked in 1964 next to the bottom among the thirteen western states in average salary paid to elementary and secondary teachers.

When the state's basic plan for providing aid to local school districts, the
so-called Foundation Program, was adopted in 1949, it omitted any reference to
school district reorganization. The issue has arisen again as a result of a study of
school organization completed in 1958.[9] The report has not been acted upon by
the Legislative Assembly, but increasing needs for funds for education plus an
active campaign among education groups seem likely to assure some kind of action. Meanwhile, hopefully, there has been a steady attrition in the number of
school districts.

8. Superintendent of Public Instruction, Biennial Report, 1964, p. 18.

9. Division of Surveys and Field Services, George Peabody College for Teachers, *Public Schools of Montana: A Report to Montana Taxation-Education Commission*, 1958.

Although some state aid is provided through the Foundation Program, the bulk of the financial support for schools (excepting the University system supported exclusively by the state) comes from local sources. In 1963-64, of the $98 million expended on elementary and secondary education, 73.5 percent came from local sources, 21.5 percent from the state, and 5 percent from federal funds, the latter largely for so-called federally impacted areas. A complex formula is followed in financing public education under which there are mandatory county-wide and district tax levies on property, augmented by permissive district levies and further augmented, with voter approval in the district, by voted levies, supplemented in turn by state funds derived from general fund appropriations, from interest on the permanent school fund, and from royalties secured through the leasing of state-owned lands.

A special citizens' committee was appointed by the Governor after the 1961 legislative session to study the financing of elementary and secondary education and to recommend changes. The committee report, implemented by the 1963 legislative session, retained the Foundation Program, but provided a more flexible basis for adjusting budgeting power of local school districts to meet rising costs. Although the report was accepted on a bipartisan basis in the Legislative Assembly, the new formula became a political issue in the 1964 campaign, Democrats charging Republicans with passing the buck for financing to local property tax sources and failing to augment state support. The role of the state in supporting public education will probably continue to be a political issue, inasmuch as the state ranks low (37th) in percent of aid furnished to local school systems.[10]

The desire to keep education out of politics is manifested through such devices as the nonpartisan election of members of school district boards of trustees and the requirement that the two major parties be represented equally in the appointed membership of the state Board of Education. The ideal is not fully attained, for both the state superintendent of public instruction and the county superintendent of schools are elected on a partisan ticket. Moreover, the University system has not infrequently become a center of conflict among competing sectional and factional interests. An example is afforded by the prolonged dispute over the allotment of funds from the successful 1948 University building bond referendum. After voter approval of a $5,000,000 bond issue, the money was not allocated for more than two years, while the Board of Examiners (composed of the governor, secretary of state, and attorney general) differed with the Board of Education on how the money should be distributed. The dispute focused attention on the extent to which political and sectional forces are a factor in formulating educational policy in this state.

NEWS MEDIA AND PUBLIC OPINION

Montana's geographical remoteness and its sparsity of population increase the dependence of its people on its news media. In 1964 there were 17 newspapers with a daily circulation of 179,519 and a Sunday circulation of 167,146. A total of 77 weekly or semi-weekly newspapers also are published in the state.[11] In 1957 a daily was circulated for each 3.9 persons, as against the national average of one

10. *Christian Science Monitor*, June 29, 1965, p. 9.

11. N. W. Ayer & Son, *Directory Newspapers and Periodicals 1965* (Philadelphia: N. W. Ayer & Son, 1965), pp. 607, 1261.

newspaper for each 2.9 persons. The circulation of weekly newspapers in the state helps to alleviate this discrepancy.

Montana relies heavily upon radio and television as media of communication, although television to some extent is hampered in the western section by the mountainous terrain and throughout the state by the problem of distance. Radio service began in 1922 with the establishment of a station in Great Falls. Forty-five stations now broadcast in the state, many of which are affiliated with networks, and eight television stations operate.

A discussion of the role of the press would be incomplete without reference to the era of the Anaconda Company in journalism through the medium of the so-called "company press."[12] Until June 1, 1959, Anaconda had published eight daily newspapers in the state, some for more than fifty years. Anaconda's control of these newspapers was maintained through a publishing subsidiary, the Fairmount Corporation. The company-owned newspapers, including all dailies published in four of the five largest cities, were the *Billings Gazette*, the *Livingston Enterprise*, the *Daily Post* and the *Montana Standard* (both published in Butte), the *Anaconda Standard*, the *Helena Independent-Record*, the *Daily Missoulian*, and the *Missoula Sentinel*. The company papers had about 55 percent of the total daily newspaper circulation and about 60 percent of the total Sunday circulation.

How and why the Anaconda Company acquired control of its newspapers is shrouded in mystery. It was not definitively known even until 1951 just which newspapers were company-controlled, although many uneducated guesses had been made over the years. The *Anaconda Standard* was established in the 1890's by the founder of the Anaconda Company, Marcus Daly, and the company acquired the remainder of its chain of newspapers between 1906 and 1929. The disturbing episode early in the century when F. Augustus Heinze challenged the position of the Amalgamated Copper Company (Anaconda's predecessor) through dramatic appeals to public opinion probably was a factor convincing the corporate leadership of the wisdom of its journalistic course. It is not without significance that Anaconda's acquisition of a substantial part of the Montana press coincided with growing concern on the part of America's business enterprises with their corporate "images." The Anaconda Company has long served as a convenient "whipping boy" for discontented elements in the state, and control of the press offered a means of improving the company image through effective news management.

Policies of the company press varied considerably over the years of company control. While it was stoutly maintained by corporate officials that each paper's editorial policy was determined locally, it was evident that whether by instinct or pipeline, each paper followed essentially the same course with respect to the treatment of political news and editorial policy. During the 1920's, when the company's political hegemony was seriously challenged by a series of able gubernatorial candidates, its press struck out vigorously with "no holds barred." Its attacks on Governor Joseph M. Dixon were especially noted for their vituperation.[13] Former Senator Burton K. Wheeler, who in his earlier years in the Senate had incurred the wrath of the company more than once, reflected liberal sentiment of the era

---

12. See Richard F. Ruetten, "Anaconda Journalism: The End of An Era," *Journalism Quarterly* (Winter 1960), pp. 3-12, 104.

13. Shirley Jean DeForth, "The Montana Press and Governor Joseph M. Dixon, 1920-1922" (Master's thesis, Montana State University, 1959).

when he remarked: "If you ever see my picture on the front page of the Company Press you'll know I've sold out."[14]

Beginning with the 1930's, however, the Anaconda-owned papers underwent a marked change in their editorial politics and in their treatment of political news. Controversial news was often suppressed entirely, when it was not buried on an inside page. The announcement by a Great Falls legislator, for example, that he would introduce a bill to label silicosis an industrial accident was not reported in the company papers. Editorial policy became not only neutral, but sterile as well. A variety of historical, exotic, or otherwise irrelevant topics graced the editorial pages, constituting in all probability the blandest diet of editorial comment ever served to any group of American newspaper readers.

While the editors of the company press carefully avoided printing stories that might put Anaconda or its friends in a bad light, they were generally fair to both major political parties and all candidates in political campaigns. Studies of recent campaigns indicate that the papers gave approximately equal space to the candidates of both parties. The selection of syndicated columnists and cartoonists, however, reflected a decidedly conservative bias. For years the *Daily Missoulian*, for example, subjected its readers to a steady fare of David Lawrence, Westbrook Pegler, and George Sokolosky. Residents of communities served by company papers experienced the disinterest of their newspapers in community affairs and projects. A reader of a company paper was likely to be better informed on national and international developments than he was on state or local issues. Nor was the safety-valve device of a letters-to-the-editor column available; the owners seemed to assume that all would be better off without such a column. In sum, readers of the company press were without a forum to serve as the market place for ideas.

Rumors in 1958 that the Anaconda Company planned to sell its newspapers were confirmed with the June 1, 1959, announcement that all of the papers had been purchased by Lee Newspapers, Incorporated. Headed by Lee P. Loumis of Mason City, Iowa, the chain is noted both for its successful business operations and for the relative autonomy in editorial policy it allows each of its member newspapers. Montanans of both liberal and conservative persuasion applauded the sale. A number of important changes in publication policy have occurred. Each paper now takes editorial stands on community as well as national issues. Each has strengthened considerably its local news coverage. Some have added letters-to-the-editor columns and liberalized somewhat their choice of syndicated political columns. Each paper is apparently entirely free to pursue its own editorial policy. Managed political news is a thing of the past.

There have always been some independent newspapers in Montana speaking both for the political right and the political left. Until its recent sale the major independent, the *Great Falls Tribune*, had gained the reputation of providing the best news coverage of state affairs available. Long owned by the noted Warden family, its sale on April 30, 1965, to the Minneapolis Star-Tribune Company leaves Montana without a single major home-owned daily. In the weekly newspaper field publications do represent most points on the political spectrum. Generally well to the left of center are the *Western News*, published in Hamilton, and the *People's Voice* of Helena. The *Voice* staunchly supports the liberal wing of the Democratic

14. Joseph K. Howard, "The Decline and Fall of Burton K. Wheeler," *Harper's Magazine*, 194 (March 1947), 227.

party and is militantly pro-family farm, pro-labor, and anti-company in its editorial outlook. Montana's most successful and distinguished weekly, the *Hungry Horse News*, is published by Mel Ruder in Columbia Falls. Dedicated to thorough, factual reporting, it has repeatedly attracted national attention and was the recipient of a Pulitzer Prize for its reporting of the 1964 floods. The voice of conservatism on a statewide basis is heard most clearly in the columns of the *Montana Citizen*, published by the Montana Chamber of Commerce. A 1965 venture, the *Hellgate Herald*, which purported to speak for the extreme right proved unsuccessful, possibly because it attempted to support itself by advertising alone. The only out-of-state newspaper with a significant circulation in Montana is the Spokane *Spokesman-Review*, which blankets a goodly portion of the state west of the Continental Divide.

Public opinion in Montana has a mercurial and evanescent quality. In a state with vast distances, sparse population, and generally inadequate facilities for mass communication, there is a tendency to rely heavily on the informal processes of grapevine and rumor. Typically, Montanans are better informed on national affairs than on state and local issues. As a result, a substantial amount of apathy exists, as far as public opinion at the grass roots is concerned. For longer than most people can remember the shadow of Anaconda's power has hovered forebodingly over the political horizon. A sense of pessimistic fatalism has resulted in which failures and inaction are excused, far more than is warranted, by fixing all blame on a convenient company "scapegoat."[15]

If public opinion is registered ultimately through election results, these are a poor guide in Montana which, like most of her western neighbors, prefers splitting tickets and "voting for the man" rather than for the party. In only four of the past thirteen legislative sessions, for example, has a single party controlled simultaneously both houses of the legislature and the governorship. And during the same period it has been normal for the elected governor to find himself in the political minority on the three-member Board of Examiners, which possesses much of the actual executive power which elsewhere is the prerogative of the governor. The practical consequence of "voting for the man" thus is often the creation of an irresponsible governing arrangement—one in which neither party can point to a clear mandate of public opinion or be held fully accountable by the public.

The formation and expression of opinion are hampered by an inadequate system of communication and a kind of voter and party irresponsibility. Moreover, means for the measurement of opinion do not exist. No opinion polls are maintained aside from infrequent and sporadic samplings by members of the academic profession. Newspaper editorial comment has been so sterile in the past as to have little value as a gauge of opinion. The closest measurement occurs in popular votes on referenda and initiative measures which, however, are possible only at two-year intervals. Between elections no reliable indices of actual opinion exist although the seasoned politician will sense the broad currents through his conversations, contacts, and correspondence.

15. Typical of Montana skepticism toward the Anaconda Company's professed benevolence is the tale, widely repeated, of two Butte miners who were discussing the imminence of war. A heated argument ensued with one miner asserting, the other denying, that war would occur. The latter finally advanced this clinching argument: "Everybody knows that the only enemy would be Russia. If they attack us they will come down through Alaska and Canada to invade Montana. And everybody knows the Company won't let them into Montana!"

NOMINATIONS AND ELECTIONS[16]

Political parties decide through the nominating process which candidates they will support in the general election. In Montana all nominations by a political party which polled 3 percent of the popular vote at the preceding election must be made through a direct primary, a provision insuring that both major parties will choose their nominees exclusively by this method. Anyone eligible to vote may vote in the primary, although in practice the turnout is always considerably less than in the general election. A 1965 law, which sought to shorten the duration of political campaigning by fixing the late primary date of the first Tuesday after the third Monday in August, resulted in the lowest primary vote turnout, 41.9 percent. The 1967 session of the Legislative Assembly promptly remedied the situation by legislating a return to the traditional date for Montana primaries, the first Tuesday in June.[17]

The law prescribes the use of the open primary, rather than the closed primary found in most states. Its distinguishing feature is that a voter is not required to reveal his political party affiliation nor to offer any promise to support the nominees of his party in the general election in order to participate in the primary. That party affiliation will remain secret is assured by the requirement that the ballot of each party entering candidates in the primary be given to the voter who, in the privacy of the voting booth, selects one and marks it, and then folds the ballots separately, depositing the marked one in the ballot box and the unvoted one in another receptacle provided for the purpose.

This procedure minimizes party responsibility and voters may and do cross from one party to the other with impunity. However, any candidate expecting to compete seriously for the nomination, normally must have a recognized standing within his party. Neither party endorses an "organization slate" in advance of the primary, but there is a tendency for organization support to coalesce about that candidate who informally has secured the blessing of party leaders. The extent to which members of one party may invade the primary of the opposition to vote in a spirited contest is not known. It has been demonstrated repeatedly, however, that the outcome of a general election cannot be gauged by the size of the vote in the respective party primaries. In the 1964 gubernatorial primary, for example, the total vote cast for the two Democratic aspirants was 128,677, more than twice the vote received by Governor Babcock, who was running unopposed in the Republican primary. Yet Governor Babcock defeated his Democratic opponent in November 1964 by more than 7,000 votes.

The state's delegates to national presidential nominating conventions, except in 1956, have been chosen at state conventions. After the 1952 Republican national convention, in which most of the Montana delegation stayed with Taft to the bitter end, the Legislative Assembly in 1953 adopted a measure providing for a presidential preference primary law. The presidential primary was employed in 1956 without generating a great deal of enthusiasm in either party. Consequently, it was repealed outright by the 1959 Legislative Assembly, which reinstated the old procedure.

Montana employs a system of permanent registration of voters. Once regis-

16. In this section data regarding election procedures are derived chiefly from *Election Laws of the State of Montana 1962* and the *1963 Supplement* (Helena, Montana: Secretary of State, 1962 and 1963).

17. *Laws of Montana* (1965), chap. 156; and *Laws of Montana* (1967), chap. 151.

tered, the voter may miss primary and local elections but if he fails to vote in a general election he must re-register. In addition to the usual eligibility requirements, the further qualification is prescribed for voting in elections authorizing the incurrence of public debt or the levying of additional taxation that one must be a tax-payer upon property, real or personal, within the state.

The administration of elections is decentralized, the conduct of election machinery being largely in the hands of each county's board of commissioners and clerk. It is the responsibility of the county commissioners to draw the boundaries of the election districts or precincts and to serve as a board to canvass the results of the election. The county clerk registers voters, prepares the official registration lists and poll books, supervises the preparation and distribution of ballots, and receives the official returns from the election officials in the various polling places.

On the ballot, names of candidates are grouped by office sought rather than by party column. Party designation of each candidate is specified, but in order to vote a straight ticket one must mark separately the square of each candidate of the party; it is impossible to vote a straight ticket by marking a single square. Split-ticket voting is facilitated if not actually encouraged by this ballot form. Six counties now employ voting machines, and the trend toward their use is likely to continue in the urban counties. The 1965 session of the Legislative Assembly enacted legislation permitting the use of electronic voting systems, which have been adopted in three counties.

Like her sister states, Montana has a great deal of "corrupt practices" legislation on the statute books, pertaining largely to the role of money in election campaigns. One may assume in the absence of instances of prosecution of violators that such legislation is more often honored in the breach than in the observance. Among specific corrupt practices legislation provisions are those outlawing the intimidation or deception of voters, the bribing of members of caucuses or conventions, betting on elections, employer coercion of employees, and fraudulent registration or voting. A candidate may spend no more than 15 percent of the annual salary of the office he seeks in his campaign for nomination and no more than 10 percent in his campaign for election. Exempt from the above limitations are expenditures for travel, office rent, advertising, and campaign literature. Corporations and public utilities are expressly prohibited from making any contribution toward the political candidacy of any individual.

Every candidate is required to file with the secretary of state or county clerk within fifteen days after the election an itemized statement of all monies received and expended in behalf of his candidacy. Failure to file such a statement makes a candidate liable to civil or criminal proceedings. No instance has been reported in which legal proceedings have been instituted against a delinquent candidate although instances of delinquent reporting, while uncommon, do occur. It is, indeed, exceedingly difficult to observe this process continuously, inasmuch as reports are not kept permanently, and a casual scrutiny of reported expenditures in a campaign leads one quickly to conclude that a full story of what actually was expended cannot be constructed from such reports.

PARTY ORGANIZATION AND PARTY LEADERS

Those who think of political parties as disciplined and responsible bodies learn quickly that such concepts are not applicable in Montana. Moreover, the state is not, nor has it been, frequented by identifiable political bosses. It is well known that the monolithic economic giant, the Anaconda Company, often in consort with the Montana Power Company, does take a lively interest in political affairs, but one is far from the mark in describing "the Company" as a political boss. On the whole, Montana resembles a catch-as-catch-can land in which personalities and personal followings are of more importance than traditional organization.

This is not to say that party organization can be disregarded. Indeed, it is carefully prescribed, at least in outline, by the statutes.[18] At the bottom of the organizational structure are the precinct committeeman and committeewoman who are chosen for two-year terms at the primary. Meeting together they comprise the party's county central committee which selects a chairman who becomes the local leader and spokesman of his party. Among the principal functions of this committee are the coordination of the work of the party in the county and the all-important task of finding financial sources of support. In theory each precinct is manned with workers engaged actively in promoting the fortunes of the party. In fact, however, local organization is mostly a hit-or-miss arrangement in which a small band of the faithful, spread far too thin in both parties, struggle valiantly to plug the numerous leaks in the organizational dike.

At the next level is the central committee, composed of a state committeeman and committeewoman from each county chosen by its central committee. The state central committee in turn selects the state chairman who, in the party of an incumbent governor, normally is the governor's choice. Because it is too large to meet frequently the state central committee chooses a smaller executive group to act in periods between its meetings. The state committee assumes the tasks of coordinating party activities and maintaining party harmony, speaking for the party between conventions, raising funds to finance party activities, and supporting the campaign for victory at the biennial general election. It also selects the national committeeman and committeewoman for four-year terms. These influential leaders carry much weight in state party councils in addition to having a voice in national party affairs.

The position of state party chairman has not, until recently, been regarded as a full-time job. Typically, each party in the past has maintained a headquarters in Helena, with a small secretarial staff to handle correspondence. During election campaigns the staff has been expanded. Recently, there has been a tendency in each party to strengthen its organizational leadership between campaigns. Initially, the parties followed different routes, the Republicans instituting the practice of appointing a full-time, salaried state chairman. At this writing both parties have chairmen who devote only a part of their time to party duties, but both have provided their chairmen with a full-time executive secretary who, under the direction of the chairman and the central committee, carries on the management of party affairs on a day-to-day basis.

Ultimate authority to speak for the party at the state level is vested in the convention. There are actually two which meet in presidential years. It is the task of the first to select delegates to the national convention. A short time after the primary a second convention meets to formulate a state platform. It consists of members of the state central committee as well as nominees of the party for all statewide elective offices. Legislation adopted in 1965 permits each party to

18. See *Laws of Montana* (1965), pp. 201-3 and *Revised Codes of Montana*, 1947, 23-929.

make its own rules and regulations.[19] Subsequently, both major parties have adopted new ones.

Discussion of the formal aspect of party organization tends to obscure the vital behind-the-scenes conflicts for control. While these can be known intimately only to insiders an occasional explosion may reveal something of the power structure. Both parties are coalitions of important economic interests within the state, some major interests being content to avoid taking sides and to work with both organizations. Within each party there appears to be a liberal-conservative division:[20] the "liberals" generally possess the whip hand in Democratic circles while the "conservatives" appear to be in the ascendancy on the Republican side.

The dominant liberal group in the Democratic party is made up of a coalition of organized labor and the Farmers Union, the leading farm group in the state. Practically every active leading Democrat is currently identified to some extent with the liberal coalition, although the senior senator, Mike Mansfield, has built a nonpartisan "image" for himself which has proven attractive to many independent and Republican voters. Senator Metcalf, on the other hand, is out-and-out identified with the liberal wing and makes no bones about it. Since the defeat of Senator Wheeler in 1946 it has become increasingly difficult to locate conservative Democrats although some, mainly in the professions or small business circles, do exist.

The Republican party remains today as it has been since statehood—a coalition of stockmen and business, professional, and financial interests. The rising oil interests appear to have gravitated strongly toward the Republican side, especially in the 1956 gubernatorial campaign, while major mining interests, notably Anaconda, carefully cultivate friendly relations at all points in the political spectrum. Since Governor Dixon's retirement from politics in 1924 there has seldom been an effective spokesman for the liberal or moderate wing of the Republican party. Practically every Republican candidate during the past twenty years has presented an ultraconservative viewpoint. An exception of sorts may be noted in the flurry of pro-Eisenhower activity before the 1952 convention among younger Republicans but little of this zeal has been carried over into the hard core of the organization.

The last quarter-century of Montana politics may be treated conveniently in four periods: (1) from 1940 to 1946; (2) from 1946 to 1952; (3) from 1952 to 1960; and (4) since 1960. During the first period, Democratic Senator Burton K. Wheeler, overwhelmingly re-elected to his fourth term in the Senate in 1940, gained a considerable measure of bipartisan power through an alliance with his good Republican friend, Governor Sam C. Ford. His relations with another powerful Republican, Wellington D. Rankin, were also close, and the Wheeler-Ford-Rankin triangle appeared to be a formidable political combination. However, the triangle collapsed with the successive political defeats of Rankin in 1942, Wheeler

19. *Laws of Montana* (1965), chap. 156.

20. As used here the admittedly amorphous terms "liberal" and "conservative" refer to orientation toward domestic social legislation and governmental intervention in the economy and toward involvement internationally in foreign aid and international organization. As one surveys political orientation along a continuum, one finds greater advocacy of government action toward the "liberal" side and of government abstention from action on the "conservative" side. Thus "conservative" Republican congressional candidate Jean Walterskirchen described the United Nations building as "a monument to folly" in the 1958 campaign, while "liberal" Democrat Lee Metcalf has advocated more federal projects for Montana.

in 1946, and Ford in 1948. Democratic Senator James E. Murray was well established by 1940 as the leading spokesman for political liberalism and, in 1942, won a third term in the Senate by defeating Rankin.

In the second period, from 1946 to 1952, the Republicans produced two new faces, Senator Zales N. Ecton, and Congressman Wesley A. D'Ewart. Both were conservatives with agricultural backgrounds. They shared the political spotlight during this period with Senator Murray, Congressman Mike Mansfield, and Governor John Bonner, on the Democratic side. This period ended in 1952 when Governor Bonner lost his office to a Republican challenger, while Senator Ecton, who has the distinction of being the only Republican ever to be elected by the voters of Montana to the U.S. Senate, bowed to defeat before the rising political star of Mike Mansfield.

The third period in Montana's recent political history was launched by the sweeping victory which carried the state for General Eisenhower in his contest for the Presidency. Simultaneously, the voters chose a Republican, Hugo Aronson, for governor, while elevating Democrat Mike Mansfield, a veteran congressman, to the Senate. The period, which has been characterized as a bipartisan era nationally, saw Montanans continue to prefer Republican executive leadership at the national and state level (Eisenhower and Aronson) while throwing their support to Democrats in congressional and senatorial races. As 1960 dawned there was no longer a single Republican in the four-man Montana congressional delegation.

The period beginning with 1960 may best be characterized as one of the changing of the political guard both nationally and at the state level. A new political generation was coming of age. Governor Hugo Aronson decided to retire after eight years in the executive mansion. Senator James E. Murray, up for re-election, withdrew from the Democratic primary after it became apparent that he would have a difficult time overcoming some of the challengers who aspired to his seat. Congressman Lee Metcalf succeeded in capturing the Democratic nomination for the seat Murray vacated, going on to win a close race in November. Republican Donald Nutter succeeded Aronson in the governor's office, only to be killed tragically in a plane crash in January 1962. Since Nutter's death his successor and the former lieutenant governor, Tim Babcock, has maintained a firm hold on the executive office. In 1960 the state followed its practice of the 1950's by casting its presidential election votes in the Republican column, but returned to the Democratic fold in 1964 in the Johnson landslide. In 1966 Senator Lee Metcalf was elected to a second term, defeating the governor, Tim Babcock.

The five men who loom largest in the past twenty-five years of Montana political history are Wheeler, Ford, Murray, Mansfield, and Aronson. There is enough color in the career of each of these men to fill a fascinating political biography. Of the five, Wheeler is easily the most enigmatic.[21] After serving for twenty-four years in the United States Senate and basking frequently in the national limelight he was defeated in the Democratic primary in 1946 by Leif Erickson. Why, is one of the unsolved riddles of Montana politics.[22] Always the political maverick, his party irregularity may have brought him finally to a political reckoning. A more plausible thesis, however, would be simply that by 1946 Wheeler had grown re-

21. See his autobiography, *Yankee from the West* (Garden City: Doubleday, 1962).

22. See Joseph P. Kelly, "Senator Wheeler's 1946 Democratic Primary Loss" (Master's thesis, Montana State University, 1959).

mote from and out of touch with Montana affairs. After his defeat he has remained in Washington and his law firm has enjoyed a flourishing practice. In 1958, his name was seriously proposed by Republican national Committeeman Wellington Rankin as a candidate for Mansfield's Senate seat—on the Republican ticket!

James E. Murray, who retired in 1961 after twenty-six years of service, earned the distinction of having been a U.S. senator longer than any other Montanan. Now deceased, Murray first entered the Senate in 1935 by winning election to the remainder of the unexpired term of the late Senator Thomas Walsh. Throughout his distinguished career Murray was unrelenting in his liberal stand, earning the friendship of labor and farm groups. Lacking the color of a Wheeler or the bipartisan appeal of a Mansfield, he managed to survive a number of extremely close races in retaining his seat. Among major legislative measures he supported during his Senate career were: the proposed Missouri Valley Authority; the Small Business Administration Act; the Full Employment Act; and compulsory health insurance.

Since his first election to the U.S. House of Representatives in 1942, Senator Mike Mansfield has risen steadily, if quietly, to the position of eminence he now occupies in state and national affairs. Moving up from the House to the Senate in 1952, Mansfield quickly won the respect of his colleagues, and, in 1957, was made assistant majority floor leader. Subsequently in 1961, when Lyndon Johnson assumed the Vice Presidency, Senator Mansfield became the majority leader of the Senate. Throughout his congressional career, Mansfield's area of greatest legislative interest has been foreign affairs, especially with reference to the Far East. He has never neglected the interests of his constituents, however. Mansfield's immense personal popularity and bipartisan appeal rest solidly on an unmatched record of concern for Montana interests, an impressive international reputation as one of America's ablest senators, and the indefatigability of a thoroughly professional office staff that leaves nothing to chance in handling the individual requests of constituents. With a political image that somehow benefits from his having worked in the Butte mines as a mucker and served for seven years as a university professor, Mansfield's political stature in Montana is generally regarded as being so lofty as to make him virtually unbeatable.

Both Republican governors of the past twenty years, Ford and Aronson, have been noted for their businesslike management of public affairs. Markedly different in background and temperament, each tended toward conservatism in outlook and policy. Governor Ford owed his victory in part to the support he received from Senator Wheeler and showed his appreciation by retaining in a number of key positions Democrats known to be loyal to Wheeler. An important episode during his eight years in the executive mansion was his feud with the Republican national committeeman, Dan Whetstone, over patronage, which led in 1948 to the ousting of Whetstone and his replacement by Wellington Rankin.

Former Governor Aronson is genuinely a self-made man in American politics. A Swedish emigrant, he rose to prominence in the Montana oil and trucking industries, and served in the Legislative Assembly prior to his election as governor in 1952. He completed his second term and announced that he would not be a candidate for re-election in 1960. As the "Galloping Swede" of Montana politics, Aronson was an appealing candidate. With his retirement the Republicans lost a popular vote-getter.

PRESSURE GROUPS

The growth and diversification of the economy of a state, a region, or a nation leads inevitably to the formation of a host of specialized group interests [23] which make claims upon the organs of government. As such groups arise naturally out of the economic and social conditions peculiar to a particular state, one finds a basis for the principal group interests in Montana in livestock, wheat, mining, petroleum, lumber, and a variety of business, professional, and labor activities.

The most conspicuous and most effective business group is the Montana Chamber of Commerce. Its major publication, the *Montana Citizen*, takes a vigilant interest in legislative proceedings, and keeps members informed on governmental developments affecting them. The Montana Taxpayers Association, which publishes the *Montana Taxpayer*, maintains a critical eye on tax and spending plans whether by local school districts, counties, cities, or the state government. In the field of transportation, the Montana Railroad Association has a reputation as an effective organized interest with able lobbyists to represent it. A proposed weight-distance tax on trucks has been powerfully and effectively opposed by the Montana Motor Transport Association. The Licensed Beverage Dealers Association is an active group which attempts to block proposals which are a threat to the prosperity of its members.

One effective business interest cannot be called, in any strict sense, a pressure group at all, but is a single powerful corporate concern, the Anaconda Company. Long known for the excellence of its lobbying activities, Anaconda's attorneys follow with keen scrutiny the course of every measure under consideration by the legislature. Its strength rests not only in its wealth and resources, but also in its elaborate network of relationships with key citizens, banks, legal firms, and business organizations throughout the state. Rare is that unit of local government—county, city, or school district—that does not have on its policy-making body a person associated, in some capacity, with the Anaconda Company. And Anaconda men are invariably among the leaders of the power structure in every large community in the state. Until June 1959, the Anaconda network was further strengthened by its control of most of the leading daily newspapers. It should be emphasized that Anaconda has used its great power largely in a negative fashion—to prevent government actions which it opposed.

The Montana Power Company has, over the years, been closely identified with the Anaconda Company on questions of public policy. Frequently, the two were referred to as "the Twins" or simply as "the Company." By 1962, however, there were reports of a growing estrangement between the two corporate giants. Uncertain conditions in Chile, where it had obtained more than two-thirds of its copper ore in recent years, forced Anaconda to look to a fuller utilization of its extensive Montana holdings in copper, zinc, lumber, and aluminum. In developing its aluminum plant at Columbia Falls in the 1950's Anaconda found it advantageous to exploit the available low-cost public power generated at Hungry Horse. Increasingly, its need for public power plus its worldwide orientation has separated Anaconda from its traditional friendship for Montana Power, a determined foe of public power. [24]

23. The writer prefers the term "interest group" partly because of the value-loaded connotation of "pressure group," but the latter term survives in both popular and academic writing on the subject of politics.

24. For an analysis of the economic factors involved, see financial section, *The New York Times*, November 25, 1962.

Labor is a force to be considered among Montana interests—always numerically significant, albeit lacking the cohesive quality of the business community. Three principal labor groupings are important—the AFL-CIO, the independent Mine, Mill and Smelter Workers Union, and the Railroad Brotherhoods. Labor's numerical advantage is vitiated by its concentration in urban mining and manufacturing centers. On the whole its voice from and for labor concerns is much stronger in Washington, D.C., through Montana's pro-labor Democratic delegation, than it is in Helena.

Of the three nationally important farmers' groups—the Farm Bureau, the Grange, and the Farmers Union—the Farmers Union, which has approximately twice the membership of the other two combined, is much the most important. As one would expect, remembering that about half of Montana's agricultural cash income is derived from livestock, associations of cattle and sheep men, notably the Montana Stockgrowers' Association, the Montana Cattlemen's Association, and the Montana Wool Growers Association, are powerful indeed. The stockmen are a force for conservatism, while the farmers, especially in wheat, tend toward a more liberal persuasion. Both have enjoyed enormous advantages over labor because of the pattern of apportionment of seats in the legislature which prevailed until the court-ordered reapportionment of 1965.

Numerous professional associations articulate their views whenever issues adversely affecting their interests arise. Among the more powerful are the Montana Medical Association and the Montana Bar Association. Among public employee groups the Montana Education Association is respected for its effectiveness. It is a revealing commentary on the prevailing power of rural areas that the County Commissioners Association is relatively strong, while the Executive Secretary of the Montana Municipal League, after a recent legislative session, lamented his inability to get a single major item of his legislative program adopted.

Methods employed by pressure groups are typical of those encountered in most states. The greatest energies are concentrated during the brief legislative sessions when as many as 300 lobbyists descend on Helena and, in turn, are aided by the thousands of constituents who either are brought to Helena for personal appearance before committees or submit their views by correspondence. Lobbying flourishes with little restriction; the sole check is an act to "Regulate and Control Lobbying" passed in 1959, with only the moderate stipulation that all paid lobbyists must register with the secretary of state and secure a license.[25] An important weapon of the lobbyist with ample resources is the social lobby, and numerous "water holes" with their free liquor are accessible to thirsty legislators. The forces of public opinion are mobilized on important issues and the powerful corporations are especially successful in getting their stockholders to communicate the sentiments of the corporation to their legislators. The better lobbies maintain staffs of experts who are not only valuable to their employer in an immediate sense but often constitute the only expertise available to counsel with ill-informed legislators.

Between sessions of the legislature a variety of techniques are employed by pressure groups, depending on their resources and size. A few maintain permanent headquarters or offices in Helena, as for example, the Montana Education Association, the Montana Chamber of Commerce, and the Montana State Nurses Association. Some engage in long-run advertising campaigns designed to inculcate a favorable opinion. Most hold annual meetings which are publicized and which furnish the occasion for the adoption of resolutions by the membership. The better

25. *Laws of Montana* (1959), chap. 157.

organized interests publish periodicals at regular intervals to rally the faithful to the cause of the group.[26]

LEGISLATIVE POLITICS

Montana voters often exhibit a kind of political schizophrenia which causes them to select liberal politicians to represent them in Congress, while often preferring conservatives in both the office of governor and their state legislature. The 1966 election points up this generalization: liberal Democrat Lee Metcalf was given a second term in the U.S. Senate, while Republicans gained added seats in the state Senate and control of the House of Representatives. This tendency to march in two directions at once is an illustration of the proposition that differing factors, indeed differing constituencies, are involved in the selection of national as contrasted with state representation. It might be added that partisan politics does not operate as a controlling factor in the liberal-conservative orientation of the legislature. Some recent sessions of the Legislative Assembly, which were not distinguished by their liberalism, saw Democrats with substantial margins in both houses.

The Republicans have controlled the state Senate three times as often as have the Democrats since the end of World War I, while control of the House has been divided on virtually even terms.[27] For the period since 1940 the Republicans have controlled the state Senate on eight occasions to six for the Democrats: control of the state House of Representatives has also rested with Republicans eight times and with Democrats six times. Ironically, in eight of the fourteen legislative sessions since 1940, a single party has simultaneously had a majority in both of the houses—the Republicans on five and the Democrats on three of those occasions, with divided party control in the other six sessions. Since 1940, the greatest margin of Democratic control in the state Senate occurred in 1959 when there were 38 Democrats and 17 Republicans; their greatest margin in the House was in the same year, 62 to 31. The Republicans enjoyed their largest margin in the 1947 Senate (41-15) and in the 1953 House of Representatives (63-32).

Party control of the Legislative Assembly has rarely been accompanied by any collective sense of party responsibility for a particular program. Indeed, until the 1959 session, when for the first time a bipartisan Legislative Council functioned, no systematic means of program planning was provided. Party control has meant chiefly the ability to determine the organization of the legislative body along partisan lines—but party lines do not appear especially significant in legislative decision-making.

26. The following groups publish their own organs at varying intervals: Dude Rancher's Association, Montana Farmers Union, Montana Education Association, Montana Department of American Legion, Montana Stockgrowers' Association, Montana Wool Growers Association, Montana Food Distributors Association, Montana Taxpayers Association, Montana Chamber of Commerce, Montana Citizens Freight Rate Association, Montana Congress of Parents and Teachers, Montana Grain Growers Association, Montana Motor Transportation Association, Montana Municipal League, Montana Automobile Association, Montana State Nurses Association, Montana Optometric Association, Montana State Press Association, Montana State Grange, Montana Conservation Council, Disabled Veterans, Montana Reclamation Association, Montana School Boards Association, Montana State Rural Electric Cooperative Association, Montana Federation of Women's Clubs, Montana Credit Unions League.

27. Ellis Waldron, *Montana Politics Since 1864: An Atlas of Elections* (Missoula: Montana State University Press, 1958), *passim.*

The Legislative Assembly, by the 1960's, had become increasingly malapportioned as the urban areas increased in population while the rural areas declined.[28] The census of 1960 shows that the eight most populous counties contained about 52 percent of the state's total population, but had less than 15 percent (one-seventh) of the representation in the Senate and 42.5 percent of the representation in the House. On the other hand the less populous counties were so overrepresented that a majority of votes in the Senate could be obtained from counties containing 16.1 percent of the population, while in the House, 36.6 percent of the population furnished a majority of the members. The so-called "variance ratio," used by the Supreme Court of the U.S. as a measure of malapportionment, revealed a disparity of 88 to 1 between the most populous and the least populous districts (counties) in the Senate, and a disparity of 14 to 1 in the House of Representatives.

Prior to the series of court decisions beginning with *Baker v. Carr* (1962) and culminating in the court-ordered reapportionment of the Montana Legislative Assembly in 1965, reapportionment had occurred at intervals of ten years and was based on the decennial census, with legislative districts confined to county boundary lines. The 1961 law,[29] following the state constitutional mandate, fixed membership in the Senate at one senator for each of the 56 counties. The representation accorded Yellowstone County, with a population of 79,000, was identical with that granted Petroleum, which had 900. An inequitable but more nearly representative pattern was established in the House where, although each county was automatically entitled to one representative irrespective of its population, a county was granted one representative for each 8,500 persons or major fraction thereof. Thus a county received two representatives if its population was 12,751, three representatives if 21,251, and so on. In earlier decades similar formulae had produced less noticeable malapportionment results. After 1920 the two major factors contributing to a growing malapportionment were the effects of the county-splitting era (1910-25), when the number of counties doubled from 28 to the present 56, and the growing urbanization of Montana's inhabitants with a corresponding decline in rural population. The proliferation of counties with few people and the continuation of the historic practice of giving each county one senator and at least one representative produced results which had become obvious by the 1950's.

Regardless of which political party controlled the legislature, a conservative orientation was characteristic normally of that body. Given the pronounced rural composition of both houses, progressive behavior was likely to be confined to a minority of the members. Farmers and lawyers, the two groups most heavily represented in the membership, have tended, on the whole, to reinforce the typically conservative outlook of the legislature. Inevitably, over the years, legislation favored by rural interests has had a more friendly reception than that favored by urban interests. On the basis of a questionnaire administered to members of the

28. Much of the material for this section is taken from the series of articles entitled "Background and Priorities for Legislative Reapportionment in Montana," *Montana Business Quarterly*, Winter 1965, pp. 37-140. The articles, which were collected and edited by Professor Ellis Waldron, include: Ellis L. Waldron, "Introduction and Summary"; "How the Montana Legislative Assembly Became Malapportioned"; "Statistical Measures of Apportionment"; "The Constitutional Obligation to Reapportion"; "What Kind of Legislature?" and "Getting the Job Done"; Douglas C. Chaffey, "Effects of Malapportionment in the Montana Legislative Assembly"; and Howard E. Reinhardt, "The Political Effects of an Equitable Apportionment."

29. *Laws of Montana* (1961), chap. 233.

1963 Legislative Assembly, Douglas C. Chaffey came to the following "cautious conclusions" on the effects of malapportionment:

1. Overrepresentation of rural counties in both houses increased the difficulty of passing certain types of legislation, including measures dealing with urban problems and finances, fish and game and recreation measures, and any measures which might adversely affect farming and ranching . . . rural opposition . . . may have killed legislation such as . . . the more extensive auto-license fee split and the property reclassification bills. . . .

2. Rural overrepresentation gave to the legislative parties a more conservative cast than they would have had in a more equitable apportionment, and contributed to lack of party cohesion.

3. Rural overrepresentation made it more difficult for urban interest groups to approach the legislature; this same imbalance facilitated the ease with which interest groups could bring pressure, especially in the state Senate.

4. Rural overrepresentation in the 1963 legislature accentuated both the Republican House majority and the Senate Democratic majority.

5. Rural overrepresentation increased the difficulty of adopting any changes in legislative structure and procedure which might have been proposed.[30]

When the Legislative Assembly convened in January 1965, Montana was one of only seven states in which no steps toward reapportionment had yet been taken. Proposals for reapportionment were being advanced from all sides, and it was widely assumed that during the session affirmative action would be taken to settle the question. Prospects for affirmative action were augmented when, early in the session, Phoebe Herweg filed a complaint against malapportionment in the federal district court in Butte against the Legislative Assembly, Governor, and Secretary of State.[31] On January 13, 1965, a special three-judge panel assumed jurisdiction but decided to defer any final action until after the legislature had adjourned, thus giving the responsible state body an opportunity to act. The two houses reached an impasse over acceptable plans, however, and the Legislative Assembly adjourned in March leaving reapportionment an unsettled issue.

The problem was then left in the hands of the special federal court panel. At a hearing on July 7, 1965, a tentative plan for reapportioning the Legislative Assembly to be effective for the 1966 election was announced and this plan, with some slight modification, was adopted on August 6, 1965.[32] Under the court-ordered plan of reapportionment, the 1967 Legislative Assembly was to be composed of a Senate of 55 members (contrasted with the previous 56) and a House of 104 members (contrasted with the previous 94). A total of 31 senatorial districts was established, each senator to represent an average of 12,268 persons. For the House, a total of 38 representative districts was established, each representative to represent 6,489 persons. In the court-ordered plan, county lines were preserved inviolate. This necessitated in numerous instances a combination of sparsely populated counties to establish an adequate population base for a district. The court also found it constitutionally impossible to prescribe single-member districts for those counties entitled to more than one senator or representative. As a consequence, the voters of the most populous county, Yellowstone, will in future elect twelve representatives and six senators at large.

Reaction to the reapportionment decree was generally more favorable than might have been anticipated. Predictions of drastic changes in the legislature, both

30. Chaffey, *op. cit.*, p. 88.
31. *Christian Science Monitor*, January 4, 1965.
32. *Great Falls Tribune*, July 8, 1965; August 7, 1965.

in composition and in legislative product, although freely made at the time, have thus far not been borne out by experience. The Legislative Assembly which convened in January 1967 was the first fairly apportioned legislature in the state's history. Its output was far from revolutionary by any standard; its notable inability to come to grips with the state's pressing fiscal problems was due in large measure to divided partisan control. The Democrats retained control of the Senate 30 to 25, while the Republicans won 64 seats in the House to 40 retained by their opponents. The pattern of political control in the 1967 session, resulting from the outcome of the 1966 elections, confirmed the basic conclusion of the author of a statistical study to the effect, essentially, that in a fairly apportioned legislature the pattern of party control would be substantially unaffected by the introduction of reapportionment.[33]

Montana's constitution sets up machinery for direct legislation. The devices of initiative and referendum may be employed, the former providing a means for enactment of legislation directly by the electorate, and the latter a means of considering and possibly reversing action already taken by the legislature. Since 1940 four initiative and sixteen referendum measures have appeared on the ballot, and seventeen proposed constitutional amendments have been referred to the electorate. In general the voter response to direct legislation measures indicates a healthy respect for the normal patterns of representative government. Only one of the four initiative measures was adopted, while all but four of the sixteen acts of the Legislative Assembly referred to the people were sustained. Thus, in only five of nineteen instances can it be said that direct legislation was needed to achieve a popular goal at variance with legislative action. Ten of the seventeen constitutional amendments proposed by the legislature were adopted.

This summary of action on direct legislation does not tell the entire story. Some referendum measures, notably the statewide mill levy to provide some of the funds for the operation of the University system, which must be resubmitted for voter approval at ten-year intervals, have survived by shaky margins, and their adoption at all is a tribute to the extensive organized citizen campaigns in their behalf. Both labor and management have, on occasion, been able to block initiative proposals which would have damaged their respective interests by squelching the measures during the petition-signing stage. In 1952, a measure which would have provided industrial accident benefits for victims of silicosis was kept off the ballot through united action by the Anaconda Company and its friends. On the other hand, labor was able to rally enough support in 1958 to keep a right-to-work measure off the ballot.

Until 1959, the legislative process was conspicuously weak in the area of budget and appropriations because of the absence of sound machinery for financial planning. In 1951 Montana began an eight-year experiment with budget preparation by a newly established independent officer known as the controller. He was required by the statute to submit a budget in which proposed expenditures would not exceed existing revenues, a patently absurd arrangement in a period of mounting costs. The controller's only recourse was the familiar "meat axe" technique in which all estimates were reduced on an across-the-board percentage cut basis, resulting in a "balanced budget" which, in practice, was deliberately ignored by the legislature. Finally, the legislature abandoned fiscal fantasia in 1959 by adopting an executive budgeting plan patterned after those in effect in most states as well as in the national government.

33. Reinhardt, *op. cit.*, p. 95.

Much of the actual work of legislative financial planning is done in the committee stage, the responsible committees being Appropriations in the House and Finance and Claims in the Senate. Leaders of the majority party seek to arrive at a ceiling on the amount the state can spend in terms of existing or anticipated revenues in conference with the party members of the committees which are responsible. How well this procedure works is, of course, dependent on party discipline, which is never complete and varies from session to session. At this crucial point in the legislative process it is evident that those interest groups which have competent technical staffs to provide information and favorable patterns of access will be most effective, especially since the average citizen is in no position to follow the maze of appropriations procedure. It should not be surprising that groups favoring the status quo have been most successful, given their superior resources of access and technical competence.

In 1957 the Legislative Assembly created its most useful agency when it established the Legislative Council. Since its inception this body has been responsible for recommending numerous significant changes in the state government. It was, for example, a recommendation of the Legislative Council which resulted in the establishment of the system of executive budgeting in 1959. The Council has often been the recipient of political "hot potatoes" too difficult to be handled effectively by other means. Often charged with being a kind of legislative overlord or "dictator," the Council is actually nothing of the sort. Because of its bipartisan composition it must work, unavoidably, in those areas in which a substantial degree of two-party consensus prevails.

The Legislative Council is comprised of twelve members chosen from the two houses of the legislature in equal numbers, with each political party equally represented. The Council in turn appoints an executive director, who is charged with directing the permanent staff of the organization and conducting research. During the first eight years of its existence, the Council enjoyed the advantages of continuity through the tenure of a single executive director; when a successor was chosen recently from the staff, continuity was preserved. Each session of the Legislative Assembly has witnessed a growing acceptance of the role of the Council. Of seventeen recommendations for legislative action of one kind or another made by the Council in 1965, ten were adopted by the Legislative Assembly.

VOTING HABITS

In fifteen of the first seventeen presidential elections in this century Montana's electoral votes have been in the column of the winning candidate. Only in 1900 and again in 1960 did the voters depart from this tradition. On the whole, the state has been a political weathervane registering the changing currents of American presidential politics. No fully satisfactory explanation of this phenomenon has yet been advanced. The mobility of population (an estimated 50 percent were not born in the state) together with the absence of either a clearly structured society or a disciplined political party system suggest themselves as partial reasons for the behavior. From the beginnings of statehood and the Clark-Daly feud down to the present, politics has usually been more personal than partisan. The organization man is not unknown, but his role has been decidedly secondary. The state has never had a political machine which could, with ruthless and impersonal efficiency, deliver its votes to a candidate irrespective of merit or personal following. On only one occasion in recent years could the charge be made that a political machine of bipartisan character was being developed. Senator Wheeler, against whom the charge was leveled, demonstrated that the machine was ineffective, if it existed at all, by losing his next primary, something a machine politician rarely does.

With the importance given to personalities by the electorate naturally goes a penchant for split-ticket voting. If any discernible trend can be said to have emerged from this display of political ambivalence, it is a general disposition, of marked proportions since 1940, to prefer Democrats in national politics while preferring Republicans in both the legislative and executive wings of the state Capitol. The Democrats have won twenty-seven of thirty-nine contests for seats in Congress (Senate or House) in this period, while the Republicans were winning twenty-two of thirty-five state contests involving the governorship or control of the two houses of the Legislative Assembly.

It might seem fruitless to search for significant geographic voting patterns in Montana; it is a truism that the only thing more uncertain than the state's weather is its politics. Some areas tend, however, to exhibit a fairly consistent partisan allegiance. The mining counties and the tier of so-called "High-Line," wheat-producing counties lying north of the Missouri River have been dependably Democratic. These are usually joined in the Democratic column by the lumber-producing counties of western Montana. The Republicans over the years have fared best in the livestock counties south of the Missouri River and in the western counties with diversified crops and irrigated farming.[34]

A review of actual political trends on an election-by-election basis must of necessity omit much interesting and important detail.[35] In presidential politics the state remained in the Democratic column in 1940 and 1944 with Franklin D. Roosevelt and continued its allegiance to the Democrats in 1948 with Harry Truman, although by a substantially reduced margin. Montana voters changed sides in the 1950's, however, and gave sizable majorities to the Republican winner, President Dwight D. Eisenhower, in the 1952 and 1956 contests. With the exception of the single six-year term of Republican Zales N. Ecton (1947-53) both Senate seats have been in Democratic hands throughout the 1940's and 1950's. Senator James E. Murray held one of them from 1935 until 1961, when he was succeeded by Lee Metcalf. The other has had three different occupants in the period. Burton K. Wheeler, who seemed politically invincible after decisively beating his Republican opponent, E. K. Cheadle, by 112,812 votes in 1940, lost in the 1946 primary. Ecton then held the seat for a single term, losing to Mike Mansfield in 1952. Senator Mansfield was re-elected decisively in 1958, and again in 1964.

Montana's voters, who generally eschew traditionalism, have displayed much consistency in voting for representatives from the two congressional districts. In the first (western) district, where lumber and mining interests are paramount, Democrats have maintained a firm hold. Through the 1966 election, they

34. See especially the political maps in Waldron, *op. cit.*, *passim.*

35. But see the series which has appeared in the *Western Political Quarterly's* symposia on Western elections. Included are two articles by Jules A. Karlin, "The 1948 Elections in Montana, 2 (March 1949), 109-13, and "The 1952 Elections in Montana," 6 (March 1953), 113-17; and seven articles by Thomas Payne: "The 1954 Election in Montana," 7 (December 1954), 610-13; "The 1956 Election in Montana," 10 (March 1957), 127-31; "The 1958 Election in Montana," 12 (March 1959), 313-16; "The 1960 Election in Montana," 14 (March 1961, Part 2), 343-46; "The 1962 Election in Montana," 16 (June 1963), 439-42; "The 1964 Election in Montana," 18 (June 1965, Part 2), 491-94; and "The 1966 Election in Montana," 20 (June 1967, Part 2), 576-80.

had carried the district in 22 of 25 contests. The second (eastern) district, which is dominated by agriculture (wheat and cattle) and oil, is almost as consistently Republican. The Republicans have won 17 of 26 contests in the second district.[36] Over the years the two districts have chosen markedly different breeds of representatives. The western district voters have shown a preference for liberal Democrats, while those in the east have expressed a fondness for conservative Republicans. Both districts have, however, known close elections, and there have been notable exceptions to the prevailing situation just described.

Miss Jeanette Rankin was the last Republican to win a seat in the first district when she was elected to a single term in 1940. Democrat Mike Mansfield captured the seat in 1942 (when Miss Rankin did not run) and held it until 1952, when he sought and won election to the Senate. Lee Metcalf, another Democrat, succeeded Mansfield, and held the seat until 1960, when he succeeded James E. Murray in the Senate. Since 1960 the western district seat had been occupied by Democrat Arnold Olsen.

In the eastern district a Democrat, James F. O'Connor, was the representative in 1940, and held the seat until his death in 1945. In a special election, Republican Wesley A. D'Ewart was elected and continued in the seat until 1954 when he relinquished it in an unsuccessful bid for Murray's Senate seat. D'Ewart was succeeded by another Republican, Orvin B. Fjare, who held the seat for a single term and was defeated in 1956 by Democrat LeRoy H. Anderson. After two terms Anderson sought unsuccessfully the Murray Senate seat, and was followed by a Republican, James F. Battin, who has held the seat since 1960.

Montanans have chosen Republican governors in six of the past seven elections. They elected Sam C. Ford to two successive terms (1941-49). He was defeated in 1948 by John W. Bonner, the only Democrat to serve in the period. Bonner in turn bowed in 1952 to Hugo Aronson, who served two terms in the executive mansion. He was succeeded by still another Republican, Donald Nutter. Upon the death of Governor Nutter in a plane crash in January 1962, Lieutenant Governor Tim Babcock succeeded to the office, and won election in his own right to a full term in 1964. The offices of secretary of state, auditor, and attorney general have, with a single exception, been monopolized by Democrats during the last twenty-five years, while Democrats and Republicans have shared on almost equal terms the offices of lieutenant governor, treasurer, and superintendent of public instruction.

IMPACT OF NATIONAL POLITICS AND TRENDS

Some Montanans may boast that their individualism and self-reliance, preserved since frontier days, enables their state to fend for itself with no helping hand from Washington. Most, however, are sensitive to national politics and trends, and often take a greater interest in what is happening in Washington than in what is taking place in Helena. In many respects national and state politics are woven inextricably into a single fabric, and personnel do move from one level to the other in party and government. National and state political campaigns occur at the same times, but as a general rule national issues are not injected into contests at the state level. This explains partially why there is so little "coat-tail" effect—Montana registers with weathervane reliability national trends in its support of national candidates, but voting behavior in national elections seems to have little to do with the outcome of state contests.

---

36. The disparity between the two districts in total number of election contests results from a 1945 by-election in the second district.

Like all Westerners, Montanans—whether they like to admit it or not—benefit extensively from the activities of the national government. For one thing, the national government is one of the largest single employers, with more than 10,000 civilian employees alone in the state. A proposal to transfer a major national field installation from Montana to another state will invariably bring protests from many segments of the population. The national government is the state's largest landholder, owning about one-third of all the area. National ownership has unfavorable consequences for local government finance, in that the property tax base is proportionately reduced. Such consequences have been offset partially through payments to local governments in lieu of taxes in some areas including, for example, proceeds from timber sales in national forests.

Federal grants have come to play an increasingly important part in governmental activities. A recent report shows that for fiscal 1965 a total of $96.2 million in such grants was received by governmental units and individuals in the Treasure State.[37] On a per capita basis, Montana received $137 for each person as contrasted with the national average of $67. Well over half of the national funds expended went for highway construction, but public assistance, health, and education were substantial beneficiaries. Montana's share of the total national expenditure for grants in fiscal 1965 was .79 percent, compared with its .32 percent share of the national tax burden in the same period. Relatively speaking, the state received more than its share on a purely population basis, and paid less than its share. The federal grant totals do not include funds expended directly by the national government in Montana. The inclusion of such figures would accent still further the fact that the state receives far more proportionately in federal largesse than it expends in taxes to the national government.

Finally, the national government is important in Montana because of far-reaching projects and activities in which it engages. The construction of major multi-purpose dams at Fort Peck, Canyon Ferry, and Hungry Horse has promoted significant agricultural and industrial development. The location of large military aviation bases near Great Falls and Glasgow also has been of importance in the expansion of the economy. The announcement of the decision of the Department of Defense to close the air base at Glasgow set off a strong reaction in the community as well as among state political leaders of both parties. Indeed, candidates in all parties seem to vie with each other in bidding for the location of additional federal projects, and in claiming credit for those which have been established already. A former Republican congressman, Orvin B. Fjare, owed his 1956 defeat in part to the belief of many of his constituents that his position was responsible for delaying the construction of Yellowtail Dam. In early 1965 when the Veterans Administration announced plans to close its Miles City hospital political leaders of every persuasion joined in a chorus of protest and succeeded in convincing the VA of the wisdom of reversing its decision.

Policies and programs of the federal government which significantly affect Montana's economy and politics include the tariff, metals policy, and price supports for basic crops. Tariff considerations are of vital concern to groups such as the wool growers, the sugar beet producers, and the copper mining interests. Few politicians in either party who were unsympathetic to these tariff concerns have enjoyed political preferment or advancement. The state has a long record of enthusiasm for causes such as free silver, populism, progressivism, and the silver purchase policies of the New Deal. Copper and zinc producers are deeply concerned

37. Prepared by *Congressional Quarterly* and published in the *Daily Missoulian*, July 22, 1965.

about the stockpiling by the federal government of these strategic metals. Montana wheat farmers have generally prospered since the 1940's, in part because of the program of government price supports to wheat.

An examination of the benefits derived from the policies and activities of the national government may provide a helpful clue to an understanding of the paradox of the state's politics which has been alluded to repeatedly in the preceding pages. It may be more than purely coincidental that voter behavior has been liberal in national politics while exhibiting a conservative orientation locally. Can these apparently opposing tides be explained or reconciled? There is support for the proposition that the same configuration of interests which benefits from political liberalism in national politics finds political conservatism in state affairs advantageous. Perhaps, then, Montana's political schizophrenia is not pathological after all. In a state with a sparse, scattered population and an economy based chiefly on the production of raw materials, a policy of restricting state expenditure where possible and seeking generous outlays of public funds from Washington may coincide with the interests of a substantial majority of the population.

NEVADA:

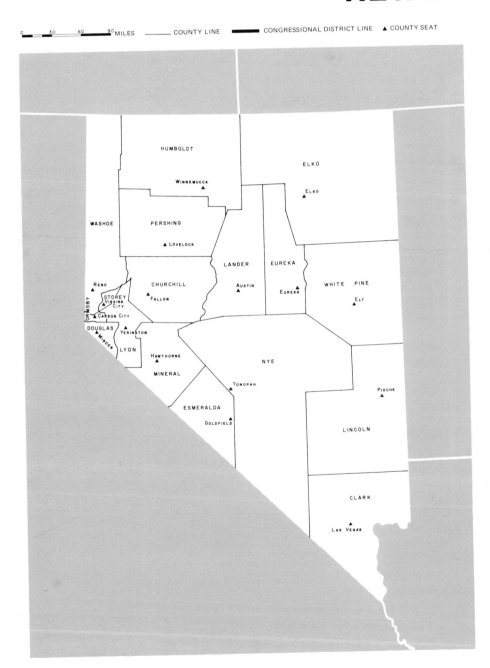

HUMBOLDT

ELKO

WINNEMUCCA ▲

ELKO ▲

WASHOE

PERSHING

▲ LOVELOCK

LANDER

EUREKA

WHITE   PINE

RENO ▲

CHURCHILL

AUSTIN ▲

EUREKA ▲

ELY ▲

ORMSBY

STOREY
VIRGINA
CITY ▲

▲ FALLON

▲ CARSON CITY

DOUGLAS

YERINGTON ▲

▲ MINDEN

LYON

HAWTHORNE ▲

NYE

PIOCHE ▲

MINERAL

TONOPAH ▲

ESMERALDA

GOLDFIELD ▲

LINCOLN

CLARK

▲ LAS VEGAS

Eleanore Bushnell

The Tourist State

Proportionately, Nevada is the fastest-growing state in the nation; the population increase exceeded 78 percent between 1950 and 1960 and exceeded 58 percent between 1960 and 1966. This remarkable growth assures that the nationwide fascination with the "population explosion" receives its full share of attention in this state; furthermore, the tourist trade has increased in Nevada, mostly because of the expanding population of neighboring western states.

Political and business leaders in Nevada cite with gratification its rapid growth: the increasing number of new residents—the increasing profits derived from a flourishing tourist trade. But the inevitable corollary to mounting population, the need for additional public services, is sometimes viewed with dismay and is sometimes ignored. A few of the same leaders who are delighted with the growth of the state turn their backs on certain of the problems caused by a burgeoning population—demands for greater expenditure on schools, roads, public welfare. Such disregard has sometimes been exemplified by failure of the legislature to broaden the revenue base even though conspicuous lacks in fundamental services were all too evident. More recently, however, legislators have faced politically uncomfortable reality and have increased taxes; the 1967 legislature, for example, raised gambling and sales taxes, particularly to improve allotments to education. The largest direct revenue-producer for the state is the over-all 3 percent sales tax, paid alike by tourist and resident; taxes on gambling and motor fuel bring in the next largest amounts. Gambling, legalized in 1931, is the main industry of Nevada, an industry that can obviously be sustained only by tourists. The rise in tourism is largely attributable to the mobile and opulent inhabitants of San Francisco and Los Angeles who regularly come in large numbers to Reno and Las Vegas. Employees of the adjunct businesses that feed upon gambling—restaurants, hotels, motels—make up a substantial part of the new resident population; their employment depends upon the continuing affluence that makes tourism the major business. In addition to gambling, other tourist attractions include the "no-wait" marriage laws and the six-weeks divorce, the latter contributing to the high incidence of attorneys as well as to the number of first quality guest ranches and hotels.

Nevada was a rich and colorful state in the 1860's, its economy geared to mining as in the 1960's it is geared to gaming. Both these occupations are oddly transient and extractive, a quality causing anxiety among some residents now as it did in the mining era. During the angriest debate in the constitutional convention (1864), when the issue was whether to tax mining property, one delegate argued for taxing mines at the same rate as any other property in order to ". . . make those gentlemen who are rolling in wealth in San Francisco, pay something for the support of our government, for the support of our common schools, and for the support of our courts."[1]

His plea was unsuccessful. Public figures in the 1960's who have the same desire to require more taxes from the gambling industry have sometimes argued with equal lack of success for their imposition. Both the executive and the legislative branches have been uneasy about increasing gambling taxes, fearing, as did their counterparts in the 1860's, that higher taxes might jeopardize the state's only real income-producer.

Nevada's rapid development from part of Utah Territory in 1850 to statehood in 1864 was caused by a congeries of political factors. The Carson Valley settlers often had antagonistic relations, based on religious differences, with the theocratic government of the Mormons in Salt Lake; so did the national government. After several adventures in attempting to have themselves annexed to California, the settlers finally won sympathetic attention in Congress, which, partly to reduce the ambit of Mormon hegemony, created the Territory of Nevada in 1861. Then, because Lincoln and his party needed more favorable votes in Congress on the pending 13th Amendment and correctly gauged the staunch pro-Union position of Nevada Territory, Nevada was admitted as the 36th state in 1864. Except for California, which was never a territory, Nevada's progress from territory to state in three years is faster than that of any other western state.

GEOGRAPHY AND RESOURCES

Nevada is the seventh largest state in area, 110,540 square miles, of which only 752 are water surface, and is the second smallest in population: 285,278 according to the 1960 census. In 1967 the Census Bureau gave the population at 444,000, putting Nevada ahead of Alaska, Wyoming, and Vermont. Eighty-seven percent of the land is owned by the national government. The state is semi-arid; lack of water is one reason for the difficulty in attracting new industries and also explains why Nevada has the fewest farms and the smallest number of acres in farm production of any of the mainland western states. In the future more water may become available because Nevada was allowed 300,000 acre feet annually as part of the settlement of the California and Arizona dispute over disposal of Colorado River water. This water is expected to reach the Las Vegas Valley during 1968. Hay is the chief farm product; alfalfa seed, garlic, barley, oats, potatoes, wheat, and cotton are grown. Stock-raising is centered in eastern Nevada, particularly in Elko County, but is scattered throughout the state except in the south.

Mining was once the main and most celebrated industry; its present dollar value is about as high as it was during the Comstock days, but its relative position as a revenue-producer has declined conspicuously. Copper is the chief mineral product, with some gold, sand and gravel, iron ore, gypsum, diatomite, manganese, mercury, lime, and magnesite. Prospects of a new mining boom based on extensive explorations and on new extractive techniques were widely discussed in 1967, a year in which geologists looked forward to a future production boom in gold, copper, lithium, and oil. Nevada's proximity to California's huge population is an inducement to production of gypsum, lime products, and diatomite.

Within its borders lie Pyramid and Walker lakes, and the state shares Lake Mohave and Lake Mead with Arizona and Lake Tahoe with California. Friction

1. *Nevada Constitutional Debates and Proceedings*, Andrew J. Marsh, Official Reporter (San Francisco: Frank Eastman, 1866), p. 356.

has developed with California because of the charge that Nevada is despoiling the natural beauty of the Tahoe basin by the construction of more and more gambling establishments on the shores of the lake; a special session of the legislature in February 1968 was devoted almost exclusively to consideration of bi-state arrangements for preserving the Tahoe basin. Nevada rivers (Humboldt, Carson, Walker, Truckee), the mountains near Reno, Las Vegas, and Elko, and the above-mentioned lakes attract fishermen, hunters, skiers, and other vacationists.

Not following the usual pattern of economic development from agricultural to industrial dominance, Nevada has moved from a mining-centered to a tourist-centered economy. Natural resources do not support the state. It does not require an expert in geopolitics to recognize that Nevada is not self-supporting. Paucity of arable land and of water determines both the economy and the political structure. Scarcity of resources translatable into revenue has brought about Nevada's reliance upon tourists for support, tourists who are mainly attracted by wide-open gambling, tourists who come in numbers exceeding twenty million a year.

The dominant political concern is to maintain a surveillance of gambling and insure that the visitor is made welcome, knows that the games are honest, and will return; it is necessary, at the same time, to insure that the tax rates on gambling are reasonably productive for the state without jeopardizing its major industry. Thus, Nevada's biggest resource lies outside the state, a resource based upon proximity to the free-spending population of California and upon the state's position on the transcontinental route for tourists. A curious century-old fact is that the first permanent settlement in Nevada, Genoa, came into being as a supply-station for the transients hurrying from the East to seek gold in California.

Gambling and its revenue-producing attendant industries support Nevada. Gambling taxes contribute the second largest sum to the treasury, with the 3 percent sales tax first and motor vehicle fuel taxes third in 1967. Much of this revenue is derived from tourists. The major occupational category in the past twenty years has been services; jobs in this category are created mainly by gambling. An indication of its tourist-based economy may be seen in Table I, which compares Nevada and Wyoming (the two states are about equal in area and population) in four significant service categories.

In three important areas Nevada differs in revenue production from the majority of states: (1) no personal or corporate income tax is levied; (2) no inheritance or estate tax is imposed; and (3) gambling is legal and is taxed by the federal government and by the state, the counties, and the cities. The gross receipts tax is the most important of the state-levied taxes on gambling; it varies from 3 to 5.5 percent, depending upon the winnings reported by each establishment. It produced nearly 17 million dollars in the fiscal year ending June 1967; other gambling taxes produced over 5 million; so that of 60 million in revenue, gambling provided 22 million, more than a third of the state's entire revenue. Two recent studies of Nevada's fiscal policy, the Zubrow and the Lybrand reports,[2] both suggest substantial increases in gambling taxes and the ability of the industry to pay more.

Inheritance and estate taxes are prohibited by the constitution. A resolution was introduced in the 1965 session of the legislature to amend the constitution to permit an estate tax, and a bill was proposed to levy a corporate income tax; nei-

2. R. A. Zubrow, R. L. Decker, and E. H. Plant, *Financing State and Local Government in Nevada* (Carson City: Legislative Counsel Bureau, 1960); and "Lybrand Report," *A Study of General Fund Revenues of the State of Nevada* (Carson City: Legislative Counsel Bureau, 1966).

ther passed. But an amendment to raise the debt limit of the state from 1 to 3 percent of assessed valuation was approved in the 1965 session, reapproved in the 1967 session, and so will be on the ballot in 1968 for decision by the voters.

Nevada is not unique in exhibiting an inextricable involvement of economic policies with politics. The first constitution was soundly defeated by the voters in 1864, in part because it imposed a tax on mining property[3] instead of restricting the tax to proceeds of mines as was done in the second, and adopted, constitution. In 1967 the urgent need for more revenue for schools, roads, and other services forced a reluctant legislature to raise taxes, a politically painful necessity.

Grants-in-aid and other support money from the national government are economically significant. Federal allocations to Nevada (1965) were $61,954,-000, a per capita average of $141 as compared with a national per capita average of $79.[4] Classified employment in the state is also a factor in the economy. About 6,500 employees (1967) were covered by the merit system. Positions are attained by examination except for a few janitorial and gardening jobs; the probationary period is normally six months but is one year for some positions.

Entry of the enigmatic Howard Hughes into the Nevada economy must be noted. In 1967 he acquired more than one hundred million dollars' worth of property in Las Vegas, including casinos, a television station, and an airport. His offer of support for establishment of a two-year medical school at the University of Reno was the deciding factor for the 1967 legislature, which had previously been opposed to such a facility. Hughes' impact on the economy is apparent. Whether he will conspicuously affect political judgments is uncertain, but his role in establishing the medical school was determinative and may be a clue to future paralegislative decisions.

TABLE I
EMPLOYMENT IN SERVICES, OCTOBER 1964, NEVADA AND WYOMING

Category	Nevada		Wyoming	
	Employed	% Employed	Employed	% Employed
Automotive dealers and gasoline stations	4,701	10.10	3,843	32.16
Retail trade—eating and drinking establishments	6,621	14.10	4,581	38.34
Hotels, other lodgings	16,610	35.38	2,901	24.28
Amusement and recreation services (not movies)	19,007	40.49	621	5.19
TOTAL	46,939	99.98	11,946	99.97

Source: U.S. Department of Labor, Bureau of Employment Security, *Employment and Wages*, 2nd Quarter, 1964 (Washington: Government Printing Office, 1965), pp. 51-60.

3. For a discussion of this and other factors causing defeat of the first constitution, see Eleanore Bushnell, *The Nevada Constitution: Origin and Growth* (Reno: University of Nevada Press, 1965), chaps. 1, 2, *passim*; (rev. ed., 1968), chaps. 2, 3, *passim*.

4. *Congressional Quarterly*, 25 (March 24, 1967), 449.

POPULATION

Nevada's enlarging population is mainly attributable to the growth of the tourist business; in the decade 1950 to 1960 the most important component of growth was in-migration. During this ten-year period the population was augmented by 125,000, of whom over 86,000 were new residents; there were 39,000 more births than deaths during the period.[5] The population growth is concentrated in the Reno and Las Vegas areas, making Nevada an urban state. In 1950, for the first time, more Nevadans resided in urban than in rural areas, 57.2 percent; in 1960 the percent of urban dwellers had risen to 70.4.[6] Using school registration figures as a measure of total population, in 1967 Clark County (Las Vegas) had 54 percent and Washoe County (Reno) had 25 percent of the state's inhabitants.

Politically, the enlarging population and its concentration in urban centers has tended to benefit the Democratic party just as students of political party alignments would expect. The proportion of voters registering as Democrats has risen from 57 percent in 1952 to 63 percent in 1967. Clark County (Las Vegas) had a strong registration superiority for the Democrats in 1967: 68 percent. There were more registered Democrats in Clark County than registered Republicans in the entire state. This county, with about 54 percent of the total population, is becoming (1967) the controlling political power in Nevada, causing some speculation that Washoe County (Reno) with about 25 percent of the population, might move toward an alliance with the fifteen small counties to offset the massive impact of Clark.

As well as being urban, the population (1960) is approximately 90 percent Caucasian. Negroes are the largest racial minority, about 13,500, of whom nearly 80 percent live in Las Vegas. Indians are the only other large non-Caucasian group; their number increased between 1950 and 1960 from 5,000 to over 6,500, but the percent of Indians in the total population decreased from 3.1 to 2.3 because of the great increase in the state's population.[7] These two minorities (Chinese, Japanese, and others totaled less than 2,000 in 1960) usually have the low-income, low prestige jobs and a rate of unemployment nearly double that of the Caucasian group; their average exposure to formal education is approximately four years less than that of Caucasian residents.[8]

Campaign appeals have not been directed toward minority groups, nor has religious affiliation (Catholics and Mormons are the two large bodies) been a dominant factor in Nevada politics; however, some examples of minority bloc-voting in recent years can be cited. In the 1964 election, incumbent Senator Howard W. Cannon (D) spoke in favor of the Civil Rights bill; his opponent for the Senate seat, Paul Laxalt (R), said he would have voted against the bill. Cannon carried twenty predominantly Negro precincts in Las Vegas by 95 percent, an achievement squarely attributed to Negro dissatisfaction with the Republican party's position on civil rights. In the 1966 election the first Negro legislator was elected from an essentially Negro residential area in Las Vegas. A factor in Paul Laxalt's winning the governorship from Grant Sawyer (D) was his success in cutting into

5. William Petersen and Lionel S. Lewis, *Nevada's Changing Population* (Reno: Bureau of Business and Economic Research, University of Nevada, 1963), p. 77.

6. *Ibid.*, p. 8.

7. *Ibid.*, p. 26.

8. Elmer R. Rusco, *Minority Groups in Nevada* (Reno: Bureau of Governmental Research, University of Nevada, 1966).

the normally Democratic Mormon vote in Clark County, in part because of his endorsement by local church leaders, in part because Governor Romney of Michigan urged his co-religionists to support Laxalt.

In 1961, after several anti-discrimination bills had been lost in previous sessions, the legislature established an Equal Rights Commission; the NAACP lobbied for this measure. The roll-call vote on creating the Commission was 12-5 in the Senate and 42-4 in the Assembly. All nine negative votes were cast by Republicans, none of whom represented either Clark or Washoe County.

The Commission, appointed by the governor, is empowered to study and investigate areas of tension and foster mutual understanding among racial, religious, and ethnic groups; it receives and investigates complaints and may conduct hearings. The Commission's activities were strengthened by additional appropriations made by the 1965 session of the legislature. Although some Nevadans showed reluctance to recognize that discrimination, particularly against Negroes, existed, an important civil rights act was passed in 1965 making it unlawful to discriminate on the basis of race, color, religion, or national origin in public accommodations or employment. Efforts to remedy the 1965 legislature's failure to include housing in the ban on discriminatory practices were not successful. In 1968 Governor Laxalt announced that unless residents rented or sold housing to minority groups on a voluntary basis he would support open housing legislation in the 1969 session of the legislature.

EDUCATIONAL POLITICS

Since the stormy period of 1952-57,[9] the University of Nevada, the only collegiate institution in the state, has been less beset with internecine differences. The legislature only infrequently manifests distrust of the administration and a temptation to interfere with management of the University. Although appropriations have been lower than requests, no consistently anti-university faction exists in the legislature nor is the school's budget affected by any political party division; state appropriations have grown from $5,868,900 for 1963 to $11,732,000 for 1967.

Despite this sturdy increase in funds, Nevada, with the highest per capita income of the western states both in fact and as projected through 1970, is conspicuously below average with respect to effort for higher education. The mean per capita state expenditure in the thirteen western states is $48.17; Alaska is highest, with $64.82, and Nevada lowest, with $24.55. The mean expenditure for higher education as a percentage of state total expenditures is 22.4 percent; Colorado is highest at 34.6 percent and Nevada second from lowest at 9.6 percent; Alaska is lowest, with 9.4 percent. Wyoming, whose similarity to Nevada in population and area was noted above, expends $50.00 per capita and 15.7 percent of total general expenditures for higher education.[10]

The governing body of the University is the Board of Regents, composed of eleven members elected for four-year terms: five from Clark County (Las Vegas), three from Washoe County (Reno), and three from the other fifteen counties. In

9. See Don W. Driggs, "Nevada," in *Western Politics*, ed. Frank H. Jonas (Salt Lake City: University of Utah Press, 1961), pp. 211-13.

10. Comparative data in the thirteen Western States is found in U.S. Bureau of the Census, *Governmental Finances in 1964-65*, Series GF-No. 6 (Washington: Government Printing Office, 1966), pp. 34-39, 52; and Selma J. Musken and Eugene P. McLoone, *Public Spending for Higher Education* (Chicago: Council of State Governments, 1965), p. 64 and *passim*.

1965 the internal organization of the University was changed with the appointment of resident chancellors for the Reno and the Las Vegas campuses. Upon the resignation of President Armstrong in late 1967, the Board of Regents considered various plans of administrative organization other than the existing president-two chancellor system. Their decision, announced in 1968, was to change titles by designating the head of the system as "Chancellor" and the resident head of each campus as "President." Greater autonomy was granted to the two campuses which were made independent of each other with respect to academic and other internal matters; responsibility for university-wide decisions and certain financial authority was vested in the chancellor.

The Desert Research Institute, founded in 1959 as the general research arm of the University, has received 6.5 million dollars in grants (January 1967); it built the world's first Atmospherium-Planetarium and has stimulated research in a number of fields.

A branch of the University was established at Las Vegas in 1951; it was authorized to grant degrees in 1964 and is co-equal with the Reno campus in curriculum and all other aspects of university management. Degrees granted by the University have increased steadily since 1962; 405 degrees were conferred in that year and 796 in 1967 including 127 at the Las Vegas campus.

Enrollment has grown continually since 1958; at that time, 2,128 students were registered at Reno and 340 at Las Vegas. The 1967-68 regular student enrollment was 5,080 at Reno and 2,784 at Las Vegas. The student body has been relatively quiescent, even apathetic, on crucial national and international issues. The only matter (1967) which seemed to arouse the students was compulsory ROTC, a requirement they opposed but the Regents favored. Important or controversial speakers on campus are very rare.

The feasibility of establishing community colleges in Nevada, a project enlisting the staunch support of Governor Laxalt, was being studied in 1968. Such a college was functioning in Elko at that time, providing mainly an adult education program.

Public schools are administered by the counties, each of the seventeen counties constituting a school district. The state superintendent of public instruction has been appointive since 1957 and is responsible to the State Board of Education. In 1966 Nevada's expenditure per pupil was $574 compared with a national average of $641; the average for Nevada public school teachers' salaries (1965-66) was $7,025 compared with a national average of $6,500.[11] This state, although ranked third in the nation in per capita income, was ranked eighteenth in percent of expenditure for public schools.[12] The number of pupils has risen sharply—180.1 percent between 1950 and 1960 and 12.2 percent from 1963 to 1964. The national percent change in the latter year was three. Nevada's pupil growth is almost twice as great as the increase in any other state in the Union; the closest to Nevada's 12.2 percent is Colorado, with a 6.6 percent increase.[13]

The politics and economics of the state's large number of new residents are clearly seen in school financing difficulties. Public officials and candidates for office of both parties uniformly express a desire to have good schools, but many express distaste for higher taxes. The 1967 session imposed a 1 percent increase in

11. *Digest of Educational Statistics*, U.S. Dept. H.E.W. (Washington: Government Printing Office, 1966) pp. 41 and 57.

12. *N.E.A. Research Bulletin*, 44 (February 1966), 13.

13. *Book of the States, 1966-1967* (Chicago: Council of State Governments, 1966), pp. 276, 283.

the sales tax, the revenue to be returned to the county of origin specifically for schools. Although the additional revenue is substantial, it has not worked equal benefits among the counties, and certain of the sparsely populated ones (Lincoln is the best example) are in a worse financial plight than before the new tax was levied. School financing is a persistent and worrisome problem to all the political leaders.

NEWS MEDIA AND PUBLIC OPINION

Journalism in Nevada is, unsurprisingly, dominated by the newspapers of the two main cities, Reno and Las Vegas, each of which has two daily papers. The *Reno Evening Gazette*, the afternoon paper, is not published on Sunday but has the highest daily circulation in Washoe County, slightly over 23,000, while the morning paper, the *Nevada State Journal*, has a daily circulation of over 18,000; its Sunday printing is about 32,000. Both Reno papers are owned by the Speidel organization; the *Gazette* tends to favor Republicans; the *Journal*, Democrats. One of the Las Vegas dailies, the *Review-Journal*, has a daily circulation of about 49,000 and a Sunday printing of 51,000; it is one of the five Nevada papers published by the Reynolds chain. The other Clark County paper, the *Las Vegas Sun*, has a circulation of over 31,000 daily and 29,000 Sunday; the editor and publisher, H. M. Greenspun, is the most "crusading" and controversial journalist in the state. Both Las Vegas papers tend to support the Democrats, although Greenspun is a Republican, who ran unsuccessfully for his party's nomination for governor in 1962. Daily papers are also published in Ely, Winnemucca, Elko, and Carson City.

Approximately thirty-five other papers, their circulation and news-coverage mainly local, are published in Nevada at intervals other than daily. Two papers, both controlled by the D. W. Reynolds chain, are published in Carson City, the capital. No foreign language papers are published in the state. The *Territorial Enterprise*, first printed newspaper in Nevada, began publication in 1858 and has been issued intermittently since. It was famous when Virginia City was the mining center and because such celebrities as Mark Twain have served as editor. Now (1968) published weekly, it is largely a tourist paper and has a circulation of less than 4,000.

The Associated Press and United Press International maintain permanent staffs in Reno, Carson City, and Las Vegas; the national newsmagazines use free lance and part-time writers to cover Nevada news.

None of the Nevada papers has any official political affiliation, and their impact upon the political process is not clear. In the tense Cannon-Laxalt campaign (1964) for the United States Senate, two editors lost their jobs. An editor in Carson City quit when his editorial supporting Laxalt (R) was removed from the paper, and the editor of the *Las Vegas Review-Journal* left in a dispute over the paper's endorsement of Cannon (D). Both of these are Reynolds papers.

The Reno and Las Vegas papers do not involve themselves in issues arising from gambling, and support conservative taxation policies.

NOMINATIONS AND ELECTIONS

Delegates to the nominating conventions for the presidency are chosen by the state conventions of the two parties; the precincts select delegates for county conventions, and from the latter come the state convention delegates. Legally, both parties can instruct their delegates to national conventions, but ordinarily they do not. With only three electoral votes, Nevada is not important in national politics; it is unlikely that a serious contender for the presidential or vice-presidential nomination could emerge from this state.

Because Nevada has the closed primary for nominations for state offices, a voter must designate his party affiliation in order to vote in a party primary; therefore, the nearly 9,000 voters who registered as Independents (1967) had a voice only in the general election, or for the nonpartisan offices in the primary. District and Supreme Court jurists, the University regents, and municipal officials run as nonpartisans. A measure to adopt the Missouri Plan, appointment of judges followed by voter approval or disapproval at a subsequent election, has failed to secure legislative approval (1968); usually, in Nevada, incumbent judges run without opposition.

Six months' residence is required for eligibility to vote. Registration is permanent as long as the voter participates in each general election, or does not change his name; he must also re-register if he votes by absentee ballot.

Voters are frequently confronted with a dismaying number of choices, forty-six in one recent election. Nine statewide offices, national and local offices, amendments, and propositions are often presented on a single ballot and require of the electorate a discouraging number of decisions. The consequence is that voters vote for the major offices but usually show a lessening interest in making choices for the minor positions and the propositions. The short ballot has been discussed in Nevada, but no real support exists for its adoption.

From 1952 to 1966 voters had to decide on seven initiative petitions, of which two were proposals to amend the constitution; on one referendum; and on eighteen amendments presented by the legislature. Twenty-one of these twenty-six propositions were approved by the voters.

The Nevada constitution is subject to amendment in two ways. The first is by majority vote of the elected members of the legislature; the proposal is then referred to the next regular legislative session, and if again approved by a majority of the elected members, it goes on the ballot for voter decision. The second method is by initiative petition; Nevada is one of only fourteen states that allows the voters to begin the amendment process. A change approved in 1962 provides that an amendment proposed by initiative petition does not go to the legislature at all, as do initiatives proposing a change in statute law, but goes on two successive general election ballots for voter determination. Such complete elimination of the legislature from the amending procedure is surely direct democracy at its apogee.

Although the closed primary precludes participation of non-affiliated voters in party choices and so may cause them to stay away from a primary election (5,000 to nearly 9,000 were non-affiliated in the period 1958-66), Nevada's record of conspicuously lower voting totals in primaries follows the pattern of most states.

Comparative participation in the primary and in the general elections is much closer in the three non-presidential elections recorded in Table II, suggesting concern by the voters in participating in the selection of their party's candidates for state officials, who are chosen every four years in the non-presidential elections years. As is expected, a higher proportion of eligible voters went to the polls in the general election when the presidency was at stake, 1960 and 1964; but a higher proportion, in the period tabulated, voted in the primary as compared with the general election when the governor and other state officers were on the ballot, 1958, 1962, and 1966.

TABLE II

PRIMARY AND GENERAL ELECTION REGISTRATION

AND VOTING, 1958-1966

Year	Primary			General		
	Registered	Voted	% Voting	Registered	Voted	% Voting
1958	112,797	69,119	61.1	117,568	87,026	74.0
1960	116,788	65,858	56.3	128,898	109,132	84.6
1962	128,437	81,062	63.1	134,350	99,340	74.0
1964	147,625	92,451	62.5	163,475	137,378	84.0
1966	175,341	110,252	62.8	183,863	139,355	76.1

No restrictions of any kind exist in Nevada respecting sources, amounts, or reporting of campaign funds. Corrupt practices legislation is slight: it is unlawful to intimidate a voter, interfere in any of several designated ways with conduct of an election, offer or receive a bribe, offer any financial inducement or reward for an appointment, or bet on an election. Unprincipled campaign techniques have occasionally been employed. In the 1964 election incumbent Senator Cannon (D) charged his opponent with a "smear" when the latter attempted to link Cannon with Bobby Baker. In 1962 incumbent Governor Sawyer ". . . was embarrassed to find flyers impeaching his opponent as an alcoholic. . . . investigation indicates they were the work of an outside group trying to discredit the governor."[14] The nationally circulated attacks on President Johnson (1964) were distributed in Nevada. But in recent elections, campaigns have not been scurrilous except for the modest incidents described.

The size of the state, the fact that the two big population clusters are 450 miles apart and that Elko, located in the third largest county, is 300 miles from Reno and 500 miles from Las Vegas makes campaigning expensive and decentralized. Election strategy requires concentration of energy and money on the voters of Clark and Washoe counties. Since there is no limit on the amount a candidate may spend, and no financial accounting at all, problems arising from the costs of campaigning have worried both candidates and students of the political process. Only negligible sums have been raised by the political parties and disbursed to candidates. Campaign costs for statewide offices are estimated at $50,000 to $250,000; some political analysts say that the latter figure is, in truth, a minimum. Candidates are dependent upon contributions from business, especially gambling, and upon private resources. Since gambling is a legitimate business, campaign funds from that source should have no more sinister connotation than from any other business source. A few legislators have acknowledged receiving contributions from the gambling industry. The immediate effect is discernible in the success with which taxation of gaming has been restricted, but a no vote on raising such taxes cannot be construed as a *quid pro quo*, since the whole state economy depends upon the vitality and cooperative attitude of that industry.

14. Fair Campaign Practices Committee, *The Fourth Biennial State-by-State Study of Smear: 1962* (New York, 1964), p. 10.

PARTY ORGANIZATION AND PARTY LEADERS

The state has produced several important political figures.[15] In the 1960's the major Republican is Governor Paul Laxalt, who, when he won the lieutenant governorship in 1962, was the only Republican elected to a statewide office. The major Democrats are U.S. Senators Bible and Cannon, Congressman Baring, and former Governor Sawyer; each of these men has his own political organization rather than depending solely on party structure for campaign support.

Sawyer, governor from 1958 to 1966, was widely known outside the state. He served as chairman of the National Governors' Conference and president of the Council of State Governments, the first Nevada governor to hold either post. He was vice-chairman of the Western Governors' Conference in 1964 and chairman of that body 1965-66. He was defeated in his bid for a third term (1966) by Paul Laxalt. A Nevada governor, elected for four years, is not constitutionally limited to two consecutive terms. But no governor has served more than two; Bradley in 1878, Russell in 1958, and Sawyer in 1966 attempted unsuccessfully to attain third consecutive terms. Other facets of this campaign are sketched below.

Further evidence that the Democrats may be in trouble in coming elections, despite a voter registration advantage of 64 percent, is the fact that the two big counties showed dramatic changes in 1966 in their otherwise quite predictable voting behavior. For example, Clark County delegations to the state legislature, 1950-64, were 87.3 percent Democratic and Washoe, 59.8 percent Republican.[16] As a consequence of the 1966 election, the Clark delegation dipped to 75 percent Democratic and the Washoe delegation rose to 72 percent Republican, a gain of 12 percent for the Republicans in each county.

Except for an exchange between Laxalt and Sawyer in the 1966 campaign over charges of unreported gambling winnings by some casinos, gambling, as is customary, was not a partisan nor a debated issue. Party leaders of Nevada at both the national and the state levels are quiet on the subject and particularly wish to avoid attracting any unfavorable national attention to the state's main industry. At the national level one indication of the political consequence of legalized gambling is the fact that Nevada senators usually vote against imposing cloture. In 1965 both Senators Bible and Cannon voted against cloture on the voting rights bill though neither took a position against its substance; with Senator Hayden, they were the only Democrats outside the South to do so. Perhaps Nevada senators reason that should gambling ever become an issue in the Senate, they would want as much support as possible to maintain a filibuster; they hope to store up goodwill for such a contingency.

PRESSURE GROUPS

Efforts of interest groups to influence legislation are mainly negative: to prevent unwanted bills from being passed rather than to work for some desired new measure. Banks, insurance companies, the gambling industry, public utilities, railroads, and mining interests have representatives at legislative sessions whose main energies are devoted to stopping unwanted regulatory measures or the imposition of higher taxes. Labor is weak in Nevada both in numbers and in legislative effectiveness, as the right-to-work conflict (sketched below) attests.

15. Driggs, *op. cit.*, pp. 214-15 for a summary of pre-1960 politicians.
16. Elmer R. Rusco, *Voting Behavior in Nevada* (Reno: University of Nevada Press, 1966), p. 16.

Nevada's right-to-work law was the cause of hectic voter participation in the legislative process. An initiative petition providing for the open shop reached the ballot in 1952 and was passed by a slender 50.6 percent. Labor summoned support for an initiative to repeal the law; the repeal initiative, on the ballot in 1954, lost by 51.3 percent. In the 1956 election, two other repeal efforts lost. The first, a constitutional amendment to affirm the union shop, was defeated by a 56 percent majority; the second, another initiative petition to repeal right-to-work, was defeated by 53.9 percent. This activity led supporters of right-to-work to successful passage of an amendment in 1958 tightening the initiative process by changing the requirement that 10 percent of the electors of the state must sign an initiative petition to the requirement that 10 percent of the voters in thirteen counties must sign; this revision eliminated the opportunity to obtain the necessary signatures in only Clark or Washoe counties, where labor is organized. The amendment was passed in every county, suggesting that the voters in Clark and Washoe either did not understand that they were depriving themselves of an advantage accruing to their being the two population centers, or that they did not care. This episode, involving five occasions when right-to-work was on the ballot, is evidence of the non-industrial character of the state and of the political strength and acumen of the agricultural and business interests. That labor continues to be a negligible force in the political process is attested by the fact that of sixty members in the 1967 legislature only one identified himself as having any connection with organized labor.

Educational lobbyists, unlike their industrial counterparts, seek to secure favorable legislation; their major effort is to improve appropriations, mainly for buildings and for salaries. A proposal to raise the sales tax to 3 percent, the additional money to be used for schools, was the subject of a special election in 1963. It lost in all seventeen counties. So total a defeat might suggest that the educator groups were very unconvincing in presenting their case to either the legislature or the public. But one factor in the defeat was that the 2 percent sales tax included food and prescription drugs; these necessities were not exempted in the proposal to raise the tax. Dislike of the all-encompassing application of the sales tax rather than unconcern for the schools is the probable cause for the loss. Because the increase in the sales tax was defeated, a special session of the legislature was called in 1964 to relieve the hard-pressed school districts; the session voted 1.8 million dollars to the schools.

The voters' unequivocal rejection of an increase in the sales tax brought the legislature to an unusual action. Nevada's constitution stipulates that any law created via the initiative petition method can be changed or revoked only by direct vote of the people. The sales tax was such a law and the people had refused to modify it. Thus, the 1967 legislature, faced with the need for more revenue, passed a one cent county sales tax for local school support, the money so raised to be returned largely to the county in which it was collected. Labor and local government officials lobbied in vain against the bill. It was passed 13-7 in the Senate and 29-6 in the Assembly; the roll-call vote shows neither a partisan nor an urban-rural flavor. The state Supreme Court upheld the constitutionality of the law, 2-1, upon the ground that because it was a school tax complete in itself and not amendatory of the sales tax, it did not require voter approval. The dissenting opinion advanced the position that the legislature had done indirectly what it could not do directly: raise the sales tax to 3 percent. This instance of legislative politics also illustrates labor's lack of power.

The NAACP was active in support of the civil rights measures that the legislature passed in 1961 and in 1965. Certain legislators who expressed no interest in the substance of the bills said they voted for them in fear of investigation by the national government of alleged civil rights violations should the state fail to act. The impact of the NAACP and allied groups in this matter is unclear.

No consumer organization exists in Nevada.

Lobbyists are not required to register; they are viewed by most legislators as friends and welcome adjuncts to the business of legislation. They are sources of information and assistance. Some dark talk may be heard of improper lobbying, but no flagrant cases of unethical conduct have become public knowledge since the days when the railroads were conspicuously active in the Nevada legislature. Legislators are treated to lavish entertainment by the gambling and other industries; at least, such entertainment is available to those who wish to accept it. It is believed, and certainly logically, that various interest groups make important contributions to political campaigns; the absence of reporting procedures leaves the extent of such contributions in the realm of "reasoning by sign."

Efforts in the 1960's to create the Great Basin National Park near Ely in White Pine County show competing pressure groups in action. The Interior Department wanted a park of about 123,000 acres to preserve important geological and wildlife specimens; a bill providing for this was introduced by both Nevada senators. Some groups, mostly in White Pine County, favored a small, 53,000 acre park, or no park at all. Supporting establishment of a small park were the Nevada Fish and Game Commission, White Pine grazing and mining groups, sportsmen, mill and smelter workers, and, politically most powerful of all, Congressman Baring. However, these groups appeared to be more anti-park than pro-small park.

Sawyer, at that time governor, and several organizations throughout the state, including the White Pine Chamber of Commerce and Mines, formed an association to work for a park without taking a stand on size. The association sought to reconcile the opposing positions. Sawyer said the desire was to establish ". . . a national park of any size which will preserve this outstanding example of Great Basin physiography for scenic and recreational values . . . and at the same time guarantee the rights of miners, ranchers, and other users of the area."[17] The Nevada Wildlife Federation opposed a national park because the members feared the lack of provisions for multiple use.

LEGISLATIVE POLITICS

Nevada's original constitution, like that of the majority of states, provided for both houses to be apportioned on a population basis; the state's constitution stipulated that the census should be the ". . . basis of representation in both houses of the Legislature."[18] When, in 1950, the constitution was amended to provide one senator per county, this clause was not repealed, thus creating a logical incompatibility. The constitution also requires reapportionment of the Assembly following each decennial census, stipulates that the number of senators may not exceed one-half nor be fewer than one-third the number of assemblymen, and sets the maximum size of the legislature at 75.

The last pre-reapportionment legislature, 1965, was composed of 37 assemblymen, serving two-year terms, chosen essentially on a population basis, with

17. *Nevada State Journal*, June 11, 1965, p. 8.
18. Art. XV, sec. 13.

each county entitled to at least one assemblyman; and of 17 senators, serving four-year terms, one from each county. A bare 8 percent of the voters were able to elect a majority (9) of the Senate; Clark and Washoe counties, with three-fourths of the population, had just two votes. In the Assembly, Clark County had twelve seats and Washoe nine; combined, they had not quite 57 percent of the voting strength.

Fear and dislike of reapportionment pervaded the 1965 legislative session and paralyzed the legislators. Six measures concerning reapportionment were introduced, of which one was passed; it requested Congress to propose an amendment permitting one house of a state legislature to be based on other than population factors if the voters of the state approved. Of the measures that attempted to adjust the Nevada legislature to the requirements of the "one man one vote" rulings of the United States Supreme Court, only one received serious consideration. It proposed a seventeen-member Senate, in which Clark County would have seven senators and Washoe County, five; the remaining fifteen counties, reconstituted into five electoral districts, would have one senator for each of the new districts. The Assembly would be composed of thirty-five members, fifteen from Clark, ten from Washoe, and two from each of the five new electoral districts.

This bill would probably have been construed by a court as being close enough to a mathematical reflection of the state's population in the legislature to be acceptable. That it was not politically acceptable is evidenced by its defeat in the Assembly and by the fact that the dominantly rural Senate declined even to consider reapportionment. Thus the 1965 session, aware that the matter would be brought before the federal district court unless action was taken before April 15, 1965, abdicated the legislative responsibility for reapportionment to the judicial branch.

The federal district court in which two residents of Clark County had filed suit requesting relief from alleged malapportionment took cognizance of the case because of the legislative inaction sketched above. In *Dungan v. Sawyer*[19] the court ruled that (1) Nevada's Senate and Assembly were invalidly apportioned under the equal protection clause of the Fourteenth Amendment; (2) the clause in the Nevada constitution stipulating that the number of senators shall not be less than one-third nor more than one-half of the members of the Assembly and the clause limiting total legislative membership to seventy-five were unconstitutional only if they prohibit the adoption of a valid system of apportionment; (3) the requirement of one senator per county and at least one assemblyman per county was unconstitutional as long as population inequalities exist among the counties; and (4) present apportionment was unconstitutional.

The court ordered that the governor convene a special session by October 30, 1965, to reapportion each house in conformity with the *Dungan* decision, said reapportionment plan to be submitted to the court not later than November 20, 1965. Should the legislature fail to adopt a valid plan by the stipulated date, the court would either reapportion the state or would direct at-large elections.

A special session was convened, and despite many expressions of grief and outrage, it adopted a reapportionment scheme. The newly-constituted Senate is made up of twenty members and the Assembly of forty, an increase of three in each chamber. Clark County (Las Vegas), containing 44.5 percent of the state's population (based on the 1960 census), was given eight senators and sixteen assemblymen, thus securing 40 percent of the seats in both houses. Washoe County

19. 250 F. Supp. 480 (1965).

(Reno) was combined with Storey County (Virginia City) for electoral purposes. This district, containing 29.8 percent of the population, was assigned six senators and twelve assemblymen; it elects 30 percent of the members in each house. Elko County's 4.2 percent of the population choose one senator and two assemblymen—5 percent of the seats in both chambers. The remaining thirteen counties were grouped into five electoral districts, each newly-created district receiving one senator and two assemblymen. The maximum population variance ratio in the Senate is 1.47 to 1 and in the Assembly is 1.5 to 1.

Under this apportionment, 49.7 percent of the population could elect a majority in the Senate as compared with 8 percent under the former pattern; 46.8 percent could elect a majority in the Assembly as compared with 29.1 percent under the preceding apportionment formula.

In November 1965, following the adjournment of the special session on November 13, the act adopted in the session was presented to the federal district court as required by the *Dungan* decision. An agonizing wait ensued. It was not until March 21, 1966, that the court announced its unenthusiastic approval of the reapportionment scheme, unenthusiastic because the court believed that although the new apportionment was constitutionally permissible, it ". . . is not the fairest and best plan that the Nevada Legislature could possibly enact."[20]

Dramatic consequences to the political process in Nevada are not expected from reapportionment. The Democratic party achieved only a one-vote majority in each house in the 1966 election—another instance of the Democratic slippage characterizing that election. Conceivably, the new urban majority in the legislature may prove to be more receptive to urban-centered needs (housing, transportation, welfare). But no profound change in policy has been predicted, nor is there any significant clue from the action of the 1967 session that the conservative outlook of the legislators will change.

The Democratic party has controlled the Assembly since 1931; in the 1967 session the Democrats had 21 seats, the Republicans, 19. The Senate was controlled by the Republicans from 1937 until the 1965 session, when they were evenly matched with their opponents; one seat was held by an Independent, who chose to vote with the Democrats. In the 1967 session, Democrats achieved a one-seat majority.

Within the legislature, party issues and reliable party voting have been rare. Studies of roll-call votes generally confirm that conservative-liberal splits, and voting on a constituency or interest-group basis have characterized the legislative voting pattern. The dominant note has been limitation of the ambit of government, especially in respect to taxation; this conservative position was fortified by the long service of many legislators, particularly legislators from rural communities. With Clark County's control of the legislative process, the tendencies sketched above could change conspicuously; some shift to greater party regularity in voting could occur, as well as greater willingness to provide more government services with the probable consequence of higher taxes.

Because of reapportionment, the entire Nevada legislature was newly elected in 1966. Democrats gained three Senate seats and Republicans, one; Democrats lost four Assembly seats and Republicans gained seven. A woman was elected to the Senate for the first time and a Negro was elected to the Assembly, the first member of his race to serve in the legislature.

The Senate elected in 1967 was an unusually experienced body. Of twenty

20. *Ibid.*, 253 F. Supp. at 358 (1966).

members, fifteen had served in the immediately preceding session and seventeen had had former legislative experience, leaving only three who were freshmen. Eleven senators had previously served in the Nevada Assembly. One man had been a senator since 1951, one since 1955; six had attended four or more sessions of the legislature as members of the Senate. Only three members were practicing attorneys and the rest were in various professions and business occupations; none mentioned any labor union connections. The oldest senator was 69, the youngest 38; the median age was 52. Six were born in Nevada; thirteen had attended college, five having attended the University of Nevada.

TABLE III
PARTY COMPOSITION OF LEGISLATURE

Year	Senate			Assembly	
	D	R	I	D	R
1959	7	10		33	14
1961	7	10		32	15
1963	8	9◇		25⊕	12
1965	8□	8△	1	25	12
1967	11	9		21	19

◇The Republicans lost Eureka County to the Democrats.
□The Democrats lost Nye County to an Independent, but he chose to vote with the Democrats to organize the house.
△The Republicans lost White Pine County to the Democrats.
⊕This session is the first after the reapportionment following the 1960 census, which reduced Assembly seats from 47 to 37; though retaining control of the Assembly, the Democrats lost 7 seats; the Republicans, only 3.

An analysis of the composition of the first Assembly under reapportionment shows this chamber to be relatively inexperienced, with twenty-one freshmen in the forty-member body. Fourteen assemblymen had served in the immediately preceding session and thirteen had won three or more elections to the lower house. One member had served continually since 1947 and one since 1957. Six of the forty assemblymen were practicing attorneys; only one man identified himself with organized labor. The oldest assemblyman was 62, the youngest 29; the median age was 46. Ten of the members were born in Nevada; twenty-five had attended college, seven having attended the University of Nevada.

Republican Governor Paul Laxalt is less directly activist in attempting to influence the legislature than was his predecessor, Grant Sawyer. He did not have a majority in either house (1966-68) and maintained a modest and pleasant relationship with most of the legislators; his emphasis was upon the doctrine of separation of powers. He was rebuffed in his plan to lower the voting age to eighteen, but in general fared well from the legislature. Six hundred eighty-nine bills were passed in the 1967 session and signed by the governor; he vetoed only five bills. These vetoed bills were sent to the secretary of state, as required when the legislature has adjourned, and will be presented by him to the next regular session of the legislature, where a two-thirds vote is needed for their repassage. The Nevada governor does not, then, have a "pocket veto"; neither does he have an item veto.

The speaker is ordinarily the most powerful member of the party that controls the Assembly. He is the presiding officer and usually commands the machinery of the Assembly: he appoints the personnel of the twenty committees, but he does not refer bills to committees, that authority belonging to the introducer.

The lieutenant governor presides in the Senate and formally appoints the members of the twelve committees. In the 1958 and 1962 elections, in which Sawyer (D) won the governorship, the voters chose two Republicans as lieutenant governor: Rex Bell in 1958 and Paul Laxalt in 1962. In 1965 Laxalt presided in a Senate over which his party had lost control; even so, he was an influential figure in the session, notably successful in delaying action on reapportionment. Edward Fike (R), also presiding over a Senate controlled by the opposing party (1967), earned the respect of the senators for his parliamentary ability. The lieutenant governor may vote only to break a tie. However, because the state constitution requires a majority of the elected members (11) to pass a bill and because the lieutenant governor is not a member of the Senate, it has become a tradition for him to cast a tie-breaking vote only on motions or resolutions, not on bills.

The legislature meets in the odd-numbered years, and members are paid $40 salary a day and $25 per diem expenses. After the 60th day, salaries cease; originally, per diem was then reduced to $15, but the 1967 legislature increased it to $25. This arrangement allows the legislature to continue in session as an official body as long as necessary but discourages delaying tactics.

In the period 1958-68 the legislature met eleven times. Regular biennial sessions were held in 1959, 1961, 1963, 1965, and 1967; special sessions were convened in 1958, 1964, 1965, 1966, and 1968. A special session is called by the governor and is restricted to topics presented by him; salaries stop after the twentieth day. The session in 1960 was Nevada's single experience with a regular annual session.

The history of the vain effort to establish annual sessions is curious. In 1958 an amendment instituting regular annual sessions was passed by 60 percent of the voters. Before the first session authorized by the new amendment had even met (1960), a petition revoking the amendment had been circulated and had received the necessary signatures; at the 1960 general election 57 percent of the voters voted to return to biennial sessions. Some people, including a few legislators, believe that dilatory tactics of the 1960 session had some part in this reversal; but the main reason for it was the belated realization of many business groups that annual sessions would raise legislative costs, might result in more taxes, and would double lobbying expenses.

In 1963 the legislature, still believing that annual sessions were imperative, passed a proposed amendment providing for regular sessions in the even-numbered years, such sessions to be restricted to the budget. As required by the constitution, the proposed amendment was re-introduced in the 1965 session. It died in committee, probably a victim of the inertia caused by the reapportionment issue, an inertia that afflicted the whole session. If the need for annual sessions becomes crucial, the device of the special session will have to continue to be employed; meanwhile, the lengthy amendment procedure was started once more in the 1967 session.

The Legislative Counsel Bureau was established in 1945 to assist legislators, government officials, and the public in bill drafting and research; additionally, it is responsible to the legislature in certain financial and accounting matters. A commission elected by the legislature and composed of four senators and four assemblymen, two from each party from each house, directs the work of the Bureau, appoints the division chiefs, and fixes their salaries. In 1963 the Bureau was reorganized into Legal, Audit, and Research divisions, each with a director; one of the three division directors is appointed by the Legislative Commission to be executive head of the Bureau. The Bureau functions throughout the year.

All bills are drafted by the legal division; a post-audit is conducted by the fiscal division, which also makes recommendations to the legislature concerning the budget and the more efficient operation of government. The research division studies problems of government specifically authorized by the legislature or requested by the Legislative Commission, and does "spot research" for officials and for the public. Seventy-one extensive research studies have been published by the Bureau (1967).

Although the Bureau is nonpartisan and gives assistance to officials and to the public without respect to party affiliation, occasional claims of political connotation to its research studies have been advanced, particularly with reference to the timing of the release of such studies when the data reflected adversely on state agencies or the administration just before an election. Comment has also been made that the chairman of the Legislative Commission may choose subjects for investigation that could prove detrimental to the administration when it is of the opposite party. Even so, the Bureau is generally respected and is viewed as performing very important service for the state. The Bureau participates in the Council of State Governments and the National Conference of State Legislative Leaders; one of its assignments is to encourage amicable relations with the national government.

VOTING HABITS AND PARTY AFFILIATION

In registration, the Democratic party holds a great superiority over the Republicans; from 1958 through 1966 this superiority was usually evident in elections for statewide offices, although in five races during this period the results make one wary of prediction of Democratic victories.

Since President Eisenhower's victory in Nevada in 1956 by just under 58 percent of the vote, only five statewide posts have been won by Republicans. Bell in 1958, Laxalt in 1962, and Fike in 1966 were elected to the lieutenant governorship; Laxalt won the governorship and Wilson McGowan upset the incumbent Democrat to win the controller's office in 1966.

In 1958, 84,889 votes were cast; Bell won by over 10,000 votes in an election in which the Democrats won the seat in Congress by over 27,000 votes, the governorship by nearly 17,000, and the United States Senate seat by about 13,000. In 1962, 99,430 votes were cast; Laxalt won by over 9,000 while the Democrats captured the United States Senate seat by nearly 30,000, the congressional post by over 40,000, and the governorship by not quite 33,000. Both Bell and Laxalt were elected lieutenant governor in the face of a powerful Democratic current.

Laxalt, like his predecessor Bell who died in office, is an appealing and popular candidate with voter-attracting abilities of sufficient potency to cause ticket-splitting. His two victories suggest that personality remains a factor in a state in which many people boast of continuing the frontier tradition of voting for individuals, not for party. But his 1966 triumph raises some serious questions for the student of politics. In winning the governorship, Laxalt did generally less well on a county basis than he had in 1962, when he won the lieutenant governorship. But he did remarkably well in the big county, Clark, where he got a very high 49.6 percent of the vote and where his two Republican colleagues, Fike and McGowan, carried the county. This election may presage a change in voting behavior for Clark, which has been a Democratic stronghold. "The Republican gains in Clark County in 1966, then, are nothing less than spectacular. If they persist, it would be appropriate to speak of a revolution in the voting behavior of Nevada."[21]

TABLE IV

REGISTRATION AND ELECTION RESULTS, 1958-1966

	Registration				Election	
Year	D	R	I	% Demo. of Reg. Voters	% Reg. Voters Who Voted	Republican Statewide Victories
1958	73,229	39,085	5,254	62.2	74.0	Bell—Lt. Governor
1960	81,682	41,357	5,858	63.5	84.6	None
1962	85,403	42,970	5,977	63.6	74.0	Laxalt—Lt. Governor
1964	104,630	50,462	8,383	64.0	84.0	None
1966	116,643	58,281	8,939	63.4	76.1	Laxalt—Governor Fike—Lt. Governor McGowan—Controller

Another election with important consequences and one that would shatter the Democrats' complacency, if any exists, was the Cannon-Laxalt contest in 1964 for the United State Senate seat.

Laxalt had proved his vote-getting capacity in 1962, when he was elected lieutenant governor in spite of a Democratic sweep, and he was the Republican party's only hope for capturing a major office in the 1964 election. As a dynamic campaigner, he continued to prove formidable against incumbent Senator Cannon, who, though an unspectacular officeholder, had earned the respect of his colleagues in the United States Senate. Predictions that Laxalt would run a good race were common, but no evidence exists that any political analyst anticipated how close the outcome would be: Cannon won by just 48 votes. In a recount, understandably requested by Laxalt, Cannon's majority was raised to 84.

In the 1964 election President Johnson, who came to Nevada particularly to support Cannon, won by 58.5 percent,[22] and incumbent Congressman Baring (D), by 63.2 percent. Senator Cannon's extremely thin 50.03 percent was a surprise. He received fewer votes than Johnson in every county and led Laxalt in only four of the seventeen. Laxalt, obviously, ran far ahead of Goldwater, leading him

21. Elmer R. Rusco, "The 1966 Election in Nevada," *Governmental Research Newsletter* (Reno: Bureau of Governmental Research, 1966), 5, No. 3 (December 1966), 2.

22. Johnson's victory by a healthy margin of 23,245 votes may have obscured the fact that his Republican opponent, Goldwater, received 5,632 more votes than there are registered Republicans in the whole state.

in every county and securing 10,729 more votes than the Republican presidential candidate did. Even in populous Clark County, Cannon's home, with a Democratic registration of 56,402, Laxalt received 25,044 votes to Cannon's 38,680.

The closeness alone of the result[23] makes the 1964 senatorial election memorable, but it also precipitated a series of events of significance. (1) For the first time in Nevada history a statewide recount was held. (2) Following the recount, Laxalt appealed to the Nevada Supreme Court regarding certain paper ballots that had been classed by the recount officials as spoiled and so invalid. The Court ruled unequivocally[24] that jurisdiction of a contested senatorial election is vested solely in the United States Senate; furthermore, the Court, in an aside reminiscent of *Marbury v. Madison*, suggested to the legislature that the statute[25] by which original jurisdiction of a contested election had been conferred on the Nevada Supreme Court might be unconstitutional. (3) The part of the election laws describing recounts, heretofore untested, proved to be silent on whether a Supreme Court canvass, which is required to certify a regular election, is necessary to make the result of a recount official; no canvass followed the Cannon-Laxalt recount, but the secretary of state issued a supplementary certificate of election showing Cannon to have won by 84 votes. It is not clear whether the official margin of victory is the 48-vote lead of the general election or the 84-vote lead of the recount. (4) Because of the confusion over what constitutes a valid ballot, the legislature in its 1965 session passed a law establishing a uniform ballot throughout the state.

As noted, Laxalt put his campaign experience to good use in his race against incumbent governor Grant Sawyer in 1966. Each man was the key figure in his party; both are formidable campaigners.

Haunting the campaign was the apparition of the Nevada tradition against a third term: two previous incumbent governors had tried without success to combat this prejudice. Additionally, widespread displeasure with the Johnson Administration resulted in seepage throughout the nation to Republicans, and so aided Laxalt. The favorable political climate for Republicans that characterized the 1966 elections was marked in the western states.

But in accounting for his victory Laxalt cited meticulous organization and reliance upon skilled professional politicians as the factors overriding all others in his triumph; he and his managers decided to disregard issues and to concentrate on thorough and extensive organization. Laxalt announced his candidacy more than a year before the election and began at once to seek support in populous Clark County (Las Vegas), which has over 50 percent of the registered voters in Nevada. His task was redoubtable: (1) 70 percent of the registered voters in Clark County are Democrats; (2) this county has more registered Democrats than there are registered Republicans in the entire state; and (3) the voting behavior of the county has been conspicuously Democratic since 1920. Laxalt's organizational strategy was a success: in Clark County he held Sawyer to a win of only 50.4 percent, a mere 487 votes.

Republican capture of three statewide offices belies the suspicion that Nevada was moving into a non-competitive "one-party" status. One other aspect of the 1966 election shows a habit of the Nevada voter: continuing the incumbent in

23. The 1964 election was the closest since 1910, when another incumbent Democrat, Senator Newlands, won by just 40 votes.

24. *Laxalt v. Cannon*, 80 Nev. Rep. 588 (1964).

25. *Nevada Revised Statutes*, 293.407.

office, a habit which, in this election, also exemplifies ticket-splitting. The State Printer won a seventh term; the Secretary of State, a sixth; the Inspector of Mines, a fifth; the Attorney General, a third. The Treasurer, running unopposed for a second term, secured the highest total of votes ever cast in Nevada. All of these officeholders are Democrats.

Nevada has one seat in the House of Representatives, to which Walter S. Baring has been elected eight times; in 1964 he was the largest vote-getter in the state and defeated his opponent by the greatest number of votes. He carried all seventeen counties. Again in 1966 he carried all the counties and defeated his opponent easily (67.6 percent) in an issueless campaign. His total vote was second highest among the partisan, contested races; John Koontz running for his sixth term as secretary of state had only token opposition from another Democrat and secured more votes than Baring did.

Baring has a curious political history[26] to which insufficient study has been given to insure any firm comments on his amazing electoral powers. He entered office as a pro-labor, New Deal Democrat and has evolved into what he calls a "Jeffersonian States' Rights Constitutional Democrat" who acts and votes like a conservative Republican. He does not always have the backing of the Democratic party organization in the state. He opposes foreign aid, federal encroachments upon states' rights, the poverty program, and kindred excesses, as he sees them, of the Administration. Although he resides in Reno, he is the exemplification of the rural-based, conservative Democrat, who holds his own party's vote and secures a very large vote from the Republicans.

Since entering the Union in 1864, Nevada has conducted twenty-seven elections for governor; eleven were won by Republicans, twelve by Democrats, two by Silver-Democrats, and two by the Silver party. In elections for the governorship in the twentieth century, the dominance of the Democrats is marked. Only four Republicans have won the governorship: Oddie in 1910, Balzar in 1926 and 1930, Russell in 1950 and 1954, and Laxalt in 1966. Thus, of seventeen contests in the twentieth century, the Republicans have won six; the Democrats, nine; and the Silver-Democrats, two.

Even greater Democratic party dominance shows in choices for other state officials since 1900. Of the offices that remain elective[27] Republicans have won since 1900 in only the following elections: lieutenant governor, six times; secretary of state, twice; treasurer, three times; controller, seven times; state printer, once; inspector of mines, five times; and never in the twentieth century have the Republicans elected an attorney-general. Since the 1906 election, no Republican has been chosen as secretary of state or as state printer. The Democrats won every state office in the New Deal period; in the elections of 1934, 1938, 1942, and 1946, no Republican was elected to any statewide office.

The hypothesis that urbanization tends to strengthen the Democratic party is borne out in Clark County (Las Vegas) and in Washoe County (Reno) in respect to registration preferences.

But the two counties differ in respect to voting in accord with their expressed party preference. The Washoe Democrat is much more of a maverick than

26. In the 1962 election in which he was the largest vote-getter, Baring was repudiated by the Democratic State Convention. For a review of his pre-1962 record as a New Deal, pro-labor, administration Democrat, see Erwin A. Jaffee and Stanley A. Pearl, "The 1962 Election in Nevada," *Western Political Quarterly*, XVI (June 1963), 443-44.

27. Judicial and school offices became nonpartisan in 1918; the surveyor-general was eliminated from elective office in 1954; the inspector of mines became elective in 1910.

the Clark Democrat. In the major contests (16) during the period tabulated above (President, United States Senate, House, governor, and lieutenant governor), the Republican candidate won eight times. In the period 1920-64, Democratic victories in statewide elections in Washoe County were only 43 percent and in contests for the state legislature, just over 40 percent.[28] Two observations may be made on Washoe's voting behavior: (1) that the county has voted primarily for Republicans and (2) that if the election of 1966 marks a trend, the Republicans will not only do well in Washoe County despite the registration preference for the Democrats but may continue to improve their electoral superiority—in 1966 the Washoe delegation to the state legislature was 72 percent Republican, a gain of 12 percent in that party's representative strength.

TABLE V

CLARK AND WASHOE PARTY REGISTRATIONS, 1958-1966

Year	Clark			Washoe		
	D	R	% D	D	R	% D
1958	33,837	11,013	75.44	18,152	15,409	54.08
1960	38,001	11,822	76.27	21,722	16,893	56.25
1962	41,329	13,920	74.79	22,017	16,679	56.89
1964	56,402	18,965	74.83	25,234	18,264	58.01
1966	64,527	23,793	73.06	26,752	19,934	57.30

The Clark County Democrat may be the ideal of every party leader; in the 1958-66 period the Democratic candidates won all but three statewide contests. Republican candidates secured the lieutenant governorship in 1958 and 1966 and the controller's post in 1966. The last Republican to win national office in Clark County was Eisenhower in 1952. Therefore, in that county the registration preference and voting behavior are very close; because Clark is the fastest growing area in the state and because the dominance of the Democrats in the county is so marked, some observers have speculated that Nevada may be developing into a one-party state and that "as Clark goes, so goes Nevada." Yet the good showing of Laxalt in Clark County in 1966, the persisting Republican voting habits of Washoe County, and the tight Cannon-Laxalt contest in 1964 with its reminder of the imponderables of voter loyalty to party in the face of a pleasing candidate prohibit any prediction that the Republican party will ineluctably dwindle in this state as the power of Las Vegas and Clark County swells. On the latter topic, Laxalt commented (1965) that the Republicans must broaden their base to attract labor and minority groups and that survival of the two-party system in the state was seriously threatened unless the Republicans did well in the 1966 election. They did do well, they did make an effort to attract labor and minority support,[29] and they did win three statewide offices.

28. Rusco, *Voting Behavior in Nevada*, pp. 9, 16.
29. Eleanore Bushnell, "The 1966 Election in Nevada," *Western Political Quarterly*, XX (June 1967), 581-82.

IMPACT OF NATIONAL POLITICS AND TRENDS

Of the twenty-six elections in Nevada for President of the United States, thirteen were won by Democrats, twelve by Republicans, and one by the Populist candidate when silver was the overriding issue in the state. Nevada usually follows the national pattern; in twenty of the presidential elections the successful candidate also prevailed in this state. In the twentieth century the Democratic candidate won eleven of the seventeen presidential contests. Yet in 1952, when 57 percent of the voters were registered Democrats, *all* the Republican candidates for national office (President, Senate, House) were elected in Nevada; and in 1954, when Democratic registration had risen to 59 percent, a Republican was chosen for Nevada's one seat in the House of Representatives. Republican success in these two elections in Nevada was a reflection of the national support for Eisenhower. The 1954 election was the last one in which President Eisenhower's popularity aided a Republican candidate in attaining office in the state; his re-election to the presidency in 1956 marks the last time Nevada chose a Republican candidate for a national office in the period 1956-67.

In the twentieth century, twenty-three contests for United States Senator have taken place; Republican candidates have won just five of these contests. Thirty-four elections for the House of Representatives have been held since 1900, with the Republicans winning only eleven. A serious question arises as to whether the Democrats make up the only effective party for securing national office in Nevada; without respect to individual preference, political analysts must consider whether Republican victories in this state are bizarre occurrences rather than the expected interchange of office that characterizes the two-party system.

Nevada's congressional delegation (1967) was composed of Senators Bible and Cannon and Congressman Baring, all Democrats. The senators are frequently on the same side on important issues and usually support the administration; Baring is often on the opposing side. The three have been, however, together in their support of mining interests, together in opposing legislation that could affect gambling, together in working for more water for Nevada, together in opposing reduction of silver in coins, and, to a lesser degree, often together in support of states' rights.

Baring, with his eight victories for the House of Representatives, was (1967) Nevada's most entrenched political figure; he ran ahead of the presidential candidate in the elections of 1960 and 1964 and led the ticket in 1958, 1962, and 1966 for offices that were seriously contested. His voting record in Congress in 1965 was approved by the Americans for Democratic Action 5 percent of the time and by the American Farm Bureau Federation 100 percent.[30] On issues in which a yes vote supported a larger federal involvement, Baring voted no on well over half the roll calls. On 61 House roll-call votes in which the Democrats were split between northern and southern positions in 1965,[31] Baring was recorded in agreement with the southern Democrats in every instance and never at any time with the northern Democrats.

Perhaps an even clearer indication of Congressman Baring's position is his identification with the "conservative coalition," a grouping of Republicans and southern Democrats against the northern Democrats in Congress. This "coalition" is identified by *Congressional Quarterly* as less an organized and directed voting bloc than as an outlook, an exemplification of a political philosophy. Its

30. *Congressional Quarterly*, XXIV (February 25, 1966), 473.
31. *Congressional Quarterly Almanac*, XXI (1965), 1097.

strength in 1967 is attested by its voting twenty-nine times against the expressed position of President Johnson and winning seventeen of these votes; it helped to defeat Johnson on such measures as foreign aid, crime control, and rat control. Baring is comfortable with this conservative group; he voted with it 80 percent of the time in 1967 and is one of three Democrats from the West with the highest conservative coalition support score.[32] Thus, Baring may be viewed as a conservative Democrat who votes with the Republicans and with the southern wing of his party; that he pleases his constituents is overwhelmingly and unimpeachably evident.

Nevada's senators show a somewhat, but not remarkably, different pattern from Baring's. Bible's 1965 voting record was approved by Americans for Democratic Action 47 percent of the time and by the American Farm Bureau Federation 20 percent; Cannon received 59 percent and 40 percent approval respectively from the two groups.[33] Ninety-nine Senate roll calls were recorded in 1965 in which there was a split between the northern and the southern wings of the party. Bible voted with the South forty-two times and with the North fifty-three; Cannon voted with the South thirty times and with the North forty-eight.[34]

With respect to degree of support for positions in which the majority of Republicans and southern Democrats voted together in 1967—the "conservative coalition" sketched above—Bible voted with the group on 68 percent of the roll calls and Cannon voted with it on 45 percent. Both Cannon and Bible were listed among the six northern Democrats who voted most consistently with the Republican-southern Democrat position in 1967.[35] Both Nevada senators may be appraised as conservative. Neither has the hold on the voter that Baring has; however, Bible won re-election easily in 1962 against a very conservative Republican who carried only Douglas County; Cannon's difficulties and meagre win in 1964 have been described.

In the matters summarized above and on other issues not presented here Nevada's representation at the national level is conservative. The "coalition" support score as tabulated by *Congressional Quarterly*[36] lists the fifteen northern Democrats in the Senate and House who have the highest record of consistent voting identification with the "coalition"; three of the fifteen are the representatives from Nevada—the entire delegation. This distinction is unique among northern Democrats. The only other western state with representation among the fifteen (1967) is New Mexico, with one senator and two representatives on the list.

In the late 1960's, despite the fact of a forced reapportionment, Nevada continues to reflect conservative, non-metropolitan political preferences at both the local and national levels. Some observers speculate that as the dominance of Clark County (Las Vegas) makes itself felt in elections, the conservative bias of the state may change and that welfare, roads, schools, and other population-created needs will be met with greater alacrity. To achieve success in either a national or a state election, the candidate will need to secure Clark County or receive a high proportion of the vote there. Such a requirement gives Democrats a powerful advantage; but a strong Republican, like Laxalt, with basic support from Washoe County (Reno) and from the small counties, has demonstrated that Republicans can win

32. *Congressional Quarterly*, XXV (December 29, 1967), 2652.
33. *Ibid.*, XXIV (February 25, 1966), 474.
34. *Congressional Quarterly Almanac, op. cit.*
35. *Congressional Quarterly*, XXV, (December 29, 1967), 2652.
36. *Ibid.*

and that the party is not moribund. As the population continues to rise in the Las Vegas area, the very lopsidedness of Clark County's dominion might summon forth new political alliances. Nevada, because of its phenomenal growth, its nearly total dependence on tourists, and the strains on government that these forces bring is an interesting exhibit for the student of the political process.

NEW MEXICO:

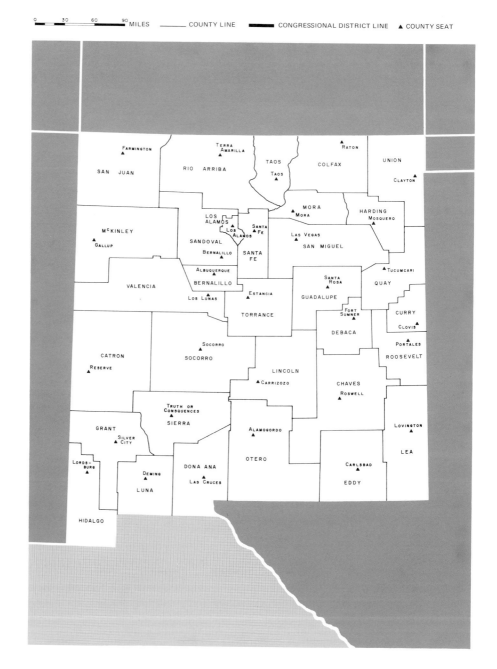

Farmington ▲

TERRA AMARILLA ▲

TAOS
TAOS ▲

RATON ▲

UNION

CLAYTON ▲

SAN JUAN

RIO ARRIBA

COLFAX

MORA
MORA ▲

HARDING
MOSQUERO ▲

McKINLEY

GALLUP ▲

LOS ALAMOS
LOS ALAMOS ▲

SANTA FE ▲

LAS VEGAS ▲

SANDOVAL

BERNALILLO ▲

SANTA FE

SAN MIGUEL

ALBUQUERQUE ▲

BERNALILLO

SANTA ROSA ▲

QUAY

TUCUMCARI ▲

VALENCIA

LOS LUNAS ▲

ESTANCIA ▲

GUADALUPE

FORT SUMNER ▲

CURRY

CLOVIS ▲

TORRANCE

DEBACA

PORTALES ▲

SOCORRO ▲

ROOSEVELT

CATRON

RESERVE ▲

SOCORRO

LINCOLN

CARRIZOZO ▲

CHAVES

ROSWELL ▲

TRUTH OR CONSEQUENCES

SIERRA

ALAMOGORDO ▲

LOVINGTON ▲

GRANT

SILVER CITY ▲

LEA

LORDS-BURG ▲

DEMING ▲

DONA ANA

LAS CRUCES ▲

OTERO

CARLSBAD ▲

EDDY

LUNA

HIDALGO

Harry P. Stumpf
T. Phillip Wolf

The Political State

One of those stories that grows with the telling has it that a tourist visiting New Mexico a few years ago purchased ninety-eight dollars worth of silver jewelry in a Santa Fe shop. When asked whether the import duty could be paid on the spot rather than at the border, the shop's proprietor promptly replied, "Yes, that will be just $9.80 more!" In the same vein is the experience of a retired admiral, now an Albuquerque resident, who was sent a *Tax Guide for U.S. Citizens Abroad* from the Internal Revenue Service. As one commentator put it, "New Mexico must keep up the struggle to 'stay put' in the Union. . . ."[1] Such tales are suggestive of a more general (and more significant) set of conditions one perceives in studying the affairs of the forty-seventh state, for New Mexico indeed seems to be searching for identity in more dimensions than simply the geographic.

With fewer first and second generation Mexican-Americans in the state than in three others,[2] and with the percentage of Spanish-American surnames dropping steadily (45 percent in 1940, 37 percent in 1950, and 28 percent in 1960), one can hardly characterize New Mexico as the land of *manana*, of *poco tiempo*. Indeed, attempts to isolate the Hispanic variable in the state's politics have increasingly emphasized its diminution, at least in terms of current political power. Nor is the American Indian element in the state's demographic make-up (steady, at roughly 6 percent) very helpful in understanding political New Mexico.[3]

Earlier commentators have been fascinated with the old Spanish *patron* system and its offspring, an effective statewide patronage system. But the 1961 and 1963 State Personnel Acts are working to erase this feature of politics in New Mexico. Educational excellence can be one small measure of a state's total political and economic profile, but even here, where New Mexico can boast of national records as measured by the ratio of income to expenditures, economic realities continue to disadvantage the state as compared with its neighbors. Whether one selects tourism, mining, agriculture, defense production, over-all growth rate or

Note: The authors gratefully acknowledge the assistance of Jack E. Holmes, University of Tennessee, Dorothy I. Cline, University of New Mexico, and the late Frederick C. Irion, University of New Mexico. Professor Irion gave permission to use portions of his chapter appearing in *Western Politics* (Salt Lake: University of Utah Press, 1961).

1. *Albuquerque Journal*, February 21, 1965.

2. *Congressional Quarterly Census Analysis: Congressional Districts of the United States*, Weekly Report No. 34, August 21, 1964 (Washington: Congressional Quarterly Service, 1964), p. 1870. The 1960 figures are: California, 695,643; Texas, 655,523; Illinois, 63,063; and New Mexico, 34,459.

3. Estimated from data presented in Paul Walter, Jr., and Ross Calvin, *Population Trends in New Mexico* (Albuquerque: Division of Government Research, University of New Mexico, 1947), pp. 13-17.

levels achieved, the New Mexico economy is neither distinguished nor easily distinguishable from that of many other western states.

If New Mexico and its politics are thus not easily defined, distinctive features are nonetheless present. A tradition of inefficiency combined with patience, a storied emphasis upon political skills, and an almost unspoken commitment to individual liberties and civil rights—these are but a few ingredients of the political formula of the state. The next several pages attempt to explicate and explore these and other factors which help to identify New Mexico's political styles.

THE VARIABLE OF HISTORY

Historical influences are perhaps the most difficult kind of variable to relate empirically to current patterns of political behavior. The relationship is notoriously easy to assert, but difficult to prove. Yet, there are some characteristics of New Mexico politics which are impossible to understand without reference to the history of the region—a history which is distinctive chronologically, culturally, and politically.

Twenty-five centuries ago, when Greece won freedom for Western Civilization at Marathon and Salamis, the ancestors of the Pueblo Indians were performing their ceremonial dances, some of which have been virtually unchanged for one thousand years. It is likely that "these surviving Pueblo communities constitute the oldest republics known."[4]

As for European origins, New Mexico's political life begins with Coronado's expedition of 1540-42. There has been an uninterrupted line of governors since Onate was appointed on October 25, 1595. This line of succession is longer than that of any other state in the Union.[5] Even discounting Pueblo history and the early explorations, New Mexico still has long-standing political institutions. For instance, in the establishment of Santa Fe, probably in 1610, the first European form of government came to New Mexico.[6] Santa Fe, with the oldest public building in the United States (the Palace of Governors), was the northern terminus of America's oldest highway, El Camino Real, from Mexico City.

The Inquisition came to New Mexico in 1626.[7] It was active during much of the seventeenth century and apparently had some influence during the eighteenth. The Pueblo Revolt of 1680 saw the Spanish driven out until the reconquest of 1692. New Mexico became a province of Mexico in 1821, the year which also marks the opening of the Santa Fe Trail. General Kearny raised the American flag over the Palace of Governors in 1846. From 1846 to 1851, New Mexico had a temporary government. It was then ruled by a territorial government until 1912, when it was formally admitted to statehood, under a constitution which had been drawn up two years earlier.

4. Edgar L. Hewett, "My Neighbors, the Pueblo Indians," *Art and Archeology*, XVI (July-August 1923), 10.

5. Lansing B. Bloom, "The Governors of New Mexico," *New Mexico Historical Review*, X (April 1935), 152-57. See also Dorothy Woodward and John H. Feth, *New Mexico—Land of Enchantment* (Washington: Government Printing Office, 1941); 77th Cong., 1st sess., S. Doc. 91.

6. Lansing B. Bloom, "Beginnings of Representative Government in New Mexico," *New Mexico Historical Review*, XXI (April 1946), 127.

7. France V. Scholes, "The First Decade of the Inquisition in New Mexico," *New Mexico Historical Review*, X (July 1935), 195-229.

Between this long history of Spanish rule (combined with frequent and continuing contact with both the Anglo and Indian cultures) and the current political styles of New Mexico politics there exists that elusive cause and effect relationship referred to above. Regarding the marriage of the Spanish and Anglo cultures, Jack E. Holmes writes:

Both groups were European, both Christian, and they shared more basic conceptions than they disputed. This new confrontation of the Protestant and Catholic ethics involved no severe strain, for the modes of resolving that issue had already been worked out elsewhere in Europe and in the United States.

Conflict was present, of course, but it was not so serious that it prevented the evolution of a political system incorporating and merging factors important to both groups. There evolved, rather, a notable emphasis upon political institutions and processes—an emphasis probably not at all incompatible with central elements of the Hispanic subculture.[8]

Attempting to pinpoint the origin of that extra measure of political skill often alleged to characterize New Mexico politics, Holmes relies upon Melville Herskovitz: "Not all aspects of a culture (as in a vocabulary) are given equal emphasis. . . . The things that outstandingly mark the culture of a people . . . also tend to dominate their lives. Because such matters are important to them, people will think and talk a great deal about personalities, events, and possibilities lying in this aspect of their culture."[9] Here the argument becomes circular and fuzzy, cause and effect being interchangeable. It is indisputable that politics was a highly significant aspect of the Spanish settlements and the *patron* system and that political skills and endeavors constituted a stock-in-trade as compared with modern American experience.[10] The precise reason for this is much less clear. That interest in and knowledge of political relationships remains high, especially among the Hispanic peoples of New Mexico, is also in evidence, although not well documented. A partial explanation of the endurance of this tradition, as well as that of civil liberties, may lie in the concept of cultural assimilation. Some understanding of the ethnic accommodation and assimilation achieved in New Mexico may be gained by contrasting it with the Texas experience. In writing of the Spanish-Americans living along the Rio Grande on the Texas side, V. O. Key says:

The Mexican-American voters have been managed in the same way as national minority groups in the major urban centers. For the most part they remain unassimilated into the cultural pattern of Texas. Many of them do not speak English, have meager schooling, and have only the most remote conception of Anglo-Saxon governmental institutions. Often of low economic status, they are subject to the coercive influences usually brought to bear on depressed groups. Their social status lies somewhere between the "white" and the Negroes. Their group pride contributes to political cohesiveness and makes easier the task of the politician who would manage them. Mexican-Americans suffer unmistakable discrimination and

8. Jack E. Holmes, "Party, Legislature, and Governor in the Politics of New Mexico, 1911-1963" (Ph.D. thesis, University of Chicago, 1964, Thesis No. T 10646), p. 37. This 340-page work is a near-encyclopedic treatise on political change in New Mexico since statehood. Using the V. O. Key model, Holmes relies heavily upon election data to analyze party and legislative trends, county-by-county and region-by-region, and to attempt to isolate the ethnic and historic factors in the state's political development. Though not sharply focused, the study may be viewed as the best and most comprehensive work on New Mexico politics to date, and is especially valuable in its attempt to anchor New Mexico data to the recent scholarly literature on state and local politics. Holmes served as director of the state's Legislative Council Service from 1951 to 1959, and is now with the University of Tennessee. A revised version of the thesis is Jack E. Holmes, *Politics in New Mexico* (Albuquerque: University of New Mexico Press, 1967); citations that follow are from the original thesis.

9. *Ibid.*, citing Melville J. Herskovitz, *Man and His Works* (New York: Knopf, 1948), pp. 543-45.

10. See Holmes, *op. cit.*, pp. 22-30, and the sources cited therein.

some forms of segregation, though not to the same extent as Negroes. As might be expected, there occurs among the Mexican-Americans a high incidence of political indifference, ignorance, timidity, and sometimes venality.[11]

The role of the Spanish-American in New Mexico has been almost the exact opposite of this, although perhaps not as much so as most New Mexicans would like to think. Relying partially upon data from V. O. Key, Jack Holmes notes that the Hispanic peoples living in the same valley in New Mexico have, for sixty years, produced a significantly and consistently higher voter turnout than just across the border in Texas.[12]

From statehood, and before, ethnic differences were approached from a different point of view in New Mexico, and there evolved a positive racial affinity, delightfully summed up by David Boroff, who visited the state in the early 1960's. " 'Ethnic' is something of a cult word in New Mexico. It bespeaks respect—even reverence—for other cultures in the area. It means liberalism, sophistication, the charms of the primitive."[13] And speaking of the New Mexican's self-image and of his *Kulturkampf* with Texas, Boroff writes:

There are those who view New Mexico as an island of liberalism hemmed in by Goldwater country, Texas (a curse word), and conflict-ridden Colorado. And the graceful coexistence of the three cultures—Spanish, Indian, and Anglo—is an article of faith. . . . New Mexicans see themselves as less self-aggrandizing and more humane, and they point to the inferior status of the Spanish—the Mexicans—in the adjoining state.[14]

Hence, whatever its exact cause, a high degree of cultural assimilation in New Mexico has itself encouraged the perpetuation of the twin traditions of political finesse and commitment to civil liberties. Current evidence of the former is seen less in voting turnout[15] than in other forms of political participation—at the precinct and county levels, especially in the Spanish villages and towns of the northern and western counties. In New Mexico, politics is more often viewed as a fascinating game than in terms of a "dirty business" so common in American thinking generally.[16]

Evidence of a strong tradition of civil liberties in New Mexico is much more easily presented. Aside from the impressionistic testimony of visitors such as Boroff, the state's constitution of 1910 contains a rather remarkable provision for its day. Article 7, Section 3 states:

The right of any citizen of the state to vote, hold office or sit upon juries, shall never be restricted, abridged or impaired on account of religion, race, language or color, or inability to speak, read or write the English or Spanish languages except as may be otherwise provided in this Constitution; and the provisions of this section and of section one of this article shall never be amended except upon a vote of the people of this state in an election at which at least three-fourths of the electors voting in the whole state, and at least two-thirds of those voting in each county of the state shall vote for such amendment.

11. V. O. Key, Jr., *Southern Politics in State and Nation* (New York: Knopf, 1949), pp. 271-72. This excerpt is from the Random House Vintage Books edition.

12. Holmes, *op. cit.*, p. 22.

13. "A New Yorker's Report on New Mexico," *Harpers*, 230 (February 1965), 76.

14. *Ibid.*, p. 75.

15. See below, Table II, for the state's electoral participation.

16. The fact that so much is said about "politicized" New Mexico but so little evidence is available may suggest that we are dealing with a myth. Yet, myths are a part of politics, too, and are known to be movers of men—and events. The easy (but correct) answer is that more research is needed. For instance, by holding constant the major variables associated with political participation, a study of voting turnout in New Mexico as compared with other states might yield the hard evidence now lacking.

That such strict insistence upon minority rights should be found in the document is less remarkable than the fact that little opposition to such provisions was in evidence during the 1910 constitutional convention.[17] As previously suggested, further evidence of a strong civil rights tradition in New Mexico politics is the very absence of the issue. Except in terms of national politics, one seldom hears civil liberties discussed. Even among conservative Republican leaders, McCarthyism found virtually no support in the state.

The constitution itself, still in effect, was drawn up by Republicans of a conservative bent.[18] Although not in the extreme as compared with some other states, the document is replete with the all too common minutiae and complicated provisions. As one scholar has put it, "any lawyer with an imagination can challenge (as unconstitutional) . . . nearly any law or executive action."[19] Although amended fifty-five times since statehood, the constitution contains the above-mentioned extraordinary amending requirement for certain educational as well as voting provisions. One practical result of this has been to prevent, time and again, absentee voting in New Mexico. The eleventh referendum to establish absentee balloting easily won majority approval in November 1967. It did not gain the extraordinary majority of two-thirds approval in each county and three-fourths statewide which the state constitution required to change voter qualifications. The Attorney-General then filed suit to have this restriction in the state constitution declared in violation of the equal protection clause of the U.S. Constitution's 14th Amendment. On February 3, 1968, the New Mexico Supreme Court upheld this position, clearing the way for legislative action. The legislature, then in session, quickly approved absentee balloting. When the governor signed the bill, New Mexico lost its unique status of not permitting absentee balloting for state and local office.

In 1963 a Constitutional Revision Commission was established, consisting of eleven members and four legislative advisors. The Commission continued its work through 1966, culminating in a 1967 report that presents an article-by-article proposal for revision of the constitution. The 1968 legislative session put on the November 1968 ballot a referendum for a constitutional convention. If approved, the convention could be held in 1969 or 1970.

POPULATION AND OTHER RESOURCES

The state's population growth has been quite uneven. Although it has more than tripled since 1910 (from 327,301 in that year to an estimated 1,041,300 in

17. Holmes, *op. cit.*, p. 62, footnote 1. On page 63 Holmes labels such constitutional provisions the first formal expression of Calhoun's doctrine of concurrent majority governing ". . . a major aspect of politics *within* a state." The U.S. Congress was more reactionary on the civil liberties issue than the state constitutional convention. The Enabling Act of 1910 required proficiency in English for officeholding but Congress later rescinded its position on this matter.

18. As one father of New Mexico's constitution wrote: "We [the Republicans] are sure to have a two-thirds majority in the convention, and we are better able to make a good constitution than the Democrats. We know that they would not hold a nonpartisan convention if they were in the majority. To make it nonpartisan means that we would have to give away some of our strength, and I do not believe any political party can succeed by surrendering a part of its strength." Letter of T. B. Catron to Wm. H. H. Allison, June 28, 1910, as quoted in Thomas C. Donnelly, *The Government of New Mexico* (Albuquerque: University of New Mexico Press, 1953), p. 43.

19. Charles B. Judah and Frederick C. Irion, *The 47th State: An Appraisal of Its Government* (Albuquerque: Division of Government Research, University of New Mexico, 1959), p. 23.

1966), its distribution throughout the state has shifted appreciably. Especially significant from a political point of view is the changing demographic role of Bernalillo County (Albuquerque and environs), the state's only Standard Metropolitan Statistical Area. Now well over 300,000, the county has consistently been the locale of the greatest population growth. In 1950, Bernalillo County accounted for barely 20 percent of the state's population while the proportion is now approaching one-third (30 percent in 1964). The county's closest rivals by this measure are Dona Ana County (Las Cruces), with 6 percent of the state's population, and Chaves County (Roswell), with 5 percent.[20] Bernalillo County is also the current leader in rate of growth (18 percent in 1960-64), although economic and industrial conditions have at times given other counties rapid changes. Los Alamos, although atypical, grew 4,265 percent from 1940 to 1950, and its rate of growth is still high. Another example is again Dona Ana County, the location of fast-growing New Mexico State University. This county's 1960-64 growth rate is estimated to be 17 percent.

Nevertheless, several counties have consistently lost population, both relatively and absolutely. In the fifty-year period 1910 to 1960, eleven counties had absolute losses, ranging up to 49 percent. Some of these are among the lowest per capita income counties in the nation.

The fundamental basis in the past for New Mexico politics has been a rural population. Measured by the old census definition (urban defined as incorporated places of 2,500 or more), the state was nearly 86 percent rural in 1910, and as late as 1950 the state was still predominantly rural (54 percent).[21] New Mexico moved from rural to urban status in the early nineteen-fifties. Employing the new definition of urban (incorporated and unincorporated places of 2,500 persons or more and densely settled urban fringe areas), the 1960 population of the state is nearly 66 percent urban. A measure of urban-rural change in New Mexico may also be taken from the growth of Bernalillo County, described above.

One problem facing the state in the shift to metropolitan areas is that municipalities are not prepared for growth. The Bureau of Business Research of the University of New Mexico concludes:

It is fairly clear that most New Mexico municipalities are financially unable to provide the services expected of modern cities, that the over-all problem of city financing has never been attacked, that the financial procedures are archaic and confused, that the structure of revenues and expenditures is a make-shift arrangement which has been built on expedience, and that a complete overhauling is urgently needed to prevent civic decay and provide a sound basis for economic development.[22]

New Mexico's rapid population increase is also causing a drastic shift in the state's ethnic composition. Myths aside, the best data available indicate that measured both by the percentage of Spanish surnames and by absolute numbers of first and second generation citizens of Mexican stock, the state is very rapidly becoming "Anglosized." Prior to the state's first congressional districting in 1968, New

20. Ralph L. Edgel and Eldon G. Marr, *Estimates of the 1966 Population of New Mexico Counties*, Business Information Series No. 45 (Albuquerque: Bureau of Business Research, University of New Mexico, January 1967), p. 6, Table 8.

21. Arthur A. Blumenfeld, *New Mexico's Population Since 1910*, Business Information Series No. 40 (Albuquerque: Bureau of Business Research, University of New Mexico, November 1962), p. 5.

22. Arthur A. Blumenfeld, *Some Aspects of Municipal Finance in New Mexico* (Albuquerque: Bureau of Business Research, University of New Mexico, 1959), p. 14.

Mexico ranked twelfth among congressional districts in portion of Mexican stock.[23] The state's Indian population, now standing at about 57,000, is neither numerically nor politically significant. Although in *Trujillo v. Garley* (U.S. District Court for New Mexico, August 11, 1948, not reported) the Indian received voting privileges, the degree of participation (except for the Navajos) has been very low.[24] Negroes constitute the only other notable ethnic group, numbering 17,063 in 1960.

Important political implications are to be found in the age distribution of New Mexico's population. Although the state can still claim the lowest median age in the nation (22.8 years in 1960), this is probably of less significance than the changing distribution. As shown in Table I, the number of persons over sixty-five

TABLE I

NEW MEXICO POPULATION BY AGE GROUPS
1910 - 1960

	1910	1920	1930	1940	1950	1960	% Change 1910-1960
Total Number	327,301	360,350	423,317	531,818	679,425	951,023	
% Distribution							
Under 6	16.5	15.5	15.4	14.4	16.5	17.0	199
6 - 13	18.3	19.4	19.1	17.9	16.8	19.1	222
14 - 17	8.0	7.9	8.2	8.3	6.9	6.9	149
18 - 20	5.9	5.8	6.0	5.9	5.1	4.3	113
21 - 44	35.2	34.2	33.5	34.6	35.0	32.2	166
45 - 64	13.1	13.8	13.8	14.5	14.8	15.1	234
65 & over	3.0	3.4	4.0	4.4	4.9	5.4	440
TOTAL	100.0	100.0	100.0	100.0	100.0	100.0	

23. *Congressional Quarterly Census Analysis*, p. 1872. Liberals, Spanish-Americans, and Republicans were proponents of congressional districting; each thought that action would increase the likelihood of one from their respective groups winning a seat. As it turned out, the election opportunities of none of these groups were served. Initially, it appeared the legislature had taken a swipe at the incumbent congressmen, both of whom were placed in the same district. But this first congressional districting act in the state turned to the incumbents' benefit when E. S. (Johnny) Walker quickly changed his residence from Santa Fe to Las Cruces. In District 2, his portion of the two-party vote in 1964 and 1966 was 53 percent and 54 percent, respectively, while statewide he got 51.6 and 50.6 percent in those years. (In District 1, Walker had 50 and 48 percent of the vote.) This improved position of Walker's combined with the election record of Thomas Morris, who runs well throughout the state, indicates both incumbents will continue to be elected.

24. See Holmes, *op. cit.*, pp. 106-12, and sources cited therein for a good analysis of the Indian political role, present and prospective.

continues to increase faster than any other group, while the age groups represent-ing the bulk of the labor force, present and in the near future, are growing at a much slower pace. At the very least, this suggests a heavier welfare, health, and personal services burden for a relatively smaller portion of the state's population.

Over-all, a significant trend is the movement away from agriculture. Al-though a familiar phenomenon nationally, this shift has been particularly dramat-ic in New Mexico. To illustrate, in 1954, 9.8 percent of New Mexico employment income was from agriculture, this figure dropping to only 4.4 percent in 1964.[25]

In contrast, government, particularly the federal sector, continues to expand its already major role in the state's economy. There are several ways of stating this phenomenon, but they all point to one conclusion: the federal government is the critical backbone of the state's economy to an extent which would distress the Chamber of Commerce Diversification Committee of most states.

Since the first atomic bomb was exploded at Trinity Site near Alamogordo on July 16, 1945, nuclear research, manufacturing, and related military activities have come to account for over 16 percent of persons employed in New Mexi-co.[26] The federal government's annual expenditure in the state now exceeds one billion dollars, which is more than four times the total federal taxes from the state each year, or approximately one thousand dollars per New Mexican. Federal wage employment in 1964 accounted for nearly 12 percent of the state's total, as com-pared with 4 percent for the nation as a whole.[27] Including all governmental activ-ity, federal, state, local, civilian as well as military, the proportions in 1964 are even more impressive: 27 percent of the total number employed in the state (up nearly one-third within the last ten years) and 28 percent of personal income, almost double that of ten years ago.

Despite these significant inputs, the rate of the state's economic growth in terms of *Business Week*'s index has been lower than that of the nation seven of the seventeen years, 1948-64, which is contrary to the impressive growth rates in most other western states.[28] The state's family income thus continues to remain at a relatively low level, falling in the lowest one-half of the 435 congressional districts.[29] Per capita income stood at $1,928 in 1964, lower than that of any other Mountain or Pacific state.

The extreme contrast of per capita income by counties indicates another politico-economic problem of New Mexico. In 1963, the people of Sandoval County averaged only $783, while those of Los Alamos averaged $3,456, the highest in the state. More typical is Bernalillo County's $2,314 in 1963 as con-trasted with San Miguel's $1,115.[30]

Although comparative data from other states are not readily available, there is considerable evidence to suggest that tax evasion in New Mexico must also be added to the list of the state's politico-economic liabilities. Based on a comparison

25. *New Mexico Business* (Albuquerque: Bureau of Business Research, University of New Mexico), March 1965, p. 4.

26. *Ibid.*, p. 3. This percentage does not include that portion of construction employ-ment working on defense and space projects.

27. "Albuquerque: The City Uncle Sam Built," *Empire Magazine* (*Denver Post*), April 4, 1965, p. 10.

28. *New Mexico Business*, March 1965 (Source, Table IV), p. 1.

29. *Congressional Quarterly Census Analysis*, p. 1837.

30. These data are based on estimates supplied by the Bureau of Business Research of the University of New Mexico.

of federal and state income tax returns, the State Revenue Bureau estimated in 1965 that there were some 90,000 evaders, or about 15 percent of New Mexicans who filed federal returns.[31] The incidence of nonpayment of property taxes as well as municipal sales taxes may be even higher, although assessment laws and their administration appear to be partially responsible, especially for property tax evasion. Efforts to improve tax administration have centered on tighter enforcement of state income tax laws and property reappraisal. In late 1967, twenty-six counties had begun (two had nearly completed) county-wide programs of property reappraisal; two of the remaining six were about to initiate these programs.[32]

One conclusion suggested by the foregoing discussion is that despite the contributions of the state's traditional economic base (agriculture, mining, oil and gas), as well as a growing tourism and convention industry, an end to the cold war would confront the state with major problems of economic adjustment. While community and state spokesmen are prone to emphasize that the nature of federal spending in the state is more long-range and research-oriented than that involved in the less exotic defense manufacturing elsewhere, it is nonetheless true that the state's economy is tied directly to the federal budget in a critical way—primarily because there are few alternatives.[33]

PUBLIC OPINION

Whether viewed as an environmental factor or as a part of the political process itself, public opinion and its conduits as well as the broader ideological context within which they are found comprise a variable near the heart of any political system, and it is here that New Mexico's historical roots are most in evidence. In this sense, the discussion to follow is a continuation of the historical data presented above.

New Mexico's political system has weathered quite well the population increases and shifts, the utilization of new resources, the vast differences in per capita income, the influx of governmental and military personnel—the forces, that is, which have revolutionized lifeways in less than a decade-and-a-half. Apparently two different sets of mores now exist side by side. The old system is based on a rural consensus with a heavy Hispanic flavor, and is the system which has upheld civil rights in New Mexico. A new system, based on largely "Anglosized" public opinion, which is now beginning to make itself felt, is destined to take over the politics of New Mexico.

While a distinctive feature of New Mexico's politics would appear to be the Hispanic element, a significant degree of political cohesiveness is simply not present.[34] Any interpretation of the state's politics in terms of, say, the New England

31. *Albuquerque Journal*, January 6, 1965.

32. See *ibid.*, September 2, 1967; for comments on the tax evasion problem see *ibid.*, April 16, February 20, and May 28, 1965.

33. Data on the state's resources are summarized in Frederick C. Irion (ed.), *New Mexico and Its Natural Resources, 1900-2000* (Albuquerque: Division of Government Research, University of New Mexico, 1959); Dorothy I. Cline and Joel V. Barrett, "Concepts and Planning in the Use and Conservation of Natural Resources," *New Mexico Business*, December 1964, pp. 1-10; and New Mexico State Planning Office, "A Design for Development Decisions" (Santa Fe: State Planning Office, 1962).

34. See Holmes, *op. cit.*, chap. II, on the role of the Spanish-American in New Mexico politics.

pattern of candidate selection related to race, religion, and similar factors can only obscure what goes on in New Mexico. Of course there is in the state a balancing process in the selection of candidates, and certainly there are many communities with a preponderance of Spanish-Americans. But such communities have their own particular needs and make their own particular political demands. These needs and demands are better understood in terms of community or regional rather than ethnic differences.[35]

The Spanish-Americans belong to both parties and split on many issues; this is their strength as well as their weakness. Their interest in politics constitutes both a vocation and avocation. There is a political hierarchy, of which the Spanish-Americans are much more aware than the Anglos. This hierarchy, from the precinct up, is admired by the Spanish-Americans. To be a part of it confers prestige. Therefore, there is a continuous conflict—fought out with verbal ferocity— among the "ins" and "outs." As previously suggested, the typical Anglo distaste for things political is much less prevalent within the Spanish-American community of the state.

In Spanish-American areas, the Anglo often keeps out of precinct politics, although he is normally welcome if he wishes to participate. The view is that an Anglo vote is just as good as any other vote. In predominantly Spanish-American communities or counties, the superior political leader of either group may strive for a position in the political hierarchy above the precinct level. Both Spanish-American and Anglo politicians are "realists." They recognize and work with political leaders from each other's areas. They want any support.

The Spanish-American concept of the family is both broader than and somewhat different from the Anglo concept. As developed historically, the Spanish-American feels an intense personal responsibility for family and friends. Recognizing this, the Anglo politician usually has cooperated actively in seeing to it that the Spanish-American politician gets his share of the patronage when he wants to put his family or friends on the public payroll.

This presentation may seem to be at odds with the attempt of the Spanish-American protest organization, the *Alianza Federal de Mercedes*, to seize a portion of Kit Carson National Forest in 1966, and its escapade at the Tierra Amarilla courthouse in June 1967. A closer look at the status of Spanish-Americans in New Mexico should put these incidents in proper perspective. First, there is no question that Spanish-Americans have played and do play an important role in the state's public affairs. The Mexican-American Study Project at UCLA reports that the 1967 legislatures in the five southwestern states contained forty-eight Spanish-Americans; thirty-three of those were in New Mexico (none in California, one in Colorado, four in Arizona, ten in Texas).[36]   For decades, Spanish-Americans have held prominent state and national office in New Mexico, including the U.S. Senate's only current Spanish-American member, Joseph M. Montoya. Second, there is an undercurrent of discrimination against Spanish-Americans. Candidates with Spanish surnames traditionally trail their tickets in the southeast corner (the "Little Texas" counties) of the state and in the Anglo (or "Heights") districts of

35. *Ibid.*, p. 66.

36. *Progress Report: Mexican-American Study Project* (Los Angeles: Graduate School of Business Administration, UCLA, No. 9 (May 1967), p. 3. This project is a valuable source of information on the status of Spanish-Americans in the Southwest, although *Mexican-American* is a pejorative term among New Mexicans; more acceptable is Native or Hispano.

Albuquerque. In 1966, not a single candidate with a Spanish surname won state-wide office. (Some Spanish-Americans with Anglo names did.)

Third, Spanish-Americans as a group have lower indices of economic attainment than the population as a whole. These lower indices are particularly characteristic of the state's northern counties, which have chronically depressed economies; Kit Carson National Forest and Tierra Amarilla are in the northern area. Although the protest movement led by Reies Tijerina bases its claims on historic legal grounds—treaties and land grants—the relevant sources of the protest are economic. The details of the *Alianza* argument are too involved to discuss here, but it is clear that history cannot be turned back. Moreover, to apportion the ancient land grants among the proclaimed descendants of the original grantees would produce holdings that are economically inefficient. Tijerina's proposal for a separate state is no more likely to resolve the difficulties of Spanish-Americans than those of American Negroes.[37]

Fourth, genuine efforts have been and continue to be made to alleviate the economic disadvantages of the Spanish-Americans. David F. Cargo, who was elected governor in 1966, has made such a deliberate practice to appoint and employ Spanish-Americans that he has been criticized by his fellow Republicans, as well as by Democrats. In 1966, Spanish-Americans in federal employment were actually overrepresented as a percent of the state's work force.[38] Much needs to be done to improve economic opportunity for Spanish-Americans, but this is true for citizens of the state in general, regardless of their ethnic origins.

Finally, the state's major political figures of Spanish-American background have all chosen to disassociate themselves from Tijerina and the *Alianza*. In fact, some of his sharpest critics have been Spanish-Americans who could make equivalent or stronger claims as land grant heirs. These persons have preferred to follow the proven political pathways of the state.

The actual working out of these political accommodations is complicated. But the fact is that the Spanish-Americans and the Anglos over many generations have continuously developed successful operating arrangements to the satisfaction of the politically ambitious of both groups. The patterns of accommodation have been stable. The essential fact is that votes count. The prevailing view has been that there is little to be gained from pitting one bloc against another. Everything is to be gained from working with the political machinery that has been functioning smoothly for many decades.

37. For additional background on the land grant problem, see these issues of *New Mexico Business*: Clark S. Knowlton, "Land-Grant Problems Among the State's Spanish-Americans," Vol. 20, No. 6 (June 1967) and Wayne S. Scott, "Spanish Land-Grant Problems Were Here Before the Anglos," Vol. 20, No. 7 (July 1967). Professor Knowlton is head of the Department of Sociology, University of Texas at El Paso, and taught for several years at New Mexico Highlands University in northern New Mexico; Scott is a veteran reporter for the *Albuquerque Journal*.

38. *Progress Report*, No. 8 (February 1967), p. 3. Of the state's work force, 23.7 percent were identified as Spanish-American in 1960; 26.6 percent of federal employees in the state were identified as Spanish-American in 1966; it should be recalled that the portion of Spanish-Americans in the state has probably declined since 1960 unless a trend of several decades has ceased. The state compares well with Colorado and Texas which overrepresent Spanish-Americans in federal employment. The same *Report* (p. 4) shows New Mexico has essentially numerically perfect representation of Negroes in federal employment (1.8 percent in 1960 work force; 1.7 percent in 1966 federal service); California and Colorado are easily the leaders in federal employment of Negroes among the five states.

Reflecting the development of urban opinion in New Mexico are Albuquerque's two newspapers, the *Journal* and the *Tribune*. The *Santa Fe New Mexican* also has considerable statewide circulation. The *Albuquerque Journal*, which has the largest circulation in the state, consistently deplores the control of government by special interests and can be expected to espouse the cause of the oppressed taxpayer against bureaucratic inefficiency in all its forms. By any currently relevant conservative-liberal scale, this morning newspaper and the columns it carries (e.g., Holmes Alexander) could be located in a category of newspapers characterized by the *Chicago Tribune* and opposite such western papers as the *Denver Post*. Although never formally endorsing Senator Goldwater's candidacy for President, the *Journal* took a very strong pro-Goldwater stand, endorsed the Goldwaterite, Ed Mechem, for the U.S. Senate, and was found to have devoted almost twice the amount of prominent coverage to Republican candidates as to Democratic candidates during the 1964 election campaign.[39] Its façade of independence was not very convincing.

The *Albuquerque Tribune* (Scripps-Howard) and the *Santa Fe New Mexican* evening papers, are also self-styled independents, and are usually Democratic-liberal in editorial policy.[40] However, they tend to join with the *Journal* in opposition to special-interest influence in the legislature. With the possible exception of the *New Mexican*, adverse comment on the over-all quality of the state's three leading newspapers is widespread, especially from out-of-state visitors.

NOMINATIONS AND ELECTIONS

New Mexico began its statehood in the Republican camp, teetered between the Republican and Democratic parties at the congressional and gubernatorial levels for about two decades, became overwhelmingly Democratic during the Depression, and has remained mainly Democratic since.[41] New Mexico has always voted for the winning presidential candidate, and in doing so has failed but twice (1924 and 1960) to elect a governor of the President's party. Republicans have elected governors in 1918, 1920, 1926, 1928, 1950, 1952, 1956, 1960, and 1966. The legislatures elected from statehood through 1930 were solidly Republican, except for the 1923 and 1925 sessions which saw Democratic majorities in the House. Except for the one-vote Republican House margin in 1952, the state legislature has been solidly Democratic since New Deal days. New Mexico voters have not sent a Republican to Congress since 1935.

Whether this brief description of party fortunes classifies New Mexico as a one-party or two-party state depends upon the measure one wishes to employ. On

39. This finding is based on a content analysis of 10 randomly selected issues of the *Journal* in September of 1964. The analysis was undertaken by staff members of the *New Mexico Lobo*, student newspaper at the University of New Mexico, and included only those items pertaining to the candidates which were printed as a result of editorial judgment. Aside from the column-inch indicator, which revealed a 348 to 190 ratio for the Republican candidates, the analysis also uncovered a pro-Republican bias in terms of location of the coverage in the *Journal*'s format, multi-column headings, straight wire service reportage versus argumentative statements, and editorial treatment. See *New Mexico Lobo*, September 23, 1964, p. 2.

40. In late 1967, the *New Mexican* changed from an afternoon to a morning paper. After an eight-day trial, the newspaper returned to an afternoon delivery practice in November 1967.

41. Charles B. Judah, *The Republican Party in New Mexico* (Albuquerque: Division of Government Research, University of New Mexico, 1949).

the one hand, Jack Holmes presents some convincing data to document the state's historic close and stable two-party balance.[42] For instance, in the first thirteen non-presidential year gubernatorial races after statehood, New Mexico voters awarded an average winning majority of only 53 percent, while the range of electoral margins from the weakest to the strongest candidate was only 11 percentage points.[43] Measured by Democratic percentage (excluding third parties) for governor, the variance has been only 13 percent since 1912; as Holmes states, "the Democratic trend line gain in the fifty years is only one-half of a percentage point in going from 51.3 to 51.8 percent."[44]

On the other hand, the state's long-standing Democratic orientation in both gubernatorial and legislative elections has led some scholars to classify it as "modified one-party Democratic." For example, using the Dawson-Robinson formula, which considers frequency and duration of one-house, two-house, gubernatorial, and over-all party dominance of state offices, Austin Ranney found that New Mexico's "index of party competitiveness" is .7023, the lowest (weakest) of the modified one-party Democratic states.[45] This is probably the most accurate and useful summary statement of current party balance in New Mexico, and upon examination, is not at odds with the conclusion of Holmes.

Electoral participation in New Mexico has not been high, as evidenced by the data of Table II. For comparative purposes, one can derive from this table the average state gubernatorial vote turnout for the non-presidential years, 1954 and 1958, which is 44.5 percent. Lester Milbrath arrived at a similar figure when including the senatorial vote as well.[46] Milbrath ranks New Mexico thirty-second among the forty-eight states in electoral participation, the same position indicated by the data of Table II. In a similar manner, another scholar has ranked the state thirty-third among the states in electoral participation in 1952 whereas the data of Table II would place the state thirty-fourth that year.[47]

Whatever New Mexico's exact rank, the important fact is that it is clearly among the lowest two or three western states in voting participation, and is just above that group of states (Middle and Deep South) with the lowest sectional turnout in the nation.[48] In the absence of research on specific New Mexico factors, this can be explained only by the familiar variables associated with electoral participation—in this case, undoubtedly socio-economic rather than politico-legal

42. Holmes, *op. cit.*, p. 4. See also his pp. 1-7, Table I and Figure 1, supporting this conclusion.

43. *Ibid.*, p. 2.

44. *Ibid.*, p. 4. The 1964 and 1966 elections do not substantially change this 1912-62 pattern.

45. Austin Ranney, "Parties in State Politics," *Politics in the American State: A Comparative Analysis*, eds. Herbert Jacob and Kenneth N. Vines (Boston: Little, Brown, 1965). This index is explained on pp. 63-67. Of the remaining twelve western states, eleven are classified as two-party while Arizona is given the same label as New Mexico, modified one-party Democratic.

46. Lester W. Milbrath, "Political Participation in the States," Jacob and Vines, *op. cit.*, p. 40.

47. Hugh A. Bone, *American Politics and the Party System* (2nd ed.; New York: McGraw-Hill, 1955), p. 562. Although it is clear that neither the Bone nor Milbrath data are perfectly comparable with Table II (Bone, for example, does not say what sort of electoral participation he is talking about), the comparison is thought to be close enough to be mutually supportive.

48. See Milbrath, *op. cit.*, pp. 38-40, for sectional classifications. Milbrath classifies New Mexico as a border state, with Kentucky, Missouri, Arizona, Maryland and Oklahoma.

variables. Income, education, degree of rural orientation, unemployment, geographic mobility, etc., would be explanatory factors.[49]

New Mexico's political leaders have experimented with various nominating devices, the subject being frequently in the forefront of party and broad-scale public debate for some thirty years. From 1912 to 1938 the state employed the party convention, but due more to party than to general public pressure, this was replaced with a primary system of nominations, which went into effect with the 1940 elections. The law required nominations by direct closed primary for all elective offices except those of municipalities and those chosen by special elections to fill vacancies.[50] After five tries with the primary, an effort was made to modify it.

Accompanied by a storm of emotional debate, the 1949 New Mexico legislature adopted a rather complex pre-primary system of nominating statewide candidates. Spearheaded by the state's press, especially the *Albuquerque Journal*, a petition to suspend the legislation got enough signatures to place the issue before the voters in the election of 1950.[51] When the constitutionally required 40 percent of

TABLE II

PARTICIPATION IN NEW MEXICO
GUBERNATORIAL ELECTIONS, 1946 - 1966

Year	Population	Total Votes for Governor	% Population Over 21	% Eligible Voters Voting for Governor
1946	556,000	132,630	54.4	43.8
1948	592,000	189,992	54.7	58.7
1950	681,187	180,205	55.1	48.0
1952	718,900	240,150	54.6	61.1
1954	776,800	193,956	54.1	46.7
1956	829,500	251,751	53.6	56.6
1958	912,300	205,048	53.1	42.3
1960	951,023	308,542	52.6	61.6
1962	986,100	247,112	52.1	48.0
1964	1,026,700	318,037	51.6	59.7
1966	1,041,300	260,212	51.2	48.7
			AVERAGE %	52.3

49. *Ibid.*, p. 52.

50. See Charles B. Judah, *Aspects of the Nominating System in New Mexico* (Albuquerque: Division of Government Research, University of New Mexico, 1957).

51. *Ibid.*, p. 11. Professor Judah quotes an *Albuquerque Journal* editorial of March 13, 1949: "The primary no longer will be a primary in fact. . . . The delegates to the conven-

those voting did not vote on the measure, the referendum failed and the pre-primary system was adopted. The new law, providing for pre-primary designating conventions, survived two stormy election periods, 1952 and 1954. Both parties then pledged to return to the direct primary, and the 1955 legislature redeemed the pledge. Hence, from 1956 through the 1962 elections the direct primary was in force.

Enough was not enough, however, and in the regular session of the 1963 legislature a new pre-primary endorsing convention law was passed. While the new law rearranged most of the state's election machinery, its central features dealt with nominations for the leading state and national elective offices. As summed up by one writer, the legislation provided the following:

> Nominees were to earn a place on the primary ballot through one of two channels. The first method was selection by an endorsing convention of one's party. Delegates to that convention were selected by county conventions as prescribed by party rules. A candidate receiving 20 percent of the votes from the endorsing convention on any ballot won a slot on the primary ballot. To determine position on the ballot, the delegates continued voting for each office until one nominee received an absolute majority. That nominee was placed at the top of the list for that office. The second method of nomination required a candidate to secure petition signatures: (1) in one-half of the counties; (2) equal to 3 percent of the vote cast in the last general election for the office sought. Petition nominees would be placed on the ballot below convention nominees.[52]

The difficulty of getting on the ballot via petition suggests the lawmakers intended this latter method to be *pro forma*, rather than a meaningful alternative.

True to form, yet another petition drive to repeal the new legislation was waged in the summer of 1963; again the opponents of the pre-primary concept were successful in placing the law on the November 1964 election ballot, and again, the required 40 percent of those voting was not achieved.[53] Subsequent to the 1964 elections, which at times seemed swamped by the pre-primary issue, the scene of combat shifted back to Santa Fe where, on March 16, 1965, repeal of the 1963 law failed by one vote in the Senate. The only major alteration in the law, coming during the final week of the 1965 legislative session, eased the required absolute convention majority for determining ballot position. Nominees were now to be positioned according to the convention vote they received above the 20 percent minimum. The major reason for this amendment was the nearly all-night Democratic session in 1964 required to achieve a majority convention vote for Congressman E. S. (Johnny) Walker.[54]

The 1966 elections used the pre-primary system, but the 1967 legislature

tion will be named at precinct mob caucuses. . . . The people will have to march to the polls for the political-favored candidates much in the style that voters in Communist Russia have to do."

52. This excerpt is taken from T. Phillip Wolf, "The 1964 Elections in New Mexico," a paper delivered at the Southwest Social Science Association meeting, Dallas, Texas, April 15-17, 1965. The paper contains a detailed account of how the law worked in 1964 and of the continuing controversy over the issue.

53. The forces working for repeal included the press, particularly the *Albuquerque Journal*, elements of the rank and file in both parties, and generally led by Republican spokesmen and the Young Republicans of the state. Democratic Senators Clinton P. Anderson and Joseph M. Montoya strongly opposed repeal, the former being accused of unjustified meddling in state party affairs. See *Albuquerque Journal*, March 4, 1965, March 14, 1965; also, the *Albuquerque Tribune*, March 18, 1965. Wolf explains the position of the press not only in terms of the less influential role it is likely to have in a pre-primary system but also perhaps because of loss of revenue from political advertising. Wolf, *op. cit.*

54. *Albuquerque Tribune*, June 24, 1965.

repealed that method of nomination and returned to the direct primary, moving the nominating election from May to the last Tuesday in August.

Voter registration in New Mexico is another aspect of the state's election machinery deserving comment. Underlying the classification of the state as modified one-party Democratic is a current two-party registration ratio of roughly 2.6 to 1 Democratic. In only one county (Mora) did the 1964 Republican registration exceed that of the Democrats, but even here, significantly, the two-party registration is the most evenly divided of any county in the state, and, moreover, is rapidly moving to the Democratic column. The statewide registration figures for 1960, 1962, 1964, and 1966 are presented in Table III.

TABLE III

NEW MEXICO VOTER REGISTRATION
1960, 1962, 1964, 1966

Year	D	R	I	Other	Total
1960	285,577	114,748	13,379	9,561	423,265
1962	277,775	111,357	6,914	13,952	409,998
1964	316,462	125,465	8,123	14,861	464,911
1966	308,802	121,698	9,733	11,307	451,540

There is little reason to question the over-all preponderance of Democratic voting power in the state. Yet, specific county registration figures are so far from reality as to have become the butt of public jokes. Thirteen counties of the state are shown to have had more people registered in 1960 than population over twenty-one years of age, and one county (Guadalupe) boasted a larger 1960 voting turnout than number of people over twenty-one. The 1964 Rio Arriba County registration exceeded the county's *total* estimated population by about 600.[55]

Such data have provided the minority Republican party with an appealing campaign issue. Edwin L. Mechem, former Republican U.S. senator and governor, has termed this gravestone competition "a consistent studied political conspiracy" and former State Republican Chairman Merle Tucker insisted his party was "serious" about filing a suit to obtain statewide voter re-registration.[56] Grounds for such action would be the alleged undermining of the United States Supreme Court's "one man, one vote" doctrine.

As the poll books were closed in the fall of 1966, the Bernalillo County Republican party brought forth a list of several thousand names which the party

55. This information is taken from figures published by the Legislative Council Service, Santa Fe. The Secretary of State and County Clerks continue to work on the registration problem. A purge of registration rolls after the November 1967 election deleted 42,838 names in thirty-one counties. The remaining county, Bernalillo, was checking the registrations of 47,875 persons. *Albuquerque Journal*, February 18, 1968.

56. *Albuquerque Journal*, May 30, 1965, and *Albuquerque Tribune*, May 29, 1965.

claimed were fraudulently registered in the county. The main basis of the charge was that these persons no longer lived at the addresses listed. Under existing registration practices, this was quite likely; as long as one continued to vote in a precinct where he once lived, his registration would not be purged. It is this practice that underpins inflated registration totals around the state. After a judicial hearing, the Republican position was upheld and policies were enacted to purge such registrants. Bernalillo County has modernized its electoral and registration practices; many records are now stored in computers. This kind of election administration is not typical throughout the state, although voting machines are widely used.

Speaking for the Democrats, Senator Joseph M. Montoya has questioned the sincerity of the Republicans, charging them with wanting to disfranchise voters throughout the state for their own relative advantage.[57] Since the precise outcome of re-registration is highly unpredictable, and since, in any case, a county-by-county purging of the rolls would be a relatively easy matter if anyone wanted to accomplish it, the sincerity of both parties is open to serious doubt.

If registration is generally chaotic in New Mexico, the last decade has produced a considerably improved set of election procedures. A spectacular climax of the old practices was reached in 1952 when U.S. senatorial candidate Patrick J. Hurley challenged the election of his incumbent Democratic opponent, Senator Dennis Chavez. The faults and difficulties of New Mexico's election laws and procedures were aired in detail in the local press and were given national publicity. Senator Chavez was eventually sustained, but not until a number of voluminous Senate documents were released.[58] Since then, numerous procedural changes have been effected, including a wide-scale adoption of voting machines, the use of data processing equipment, judges, emergency procedures in the event of voting machine failure, and a tightening of the law relating to voter assistance at the polls.[59]

To the student of New Mexico politics, party finance has proven an elusive aspect of the political system. A hint here, a shred of evidence there, combined with a reasonably coherent picture of past practices—such is the present state of our knowledge. In his textbook on New Mexico government Donnelly states:

> The sources of campaign funds in New Mexico are the usual ones tapped in other states. The party in power at Santa Fe often levies a regular monthly assessment (2 percent usually) on the salaries of all politically appointed employees to finance its activities, and special assessments are sometimes made in campaign years. Contributions from those who are receiving, or hope to receive, favors from the state administration help to swell the funds of the party in power. The party out of power has to depend largely on the contributions of its adherents, and aid sent it from national party headquarters. Contributions from the candidates and their friends also are an important source of funds to both parties.[60]

57. *Albuquerque Tribune*, June 4, 1965.

58. *Senator from New Mexico. Report of the Subcommittee on Privileges and Elections to the Committee on Rules and Administration, Eighty-third Congress, Second Session, Relative to the Contested Election of November 4, 1952.* Report 1081, Part 1 (majority), Part 2 (minority). Also published under the title of *Senator from New Mexico* were the *Hearings . . . on the Contest of Patrick J. Hurley v. Dennis Chavez . . . April 27, May 1, 7, 11, 27 and August 12, 1953* (Washington: Government Printing Office, 1953).

59. See *Albuquerque Tribune*, June 24, 1965. The acquisition and maintenance of voting machines has been a source of political controversy; see T. Phillip Wolf, "The 1966 Elections in New Mexico," *Western Political Quarterly*, XX (June 1967, Part 2), 589.

60. Donnelly, *op. cit.*, p. 87.

The Republican administrations of 1951-54 and 1957-58 seem to mark a transition period in which the collection of funds from state employees became less direct. In 1959, when a Democrat became governor, it was claimed the party tried to institute a 1 percent payroll levy. At least partly because of public protest, the compulsory assessment was cancelled.

When the Democrats were not in the governor's office, a system of "note signing" was developed by about ten Albuquerque Democrats who controlled the entire state Democratic organization. These note-signing Democrats would borrow money for campaign purposes, then sell banquet tickets to Democratic office-holders. Such banquets were well attended, and the profits could be relied upon as often as necessary to pay off the debt.

With the enactment of the State Personnel Acts of 1961 and 1963, direct patronage funds were presumably diminished. However, state "positions" can often be created, as they frequently are for county chairmen and other party functionaries. Such practices are but new variations of an old theme in New Mexico, for until 1945 it had been common to place state legislators on the payroll.[61]

In the current era of relative prosperity, large individual contributions,[62] state payroll sources, and gifts from business licensees such as building and highway contractors and liquor dealers[63] probably constitute the major sources of party funds.

The organization of political parties in New Mexico can be summarized briefly. The precinct, county, and state echelons function mostly in accordance with tradition. Party rules and regulations usually are vague and ambiguous and therefore can be easily interpreted in a way convenient to those in control. The New Mexico Assembly on State Government (jointly sponsored by the American Assembly of Columbia University and the University of New Mexico) reached the unstartling conclusion that:

New Mexico's party system is unhealthy. . . . Parties adopt platforms that reflect few or no policy differences between them and that result in empty statements of purpose. The parties' candidates, having no meaningful platforms on which to stand, tend to run on their personal platforms. This situation destroys party lines, discourages party responsibility, and makes party discipline almost impossible. Unless parties become accountable to those who support them, their members have no remedy for inaction or irresponsible conduct.[64]

61. See Holmes, *op. cit.*, pp. 245-48, for a description of party financing mechanisms.

62. For example, it is known that the Republican party has long looked to such individuals as former Governor Tom Bolack of Farmington and Robert Anderson of Roswell for aid in campaign fund-raising. Sometimes called the "financial Angel" of the Republicans, Anderson is probably the wealthiest individual in the state and is said to own more land than anyone in the United States. See *Albuquerque Tribune*, April 5, 1965.

63. Some graphic detail regarding the role of liquor money in party financing was provided some years ago by the *Carlsbad Current Argus*. As presented in an *Albuquerque Journal* editorial of October 9, 1948. "In November of last year [1947] state liquor inspectors called on liquor dealers in Eddy Company for $100 contributions to the Democratic party. Carlsbad liquor dealers raised a fuss over having to pay. But most of them . . . kicked in with the money. The $100 entitled the liquor dealers to membership in a so-called 'State Democratic Club.' But now it develops that the membership cards—although sold last November—expire this month (October). And the state liquor men are back putting the bite on the defenseless liquor dealers for campaign contributions again." Whether such arrangements still exist is uncertain.

64. As presented in Charles B. Judah and Frederick C. Irion, *The 47th State—An Appraisal of Its Government* (Albuquerque: Division of Government Research, University of New Mexico, 1959), p. 61.

PARTY LEADERSHIP

As in a good many other states, meaningful issues are conspicuously missing in most New Mexico political contests. This fact renders more useful a political profile of the state in terms of individual personalities and performances, past, present, and prospective.

The state's delegation to Congress since 1940 (when New Mexico first gained two representatives) may be broadly characterized as ideologically mixed.[65] Carl A. Hatch, Democrat, was appointed to the Senate in 1933. He was elected and re-elected until he retired in 1948. He was a reformer of the old school and sponsor of the Hatch Acts. His successor, Clinton P. Anderson, Democrat, is a well-known liberal policy-maker, and he is one of the most important figures on Capitol Hill.[66]

Dennis Chavez, Democrat, was appointed to the Senate in 1935 to take the seat of Republican Bronson Cutting, and continuously served in that position until his death in late 1962. Senator Chavez had an outstanding liberal record. His entire public career showed a decided sympathy with the underprivileged.[67] Events since his death suggest that the Chavez image is becoming a legend in the state.[68]

Upon the death of Senator Chavez, Governor Edwin L. Mechem stepped down to have himself appointed to the Senate, but his tenure was short-lived. Mechem, regarded as Mr. Republican in the state, had served four terms as governor, and had been his party's leading vote attraction. Nonetheless, his strong pro-Goldwater stand in 1964 helped unseat him in favor of Joseph M. Montoya.[69]

Montoya had won a seat in the state legislature when he was still a law student, had served as lieutenant governor, and was finishing his third full term in Congress when he announced for the Senate. As a congressman he had been a strong Administration supporter and, aside from his Hispanic advantage, enjoyed the support of prestigious Senator Anderson as well as of state labor interests. His present assignments on the Senate Public Works, Agriculture, Government Operations, and Small Business committees plus his role as champion of Hispanic interests give him an unusually strong position from which to influence New Mexico politics, locally and nationally, for some years to come. These factors made the Mechem-Montoya race the most significant and interesting one in New Mexico in 1964.

65. The following analysis is based on the *Congressional Quarterly Almanac*'s party unity rating system, on the *New Republic*'s liberal-conservative rankings, on voting records and similar data.

66. See "These 14 Men Will Shape Your Future," *Nation's Business*, XLIII (March 1955), 85. Senator Anderson is chairman of the Aeronautical and Space Committee, and a member of the Interior and Insular Affairs, Finance, Joint Atomic Energy, and Democratic Steering committees. The federal role in New Mexico's economy could probably be explained by these facts alone.

67. See Edward Lahart, "The Early Career of Dennis Chavez" (Master's thesis, University of New Mexico, 1959).

68. A bronze likeness of Senator Chavez is New Mexico's first entry in Statuary Hall in Washington. See *Albuquerque Journal*, May 30, 1965.

69. The 1964 campaign is described in Wolf, "The 1964 Elections. . . ." Mechem's political coloration is described by *Congressional Quarterly* as "Unflinchingly conservative"—a man who "warmly embraces the candidacy of Barry Goldwater." While in the Senate, Mechem voted against the 1964 Civil Rights Act and the Test Ban Treaty. See *Congressional Quarterly*, *Weekly Report*, No. 42 (October 16, 1964), Part I, p. 2434.

Antonio M. Fernandez, Democrat, was first elected to the United States House of Representatives in 1942, where he remained until his death in 1956. He was moderate to conservative in his voting record and was replaced by the liberal Montoya.

Mrs. Georgia Lusk, Democrat, served in the House in 1947-48. Her record was moderate-conservative. John E. Miles, Democrat, who served in 1949-50, was very conservative, as was John J. Dempsey, Democrat, who took his seat in the House in 1951, where he remained until his death in 1958. Thomas G. Morris, Democrat, followed in 1959. Morris has the most conservative voting record of the present New Mexico congressional delegation.

E. S. (Johnny) Walker, former state land commissioner, was narrowly elected to the House in 1964 and again in 1966. Walker replaced Montoya in position No. 2 and has thus far demonstrated a voting record similar to that of his predecessor.

In 1964, Walker was opposed by Jack Redman, popular Albuquerque physician, who had run a surprisingly strong race as a political unknown in 1962 against the then Congressman Montoya. Walker's 1966 opponent was Robert C. Davidson, Albuquerque insuranceman and former Republican chairman of Bernalillo County. Both men are likely to run again for major office. Redman's prospects are especially promising and are undoubtedly enhanced by his widely publicized 1967 volunteer medical service in Vietnam.

Other prominent Republicans include former Texas Congressmen Ed Foreman, a flamboyant spokesman for conservatism, and Schuble Cook, who ran against Morris in 1966. Lieutenant Governor Lee Francis, Grants rancher and former party official, held the second highest office occupied by a Republican after the 1966 elections. Anderson Carter, former Democratic legislator and Goldwater conservative, made a strong electoral challenge to Senator Anderson in 1966. Carter replaced Ed Mechem as national committeeman in late 1967. Tom Bolack, Farmington oilman and rancher, served as interim governor when Mechem resigned in 1962 and has repeatedly been asked to run for office since. Joseph Skeen, state senator from Lincoln County, has indicated he will seek major office in 1970.

The unquestioned leader of the state's Republicans for many years was Edwin L. Mechem of Las Cruces. In 1950, he broke a twenty-year Democratic hold on the governor's mansion. He was re-elected in 1952, won again in 1956 and 1960. As governor, Mechem, at least initially, brought a whiff of fresh, clean air into state politics. Later as U.S. senator, he was unable to win election in 1964. After that defeat, he served as national committeeman and in late 1967 was suggested by Governor Cargo as a member of the controversial State Highway Commission. The 1966 election was the first general one since 1948 in which Mechem did not run for major office. (He lost races for the U.S. Senate in 1954 and for governor in 1958 and 1962.)

Turning to the state level, the apparent but not unchallenged Republican leader after the 1966 elections is David F. Cargo, native of Michigan, Albuquerque attorney, and former state representative. Cargo, who became well known as an advocate of reapportionment and equitable representation for Bernalillo County, was nominated in face of opposition from the established party organization. His general election victory was achieved by an unprecedented plurality in Bernalillo County. Regarded by many as a liberal, he had exceptional support from labor in his campaign and has made a persistent appeal to the state's Spanish-Americans. Cargo uses the press skillfully to keep his activities before the public. This skill and the enthusiastic support of major news media, especially the *Albuquerque Tribune*, was a major asset in his campaign; some of the enthusiasm faded after he took office.

Although he was the leading 1966 Republican vote-getter, Cargo has not established rapport within his party. His candidate for vice chairwoman of the state central committee was defeated. In the summer of 1967, the state auditor, a Republican, publicly called the governor a liar. During the 1967 legislative session, the minority leader of the state Senate, Joseph Skeen, characterized the governor as a "Mickey Mouth."

Despite Republican squabbling, Democrats have not been able to capitalize effectively upon the opposition's feuding. Although Clinton Anderson is the unquestioned leader, there has been no recognized spokesman for the party at the state level since the 1966 elections. Among those who may lay claim to that position are: Jack M. Campbell, former governor (1963-66), state representative, and Roswell attorney; T. E. (Gene) Lusk, son of Georgia Lusk, former state senator, and loser to Cargo in 1966; Bruce King, Santa Fe rancher and state representative, including service as speaker of the House; and Mack Easley, Campbell's lieutenant governor and state senator. Former governors John Simms (1955-56) of Albuquerque and John Burroughs (1959-60) of Portales are elder statesmen of the party but are unlikely to seek office, especially Burroughs after his crushing primary loss to Lusk in 1966.

From the early 1930's until 1966, only two Republicans, Ed Mechem (four times) and Tom Bolack (once by a disputed margin that took two years for the court to affirm), won statewide office. In 1966, four Republicans were elected to state office: state treasurer, state auditor, and governor-lieutenant governor. (Voters cast a single vote for the latter offices just as they do for U.S. President and Vice President.) In addition, Republicans were narrowly defeated in races for secretary of state and one congressional seat. The GOP made sharp gains in both houses of the legislature and won a slight majority of the total vote for all *contested* races of the two chambers. All of this took place in a year when the party's ticket-leaders in recent years—Ed Mechem, Tom Bolack, and Jack Redman—did not run. These results are significant for several reasons. First, Republican victory does not rest on Mechem or his coattails. Second, the base of Republican votes that customarily ran 40 percent throughout the 1950's can be augmented for occasional if not regular electoral majorities. Third, the core of Republican voting strength is in the urban areas, especially Albuquerque and Roswell, at a time when these areas constitute an increasingly large portion of the total state vote.

For both parties 1968 is a critical year. The Democrats must find a leader to coordinate their party's disparate wings. The old-line party regulars have been challenged by the "Grass Roots Democrats" (or collectively the New Mexico Democratic Council, a counterpart of the California Democratic Council but much smaller in number) in some counties. The "Grass Rooters" and liberal Democrats in general in the state were obviously disheartened in 1966-67 by President Johnson's Vietnam policy.

Republicans, having savored success, must avoid consuming themselves in competing for further electoral delicacies in 1968. There is definitely an anti-Cargo wing in the party. In late 1967, this wing seemed content to use oblique tactics rather than a frontal assault on the governor himself. In addition to the incidents mentioned above, this group defeated Cargo's nominee to succeed Mechem as national committeeman. Despite factionalism, fund raising and organizational work began in 1967 for the 1968 campaign. Rex Mattingly, Bernalillo County chairman in 1966, and his assistant Eddy Mahe, who engineered the amazing Republican vote totals in that county, were promoted to head the state central committee. Whether they can create a comparable precision operation statewide is problematic.

PRESSURE GROUPS

In his recent comparative analysis of state interest groups, Harmon Zeigler suggests that pressure group strength in state politics correlates positively with relatively backward, agrarian socio-economic systems and with weak, non-cohesive party systems.[70] The New Mexico experience supports this hypothesis, for one could hardly ask for a more fertile field for studying interest groups at work than in Santa Fe.[71] Although the day of railroad corruption and control in New Mexico politics has long since passed, new and highly successful interest groups have emerged to continue the tradition, albeit in greatly modified form.[72]

One goal of interest groups is to achieve for themselves a favored position within the economy. This goal has been widely pursued and frequently realized by New Mexico interest groups. A consequence is that a considerable amount of business activity is essentially noncompetitive. Not only do fair trade laws establish the price of alcoholic beverages, but transportation, utilities (as is common throughout the nation), and a host of other enterprises also use the state's many commissions and boards to fix prices. Through a growing number of licensing laws, an inordinate number of professional and trade groups have established themselves, their practices, and often their prices and fees.

The *New Mexico Bluebook of 1965-66* lists 136 state departments, boards and commissions, many of which regulate trades or professions traditionally in the private sector. Examples are the Liquefied Petroleum Gas Commission, the Peanut Commission, the Board of Examiners in the Basic Sciences, the Dry Cleaning Board, and the Plumbing Administrative Board.[73] Writing during the 1965 Legislative Session, Wayne S. Scott of the *Albuquerque Journal* noted: "Youngsters who sell newspapers and rake leaves . . . may have to secure state licenses if

70. Harmon Zeigler, "Interest Groups in the States," Jacob and Vines, *op. cit.*, pp. 113-15. Party cohesiveness in the legislature is discussed below.

71. A few visits to the state capital may suggest to the reader, as it has to these writers, that the term "lobbying" might well have originated in the lobby and bars of the La

72. For an analysis of the role of the railroad interests in early lobbying practices, see Edgar Lane's *Lobbying and the Law* (Berkeley: University of California Press, 1964), pp. 20-25, and sources cited therein. Lane lists New Mexico as one of those states in which interest group access is enhanced by the frequent division of decision-making between the parties. See p. 112.

73. *Bluebook*, pp. 59-67. In 1967, Governor Cargo said the more than 200 state boards, agencies, and commissions in existence when he took office should be drastically reduced in number. Through executive order, legislative action, and constitutional revision, he hoped the number could be reduced to less than 20; *Albuquerque Journal*, September 1, 1967. Following the recommendation of his Committee on Reorganization, Governor Cargo combined the boards of the various state hospitals into one board in the fall of 1967; this action was approved by the 1968 legislature, which rejected the governor's proposal for a State Department of Labor. Acting upon previous legislative authorization, the governor also Fonda Hotel in Santa Fe, for during the legislative sessions these pleasant environs reek with legislator-lobbyist bargaining. For a bit of the flavor of Santa Fe during these times, the reader is referred to the columns by Will Harrison, appearing in the *Albuquerque Tribune*, among other papers. See especially February 24, 1965, *Albuquerque Tribune*.
combined the Departments of Public Health and Public Welfare into one agency.

the current trend of legislation continues."[74] Scott commented that the legislature had just approved two more licensing boards (for psychologists and photographers), had a third vetoed by the Governor (to license septic-tank cleaners), and was then considering licensing TV repairmen, piano players, marriage counselors, and pesticide applicators. A measure to license ambulance drivers was killed during the session.

One result of this policy is that government plays an even larger role in the state's economy than employment and income data suggest. When activities which are protected from direct price competition are added to those actually undertaken and financed by government, perhaps only one-fourth to one-third of New Mexico's economy operates in terms of traditional free enterprise. The question may properly be asked if New Mexico does not have a kind of economic socialism for private gain.

The most controversial aspect of this whole policy has been the 1939 guaranteed minimum mark-up law on liquor. Judging from the coverage by the two Albuquerque newspapers, this has been the most significant public question in the state in recent years. Despite frequent and outraged opposition, liquor fair trade laws have been in effect nearly thirty years. Support for the laws has come from two groups with contrary views on the consumption of alcohol. On the one hand, liquor wholesalers and retailers have avidly defended the laws which, with the restricted number of liquor licenses, guarantee a return on liquor sales. On the other hand, the forces of temperance and abstinence have supported the laws as a means to inhibit the use of alcohol and the adverse consequences of that use.

Over the years, this issue of liquor laws has played a much greater role in New Mexico politics than it deserves. First, to protect themselves from repeal of the minimum mark-up, individuals associated with the liquor industry have been exceedingly active in party politics, especially in the Democratic party. Many precinct elections through the years have been fought over this issue. In the selection of party officials and candidates, the decisive factor was often their stand on the liquor question rather than their views upon economic development or some other issue of genuine consequence. Second, an inordinate amount of legislative time, especially in the 1960's, has been spent on this issue.

Perhaps the turning point in the long drive for repeal came during the 1963 legislative session when a spokesman for the liquor industry allegedly said he "owned" the legislature. An impressive battle for repeal was made in the 1965 legislative session, but the liquor lobby, trying to be less conspicuous than before, saw the state Senate kill repeal by a 12-20 vote.[75] As a leader of the repeal forces, state Senator Sterling Black (son of the U.S. Supreme Court justice) saw it, the 1965 struggle would be the last victory for the liquor forces.[76] By the middle 1960's, individual clergymen, even from "dry" denominations, were publicly opposing the liquor fair trade laws. In the 1966 election, both candidates for governor said the issue was no longer important and repeal of these laws was inevitable. But the history of more than three dozen attempts at repeal plus the alleged role of liquor sources for party finance do not indicate that the minimum mark-up will

74. *Albuquerque Journal*, February 21, 1965.

75. Columnist Will Harrison said that 1965 was the driest legislature in memory, the industry refusing to stock the closets of legislators' hotel rooms with cases of their favorite brands, as they had done in the past. *Albuquerque Tribune*, February 18, 1965.

76. *Ibid.*, March 2, 1965.

quickly disappear.[77] On the eve of the 1966 general elections, the State Supreme Court declared the minimum mark-up illegal. In December 1966, the Attorney-General intervened, requesting a delay and clarification, before the court's decision was enforced. This was denied but prices did not decline. The 1967 legislature, in its closing hours, came to the rescue by deciding that wholesale prices in New Mexico could be no higher than those in any other state. As in New York, which has a similar law, this did not have the presumed effect of lowering prices. After the passage of this new law, liquor prices were unchanged, uniformly high, and New Mexicans continued their custom of traveling to Colorado and Mexico to purchase large stocks of spirits. The 1968 legislative session was the first in recent years in which the liquor issue was not raised. At the same time, the initial crack in the liquor price structure occurred when in February 1968 an Albuquerque retailer advertised lower prices.

The political role of the liquor industry is but one example of interest groups in operation in New Mexico. It is notable that this industry points to the state's fair trade liquor law as a model for other states to follow. The trucking industry has been similarly successful in what is popularly known as the "big truck law," a favorable arrangement for truck weights, and in what the industry considers to be a desirable tax structure. Two other strong lobbies in New Mexico are the Taxpayers' Association and the Oil and Gas Association.

Anyone familiar with western state politics is aware that the long and steady decline in agricultural income and population has generally not been accompanied by a corresponding decline in agrarian influence in the state legislature. New Mexico is no exception to this generalization. While there is no evidence that the cattlemen are quite as entrenched in the state legislature as they are in some other western states,[78] their influence is nevertheless great. In his annual report of 1957, the president of the New Mexico Cattle Growers Association claimed: "Your association and agriculture in general had better representation in the State Legislature than in any time in recent years. Of the 32 members of the State Senate, 14 were members of the association, and of the 66 members of the House of Representatives, 23 were members of the association."[79] In the mid-1960's, the Association was successful in the passage of legislation requiring the labeling of foreign meats and in persuading the lawmakers to approve the resolution calling for a federal constitutional convention to overturn the Supreme Court's reapportionment edict. While much legislation was bogged down in the 1965 legislature, seven of the first eleven bills signed into law dealt directly with livestock.[80]

77. *Ibid.*, March 10, 1965.

78. In Colorado, for example, see Lowell H. Watts, "The Colorado Cattlemen's Association: A Case Study in the Organization of an Effective Political Interest Group," and "The Colorado Cattlemen's Association: A Case Study." Mr. Watts is currently Director of the Colorado Agricultural Extension Service, Colorado State University. The latter study is a student effort sponsored by the Rocky Mountain Center for Education in Politics and the Department of Political Science, CSU. It is available from that department.

79. "President's Annual Report," *New Mexico Stockman*, XXII (April 1957), 20.

80. See *Albuquerque Tribune*, February 23, 1965, and *Albuquerque Journal*, February 23, 1965. Reversal of the reapportionment rulings has been a key goal of cattlemen's associations everywhere. At the state association's annual convention in March of 1965 in Albuquerque, an executive vice-president of the American National Cattlemen's Association stated that "legislatures based on population alone would tend to ignore the obligations of property and resource development in favor of more tax-and-spend schemes." *Albuquerque Tribune*, March 30, 1965.

Attempts by the Rocky Mountain Farmers Union to establish units in New Mexico have given rise to a rift among farm forces. In March of 1965 the Farm Bureau's organ, *New Mexico Farm ànd Ranch*, carried an editorial which alleged that such moves were caused by "certain highly placed politicians and agencies of the U.S. Department of Agriculture." Due to the Union's "close ties with organized labor," continued the editorial, "We believe New Mexico farmers and ranchers will shun a group with goals and objectives known and rejected by most Americans."[81]

Such viewpoints help to explain why organized labor has not been more influential in the state. Another reason is the state's lack of basic industry and manufacturing. Whatever the cause, it is clear that the power of organized labor is just beginning to be felt in the state's politics and is perhaps fifty to seventy-five years behind the significant role it plays in our most highly industrialized states. Holmes sums it up by saying:

> Organized labor is of considerable importance in the politics of the mining communities in the peripheral areas of the state, but in Albuquerque and the defense and research towns along the Rio Grande its importance is largely limited to activity in the Democratic primary. And there its structure and membership is such that it can be of considerable weight only when it is aligned with the dominant local faction. The place occupied in many areas by medium and heavy industry, and the corresponding organized trades, is largely filled by government in New Mexico.[82]

It is true that right-to-work legislation is biennially defeated or side-stepped in the New Mexico legislature, but this is due more to the state's general ideological orientation than to any concerted action by New Mexico labor.

On occasion, the Catholic church has spoken for labor interests in this regard, and in a manner more eloquent than that of labor spokesmen. For example, Archbishop Edwin V. Byrne strongly urged the rejection of a proposed constitutional amendment in 1948 which would have banned the closed shop, saying:

> As one desirous of industrial peace and desirous to aid in the prosperity of my State and my Country, as a friend of the workingman, I cannot approve this proposed amendment, which, if it does not outlaw unionism, deals it a death blow. Rather it seems to me that it should be opposed by men of good will and peace, who reverence the individual dignity of man and the spirit of the Constitution of the United States.[83]

If speechmaking is any indication, students of New Mexico politics can expect an intensification of the political activity of religious bodies in the state's public affairs. On March 29, 1965, The Most Reverend James Davis, Archbishop of Santa Fe, told his flock of 250,000 that they must "close ranks and mobilize" and become more involved in politics. The Archbishop insisted that "the Church is not interested in politics, but its men should be."[84] The precedent-breaking affiliation of New Mexico Catholics with the New Mexico Council of Churches provided a good start, as did the Archdiocesan sponsored and led picketing in March

81. *Albuquerque Journal*, March 16, 1965.

82. *Op. cit.*, pp. 104-5. See Lucien A. File, Business Manager of the State Bureau of Mines, "Labor Unions in New Mexico's Nonferrous-Metals Mining Industry," *New Mexico Business*, October 1964, pp. 1-14. File attributes the lack of unionization to the Spanish *patron* system, proximity to cheap migratory labor, and the nature of New Mexico's natural resources.

83. *Albuquerque Leader*, June 2, 1948.

84. See A. C. DeCola, "Catholics Urged To Take Large Roles in Politics," *Albuquerque Tribune*, March 29, 1965.

1965 of the state legislature for its refusal to approve a memorial directed against Alabama's racist policies. The New Mexico House "failed to uphold the principles of this country and of God," declared Reverend Father Luis Jaramillo, Vice-chancellor of the Santa Fe Archdiocese.[85] Militant statements from Protestant groups are also in evidence,[86] and the role of religious spokesmen in the liquor controversy has already been noted. In other states, such data would be of little more than passing interest; in New Mexico they are believed to signal a turn in the road for organized religion in the state.[87]

Los Hermanos Penitentes, legendary lay religious organization of northern New Mexico and southern Colorado, is still not to be completely discounted in state politics.[88] Not more than three decades ago the Republican party of San Miguel County could rely upon 2,000 to 3,000 bloc Penitente votes for its cause, although not all of these were actual members of the Brotherhood.[89] Voting data analyzed by Holmes suggest that although Penitente strength is now more evenly divided between the parties, the strong tradition of Republican loyalty of these voters could still be of significance in a close statewide race. The Chapel (*Morada*), still the center of Penitente political activity, has come to reflect this bipartisanship, and in many communities there are now two such Chapels. For example, "in the village of Abiquiu, New Mexico, one chapter house is now known as the 'Morada Republicana,' the other as the 'Morada Democrata.' "[90]

It is the New Mexico Education Association, however, rather than any of those mentioned above, which is usually referred to as the most powerful lobby in Santa Fe. Its success in maintaining state educational expenditures at record levels, in retaining its payroll deduction system for dues but denying the same arrangement to the American Federation of Teachers, and in helping to elect policy-makers sympathetic to its aims are but a few indicators of the political power of this group and of the interest it represents.[91]

EDUCATIONAL POLITICS

New Mexico is generous in its treatment of young people, at least in terms of formal education and in relation to its ability to pay. Numerous indicators point this up. The 1962 Census of Governments shows that despite New Mexico's rank

85. *Albuquerque Journal*, March 16, 1965.

86. *Ibid.*, May 29, 1965.

87. Readers may note the statement made in *Western Politics* (Salt Lake City: University of Utah Press, 1961) that "except in certain specific labor matters, the Catholic Church in New Mexico almost always keeps out of politics." Such does not now appear to be the case.

88. The society is thought to have originated in the early nineteenth century when the Franciscan padres were forced to leave New Mexico. Geographically and spiritually isolated, these people developed their own form of worship which included highly politicized chapel self-government and flagellation. For a historical and political profile of the Penitentes the writers are again indebted to Jack Holmes, *op. cit.*, pp. 41-60. For scholars seriously interested in the Brotherhood, documentary materials are available in the library of New Mexico Highlands University, Las Vegas, New Mexico.

89. Such bloc voting seemed to come via low-pressure negotiations rather than by outright purchase. See *ibid.*, pp. 48-49 and the many sources cited by Holmes on this point.

90. From a manuscript in the library of New Mexico Highlands University. Holmes estimates that the actual membership of the Brotherhood in New Mexico is now about 2,000 to 3,000. Holmes, *op. cit.*, p. 46.

91. Regarding the dues-deduction controversy and other issues on which the NMEA has taken a position, see the *New Mexico School Review*, October 1964, pp. 10-14 and 35-42.

of fortieth among the fifty states in per capita income, it ranked eighth in the proportion of full-time equivalent employees in education and first in the nation as to its educational expenditures per $1,000 of personal income.[92] This may be contrasted with the state's general expenditure for governmental operations, ranking thirty-eighth nationally in this respect.[93]

Another revealing indicator of the role of education in New Mexico's expenditures is seen in the "effort index" developed by Congress in drafting the primary-secondary education bill (PL 89-10, April 11, 1965). The index measures a state's expenditure per school child as related to per capita income. Again, New Mexico topped all other states with a 6.57, the national average being 4.6.[94] The final formula employed by Congress was 50 percent of each state's average expenditure per school child times the number of school children whose parents earn less than $2,000 per year.[95] For New Mexico, this resulted in funds totaling nearly nine million dollars, allotted for some 38,000 students or 14 percent of the state's total number of school children. A National Education Association representative said the state had the greatest proportionate need of any of the thirteen western states.[96]

The continuing ability of New Mexico to support education at these peak levels is attributable in part to unusually strict statewide budgetary controls which have characterized educational politics almost since statehood.[97] State-directed consolidation and reorganization of structures and functions has also helped.

In spite of these rather remarkable achievements, the reverse side of the coin is not quite so shiny. The quality of the product purchased has not been uniformly high, as evidenced by the ninety-five high schools throughout the state (over 60 percent) not yet regionally accredited. Continued double sessions, the absence of kindergartens, controversy about teachers' salaries, tuition charged for summer programs, and increases in out-of-state tuition for the state's colleges and universities—these factors and others suggest the difficulty the state is having—and will continue to have—in competing with more well-endowed states.

A struggle between the National Educational Association and the American Federation of Teachers broke out during the 1965 session of the New Mexico legislature. The small but growing AFT, headquartered in Albuquerque, sought passage of legislation to prohibit local retribution against its members. The Federation's spokesmen documented their charge that official pressure had been used to persuade certain teachers to discontinue their union activities and join the offically sanctioned New Mexico Education Association.[98] Bitter opposition came

92. U.S. Bureau of the Census, *Census of Governments*, 1962, Vol. VII, No. 31, *Government in New Mexico* (Washington: Government Printing Office, 1964), p. 8.

93. *Ibid*.

94. See Paul R. Wieck, "Formula Could Reward New Mexico under Pending School Bill," *Albuquerque Journal*, March 5, 1965.

95. *Congressional Quarterly, Weekly Report*, April 16, 1965, p. 665.

96. *Albuquerque Tribune*, May 12, 1965.

97. For an extensive description and analysis of this phenomenon, see Tom Wiley, *Public School Education in New Mexico* (Albuquerque: Division of Government Research, University of New Mexico, 1965).

98. See the series of articles by Don Graydon, UPI, appearing in the *Albuquerque Journal*, February 28, March 1, and March 2, 1965. The AFT membership in New Mexico is variously estimated at between 150 and 500, depending upon who tells the story. NMEA membership is now approximately 11,000.

from NMEA, whose Executive Secretary, Mr. Charles Wood, called the bill an attempt to give "unequal representation." Other NMEA representatives said the bill would "create a monster" by encouraging expansion of labor unions in education.[99] The bill was itself a counterthrust to an NMEA-backed proposal to create a state professional practices commission as advisory to the State Board of Education. All of its members were to be nominated by teachers, presumably mostly NMEA members.

Although the two groups might have followed paths of bitter antagonism, they presented a common policy to the 1967 legislature. The increasing militancy of the National Education Association has enabled NMEA and AFT generally to reconcile their former differences.

A crisis developed in February 1968 when public school teachers in Albuquerque and some other communities "withheld their professional services," i.e., went on strike. This action was a response to the legislature's failure to meet NMEA demands for increased public school finances. The background of the strike is complex but its main outlines can be summarized. First, many educators and politicians agreed that the basic formula for distribution of state monies to school districts needed to be replaced. The approach used for several years, the Greer formula, named after State Senator Al Greer who devised it, discriminated against large school districts, especially the Albuquerque district. The new approach would be a foundation plan, providing for a basic level of educational support in each district. This foundation level could be augmented in any district by raising additional revenues in the district. Second, Governor Cargo presented to the 1968 legislature his foundation program, P.I.E. (Program for Improved Education) but with no provision for tax increase. The Democratic legislature maintained a tax increase was necessary; it rejected P.I.E., continued the Greer formula, and added less than five million dollars in new taxes. Third, the education lobby was ineffective for several reasons: NMEA had a foundation program; one so complicated few understood it and it was not drafted as a bill. Moreover, the educators were divided. Some school districts were very satisfied with their allotments under the Greer formula and opposed any potential change in their favorable position. NMEA opposed P.I.E. but had no ready alternative to the Greer formula. Finally, the issue must be seen within the context of a legislature serving without pay (only per diem and mileage), meeting for only thirty days, and with very limited staff (none for individual members). In these conditions, effective lobbyists must gain the confidence of legislators by extensive personal contacts and be able to provide staff skills, e.g., research and bill drafting. The education lobby did not adequately meet these tasks for the 1968 legislative session. The strike was called to compel Governor Cargo to call the legislature into special session, which would be devoted exclusively to public school finances.

Higher education in New Mexico, though supported by the same "effort index" as above, probably compares more favorably with that of other states than do the primary and secondary systems. Perhaps the crucial factor in evaluating

99. *Albuquerque Journal*, February 25, 1965. Not to be overlooked in the discussion of educator organizations are the associations of classroom teachers found in nearly every county. The associations have strengthened the position of the classroom instructor at the same time administrative pre-eminence is decreasing in the NMEA; see Wayne S. Scott, "NMEA About-Faces, Will Submit Program," *Albuquerque Journal*, February 25, 1968. It was the Albuquerque Classroom Teachers Association (ACTA) that called the first teachers strike in 1968.

higher education in New Mexico is to realize that it is overwhelmingly public rather than private. In the fall of 1967, there were six publicly financed institutions of higher education, the University of New Mexico (Albuquerque), New Mexico State University (Las Cruces), Eastern New Mexico University (Portales), Western New Mexico University (Silver City), New Mexico Highlands University (Las Vegas), and the New Mexico Institute of Mining and Technology (Socorro). Four institutions were privately financed: the two Roman Catholic schools, the University of Albuquerque (formerly the College of St. Joseph on the Rio Grande) and the College of Santa Fe (formerly St. Michael's College); and St. John's of Santa Fe (a sister college to St. John's of Annapolis, Md.) and the College of Artesia (patterned after Parsons College of Fairfield, Iowa). The total enrollment of the public universities in 1967 was about 30,000; the private institutions enrolled about 3,000. In addition, the public sector includes the New Mexico Military Institute, which offers a combined high school-junior college curriculum, and New Mexico Junior College (Hobbs). Studies are under way to ascertain the desirability of junior colleges in Albuquerque and in Valencia County; these could be in operation by 1969.

Although there is no master plan for higher education and no common Board of Regents, there is an instrument for coordination of the public institutions. The Board of Educational Finance, established in 1951, has responsibility for evaluating the over-all priorities of higher education. The Board has kept inter-university competition within reasonable bounds. By a policy of what might be called "highly selective emphasis," the limited financial resources of the state have been utilized to achieve excellence in particular academic areas.[100]

In recent years, well over 50 percent of the state general fund has gone to education (closer to 70 percent for all levels of education). One wonders whether this will continue, especially in view of the predictable intensification in the struggle for funds. The Statewide Commission on Higher Education has been highly optimistic, saying that the state "can reasonably expect to meet educational costs which will produce a fine higher education system."[101] Other observers are much less sanguine.[102]

LEGISLATIVE POLITICS

The struggle of the New Mexico legislature to secure independence from the governor's control is perhaps the single most significant aspect of formal policy-making in the state. A benchmark was reached in this conflict in 1945 when the legislators forbade the practice of having themselves placed on the state payroll subservient to the governor. This event, however, was itself a reflection of the changing party balance wherein Democratic factionalism was beginning to overshadow interparty competition as a major political cleavage in legislative politics.[103] Additionally, legislative independence has been a by-product of the high

100. For a fuller discussion of higher education in New Mexico, see Harold L. Enarson, "Profile of the University of New Mexico," *New Mexico Business*, February 1965, and Allan R. Richards, *Some Aspects of Higher Education: Arizona, Colorado, and New Mexico* (Albuquerque: Division of Government Research, University of New Mexico, 1961).

101. As quoted in Enarson, *op. cit.*, p. 11.

102. *Albuquerque Tribune*, May 18, 1965.

103. These changes are rigorously and richly documented in Holmes, *op. cit.*, chaps. VIII and IX.

degree of competition for the governorship. Frequently faced with a chief executive of the opposing party, the legislative majorities have had to develop independent sources of support.

As one might expect in a modified one-party state such as New Mexico, party cohesion in both chambers of the legislature has been low, and this fact, too, may be seen as a further indication of legislative autonomy vis-à-vis the governor.[104] Using the Rice index of cohesion, Holmes found that while the Republicans have generally formed a more cohesive bloc than the Democrats in legislative voting, both parties have historically demonstrated an unusually low level of cohesiveness as compared with other states.[105] That this should be so is not surprising, however, in view of the traditional absence of a sharp urban-rural split in the state's politics.[106]

All of this would suggest a relatively weak office of governor for the state, which is largely the case. To begin with, his two-year term with but one re-election permitted is a serious limitation as compared with every other western state. [107] This combines with his limited appointive, budgetary, and veto powers to render the office the weakest in terms of formal power of any western state except Arizona.[108] This has meant that informal roots of power have had to be cultivated if New Mexico governors were to retain an efficacious hand in dealing with the legislature and other decision-making bodies. The vast array of boards and commissions has been one technique, as has an attempted dominance over party finances. The legislative-executive relationship in New Mexico may be summed up as one of balance, with the legislature having achieved a favorable redress only after decades of executive dominance.[109]

It may be that as a consequence of the state's emphasis on politics, an added measure of prestige is attached to the office of state legislator. Certainly the pleasant, well-liquefied atmosphere in Santa Fe would lend credence to this proposition. Yet, this view of the legislative role is difficult to document, and the weight of contrary evidence is quite impressive. For example, the rate of turnover of legislative seats in both the House and the Senate since 1912 has been unusually if

104. As Holmes points out, low cohesive indices indicate "unified, a-partisan, internally-regulated bodies making their own resolutions of conflicts coming before them, and determining as well which matters become issues." *Ibid.*, p. 337. Holmes has a considerable amount of data and measures regarding party cohesion in New Mexico and comparatively.

105. Currently, the New Mexico legislature would rank at or near the bottom of the group of states Malcolm Jewell studied in *The State Legislature: Theory and Practice* (New York: Random House, 1962), pp. 50-52. *Ibid.*, p. 331.

106. The authors noted earlier that growing urban areas such as Albuquerque do not fit the traditional pattern of New Mexico politics, which has been rural and small-town oriented. In his chapter on state political parties in Jacob and Vines, *op. cit.*, Austin Ranney notes that "where party divisions do not coincide with metropolitan-small town conflict . . . party cohesion [in the legislature] tends to be lower even where party competition is close." See Ranney, *op. cit.*, p. 89.

107. The office in nine western states carries a four-year term with no restraints on re-elections, in two (Alaska and Oregon) a four-year term limited to one renewal, and in one (Arizona) a two-year term with no restraints on re-election. See Council of State Governments, *Book of the States*, 1962-63 (Chicago: Council of State Governments, 1962), p. 139.

108. Joseph Schlesinger awards the New Mexico governor a formal power index rating of eleven, the lowest states having seven (including Arizona), and the highest, nineteen. No other western state is given a rating of less than fourteen. See Joseph A. Schlesinger, "The Politics of the Executive," Jacob and Vines, *op. cit.*, p. 229.

109. Holmes, *op. cit.*, p. 303, has a summary view of this relationship.

not astoundingly high. New Mexico legislators have been found to be considerably less experienced than those of any state studied, although tenure is substantially up from the pre-New Deal era and may be expected to continue to rise. [110] Since the best evidence indicates that financial remuneration is not the most important factor in explaining tenure and turnover, [111] one must conclude that legislative service in New Mexico, far from being regarded as particularly prestigeful, is viewed rather as an onerous enterprise.

Lacking complete and reliable data concerning the socio-economic backgrounds of New Mexico's legislators, only a brief statement can be made in this regard. Small towns and rural legislators dominate the scene, with an apparent preponderance of business and agrarian interests being represented. Although each session usually has a good many lawyers, the legal profession is far from dominant. This general picture suggests that the body is composed in a manner not unlike most other states of the Rocky Mountain and Southwest regions.

The New Mexico legislature moved to regular annual sessions in January 1966. The enabling constitutional provision, adopted in November 1964, limits sessions in odd-numbered years to sixty days and in even-numbered years to thirty days. [112] In even-numbered years, substance of legislation is limited to: (1) budgetary, appropriations, and revenue bills; (2) bills drawn pursuant to special messages of the governor; and (3) bills of the last previous regular session vetoed by the governor. The limitations are not very limiting.

As in most states, a critical legislative issue for New Mexico in the 1960's has been reapportionment. When the United States Supreme Court decided *Baker v. Carr* in March of 1962, the New Mexico Senate ranked among the nine most malapportioned upper houses in the nation, only 14 percent of the state's population being necessary to elect a majority to that body. The House of Representatives, on the other hand, found itself in a slightly better position, being classified in a group of twenty-two states in which at least 40 percent of the population was required to elect a majority of representatives. [113] Measured by the degree of malapportionment in both houses combined, New Mexico fell in a group of sixteen

110. *Ibid.*, pp. 273-78. Holmes found that turnover of New Mexico legislators exceeded that of the ten states Charles Hyneman studied as well as the states covered by Wahlke and Epstein. See John C. Wahlke *et al.*, *The Legislative System: Explorations in Legislative Behavior* (New York: Wiley, 1962), p. 49; Leon D. Epstein, *Politics in Wisconsin* (Madison: University of Wisconsin Press, 1958), pp. 104, 198-99; Charles S. Hyneman, "Tenure and Turnover of Legislative Personnel," *Annals of the American Academy of Political and Social Science*, Vol. CXCV (January 1938). New Mexico also has a higher turnover rate than Washington. See Paul Beckett and Celeste Sunderland, "Washington State's Lawmakers: Some Personal Factors in the Washington Legislature," *Western Political Quarterly*, X (March 1957), 184-85.

111. New Mexico legislators, by constitutional provision, receive twenty dollars for each day in session and ten cents per mile for one round-trip to Santa Fe each session. A proposed constitutional amendment, defeated by the voters in September 1965, would have set the pay at $200 per month. The legislators have also provided themselves a moderately attractive pension plan, which may be a factor in encouraging longer service. The constitutionality of the pension has been questioned but its legality has not been given a judicial test.

112. *New Mexico Constitution*, Article IV, Sec. 5(a).

113. *New York Times*, April 1, 1962, as contained in Robert K. Carr, Marver H. Bernstein and Walter F. Murphy, *American Democracy in Theory and Practice* (4th ed.; New York: Holt, Rinehart and Winston, 1963), p. 902. The New Mexico lower house percentage figure was 42. For a survey of reapportionment in New Mexico prior to *Baker v. Carr*, see Inez Bushner Gill, *Legislative Apportionment and Congressional Districting in New Mexico* (Albuquerque: Division of Government Research, University of New Mexico, 1953).

states which were termed "Equivalent of Federal Plan," meaning population was the least significant factor of legislative apportionment of four categories of states.[114]

The initial response of New Mexico legislators to the Tennessee decision was one of evasive resistance. With the convening of the Twenty-Sixth Legislature in January 1963, several reapportionment measures were introduced. However, as might be expected, the impetus came from urban interests, especially from Bernalillo County legislators; and in the absence of direct judicial intervention chances of success were low. Bernalillo County clearly had the most to gain by reapportionment. With roughly 30 percent of the state's population, it had only 14 percent of the House seats (nine out of sixty-six) and about 3 percent of the Senate seats (one out of thirty-two). The result of the session, however, was to pass no redistricting legislation but to appropriate $25,000 to fight court suits, then pending.[115]

On August 27, 1963, New Mexico District Judge Caswell S. Neal, responding to a suit brought by State Representative David F. Cargo (Republican, Bernalillo County) and others, asked Governor Campbell to call a special session of the legislature, specifically to reapportion the lower house.[116] Meeting in November of that year, the legislature adopted a bill to increase the size of the House to seventy-seven members, each county having at least one representative, and the more populous counties having their votes on most measures weighted in proportion to their population.[117]

In January 1964, Judge Neal, contrary to most expectations, held the weighted voting system null and void as violative of eleven separate sections of the New Mexico Constitution.[118] He also nullified sections of the state constitution as contrary to the Fourteenth Amendment. The actual geographic districting portions of the new law were left intact, and it was under this legislation that the 1964 state elections were held.

Following the second bombshell of *Reynolds v. Sims* in June of 1964, another suit was brought in Federal District Court, alleging that the State Senate was unconstitutionally apportioned. However, the special three-judge federal tribunal constituted to hear the case decided to postpone a decision until the 1965 legislature could act.

114. See Paul T. David and Ralph Eisenberg, *State Legislative Redistricting* (Chicago: Public Administration Service, 1962), p. 10. Other western states which fell into this "most malapportioned category" were Arizona, Hawaii, Idaho, Montana, and Nevada.

115. See *Albuquerque Tribune*, February 9, 1963; also, see Wolf, "The 1964 Elections . . . ," pp. 1-4.

116. *Judges Memorandum*, State of New Mexico, County of Santa Fe, Civil Action No. 33237. It should be noted that the memorandum included a 1,000-word stinging indictment of the United States Supreme Court and its "judicial legislation of a type which in recent years, has invaded the rights of the states and the people thereof. . . ." After finding that the Fourteenth Amendment was adopted "by highly dubious and devious means," the judge concluded his remarks with this: "Be these things as they may, I suppose it is too late in this high noon of the Twentieth Century to dwell longer upon this depressing subject."

117. See Frederick C. Irion, "Apportionment of the New Mexico Legislature, 1850 to June, 1964, Including an Analysis of the Weighted Voting Plan of the House" (Albuquerque: Department of Government, University of New Mexico).

118. *Cargo v. Campbell*, District Court for the County of Santa Fe, No. 33237, January 8, 1964.

The March 1965 apportionment of the Senate increased that body from thirty-two to thirty-seven members, with Bernalillo County receiving the added representation. The Senate then followed the House precedent by adopting weighted voting. Five hundred and nine weighted votes were apportioned among the thirty-seven proposed Senate seats according to the population represented by each. The law, to go into effect in January 1967, was considered constitutional by almost no one, but the federal court decided once again to postpone a decision. The legislation was accompanied by a proposed state constitutional amendment designed to permit weighted voting; the amendment was rejected by the electorate in a special election in September 1965.

Again the court ordered the legislature to reapportion its Senate. The 1966 legislature came close to doing this to the court's satisfaction. A Senate of 42 members was designed. Seven multi-county districts and one inter-county district (Los Alamos and part of Santa Fe) were created with the remaining seats drawn from districts within single counties. Immediately after the session, the federal court was presented the apportionment plan, which was subsequently declared invalid. The court's alternative is not too dissimilar from that prepared by the legislature; the number of seats is 42 but the deviations from the population norm are slightly less.

The 1965 House apportionment established a seventy-member body, some elected from five multi-county districts with each member representing an average of 13,568 persons. Only seven House districts exceed or fall below this average by more than 15 percent. Both chambers of the legislature now meet judicial tests of fair apportionment; it is unlikely either house will be apportioned again until the 1970 census is available.[119]

If the state's lawmakers have shown their ingenuity and innovative skills in the crisis of reapportionment, it can at least be noted that they have also done so with respect to the legislative process generally. As Holmes has written: "A number of legislators have so consciously sought for the means to improve legislative mechanics and organization that the fact, as well as the results, of their searching could well be a source of gratification to their former teachers of civics and government."[120] Among the recent innovations are a legislative council, financial and budgetary reform, and a more precisely defined and more highly centralized committee system.

Budgetary reform resulted in at least two sub-institutions of considerable importance: the State Board of Educational Finance, which has helped to achieve more reliable and responsible educational cost estimates; and the Legislative Finance Committee, which reviews costs and financing of governmental operations generally. The Finance Committee has succeeded in eliminating most pockets of untouchable "earmarked" funding, forcing many agencies and departments to justify expenditures on their merits. Yet, such concepts as a performance budget have not become fully operational in state financing.

The New Mexico Legislative Council, established in 1951, is composed of thirteen members: the president *pro tempore* of the Senate, the speaker of the House, five senators, and six representatives. The primary function of the Council

119. For more detailed examinations of reapportionment in the state, see: Richard H. Folmar, *Legislative Apportionment in New Mexico, 1844-1966* (Santa Fe: New Mexico Legislative Council Service, 1966) and Harry P. Stumpf, "Reapportionment in New Mexico: Inventive Evasion" (forthcoming).

120. Holmes, *op. cit.*, p. 310, note 2.

is the supervision of its research and service unit, the Council Service. The latter, currently directed by Clay Buchanan, has developed into a major research and bill-drafting agency and has every appearance of having won the support of a majority of lawmakers. Though its staff is still quite small, the Council Service now drafts an overwhelming majority of bills introduced, manages an indispensable collection of documents and other library materials, and has undertaken some broad-scale research projects.[121]

The citizens of New Mexico possess neither the power of initiative nor recall, but there is a provision for a popular referendum on laws enacted by the legislature. However, the referendum is rendered almost meaningless by removing from its scope, by constitution and by judicial interpretation, laws providing for public health, peace, safety, and related matters. The only recent uses of the referendum have been discussed in connection with the pre-primary candidate selection systems.

A NOTE ON JUDICIAL POLITICS

Reorganization of New Mexico's judicial establishment is a major political issue and can be expected to generate a good deal of heat within the next few years. The present structure consists of a five-member Supreme Court, eleven District Courts of from one to six judges, and approximately 220 justices of the peace. All judicial personnel are elected on partisan ballots—to the Supreme Court for eight years, to the District Courts for six years and to the JP courts for two years. The state also has a Juvenile Court in each judicial district as an adjunct of the District Court, a Probate Court in each of the state's thirty-two counties, and one Small Claims Court in Bernalillo County. The latter two courts have elective terms of two years. There is also a Municipal Court in each of the state's eighty-seven incorporated municipalities.[122]

Major controversy has recently centered around four key aspects of reform: (1) an alteration in the selection procedures; (2) abolishing the JP's and their fee-system, replacing them with salaried magistrates; (3) creating an appeals court between the District and Supreme Court; and (4) court financing.

In 1952 voters turned down a constitutional amendment which would have given the state a modified Missouri Plan for the selection of judges.[123] Sporadic attempts at reform during the late fifties met with little success. In 1959, however, the State Judicial System Study Committee was created, headed by State Senator Fabian Chavez. Its reports and recommendations have served to rekindle interest in reform. Yet, in the 1965 legislative session a complex, omnibus reform proposal was chopped to pieces by the lawmakers.[124] All that survived was a pro-

121. See New Mexico Legislative Council and New Mexico Legislative Council Service, *Biennial Reports* (Santa Fe: New Mexico Legislative Council Service).

122. State Judicial System Study Committee, *Survey of the Judicial System in New Mexico*, 1965, by Philip T. Manly (Santa Fe: Legislative Council Service, 1965).

123. Glen R. Winters, "The New Mexico Selection Campaign—A Case History," *Journal of the American Judicature Society*, XXXV (April 1952), 166-76.

124. Lynn A. Buckingham, Benjamin L. Crosby, III, and Joseph L. Martinez, "Judicial Reform in New Mexico" (unpublished research paper, Department of Political Science, University of New Mexico, May 1965). This paper summarizes the major aspects of judicial reform in the state and attempts to identify the sources of support and opposition. See this paper for the contents of SJR-5, the 1965 reform proposal, which originally included a modified Missouri Plan for judicial selection, the California method of discipline and retirement of judges, and a centralization of judicial administration in the hands of the chief justice.

posal to replace the JP's with salaried magistrates and to create a Court of Appeals to relieve the work load of the Supreme Court.[125] The former was approved by the voters on the 1966 ballot, the latter in the September 1965 special election.

A member of the State Supreme Court, David W. Carmody, has taken special interest in reorganizing and centralizing judicial administration, but has by no means achieved the full support of the state bar association.[126] The legislature has also proven lukewarm to most proposals, especially those seeking to make judicial office appointive rather than elective. In this sentiment they have generally been supported by the state's congressional delegation.[127]

The justice of the peace system in New Mexico became one of the first subjects of study of the State Judicial System Study Committee.[128] The Committee's 1961 report revealed grotesque conditions throughout the state, including kickbacks by JP's to police officers, net incomes from the fee system from $12,000 to $18,000 per year in some cases, JP's who could never remember having found anyone innocent, "court" held in filling stations, bars, and coal mines, and some totally illiterate JP's.[129] Apparently this exposure was sufficient to prod the legislators into action in 1965, but not without considerable protest from the JP Association.[130]

Judicial reform is under way. In the September 1965 special election, a constitutional amendment was approved to create a new appellate court. Implementing legislation, which established a four-judge court at this level, was passed in 1966. An amendment to abolish the justice of the peace system was ratified in the 1966 elections. The 1967 legislature passed the initial legislation to systematically replace the justices of the peace with a set of magistrate courts. After voters approved the enabling constitutional amendment in November 1967, the 1968 legislature established a system of paid magistrates, who were required to be lawyers in some counties. Ultimately, it is expected all magistrates will be full time and lawyers. The November 1967 referendum included the establishment of a board to review complaints against judges, along the lines of the California arrangement.

125. *Ibid.*, pp. 18-19.

126. The Supreme Court justice with the shortest term to serve is automatically the chief justice. See Carmody's views of the judicial process and the Missouri Plan in "Non-Political Justice," *Western Review*, II (Summer 1965), 57-58. Justice Carmody's desire to take politics out of judicial politics and his alleged attempts to enhance his own power within the judicial hierarchy have brought him criticism, although mostly of the sub-surface variety, and some from legal circles simply opposed to change.

127. Buckingham, Crosby and Martinez, *op. cit.*, p. 7. See also the *Albuquerque Tribune*, March 1, 1965, and the *Albuquerque Journal*, March 2, 1965.

128. State Judicial System Study Committee, *The Courts in New Mexico* (Santa Fe: Legislative Council Service, 1961).

129. *Ibid.* See especially chap. 1, "The Justice of the Peace Story as Told by the JP's Themselves."

130. One JP defended the system, saying, "I do not know why that the proponents of getting rid of us are working so hard and evading the issues." He protested that "No JP has been convicted of stealing or any other serious crime in over three years. . . ." Letter to the Tribune Public Forum, *Albuquerque Tribune*, February 27, 1965. He almost spoke too soon, however, for Lorenzo C. Duran, JP for Precinct 35, was arraigned July 19, 1965, for "turning his . . . office into a horse betting parlor without a wagering stamp." However, an IRS spokesman said the bets were only "on a small scale." *Albuquerque Journal*, July 20, 1965.

TRENDS AND ISSUES

The political system that is New Mexico may be described and analyzed either in terms of the colorful, the unique, the elusive, or via the hard data of voting trends, party cohesion, and socio-economic indices. That both approaches can be combined to serve both scholarship and general readership is an explicit and obvious assumption underlying this essay.

New Mexico is a political system grounded in an enviable tri-ethnic harmony and accommodation, wherein participation in its manifest forms is low, corresponding to a low per capita and family income and relatively high unemployment and welfare benefits—a relationship found to exist in other states. Despite these latter burdens, the state has a demonstrated commitment to educational attainment; it also has the most Ph.D.'s per capita of any state.[131]

The state's growing urbanization, combined with legislative reapportionment, suggests a redress of party balance in years to come.[132] Areas of highest per capita income are the growing areas of the state—and growing Republican; whereas Democratic strongholds tend to be losing population—and prosperity.[133] In the immediate future, however, Democratic dominance of official decision-making can be expected to continue, if not intensify, although this is likely to be punctured now and again by house-cleaning Republicans.

When the variable of party balance is added to a slowly improving economy and educational system, there exists a set of conditions likely to produce an increased sensitivity to both state and national issues—this in a state whose affairs are already linked to those of the nation in a particularly acute way.

If not for moral, then for practical political reasons, New Mexico policymakers must come to grips with their proclivity for influence dealings, for both economic and political tolerance levels are now visible. The forced start in the 1961 and 1963 Personnel Acts has yet to be matched with further steps, a next logical one being in state highway construction and maintenance.[134] (Attempts to bring the Highway Department under the employment aegis of the state personnel director have been delayed.) This particular policy area has been the source of some of the state's darkest and most embarrassing days, and although some improvement has been seen since the scandals revealed in the 1961 Blatnik report, the State Highway Commission's image in the eyes of the electorate is tarnished.[135]

131. "Boom in the Desert—Why It Grows and Grows," *U.S. News and World Report*, 56 (May 25, 1964), 49. The ratio is one Ph.D. for each 350 persons.

132. See Wolf, "The 1964 Elections . . . ," p. 3, wherein the Republican advantage in Bernalillo under the 1963 House redistricting law is described.

133. Holmes, *op. cit.*, p. 317.

134. The precise impact of the merit system adopted in 1961 is not yet clear, but if changes at the state mental hospital are indicative, one can expect vast areas of improvement in administrative efficiency in New Mexico. A study of the changes wrought at the state hospital is Robert S. Landman, *New Mexico State Hospital* (Albuquerque: Division of Government Research, University of New Mexico, 1965).

135. See U.S., Congress, House, Special Subcommittee on the Federal Aid Highway Program of the Committee on Public Works, *Hearings, Highway Construction Practices in the State of New Mexico*, 87th Cong., 1st sess., 1961. Known as the Blatnik report, these hearings and findings revealed some aspects of the long-standing relationship between politics and highway construction in the state. See also a synopsis of the sub-committee's findings in *Albuquerque Journal*, July 15, 1962.

On the other hand, long-range state planning and the explicit policy developments one hopes will flow therefrom constitute an optimistic element in the
system, as does the considerably improved administration in health and welfare
services over the past decade. The still unsolved problem of the state's perpetually
depressed areas has been the recent target of federal programs. This, plus an improved state capacity to administer efficiently such aid should result in at least a
partial solution within the decade ahead.

More than twenty-five years ago, Thomas C. Donnelly wrote of his state:

As one considers the various forces at work in New Mexico politics today, they add up to
the conclusion that the state is a political democracy on the march, that it is interested in
progressive governmental policies, and that it is unafraid of the future, for it expects much
from it. Consequently, leaders and parties must promise to go ahead rather than call a halt or
beat a retreat.[136]

Progress made since that time and recorded in this essay underscores both the
appropriateness of Donnelly's remarks and the major lesson to be derived therefrom: that the land of *manana*, of *poco tiempo*, is no more.

136. *Rocky Mountain Politics* (Albuquerque: University of New Mexico Press, 1940),
p. 251.

OREGON:

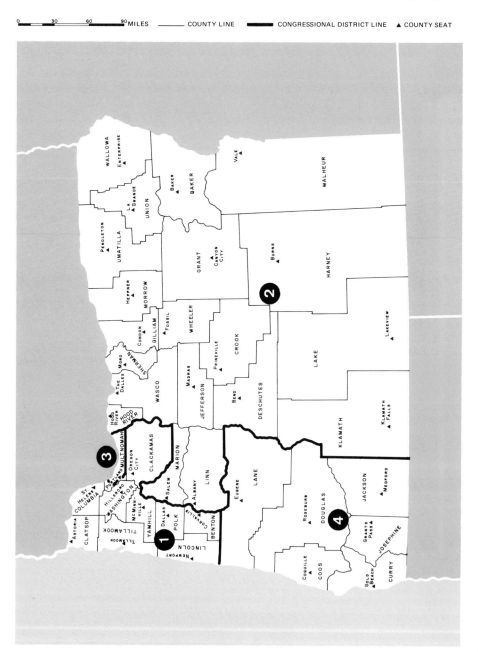

John M. Swarthout
Kenneth R. Gervais

Political Experiment Station

For one of the smaller states, carrying no great weight in the nation's electoral and congressional scales, Oregon has found itself the focus of national political attention surprisingly often throughout its century of statehood. Admitted to the Union on the eve of the Civil War, as a pawn in the explosive political struggle of that time of animosity; its few electoral or congressional votes a frequent key factor in the harrowing post-Civil War political balance; its driving reform movement at and after the turn of the century such as to bring it recognition as the "political experiment station of the nation"; its contested internal innovations during the first three decades of the 1900's the source of such signal and basic constitutional law cases as *Pacific States Telephone & Telegraph Co. v. Oregon* and *Pierce v. the Society of Sisters*—Oregon has regularly earned more political notice than its size has warranted.

In the election years since World War II, the state has continued its upstage ways. Virtually every postwar election has seen Oregon, if not in the sun, at least in the national spotlight. It was the Oregon primary of May 1948 that destroyed Harold Stassen and made Thomas Dewey a second-time Republican presidential candidate; and four years later, it was Eisenhower's resounding Oregon primary victory over Taft that gave the impetus necessary to Ike's success in the Republican convention of 1952. In 1954, Dick Neuberger's 2,500-vote defeat of incumbent Guy Gordon, undecided and unpredictable until twenty-four hours after the polls closed, enabled the Democrats to organize the United States Senate; and in 1956, the Wayne Morse-Douglas McKay senatorial race was generally accepted by both national parties as that year's vital test between them. The selection in 1958 of young Republican Mark Hatfield as Oregon's governor in the face of a general Democratic sweep both in Oregon and elsewhere raised eyebrows countrywide and influenced markedly the "new look" national Republicans assumed in 1960. And if the Republican national convention of 1964 slapped the face of Oregon's Republicans, who had handed Barry Goldwater a resounding defeat in a more or less hotly contested primary, Oregonians were certainly vindicated in November.[1]

---

1. The 1966 senatorial race put Oregon again in the national eye, as the primary campaign was turned into a stage show for the country's debate on the war in Vietnam. The actors on the senatorial platform were Republican Governor Mark Hatfield, who questioned—or seemed to question—the Administration's Vietnam policy; Democratic Congressman Robert Duncan, who vigorously championed Johnson's actions (thus assuring presidential support); and Democrat Howard Morgan, former Federal Power Commission member, who strongly attacked the President (and who was roundly beaten by Duncan in the primary). But walking and talking offstage—sometimes loudly—were Senator Wayne Morse, President Johnson, Mao Tse-Tung, Ho Chi Minh, and Nguyen Cao Ky—none of whom was a candidate but any or all of whom may actually have determined what happened in the election. The candidates placed themselves at the mercy of an international crisis over which

Indeed, as if in recognition of its birth in the midst of the nation's most violent political controversy, Oregon seems to have been assigned by that part of Providence that watches over American government to a continuing dramatic role as a much fought-over battleground of American politics, a sort of political Shenandoah Valley or Manassas Plain of the mid-twentieth century. At regular intervals, the campaign troops come into the state from all over the country to fight out battles of national import. And the reporters follow them.

Yet it can be ventured that most Oregonians have generally been, and to a degree still are, primarily inward-looking, more than usually concerned with state and local than with national affairs and more interested in the effects of their votes on state and local than on national government and politics. Indeed this parochialism (or sturdy local independence, as you wish to view the matter) is one of the distinctive traditional features of Oregon politics, a fact responsible in part for Oregonians' willingness to experiment (in some seasons, at least) with their own governmental arrangements, as in the "Oregon System," without regard to national opinion. This internal concentration has contributed as well to those characteristics of Oregon elections most puzzling to outsiders: the wanton disregard Oregonians have often shown for national party trends in the selection of their state and local leaders, the frequent willingness of Oregon voters to split their tickets in terms of national party labels, and their occasional paradoxical tendency to favor in the same election "liberal" national senators and congressmen and "conservative" state governors and legislators.

In considerable contrast to its West Coast neighbors, California and Washington, Oregon has a record of abnormal historical continuity in its social and economic structure,[2] a continuity interrupted only infrequently by upheavals of any measurable consequence. Waves of immigration have come to the state ever since "The Great Reinforcement" of 1840, but at least until World War II, these massive intrusions have commonly merged into and bolstered the existing hierarchy of interests. This fact of social continuity forms even now a further important element in the state's political atmosphere and makes a consideration of Oregon political and social history more than usually important to an understanding of the state's current politics.

Oregon's social pattern was early established. The pioneers who settled the Willamette Valley in the 1840's and 1850's were homogeneous in their occupations and economic status, not seekers after gold or other sudden fortune. To be sure, they were heterogeneous in their origins, coming from states both North and South; but once they had surmounted the disruptive effects of the Civil War and the overriding issue of Negro status, the Oregon citizenry crystallized into a socially stable community, at once economically conservative and politically liberal, almost after the Jeffersonian ideal, firmly based on the small home-owned farm and the small home-owned business. The governmental structure set by the 1859 constitution and the standard two-party system that accompanied it, both borrowed from older sister states,[3] seemed as suited to this society as to any. Repub-

they had no control. Hatfield came out victorious in the close contest with 51.8 percent of the votes. See Donald G. Balmer's evaluation of "The 1966 Election in Oregon," *Western Political Quarterly*, XX (June 1967, Part 2), 593-601.

2. See on this point Pollard Lancaster, in *Regionalism in America*, ed. M. Jensen (Madison: University of Wisconsin Press, 1952), pp. 196 ff. More recent studies find little change from the conditions that intrigued Lancaster.

3. Almost every provision of the Oregon constitution was taken, often verbatim, from existing state constitutions, especially those of Missouri and Kentucky.

licans took over the state's politics with the Civil War and early won for themselves that "monopoly on respectability" that seemed a built-in characteristic of
Oregon party politics until very recent years.

But as the last decades of the nineteenth century wore on, Oregon's borrowed political system seemed to fail its solid citizens, as they found themselves
faced, to an increasing degree, by the corruption that marked the "Gilded Age"
throughout the country. The Oregon legislature in the 1880's and 1890's established for itself a reputation surely exceptional if not unique. The state's more
powerful moneyed interests, controlling the nominating caucuses and conventions and thus the parties, dominated the legislative halls and filled them with
"briefless lawyers, farmless farmers, business failures, barroom loafers, Fourth-
of-July orators, and political thugs."[4] Drunkenness and debauchery commonly
surrounded the legislative sessions in Salem, and reform measures backed by overwhelming popular support—like the Australian ballot and the voter registration
law—were sidetracked for years, while attention was given to matters of political
control, like the election of United States senators,[5] or to bills supported by the
powerful lobbies.

Into this unhealthy atmosphere, the reform doctrines of the Populist movement came like a cool and cleansing breeze. Oregon's political consciousness had
been already pricked into irritated awareness by the needle of economic misfor-
tune, for the state's farmers and farm-suppliers, like those of the Midwest where
the Populist movement was born, suffered from a monopolistic out-of-state domination of their economy that came in the wake of the corporate revolution. Railroads, bankers, and land speculators controlled transportation and farm prices,
interest rates, and land sales. Oregon early produced a strong Grange movement,
and within its organization anti-monopoly, anti-railway, anti-privilege, and progressive taxation sentiment swept the farms and villages of the state. Since economic reform seemed impossible of achievement within the existing political
structure, sentiment for political reform, "returning to the people the power to
govern," grew rapidly. The Australian ballot, voter registration, the direct primary, corrupt practices legislation, the initiative and referendum, the recall—all
became part of the reform movement, the long-range goals of which were for the
most part economic. Sudden successes of the Populists at the polls in 1894[6]
served as a sobering threat to Republican and Democratic leadership, and accordingly the major party leaders, chastened and reoriented, themselves reluctantly

4. Burton J. Hendrick, "The Initiative and Referendum and How Oregon Got
Them," *McClures Magazine*, XXXVII (July 1911), 240. Testimony on this score by men
then engaged in Oregon politics is legion. See, e.g., G. A. Thatcher, "The Initiative and Referendum in Oregon," *Proceedings of the American Political Science Association*, IV (1907),
201; Joseph Gaston, *Centennial History of Oregon*, 1811-1912 (Chicago: S. J. Clarke Pub.
Co., 1912), pp. 654-55; (Governor) T. T. Geer, *Fifty Years in Oregon* (New York: Neale
Publishing Co., 1912), pp. 476-78.

5. Geer reports that "out of seven elections for United States Senators, five of them
required the entire time of the session—two of these resulting in no election at all, and one
of them in no organization of the House, with no legislation on any subject whatever." *Op.
cit.*, pp. 476-77.

6. The Populists won 13 of the 60 seats in the House and 3 of the 30 in the Senate.
In the succeeding legislative session the Populists in the House held the balance of power
between antagonistic Republican factions competing over the selection of a U.S. senator and
of a House speaker; their attempt to use their weight as trading material in bringing about
the reforms they favored led to the famous "hold-up session" of 1895, during which the
House met for seven weeks of astonishing impasse before adjourning without even organizing
itself. No state business whatsoever was accomplished.

succumbed to the reform program. With the initiative and the referendum adopted in 1902, they opened the door to all the great features of the "Oregon System."[7] In so doing they virtually revolutionized Oregon government and politics, destroying almost at a stroke the "strong-party system," reducing immensely both their own power and that of the moneyed interests allied with them, raising new interest groups (like the Grange) to positions of great strength, and opening up a new non-party political arena that became for a while virtually the center ring in the Oregon political circus. This arena remains to this day a matter of much consequence insofar as internal state politics is concerned.

Indeed, for the first two decades after the adoption of the Direct Legislation amendment, the decisive battles of Oregon politics were fought out almost entirely apart from party labels and without the intervention of party machinery at all. Throughout this heyday of the initiative and referendum,[8] the major issues of political reform (e.g., the direct primary, the presidential primary, the corrupt practices law, municipal home rule, and legislative and judicial reorganization) and of economic regulation (e.g., taxation and regulation of railroads and other utilities) were contested principally as direct legislation measures and settled by the people (as nonpartisans) at the polls rather than by their partisan representatives in the legislature. The "platforms" adopted by organizations like the Grange and the Farmers Alliance, with wide but close-knit membership, were likely to be of much more importance to the state's political course than were positions taken by the parties; and a unique body called the "People's Power League" (led by the redoubtable William S. U'Ren, who had earlier "fathered" the initiative and referendum through a variety of devices)[9] provided for over a decade a leadership in the "popular branch of the legislature" more influential than that of either party.[10]

7. The Australian ballot was adopted by the Oregon legislature in 1891, but only after a long and hard-fought battle. The state's first registration law was finally passed in 1889. The initiative and referendum provision (on state measures) was initiated in the legislature by heavy majorities in the session of 1899 and reapproved, as then required, in the session of 1901, unanimously in the House and with but one dissenting vote in the Senate; it carried at the polls by 62,024 to 5,668, almost 11 to 1! Direct legislation permission was extended to local governments by a constitutional amendment proposed by the initiative in 1906. The direct primary was brought in by popular vote on initiative petition in 1904, and a corrupt practices act adopted by the same device in 1908.

8. The general elections of 1910, 1912, and 1914 formed the high mark of direct legislation in Oregon, 32, 37, and 29 state measures appearing on the ballots of those years. During the first two decades after 1903, the people were faced with an average of 20.2 measures per biennium; in the last 40 years the average has been only 12.5.

9. U'Ren's methods in the fight for direct legislation deserve study by any serious and ambitious political manipulator. Until his death in 1927, he insisted that direct legislation and the other political reforms he espoused were designed entirely as "tools of the mechanic" for the accomplishment of economic and social legislation; the single-tax, the reform he most wanted, he was never able to bring about.

10. The People's Power League developed from a circular letter sent out on September 6, 1906, to some 1,000 representative citizens of Oregon to "get their opinion of the wisdom of submitting certain amendments to popular vote." The letter was signed by seventeen Oregon political leaders, headed by Thomas A. McBride, shortly to be Chief Justice of the Oregon Supreme Court, and requested replies be sent to U'Ren. Leaders of the organization included most of the group that had led the Direct Primary League, which had spearheaded the movement which won the primary in 1904, and before that of the old Non-Partisan Direct Legislation League. In the election of 1906, the PPL offered five measures—the extension of direct legislation to local units, municipal home rule, the requirement of a popular vote for the calling of constitutional conventions, statutory regulation of the office of State Printer (long a hotbed of graft), and provisions to prevent the use of free railroad passes for corrupt purposes—all of which passed comfortably. Four more PPL measures, in-

But Oregon's party history, even since 1920, is not an entirely straight-line affair. Republicans generally dominated state politics until after World War II, but the appellation "The Vermont of the West" was never fully justified, even when Republican registration was highest in the 1920's. The early and middle Oregon record is full of militant third-party movements—Populist, Progressive, and "independent"—all of which drew membership predominantly from the Republicans. Democrats more than occasionally benefited. They elected two governors and two U.S. senators during the period of Populist Progressive-Republican upheaval in the 1900's and the 1910's, and two more governors when Populist-minded Republicans broke ranks in 1922 and 1934.[11] Republicans generally enjoyed overwhelming control of the state legislature until the 1950's, but even within the legislature Republican factions often bolted to join the Democratic minority or acted as nonpartisan legislators.

In more recent years, Republican control slipped. Republican registration fell dramatically during the Depression (from almost three-fourths of the total in 1930 to only a few percentage points over one-half in 1940), climbed part way back during World War II, and then began a gradual decline that has made the GOP the state's minority party since 1954. In 1964, Democrats registered 56 percent of the state's vote.[12] Furthermore, Oregon citizens, who used to vote more Republican than they registered (whenever the party held together), no longer seem to do so with the same consistency; and Democrats have won their share of offices

cluding proportional representation authorization and a long corrupt practices act, passed in 1908. After 1910, the PPL offerings began to include proposals for increasingly drastic— "radical"— reforms; its four measures in 1910 included not only the presidential primary, which passed, but also a confusing judicial reorganization amendment (which passed), an amendment for complete reorganization of the legislature, with a proportional representation (which failed), and an amendment to establish a "Board of People's Inspectors," to publish findings in an *Official Gazette* (which failed). The 1912 PPL program included the "U'Ren Constitution," completely reorganizing the whole state government, abolishing the Senate, etc., which was roundly defeated. In 1914, a PPL measure for thorough legislative reorganization, with proportional representation, failed again, along with 24 more of the 29 measures on the ballot. It was of this election that the *Oregonian* editorialized: "It is Oregon's message to the world that the disastrous U'Ren epoch is passed." (November 5, 1914, p. 10.) After 1916 the PPL's influence and activities declined.

11. Governors George Chamberlain (1902 and 1906) and Oswald West (1911-15), Walter Pierce (1922), Charles Martin (1934); and Senators Chamberlain (1908) and Harry Lane (1913).

12. Democratic gains have been statewide, appearing in almost every county. By 1966, only seven of the state's thirty-six counties registered Republican majorities, and in all but two of these, Benton and Marion, the majorities were paper thin. Recent registration figures follow:

Year	R	% R	D	Total
1948	347,175	50.9	334,784	681,959
1950	361,158	48.8	378,357	739,515
1952	421,681	50.3	416,589	838,270
1954	402,283	49.9	404,694	806,977
1956	413,220	47.9	450,122	863,342
1958	413,659	47.8	451,179	864,838
1960	405,195	45.7	480,588	885,783
1962	395,351	45.4	475,561	870,912
1964	402,336	44.0	511,973	914,309
1966	412,884	45.5	518,749	950,659

lately, even winning both houses of the legislature in 1958 for the first time since 1878. But the Republicans staged a comeback in 1964 and 1966, gaining firm control of the House, a U.S. Senate seat, two congressmen, and retaining the governorship, despite superior Democratic registration (54 percent). Oregon accordingly now fully deserves to be classed as a two-party state in good standing. It seems very likely that the third-party proclivity that marked the Republican years has waned to the point of no return, and by all precedent, there ought to be resulting increased orthodoxy in Oregon's party behavior.

But despite the two-party renaissance, the legacies of the "Oregon System" remain, and it would be a serious error to ignore the fact that unalloyed party politics forms even today a lesser segment of Oregon politics in general than is true in most states. Except for appropriations, usually left untouched, it is a rare major measure that is settled in the state legislature alone, escaping the referendum. Important policy bills appear by initiative petition every biennium, to be settled by the largely nonpartisan politics of direct legislation. Further, the direct primary, jealously protected and zealously used by Oregonians, has made personality a matter of unusual moment in Oregon's partisan elections, and a party label on a candidate is not a guarantee of the candidate's faithful adherence to either party leadership or party doctrine. Nor is there any guarantee of the voter's loyalty.[13] The Oregon voter, schooled in classrooms built in the Era of Reform, continues to guard his right to be perverse on party matters, to nominate men at outs with party leadership, to split his ticket between factions in the primary and between parties in the general election, and to take issues that are close to his heart—like the sales tax or other tax bills, daylight saving time, liquor control, or the regulation of fishing—altogether out of party hands and directly into his own at the polling place. "Politics in Oregon" must mean as much the "politics of direct legislation" and the "politics of personality" as "the politics of party."

GEOGRAPHY AND RESOURCES

It takes no economic determinist to recognize the important degree to which Oregon politics has been shaped by economic factors. The peculiar characteristics of the society, from which the political pattern emerged, were substantially influenced by the state's geography. The state's location and resource base have always had much to do with the nature of its predominant political issues and the attitudes of its voters about them.

Throughout its early years, Oregon was nearly the most isolated of the states. Off the beaten track to California—and to almost anywhere else, for that matter—and virtually without gold, Oregon attracted immigrants who came only to settle and to work, with resulting unusual singleness of purpose and outlook. Since outside aid was far away in terms of distance or of time, local self-sufficiency was imperative and an inward focus of attention almost inevitable. Recent developments have swept Oregon increasingly into the national economic complex and enlarged drastically the local impact of national economic regulation, but the psychological effects of relative isolation remain. Distance from primary markets and production centers makes transportation policy a vital issue to today's Ore-

13. Recent political developments elsewhere in the nation make it worth speculating whether in this respect Oregon may not be a leader for American state and national politics rather than a laggard with a party system that still lacks "maturity." The recent election of John Lindsay as Mayor of New York City is only one straw in the wind of this very possible trend toward the "Oregon System" in the settled and mature East.

gon citizens as it was to their Populist forebears. The almost catastrophic effect of recent boxcar shortages—increasingly a problem since 1960—on the state's lumber and grain industries is enough to illustrate the dependence of Oregon on national transportation.

Internally, Oregon is divided roughly into a series of north-south belts by the effects of two mountain ranges: the Coast Range separates a narrow coastal plain from the valley of the Willamette River, which rises in the mountains to the south and flows due north into the Columbia at Portland; the higher Cascades in turn divide the Willamette Valley from the wide-reaching plateau country of eastern Oregon. The Cascades catch most of the ocean moisture that the Coast Range misses, and accordingly Oregon west of the Cascades enjoys a Mediterranean-type climate, moist and green in the winter, though comparatively rainless in the summer months, with very moderate temperatures. Eastern Oregon, by contrast, is largely dry country with somewhat greater temperature extremes; some degree of precipitation plus good streams for irrigation in the plateau and mountain areas of northeastern Oregon makes for some fine cattle, wheat, and other large-scale farming, but toward the southeast corner the land turns increasingly dry and barren, suitable throughout much of its large reach for sheep or nothing. The state's heart lies in the relatively narrow, immensely fertile Willamette Valley, in which two-thirds of all Oregonians live and in which the principal urban centers lie.

Despite its 96,981 square miles, almost equaling Illinois and Iowa together, Oregon is not blessed with a rich variety of resources. Its mineral wealth is almost negligible, and the state has depended in the past principally on three gifts that it has in abundance: agricultural land, timber, and its rivers. Farm produce led the Oregon economy until World War II, but since 1946, timber and lumber-based industries have been increasingly dominant. Its timber production has led the nation since the late 1930's; half of the nation's plywood and one-fourth of its softwood lumber come from Oregon. Almost half of the state's area is forested, and in 1964 timber-based industry employed more people than any other, using 48.7 percent of Oregon's industrial employees and providing 47.6 percent of its manufacturing payroll.

Since early settlement, Oregon's rivers have represented both a great resource and a problem. Once vital for transportation (and still important, especially the down-stream Columbia, which makes Portland the West's only inland and largest dry-cargo port, serving a huge hinterland), they now act as the state's only local source of power,[14] provide the irrigation necessary to much of its farming (especially east of the Cascades), make possible timber and food processing industries, and furnish a tourist attraction and recreational resource. But they are seasonally irregular by nature, having heavy winter and spring run-offs and a greatly reduced summer flow. Without artificial control by dams, floods have created havoc in the one season, and drought has done so in the other.[15]

Still heavily dependent on the products of its farms and forests, Oregon recently has begun to diversify its production somewhat. Manufacturing output tripled between 1939 and 1954 and increased 66 percent between 1954 and 1963,

14. Oregon's per capita consumption of residential electric power is two and one-half times the national average; 98 percent of this power is hydroelectric.

15. Floods have been traditional in January and February west of the Cascades and in late spring to the east, where some streams go dry in late summer. Both the Willamette and the Columbia have caused immense damage. The Columbia Flood of 1948 wiped out the settlement at Vanport, and caused damage above $100 million. The Willamette's Christmas Flood of 1964 was the worst disaster in Oregon history, causing $242 million damage.

and a modest rate of growth continues. Though much new industry is in food processing, lumber products, and woolen goods, a significant portion is now in other fields, especially aluminum (which takes quantities of cheap power) and electronics (which depends on literate, trainable labor rather than on heavy raw materials and which turns out products of high value relative to weight and corresponding shipping costs). Most manufacturing is centered in and around Portland and in the middle and lower Willamette Valley.

POPULATION

Like all the western states, Oregon has a history of population explosion, but, unlike most of its neighbors, its growth has slowed considerably during the last decade and a half.[16] The general mobility encouraged by World War II and comparative prosperity in Oregon brought the state's population from a million to a million and a half between 1940 and 1950, but immigration began to slow markedly in 1952, and Oregon finished the ten years ending in 1960 with an absolute gain of only 57 percent of that of the ten years before;[17] its growth since 1960 has been at a rate just above the national average, but below that for the other western states. The slowdown in the 1950's resulted primarily from a creeping decline in a farm- and lumber-based economy, when unemployment and income figures in Oregon, unusually favorable in the 1940's, looked less healthy than they did elsewhere in the nation. In the last few years, with revitalization of the forest products industry and some diversification in manufacturing otherwise, these trends have been emphatically reversed,[18] but immigration has not yet fully responded.

Oregon's population has historically been concentrated in the middle and lower Willamette Valley, increasing in density closer to Portland, at the Willamette's mouth. Multnomah County (in which most of the city of Portland lies) contains almost 30 percent of all Oregonians, and the suburban counties of the metropolitan area, Washington and Clackamas, another 13.5 percent. Most of the state's other principal cities, including second-place Eugene and third-place Salem, lie farther up the Willamette, though clusters of people live along the sea coast, up

16. Oregon had just over 50,000 people when it became a state in 1859, and over 400,000 by 1900. Its subsequent growth by decades follows:

Date	Population	% Annual Increase	Date	Population	% Annual Increase
1900	413,536		1940	1,089,684	1.4
1910	672,765	6.3	1950	1,521,341	4.0
1920	783,389	1.6	1960	1,768,687	1.6
1930	953,786	2.2	1966	1,907,000	1.3

17. Before 1950, in-migration consistently accounted for well over half of Oregon's population increase. Between 1950 and 1960, by contrast, net in-migration was responsible for only 13.6 percent of the state's growth.

18. Oregon's per capita income, as a percentage of the national figure, dropped steadily from 115.3 in 1947 to 99.3 in 1958. Since then, it has climbed again to 103.7 in 1964. The state's unemployment ran well above the national average between 1952 and 1958—reaching 9.1 percent in May of the latter year—but it has been consistently below the national rate since the beginning of 1959.

the Columbia, just east of the Cascades, and here and there in the more sparsely settled northeast. Within most counties the trend toward urbanization is apparent, as the rural population, over half of the whole in 1930, dropped to well under 40 percent in 1965.[19]

Sociologically speaking, despite recent immigration and urbanization, the Oregon population remains unusually homogeneous. Income extremes, though spreading, are still comparatively narrow. Racially the state is nearly all white—97 percent—with what amounts to handfuls of persons of Negro, Chinese, Japanese, Arabic, and Indian ancestry, largely clustered in Portland. Oregon directories indicate Caucasians from all parts of Europe, but except for a notable Finnish community—the largest in the United States—in the "salmon city" of Astoria, there are no real European "colonies" of consequence. In religion, the state is overwhelmingly Protestant, with a Catholic population of only around 10 percent and a very small Jewish community;[20] "fundamentalist" faiths are especially strong, with unquestionable political consequence. The literacy and educational levels are very high,[21] and the climate of opinion in the state has been traditionally favorable to academic freedom and encouraging to education generally.[22]

Two other factors in the composition of the population, age and sex, have political consequences in some degree. Like most other states, Oregon is short in people in the productive middle age brackets, made up of persons born in the small-family days of the depressed 1930's, and long in people at both ends of the age scale. By 1965 figures, less than half of all Oregonians were between 15 and 54, with roughly 30 percent—almost a third!—under 15, and 20 percent 55 or over. In sex distribution, the Oregon population since 1950 has been passing rapidly from the masculine domination common to a "pioneer" state, with heavy (and predominantly male) immigration, until in 1965 the state's women slightly exceeded its men in numbers.[23] All these factors have in the past tended to produce a pattern of economic conservatism and political individualism.

But the state is changing, as its shift from a Republican to a Democratic registration majority indicates. The social composition of the population was more heavily affected, probably, by the flow of immigration that almost submerged Oregon during and just after World War II than by any of the previous waves that have hit the state since the time of the pioneer migrations.[24] Continuing modifica-

19. Oregon, which had only two cities over 10,000 in 1910, now has 15. Even in the most sparsely populated of the state's counties, the rural population has declined and the urban population has grown in the last quarter century.

20. Catholics constitute 28 percent of Oregon's listed church members, against a national average of 40 percent; Jews make up but 2.2 percent against 6 percent nationally. Conservative and moral Oregon ranks very near the bottom among the states in church membership as a percentage of total population, probably because Protestants are not very good churchgoers.

21. The median Oregonian has completed 11.8 years of school—the ninth highest figure in the U.S. Oregon ranks second in percentage of population with at least five years of education, seventh with four years of high school, and third in the percentage of its population which is literate.

22. It never had a purgative oath for teachers. It has had, and has, its anti-intellectual fringe, but its public is generally respectful of education at all levels; Oregon voters, notably conservative about government spending, are usually somewhat more generous to school-support measures than to others requiring tax money. The state ranks sixth in per capita expenditures for education.

23. In several recent years, Oregon has had almost 150 male deaths for every 100 female deaths.

24. Large numbers of workers moved in to man the booming Portland shipyards during World War II; many stayed to work in urban industry or in the woods; more recently the

tions in the structure of the Oregon economy, acting to reduce steadily the proportion of the farm and village population and to increase the numbers of landless blue-and-white-shirt industrial and service employees, have tended to multiply the effect so begun, and they bid fair to do so even more in the future. Further social restructuring seems inevitable as the age pattern shifts—today's large group of senior citizens passing from the scene, the small class of middle-aged replacing them, and the huge mass of youngsters growing into youthful voters.

One further fact must be noted. The recent and continuing changes in social structure are not being felt equally in all parts of the state, and the resulting differential has consequences for the state's political behavior. A rapid survey of the state's disparate areas is in order.

The Portland Metropolitan Area. The Portland metropolitan area includes Multnomah County, in which most of the city of Portland lies, and the suburban counties of Washington and Clackamas.[25] Containing 41 percent of the state's population, the metropolitan area was long the victim of the state's principal gerrymander, and even now such underrepresentation as the state permits is felt principally in the city. Increasingly commercial and cosmopolitan, Portland is no longer an overgrown town. It is beginning to share with eastern cities the sociological results of the "flight to the suburbs" and other problems, and to take on a comparable social and political complexion. As in other metropolitan areas, Portland's city core and its suburbs are politically at some odds: in 1966, Multnomah County registered 61 percent Democratic, while Washington county registered 51.9 percent Republican and Clackamas County but 55 percent Democratic.

The Willamette Valley. It was in the Willamette Valley that the bulk of the pioneering farmers settled, and the Valley is still mostly diversified small farm and small city territory. Long the heart of Oregon's "black Republicanism," it is no longer "safe" country even for more moderate GOP candidates, and for full-blown conservatives it may be a wilderness; in 1964, Barry Goldwater failed to carry a county in it, either in the primary or the general election.[26] Industry and commerce are beginning to replace the area's long dominant farm interests, with obvious sociological and political effects.[27]

The Coast. Oregon's coastal region is largely oriented to its lumber industry, though fishing and dairy farming—Tillamook County makes a famous cheese—continue to be significant economic interests and the tourist trade is looking up. The northern coastal counties, near the mouth of the Columbia and historic Astoria, have had a fairly stable population, though the beginnings of industrialization and urbanization may soon change that fact. The counties to the south, particularly Coos, by contrast, have received large influxes of Southerners in the last

timber firms have been bringing in woodsmen, chiefly from the Democratic South, who are unlike the earlier agricultural settlers.

25. It includes also Clark County, Washington, just across the Columbia River, making Portland a two-state city. The two states' different tax patterns—Washington with high sales and cigarette taxes and Oregon with neither, but a high income tax—have encouraged some people to live in Clark County and shop in Multnomah. Until 1966, when a small cigarette tax finally won in the Oregon primary, store sales records *seemed* to indicate that the smoking rate in Clark County was less than one-fifth that in either Seattle or Portland!

26. Even Benton County, the home of Oregon State University and unique west of the Mississippi in having never voted for Franklin Roosevelt, went Johnson in 1964, although it remains Republican in registration.

27. The Valley's cities are beginning to reach out north and south along the straight Portland highway, to form the embryo of what will very probably become a 150-mile megalopolis not unlike those common in the East and in California. Portland is spreading east and west along the highway south of the Columbia, to form the crossbar of a "T."

two decades. Lumber continues to be the dominant interest in the southern counties, though the nature of this industry, and consequently of the people it employs, has changed considerably in recent years as the more sophisticated products of plywood and composition board have replaced the traditional bare lumber in the market. Long an area subject to boom and bust, the Oregon coast is still much affected by the vagaries of the building market, even though sustained yield harvesting of forest products has given it today a somewhat more even economic base, less touched by the effects of logged-out forests than in the past. Much work in the woods continues to be seasonal, with little logging in the winters; high seasonal unemployment rates, therefore, tend to persist. Businessmen in the area look to the Pacific, both to Japan and (though quietly) to China, for an expanding future in commerce. There is a strong push for vastly better access roads across the mountains to the interior so that the coast can serve, as it now cannot, as seaport for the entire state.

Once a Republican stronghold, the coast now shows a substantial Democratic majority in every county, with Coos a virtual stronghold. Democratic registration for the coastal area is now about 60 percent of the total.

The Central Southern Section. As an extension of the state's major valley, this area has much the same farming conditions as does the Willamette Valley, though the colder winters of the southern mountains make for somewhat more concentration on fruit crops. Lumbering and forestry are also important to this region, and accordingly the area is similar to the southern coast in that its population has been increased by fairly large numbers of migrants from the South. What it does not yet have is industry in quantity. The three counties which compose it, Douglas, Jackson, and Josephine, had a combined Democratic registration of 54.6 percent in 1964, but its voters are a different breed from those to either north or west. The farmers of the region, still little touched by industrialization, tend to be a good deal more conservative than their northern counterparts on questions like civil rights and labor legislation.[28]

Eastern Oregon. The broad, dry reaches east of the Cascades encompass more than two thirds of Oregon's land area and less than 15 percent of its population. The region's northern half is principally large-farm, wheat, and cattle country; potatoes and grains grow along the California border near the Cascades and along the Idaho border near the Snake; sheep graze the barren southeast corner; and scattered timber is found here and there. Eastern Oregon reacts nationally to farm (especially grain and cattle) and water-use policy, and on the state level to all urban-rural issues. During and since the Eisenhower years, it has turned Democratic (56 percent by registration in 1966) from a once close party balance. Always sparsely populated, it is growing less rapidly than any other part of the state; only along the Columbia, especially near new dams, is it keeping up. Its social composition has accordingly been more static, and unless new hydropower sources bring industry to it, probably Portland and the West will grow steadily apart from it in outlook.

NEWS MEDIA AND PUBLIC OPINION

As in most one-metropolis states, journalism in Oregon is largely dominated by the big city press. Historically, the Portland *Oregonian* has been by all odds the

28. Josephine has lately seemed to be becoming the conservative refuge in the state. It was one of four Oregon counties to favor Goldwater in the 1964 primary and, despite its

most important journalistic factor, and though the *Oregon Journal* (Portland's evening paper) seems to have been gaining in influence, the *Oregonian* retains its top position by a comfortable margin.[29] Of the down-state papers, the Salem *Statesman* and the Eugene *Register-Guard*, are the most influential, the *Statesman* in particular being accorded respect.[30]

On balance, the Oregon press is hardly a nonpartisan force. The *Oregonian* admits to being "an independent Republican newspaper," with a consequent usual partisan position, and the *Journal*, though it emphasizes its party independence more, normally finds Republican candidates most appealing. Indeed, throughout the state only three significant daily newspapers are consistently on the Democratic side—the Medford *Mail Tribune*, the *Coos Bay World*, and the Pendleton *East Oregonian*. Not surprisingly, the state's press as a whole leans toward the conservative in editorial policy, and both "liberal" measures and "liberal" candidates commonly find themselves fighting without much newspaper support.[31]

But the influence of the press in Oregon, though conceded to be considerable, is far from overwhelming, and both candidates and measures may win against it. Wayne Morse, journalistically treated throughout the state with a roughness amounting to rudeness, still won his way to the Senate in 1956 by almost as large a margin as that Oregonians gave to Eisenhower, and Dick Neuberger won a Senate seat in 1954 and Bob Holmes the governorship in 1956 with only a very few papers, all down-state, behind them. On questions of direct popular effect, like daylight saving time, liquor control, or local bond issues, the voters seem often to ignore the newspapers entirely.

One new element, if not added, has been expanded in the state during the past few years. Oregon's TV coverage of the the news is both good and extensive, and in the Portland area, at least, it is accompanied by better than average analysis, both national and local.[32] The consequent broadening of public interest and understanding is unquestioned.

NOMINATIONS AND ELECTIONS

Oregon's election system, by the standards of the western states, is pretty orthodox. Each biennium the state nominates by party primary the normal complement of state and some local officials, and by nonpartisan primary its judges,

Democratic registration majority, one of only two—barren Malheur being the other—to vote for him in November. In the primary, its Democrats produced the highest percentage for Alabama's Governor Wallace (by write-in) in the state.

29. The *Oregonian* was founded in 1861, and by 1902, when the *Journal* began publishing, it was already accepted throughout almost the entire state as "the family paper."

30. The *Statesman* is owned, published, and edited by ex-Governor Charles Sprague, whose editorial expressions are highly regarded and widely republished. Sprague, a Republican, has an independent and moderate point of view, and he does not hesitate to praise and support Democrats he believes to be deserving.

31. Edith Green, the Third District's Democratic congresswoman, has won both *Oregonian* and *Journal* endorsement against weak opposition in the last several elections, and a few other Democrats have sometimes gotten scattered press support. It needs to be noted that "reactionaries" receive no better treatment than do "radicals" in Oregon's journals, and even Barry Goldwater went without support from either the *Oregonian* or the *Journal*. The Portland papers lean gently toward the conservative, but they do not fall over that way.

32. Tom McCall, formerly Oregon Secretary of State and 1966's Republican winner of the governor's chair, was until his election in 1964 KGW-TV's news analyst. His replacement on KGW, Forrest Amsden, has by now won a sizable following of his own.

the state superintendent of public instruction, county superintendents of schools, and a scattering of city and county officials as determined by home rule. A voter who participates in the electoral act, if he is new, has moved, or failed to vote two years before, must register at least 30 days before the election; to register, a person must be 21, a U.S. citizen resident in Oregon for at least six months,[33] literate, and not mentally diseased, an idiot, or a convicted felon.

Oregon uses a typical closed primary, held the third Tuesday in May each even year. Any registered party member may file for nomination by his party for any partisan office for which he is otherwise eligible, either by simple personal declaration or by a petition signed by a specified number of registered members of his party.[34] Filing must take place at least 70 days before the primary, and "filing day"—the last possible day—is often an exciting time in Salem, as hopeful candidates wait each other out or jockey for position.[35] Minor parties[36] not eligible for primary participation may nominate by petition or by convention.

The Oregon presidential primary has its own twists that make it about as thoroughgoing as any in the country. Delegates to national conventions are chosen in the primary, two from each congressional district and the remainder at large. Party voters likewise express in the primary preference among the party's national presidential candidates, and delegates are pledged to support the voter's choice through at least two convention ballots unless the candidate releases them or fails to muster 35 percent of the convention votes on the first ballot. But the principal twist appears in a law adopted in 1959, under which the secretary of state, at his sole discretion, places on the preferential ballot the name of each willing or unwilling person whose "candidacy is generally advocated or recognized in national news media throughout the United States" unless that person files an affidavit stating that he is not and does not intend to become a candidate at all. Oregon primary voters are thus assured a wide range of choice, and they are happier about it than are the candidates, who *must* make a race of it or lose face nationally. The effects of this law on primary campaign costs, were it to be widely copied elsewhere, seem almost incalculable.

Other election procedures are less unusual. Oregon issues a sizable, state-printed *Voters' Pamphlet*, in which candidates and proponents and opponents of

33. Citizens may cast a ballot for President if they are residents by the day filing closes.

34. Generally 2 percent of the party's vote for President in the district involved in the last general election, but not over 1,000 for statewide office or congressman and not over 500 for other offices. Signatures must be geographically distributed according to formula depending on the office.

35. In 1960, for instance, several top Democrats reputedly waited to see if Mrs. Neuberger intended to file for the Senate seat but recently vacated by the death of her husband; when she did so, late on the last day, they filed for other offices, starting a chain reaction that affected lesser fry down the line. This sort of development is fairly common. The Ides of March 1966 saw the first working of a new law which requires candidates to file by numbered positions where there is more than one to be elected in the same constituency for the same office—principally seats in the state legislature. A candidate may change as many times as he wishes as long as he first withdraws his name from previous filings. The coup of the day was scored by a popular Republican incumbent in the State House: when his numbered position was shunned by lesser known opponents, he withdrew at the last minute and filed in another position for the same district, opposite those who had tried to avoid running against him. This action made it possible for a relatively unknown woman to file, by previous arrangement in his abandoned spot, in a safe Republican district. Since the primary is virtually tantamount to election, she was in effect coopted by her helpful colleague.

36. A "major political party" is defined by law as one receiving at least 20 percent of the vote in the last presidential election.

measures are allotted space—one of the earliest and most complete such publications in the country. Direct legislation makes the ballots relatively long, but not abnormally so, except in a rare year when an unusual number of state and local issues appears. The state permits the use of voting machines, and their use is spreading rapidly, especially in the metropolitan and other urbanized areas. Hand-punched IBM cards and machines to count the traditional paper ballots are being tried by some counties in the state. Hand counting in the past has often resulted in a slow count which has left a major race[37] in doubt for 24 hours or so after the polls close. Even when the results are tabulated, the totals are unofficial, compiled by the news media; the official tabulation is not completed for several weeks after the election.

The state's Corrupt Practices Law, early adopted, is strict, but as in most states, it is not easy to police.[38] It needs to be stated, though, that Oregon elections are unusually free from corruption, or at least corruption has been a very rare charge and one even more rarely proven. Most analysts, for good reasons or bad, have traced the comparative honesty of the state's elections to the general public attitude, more puritan than most; a hint of scandal brings a public outcry that comes from outraged virtue in the heart.

PARTY ORGANIZATION AND LEADERSHIP

Oregon's major parties in the 1950's and 1960's are in the midst of a state of flux that may be a mark of transition. Weakened almost to the point of no return by the developments of the Reform Era, their power made suspect and controls within them decentralized by the long period of one-party dominance, their internal cohesiveness repeatedly shattered by the persistent independence of the Oregon voter—they faced the recent dramatic appearance of two-partyism unsuitably organized to play much of an active role. Somewhat reformed and strengthened by 1959, each remains in large part today a loose and uncertain structure, providing principally a basis for grouping primary voters and a shadowy symbol to bind together diverse (and sometimes antagonistic) candidates who choose to run under it.

The coming of the 1950's two-partyism, for which changes in the social and economic structure had ploughed the ground, was certainly encouraged, if not made inevitable, by shifts in the orientation of state party leadership in the late 1940's. Both major parties in Oregon have historically had split personalities reflecting in microcosm national party schizophrenia, the result in large part of their origins in a pioneer state that got its earlier voters from elsewhere all over the nation. Geographic isolation and political insularity for long kept Oregon parties from changing rapidly to follow new national models, and even today both parties have an old-style core, veneered over by the new, with some puzzling results. An old-style Democrat may look like a new-style Republican and vice versa.

Thus Republicans throughout the state's early and middle years were always strongly tinged with the liberal colors of the Populist-Progressive movement.

37. Like the 1956 Neuberger-Cordon election, nationally watched because it decided control of the U.S. Senate, and unsettled for fully 24 hours after the polls had closed.

38. It limits personal expenditures by a candidate to 10 percent of the annual salary of the office for which he runs, with a minimum allowance of $250, and requires that he and every other person or political committee spending campaign money file a detailed statement showing contributions and expenditures. It forbids such practices as promising appointment, making payment, or using "undue influence" to gather support. Giving anything of value, even a match book, is illegal.

Through the 1930's this tinge persisted in strength, as party leaders like Charles McNary led the fight for Columbia River development and comparable programs. But in the late 1940's, as Oregon's society was beginning its own remodeling, Republican leadership slipped into the hands of men like Douglas McKay and Guy Cordon, archetypes of the classical conservative. The new party leadership essayed some partly successful housecleaning of liberal members shortly thereafter, virtually forcing Wayne Morse from the ranks after the Eisenhower nomination in 1952 and disposing of such men as Homer Angell, long-time labor-backed congressman from the Third District, defeated in the primary in 1954.

Oregon's Democrats, meanwhile, had a very spotty record until the 1950's. As much as the Republicans, the Democrats were split by their origins and early history, for the party was born among southern immigrants and steadily reinforced by new waves from the South. Meanwhile, as a decided minority offering small chance of victory to its aspirants, the state's opposition party for years found only an occasional respectable candidate willing to run, and the party's leadership in the 1940's had won a reputation for incompetence, corruption, and even debauchery; many of its candidates were far more conservative than their Republican opponents. Not until the postwar Republican reorientation did a group of determined young men, spawned by the New Deal, arise to remake the party's image. Monroe Sweetland, who won as national committeeman, Howard Morgan, who became state chairman, Multnomah County's Alfred Corbett, and others took over internal Democratic control shortly after 1950, and by 1954 the transition began to pay off in respected new candidates as Dick Neuberger became Oregon's first elected Democratic senator since 1914 and Edith Green, the first Democrat sent by Oregon to the national Congress in over a decade. In 1956, newly Democratic Wayne Morse disposed of Douglas McKay as Richard Neuberger had of Cordon, Democrat Bob Holmes won the governorship, two of the remaining three congressional districts went Democratic, and despite the loss of the state's electoral vote to Eisenhower by 55.3 percent, the party generally had a field day.[39]

This debacle made a shambles of the Republican organization. Criticism by younger Republicans, barred from the party's policy councils, often even at county level, was rife, and reorganization to match the Democrats was obviously in order. It came after 1958, under the soaring banner of thirty-five-year-old Mark Hatfield, who took the gubernatorial nomination from the conservative wing's Sig Unander and went on, with a highly personal campaign,[40] to win the election from Holmes by a percentage equal to Eisenhower's two years before. Although Hatfield, elected to the U.S. Senate in 1966, is now the party's recognized public figure, he has not molded a cohesive party unit by personal direction, preferring

39. The only statewide offices the Republicans salvaged were those of secretary of state and state treasurer, won by Mark Hatfield and Sig Unander, respectively. Though both were relatively young, Unander was by all odds the more conservative.

40. Hatfield virtually ignored the party organization. His campaign deliberately emphasized the nonpartisan needs of the governorship. His advertisements contained no mention of the Republican party, and he did not encourage the entry of supporting national party figures into the state, at least after an early speaking appearance by Vice President Nixon that led to adequate campaign contributions.

This pattern has become almost standard for rising liberal Republicans, as its reverse has for Democrats. Tom McCall, Republican (and thus minority party) candidate for governor in 1966, avoided party labels wherever possible; his Democratic opponent, Robert Straub, made much of them. McCall's well-financed campaign paid off when he won the office by carrying all but three of Oregon's thirty-six counties.

apparently to be "above politics," exerting influence on the party through intermediaries. This fact has left something of a vacuum within the party and an absence of cohesion among its three major elements, the radical right, responsible conservatives, and young liberals. Nevertheless, it is the last of these groups which seems to have caught the rising star in Oregon politics, as in an earlier, Populist day.

Indeed, the "new Progressives" have emerged in the '60's as an impressive array of young and aggressive leaders. The emergence has had its geographic center in the Portland area and its ideological origins among the Young Republicans, though Mark Hatfield's consistent election as a liberal surely provided some of the inspiration. In any case, these newer and younger figures in Oregon Republicanism have for several years shown an unusual capacity for recruiting attractive candidates, promoting them, and even raising some money for their use. This active recruitment and support is generally regarded as the principal factor behind Republican success in winning control of the Oregon House of Representatives in 1964 for the first time in a decade, and increasing their margin two years later. The divisive thrust of the radical right among the Republicans in 1964 resulted in placing some of the more responsible conservative party elements in a position of supporting the new young leadership, and it may well be that the threat from the right has brought some Republican cohesion behind the party's left. Certainly the party presented a united front in 1966 and evidenced a marked resurgence.

Democratic leadership, meanwhile, like that of the too-successful Republicans before it, appears nearly to have broken apart in personal controversy under the pressure of victory. Since the death of Dick Neuberger, Wayne Morse and Edith Green are the strongest Democrats, with Congressman Robert Duncan and State Treasurer Robert Straub rising behind them, but neither has widespread control of party machinery as such.

Duncan lost the Senate race to Hatfield, and Tom McCall, the Republican secretary of state, defeated Straub by a wide margin in the 1966 gubernatorial contest. Some old-line conservative Democrats are back in the limelight—and worse, coalitioning with Republicans in the legislature and elsewhere—and not all the Young Turks are satisfied with the party's position. The party's internal cohesion seems badly in need of rebuilding, but at the moment the unifying force does not appear in sight. The sizable Democratic registration majority led to more complacency than the party, as party, could easily stand; and the Democrats have not yet demonstrated that they can so dominate the state that their unity is of little moment, as the Republicans did before the war. They proved that internal division and inferior organizational and financial resources spelled defeat in 1966.

Oregon's formal party organization, largely specified by law, itself makes the unified use of party difficult. The national committeeman and committeewoman are chosen in the statewide primary, but the rest of the structure is hierarchical, rising from an unrepresentative geographic base. Precinct committeemen and committeewomen, locally elected, form the county committee in each of Oregon's 36 counties and choose the county chairman and other officers; county chairmen and vice-chairmen form the State Central Committee, insuring its control by the party's rural elements.[41] Among both Democrats and Republicans, conflicts between the State Central Committee and county committees, espe-

41. To illustrate, Eastern Oregon's eighteen counties hold half the State Central Committee's voting strength. Little Sherman County, with a static population of 2,300, is represented equally with Multnomah.

cially in populous Multnomah, have been traditional,[42] and the state organization has enjoyed only such powers as prestige might bring and county committees choose individually to recognize.[43] Further, conflicts have developed regularly between national committeemen and state chairmen, chosen by very different constituencies.

In any event, the great bulk of candidates for high and middle posts in Oregon form their own campaign organizations for primary battles and continue them through the general election. Party funds, especially with the Democrats, are limited and used mostly to support the state organization and to campaign in a limited way for the party's whole slate. Only occasionally does a candidate depend heavily on party workers as such and receive significant support from party coffers. The independent behavior of top officeholders suggests they will not help in the organization of a stronger party and in fact, have resisted efforts to do so. The most significant party functions are those of insuring that all proper voters register and turn out to vote.[44]

PRESSURE GROUPS

Oregon's interest groups, like those of other states, vary considerably in size, strength, and methods, but as elsewhere they are constantly active and the number of them that are well organized has steadily grown. Among economic groups, agriculture (speaking particularly, though not exclusively, through the Grange), and lumber are especially strong. Labor's power (organized in such unities as the AFL-CIO and the Central Labor Council of Portland) has expanded considerably with the industrial explosion since World War II, especially in the Portland area; and the general voice of industrial and commercial ownership and management has increased in volume too. Railroads and truckers exert the considerable pressure to be expected in a geographically large state that imports and exports a great deal. The voices of commercial fishing interests are still heard but much less plainly than they used to be, and sportsmen, tightly knit in the Isaak Walton League and the Oregon Wildlife Federation, often overpower them now. Liquor, horse- and dog-racing, theater, and similar interests are present and ever-watchful. Professional associations like the AMA, the Bar Association, and the organizations of accountants, social workers, and so on, have increased their organized pressure markedly in recent years, sometimes reaching a high enough pitch for effective-

42. Under County Chairman Robert Jordan in 1958 and 1959, for instance, Multnomah's Democrats nearly parted from the state organization entirely over such issues as the division of funds raised by high-priced dinners held in Portland with speakers like Truman.

43. Monroe Sweetland as Democratic National Committeeman in 1950 used great power gained from control of national patronage from a Democratic president to force state party reorientation, but in other times, with two Democratic senators and three congressmen to satisfy, no such power has been available to the office.

44. The Democrats lately have been trying, with limited success, to expand the party's role through fairly extensive use of a State Executive Committee. Beginning in 1960, the Democrats have conducted in each election year a "platform convention" to prepare a document intended to serve as a guide to party candidates and voters; the Republicans have followed a similar procedure but on an unofficial basis, holding in each recent election year a "Dorchester Conference" in an effort to articulate a "Republican" position. It is problematical whether the voters pay any attention to either party's documents. The Democrats (particularly in Multnomah County) have sometimes attempted to get candidate commitments to their platform, and at one time or another each party has tried to utilize a pre-primary endorsement to penalize those who have refused to go along. These efforts have generally failed, being widely labeled as "boss-ism," a strong disapprobation in Oregon.

ness; the Oregon Education Association (representing the public school teachers), as will later appear, is sometimes called the most powerful lobbying group in Salem. Veterans are organized, as everywhere, but seem less active than in most other states. "Idea" groups, like the Oregon Council of Churches, the WCTU, the League of Women Voters, and the Federation of Women's Clubs consistently take positions on measures and occasionally on candidates.

Lobbyists are not required to register in Oregon, but they do prepare a voluntary list themselves. For good reasons or bad, or for no reason at all, Oregon lobbyists are generally respected by legislators, the press, and each other. The public, meanwhile, appears to be generally unaware of their existence at all. Careful avoidance of scandal has kept the system largely from afflicting the public eye, and the rare lobbyist caught *in flagrante delicto* is likely to attract the ire of his peers accordingly.

Because of the importance of direct legislation in the state, Oregon pressure groups are faced with a double task: not only must they keep a careful eye on the legislature and a hand in its operations, frequently they must gird their loins for a battle at the polls. The more powerful of them are well set up, on a standing basis, for the former of these functions, working (though sometimes surreptitiously) for the election of "right candidates" and maintaining active, party-throwing lobbyists during legislative sessions;[45] the less powerful appear on call, so to speak, when their welfare is at stake. For the second function, influencing the public when a "final decision" at the ballot box is at issue, they are likely to operate with all stops out either directly, or, more commonly, behind the scenes; popular legislation, after all, represents a direct battle among interests, without the intervening influence of party or legislative structure. Interest groups often are the driving force behind an initiative or referendum petition at the outset.

Among economic groups, the Grange has historically been especially active and influential. Since well before its performance of a central role in the establishment of the Oregon System, the Grange has taken a dynamic part in Oregon politics. Far from limiting itself to matters directly affecting farm interests, the Grange has involved itself in a wide variety of issues, both in the legislature and out. Today Grange influence seems on the downward path, as Oregon's farm population gives way to a preponderance of urban residents, and lumbering and other industrial, commercial, and professional interests grow in size and authority. Grange voters alone can now be overwhelmed on issues settled by direct legislation; and Oregon's new reapportionment system, though it continues the overrepresentation of rural counties somewhat, has reduced drastically the power of rural constituencies in the legislature. A new alignment of dominant interests is obviously in the making, with lumbering, labor, education, and transportation emerging as the apparent "big four."

EDUCATION IN POLITICS AND VICE VERSA

In the past few years, meanwhile, as these four voices have been working their way forward in the interest-group choir, no voice in the quartet has strengthened more rapidly than that of education. As indicated earlier, Oregonians have always been concerned with educating their young, and the Oregon record on schools has not been at all bad. But until very recently the state's teachers have

45. Some of Oregon's underpaid legislators amplify their income by serving as "representatives" for professional and other interest groups, being permanently retained as legal counsel or in other association office.

been mostly decorous in their political behavior, pressing school boards and the legislature through organizations like the Oregon Education Association and the American Association of University Professors chapters in a generally genteel way; board members and legislators have responded in kind. Pressures from educational interests, however, have lately grown, generating more vigorous counter-pressures, and the field of educational politics now looms as a battleground for especially strident conflict.

Structurally, Oregon education is organized much as elsewhere in the West, with a few important variations. Public higher education, involving some seven institutions,[46] is controlled by a single nine-member appointive Board of Higher Education, which employs a chancellor as its executive officer; the chancellor's staff has grown lately and is now quite substantial, reaching into most functional areas of administration. The single-board structure has resulted in the transference of most inter-institutional politics from the legislative halls to the chambers of chancellor and Board; matters ranging from division of the single-budget appropriation and assignment of building priorities to curricular allocations are regularly settled by Board decision on recommendation by its executive. Only occasionally does the legislature actively insert its authority in detailed internal State System affairs, as it did in 1955 in directing the establishment of Portland State College and as it has done more recently in appropriating special funds for graduate work at that institution. State System academic people are sometimes of two minds about the system, and occasionally those at one school or another threaten or try direct appeals to friendly legislators, but for the most part they fear the possibility of stimulating a habit of legislative interference more than they hope to gain from it. Accordingly, their approaches to the legislature are usually pretty well disciplined and directed toward the support of unified and agreed-upon budget and program requests—especially for salary improvements—submitted by the Board.

The lower public schools, as almost everywhere, are organized in school districts and largely controlled by local elective boards. Oregon's record in enlarging its districts and thus reducing their numbers is fairly good, and there are now only a few districts in the state too small for efficient education; some, like District No. 1, Portland, are very large. A state Board of Education, with members appointed by the governor, sets only broad teacher certification and other standards. Sharing its limited authority is the state superintendent of public instruction, an elective officer; a constitutional amendment to give the Board authority to appoint its own executive was voted down by the people in 1966 after a quite bitterly contested campaign. In any event, power over the lower schools is obviously in the hands of the local boards, and it is in their chambers that the great part of school politics takes place.

One good measure of the importance of education in Oregon politics is surely the amount of money spent on schools, and it is considerable. The public schools are largely supported by local property tax funds, but even so, over half the state budget—53.5 percent in 1967-68—goes for items included under "education,"[47] and another 6 percent is dedicated to "relief" of local property taxes,

46. The University of Oregon (Eugene), Oregon State University (Corvallis), Portland State College, Oregon College of Education (Monmouth), Southern Oregon College (Ashland), Eastern Oregon College (LaGrande), and Oregon Technical Institute (Klamath Falls). These institutions generate their own local support, of course, introducing factors of regional politics at both Board and legislative levels.

47. Altogether $315 million, including $155 million for basic school support, $127 million for higher education, $15 million for community colleges, and lesser amounts for

three-fourths of which are in turn for schools. Direct state support for local schools is the largest single item in the state budget, taking over 25 percent of the total, but it furnishes only about a third of local school support. It is distributed to local districts by a complicated formula that takes into account the relationship of the numbers of school-age children to the amount of taxable property, an arrangement that Portlanders believe results in siphoning off their state income-tax money to subsidize poorer areas. Both the amount of state support and the formula are subjects of great dispute, and Oregon politics is the fuller for them. Among the more significant ramifications of the school-support struggle since 1966 has been the real threat of an initiative petition to limit local property taxes drastically—perhaps to 1.5 percent of market value—the success of which would force either drastic upward revision of state support, with radical side-effects on the rest of the state budget, or widespread reduction of schooling.[48]

Oregon teachers and administrators in higher education lobby and otherwise politic with chancellor, Board, and legislature. Their counterparts in the public schools do the same with local superintendents and boards and the legislature.[49] They have been organized for the purpose for many years, but both organization and means seem to be changing.

The changes are most noticeable in the public schools, and particularly in those of Portland. The traditional agency of teacher action in Oregon has been the Oregon Education Association,[50] with its Portland affiliate the Portland Association of Teachers. The OEA has never been primarily an agitation organization. Historically its focus has been on "teacher services," like the provision of information on educational trends and the holding of conferences on subject matter and method. It has for years maintained an active lobby at the legislature—sometimes called the most powerful lobby in Salem—and its local chapters, especially the PAT, have spoken for their members before local boards. But it has never been militant in the labor organization sense, at least never until lately.

What has brought about, or at least threatened, metamorphosis during the last four years has been the American Federation of Teachers, AFL-CIO, through the Portland Federation of Teachers. The AFT's success in the East has not been matched as yet in Portland, but the rapid recent rise in the PFT's original tiny membership has quickened the pulses of the PAT, the Portland Board, and the Oregon legislature alike. The PAT and the OEA, with the great majority of Oregon teachers still supporting them, have been, probably, the biggest guns behind teachers' recent gains in Oregon, but the PFT has triggered their actions.

Increased teacher activity has taken several new forms. Under pressure, the state legislature in 1967 passed a Teacher Negotiation Law which allows direct negotiation with school boards on salaries and working conditions—an undreamed of practice as recently as four years ago; labor-management practices are

such items as the School for the Blind and Deaf, the Department of Education, and the State Library.

48. In the fall of 1967, the threat appeared so imminent that the legislature was called by Governor McCall into special session to deal with the problem of property tax relief. After three weeks of dispute over state tax measures to provide the necessary money—repeating the debates of the regular session of a few months earlier—the legislature adjourned without action.

49. Oregon teachers at all levels engage in broad political action among themselves and with their institutional administrators, and this internecine exercise of and struggle for power is increasingly vigorous and overt. It is, however, beyond the scope of this study.

50. An affiliate of the National Education Association. The OEA had in 1967 some 24,000 members.

now developing in Portland and elsewhere. Teachers are now permitted by law to engage actively in politics, and many are doing so; to facilitate the practice, the OEA recently organized a "political arm," supported by voluntary contributions. Though Oregon law prohibits strikes by public employees, the PFT talks openly—and loudly—about strike use in Portland, matching that in eastern cities, if teacher demands are not met, and even the OEA today concedes the validity of a strike call if "conditions of severe stress cause deterioration of the educational program" when "good faith attempts at resolution have been rejected." Teacher revolt meeting tax revolt in the last years of the 1960's may make for some fascinating fireworks.

Meanwhile, there are some new and unusual rumblings in the ranks of higher education also. The volume is as great as that heard in the public schools, but the tune is somewhat different. Oregon has never supported its colleges and universities in the manner that the academic people would like—aspiring mostly only to hold its own in the middle of the pack and lately slipping even from that modest goal—but it has done reasonably well most of the time. Accordingly, college teachers have commonly pressed their personal interests through administrators, buttressed by the reasoned tones of the AAUP. Now, with the state hit on the one side by the depressing effects of a housing decline and on the other by the strident cries of local property-taxpayers and public schools, college faculty have talked some of unionization, strikes, and general militancy to bring support levels "back to parity and on to excellence"—but they have done little else.

It is on another front that faculty, and especially younger ones, have exploded: bidding rather for power inside the institutions they serve. The college battles of the last few years have been real and very earnest, but they have swirled principally around such issues as curricular policy, recruiting on campus, protests, and pornography, and the right to set policy on these matters. As a result, they have been directed more at college administrations than at Board and legislature. Why salaries have been neglected in the movement to militancy is moot: perhaps college teachers *are* more interested in "principle" than profit; perhaps they *are* more professionally oriented than their public school brethren. Or perhaps they are just practicing—girding their loins for the larger battle against the forces beyond the campus. In any event, there are uneasy sounds from some of Oregon's more conservative legislators, anti-educational rumblings that may indicate that the pleasant days of gentlemanly diplomacy may be ending.

LEGISLATIVE POLITICS

Since the adoption of the initiative and referendum amendment, the "legislative department" of Oregon's state government is something more than bicameral; it consists, says the Oregon Supreme Court, of "two separate and distinct lawmaking bodies." The department operates, says the Court, in ways "different from before—one method by the enactment of laws directly, through that source of all legislative power, the people; and the other, as formerly, by their representatives."[51] Legislature and people are thus co-equal legislative organs, each able to make, repeal, or modify law on its own. Legislative politics in Oregon applies to both, and interest groups must gear their machinery of influence accordingly.

Oregon's Legislative Assembly consists of a sixty-member House of Representatives, with a two-year term, and a thirty-member Senate, with a four-year

51. *Straw v. Harris*, 54 Or. 424, 430 (1910). See also, *Kalich v. Kapp*, 73 Or. 558 (1914).

term. It meets biennially, in January of odd years, for four months or so; its members draw salaries of $250 per month plus $20 a day for the first 120 days during the session.

As in all states, legislative apportionment in Oregon has been a knotty problem of political power, frequently fought over. The Oregon legislature is not perfectly representative of people in numbers, but it is as nearly so as in any state. The state constitution provides for decennial apportionment of each house by counties according to population, adding that a county with over half the necessary ratio for the appropriate house shall have a seat therein; one that fails to muster this number shall be attached to some adjoining county or counties for senatorial or representative purposes.

For many years the rural counties, especially in eastern Oregon, were able to maintain a "silent gerrymander," preventing legislative reapportionment action of any consequence from 1910 until after 1950, while the forces of urbanization brought radical shifts in the balance of population. In 1952, however, the preponderant urban vote, in the one-to-one balloting of direct legislation, pushed through an amendment for "automatic reapportionment,"[52] specifying meanwhile (until after the 1960 census) a legislative composition that remedied in part the accumulated errors, increasing representation from Multnomah and other urban counties and reducing that from the rural back country. Fearful and frustrated farm folk tried in 1952 for drastic revision, offering by initiative an unsuccessful amendment for a "federal" system representing counties equally in an enlarged thirty-six-member Senate; a similar proposal was given a resounding 62 percent "No" vote in 1962. The 1961 reapportionment with minor revision in 1963 places the Oregon House and Senate as close to perfect population apportionment as any in the country. To carry apportionment reform to the national level, a 1965 change in the boundaries of Oregon's four congressional districts resulted in a discrepancy of less than 9 percent in the most malapportioned district; this one, southwest Oregon's Fourth District, is only 38,007 votes below the optimum 442,172.[53]

The party organization of the legislature still carries over the effects of the many years of one-party dominance. Until the 1950's (except in rare sessions in the 1930's) both houses were so overwhelmingly Republican[54] that partisan con-

52. The amendment requires that in the absence of legislative action by July of the session year following a census, the secretary of state shall by August 1 file a plan with the governor. The State Supreme Court is given original jurisdiction to compel the mandatory action or to review the plan presented by the legislature or by the secretary of state, ordering a redraft if necessary. This system seems as "automatic" as any in use in the United States and calls for the largest judicial participation found in any state except, perhaps, Arkansas.

53. The redistricting of 1965 was designed principally to remedy the discrepancy that resulted from the fact that Multnomah County, the Third District, had grown to include 30 percent of the state's population and the northwest's First District had likewise increased; while eastern Oregon, the Second, had declined proportionately. The struggle over details was more personal than party: Congresswoman Edith Green, happily occupying the seat from solidly Democratic Multnomah, disliked losing the overwhelming Democratic eastern part of the county; Al Ullman, Democrat from eastern Oregon, wanted to add precisely that area or nothing; Republican Wendall Wyatt, from the First District, opposed any loss of the Republican part of the Willamette Valley, to leave the Democratic northwest coast dominant in his constituency. In the final compromise, the Republican western corner of Multnomah went to the First District, which gave up Republican Marion and Democratic Linn counties to the Second—a victory for Mrs. Green, a stalemate for Mr. Wyatt, and a slight loss for Mr. Ullman.

54. As recently as the 47th Session in 1953, the House was controlled 49-11 by the Republicans and the Senate, 26-4.

siderations were virtually ridiculous; and in the early 1960's when the Democratic renaissance brought about a nearly balanced body, its procedures took little account of party. The House once again now has a Republican majority, while the Senate is still nominally in Democratic hands. But a coalition of Republicans and conservative Democrats continues the pattern of cooperation in that body which has existed for the past decade. Formal caucuses play little role, even for organizational decisions, and the presiding officer (though by mutual understanding a member of the majority) is elected by a personal vote that does not follow party lines.[55] Committees are appointed and their chairmen chosen by the presiding officer, who may or may not consult other party leaders on the matter. Each party has its conservative and liberal legislators; members on both sides normally behave, debate, and vote as individuals, irrespective of partisan considerations, and are treated as such. Democrats—what there were of them—were frequently assigned committee chairmanships during the era of Republican dominance, and a Republican may be accorded the same recognition under Democratic organization.[56] "Party responsibility," legislatively speaking, is strictly a euphemism in Oregon.

Working conditions and staff for Oregon legislators can only be described as miserable. Each member is allowed one secretary (often his wife). He has little other staff support, although most of the committees usually employ some professional help, at least on a part-time basis. The Legislative Council is a highly qualified bill-drafting agency, but it, like the committees, is understaffed. A legislative fiscal officer is appointed by the legislature to provide some independent information about the budget.

The popular half of Oregon's "legislative department" is nonpartisan altogether. As vital a force in the state's law making as the legislature, its one-person-one-ballot voting formed a counterweight to the state's gerrymandered apportionment during the years before 1952, and it still serves this function, with less need, now. The reapportionment amendment was achieved by initiative petition and popular vote, after decades of legislative inaction.[57]

Oregon's direct legislation program is extensive. It permits the initiative, the referendum by the legislature, and the referendum by petition. An initiative petition requires the signature of 8 percent of the legal voters for a measure or 10

55. In both the 1963 and the 1965 sessions, the Democrats, who enjoyed a two-to-one Senate majority, were unable to elect as president the choice of the Democratic caucus; in each case, a coalition of Republicans and conservative Democrats pushed through instead a conservative Democrat from east of the Cascades—in 1963 from Hood River and in 1965 from Klamath Falls.

The results have been of a good deal of consequence in committee appointments, a matter often decisive for major legislation and especially for appropriations. As a potent illustration, the 1965 legislature's Emergency Board (a body of nine legislators authorized to act for the whole legislature between sessions in making emergency appropriations up to a several-million dollar total) included not one member from the Portland metropolitan area or from one of the larger cities of the Willamette Valley and not one who could be classed as a liberal. Five members were appointed by the Republican speaker of the House and four by the Democratic president of the Senate.

56. For many years the Senate used thirty committees—for 30 senators!—and each member, Republican or Democrat, got one committee chairmanship, with the accompanying perquisites in secretarial aid and so on. Walter Pearson, president of the Senate in its 1959 session, appointed Republican Tony Yturri chairman of the important Interim Committee on Highways, with resulting outcries from some Democrats.

57. This was also the case in Washington (1956), Colorado (1932), Arkansas (1936), and several other states.

percent for an amendment; a referendum petition takes 5 percent only.[58] Excepted from the referendum are bills tagged by the legislature as "emergency measures"; the legislature's discretion[59] in this regard is limited only in that it may not so treat "any act regulating taxation or exemption." To permit time for referral, non-emergency measures of the legislature do not become effective for ninety days after the end of the legislative session; those passed at the polls become law as of election day.

Oregonians have used their direct legislative power pretty freely. In the 62 years from 1903 through 1964, they had dealt with 452 statewide bills (including 241 constitutional amendments). Of this total, though 201 came during the first two decades—an average of 20 per biennium—more recently the number at each election has been held to more manageable proportions, usually 10 to 14. Almost half the 62-year total have been submitted by initiative petition, though the proportion of initiatives has fallen dramatically since the experimental days of the great Reform Era, and today legislative submissions are more common.[60] Not surprisingly, perhaps, adoption records, especially lately, are a good deal better for bills referred by the legislature itself than for those initiated or referred by petition.[61]

The measures that have adorned the Oregon ballot have dealt with almost every sort of issue, from the banning of cigarette sales to the prevention of picketing, from Sunday closing to the direct primary, cabinet government and the compulsory retirement of judges. Some areas of controversy have become old and familiar battlefields to the voters; legislative compensation, income, sales, and cigarette taxes, the regulation of liquor and fishing, and aspects of local home rule have had an almost constant ballot spot.[62] Some issues have opened up for awhile

58. The numbers required are reduced in fact by the definition of "legal voters" as those who voted for justice of the state Supreme Court in the last election. The number of those voting for the office of justice in any election usually comes to less than 75 percent of the ballots cast. No one may be paid for signing *or* for collecting signatures. Signatures must be those of qualified voters, but they do not have to be legible, says the state Supreme Court: "Many of our best citizens habitually sign their names in a form illegible to anyone not familiar with their writing, and it would be unreasonable to deny such voters the right of referendum because of their chirographical idiosyncrasies." *State ex rel. Hill v. Olcutt*, 62 Or. 217, 219 (1912).

59. The Constitution (Article IV, section 1) defines an emergency measure as a law "necessary for the immediate preservation of the public peace, health, or safety." The state Supreme Court will examine a bill to see if it involves taxation, but otherwise it regards the decision involved as purely legislative, adding that "the courts have no more right to distrust the legislature than it has to distrust the courts." *Kadderly v. Portland*, 44 Or. 118, 150 (1903). The legislature has often been criticized for declaring emergencies in law where none existed in fact.

60. Initiatives, 196; legislative referrals, 206; and referrals by petition, 50. The over-all decline since 1932 has been almost entirely in initiatives, from an average of 11.7 per biennium to 3.2. Legislative submissions have remained fairly steady at something over six, and referrals by petition at less than two.

61. Altogether, only 33.2 percent of all initiative bills have passed, and only 38 percent of those referred by petition, against 58.3 percent of those the legislature has submitted. In the period after 1923, adoption percentages are but 27.8 for the initiative, 30.3 for referrals by petition, and a spectacular 62.3 for legislative submissions. Proportionately more amendments have passed (51 percent) than statutory measures (37.9 percent)—not surprising since *all* amendments must be submitted to popular vote and only more controversial statutes are likely to be. Between 1944 and 1964, 62 percent of all measures passed, in marked contrast to earlier years.

62. The sales tax has been on the ballot five times since 1933 and been defeated by votes between 63 and 83 percent. The cigarette tax in six tries in 36 years also lost each time, though by lesser margins; in its seventh appearance in 1966 it finally won. Amendments to raise legislative pay failed ten times before passing in 1946; after another success in

and then died down (as with veterans' legislation after the two world wars and daylight time from 1950 through 1962); others have but shifted their focus (as with taxation, from the single tax to the income tax to sales and cigarette taxes and back to the income tax again). But always there is variety.

The politics of direct legislation in Oregon is as intense as its counterpart in the legislature. However law is made, the same interest groups are affected by it, and they involve themselves equally, if in different ways.

Organization is a first imperative, particularly in a state in which payment for petition-hawking is forbidden. If an existing organization can be interested and used, it is: the Grange, the Council of Churches, the Oregon Wildlife Federation, the State Federation of Labor, University (and other) Alumni Associations, and countless standing business and professional organizations have actively sponsored or opposed proposals affecting or of interest to their members. If no such potent organization is handy, or if it is better left undercover, a special organization may be created; the Oregon record is full of an astonishing assortment of associations, leagues, and committees bearing such exalted titles as the "Oregon Tax Reform Association" (for exemption on personal property, 1908), the "Oregon Merchants Legislative League" (for the "punchboard bill," 1940), the "Affiliated Milk Campaign Committee" (for milk control repeal, 1952), the "Highway Protection Committee" (for billboard control, 1960), or "Salmon for All, Inc." (for limitations on commercial fishing on the Columbia, 1962). Most hotly contested issues have found special organizations of this sort springing up on both sides: the "Eight-Hour League" sponsored the eight-hour day in 1914 and the "Non-Partisan League" fought it; the "Taxpayers Equalization League" proposed the School Moving Bill of 1932 and the "School Tax Saving Association" opposed it; the "Public Welfare Education Committee" supported the pension bill of 1950 against the "Needy Aged Persons Referendum Committee"; the "Workmen's Committee against Unfair Practices" battled for the workmen's compensation amendment of 1964 against the "United Citizens for Sound Government."

Very often interest groups directly concerned have buried themselves in a special organization of this sort. Liquor, ice, and soda water interests have hidden—with others doubtless more disinterested—in such societies as the "Equal Right to Home Industry Committee" (1916), "Common Sense, Incorporated" (1940), the "Citizens 317 NO Committee" and "Let's Tell Them the Truth Committee" (1950), and the "Buy Less than the Bottle Committee" (1952). Commercial fishermen have worked through such groups as the "League in Opposition to Water and Fish Bills" (1928) and the euphemistically named "Oregon Fish Protection Association" (1942). Private utilities have hidden in the "Association to Preserve Oregon's Credit" (1932) and the "Oregon Electric Consumers' Council" (1958). "Big business" masked itself behind the protective façade of the "Associated Farmers of Oregon, Incorporated," to sponsor and campaign for the strong Anti-Picketing Bill of 1938.[63]

Groups involved in fights over issues employ all the campaign tactics of politicians running for office. Not a medium of mass communications goes unused.

1950, legislators were disappointed three more times before finally winning constitutional authorization to set their own salaries in a light vote at the primary of 1962.

63. This group was supported by business interests. Richard Neuberger charged (and apparently no one bothered to deny) that of over $40,000 spent in support of the Anti-Picketing Bill, $4.65 was contributed by farmers! "Liberalism Backfires in Oregon," *Current History*, Vol. L (March 1939). See also Neuberger, "Who Are the Associated Farmers?" *Survey Graphic*, XXVIII (September 1939), 517-21.

Before election time, Oregon billboards blossom, newspapers burst with ads and inspired stories, speakers address audiences wherever found, radio and TV are alive with paid commercials. The organization with money hires a professional campaign manager. The poorer group does without, and limits its activities to those possible with volunteer workers.

Some sponsors of proposals on the ballot have borrowed techniques from successful legislative manipulators in their attempts to secure support in the popular half of the Oregon legislative department. The ancient and honorable legislative tactic of logrolling, for instance, has on more than one occasion found its way into Oregon's elections, sometimes successfully and sometimes not. Generally direct legislation logrolling has taken the form of tying none too popular programs onto others that have solid support among certain segments of the population. Income, sales, and cigarette tax measures have thus been coupled to old age welfare, educational support, or property tax relief,[64] both by the legislature and by private sponsors of initiative bills. Pro-gambling forces have sought "outside support" by tying proposed gambling revenues to pensions. By way of turnabout, perhaps, anti-gambling elements used a sort of reversed form of this same tactic in 1952 in running a bill "Prohibiting Lotteries, Book-making, [and] Pari-Mutuel Betting"; lotteries and bookmaking have been prohibited in Oregon for years!

Another not uncommon tactic in Oregon's direct legislation politics had been the use or threat of the "backfire bill," employed by a group endangered by petition to obscure the issue or to threaten its opponents in turn. Thus fish-netters and fish-wheelers petitioned each other nearly out of existence in 1908. The income tax was repeatedly (and successfully) met in the 1920's by the use of competing bills designed to divide the affirmative vote.[65] Trucking interests faced with statutory bills increasing truck taxes came up with their own bills in 1926 and 1952; and both pro- and anti-liquor forces have several times brought backfire bills to the ballot.

VOTING HABITS

As repeatedly indicated earlier, Oregon voters are an independent lot, likely to follow their own course against a national trend or, indeed, to seem to go on diverse routes at a single balloting—galloping off, like Stephen Leacock's notorious knight, in all directions at once. Though they have not lived in a one-party state for fifteen years, they still tend to act as if they did in the attention they give to personality and to issues over party.

Whatever the influences that activate them most, they *do* register and vote in fairly large numbers, and Oregon regularly has ranked respectably near the top among the states in voter participation. As everywhere, participation falls off down the ballot: almost everyone who goes to the polls votes for the Presidency, and nearly the same number ballot for the governorship or the national Senate; lesser state offices attract 85 to 95 percent and judges often as few as 65 percent. Participation on measures varies within similar extremes depending on the subject: the average bill over the past 62 years has received attention from just under

64. The sales tax, passed by the Legislative Assembly in 1935 and referred, was made the sole support of the old-age pension program; pension funds were transferred to "relief." The cigarette tax in 1945 was tied to educational support, the sales tax in 1947 to school, welfare, and "governmental" purposes, and the cigarette tax in 1966 to property tax relief.

65. The Grange graduated income tax bill of 1922 was met by one calling for a flat rate, and that of 1926 by one with a property tax offset.

80 percent of those appearing at the polls; but one on a matter close to the popular heart—the sales tax, liquor control, or daylight time—will be marked by 90 percent or over (more than the vote for attorney general), and one on a dull question of governmental procedure may draw even fewer votes than a judgeship.

It is in dealing with candidates carrying party labels that Oregonians get perverse. They long voted more Republican than they registered, as the charts indicate (note especially 1950: Democratic registration increased, as did the Republican vote), and even now they do so more often than not; yet they gave the state's electoral vote four times to Franklin Roosevelt, by sizable majorities, and a Democrat who appeals to them may sweep the state. In the Populist-Progressive tradition, they are more affected by personality and by issues than by party—yet what two men seemed more apart in personality and point of view than Dwight D. Eisenhower and Wayne Morse? Oregonians on the same day in 1956 gave 55.3 percent of their vote to Eisenhower for the Presidency, and 54.3 percent of it to Morse for the U.S. Senate! And in 1962, to prove the constancy in their inconsistency, they voted 54 percent for Senator Morse and 56.6 percent for his arch-rival, Governor Mark Hatfield.[66]

What, then, guides them as they place their X's on election day? Looming large for major offices, certainly, is the candidate's public image, created through the press, the platform, and TV, compounded of his apparent character and wisdom and the plausibility of the positions he expounds.[67] It is not coincidental, surely, that the farther analysis goes down the ballot, into the lesser local posts where candidates are faceless and unknown, the more the pure effect of party appears; a Republican coroner sweeps Republican precincts, whatever his personality or point of view, and his Democratic opponent wins wherever his party has the registration edge.[68] Offices not worth the large expense and heavy effort the creation of an image demands *do* go by party ballot. The split tickets that characterize the ballot's top stand out the more sharply for the contrast.

But whatever his behavior in treating candidates, in dealing with measures the Oregon voter comes into his own. To be sure, he has taken some admittedly unfortunate actions during his six decades of experience,[69] but in all honesty it is difficult for anyone but the most violent partisan to hold, after full review, that he has done so often. And his obvious mistakes have been soon rectified, by himself or (with his tacit approval) by the legislature.

If there is any characteristic that marks the whole Oregon direct legislation record, it is moderation, carried sometimes to the point of caution. With very few

66. In 1956, Eisenhower lost in only four of Oregon's thirty-six counties, and Morse in but seven. Wallowa County, one of the thirteen left with a Republican majority that year, was the *only* county in which the Democrats carried their entire slate. In 1962, Hatfield won in all but three counties and Morse in all but six.

67. Explaining Wayne Morse is among the more popular pastimes of Oregon analysts, for Morse regularly wins big, while the other candidates he vigorously endorses lose badly more often than not. Most plausibly, even the large number of Oregonians who disagree with Morse's point of view applaud the way he "stands up to those politicians in Washington," something most prickly Oregonians would like to have the ability—and the courage—to do. Senator Morse is likewise meticulous in his attention to the individual problems of constituents who ask his help.

68. In populous Multnomah County, party slates regularly win. Frequently fellow-party members of nearly opposite images and points of view receive vote totals that are almost identical.

69. As in the "hold-up" of University appropriations in 1912, the passage of an outlandish pension bill in 1948, and the rejection (twice in the last 15 years) of routine transfers of surplus funds.

exceptions, it is impossible to find any extreme departures achieved by the people's rule, unless the features of the Oregon system are themselves regarded as extreme. Independent-minded conservatives the folk of Oregon were when they approved the initiative and referendum so overwhelmingly in 1902; independent-minded conservatives they have remained in their use of the instruments of the people's power. The U'Ren constitution, cabinet government, the abolition of the Senate, the Board of People's Inspectors, the single tax, proportional representation, University moving, the discontinuation of military training, relaxation of medical standards—even the sales tax, the establishment of the post of lieutenant governor, school consolidation, and making the superintendent of public instruction appointive: all these have gone down before the Oregon electorate in cautious mood.

Moderation in almost everything. If the Anti-Picketing Law placed restrictions on labor, other successful measures have given workers increased freedom. If punchboards have been abolished, pari-mutuel betting has not. If the state-store liquor system has been retained, prohibition has been rejected. If appropriations for public power development have been sometimes refused, so was the private power bill of 1948. If People's Utility Districts (for power sales) have been accepted, public railroads and banking have been turned down. And if (in the 1966 primary) the voters refused to make the office of superintendent of public instruction appointive rather than elective, they then voted for the moderate incumbent who advocated appointment and against the extreme conservative who opposed it. Neither radical nor reactionary can point with much pride to the Oregon record in proof of effective operation. And only radical or reactionary can find in that record much to view with alarm.

IMPACT OF NATIONAL POLITICS AND TRENDS

Oregon's coincidental impact on national politics has been greater, surely, than the size of the state's population would justify. It has also, sometimes, been different from what Oregon voters themselves have intended. The Oregon habit of voting "the man" rather than "the party" into office has made a kind of sense in state politics not so easily transferred to Washington, D.C. Accordingly, what has appeared locally as sturdy independence, with the emphasis on moderation and imposition of purely personal responsibility on officeholders in Salem, has sometimes seemed to contribute on the national scene to political confusion compounded. To be sure, Oregonians themselves have had reason for some confusion when confronted with national elections, for in terms of national party politics, their decisions have not been easy, and a shifting environment has caught them up in emerging demands very different from those felt by their forefathers.

Traditionally, as earlier indicated, Oregonians have directed their principal interest toward their own domestic political affairs. The original settlers came to Oregon territory in order, or at least not unwilling, to live alone and in self-sufficiency; their continued isolation, coupled with the effects of their environment in an agricultural economy and rural society, confirmed their original bent and inclined their children after them. But progress (still regarded by some old-timers as the root of most, if not all, evil) brought them willy-nilly out of themselves. Increasingly the nationally integrated, industrial, corporate-type economy of the twentieth century has forced their concern to national policy in a number of areas, e.g.: (1) transportation development and regulation, a vital matter to an isolated state that depends substantially on the sale of heavy products, like lumber, in a national market; (2) the control of monopoly pricing of industrial goods, for long almost entirely imported into Oregon; (3) agricultural marketing, especially in wheat and cattle; (4) hydroelectric power development, Oregon's principal hope to escape the "economic colonialism" of the raw-material producer and to participate in the full benefits of an industrial economy; (5) national water policy, with particular emphasis on the protection of local water resources for present and future local use; (6) the encouragement of housing, upon which the health of the lumber industry largely depends; and (7) the promotion of foreign trade, to the benefit of Portland's fine and active port and producers shipping through it.

The appearance of these new demands helps to explain the apparent communal schizophrenia of the Oregon electorate in national politics. In almost exclusive part (except, perhaps, where the reservation of the state's water is concerned), Oregon interests, as state interests, call for action, not forbearance, by the national government: in railroad regulation, road building, and the improvement of navigation; in trust-busting; in farm price support; in public power construction; in housing aid; in trade promotion. Yet on principle, federal action goes against the Jeffersonian grain of the old settler and frets the *id* if not the *ego* of his descendant. Most Oregon voters feel pulled two ways, and enough of them try to vote in both. The results are to be seen in the succession of Oregonians in Congress—the stream of populist and progressive Republicans; conservative McNary, leading the fight for public power; maverick Morse (impeccable in his attention to local needs); the independent-minded, middle-of-the-road liberal Neubergers; Edith Green, in the forefront of the fight for federal aid to education; the other Democrats voted to the House in the 1950's while Eisenhower swept the state and Republicans dominated state executive offices; and lastly young liberal Hatfield, sent to tilt with a Democratic administration. These appear in the Oregonians' eager if skeptical search for some "partnership power plan," to let them eat their cake and have it too; in their ambivalent reaction to housing bills, reciprocal tariffs, and federal road programs.

It is hard to see Oregon turning back from its awakened or awakening concern with national affairs. Surely the state will become increasingly a cohesive part of the nation, economically and otherwise, and as it does so its citizenry will be more American, less Oregonian. Already there are compelling indications that the introversion of the past is gone from large citizen groups; Portland is less parochial by far than most eastern cities, and purely national questions of foreign policy, segregation, and so on incite interest and action in Oregon urban centers everywhere; Vietnam has been the overriding popular issue since 1966, in Oregon as much as elsewhere, and marches in Mississippi or riots in Watts or Chicago or Detroit excite lively debate on either side of the Cascades. The interest is generally sober and the action deliberate, it should be added, and though Oregon fringe groups on both sides are sometimes loudly vocal on national as on local questions, they seem to produce no great effect, politically or otherwise. The state's elected leaders do not give way before them, the Oregon press ponderously condemns them, after due time, and the great body of people view them with a cold eye. To this point in time, the broad Oregon view on national matters, however compounded, has been that of moderation.

So we return full circle to the starting point. As a stable folk, the Oregon citizenry was born; a stable folk, independent in its conservatism, conservative in its independence, it remains. Under the pressure of its shifting present, its future may belie the record of its past. But most Oregonians will greet the change, however golden be its hue, with an acceptance not unmarred by regret.

UTAH:

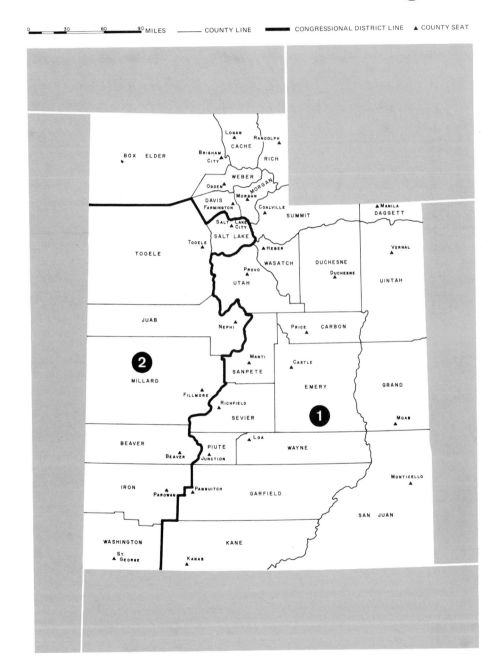

Frank H. Jonas

The Different State

In most respects the history of Utah is the history of the early western frontier with its succession of explorer, trapper, and home-seeker. Unique, however, was a new religion, commonly called Mormonism,[1] in the founding of a commonwealth. Soon after Mormon pioneers entered the Great Salt Lake Valley on July 24, 1847, in Mexican territory, they established a government which was a pure theocracy, a complete fusion of church and state, the utilization of one set of institutions for both ecclesiastical and civic affairs. The discovery of gold at Sutter's Mill on January 24, 1848, and the signing of the Treaty of Guadalupe Hidalgo ten days later, necessitated the re-establishment of a responsible civic government, since the territory was now American and thousands of gold-seekers traveled it. Consequently the Mormons created the State of Deseret in March 1849.[2]

The peace and prosperity evident under this government ended on September 9, 1850, when President Millard Fillmore signed the bill which created the Territory of Utah. Brigham Young, the Mormon colonizer, was made governor; he left office in 1857.[3] The conflict between Mormons and the Gentiles[4] which had already reached a breaking point became "so bitter and prolonged that the Mormon-Gentile complex on occasion still divides the state."[5] At least five attempts were made to enter the Union before statehood was granted in January 1896.

THE POSITION OF THE MORMON CHURCH
IN UTAH POLITICS

Relations between the Mormons and the Gentiles, with the federal government on the side of the latter, had been strained to a breaking point by 1857, the year when Johnston's army came to Utah and the Mormons retaliated, the year of

1. From April 1830 to May 1834, the name of the Mormon church was "The Church of Jesus Christ." In April 1838 it became the Church of Jesus Christ of Latter-day Saints. The popular name, Mormon, now unofficially approved by the church leaders, comes from acceptance and use of the scriptural Book of Mormon; the terms Mormons or Saints will be used throughout this chapter to designate members of the Church of Jesus Christ of Latter-day Saints.

2. See Dale Morgan, *The State of Deseret* (monograph), *Utah Historical Quarterly*, VIII (April, July, October 1940), 65-239. "Deseret" is a typical Mormon word.

3. Former United States Senator Elbert D. Thomas (Utah, 1933-51) used to relate that Brigham Young, with the traditional American concept of separation of church and state strongly in mind, sat on one side of his desk in the morning when he did state business, and then moved his chair to the other side when he did church work in the afternoon.

4. The term "gentile" is commonly used by Mormons to designate all who are non-Mormons, irrespective of their religious affiliation.

5. See William Mulder, *The Mormons in American History* (Salt Lake City: Bulletin of the University of Utah, Vol. 48, January 4, 1959).

the ignominious Mountain Meadow massacre. Tensions developed and grew in intensity in the decade 1860 to 1870. There is ample evidence to support the conclusion that the Mormon church dominated the political scene during this decade.[6] Church leaders were able to influence and manipulate the nominating and electoral procedures in the Territory. Indeed, many candidates came from their hierarchical ranks. In selecting nominees for public office, the Mormons voted almost unanimously for those selected by the church leaders. In this period not a single candidate who was selected or approved by them failed of election.

There was some opposition, however: sometimes a small number of members would refrain from voting for a particular candidate, and occasionally, there were write-in or scratch votes. In the 1858 election, a Mormon-Gentile coalition sought to run a candidate outside the "regular ticket." Although this coalition received very few votes, the effort was significant because it was the first organized opposition which developed in the Territory.

As the mining industry grew, non-Mormons were attracted to the state. More came in with the building of the transcontinental railroad.[7] In 1870, the Liberal (anti-church) party was organized by the Gentiles, while the People's party represented the church. The next year the newly established newspaper, the Salt Lake *Tribune*, developed a violent and somewhat vicious anti-Mormon policy, which it continued almost unrelentingly for fifty years.

Female suffrage, long a practice under Mormon hegemony, was done away with by the Gentiles. Test oaths were required of polygamists. Polygamous marriages were dissolved and children disinherited by force. Property worth millions at the present value of the dollar was sequestered by the government. The confiscation of homes and real property seemed necessary, apparently, to force a rival group to conform to the dominant social customs of those persons who had at their disposal the power of the federal government. Politically the two sides had aligned themselves under party banners.

National political party organization did not begin in Utah until 1872. The first Democratic club was organized November 12, 1884, and the national Democratic party, known as Sagebrush Democracy, was introduced in 1888.[8] Shortly thereafter the People's party disbanded (in 1891) as did the Liberal party two years later. The People's party had always elected the territorial delegates who sat on the Democratic side of the House of Representatives. When the party was disbanded, the church leaders, in order to enhance Utah's chances for the achievement of statehood, undertook arbitrarily to divide the membership into two parties. Several methods were used. Sometimes a church leader from headquarters in Salt Lake City attending a stake conference[9] would ask for an arbitrary division

6. See Ronald C. Jack, "Political Participation in Utah before the Formation of Political Parties, 1847-1869" (Master's thesis, University of Utah, 1967), pp. 113-15; election data by counties are found in the Appendix.

7. The Union Pacific and Central Pacific joined lines at Corrine, Utah, in 1869. Now almost a ghost town, it is slated for a centennial celebration to commemorate the driving of the "golden spike" which memorialized historically the completing of the transcontinental railroad.

8. For the growth of parties, see Stewart L. Grow, "The Development of Political Parties in Utah," *Western Political Quarterly*, XVI (September 1963), 39-40; G. Homer Durham, "The Development of Political Parties in Utah: The First Phase," *Utah Humanities Review*, I (April 1947), 122-23; Charles C. Richards, *The Organization and Growth of the Democratic Party in Utah, 1847-1896* (Salt Lake City: Sagebrush Democratic Club, 1942).

9. A 'stake" is a geographical and administrative unit, analogous to a Catholic diocese; it comprises several operating units called wards. It is presided over by a president and

of the audience down the center aisle, or an organizer might visit a small town and go from door to door assigning party membership.[10] On rare occasions, a member might express the desire to remain a Democrat, or would refuse to become a Republican.[11]

Since statehood could be achieved only by conforming to national law, the church was forced to abandon its tenet permitting plural marriage. This was made official in a pronouncement issued in 1890 by the president of the church, which became known as the Woodruff Manifesto. The church's abandonment of polygamy, the reduction of its economic power and political influence removed some of the barriers, and led to the achievement of statehood in 1896. Thereafter, politics in Utah melted gradually into the national pattern, and lost the greater part of its former distinctiveness.

From statehood to 1904 Mormons and non-Mormons shared the membership of Utah's congressional delegation.[12] The Republican party became dominant in a political development which included two factors, the advent of Reed Smoot on the scene as a political leader and a senatorial candidate in 1902,[13] and the 1904 National Democratic platform, which contained a blistering anti-Mormon plank. However, one cannot discount in any way the previous efforts of Mormon church leaders to "create" the Republican party and thereby establish the two-party system in Utah.

Party struggle continued unabated from 1902, when finally Utah slid into the Republican column by narrow margins, until 1912. By 1912 the American party, organized to fight Reed Smoot and the Mormon church, dissolved, and by 1916 Smoot's supporters had been thoroughly routed, chiefly by failure at the polls. The principal struggle was between Thomas Kearns and Smoot for control of the Republican party.

Thomas Kearns, Catholic millionaire mine owner, had become United States senator in 1901 with the help of President Lorenzo Snow of the Mormon church; when he could not obtain the same cooperation from Snow's successor, Joseph F.

---

two counselors assisted by a council of twelve men. The ward, analogous to a Catholic parish or a Protestant congregation, is presided over by a bishop and two counselors. The Mormon church has been described by G. Homer Durham, "Administrative Organization of the Mormon Church," *Political Science Quarterly*, LVII (March 1942), 51-71; and by John A. Widtsoe, *Priesthood and Church Government, 1939* (now in reprint, Deseret Book Store, Salt Lake City).

10. On one occasion an organizer from Ogden visited in Huntsville, the birthplace of David O. McKay, the present president of the church, to make the division. The story, told by Ernest McKay, a cousin, was that two McKay families, related through the mothers and not the fathers, were next-door neighbors. The organizer first visited Ernest McKay's family home. His father was an ardent Jeffersonian Democrat; he wanted to remain a Democrat. The organizer was amenable; he said that he would make the next house Republican. This was the home of President McKay's family. According to the venerable church leader the story was true, and he went on to add, "We were all ashamed in that day to be Republicans. There was only one in Huntsville and he was the town drunk."

11. The organization of the Mormon church is a mixture of democratic and authoritarian elements. Obedience is an archstone of church practice. The Saints almost invariably do what they are asked to do. This is still true to a large extent. Alternative actions or procedures to accomplish an objective are usually not considered and, above all, are not debated by the members.

12. Two of the four senators who served in this period were non-Mormons (one was a Catholic). The two others were inactive Mormons, one of whom subsequently joined the Episcopal church.

13. Smoot held the position of Apostle in the Mormon church, one of its highest offices, and was elected U.S. Senator in 1902 in which post he served until 1933.

Smith, who favored Reed Smoot, he faced defeat for re-election in 1905. Angry, he bolted the Republican party, encouraged the American party, bought the Salt Lake *Tribune*, and hired an apostate Mormon (Frank Cannon) as editor. Cannon and Kearns conducted an unprecedented campaign of vilification and vituperation against Smoot, Smith, and the Mormon church.

At the same time, Smoot's right to assume the seat which he won in 1903 was challenged; the proceedings in Washington, D.C., in the effort to unseat him became very bitter and acrimonious. The grounds for the challenge, subsequently disproved, were that Smoot was a polygamist.[14]

After Smoot was allowed to retain his seat in 1907, he became the Senate's great front fighter for a high tariff policy. The church had abandoned its policy of discouraging its members from engaging in mining. It developed the sugar beet industry as well as others which welcomed a protective tariff. The tariff became practically the sole and only real issue in the state in politics from statehood until the advent of the New Deal in 1933.

At home, Smoot gathered close to him a group of federal officeholders known as the "Federal Bunch"—sometimes derisively called the "Federal Gang." This group operated with skill and finesse from 1903 to 1910, winning at least three-fourths of the American party members back to the Republican fold. [15] Smoot used both his party and his church as vehicles to "deliver" his state to the GOP. Until 1916, according to the biographer of Smoot's political career, "God, the church, the Republican Party and Reed Smoot were all on the same side."[16]

The next four years formed an interlude of Democratic ascendancy to power and influence in the state. In the 1916 election campaign the Democrats were overwhelmingly successful. Woodrow Wilson received the state's presidential vote; Simon Bamberger, a Jew and wealthy businessman, became governor; William H. King was elected senator and the two elected representatives were also Democrats. The 1917 state legislature was overwhelmingly Democratic, and the Democrats won all five elective state offices.

From 1920 to 1932 the political scene became relatively quiet. Prohibition enforcement and the chronic depression in agriculture received considerable attention. In this decade William H. King twice defeated his Republican challenger, Ernest Bamberger, a wealthy nephew of the Governor's, who had become the GOP standard bearer in 1922 and 1928 with the aid of the Sevens Club, a secret

14. Smoot had never "taken a second wife," yet the charge remained that he was a high official in an organization which still condoned plural marriage. Although the church had disavowed the practice in 1890, it prevailed until 1904 when the church again, and finally, disavowed it. Even so, some plural marriages were consummated in Mexico until 1912 when the Mormons were driven or fled from that country. See Stanley S. Ivins, "Notes on Mormon Polygamy," *Western Humanities Review*, X (Summer 1956), pp. 229-39. Plural marriages are still performed and practiced clandestinely in Salt Lake and Davis counties and in Arizona without knowledge and sanction of the Mormon church, which considers such cases as adultery or bigamy. The one is against church rules and when exposed it brings excommunication; the other is the concern of the state and when prosecuted leads to a prison sentence and separation of families. The figure for Salt Lake and Davis counties (which may be a high since it is produced by anti-Mormon sources) is estimated at 20,000 persons living in a polygamous state.

15. R. J. Snow, "The American Party in Utah: A Study of Political Party Struggles During the Early Years of Statehood" (Master's thesis, University of Utah, 1964).

16. See Milton Merrill, "Reed Smoot, Apostle in Politics" (Ph.D. dissertation, Columbia University, 1950), p. 217. See Frank H. Jonas (ed.), *Bibliography on Western Politics* (Salt Lake City: Institute of Government, University of Utah, 1950), for published titles on Reed Smoot.

Republican political organization, led and dominated by non-Mormons. This period was also characterized by an effort to balance party tickets with Mormons and non-Mormons. In additon to the election of Senator King, the Democrats also placed George H. Dern, a Mason, in the state house as governor in 1924 and 1928.

The fact that the Sevens Club opposed Charles R. Mabey, governor from 1921 to 1925, for re-election in 1924 and supported Dern was to prove costly to the Republicans in 1928. The Sevens Club was made an issue by Republicans as well as Democrats. Mabey, J. Reuben Clark (who had an enviable national record in the U.S. State Department), and others deserted the Bamberger Republican campaign. Some prominent Republican leaders actually asked Republican voters to vote for King.

Also, the two congressional seats were divided in this period, not by party but by religious affiliation. Republican Don B. Colton, a devout and loyal Latter-day Saint, remained the representative in Utah's largely agrarian First District from 1921 to 1933. In the Second District, the seat was held successively by two non-Mormon Republicans during the same period.

Without his political machine, which had disintegrated by 1912, Smoot barely survived his re-election campaign in 1914, when he faced the electorate under the new constitutional provision for the direct election of senators. Smoot did not have an attractive political personality, but fortunately for him neither did his Democratic opponent, James H. Moyle, a distinguished lawyer, a loyal Mormon, and a founder of the Democratic party in Utah. While Smoot had displeased some voters with a boastful manner and sometimes with colorful language considered unseemly because of his high church position, Moyle remained somewhat aloof from the voters, creating the impression that he was arrogant.[17]

Smoot no longer needed a machine to win (1920 and 1926) in a nationally Republican era. He had built his reputation into a legend by cultivating an image of indispensability both to his church and to Congress as an expert on the tariff, a wizard of finance, and a hard worker who devoted himself unceasingly to detail and who kept his nose to the congressional grindstone, laboring continuously for his constituents. Except for four years of Democratic rule in the state, Smoot had served in eras of Republican administrations and had run for office with national Republican tides (except in 1914 and 1932) going with him. He was always a loyal practicing Mormon and a regular Republican.

His personality had more influence in Utah politics from 1920 to 1932 than did the Mormon church. The key to his personality was business, as it was to the personality of Heber J. Grant, who became church president in 1918,[18] and who for many years was a Democrat in his personal politics. Smoot finally won Grant

17. Moyle must be considered one of Utah's all-time political leaders. He became assistant secretary of the United States Department of the Treasury under Woodrow Wilson and U.S. Customs Collector under Franklin D. Roosevelt. Having been a Democratic candidate for public office and party officeholder on several occasions, he served his church in its early history as a capable lawyer, and just prior to the New Deal, as president of its Eastern States Mission. At his death in 1946, he was a millionaire but still a regular Democrat in good standing with the Mormon church.

18. With the death of Joseph F. Smith and Thomas Kearns in 1918, the personal symbols of a bitter political feud came to an end and opened the way for Grant, the new church president, and John Fitzpatrick, the publisher of the Salt Lake *Tribune*, to come together and assume conciliatory roles with their respective groups. Actually the conciliatory process had begun as early as 1911 (the American party won its last election in 1909) and many prominent citizens—Mormons, Catholics, and Masons—worked for a more peaceful political and business community.

over to the Republican party with the advent of the New Deal. The church leadership generally held capitalistic and conservative views. An analysis made in 1922 indicated that "the most influential men of [the] Mormon priesthood are businessmen and thus place a high value on pecuniary ideals and methods," and there was a growing tendency to take sides with the capitalistic class and with large corporations against the laboring classes.[19]

Toward the end of his career Smoot could count more heavily on many Gentile businessmen than he could on some members of the Council of Twelve (the governing body of the Mormon church). Smoot's political career and his relationship with the Mormon church has been summarized succinctly:

> Reed Smoot received some support from the Mormon church in the furtherance of his political career. The mere fact that Smoot, the Apostle, was permitted to engage in politics on the scale he did constituted an approval which may have had some political value. Throughout his senatorial years he received the unqualified and usually enthusiastic aid of two Mormon presidents who served during that time. He never received equal loyalty from other members of the hierarchy, and he frequently met determined opposition from certain of them. Except for the election of 1926 he never received on his own account a substantial majority of Mormon votes, and in all probability he received a minority of such votes in 1902, 1914, and 1932. It could not be said at any time that Smoot was the senator of the Mormon church, in the sense that he got the church vote.[20]

Actually independence characterized the Mormon and Utah vote during the Smoot era, a fact all the more remarkable because Smith, the Mormon church president during the first half of it, not only let his Republican views be known publicly in print but personally considered Smoot's remaining in office as the "will of the Lord." This independence was demonstrated in 1932 when Smoot, supremely confident and considered unbeatable,[21] lost decisively to a University professor, Elbert D. Thomas.

Smoot's crushing defeat marked the end of an era of Mormon church influence in politics, though its leaders apparently were not to realize this fact until the 1936 election, when the church thought it could influence the voters by a public announcement of its position. Angered and alarmed by Senator Smoot's defeat, the repeal of prohibition, its loss of tithing revenue, and the flocking of its members to federal relief and public works payrolls, it issued an open endorsement of the presidential candidacy of Republican Alf Landon.[22] This endorsement was to brush off negatively on all Republican candidates in Utah. Prominent life-long Democratic Mormons remonstrated with President Heber J. Grant, who took full credit for the statement.

In the elections from 1932 to 1944, inclusive, the church did appear to support only Republicans for high office, in spite of the fact that in each instance the Democratic nominees were either nominal or active Mormons, some of them having held high local administrative and general auxiliary organization positions in the church. All the Republican church-supported nominees lost at the polls. After

19. Ephraim Edward Erickson, *The Psychological and Ethical Aspects of Mormon Group Life* (Chicago: University of Chicago Press, 1922), pp. 22-79.

20. Merrill, *op. cit.*, pp. 216-17.

21. John Fitzpatrick, publisher of the Salt Lake *Tribune* and a practicing Catholic, told prospective candidates not to oppose Smoot since Smoot was invincible. Fitzpatrick's approach was different, but his objective was the same, to keep Smoot—a Republican—in office.

22. This endorsement was in the form of a statement which appeared on the front page of the *Deseret News*, the widely circulated official Mormon church news organ. As an immediate consequence, the paper lost thousands of subscribers.

their defeat they returned to their church ecclesiastical or church-compensated positions or were subsequently called to important new ones.[23] In most cases, these were mission presidencies, evidence of their high standing in the organization, and the basis for the assumptions that they had at least its tacit and unofficial support during the election.

During this same period, the Democrats held majorities in both chambers of the state legislature. A political pattern developed which can best be illustrated by the following incident. Walter K. Granger, mayor of Cedar City and a Mormon bishop, was elected to the state House of Representatives. He became the speaker. In his first two capacities he had on his hands a great many unemployed. Farmers were hard hit by the depression. They could not pay their debts and property taxes; there were many foreclosures. As a member of the legislature Granger worked hard to get an enabling statute passed which would permit the state to accept grants-in-aid from the federal government. He was met with solid Republican and Mormon church, and some Democratic, opposition. Two politically minded apostles of the church called upon him. One, a Republican, threatened him with the loss of his position in the church if he did not comply with its request that he not support his own legislation to bring federal economic relief to Utah. However, the other apostle, a former active Democratic candidate for the gubernatorial nomination (1916), delivered courteously, without any threat, the message to Granger that the Brethren were not pleased with his legislative behavior. There were several instances of this type of approach by the church to members of the legislature but none prevailed, nor was any legislative majority persuaded from its proposed course of action.

In the area of relations with the state legislature the influence of the church had waned. "Dominated" by Herbert B. Maw, a state senator for ten years, the 1937 legislature was the most liberal in the state's history. However, Maw won the gubernatorial Democratic nomination from a church-favored candidate[24] and was elected governor in 1940 over a full-time church employee. On the other hand, the 1939 session chose a church-owned property, from among several alternatives, as the new site for the state prison. It was rumored that church influence prevailed in this instance: however, the selected site was also the logical one. Another incident involving land occurred in 1947, when the legislature, this time with Republican majorities in both houses, designated a tract in Salt Lake City as a state park, and authorized condemnation proceedings. This action was bitterly protested by the largely non-Mormon landowners, who charged that there was church influence, since this project lay close to the heart of George Albert Smith, the Mormon president at the time.

In the period from 1944 to 1960, the General Authorities of the church witnessed as many measures, in which it may be assumed that they had an interest, defeated in the legislature or vetoed by the governor as were passed with their tacit or expressed approval. For example, the Sunday closing enactment, which

23. For example, Don B. Colton in 1934, Republican congressman from the First District (1921-33), was given leave from his presidency of the Eastern States Mission to run for William H. King's Senate seat. He lost. Ray Dillman lost to Governor Henry H. Blood and was immediately appointed head of the Western States Mission. In 1938 the General Authorities granted Franklin S. Harris, president of the wholly church-related Brigham Young University, a leave of absence to run as the Republican nominee against incumbent United States Senator Elbert D. Thomas. Harris lost to Thomas at the polls, and returned to BYU.

24. Henry D. Moyle, who later was elevated to an apostleship, an action which indicated his favorable standing with the General Authorities.

also had support from labor and business interests and from the Protestants, was vetoed by Governor Clyde, a Republican and an active Mormon. His action was interpreted generally as placing him in disfavor with the Mormon church in his 1960 bid for re-election. In 1967, Governor Rampton, a Democrat and an inactive Mormon, vetoed an identical measure. Neither man was a minion of the Mormon church: business and political interests invariably motivated their decisions.

In 1948 the Mormon church appeared to reactivate its interest in political candidacies. With state Republican leaders, influential Mormon Republicans settled on a single objective—to unseat Democratic Governor Herbert B. Maw. The *Deseret News* had carried on an incessant campaign against him on its editorial pages. Many influential Mormon apostles gave J. Bracken Lee, a non-Mormon, their support.[25]

Two years later the General Authorities took an active part in defeating incumbent Senator Elbert D. Thomas.[26] Visiting authorities to the local quarterly conferences let it be known that Thomas was not in "harmony with the Brethren."[27] The *Deseret News* gave Thomas some shabby news treatment, an action for which he never forgave the church which he had served faithfully all his life.

In 1952 the Mormon church "officially," as an organization, made a significant change in its political tactics. Instead of simply advising its members to vote for "good" candidates, it activated a "wake-up-the-voters campaign" and instructed them to attend the district mass meetings, where the delegates to the nominating conventions are chosen by secret ballot.[28] The results were evident. In 1954, 95 percent of all elected public officeholders, including the eighty-three-member legislature, were Mormons. Two years later, 94 percent of all candidates on the ballot were Mormons. These figures appear disproportionately high when compared with the 70 percent Mormon population in the state.

The church appeared to have suffered political reverses at the polls as a result of its open and vigorous support of two propositions on the ballot in 1954. One would have restored three junior colleges, given to the state in 1931, to the church. The other would have reapportioned representation in the legislature for the first time since 1931. Both lost by two to one, clear evidence that many Mormons had not followed the advice of their religious leaders. These losses were construed quite correctly as setbacks in politics for the church.

In the 1960 campaign both presidential candidates visited Utah and both made a strong play for the Mormon vote.[29] Usually such visitors call upon the First Presidency of the Mormon church and speak from the podium of the famous Mormon Tabernacle in Salt Lake City. Invariably they mention the courageous

25. For Lee's and Maw's relations with the Mormon church, see Frank H. Jonas, "J. Bracken Lee and the Mormon Church," *Proceedings*, Utah Academy of Sciences, Arts and Letters, XXXIV (1956-57), 109-25. See also "The Mormon Church and J. Bracken Lee," *ibid*., XXXVI (1959), 145-69.

26. See Frank H. Jonas, "The 1950 Elections in the West," *Western Political Quarterly*, IV (March 1951), 91; "Political Dynamiting," *Proceedings*, Utah Academy of Sciences, Arts and Letters, XXXIII (1956-57), 135-47; and "The Mormon Church and Political Dynamiting in the 1950 Elections in Utah," *ibid*., XL (1963), 94-110.

27. The word "brethren" is a synonym for the General Authorities in this context.

28. Two men have laid claim to having advised the church to undertake this program, Republican Governor J. Bracken Lee, a non-Mormon, and Milton Weilenmann, Democratic state chairman and a devout Mormon. The church itself made the discovery that behind-the-scenes politics could be more successful than public fanfare in the political arena.

29. For the details in this campaign, see Jonas, "The 1960 Election in Utah," *Western Political Quarterly*, XIV (March 1961), 365-72.

independence of the pioneers and then express the wish that the whole nation had more of this quality. But in this year, the appeal was somewhat different and decidedly unusual.

Before his address in the Tabernacle, John F. Kennedy called upon the L.D.S. church president, David O. McKay, who promised him that if he were elected "the church would support him." The Democrats were quite satisfied with the friendly manner in which President McKay had received Kennedy. But the highlight of the visit was Kennedy's address that evening in the Tabernacle. Well-informed Mormons stated that Kennedy sounded better versed in Mormon history and doctrine than any "Gentile" who had ever spoken in Salt Lake City. They hinted that probably an apostle had had a hand in preparing his speech. For example, he referred to "the Prophet Joseph Smith," "what Brigham had said when the Lord revealed to him," and "what the Lord said in Section 101 of the Doctrine and Covenants" (exclusively Mormon scripture). In addition, he eulogized former U.S. Senator Reed Smoot and favorably mentioned Secretary of Agriculture Ezra Taft Benson, both Mormon apostles and rock-ribbed Republicans.

Actually, the whole episode presented an excellent example of propaganda technique—a Catholic campaigning effectively for the Presidency of the United States in a state where at least 70 percent of the population were members of a different church. However, the event was not without its broader aspects for the student of politics. Kennedy did more than try to teach a lesson in religious tolerance: he tried also to point out that perhaps the United States had failed effectively to propagate abroad the role that religious liberty had played in the development of the nation. The more positive aspects of Kennedy's "sermon" were lost in the angry mood of the Republicans, both Mormon and non-Mormon, who thought that Kennedy had made some headway with the Mormon vote.

Richard M. Nixon was cordial and eulogistic but neither as specific nor as appealing as Kennedy in his reference to the Mormons. But he received what was interpreted to be the endorsement of the Mormon church. The Associated Press reported: "In Salt Lake City Monday Nixon got what sounded like the blessing of President David O. McKay of the Church of Jesus Christ of Latter-day Saints. Two weeks ago McKay seemed unusually friendly to Senator John F. Kennedy when he dropped by to pay his respects. But Nixon got more than a friendly greeting. 'I told your competitor that if he is successful in November, we would be behind him. I said today that I hope you are.' " Subsequently, however, the members of the church were told by President McKay that "Vice President Nixon is the Republican nominee for President, and as a Republican, I wish him success. This is not to be interpreted as a Church endorsement for Mr. Nixon. Members of the Church who favor Senator Kennedy should, of course, feel free to express their choice."[30]

Interest in the 1962 election campaign in Utah centered on the candidacy of Reed Benson for the Second District congressional nomination.[31] Benson, a far-right conservative, had been secretary of the All-American Society (John Birch).

30. Letter from A. Hamer Reiser, Assistant Secretary to the First Presidency of the Church of Jesus Christ of Latter-day Saints, dated November 3, 1960. Reiser was instructed by President McKay to quote him only in this manner. See Dean E. Mann's evaluation of the incident in "Mormon Attitudes Toward the Political Roles of Church Leaders," *Dialogue*, 2 (Summer 1967), 32-48. He states: "Nevertheless the conclusion of this study is that President McKay's statement had little effect on Mormon voting behavior."

31. See Stewart L. Grow, "The 1962 Election in Utah," *Western Political Quarterly*, XVI (June 1963), 460-66.

The fact that he was also the son of Apostle Ezra Taft Benson, formerly United States Secretary of Agriculture, highlighted young Benson's candidacy and evoked some strong reactions, particularly since the former Second District congressman, Sherman P. Lloyd, was also seeking the Republican nomination. The item of interest here was the statement by the First Presidency of the L.D.S. church which was carried on the front page of the *Deseret News* on August 22, 1962: "the Church has no candidate or candidates for political office. . . . It is contrary to our counsel and advice that . . . Church facilities be used in any way for political purposes. . . ." The electorate interpreted this statement, welcomed by ardent Mormon Republicans, as a rebuke of Benson.

In 1958, the preponderance of Mormon church activity in Utah politics had favored Congressman King and the Democratic candidates. In 1962 and in 1966, it did not seem to do so. There were no overt actions by the church's general or local officials, nor by the membership as Mormons in these elections. Certainly there was none which in any way could account for the Democrats' receiving an overwhelming 57 percent majority for senator, congressman, and governor in the 1964 elections, nor for the 60 percent majority the Republicans achieved for both congressmen in 1966. How then, does one account for, let alone measure in any way, the influence of the Mormon church in these election campaigns?[32]

Apostle Ezra Taft Benson on occasion has been used erroneously by the Democrats to rationalize their losses at the polls. The Democratic committeeman from Utah, Calvin Rawlings, said in 1958 that as long as Apostle Benson was active in politics, the Democrats could not win. In that election year, the Benson appearances on the Utah political scene did incumbent United States Senator Arthur V. Watkins more harm than good and contributed significantly to his loss at the polls. In 1967 the state Democratic chairman, A. Wally Sandack, resurrected the spectre of Benson, and thereby the Mormon church in Utah politics, presumably establishing a straw man to account for a prospective defeat of the Democrats in the 1968 elections. The Mormon church and its leaders have been used sometimes by both Democrats and Republicans to explain Utah's political vagaries.

The one overriding effect of the Mormon church in the 1964 election was symbolic. The sustained efforts over a period of years made by President Lyndon B. Johnson to cultivate a friendship with David O. McKay, the church president, were intensified and well-publicized in 1964 and bore extraordinary political fruit,[33] bringing the state back into the Democratic ranks. The sequence of events was as follows. In January 1964, President Johnson invited President McKay to visit with him in the White House. This visit received wide publicity. Two months later President Johnson gave permission to Secretary of State Dean Rusk to be the keynote speaker at the annual meeting of the Western Political Science Association. At this time Rusk called on President McKay at President Johnson's request. In the summer the entire Mormon Tabernacle Choir was invited to sing at the White House, an appearance which was not a part of its originally scheduled itinerary. In August of 1964, Mrs. Johnson came to Utah to dedicate Flaming Gorge Dam, the first time in history a woman has dedicated a national reclamation project. She also was the speaker at the University of Utah's August commencement

32. See Frank H. Jonas, "The 1964 Election in Utah," *Western Political Quarterly*, XVIII (June 1965), 509-13.

33. Frank H. Jonas, "President Lyndon Johnson, The Mormon Church, and the 1964 Election in Utah," *Proceedings*, Utah Academy of Sciences, Arts and Letters, XLIV (1967), 67-90.

exercises and called on President and Mrs. McKay, bringing gifts and greetings from her husband.

In the following months, September and October, President Johnson made two visits to Utah, one, a typically Johnson surprise visit, with the sole purpose of visiting with the venerable Mormon church president. Johnson's gestures of friendship for the Mormons silenced the influential and sometimes vociferous critics of the church within the Democratic party membership and leadership. He attested to the sincerity of his friendship when he again invited the Mormon Tabernacle Choir to the White House to sing at his Inauguration in January after the election. In 1967, at his personal insistence, the National Broadcasting Company included the Choir in its hour of prayer program soon after the turbulent race riots in Michigan and New Jersey. Whatever his motive the net result was a Democratic sweep at the polls in 1964.

At the present time (1968) local Democratic leaders are not wooing the church as Presidents Kennedy and Johnson wooed it from 1960 to 1965. Indeed, they are deliberately making public statements linking church leaders with the John Birch Society which arouse the anger and evoke denials not only of Mormon leaders but also of the membership generally. Mormons who would not ordinarily take any notice at all of the religious factor in politics nevertheless defend the church and its position when they feel that criticism has been unfair. Mayor J. Bracken Lee of Salt Lake City, formerly two-term governor of the state (1949-57), stated in a recorded interview that a non-Mormon can win at the polls in Utah if he does not attack the church. Himself a non-Mormon and a thirty-third degree Mason, Lee has been a candidate thirteen times for public office; he has won nine times. Much the same situation is true in other states where Catholics constitute over 50 percent of the population. Protestants win in these states because they remain on friendly terms with Catholic leaders and voters; above all, they do not alienate them as Democratic party leaders in Utah have deliberately and unnecessarily alienated the leadership and membership of the Mormon church.

What, then, may one conclude about the position of the Mormon church in Utah politics? After reviewing the elections from 1932 to 1938, the writer stated in 1940 that "although much in spirit from the period 1847 to 1896 has survived in political forms and practices, one fact is clear to the more than casual observer; the influence of the Mormon church in the politics of Utah, from the standpoint of effective pressure, is at the moment mostly a myth." After World War II it stepped up its interests in politics, with some successes and several setbacks. Because of reverses, in this period one may conclude that its alleged control was still a myth, if by control is meant that in order to gain its ends, all its leaders have to do is snap their fingers and pass the word along. Persons critical of the church's position would say categorically that the church controls politics in Utah. Devout Mormons would say unequivocally that it is not in politics in any way. Both extreme positions would seem to be in error.

In politics, however, one must distinguish between control and influence. The Mormon church does have both potential and real influence in politics, but for success at the polls or in the legislature, much depends on the circumstances in a particular situation and on its own choice of tactics. In every instance since the early days, when the church has made its position public in the press or elsewhere in print and its leaders have endorsed candidates or propositions, it has lost its cause at the polls. When it has used its organization and institutional structure, and has worked on the "inside" of these to achieve its purposes in politics, it has been more successful. Above all, the Mormon church can no longer manipulate elections as it did one hundred years ago. The situation at all times is dynamic; the position of the Mormon church in Utah politics at any one time can be ascertained only with reference to the fate of a particular legislative measure or proposition on the ballot in which it is or seems to be interested, and to the election results for a certain candidate whom it apparently wants to favor.

GEOGRAPHY AND RESOURCES

The territory of Utah was carved out of the provisional State of Deseret which included all of the present states of Utah and Nevada, most of Arizona, and parts of New Mexico, Colorado, Wyoming, Idaho, Oregon, and California, an area of 230,610 square miles. Strong anti-Mormon forces were at work to reduce the Utah Territory, adding bits to surrounding states as these were accepted into the Union. The purpose was to break up the concentration of Mormons in one area and dissipate their influence. However, it also occurred to these forces that several states could be heavily influenced and perhaps dominated by Mormon minorities because of their cohesiveness and well-knit organization. It would be better, they thought, for all the Mormons to dominate one state rather than several. Nonetheless, the territory was reduced in size six times, until by 1870 it approximated the present 84,916 square mile area of the state.

Utah offers the student of geography and geology probably the greatest possible variety of physical features of any state in the Union. Continuous ranges of mountains cut through the middle from north to south. These begin in southern Idaho and veer to the west as they approach but do not touch the Arizona boundary line. The high Uinta mountain range runs east and west in the northeast; in the northwest is located the Great Salt Lake desert; in the west central area, the Great Basin; in the southeast, the Great Central plateau; and in the northeast, the Uintah Basin. Long stretches of dry desert lands lie between the Utah mountain ranges and the Colorado Rockies on the east and the Sierra Nevadas on the west.

Most important to Utah's economy are the water resources which originate in the Wasatch range and the high Uintas. The average rainfall varies from fifty to sixty inches in the Wasatch mountains to four inches in the western desert. Water is the economic lifeblood of the state, and there is consensus that the state's future lies entirely in an accessible and adequate supply.

Water resources development in Utah has increased by leaps and bounds during the past six years. Actually the problem is related to the development of the Colorado River Basin. Two projects of interest to the state have been completed, Flaming Gorge Dam on the Green River, a subsidiary of the Colorado, in the northeast corner which backs up water to Green River, Wyoming, and Glen Canyon Dam in northern Arizona which backs up water for almost one hundred and seventy-five miles into Utah. These projects provide electrical power, recreation facilities, scenic attractions, and water flow control between the upper and lower basin states. Neither project will provide water for irrigation and for culinary and industrial uses. However, they make possible the use of feeder streams for water uses of all kinds within the state.

Other projects are underway: in 1960, the Central Utah units were started. The Stanaker Reservoir near Vernal was first. Construction of the Bonneville unit, the largest and most complex, began on May 31, 1967. Its key feature is the transfer of surplus water in the Uintah Basin to the state's heavily populated areas

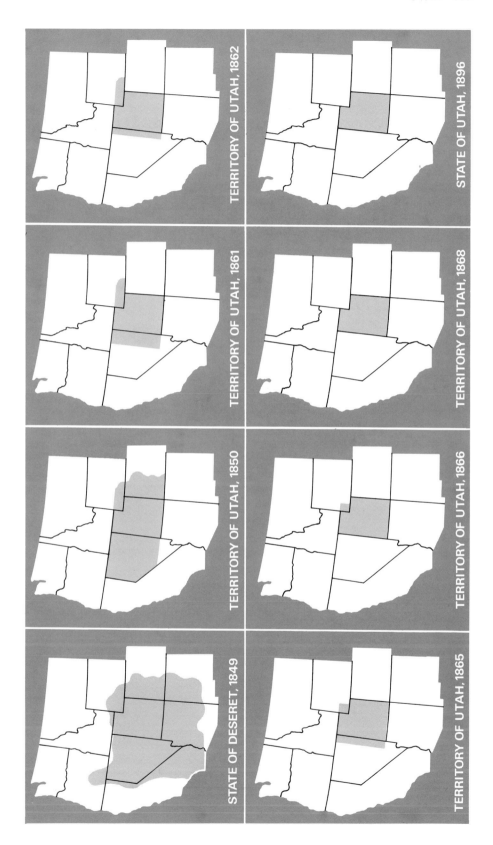

TERRITORY OF UTAH, 1862

STATE OF UTAH, 1896

TERRITORY OF UTAH, 1861

TERRITORY OF UTAH, 1868

TERRITORY OF UTAH, 1850

TERRITORY OF UTAH, 1866

STATE OF DESERET, 1849

TERRITORY OF UTAH, 1865

along the Wasatch Front. The project will deliver some 300,000 acre feet of water for municipal, industrial, and agricultural use in the two-basin area.

These and similar projects in the development of the state's resources are imperative in view of population increases and industrial expansion. Yet their implementation is slow, due to politics, not only within the state, but between the states. The struggle for water shares of the Colorado River is a political problem manifested chiefly in the sometimes desperate attempts of each party to credit its congressional delegations and state officials with initiating, developing, and completing the projects. The Democrats blamed the Republicans when Senator Arthur V. Watkins and Utah's Republican delegation in Congress failed to achieve the full package in the Colorado River Compact in 1956. The battle in and out of Congress to include the Echo Park Project was lost to the Sierra Club and the nature conservationists.

Recently a large sum appropriated for the development of the Bonneville section of the Central Utah Project was spent by the federal government on reclamation projects in other states. No reason was given, but the blame was placed at the door of the Democratic Administration in Washington and Utah's delegates in Congress. The Republicans do not oppose federal actions and appropriations for the development of water resources in Utah. What they would like is to have more credit for the development. Republican George Dewey Clyde of the Utah Water and Power Board and subsequently governor of Utah (1957-64), took the initiative in developing the Flaming Gorge and Glen Canyon dams to harness the waters of the Colorado and Green rivers for domestic and regional use.[34] However, these projects came to fruition and were dedicated under Democratic auspices. This led to even more political friction. For example, when the Glen Canyon Dam was dedicated in 1964, the Republicans complained bitterly because four of their number, former Senator Watkins, former Congressmen Henry Aldous Dixon and William Dawson, and former Governor George Dewey Clyde, were not invited.

In recent years, U.S. Senator Frank E. Moss, Democrat, and Representative Laurence Burton, Republican, First District, have been the leaders in advancing Utah's water interests in Congress.[35] Utah is a small state and can curry the favor of the national administration only through political combinations with other states. Too often the state's congressional delegation has failed to act with imagination, skill, and forcefulness in the use of political techniques.

Utah has a diversified economy, which stems from the insistence on self-sufficiency by its early settlers. Leonard J. Arrington has delimited the "different world of Utah" in economic terms and in its relationship to the West as a region. He states that (1) "the original Salt Lake settlement . . . did not depend on other western settlements for its success or growth; but in considerable measure, neighboring territories depended upon it for their success and growth"; (2) "it was planned and organized and thus did not fail"; and (3) "it and the colonies it spawned represented . . . a whole society, with many industries and types of activity. . . . That is, the Mormon community approached being an entire, well-balanced community far more capable of independent self-sufficient existence than most other western communities, which tended to be dominated by one particular type of activity—mining, lumbering, cattle-raising, or wheat raising.[36]

34. See Frank E. Moss, *The Water Crisis* (New York: Praeger, 1967).

35. Elroy Nelson and Osmond L. Harline, *Utah's Changing Economic Patterns* (Salt Lake City: University of Utah Press, 1964).

36. Leonard Arrington, *From Wilderness to Empire: The Role of Utah in Western*

Utah has mistakenly been labeled an agricultural state. In its early years the "Mormon village," with its population dwelling in the town surrounded by its cultivated areas and pasture lands on the outskirts, became the characteristic social structure.[37] Although agriculture has been since 1847 a major foundation of Utah's economy, in terms of total income it is now only 6 percent of California's or Iowa's and ranks forty-first in the nation. In the West, only Nevada and Wyoming are agriculturally smaller than Utah. The state grows few grains, used largely for livestock. Some wheat is produced, but much greater quantities are shipped in for processing and the flour is exported. Not more than 7 percent of the state's total income is derived from price-controlled basic crops. For this reason Utah's Ezra Taft Benson, former Secretary of Agriculture, was not a controversial figure in the state because of the Administration's agricultural policies.[38]

The initial agricultural and grazing activities were soon supplemented and then surpassed by mining in terms of productive wealth. Mining became not only the principal activity but almost the exclusive province of the Gentiles, since Brigham Young had cautioned the Saints against engaging in it. The Gentiles brought in outside capital to exploit metal and coal resources. Though politically Utah became known as a "silver state," gold and silver were extracted from lead, zinc, and copper ores, which could be brought out profitably only after the railroads were built. Distance and rugged terrain made transportation a great problem.

The extraction of lead and zinc ores has become increasingly expensive: they can be purchased much more cheaply in foreign markets. Utah politicians in Congress face an almost hopeless task in trying to keep this segment of the mining industry alive by public policy. But as a whole, the industry is still growing, and today pays the largest monthly wages in the state. It matches this payment dollar-for-dollar in the purchase of supplies and services. Second only to California in originating freight tonnage produced by mining, Utah is also second only to Arizona in total tonnage and value of non-ferrous metal ores produced in the nation. This glowing picture, however, has been made possible by the discovery and development of uranium, natural gas, oil, and recently, potash.[39]

With the largest open pit non-ferrous metal mine in the nation, the Kennecott Copper Corporation for many years has been the largest single taxpayer in the state. One of the largest concentrations of milling and smelting in the world

Economic History (Salt Lake City: Monograph No. 1, Institute of American Studies, University of Utah, 1961).

37. See Lowry Nelson, *The Mormon Village: A Pattern and Technique of Land Settlement* (Salt Lake City: University of Utah Press, 1952). See also Wallace Stegner, *Mormon Country*, "American Folkway Series" (New York: Duell, Sloan & Pearce, 1942), and Nels Anderson, *Desert Saints: The Mormon Frontier in Utah* (Chicago: University of Chicago Press, 1942).

38. "My stand in behalf of flexible farm support was, I am sure, favored by a good-sized majority of Utah farmers. For example, in 1958, 79 percent of Utah's agricultural income came from some form of livestock. With the exception of the dairy farmers, the livestock industry stands to lose from high price supports as a result of increased feed grain costs and higher taxes. In the last year for which figures were calculated, Utah lost $16 million in taxes for $4 million received in price support." Hon. Henry Aldous Dixon, U.S. Representative from the First District (Utah), letter to the writer, dated May 17, 1960.

39. The cumulative value of all minerals produced in Utah from 1964 to 1966, inclusive, was $10,127,222,000. Utah ranked sixteenth among the 50 states in total mineral production. Total property assessed valuation was $1,540,954,634; total property taxes paid on Utah mining property amounted to $125,365,577, and occupation or severance taxes came to $6,660,898. Employment and payrolls came to 25,213 and $185,555,852. These figures were secured from the Utah Mining Association through the courtesy of Walter Horne.

developed in the Salt Lake and Tooele County areas.[40] However, the backbone—and the symbol—of Utah's new industrial development is the big Geneva Steel Works of the United States Steel Corporation, located in Utah County approximately 35 miles south of Salt Lake City. Geneva—one of the West's largest completely integrated steel complexes—was built during World War II to serve the needs of western defense fabricators. With coal resources in Carbon County, 120 miles south and east of the plant, iron ore in Iron County, 240 miles to the south, and limestone and dolomite close at hand, Geneva's furnaces have a rated capacity of more than two million ingot tons of steel a year.

Since 1960 foreign competition from Japan, high production costs, and the long distance from large markets almost caused United States Steel to close down the Geneva plant. In an over-all effort to save the plant the railroads helped by lowering rates. Defense spending, after a serious decline in 1962, began to rise again in 1965, and employees with their families pledged, with union sanction, operation "errors zero," a campaign for greater efficiency. Had Geneva closed, Utah's economy would have suffered a serious blow. The jobs of 6,000 Geneva workers and some 20,000 other Utahns depend on this steel facility, which has a $35 million payroll and pays the state nearly $2 million in taxes.

In 1967, about 100,000 persons in Utah were employed by government. Defense spending over the previous decade increased from $242,690,628 to $331,600,000 or 26.7 percent. Some 43,000 persons were engaged in defense or in the military effort (about 20.9 percent of whom worked in missile industries). Their incomes total $257,700,000, an increase of some $90 million over the figure for 1959.[41]

In 1940, the Chamber of Commerce in Salt Lake City claimed that "Utah leads the world in smelting." In 1960, it proclaimed the state as "Missile Center, U.S.A." Although neither appellation may be valid today, the state is still very heavily dependent on defense and military spending. Any reduction now would result in challenges to both industrial leaders and politicians in a state which strongly resisted the first encroachment of the federal government at the beginning of the New Deal period.

POPULATION

Beginning in 1943, due principally to the impetus of the war, the state showed a tremendous population increase, most of it in the old Second Congressional District. By 1960, this district totaled 571,310, a gain of 40 percent over the 1950 census figure. The twenty-five counties in the old First District totaled 315,616, a gain of 10.2 percent in the decade. The total state figure of 886,926 represented a gain of 28.3. In 1967, the state's population was 1,024,000 or a gain of 13 percent over 1960. The projected figures for 1970 are 1,073,000 to 1,093,000.

Obviously, Utah's population is increasing steadily, although at a slower rate

40. Leonard J. Arrington, *The Richest Hole on Earth: A History of the Bingham Copper Mine* (Logan: Utah State University Press, 1963).

41. For the story of the defense industry in Utah see William A. Tillerman, "Federal Defense Spending in Utah," *Utah Economic and Business Review* (Salt Lake City: Bureau of Economic and Business Research, College of Business, University of Utah), XX (April 1940), 3-5; and Leonard J. Arrington and George Jensen, *The Defense Industry of Utah* (Logan: Utah State Planning Program, Economic and Population Studies, Utah State University, 1965). Employment figures were secured from the Utah State Department of Employment and Security.

than in the two previous decades. Although this rate is higher than the average for the United States (9.2 percent), it is lower than the average for the Mountain states (13.8) and for the western states as a whole (16.4). The population increase has been due to the favorable balance in birth over death rates, the strong ties of the Church of Jesus Christ of Latter-day Saints which have helped to keep people in the state and to bring many natives back from other states, and the increased industrialization which has attracted job-seekers.

Population patterns in Utah differ from those in surrounding states and the entire nation, due mainly to religious influences. Utah has been less on the move than the nation and, in every case by 20 percent or more, than all other western states; therefore, one may assume that mobility has had less effect on voting behavior. However, there has been considerable internal mobility. From 1950 to 1960 seventeen counties lost population; in the past eight years twelve continued to decrease. More than 75 percent of Utah's population now lives in so-called urban areas.[42] This compares with 50 percent in 1930, 55 in 1940, 65 in 1950. In 1960, the population was 65.4 percent urban, 23 percent rural and 11.6 percent rural farm.[43]

The four most heavily populated counties, Weber, Davis, Salt Lake and Utah, which string along the west edge of the Wasatch mountains in the northern half of the state, now form one continuous metropolitan region called the Wasatch Front. This chain of counties has become the political power base for the state.[44] It has brought about a realignment of sectional interests. This Front and not Salt Lake County alone is now attacked by the other counties in terms of possible advantages and disadvantages in the legislature.

In Utah, compared to the nation, the people are younger, males outnumber females, and families are larger. In 1955, the percentage of Mormons in Utah's population was 69.3. Five years later it had risen to 70.2 percent, or 639,420 of a total 886,926. From 1960 to 1967 the figure remained about 71 percent. In 1960 the Catholic population reached 40,541, an increase of 43.2 percent over 1950. This number was increased to 46,766 by 1964. Soon after World War II many Mormons feared that industrialization, with many Catholic labor union members coming to the state, would adversely affect the Mormon population and many non-Mormons hoped that this would be true. Neither fears nor hopes have been realized.

The percentage of Mormons has remained high because of population increases due to natural births and to net in-migration. Many Mormons migrate to Utah or return to their home state to rear and educate their children. Many non-Mormons have come to the state with the increase in the labor force and employment in defense industries. However, these increases have leveled off while the Mormons have increased in number during the past two decades.

Ethnic and minority groups have played only a small role in Utah politics. In

42. Nelson and Harline, op. cit., p. 2.

43. Recently, farmers met to discuss rural decline and what could be done about it. All they could think of was more governmental programs and more federal funds to finance them. Deseret News, December 21, 1967.

44. See Leonard J. Arrington and George Jensen, "Utah's Emerging Metropolis: The Wasatch Front" (Logan: Department of Economics, Utah State University, n.d.). "The concept of the 'Wasatch Front' really encompasses an area larger than these four counties, and includes portions of Box Elder, Wasatch, Summit, and Morgan counties. However, the only feasible means of describing the area statistically is to include only the four. These contain all the urbanized industrialized areas, with the exception now of Brigham City" (p. 9).

1950, the percentages of non-white and foreign-born white persons in the state were 1.7 and 4.3, respectively, with most of the latter in the Second District. In 1960, the 4,148 Negroes in the state constituted less than 0.5 percent of the total population. The figures for Indians, Japanese, Chinese, Filipino, and other races are negligible. Figures apparently are not assembled for other ethnic groups such as Germans, Scandinavians, other Europeans, and Latin Americans. These in Utah are substantial in number because of immigrant converts to the Mormon church from northern Europe and Latin America throughout the state's history, and from Asia and the South Pacific Islands since World War II. Immigrants from southern European countries were attracted by work in the mines and smelters and in business enterprises, chiefly in mining towns.

Since the total vote from minority groups is not large, candidates do not take them very seriously, but are careful not to antagonize them. Campaign managers will get membership lists from the Negro, Greek, Japanese, Italian, Chinese, Spanish and other similar organizations and send out propaganda, signed usually by a responsible person in each group. Some of these groups are quite easily aroused, and if they work for a candidate, they will usually vote as a bloc. Moreover, they do not generally regard politics as a "dirty" business, and once "sold" on a candidate, will do hours of work for him without pay. There are not enough "colored" or "foreign born" persons in Utah to constitute a "problem" for the vote-seeking politician.

EDUCATIONAL POLITICS

In 1939 educational problems in Utah were primarily the raising and equalizing of school funds, sectional interests in the institutions of higher learning, the office of the state superintendent, and the teachers' retirement plan. Although some water has poured over the spillway in the attempt to solve these problems during the last three decades, they are still the concern of pressure groups and of the state legislature.[45]

Utah has always ranked high in the nation in consolidation of schools and average daily attendance. Not too long ago while a neighboring state had 1,300 school districts and 750 one-room schools, Utah had only 40 and 90, respectively. Today (1968) Utah still has 40 districts; 22 of these are coextensive with counties.

The compulsory attendance law, requiring students to remain in school until the age of 18, was passed in 1919. While Box Elder County, nearly as large as Massachusetts, had 95.6 percent of its young people of high school age enrolled in its two high schools, 22 miles apart, New York had 72.9 enrolled and California, 85.8. The enrollment for Utah has remained constant during the past 30 years at approximately 95 percent.

One basic fact in educational finance is that Utah leads all other states in the percentage of its population between the ages of five and twenty-five enrolled in schools and colleges. About 50 percent of the population has completed four years of high school, and 8 percent, four years of college. It has very few parochial and private schools. Of its tax revenue, it spends one of the highest percentages in the nation for education, while at the same time it has a comparatively low expenditure per school child. The financing of education and the equalizing of educational opportunities for all children regardless of their place of birth have been

45. Frank H. Jonas, in *Rocky Mountain Politics*, ed. Thomas C. Donnelly (Albuquerque: University of New Mexico Press, 1940), pp. 19-21.

perennially major legislative tasks. In the 1967 legislative session teacher retirement, never popular with business and financial interests, became a leading problem.

Everyone would agree as to the facts in Utah education thirty years ago. For example, Jordan School District, in the heart of the mining area, had an assessed valuation of $88,000,000 while agricultural Sanpete County had one of $4,500,000. Jordan would send $528,000 to the state government and receive in return $155,000; Sanpete gave $27,000 and received $83,000. Some school boards in situations similar to Sanpete's, under pressure from local politicians and businessmen, instead of applying the extra funds to the improvement of educational conditions, would lower the tax rate in the districts, and thereby nullify the efforts of the state to equalize educational opportunities. Obviously the districts in wealthy mining and urban areas have better educational conditions than those in "America's last frontier." Those who have wealth want to keep it, or see it spent, in their own areas. The problem has given rise to a political conflict between financial and educational interests. The arena is the state legislature; the means, politics; the victims, the students and the public.

Some conditions have been corrected or alleviated by the establishment of a formula for the allocation of funds from tax revenues for a basic school program. The principal allocated sum is an amount derived by multiplying the number of distribution units for each district by $7,400 for the fiscal year ending June 30, 1968, and thereafter by $7,700. One unit is computed by dividing the average daily attendance of all full-day equivalent pupils of the district attending schools other than kindergarten and approved special and small isolated schools by twenty-seven. Other or additional units are computed for kindergarten, one- and two-room schools, and for handicapped children.

Important politically is the fact that a district cannot reduce school services while receiving school aid. If the district cannot raise sufficient funds from a mandatory minimum levy of 16 mills to pay for the basic state-supported program the state will supply the difference from its property tax. Additional contributions by the state are for libraries, extended year and summer school programs, and development of educational television.

Also, school districts have at their disposal two leeways, one a voted leeway by the district electorate and the other a Board leeway which requires no vote. The political struggle in the legislature over the latter is reminiscent of traditional sectional and urban-rural struggles for funds. In 1965 the Board of Education leeway was reduced from 12 to 11 mills and the second year to 10 mills. This action occasioned a $1,000,000 loss in revenue to the Salt Lake County districts, which cannot draw upon the wealth in Salt Lake County to pay for improved educational programs. The rural districts use this negative technique to keep the wealthier districts closer to their levels.

Controversial political actions in regard to education during the past three decades have included making the state superintendent of public instruction appointive rather than elective (1951), the creation of the Utah Board of Higher Education (1957), changing Weber College in Ogden from a two- to a four-year institution, and the discrediting of the teaching profession by a former governor, J. Bracken Lee. Lee also attemped unsuccessfully, by means of appointments to administrative boards and personal investigators on the campuses, to influence the administrations of the only two large state-supported universities.

At the present time there is a movement afoot to return the state superintendent's office to an elective status with a Board appointed by the governor. Members of the present nine-man State Board are elected for six-year terms, three being chosen each general election year. The State Board of Education is in conflict with the all-powerful Board of Examiners over the appointment and salaries of specialists. The Board of Education believes it is in the better position to determine the need for and the qualifications of specialized personnel as well as the salaries for them, since these positions are in competition with their counterparts in other states and not with other salaried state personnel. The State Board of Education also insists that it was given the function of coordinating units and functions in higher education, and that there was no need to create another board for that purpose.

Friction also exists between the University of Utah and Utah State University over duplication of course offerings and appropriations necessary to sustain them—and these frictions are voiced in the legislature by representatives who frequently are alumni of one or the other institution. Brigham Young University's graduates, while having no axe to grind for their privately supported college, tend to join forces with their brother legislators from Utah State, since many have the same rural and religious background. Also, since BYU is supported by Mormon tithing, the legislators of that predilection may well resist pressure to raise taxes in support of higher education, to which they are already contributing through their church.

This situation made it easier for former governors to resist pressure from the University of Utah lobby. Although the University of Utah has always received the larger appropriation, Utah State University has received a much higher per student allocation.

Former Governor J. Bracken Lee damaged the position of Utah schools at all levels of instruction by curtailing public revenue. In the late nineteen forties he went on an economy and tax-saving binge. Although there was then no widespread public demand for lower taxes generally and for lower property taxes in particular, he used his influence to get the 1949 legislature to lower the property tax to the extent that the Kennecott Copper Company was saved $800,000 in taxes the next year. Using this figure as a base for the measure of tax-savings by all other corporations, big and small, it appears that they were benefited by millions of dollars. This fact may account in large part for the support given by the Mormon church, probably the second largest property tax payer in Salt Lake County, to Lee in the 1948 and 1952 elections. The result of the lowered income did not become fully apparent until some twenty years later when, in 1965, the state legislature, in spite of the opposition from pressure groups representing mining and manufacturing industries and from some Republican members, bonded the state for the sum of $65,000,000 for public school building purposes. The state had not been bonded since the early days of the depression in the thirties.

In recent years the teachers have retaliated and have taken to the hustings in pursuit of their objectives for better schools and better pay. Legislative session after session has met pressure from teachers and educators by providing funds for increased salaries, but the amounts appropriated each session never brought the salary level up to that in other Rocky Mountain sister states. Lee's successor, George Dewey Clyde, refrained from petty spying activities in the schools, but in financial matters he was little better than Lee. Matters reached a head during the autumn of 1963. As early as 1955 five organizations—the Utah State Board of Education, the Utah Congress of Parents and Teachers, the Utah School Board Associations, the Utah Society of School Superintendents and the Utah Education Association—formed the Utah Coordinating Council on Education. Six years later the name was changed to the Cooperating Agencies for Public Schools (CAPS).

In early 1962, the Utah School Board Association, on behalf of CAPS, conducted a comprehensive statewide survey of Utah taxpayers called "Operation People" to determine what the taxpayers really wanted from their public schools, and if they were willing to pay the bill for improvements. There emerged almost unanimous agreement that Utah should increase its school expenditure per pupil to approximate the average of the surrounding Mountain states.

CAPS and the Governor submitted bills to the 1963 legislature. Some legislators reported that the Governor had indicated to them that he would veto any school finance program that exceeded his estimate of what should be done. The CAPS bills died in the sifting committee in the House, while the Senate Education Committee never seriously considered the CAPS program.

The 1963 legislative session was as niggardly and short-sighted in its dealing with educational problems as its predecessors. It provided the usual minimal increases for salaries and maintenance but ignored all considerations for financing so-called quality education.[46] This had been the pattern of teachers' lobbying and legislative response for decades. Business and finance pressure groups with their influence with the press and media of communication, lulled the public generally into believing that the schools needed no additional or increased taxes to finance plans for improvement. They skillfully employed the slogan "Utah has a good educational system," and the even more absurd one, "Utah has the best educational system in the nation."[47] Actually the state had neither the "best" nor even a "good" system.[48]

After the 1963 legislative session Governor Clyde appointed a twelve-man school study committee.[49] Apparently the Governor held out as long as possible in making public the committee's recommendations for the correction of certain educational conditions. The financing of these efforts was estimated at $8,000,000. He rejected the Utah Education Association's pressures for a special session of the legislature, which, it was alleged, he had promised, and became adamant and even belligerent.[50] Actually the teachers had the Governor "on the

46. Those who opposed the educators' program said over and over again that education received the greatest single appropriation (allowing up to an 11.6 million dollar increase in maintenance and operation funds for Utah education) ever given Utah schools. The fact remained that it was not enough to take the educators even half the distance from where they were to the average of the seven surrounding states.

47. At one time this slogan could have been given some credence. This was especially true in Salt Lake City in a period immediately before 1920 and extending probably to 1930. The city Board of Education, dominated by Masons, brought in the principals of the only two city high schools and many teachers, who came from New England or had received their higher education in the East. They inaugurated scientific and classical courses in high schools leading to college entrance, with the usual elective courses especially designed for those who would terminate their formal education at the end of the 12th year.

48. Teachers and educators have been as short-sighted as the legislators. They have thought mainly in terms of more money for themselves instead of devising and stressing a complete program for the improvement of education.

49. The UEA was quite pleased with the personnel of the Committee. It noted that it was not only composed of a competent group of high caliber citizens who were most certainly capable of conducting the proposed study but it also contained four professional educators, one a classroom teacher.

50. See the narrative summary of this fateful year for education in John C. Evans, Jr., *Utah School Crisis 1963* (Salt Lake City: Utah Education Association, 1963). Evans was the executive secretary of the UEA.

run." They held a political advantage in view of a more favorable public attitude toward the teachers and the UEA. Also, the 1964 election campaign was not far off and Clyde had produced no advantage for his Republican party. Then the teachers staged the most spectacular event in the history of the state's educational politics. The UEA House of Delegates voted to have its teachers take a two-day recess, not granted by the Board of Education or the superintendents. Opposing pressure group representatives called it a strike. Subsequently they petitioned the National Educational Association to apply sanctions, which the NEA did on a whole state for the first time in its history. Teachers in other states were asked neither to apply for nor take positions in Utah.

Many persons and groups in the state were dismayed and condemned the "teachers' strike." Ernest Wilkinson, president of the Mormon church's Brigham Young University, publicly denounced the UEA's action. Wilkinson's position was interpreted to be that of the Mormon church, which brought consternation to some of its devout members who were public school teachers, and who thought that the church would be vitally interested in improving Utah's public schools. The church had had a long record of encouraging education and establishing schools. Was the position of the Mormon church, and its silence, except for Wilkinson's strong negative voice, an indication that its position in politics and on public policy was on the side of those groups concerned more with the property tax than with the education of the state's children? On the other hand, the leaders and supporters of this political action by the teachers were Mormons by a great majority. But this was not the first time that the church officialdom and the majority of its members had parted company over political action and public policy.

Meanwhile, CAPS had become disorganized, and the UEA alone was carrying on the battle for the teachers, without its former allies. (The five associations are now back in a loose confederation.) In January 1964, a carefully selected group, designated as the Political Action Committee, met at the invitation of the UEA's Board of Trustees and officers to discuss the feasibility of organizing an educational political arm, analogous to AMPAC, BIPAC, or COPE in the medical, business, and labor fields. The outcome was the Utah Council for the Improvement of Education (UCIE), which set up a Board of Trustees separate as a body from the personnel of the UEA's Board, and selected a temporary director to work during the election year. Dues for UCIE of $10 a person were solicited from members of the UEA. About one-third of the members joined, giving the new pressure group an operating fund of $35,000.

Screening meetings for gubernatorial candidates were held as were training meetings for teachers to acquaint them with Utah's electoral system, of which a distinguishing feature is the so-called mass meeting described elsewhere in this chapter. Teachers were asked to attend these meetings and to use all the influence they could in each district to elect delegates to the county and state pre-primary conventions.[51]

The meetings in 1964 were the best attended in the state's history. The principal reason for this unprecedented large attendance was the fact that former Governor Lee, then mayor of Salt Lake City, had filed his candidacy for the gubernatorial nomination on the Republican ticket. This was enough to bring out the school teachers, many of whom had not attended a political meeting of any kind

51. See Frank H. Jonas, "The Role and the Responsibility of the Teacher in Politics," *Utah Educational Review*, January-February 1964, pp. 14-15 ff. See also his "Teachers in Politics," *ibid.*, November-December 1964, pp. 8-9 ff.

until this election year. Even in his home district Lee's wife was defeated as a candidate for convention delegate by a school teacher. Lee harangued the school teachers in his candidate speech at the state convention. He came in third in the balloting.

The UCIE made some enemies in 1964 when it played a significant role in the election of Democratic Governor Calvin Rampton. It appointed a permanent director for the 1966 campaign and won respect from the politicians in the legislature. Generally Governor Rampton has been friendly to education and has supported its financial objectives, although he asked the 1967 legislature for less money than the educators had programmed. In the waning moments of the session it was a Republican, Franklin Gunnell, the speaker of the House, who sponsored with success a million dollar increase for education over and above the Governor's request. The wrath of the Utah Mining Association and kindred pressure groups was turned on a fellow Republican instead of, as in former years, on the so-called Democratic liberal spenders.

NEWS MEDIA AND PUBLIC OPINION

Utah is served by five daily newspapers. In Salt Lake City, The morning Salt Lake *Tribune*, owned and managed by Catholic laymen, and the evening *Deseret News*, published by the Mormon church, are statewide with circulations in southern Idaho, southwestern Wyoming, eastern Nevada, and to a small extent in Colorado and Arizona. Conservative in policy, these two papers, though previously they raised opposition to so-called New Dealers like Governor Herbert B. Maw (1941-49) and Senator Elbert D. Thomas (1933-51), both Democrats, in the past two decades have tended to give candidates fair news treatment.

Both papers are business- and family-oriented; they cooperate generally on community projects. They are administered jointly by the Newspaper Agency Corporation. Incorporators have been two management representatives from each paper and one person not connected directly with either one. The Agency has come under fire from Philip Hansen, Utah's Attorney General, who testified in Washington, D.C., that it was in violation of the anti-trust acts, although the position of the Newspaper Agency is not precisely similar to the arrangement between the two newspapers in Tucson, Arizona, which the federal court ruled to be monopolistic.

Democratic Weber County is served out of Ogden, Utah's second largest city, by the traditionally Republican *Standard-Examiner*. This paper is owned by Abe Glassman, who also owns radio and television station KLO in Ogden and the Intermountain Network which extends into Idaho, Montana, Wyoming, and Colorado along with considerable other properties in Salt Lake and Weber counties.[52] Other dailies are the Provo *Herald* in Utah County and the Logan *Herald-Journal* in Cache County, both owned and operated by the out-of-state Scripps interests. All five dailies are Republican.

The state elsewhere is served by about fifty weekly papers, all conservative, all business-oriented, all Republican. The few nominally Democratic publishers are conservative; their papers are Republican-inclined. The sole exception is the

---

52. The management and editorial staff of the *Examiner* are manned chiefly by out-of-state importations or immigrants. The Logan and Provo dailies are also managed by personnel sent into the state by the non-Utah and outside-the-state-based owners.

weekly *Salt Lake Times*. No so-called liberal or even Democratic-inclined press has survived in Utah.[53]

Television in Utah, as elsewhere in the nation, has played an increasingly important communications role in political campaigns, but it is doubtful if it has eclipsed the printed page and personal touch for effective campaigning. In 1958, for example, Congressman William A. Dawson attributed his defeat in part to the last-minute television programming of his challenger, Democrat David S. King. King was assisted by handsome, articulate Mormon Apostle Hugh B. Brown, who was the television star, which possibly made the medium effective. But King estimated he shook at least 25,000 hands and made more personal appearances than his opponent. Also, no other form of communication could have been more effective than the four-page newspaper and the leaflets which "destroyed" Elbert D. Thomas in 1950 and drove him from public life.[54]

Politicians are somewhat wary in their use of the expensive television medium. It has boomeranged in some cases. If it can be said that a politician lost an election because of his television appearances, then this is true of William Barlocker, the Democratic nominee for governor in 1960. In a debate with the Republican incumbent, George Clyde, he made an extremely poor showing. Clyde was not a colorful personality, nor a flamboyant speaker, but he was informed and his grammatical constructions were correct. Barlocker did not appear to be informed and fumbled for words. To say the least he went to pieces before the lights. On the other hand, in conversation with a small group face-to-face he spoke quite well. Former Governor J. Bracken Lee also became a television problem for his manager, because he had poor self-control when emotionally aroused. He has made few television appearances in his recent mayoralty campaigns.

About thirty radio stations thoroughly cover the state. Salt Lake City radio and television stations cover the same territory but not uniformly. Idaho's Senator Frank Church and Wyoming's Senator Gale McGee have used KSL-TV, a 50,000 watt station in Salt Lake City, to reach voters by live telecasts in southern Idaho and southwestern Wyoming.

Sometimes the communications media will enter a vote campaign as a pressure group. This was the case in 1965 when the voters in Salt Lake County failed to pass a proposition on the ballot to implement a legislative enabling act for urban renewal. Although the newspapers, especially the powerful Salt Lake *Tribune*, stood for urban renewal the proposition was defeated at the polls. In this case, the John Birch Society, with its members knocking on doors and telling the residents that they would lose their homes if the measure passed, was more influential than the press. However, some conservative pressure groups, especially the real estate and apartment house owners associations, dragged their feet and quietly behind the scenes stood for the position of the active John Birch Society members.

NOMINATIONS, ELECTIONS, AND CORRUPT PRACTICES

Utah's election laws generally follow the American political pattern for qualifications for voting and the privileges of voters. From the first elections for state

53. Shortly before the United States entered World War II, the New Deal Democratically inclined publishers of two weeklies, the *Box Elder Journal* in Brigham City and the *Pyramid* in Mount Pleasant, were forced to sell because of pressure from the advertisers and opinion leaders in their communities.

54. See Jonas, "Political Dynamiting," pp. 135-47.

offices in 1895 until May 10, 1937, Utah operated strictly with the convention system for choosing nominees. The state used the direct primary in 1938 for the first time with a runoff for the two highest candidates. First and second class cities had primaries under the old law but no run-off primaries. In 1947, the present mixed convention-primary system was adopted. In this system, delegates to nominating conventions are elected by secret ballot in party mass meetings held in voting districts.

The term "mass meeting" has been confusing to outside-the-state observers of the Utah scene. It means that every qualified elector in each voting district may attend a biennial meeting of his party for the purpose of setting up a district party organization and electing delegates to county and state nominating conventions. The delegate positions are eagerly sought. About 25,000 citizens attend the mass meetings, now held by both parties on the same night to avoid "raiding." Over 2,000 delegates in both parties who become "important people" are elected. Frequently interest groups and party workers will "stack" the meetings or employ other devices in an attempt to control them.

Not much change was made in Utah's election law from 1947 to 1963. In 1963, however, the legislature made several significant changes designed to enhance the effectiveness of party nominating procedures. The party organization conventions were placed in the odd numbered or off-election years and the nominating conventions in the even or election years. The main purpose was to eliminate the disadvantage of electing a new party chairman and group of officers shortly before the nominating conventions and sometimes well into the election year. Under the new law, new officers now have a whole year to prepare for the campaign. However, because of the insignificant role played by party organizations in finding prospective nominees and in aiding an individual campaign, changes through law in party practices and procedures in the nominating and electoral processes have not done much to make political parties more effective in electing public officials and public policy-makers.

The 1963 legislature also changed the filing deadline to fall before the mass meetings, so that the party members would know who the candidates were. Consequently, a prospective convention delegate could not dodge questions by saying that he did not know who the candidates were and for this reason he had not made up his mind. The change made the mass meetings more significant and stimulated more attendance and interest in them.

Generally, the same persons attend both county and state conventions. According to law, the county conventions elect delegates to the state conventions. In practice, however, the delegates elected at the mass meetings to the county conventions are accepted on a motion from the floor as delegates to the state conventions. Sometimes the mass meetings will elect two separate delegates or sets of delegates for the county and state conventions. Legally this is a questionable procedure since the law stipulates that the delegates to the state convention should be chosen by the county conventions.

Primary nominees for state elective offices and for the Congress are elected at the state conventions. On the convention day, the appropriate delegates meet separately in two congressional conventions for the nomination of representatives to Congress and in several separate conventions to nominate candidates for the state Senate when the senatorial district combines two or more counties. Utah has 29 counties and 27 state senators. When the present election law was passed in 1947, the state had only 23 senators. However with the adoption of the recent reapportionment plan based strictly on population for both houses of the state legislature more counties have been combined in senatorial districts than were in 1947 or 1957.

Judges of the Supreme Court and state district courts are not nominated for the primary ballot at the party pre-primary conventions. In 1951, the legislature provided for a nonpartisan method of selecting them. The judicial candidate must take the initiative by filing his intention with the secretary of state. If a judge and more than one member of the bar file declarations of candidacy for the same office, a primary as well as a general election is held. The ballots are entitled "Judicial Nomination Ballot," and contain only the names of the candidates. The two who receive the greatest number of votes at the primary election are qualified for the general election. The voter is handed a single separate ballot at the general election. Indeed, the voter in 1964 was handed *four* separate ballots. This practice has been criticized by reformers who would simplify and standardize voting procedures in the nation. Separate ballots, in addition, may be issued for school board elections. There has been some agitation to change school board elections to the odd-numbered years when there is no regular election, except every fourth year for municipal officials.

At the nominating conventions, the delegates elect candidates for the primary. The two highest for each office then enter what in reality amounts to a "run-off" primary. One of these becomes the party nominee by a majority vote. If there are only two convention candidates for the primary then both proceed to the primary election ballot. There is no run-off in this case, nor obviously in the case of a single candidate, a position enjoyed sometimes, but not frequently, by incumbents. Party and candidate campaign workers usually like to have some opposition in the primary, especially some "sure" opposition for candidates— "sure," that is, that it will not win; it makes for a more lively and interesting convention and campaign. Nothing can make for less party and candidate interest at conventions than the "no contest" sign. Also, a primary election gives a candidate publicity he may need or certainly can use for maximum public exposure in anticipation of the final election.

Crackpot candidacies have been eliminated from serious consideration for nomination to the primary by another action of the 1963 legislature. If a convention candidate receives 80 percent of the vote, his name and none other advances immediately to the final election ballot.

Utah uses the open primary; no designation of party is necessary. The 1959 legislature was unsuccessful in its attempt to introduce partisan or closed primaries and separate ballots. However, the 1965 legislature, with narrow Democratic majorities in each house, did pass a statute providing for closed primaries. Although, at the time, 44 of the 50 states in the nation and 9 (including Utah for one election or two-year period, 1965-67) in the West had closed primaries, agitation for repeal resulted in the state's returning to the open primary in 1967. In this year, both houses of the legislature were overwhelmingly Republican. The agitation for repeal was conducted by small influential groups and their representation in the legislature.

One theme was hit hard throughout this campaign. It was said that one did not have the freedom to vote in the primaries for the candidates of his choice. The argument was naïve, for according to history and theory, the nominees are supposed to be elected by their respective party members and not by the electorate at large. Everyone is certainly free to vote for his choices in the final election. The real reason for the repeal of the closed primary was that some did not want to reveal their party affiliations, many for business reasons. Also, some officials of the Mormon church did not want to reveal their political preferences. In the sole election held under the closed primary system very few church officials registered and voted. However, some who had been at least nominally Democratic, did register as Democrats. Actually, a higher percentage of known Democrats among the church dignitaries registered than did Republicans. Some church authorities tend to obscure their private political inclinations, although if members ask for their preferences they will state them privately in no uncertain terms.[55]

Independent candidates may get on the ballot by petition. The number of signatures begins with 300 for national offices and scales down for lesser ranked positions. As a result of J. Bracken Lee's re-entry in the governor's race in 1956 as an independent after his defeat in the primary, the law was amended by the 1957 legislature to make it impossible for a person to become an independent candidate after he had "previously filed in the same year a declaration of candidacy with any political party."[56] In 1958, Lee entered the senatorial race as an independent candidate. In this instance he did not have to stand for election in the pre-primary or convention elections or in the primary election.[57]

No organized third party has entered the Utah lists since 1948, when Henry A. Wallace's Progressive party was successful in placing his name on the ballot, until 1968 when the American Independent party accomplished the same objective for another of the same name, former Alabama Governor George Wallace. To become a third-party candidate one must file a petition with the secretary of state containing 500 signatures of qualified electors before the primary and a second similar petition before the final election. Also, third-party candidates must register a party designation.

Utah election statistics for presidential elections tell the story of third parties in the state.[58] Although Communists, Socialists, and others have been on the ballot prior to 1948, none was successful in securing the 2 percent of the vote necessary to remain on the ballot for the following election. Presidential electors cannot qualify for the ballot. They are not considered candidates for public office. Presidential electors, delegates to the national conventions, and the national committeemen and committeewomen, are selected at the state pre-primary nominating convention.

All district mass meeting and convention voting in both party organizations is by secret ballot, the unique feature in this particular pre-primary nominating system. Although several significant changes have been made by the legislature

55. Consultations with a sample of stake presidents revealed that in a normal election more than 100 church members will call them for their political views. This in reality is not many persons. A stake may have as high as 10,000 members, many of whom may consult their ward bishops for political advice during an election year.

56. General Election Laws, 20-3-38, p. 24. See Frank H. Jonas, "The 1956 Election in Utah," *Western Political Quarterly*, X (March 1957), 151-60. In the only other instance in Utah's history when a candidate has come in the ballot as an independent, Harman Peery, Ogden City mayor, was snowed under as a gubernatorial candidate in the 1936 election, as was Lee twenty years later when he made a final desperate effort to win a third term. But Lee's action was different from Peery's. Lee ran twice for the same office in the same year under two party labels, which raised doubts as to his status as an independent and therefore as to the legality of his action.

57. Frank H. Jonas, "The Third Man in Utah Politics," *Proceedings*, Utah Academy of Sciences, Arts and Letters, XXXVII (1960), 103-25.

58. See Frank H. Jonas and Garth N. Jones, "Utah Presidential Elections, 1896-1952," *Utah Historical Quarterly*, XL (October 1956), 289-307.

especially since 1959, all efforts by the "professional" politicians to eliminate the secret ballot have failed. This is a barrier to increased party responsibility that has yet to be overcome. Delegates to conventions and legislators, regardless of any factors in their personal profiles, hesitate to advocate doing away with the secret ballot. They do not always seem to know the reason for their position; they just like this part of the law as it now stands. The "professionals" would like nothing better than to return to the straight convention system as used before 1937.[59]

Voting machines have not been used in Utah, although they may be used in the 1968 elections. Utah's balloting system came under severe indictment as archaic by Elmer Lower, director of the American Broadcasting Company's news service, in an address to the Salt Lake Rotary Club during the heat of the 1966 election campaign. This address, *The Way We Vote*, received national publicity.[60] However, his severest and most exaggerated criticism did not apply in Utah. Actually, ABC's highly sophisticated electronic system of getting the Utah vote results to their audiences broke down on election night in 1966, and the usual media for reporting the vote were faster than the ABC's system.

The pre-primary convention system has not produced some intended results; certainly it has not increased party responsibility. Party organizations cannot choose a candidate without causing conflicts within the party, nor can they very well back a single nominee with all their resources until after the primary, except in the case of no contest. Second, it is not less expensive than the direct primary, with its run-off. That it would be so was the overt reason for making the change in 1947. Third, it has made "liars" out of many delegates. Sometimes flattered and usually under pressure, they promise their convention vote, only to change their minds. In 1956, a gubernatorial candidate stated publicly that he had 200 convention votes "sewed up" only to learn at the voting that he had only 75.

Recently parties and candidates have used either personal visits and "deals" or the opinion poll to influence the party selection for nomination to the primary ballot.[61] What the nominating system has done is to lessen the advantages of an incumbent or a front-runner in the convention. On two occasions, the second-place convention winner for the gubernatorial nomination has defeated the first-place convention winner after they reached the primary. In 1948, J. Bracken Lee defeated Rendell M. Mabey, speaker of the state's House of Representatives, and, in 1956, George Dewey Clyde edged Lee, then the incumbent governor.

One complaint about the system is that no proxies are allowed. If a delegate is ill or unavoidably absent on the weekend of a convention, the district remains unrepresented. Though criticized on these and perhaps other grounds, the system

59. See D. R. Haddock, S. H. Pond, and J. D. Williams, *Election Law Reform* (Salt Lake City: Occasional Papers on Politics No. 2, Hinckley Institute of Politics, University of Utah, February 27, 1967). This publication takes no notice of the secret ballot as an object for reform. Idealistic in their approach, the writers had not "thought through" the problems and criticisms of the state's election procedures. This publication also contains some errors of fact.

60. Published by the American Broadcasting Company, October 18, 1966.

61. In 1964 representatives for Democrat Calvin Rampton, who aspired to the governorship, persuaded all but one of several potential Democratic candidates not to make the race. Rampton was the attorney for one candidate's business firm. One was subsequently appointed to the Finance Commission in state government, another to the Industrial Promotion Commission, and so forth. Only one, Ernest Dean, a former speaker of the state House of Representatives, was either not tapped on the shoulder or he made himself unapproachable or unpurchasable. He, another Democrat, and a Republican, all candidates, were threatened with elimination from the election because allegedly they were seeking posts for which the salary had been increased during the candidate's membership in the previous legislative session. In a special session, the State Supreme Court decided 4-5 in their favor.

seems to be accepted generally: not many persons, including the professionals and party officials, can suggest ways to improve it.

Undoubtedly a legitimate criticism can be made of the long active campaign period in Utah, which gives ample opportunity for frictions to develop and is unduly expensive. Yet, not until recently has there been a serious pre-primary fight in either party. In 1966, however, a powerful Democratic oligarchy in Salt Lake City deliberately wrecked the Democratic chances at the polls because it could not control candidates and party officials. At issue were reapportionment, the administration of the merit system, and fund-raising. Salt Lake County local politics entered into the imbroglio, with the result that no Democratic nominee won anything, and prospects for leadership in that party were dimmed for the 1968 campaign. Only Governor Rampton has survived the shambles.

Utah's Corrupt Practices Act passed in 1917 is still "dead timber," although it may continue to have some value as a "silent policeman." In 1961 the legislature removed all limits on disbursements by candidates for state office. Collections from public employees to help finance campaigns have been common in city, county, and state elections. Indeed, all Utah governors have made collections in one form or another in the capitol. This practice has become a target for attack in political campaigns at both the state and county levels. Only once did it come into conflict with law, and then this was federal and not state law.[62]

Between the 1930's and 1959 the Merit System in Utah was gradually extended to include several agencies receiving federal funds. However, until the approach of the 1963 legislature, few politicians or reformers encouraged the introduction of a state Merit System. By 1962, the Utah State Public Employees Association began an aggressive campaign calling for a Merit System to end abuses in patronage and funds solicitation. This received strong endorsement from both of Utah's major newspapers, and from members of the faculty of the University of Utah in a 1962 study of state government. The next year under a financial reorganization law the existing small Merit System was extended by executive order to include all state departments, an action which blanketed-in some 84 percent of all state employees. The 1964 campaign produced a flurry of state government employees, mostly appointive officials, who ran for political office. The Deputy State Auditor and Deputy Secretary of State, along with directors of several key agencies, were candidates in the primaries.[63]

A 1963 Merit System regulation which specified that employees covered by the System "shall take no active part in political campaigns" was held by the State Attorney General, Republican A. Pratt Kesler, to be in direct conflict with the 1963 law authorizing the Merit System which provided that "partisan political activity shall not be a basis for employment, promotion, demotion or dismissal from public employment." Highway, Fish and Game, Welfare and some Health Department employees covered by the Hatch Act were barred by federal law from activity, but regulations were promulgated by the State Personnel Office which

62. After the 1958 elections, three Republican officials in the Utah State Road Commission were found guilty by the United States Attorney General's office of violating the provision in the Hatch Act which prohibits an agency receiving federal funds from soliciting money for political purposes from its employees. When the commissioners and Republican governor refused a $42,000 penalty, the amount was withdrawn as a forfeiture. This action was sustained by the Federal District and Appeals Courts. See *Brief of Appellants*, Walter L. Budge, Attorney General, in the United States Court of Appeals, Tenth Circuit, 1960. In January 1961, the U.S. Circuit Court of Appeals decided against the appellants. Salt Lake *Tribune*, January 4, 1961.

63. *Deseret News*, April 5, 1964.

recognized that most state employees were considered free to engage in political activity and to serve as political convention delegates.[64]

The Utah State Employees Association played a vigorous role in 1964 by advising state employees not to engage in political campaigning at the state level in order to avoid reprisals if their candidates lost, and to strengthen the fledgling Merit System by avoiding behavior which "removed the political lid." The Employees Association denounced the new regulations in a 1964 Merit Council hearing and issued a challenge to the 1965 legislature to amend the Merit System law by outlawing partisan political activity.[65]

The traditional practice of soliciting funds for political parties took place in 1964 in some state agencies, but federal prohibitions allegedly banned solicitations in the Highway and Welfare Departments. The Employees Association advised employees against contributing to campaigns.[66]

With the change of administration in 1965, Utah's new Democratic Governor indicated immediate dissatisfaction with Merit coverage of assistant attorney generals and the superintendent and assistant superintendent of the State Highway Patrol and stated he would seek "Legislative permanence" for the System.[67] The 1965 Legislature passed a Merit System Act which excluded a large number of "unskilled employees" from Merit coverage and which provided for public hearings on all positions designated as "exempt" from a policy-making point of view. The Employee's Association charged the new administration with making a "wholesale patronage raid" in exempting some 1,000 or more state positions. Extended hearings on proposed exemptions during 1965 led to exchanges of political barbs by both parties over the need to "insure government efficiency."[68] The act sharply restricted political activity by state employees.

The 1966 report of Utah's "Little Hoover Commission" urged a stronger Merit System to cover over 90 percent of state employees and proposed a more restrictive political activity section than that in the 1965 Merit Law. The Employees Association urged passage of such a "model" bill and also joined forces with the County Employees Association to urge passage of a County Merit System Act by the heavily Republican Utah State Legislature.[69] Governor Rampton vetoed both bills despite considerable public concern when the legislature failed to pass a code of ethics bill the Governor had called for in his 1967 program as a corollary to a stronger Merit System.[70]

Proponents of the Merit System remain somewhat dissatisfied with the results. Personnel turnover has exceeded 25 percent in many state departments and over-all is higher than it was prior to the 1963 Merit Law despite passage of a $4.6 million state employee salary increase by the 1967 legislature.[71] Recent activity

64. *Ibid.*, April 7, 1964.
65. *Ibid.*, April 9, 1964; April 23, 1964.
66. *Ibid.*, October 9, 1964.
67. *Ibid.*, November 5, 1964; Salt Lake *Tribune*, December 31, 1964.
68. Salt Lake *Tribune*, May 13, 1965.
69. *Deseret News*, February 7, 1967.
70. *Ibid.*, March 1, 1967.
71. See Oakley Gordon, Reed Richardson, and J. D. Williams, *Personnel Management in Utah State Government* (Salt Lake City: Research Monograph No. 6, Institute of Government, University of Utah, 1962), pp. 18-23. Cf. Garth N. Jones and Frank H. Jonas, "Some Employment Practices in Utah State Government," *Proceedings*, Utah Academy of Sciences, Arts and Letters, XXXIII (1955-56), 149-60; and "J. Bracken Lee and the Public Service of Utah," *Western Political Quarterly*, IX (September 1956), 755-65. The turnover in the Public Welfare Department has been extremely high the last few years, over 30 percent at times, and has given administrators cause for considerable alarm.

has concentrated on extending Merit coverage to unskilled and semi-skilled workers. The Employees Association continues to play an active lobby role and now represents 65 percent of state employees.

PARTY ORGANIZATION AND PARTY LEADERS

Utah has been in the somewhat unusual position of having the party structure and internal procedures prescribed in the *General Election Laws* and made available as a monograph by the secretary of state to party officials and interested citizens.[72] Party officials operate with this detailed document in hand and otherwise follow a few familiar traditions and practices. Any misunderstanding which they cannot resolve is referred to the state's attorney general for interpretation and rulings. These are invariably followed.

Technically, according to law, delegates are elected to the county party organization and pre-primary nominating conventions. Dates for these conventions are set by the state and county party organizations; deadlines are established in law by the state legislature.

Each district is entitled to one delegate. The state central committees determine the number of additional delegates to be chosen in each district based on the party's voting strength in the previous congressional election. The district also elects four officers and a committee of three persons. The chairman and vice-chairman, one of whom must be a woman, become members of the county central committees. The secretary and treasurer should be two separate persons, although this provision is sometimes ignored in practice.

There is no prohibition against the district's establishing other committees. In 1964, the Republican party elected chairmen of finance committees. The collection of funds began at the mass meeting itself with a televised message from the state and county chairmen. Larger than usual total donations were collected at these meetings, which were unusually well attended. Subsequently each district finance committee or district organization chairman visited each Republican in the district who had not attended the mass meeting to solicit a donation. The Democrats confined themselves generally to collecting one dollar per person from a small attendance. Campaigns in both parties are financed principally through each candidate's separate organization which may parallel and duplicate the party organization when it does become active. Party organizations, especially of the Democratic party, can no longer be relied on to conduct adequately and support financially any candidate campaigns.[73]

In Utah there is no public identification of party affiliation. Citizens shift loyalties, obscure previous party activities to gain office on an opposite ticket, or re-enter the regular organization after they have all but wrecked it by their words and deeds. In both primary and regular elections party leaders have frequently

---

72. In Utah no rules are printed or published by political parties. During the 1964 and 1966 elections the Republican party did issue a *Utah Almanac* which included historical and descriptive data on party politics and the political divisions of the state. In no sense was it complete with rules for the party to follow in its procedures and practices.

73. Former U.S. Senator Elbert D. Thomas relied almost wholly on the party for his four election campaigns. The fourth time, in 1950, the party failed him miserably and he was defeated. Had former U.S. Senator Arthur V. Watkins relied on the Republican party in 1946 probably he would not have been elected. His own personal efforts, with those of his wife and a few personal friends, were tremendous and in very large measure accounted for his success at the polls.

turned on their own candidates and have been decisive in the other party's winning an important public office.

State party organizations find it difficult even to win the cooperation of Salt Lake County (which has over 40 percent of the state vote in either party), whose party officials have exercised more influence in party councils than state officials with whom they have often been at odds in the past two decades. The main complaint of the party officials in the thinly populated and outlying counties is that they are ignored by party councils in Salt Lake City and sometimes by nominees.[74]

Undoubtedly there have been conflicts between the state and national party organizations, but none has reached the public generally which has caused the party to develop any intra-party rifts. No national party leader has tried to dictate and control party politics in the state. This cannot be said of the new third party now eligible for the ballot, the American Independent party, the party of George Wallace of Alabama who has entered the 1968 presidential race. There was an immediate play for power in the state organization of this new party, in reality hardly a movement. "Hubert Grizzele, acting chairman . . . called for party unity and issued a warning to national AIP headquarters to 'quit meddling' in Utah party affairs."[75]

UTAH POLITICAL PARTY STRUCTURE

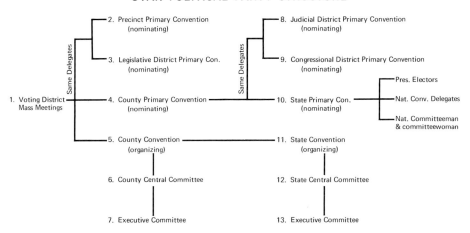

There have been instances of friction in both major parties within the state. During the past three decades, the Lee-Watkins Republican feud and the Maw-

74. There is considerable basis for this charge. For example, M. Blaine Peterson admitted that in 1960 he did not campaign in some of the areas outside Ogden City and Weber County. An axiom in Utah politics is that if a Democrat can get a seven or even a five-to-one vote superiority in Weber County over his Republican opponent, which was quite possible in the past, he can win without very much help from the other 24 small counties in the First Congressional District. This axiom may be dissipated entirely now since under the recent congressional redistricting, the third and fourth largest counties, Utah and Davis, have been added to Weber County, the second largest in the state.

75. *Deseret News*, February 12, 1968.

Moyle Democratic scrap split both parties. Undoubtedly there were other animosities and rivalries, but these two generated the greatest amount of heat.

Apparently the differences between Watkins and Lee began in 1946 when, according to Watkins, Lee failed to give him any help in his first senatorial race. In two previous elections Watkins had supported Lee. After 1952 Lee began a personal attack on President Dwight D. Eisenhower and his Administration which brought him into open conflict with Senator Watkins. Anomalous in this situation was the fact that Watkins had not always supported Eisenhower for the Presidency; but after the Mormon church's president, David O. McKay, whole-heartedly and unequivocally endorsed the General, Watkins changed his position in support of Eisenhower. Watkins was a "regular" Republican and an administration senator. Lee never did change, a stand which cost him the support of the Republican party in his subsequent political career.

He bolted the party in 1956, after he had lost the gubernatorial nomination in the primary to George Dewey Clyde, who, with all other Republican nominees

TABLE I

DELEGATES TO STATE PRIMARY CONVENTION AND STATE CONVENTION
AND MEMBERS OF STATE CENTRAL COMMITTEE, 1966-67

County	Delegates		Central Committee		County	Delegates		Central Committee	
	R	D	R	D		R	D	R	D
Beaver	7	11	2	2	Piute	3	2	2	2
Box Elder	59	34	4	3	Rich	4	2	2	2
Cache	86	41	6	3	Salt Lake	607	698	50	53
Carbon	21	47	2	4	San Juan	11	7	2	2
Daggett	1	1	2	2	Sanpete	22	21	2	2
Davis	104	77	14	6	Sevier	22	13	2	2
Duchesne	12	9	2	2	Summit	12	11	2	2
Emery	10	11	2	2	Tooele	18	37	2	3
Garfield	5	4	2	2	Uintah	22	13	2	3
Grand	11	5	2	2	Utah	158	188	13	14
Iron	22	17	2	2	Wasatch	11	12	2	2
Juab	9	12	2	2	Washington	22	14	2	2
Kane	6	3	2	2	Wayne	4	7	2	2
Millard	17	13	2	2	Weber	202	147	17	11
Morgan	6	6	2	2	TOTAL	1498	1463	144	142

Ratio: *Republicans*: Delegates—one:125 votes. Committeemen—one:1,500 votes. *Democrats*: Delegates—one:150 votes. Committeemen—one:2,000 votes.

for state and congressional offices, was elected. Two years later, however, Watkins was defeated by Frank Moss, with the GOP "renegade" Lee as an independent third man in the senatorial race. Republican politicians have asserted that Lee's presence in the campaign was the factor which defeated Watkins.[76]

The Maw-Moyle controversy was the result of long personal frictions between the two men. It assumed party significance when Herbert B. Maw, a lawyer, a state senator and leader of the liberals (1929-39) defeated Henry D. Moyle for the 1940 gubernatorial nomination; Moyle, also a lawyer, who later became an apostle of the Mormon church, represented the conservative Democrats, while Maw was a New Dealer. Maw was defeated when he attempted to hold the governor's chair for a third term, and subsequently the conservative wing returned to the Democratic fold.

The office of state chairman or national committeeman in neither party has served as a springboard for successful pursuit of public office. Utah citizens have seldom so honored a hard-hitting and rugged party campaigner. In several instances these party officials have assisted nominees who had not even held the lowly party position of district chairman. They have seldom successfully used their position at maximum potential for their own exposure. None became a successful party boss.

Undoubtedly the most influential Republican "behind-the-scenes" political leader from 1920 to 1930 was George Wilson, who never held an elective office. (His counterparts in the Democratic party in this period were H. L. Mulliner and Delbert Draper.) Yet Wilson came as close to playing the role of a "political boss" with a "political machine" as any man in the state's history, with the possible exception of former Senator Reed Smoot. Smoot remains the only member of Congress from Utah who dominated the state's politics for any length of time. Former Senator Arthur V. Watkins, who had become nationally known and respected for the significant role he played in the Senate's censure of former Senator Joseph McCarthy, almost achieved this position with the election of George Dewey Clyde as governor in 1956 and several appointments to federal office. Watkins failed both to deal conclusively with his avowed political enemy J. Bracken Lee, and to keep his previous Republican support intact, so was defeated in 1958. Congressman Henry Aldous Dixon (1955-61) in the First District was somewhat forceful in a quiet way. He served his party well in a time and under circumstances which could have wrecked it—the moral aberration of his predecessor, Douglas Stringfellow, whose two-year appearance on Utah's political stage (1952-54) was at first scintillating and then sad.[77] Senator Wallace F. Bennett, after he was released in 1958 from Watkins' domination of the Utah Republican delegation in Congress, became more active and influential in both the national and the state party.

At present the dominant Republican personality is Laurence Burton, congressman in the First District since 1962. He has shown amazing strength. In 1964, a year of overwhelming Democratic victory, Burton defeated his opponent by a 56 percent margin. The principal Democratic winners, Senator Frank E.

76. Other observers have disputed this assertion, and one prepared and published an article to sustain his position. See Jonas, "The Third Man in Utah Politics," pp. 103-25.

77. The most dramatic event in Utah's political history occurred when Stringfellow confessed, in an unexpected television appearance, that his story of personal war heroism which had landed him in Congress, was a lie. Stringfellow's story has been told by Frank H. Jonas in *The Story of a Political Hoax* (Salt Lake City: Institute of Government, University of Utah, 1966).

Moss, Congressman David S. King, and Governor Calvin Rampton, won by 57 percent. President Johnson's margin was 54 percent.[78]

As Burton stands out as a leader of the Republicans, so also for the Democrats does Governor Calvin Rampton. Each would have the best chance of any man in his party to win re-election in 1968. Both have displayed ability in their respective offices. Both would like to be senators, but each would have to run against Wallace F. Bennett, who is thoroughly entrenched in his incumbency. Bennett is wealthy and an excellent campaigner; he also has the tacit support of the General Authorities of the Mormon church.

Democratic national committeeman since 1952, Calvin Rawlings became and remained for several years the chairman of the Credentials Committee at Democratic national conventions. Indeed, as chairman of the Western States Conference, he was one of the very few delegates from the West who has been influential in national conventions.

During the Republican years from 1953 to 1957, Milton Weilenmann was Democratic state chairman and an aggressive campaigner. He has become the Democratic candidate for the senatorial nomination. Bennett, the Republican incumbent, has been assured the nomination of his party. A recent poll revealed that Weilenmann is little known throughout the state despite his previous term as state chairman. Two rivals for the party nomination are Philip Hansen, the controversial attorney general, and J. D. Williams, an articulate University professor.

From 1933 to 1951, the dominant Democratic political personality was soft-spoken and mild-mannered United States Senator Elbert D. Thomas, formerly professor of political science at the University of Utah. His strength lay in his intelligent demeanor in Congress and in his unswerving loyalty to his political credo. He served as chairman of the Armed Services Committee during the war and chairman of the influential Labor and Education Committee. During his first term he was a member of the Foreign Relations Committee. No Utah delegate to Congress since the defeat of Reed Smoot in 1932 has achieved a comparable record.

Representative David S. King (Second District), elected in 1958, gave promise of becoming a party leader. King could never stomach the stress and strain of a heated campaign. After four years in Congress, he lost his bid for the Senate in 1962. He was elected congressman for the third time in 1964, but again lost in 1966 to a previous opponent, Sherman Lloyd, who had served from 1963-65. Lloyd, like King, abandoned his House seat to try unsuccessfully for the Republican senatorial nomination in 1964. From 1953 to the present the Democrats have held District I for only one term, 1961-63.

United States Senator Frank E. Moss has overcome many obstacles since his election in 1958 to become virtually the leader of his party outside of the state organization in which no one has dominant control. He is a politician respected by his opponents, and an excellent campaigner. He worked hard to achieve Utah's share in the development of the Colorado River Basin. He does not let petty rebuffs interfere with his progress toward a goal whether these come from his three Republican colleagues in Congress or from the influential Democratic oligarchy which has now captured the party's state organization.

78. The 1964 election year in Utah revealed graphically how both Republican and Democratic nominees manage their own campaigns almost entirely apart from the party organizations. For example, Rampton attached himself to the President's campaign but disassociated himself in his poster advertisements and appearances from King and Moss. There appeared to be even less liaison between their counterparts in the Republican party and the state and county party organizations. See Jonas, "The 1964 Election in Utah," pp. 509-13.

Several women have played significant roles in Utah politics. In an earlier period there were such names as Mrs. Burton Musser, twice appointed by President Franklin D. Roosevelt as a delegate to Pan American conferences, and Mrs. James H. Wolf, Democratic national committeewoman.[79] Reva Beck Bosone, Democrat, won two elections to Congress, 1948 and 1950, and thereby became the only congresswoman Utah has produced. In 1959, Ivy Baker Priest was her opponent. Mrs. Priest became Republican national committeewoman and was placed in charge of Women's Activities on the National Republican Committee. In 1953 she was appointed Treasurer of the United States. After this eight-year service she established residence in California and was elected state treasurer.[80] More recently Esther Peterson, Democrat, was appointed by President Johnson as Assistant Secretary of Labor.

Third parties have never fared well in Utah. Their best year, with the exception of the substantial vote for Robert LaFollette in 1924, was in 1932.[81] The Progressive party in 1948, with Henry A. Wallace and U.S. Senator Glen Taylor as candidates in the presidential campaign, placed these nominees on the ballot. Sharing the ballot as third party candidates were the Socialists, Farrel Dobbs for president and Grace Carlson for vice-president. In 1950, a group which called itself the National Economy party, and in 1952 two groups, the Christian Nationalist party and Socialist Labor party, tried but failed to qualify for the ballot. Since 1948 no third party has qualified until George A. Wallace's party won a place in 1968.

In summary, when political parties in the state have had excellent leadership, good organization, competent candidates, and sufficient money they have won. When any one of these factors—especially good party organization or leaders—has been lacking, the party has lost. When these factors have appeared strong and in combination, what may be called a trend has seemed to be present to account for victory at the polls. Invariably a trend sets in after a substantial victory. The victorious party relaxes and the losers work hard to produce what is necessary for victory in a not-too-far-away election. Since 1948, with the exception of the years 1958 and 1964, the Republican party has been more successful at the polls than the Democratic party. It has not had superior candidates and potential leaders, but it has had fewer intra-party divisions and struggles. Those which have appeared have been dealt with more expeditiously and decisively. In both parties, however, the real incentive and the best results in campaign organization and activities, including fund-raising, have come from individual candidate campaigners. In this area, Senator Wallace F. Bennett and Senator Frank E. Moss have produced the best results for themselves and for their parties as a whole. Party organization in Utah simply is neither strong nor continuous.

PRESSURE GROUPS

Political parties in Utah, as elsewhere, are made up mainly of pressure groups whose interests in most instances are economic. The most influential groups

79. See Jonas, in Donnelly, *op. cit.*, pp. 27, 30.

80. Mrs. Priest has documented much of her political career in her autobiography, *Green Grows Ivy* (New York: McGraw-Hill, 1958).

81. For the record of third parties who achieved ballot status see Jonas, "Utah Presidential Elections, 1896-1952," *Utah Historical Quarterly*, XXIV (October 1956), 289-307. This article contains the election results for presidential candidates including those of third parties on the ballot. The only state or local party to achieve ballot status was the American party, 1904-12. This story has been told well by Snow, "The American Party in Utah."

which apply pressure in Congress and in the state legislature are those which represent the state's dominant industries and business enterprises. Though not listed precisely in their order of influence, these are the Salt Lake City Chamber of Commerce, the Utah Manufacturers Association, the Utah Mining Association, the Utah Industrial Council, the Utah Farm Bureau Federation, and the Utah Taxpayers Association.

In any consideration of pressure groups in Utah, one cannot ignore the Mormon church. Now over 2,500,000 in membership, it is significant as a religious institution, but in all candor one must say that it is also a pressure group, even when it acts on moral grounds to influence legislation. On the other hand, all sects, denominations, and churches are interest groups, and at times they are pressure groups on moral and even temporal grounds. Legislators and citizens generally have been somewhat surprised to see the number of lesser publicized religious groups which come forward when a Sunday closing bill is put into the hopper; usually they are in opposition to it. The Mormon church has substantial property holdings and operates a number of commercial enterprises. Consequently, it is a member, directly or indirectly, of the usual array of pressure groups representing economic interests. Also, because of its high taxpaying position, it is willy-nilly catapulted into politics, and as a result it is vitally interested in public policies affecting its temporal interests.

Other groups representing banking, finance, insurance, real estate, and construction interests are influential, as are those which represent fuels (oil, gas, and coal), utilities, the usual assortment of small business and retail enterprises, and professional and allied interests. There is also the array of groups representing agriculture and livestock interests, cattle, wool and fowl.

For the most part all of these groups have associated themselves with the Republican party which has become known in Utah, as elsewhere, as the party of big business.[82] On the other hand, the Democratic party has become identified with labor unions. Labor has endorsed almost exclusively Democratic candidates, but it has not always been successful in electing them, and on occasion, segments of labor have supported a Republican. Also, in some cases, Democratic politicians, especially legislators, have run on platforms which invariably have included planks favorable to labor, and have accepted labor union aid, only to act and vote in the legislature contrary to labor interests. This is another form of duplicity in Utah politics.[83]

In the 1950's labor unions increased their total influence in the state by becoming organized and strong in eastern Utah. Construction enterprises, especially the Flaming Gorge and Glen Canyon dams, and the tremendous upsurge in uranium and oil mining in this area gave labor additional votes and influence in the First Congressional District where traditionally it has been strong: in Ogden and Weber

82. United States Senator Arthur V. Watkins reportedly admitted his reliance on big business for financial support when he refused to hear out the plea of the Utah Petroleum Dealers for an amendment to the Robinson-Patman Act. Consequently, the only published endorsement in the 1958 election made by the Republican petroleum dealers in their house organ was for Watkins' Democratic rival, Frank E. Moss.

83. True, one may be aware of the textbook conception of the representative's position. He should "represent himself," not a party, not an interest group. This role cannot always be practiced. Politicians should at least try in their campaigning to be as honest as they possibly can; but it does happen that they can change their minds after the campaign. However, in the cases alluded to in this context, the candidates appeared deliberately to falsify their true feelings in the interest of getting votes; they never intended to be honest in the first place.

County, railroading and manufacturing are the chief industries, and in Carbon County, coal mining and natural gas.

Labor registered its best record in the state's history in getting its members to the polls for its endorsed candidates in the 1958 elections.[84] Several reasons account for the fact that it has seemed to lose ground since that banner year. Actually, Utah has not been nor has it become to this day a "labor state," and Salt Lake City has not been a "labor town." Right-to-work legislation, passed in 1954, has helped to frustrate strong labor organization. Attempts have been made in every legislative session since 1954 to repeal this legislation but none has been even moderately successful.

In agriculture, the Republican farmers generally tend to join the Farm Bureau Federation; the Democrats, the Farmers Union. The Grange is not organized in Utah. Though not large in membership, the Farmers Union has espoused the cause of the small farmer. For example, it has opposed raising assessments of farm lands in metropolitan areas like Utah and Salt Lake counties. If these were assessed at the same figure for which they could be sold, the owners could no longer afford to farm them. The small pioneering typical 20-to-80-acre farmer in Utah, in both metropolitan and non-metropolitan areas, cannot make a living on this or even a substantially larger farm unit. The Farm Bureau approaches this problem realistically; it supports the big farmer. The Farmers Union exploits the problem politically with attempts to secure federal supports and subsidies. Other pressure groups represent the livestock people, principally cattle and sheep, and the dairymen and poultry raisers.

Only in recent years have teachers acted politically in their own interests. The Utah Education Association is considered by many pressure groups representing industry and finance as the strongest—and at times the most obnoxious—pressure group in the state. Other lobbying groups in this field are the School Boards Association, the State Department of Public Instruction, and the Utah State Congress of Parents and Teachers. The Utah Council for the Improvement of Education has limited itself to the election of legislators and governors.

Women's groups in Utah politics are the Utah Federation of Women, the League of Women Voters, the Women's Legislative Council, the League of Business and Professional Women, and the Daughters of the Utah Pioneers. If confronted, these groups would deny that they were pressure groups, but each one has behaved politically at times to merit the designation according to the textbook descriptions of such groups and their methods.

LEGISLATIVE POLITICS

Legislatures in Utah generally have been conservative, except during the New Deal period. This statement is true in spite of the statistical fact that from 1929 to 1967, the Democrats had 246 members in the state Senate and 697 in the House of Representatives; the Republicans had 215 and 526, respectively. In the twenty legislatures, eleven of the Senate and eight of the House sessions were Republican.[85] The Democrats were overwhelmingly in control from 1937 to 1943. In 1945 they retained the House but the GOP took the Senate, both by overwhelming margins. With such ratios as 22:1 in 1937 and 21:3 in 1939 in the Sen-

84. Jonas, "The 1958 Election in Utah," *Western Political Quarterly*, XII (March 1959, Part 2), 348.

85. In 1951, the House was tied 30 to 30.

ate, for example, the 56:4 in the same years for the House, and with all state and national offices filled with party members, the Democrats were in the saddle. The Republicans have never matched these membership figures when the tide has run their way, until 1967, when they seated 23 of the 28 senators and 59 of the 69 representatives.[86] But to expect so-called liberal social legislation or political reform on the basis of party labels would be erroneous. Many Democrats are conservative in their views and voting; when the party's margin has not been overwhelming, the results have been decisively Republican and conservative.

It was believed, prior to the 1959 session, that Republicans vote more often as a bloc than Democrats and that individual Democrats are more likely to defect to the Republicans when voting on social legislation than are individual Republicans to the Democratic side. Also, it appeared that Republican party leaders outside the legislature controlled the votes of their representatives better than their Democratic counterparts did. These hypotheses were dispelled to a great extent by a quantitative study made of the sessions from 1959 to 1963.

The study revealed that there was more party solidarity than is generally recognized in Utah. Republicans failed to muster at least 67 percent of the party vote on only two of the bills which were examined. They maintained a party loyalty of 85 percent over-all. The Democrats split on three bills; they averaged an 80 percent party vote. This was a limited analysis, but it did show that political affiliation was a major influence on the members of the Utah legislature and that both parties commanded approximately the same degree of loyalty.[87]

Observation of the 1965 and 1967 sessions would not alter this conclusion. Indeed, the Democrats showed more party solidarity in 1965 than in any previous session since World War II. To account for this, one must cite the leadership in the governor's office and in the two branches of the legislature. In 1965 the Senate was composed of 15 Democrats and 12 Republicans. A shift of two Democratic votes on any measure could tip the scales in favor of the Republicans. The margin in the House was 39 to 30, not quite so close, but equally precarious because of the tendency of conservative Democrats to vote with Republicans on financial and social measures. Democratic Governor Calvin Rampton had excellent support from two stalwarts, Kay Allen, speaker of the House, and Bruce Jenkins, president of the Senate. Allen handled the gavel extremely well, and did not antagonize anyone. O. N. Malmquist, Salt Lake *Tribune* political reporter for almost forty years, said of Jenkins that he was the most astute and able president of the Senate he had observed during his career of reporting the legislature. Jenkins was especially effective in keeping the 15 Democratic votes intact on the measure to bond the state for $65,000,000 for building purposes. For once, if not precisely for the first time, there was no split among the Democrats along political, social, or religious ideological lines.

In 1967, the legislature was preponderantly Republican. The handful of Democrats in both houses did not demonstrate any competent opposition or leadership in the aftermath of the self-destructive antics of their fellow members in the 1966 elections which had virtually wrecked the party.

The Legislative Council, created in 1947, has had only one director during its

86. From 1961 to 1967 two sessions were Republican and two were Democratic. During this period the Republicans elected 151 House members to the Democrats' 115, and 59 to 46 Senate members. The over-all figures for both Houses were 210 Republican and 161 Democrats.

87. Rodney O. Julander, "The Composition and Voting Record of the Utah State Legislature, 1957-63," *Western Political Quarterly*, XVII (September 1964), 88-90.

life to date. Both he and the council have compiled good records of service and achievement. At times the members have attempted to serve the economic interests of their employment and professional occupations, acting more as lobbyists than as legislative representatives. In some instances the members have used their Council positions as springboards for public office. In 1948, at least five of the thirteen members filed for elective office. Ten years later, a veteran state senator, Sol Selvin, noted with considerable anguish that this condition had not changed. Whether the effectiveness of the Council for creative work has been hampered by this situation might be debatable.[88]

Politics has never been absent from the Council. On the first Council there were seven Democrats and six Republicans. But every vote on a controversial question in social legislation or a tax proposition came out as 10 to 3 for the Republicans. The members were voting along ideological and not along party lines.

In an extraordinary move the legislature designated the Legislative Council in the statute as the advisory council to the State Department of Public Welfare. Former Governor Herbert B. Maw was accused by Republicans and many influential conservative Democrats of using this Department as a pawn in his efforts to win a third term in 1948.[89]

Until 1965 the Legislative Council was made up of thirteen members: five state senators appointed by the president of the Senate; five representatives appointed by the speaker of the House; and three laymen, one each appointed by the speaker, the Senate president, and the governor.[90] In a special session of the legislature in 1965 the total membership was increased to sixteen: eight state senators and eight representatives. It was also changed at this time to become strictly a research committee. It still performs the duties of the Commission on Interstate Cooperation. This change is not likely to decrease the political role the Council has played in the past; it will only limit political activity to the members of the legislature from which most of the previous political activities emanated in the first place.

From its inception in 1947 the membership of the Council has closely reflected the economic character of the legislature. During the first twelve years attorneys and businessmen were the overwhelming majority of those appointed, mirroring the era when voting control was exercised by these two groups regardless of party label. Since 1961, the emphasis has not shifted very much. The appointees fall into the following categories: businessmen, 19; attorneys, 12; educa-

88. Indeed, in 1960, Sherman Lloyd, Senate president and Council chairman, won the Republican Second Congressional District nomination but lost the election. He won the office twice in overwhelming Republican sweeps in the state (1962 and 1966). He has been the most successful politician to use his position on the Council and his service in the state Senate as propaganda for higher office. Sheldon Brewster, Democrat, former vice-chairman of the Council, and Rendell Mabey, Republican former chairman, both speakers of the House of Representatives at the time, tried unsuccessfully to gain their party's nomination for the governorship.

89. The Legislative Council's Welfare Committee was constituted of four instead of the usual three members. Two were considered liberals and two actually were radical right-wingers, opposed to the purpose of the Department as well as to its administration. Each vote of the committee came out a tie of 2 to 2. Thrown back into the plenary Legislative Council the vote would be 10 to 3 for the dominant anti-welfare interests.

90. There were twelve committees with each member a chairman of one and a member of a second. A farmer-businessman was appointed chairman of the education committee. He fought every suggestion of an increased appropriation for the University of Utah. An educator was appointed chairman of the agriculture committee. His attempt to organize a Department of Conservation stands as a monument in the early efforts to reorganize state government in the postwar period.

tors, 5; newspapermen, 3; real-estate men and ranchers, 2 each; a radio station owner, a farmer, and a housewife. Businessmen included insurance and automotive personnel, a Geneva Steel employee, a petroleum distributor, and the owner of a hardware store.

An occupational count made of the three legislative sessions from 1959 to 1963 revealed that business comprised the largest category, 31 percent. Others were as follows: farming and ranching, 18 percent; retired, 16 percent; education, 11 percent; law, 8 percent; and miscellaneous, 9 percent.[91] In the 1965 and 1967 sessions businessmen led with 41 percent, followed by farmers and ranchers, 10 percent, and attorneys, 9 percent. About six occupations were represented by two members each in each house. All other occupations (about 27) were represented by only one each in each house, with the exception of four retired persons and four educators in the 1965 House of Representatives. The presence of teachers and educators was interesting to note in these two sessions. In 1965, as a result of intense teacher activity, there were fourteen educators in both chambers, thirteen of them in the House. In 1967, however, the number dropped to five. Other categories showed very little or no change from session to session. This was true when these averages were compared to the figures for single sessions in previous and subsequent years.

The number of freshmen did not change much over the years. In the period from 1959 to 1963 an average of 48 percent of the legislators were elected for the first time. The greatest number in a single session came in 1967, the first legislature elected under the new reapportionment on the basis of the one man, one vote formula. Forty-six out of 69 members (66 percent) in the House and 20 of 28 (70 percent) in the Senate were novices. Ordinarily the Senate turnover would be much less than in the House because of the four-year staggered terms, but everyone in 1966, due to reapportionment, ran from scratch.

Two categories, personal income and religious affiliation, have remained quite constant throughout the years. In the period 1941 to 1959, the religious composition was as follows: Mormon, 729; Catholic, 12; Presbyterian, 9; Episcopalian, 8; Christian, 5; Unitarian, 4; Methodist, 3; Greek Orthodox, 3; Baptist, 2; Congregationalist, 1; nonsectarian, 41; unknown, 2. Mormons occupied about 95 percent of the total seats in both houses during this period. In 1965 and 1967 their percentage figures dropped to 93 and 88, respectively. However, the religious affiliation of 11 members was not determined. These figures in any event can be decidedly misleading for they do not reflect the shades of personal faith or sectarian loyalty. Many Mormons are lukewarm or inactive in the church.

Two areas covered in the survey from 1959 to 1963 showed some change over the three terms. The educational level fluctuated, and there was significant change in the ages of the legislators. In 1967, of the 97 members 48 were college graduates, 16 had attended college, and 8 had attended business college. In 1959 and 1961, 55 percent of the members were over 50 years of age. In 1963, the percentage dropped to 26. The average age in the 1967 session was 48 in the House and 51 in the Senate.

All factors surveyed in this period remained fairly constant during the following two sessions, 1965 and 1967. No significant change, except in party affiliation, was noted. The few variations in age and educational levels certainly could not have accounted for any significant change in the types of bills passed or in the

91. Because of average percentages over several years in each category, these do not total 100 percent.

political ideology of the legislature. Rather, changes resulted from sheer pressure from various outside sources, such as education in the instance of the bonding program, the federal government in that of reapportionment, and the social ferment in the entire nation in the case of the two civil rights measures which were passed. These realities, more than any factors in the composition of the legislature, will cause both Republican and Democratic legislators to be a little more aware about social change which has a tendency to sweep everything before it. All that any policy-makers can do or even hope for is to stay at the head of a movement and perhaps to some extent determine its direction and the nature of the institutional forms which may finally emerge.

No real division has developed between urban and rural or between northern and southern areas. The only significant bloc voting from these groups appeared when legislators from the southern part of the state supported the Republican-sponsored education bills. This grouping has been a traditional pattern in the entire history of the state's legislative voting. The representatives of the property-tax-minded farmers have always worked with the representatives of property-tax-minded big (and small) business and financial interests headquartered in the northern cities along the Wasatch Front.

Generally, the Republicans have sponsored the tax and education bills designed to give the teachers only enough to quiet them for another two years. In 1964 many Republican teachers voted Democratic in the belief that the Democrats in the legislature have been more favorable to education. Democratic politicians have done little or nothing to keep this image alive. As a result of the fact that the 1967 Republican legislature appropriated more for education than the Democratic governor had asked for in his budget, the Republican party may be the chief beneficiary of the teacher vote in the 1968 election. Much will depend on the ability of Republican politicians to exploit this advantage for campaign purposes. Of interest will be how the educational politicians will interpret and exploit the entire situation. Any of these three groups, Democrats, Republicans, and teachers, which permits an outmoded ideology to become a stumbling block will lose out in this game of politics involving both political parties and pressure groups.

Several occupational groups consistently have voted together. The lawyers and farmers have voted in blocs and both have voted with the Republican leadership, again because of the property tax. Educators and labor members have shown solidarity in their votes and have voted with the Democratic leaders. Surveys dating back to 1956 have shown that over 60 percent of the individual teachers and educators are Republican by their own admission. The educators are a conservative influence in society as strong or even stronger than their legal and medical brethren. However, in all these professions, as with other segments of society, the money and the financial advantages that can be bestowed by politicans through public policy still form the dominant political motivation.

Personal income seems to have voting significance. Representatives earning less than $5,000 per year followed the Democratic vote more than their party membership indicated. Those earning $20,000 were fairly consistent in supporting the Republican administration.

Utah's constitution provides for legislative reapportionment following each decennial census and for an enumeration by the state to be taken every ten years beginning in 1905. The state has never taken an enumeration and only twice has the legislature reapportioned its seats at "the session next following" the federal census.[92] For this reason, the charge has been made that Utah lawmakers have "violated the Utah constitution regularly since 1905."[93]

Reapportionment has taken place six times in Utah history, 1901, 1921, 1931, 1955, 1963, and finally in 1965. A proposed constitutional change was placed on the ballot in 1954 in the form of a referendum, which would have reduced urban representation by giving one senator to each of the 29 counties while increasing this representation by raising the number of House members from 60 to 75. The campaign for the amendment, waged principally by Mormon church officials, the Farm Bureau Federation, and rural civic leaders, once again revealed the political, religious, economic, and social forces in state politics and temporarily brought about their complete realignment. Big business, the Catholic church, the Masons, and the labor unions—strange bedfellows indeed—stood together in opposition. The Salt Lake *Tribune*'s publisher, John F. Fitzpatrick, a practicing Roman Catholic lay leader, stated that the Catholic church opposed the proposition; further, he said that had the referendum succeeded it would have given *one* group too much power. The compromise arrangement passed by the 1955 legislature and subsequently upheld by the Utah Supreme Court increased the Senate membership from 23 to 25 and the House membership from 60 to 64.

In 1961, a Democratic legislature passed a reapportionment measure but the Republican governor vetoed it. Two years later a Republican legislature passed a reapportionment act which did not satisfy in the least the advocates of the federal formula of "one man, one vote." Suit was filed by three Salt Lake County residents to test the act on the grounds that a proper reapportionment had not been made as required by the Utah constitution and the new enactment did not correct an invidious discrimination on the part of the legislature. Under the 1961 act, populous Salt Lake County was to have an increased representation in the House of Representatives from 21 to 24, and in the Senate from 6 to 7. This slight increase was not considered sufficient to quiet the complaints about unequal representation. Under the 1963 act the Senate would be increased to 28 members and the House to 69. The counties would retain the minimum constitutional requirement of at least one representative for each county. On June 15, 1964, the United States Supreme Court handed down its famous decision in *Reynolds v. Sims*, "one man, one vote."[94] The question in the 1965 legislature resolved itself to the sole consideration of whether the representatives should do the reapportioning in compliance with the federal court decision or whether they should allow the court to do it; they chose to do it themselves. The legislature now has 28 senators and 69 House members.

Utah also realigned its two congressional districts in March 1965 on a nearly equal basis. In this year the two old districts had a population spread of 254,681; in the realigned ones the spread was only 13,101. Two populous counties (Davis and Utah) were transferred from the old Second District to the new First, and

92. "The Struggle for Reapportionment in Utah" has been told by Kenneth Mitchell in a Master's thesis by that title (University of Utah, 1960), and by Brad Hainsworth, "Reapportionment in Utah, 1954 to 1965," (Master's thesis, University of Utah, 1966). Mitchell covered the early period, 1896 (statehood) to 1955, and Hainsworth the later period.

93. See Jerome K. Full, "Rural vs. Urban Vote: Ratio Stays at Illegal 1 to 45," Salt Lake *Tribune*, December 13, 1959. State Senator Orval Hafen ("Dixie Solon Defends Apportionment of Legislature," Salt Lake *Tribune*, December 20, 1959) denied the constitution had been violated, except that the legislature had "not acted as often as provided in the Constitution." He defended the 1955 reapportionment act, upheld by the state's Supreme Court (*Parkinson v. Watson*, 4 Utah 2nd 191, 241 D. 400, 1955), on pragmatic grounds.

94. 377 U.S. 522 (1964).

were replaced by five lightly populated counties from the old First District. Since each District has over 500,000 population, both congressmen are entitled to equal expense money for their office staffs. Twenty-two counties now comprise the First District and seven the Second. Although these seven cover only 31 percent of the land area, they contain 55.2 percent of the population, and 54.2 percent of the state's assessed valuation. It is suggested that the redistricting helped the Republican cause.[95] Laurence Burton (R) retained his congressional seat in 1966 with 64.1 percent of the vote, while David S. King (D) lost heavily in the Second District, gaining only 38.9 percent. However, it is unrealistic to predict a pattern on the basis of one election, or even to conclude that these results were due to redistricting.[96]

With the disclosure on February 7, 1965, that they would support an amendment to the national Constitution designed to alter the ruling in *Reynolds v. Sims*, the Utah Democratic delegation, Representative David S. King and Senator Frank E. Moss, opened a schism in the Democratic party which was not healed by the 1966 elections. King indicated that, though the decision in *Reynolds v. Sims* was "perfectly fair by strict legal standards," it was nonetheless not in accord with the tradition that the "founding fathers in their great wisdom built into our system."[97] Politicians noted that King was making a play for conservative votes. Influential liberal Democrats, however, opposed him, fully realizing that the amendment would probably never become a part of the Constitution. Senator Moss felt that the question should go to the people in a referendum. When Representative Sherman P. Lloyd (R) said, "It is the people, not the states, not the federal government, not the Supreme Court, not the Congress, which have the final say about the business of running a democracy,"[98] he was talking more as a politician than as the lawyer he is in private life. Senator Wallace F. Bennett (R) was a co-sponsor with Senator Everett M. Dirksen (R-Ill.) who offered the amendment.

While the Utah constitution does not provide for the recall of public officials, it does provide for impeachment, with the usual procedure of charges being brought in the House of Representatives and the trial taking place in the Senate. However, there have never been any impeachment proceedings in the state's history.

Legal voters may by petition initiate legislation which appears on the ballot in the form of a referendum or the legislature can place a measure on the ballot in the next regular election after the session. Any legislative enactment, except when

95. Gov. Calvin L. Rampton (D) recommended that Salt Lake County be combined with solidly Democratic Tooele County. On a straight party vote the Senate (12 Republicans, 15 Democrats) passed Rampton's plan. Meanwhile the House (Republicans 30, Democrats 39), the same day, had passed a plan identical to the final one. Legislators of both parties in the House objected to the Governor's plan for two reasons: they felt it was obviously an attempt to create a "safe" Democratic district; and they wanted to make both districts represent a cross-section of the state's total population. Another factor was the tremendous size of the current First District, which made campaigning difficult and expensive. Various industries and other interests were quite dispersed in both districts.

96. See Frank H. Jonas, "The 1966 Elections in Utah," *Western Political Quarterly*, XX (June 1967, Part 2), 602-6. The fact that the 1966 election was a complete reversal of the 1964 election upset all past patterns of trends in the state's voting. In 1964, Democrats won all three national offices with an average of 57 percent. In 1966 Republicans won the two congressional seats with an average of 62.5 percent. In 1964, the Democrats won all state offices, the state legislature, and the important county commissioner posts. In 1966, the Republicans won, in addition to the national offices, all the important county seats.

97. Salt Lake *Tribune*, May 2, 1965.

98. *Ibid.*, July 25, 1964.

it is passed by a two-thirds vote in each house, may be referred to the voters before it takes effect. The mandatory requirement that "a majority of all counties of the state must each furnish signatures of legal voters not less in number than the required percentages" discourages use of the initiative procedure. The usual figure is 5 percent, but to secure it in 15 of the 29 counties requires considerable organization and is especially difficult when a measure applies principally to a limited area. If a petition measure is not enacted by the legislature, it shall be submitted to the people for vote at the next election, but in this case the number of signatures required is raised to 10 percent of all votes for all candidates for governor at the preceding election. Only the most controversial measures or those with a great deal of organizational support have made the ballot, and only those with comparable organizational effort or popular support have succeeded.

Since 1930, 52 propositions have appeared on the ballot, 40 percent of them in the past decade. The most controversial before 1958 were the tax on chain stores, defeated in 1942, and reapportionment, defeated in 1954. In those two years the referenda provided the only real issues in the elections. The chain store tax was watched closely throughout the nation as a test case for this kind of legislation. The defeat of the Utah measure put the brake on prospective similar movements elsewhere in the nation.

In the last decade, twelve of the propositions which appeared on the ballot were defeated and nine were passed. In the 1966 election eight, the total number on the ballot, were defeated. These dealt with recommendations of a special committee, established by the 1965 legislature, to reorganize the state government. However, the most unpopular with the Establishment in Utah and the entrenched wealthy interests was the proposition to call a convention to rewrite the state's constitution. These same interests would have liked the voters to have approved three or four specific recommendations, but their propaganda against propositions in general boomeranged on this occasion. The voters found it difficult to understand the recommended changes and the reasons therefor, and they had been urged by the newspapers to vote "no" for a proposition they did not understand. Referenda and initiatives have appeared on the ballot in thirteen of the last nineteen elections. Seven of these elections had three or less on the ballot in any one year. The largest number was eight, both in 1946 and in 1966.

If politics is the making of public policy, then its center is the Joint Appropriations Committee which meets biennially late in each legislative session. Here are gathered all the representatives of all the interest and pressure groups who want something from the public till and all those who want to keep them from getting it. Symbolical of these two sides are the Utah Educational Association and the Utah Mining Association. In this political arena these two groups, with their cohorts lined up on either side (but with most of them wanting to keep others from dipping into the till), could be at each other's throats, given the ingredients which might trigger violence.

One budgetary political problem has been present since the state government was reorganized in 1941 under Governor Herbert B. Maw. In this year a bipartisan three-man Finance Commission was established for the purpose of bringing "state finances under executive control in terms of broad spending policy, after legislative appropriation, and to facilitate and expedite procurement of material, supplies and also to a degree, personnel."

These functions have brought the Finance Department which includes the controller, the budget director, the purchasing agent, and the personnel manager, into conflict with the elected state auditor, the governor, and the powerful Board of Examiners, constituted of the governor, the secretary of state, and the attorney general. Conflicts and problems are compounded when one member, the governor, is not of the same political party as the other two.

During the past three decades the governor has found himself either handicapped or hamstrung in his relations with the Finance Commission. Under Governor Maw, the Commission, instead of being an auxiliary or staff agency, gained a position in state government far stronger than intended. Governor Lee managed the situation better than his predecessor. Some citizens objected to Lee's placing his "cronies" or "lodge brothers" in so many high offices in the capitol, but when he said he must have persons in these offices he could trust, he was substantially on solid ground, since at that time there was no state merit system. By these appointments and by keeping the lid tight on every department, he minimized his difficulties or kept them from breaking out into the open.

Although the governor is responsible for the construction of the budget, he still has difficulties in this area. The legislature wrested an advantage from him when it created the position of "legislative analyst" whose main function seems to deal almost exclusively with budget, tax, and revenue matters. The governor's office is the weak executive type, and the budget director is not on the governor's staff. The 1965 legislature provided for a committee to consider closely the reorganization of state government. Some reorganization, based on this committee's report, was effected by the 1967 legislature.

The chief accomplishment was the re-grouping of state agencies in compatible clusters. For example, the State Health and Welfare Departments have been combined into one division with a single head. However, each department has retained its own director. The division director deals directly with the state's auxiliary agencies and the legislature. He need not report to the governor. The Board of Examiners was left untouched and, if anything, it was strengthened in its anomalous position in the state government. It has been a constant troublemaker in asserting its right to be the final arbiter in the administration of state finances.[99]

Governor Calvin Rampton's recommendations for a cabinet government were ignored by the 1967 legislature. The Republicans in control were not about to give a Democratic governor his wish; it is doubtful if they would have given a Republican this kind of organization. Nor is it likely that the Democrats, were they in control, would act any differently. All politicians shy from strengthening the executive branch of government. So far, their intended reforms have only weakened it.

VOTING HABITS AND PARTY AFFILIATION

Some western states, such as Alaska, California, Oregon, Arizona, and New Mexico, have developed into two-party states. Utah has been one from statehood to the present time. Usually the results at the polls show a narrow margin of victory between the two major parties, which has widened only when a party has been at its height nationally. For example, Utah gave Franklin D. Roosevelt in 1936 and Dwight D. Eisenhower in 1956 comparably large majorities. Any speculation

99. Particularly it has been in hot water by attempting to assert its control over the State Department of Public Instruction and institutions of higher learning by its attempts to bring the salaries of educational specialists and of University personnel under the merit system. Ostensibly its chief function has been to review and pass upon claims against the state, but it has overstepped its bounds.

as to the influence of the Mormon church would have to take into account the discrepancies which these two elections show: their results cancel each other. In 1936, the church had little or no influence; in 1956 it seemed to have a great deal. Politics and economics—not religion—have determined election results in Utah. The role of religion has diminished as a factor determining voting behavior in the state.[100]   Both Mormon and anti-Mormon leaders would prefer to have it popularly understood that the church has a great deal of control. It is useful propaganda for both sides. Mormon leaders do not want publicized that they do not have the control their predecessors had either in the later territorial days or in the early period of statehood. The anti-Mormons want to use the alleged power of the church in politics to turn persons, both Mormons and non-Mormons, against the institution in order to minimize the influence which it can or does exert in Utah politics. Both Mormon and non-Mormon representatives of pressure groups will decry the so-called interference of the church in politics when it is to their advantage to do so, but if they think it to be to their advantage to have the support of the church, they will deliberately seek it.

Probably in no other state in the nation did the two major parties start out at statehood so equally divided and matched as in Utah. Democratic blunders, the same sort the Democrats are making today, and Republican economic policies were influential in tipping the scale for the GOP up to 1912.[101]   Three times the state went against the national trend in presidential elections: in 1896, when William Jennings Bryan received over 82.7 percent of the vote; in 1912, when Taft received a plurality;[102] in 1960, when Nixon won over Kennedy. Since statehood, however, Utah has voted nine times for a Democratic president and nine times for a Republican one.

National political and economic trends seem to reach and enter Utah later than other states. As recently as 1956, the Democratic trend, which had begun shortly after 1952, stopped dead at the state's borders; it did not become a factor until the Democratic success in 1958. However, the pattern in Utah is contrary to that which prevails elsewhere: the party out of power does not make significant gains in off-presidential election years. Only in 1966 was this pattern upset. The Republicans made a clean sweep in the 1966 elections after a comparable Democratic sweep in the 1964 presidential election.

United States Senator Reed Smoot, Republican, survived the Democratic years from 1912 to 1920, as his junior in the Senate, William H. King, Democrat, survived the Republican era from 1920 to 1932. Since statehood, seven Republicans and five Democrats have been elected to the United States Senate. Including the year 1968, the Republicans have served 82 years and the Democrats 64 years. In the same period twelve individual Republicans and nine individual Democrats were elected to the House of Representatives, the Democrats serving 60 years, the Republicans 71. Utah was granted a second representative in 1912. In the same

100. For a review of the titles on this subject and for an excellent account involving the Mormon church in this category see Mann, *op. cit.*, pp. 32-48.

101. From 1896 to 1912 the Republicans won the gubernatorial elections and 8 of 11 congressional elections. All of the Democratic successes were before 1900.

102. In this year, Woodrow Wilson, the Democratic victor, came in second. Theodore Roosevelt, who had visited the state and West several times in previous years, expressed himself as disappointed over the result. The fact is that Roosevelt had used the power of the White House in 1907 to help Senator Reed Smoot retain his seat. Smoot supported Taft. Smoot was always a "regular" Republican and always supported the party and administration in Washington, D.C. He never once in his career showed any independent tendencies.

period six Republican governors served 41 years and five Democratic governors 32 years. Although Republican governors served from 1896 to 1917, a period of 21 years, Democratic governors served from 1925 to 1949, a total of 24 years. Although three Republican and two Democratic governors aspired to third terms, none has managed it. Seven governors, four Republicans and three Democrats, have served two terms or eight years each. Two Republicans and one Democrat served one-year terms. The incumbent, Democrat Calvin Rampton, will have completed one term in January 1969; he is a candidate for re-election in 1968, being the only Democrat on his party's ticket who has a chance to win.

If these results are computed for the years 1912 through 1966, the party results appear somewhat differently. Since 1912, Utah has elected members to the House of Representatives 56 times, 28 times for each party. In the 18 senatorial elections since 1912 Utah voters have sent Democrats to Washington 8 times and a mixed delegation 10 times. In the last 16 legislatures, both houses have been controlled by the Republicans 5 times and by the Democrats 8 times. Twice party control has been divided and once, in 1951, the Democrats held the Senate but the House was evenly divided (30 to 30).

After reviewing Republican and Democratic success at the polls in the past decade, one can conclude that "the strength of the two parties in Utah is now so evenly balanced that elections are usually won or lost on the attractiveness of the candidates, the efficiency of campaign organization and techniques, and the influence of national trends and state conditions."[103] One might add the availability and adequacy of funds. The successful senatorial campaigns of Bennett (R) in 1962 and Moss (D) in 1964 were characterized by the fact that both had ample funds in addition to excellent organizations—and also a tide that was carrying them along.

No studies are available to indicate how Mormons, or members of any other group for that matter, have voted in Utah elections. A specialized study made in 1957 of Mormon political characteristics revealed that in Utah, 89 percent of the stake presidents acknowledge Republican party affiliation or sympathy.[104] In this study the samples were divided into rural small towns, and urban-industrial groups. Only Republican and Democratic sentiments were reported by the stake presidents, but the bishops reported 55 percent Republican, 22.5 percent Democratic, 13.9 percent independent, and 8.3 percent none. No Mormon official acknowledged any "other" position. A less ambitious comparable study was made in 1967 with no appreciable variations in these figures. Mormon party affiliation was divided almost equally, Republicans having a slight edge. The percentages for the rural areas were 43.3 Republican, 37 Democratic, 8.6 independent, 10.2 none, and .08 others, and for the urban-industrial areas, 36.2, 34, 15, 6.3 and 6.6 respectively.

The political characteristics of the entire membership were classified according to seven degrees of church activity, holding some responsible administrative, supervisory, or teaching position. It was found that more Mormons who were in each of the three highest degrees of activity were Republicans and that more in each of the four lower degrees were Democrats. A more plausible reason for the Republicanism of the local leadership, bishops and stake presidents, would be its

103. See Grow, "The Development of Political Parties in Utah," pp. 39-40.

104. J. Kenneth Davies, "A Study of the Development of a Labor Philosophy Within the Church of Jesus Christ of Latter-day Saints" (Ph.D. dissertation, University of Southern California, 1960), p. 296.

occupational characteristics. The church has a lay priesthood. Local Mormon leaders tend to be owners of, or to hold supervisory positions in, business. Members tend to be skilled and unskilled workers; and farmers, teachers, and salesmen tend to be divided equally between leaders and members. In other words, Mormons tend to be Republican for the same reasons that other classes of persons are Republican. The personal views and private business interests of the General Authorities, who have been approximately 90 percent Republican and 100 percent conservative during the past four decades, would bring them into the conservative orbit of the Republican party regardless of any religious considerations.

It should be recalled at all times that the Mormon officials bring their personal party preferences and ideologies into the church and to the positions they hold: they do not receive their political philosophies from the church. Democrats who have become general and local authorities in the church usually remain Democrats, although they may become politically inactive. They do serve the church in any event. If a Democrat lobbies for a policy or a position that appears to favor the Republican party, it is because his actions are in the interests of the church.

The Catholic vote is divided between the two parties. The small Negro vote is generally conservative, as is the Greek ethnic vote. German immigrants, who 60 or 70 years ago would have been Republicans, are now either politically indifferent or have become Democrats in at least equal numbers.

Local labor leaders recognize the rugged individualism of Utah citizens and quarrel often with national leaders over the use of specific tactics. Organized labor in Utah has found it difficult to hold its members in a bloc for voting purposes. Utah politicians, especially Republicans, have been able to ignore labor unions entirely during a campaign. The Utah citizen wears neither a party nor a labor union yoke. He is independent, somewhat unpredictable, and has few strong party ties.

NATIONAL POLITICS, IMPACT AND TRENDS

Any division of a state's political history would be somewhat arbitrary. The period which brought about the most significant changes, however, in Utah's political involvement with the Nation is from 1932 to the present. This is best seen in the reactions to the New Deal, especially by the Mormon church. However, non-Mormon businessmen generally and almost completely reacted in much the same way, *against*.

Early in the New Deal period and as late as the election of Dwight Eisenhower, the Mormon church and entrenched business and commercial interests resisted every move of the federal government with its grants-in-aid and financial subsidies.[105] During the depression years chronic unemployment forced many reliable citizens to turn to their church, their city and their county agencies for the very necessities of life. Local agencies could not meet these needs. The Mormon church saw the handwriting on the wall. Tithes and donations were falling rapidly. It donated its junior colleges to the state and abandoned its high schools. It then devised its much advertised Welfare Plan, which provided both employment and commodities for its members who needed aid.

In the meantime, Utah received considerable help from the federal government. Although the church boasted of taking its members off or keeping them from government relief rolls, it became known that by 1939 the state had received

105. See Jonas, "Utah: Sagebrush Democracy," in Donnelly, *op. cit.*

more money for relief per capita than the majority of the states in the Union.

The majority of the young persons who voted for the first time during the depression gravitated to Democratic ranks. Conservative Democrats, not the recipients of federal benefits, and who resented them, turned to the Republican party, but without appreciably swelling its voting strength, since they were few, mainly bankers, corporation executives, and lawyers. After 1936, the Republicans did make some small but perceptible gains in each successive election, but it was not until 1946 that they elected a member to Utah's congressional delegation. They won the governorship in 1948, all the congressional seats in 1952, and both houses of the state legislature the following year.

One feeling which developed and has continued to grow was that it behooved a person to get what he could for himself regardless of traditional belief, the plight of others, and the social consequences. He who tried to maintain his independence remained outside the pale of New Deal paternalism. New Deal ideology stood in contrast to the *pioneer spirit*, and the people of Utah underwent a change in *Weltanschauung*. In the ensuing years, this psychological shift was reflected in party orientation; indeed, it was evident in those who voted for either party.

During the Eisenhower period there was no break in the continuity of New Deal policies. All that happened was that the management was changed. The 1956 elections did not necessarily demonstrate a drift either away from or toward what has become known as the New Deal. They represent, rather, *a continuity in history*. The New Deal denoted the American nationalistic expression of a world revolution which was taking place in various parts of the globe with varying results. In the United States it meant a closer relationship between central and local government units and greater participation of government in the affairs of the individual. The same continuity which has been found in the Roosevelt-Truman-Eisenhower-Kennedy and Johnson foreign policies might also have been found in domestic legislation during more than three decades after the Great Depression.

In Utah, the Mormon church shifted, albeit reluctantly, from an apparently irreconcilable anti-New Deal position to a tacit acceptance of legislative measures and governmental action which in an earlier period it would have categorically rejected as contrary to the official interpretations of its basic tenets. It unequivocally supported President Eisenhower and the regular Republican organization in both Utah and the Nation. For the reason, however, that the church has actually made this shift in its political outlook since 1952, Secretary of Agriculture Ezra Taft Benson could accept and support a "soil bank," and United States Senator Wallace F. Bennett could campaign on the Republican record of having extended social security benefits.

The first major step in the apparent shift in Mormon political thinking probably was made when David O. McKay became the church president in 1951. His first action was to "demote" J. Reuben Clark, a politically-minded straight Republican and a strong conservative, from first to second counselor in the First Presidency.[106] Secondly, President McKay permitted Apostle Ezra Taft Benson to join President Eisenhower's cabinet. McKay's third action which suggested that

---

106. This is a body of three or more men, who together with the Council of Twelve Apostles, determine the policies of the church.

Clark's conservative views are spread through his many published public addresses. These were summarized and presented to the Utah Academy of Sciences, Arts and Letters by Frank H. Jonas. See "Mormonism and the Theory of Conservatism," Proceedings, XXIV (1948), 205.

a realignment was taking place in Mormon attitudes toward government was to give permission for the use of the Mormon Tabernacle in October 1954 for the celebration of United Nation's Week, which previously had gone unobserved in Utah. Not only did he himself and other Mormon officials attend the meeting, but the guest speaker was Henry Cabot Lodge, Jr., whose father, as chairman of the Senate Foreign Relations Committee, had been instrumental in preventing the United States from entering the League of Nations. Top play was given to the story covering Lodge's speech by the *Deseret News*. What seemed important in this incident was the change in the editorial position of the *Deseret News* on foreign policy. Still critical on some points, it had taken a generally favorable stand in this field toward the Eisenhower Administration. In the single instance when this paper had criticized President Eisenhower, the editors had been severely reprimanded by the publisher, President McKay. So by 1956, the Mormon church newspaper had completely reversed its previous support of Governor J. Bracken Lee's strong opposition to United States foreign policy.

Subsequently President McKay observed that he could no longer accept the isolationist position of his second counselor, J. Reuben Clark. How could the church be isolationist, he asked, with over 10 to 20 thousand missionaries in the field, a large percentage of these in many foreign lands? From then on the church relinquished its former isolationist position and its antagonism toward foreign and domestic federal aid.

A shift in thinking is evident in the change of position of the Salt Lake City Board of Education toward federal aid to education. Voting 12 to 0 or 11 to 1 against every new federal aid program for schools since and before the war the Board made a dramatic shift in 1965 when by a 7 to 5 vote it changed its chairman and then accepted two federal aid propositions, losing only one other by a tie vote. Every school district in Utah accepts federal aid in all possible categories for which it can qualify.

Utah's delegation in Congress pays lip service to the influential anti-federal aid voices in Utah, but it does not take them seriously; no small state like Utah can assume effective leadership in opposing the national trend of government centralization in Washington. Public Welfare with federal matching funds, especially medical aid to the aged, is hardly contested in Utah. Recently, when the State Department of Public Welfare threatened to reduce grants to the recipients of medical aid in order to prepare for a possible several million dollar deficit by the end of the fiscal year, the group who opposed the cuts were the doctors and the medical associations.

The participation of the federal government in the affairs of the people and the functions of state agencies still remains a political issue in the state, but neither the politicians nor the people really wish for the return of these functions, nor have they made any effort to take them back. In this sense, Utah is not so different from other states.

Enabling legislation for urban renewal was not passed in Utah until 1965. The incentive for its passage came from some of the most entrenched property elites in the state, principally in Salt Lake County. The motivation was a multi-million dollar civic auditorium complex which would be financed from bonds and taxes. By bringing this construction within the scope of urban renewal the County could have saved a million dollars. The proposal was referred to the people in 1965. Although the Salt Lake area Chamber of Commerce, the Mormon church, and other property interests appeared to support the referendum, it was defeated at the polls. Actually, the John Birch Society, with a carefully laid plan, covered the county house by house, beginning every conversation with the question, "Do you want to lose your home?"[107]

The Republican sweep in 1966 could have been the result of a rather widespread reaction to President Johnson's domestic programs and the Vietnam War. The Administration's so-called poverty program found very little receptivity in Utah. "Head start" had acceptance and some success. There was no very real need for the poverty program. It had been determined by welfare workers that some welfare applicants were incapable of rehabilitation and that others were being provided with sufficient opportunities by the county welfare departments. Certainly President Johnson's program could be of benefit to the impoverished, but it was thought that it should be administered by creative leadership, the will to come to grips with realities, and the willingness to administer details over a long period of time.

A doctrinal problem arose for the Mormons. The church does not permit Negroes to be ordained members of the priesthood.[108] The doctrine of the Negro was stated by Joseph Smith, the first prophet and president of the church. This belief in the position of the Negro had been linked with the civil liberties. One informed writer has stated that "there is no evidence of a carryover of the Mormon doctrine on the Negro into secular life; in fact, there is evidence to the contrary. No matter how much racism you think you see in Utah, you can't be sure it has anything to do with Mormonism. It might be related to the rural and small-town environment in much of the Mountain West (as in other parts of the country), or it might be the sickness of individual Mormon bigots, who would find some *other* way to rationalize their racism, even if the Mormon church were without its peculiar 'Negro doctrine.' "[109] Regardless of the separation of the Mormon Negro doctrine and the civil rights movement the problem has plagued the church. It has made some members uncomfortable and it has embarrassed Utah's delegation in Congress who are Mormons. It has given non-Mormons another reason to attack the church. The church has been urged to take steps to eliminate or modify the doctrine. President Hugh B. Brown, first counselor to President David O. McKay, has stated recently, "I think it unwise at this time to venture an opinion on the Church's policy on the Negro question but think that in the not too distant future we will see some modification."[110]

The candidacy of George Romney for the presidency has done much to bring the church's position on the Negro question and on civil rights into the open. Romney, an active Mormon and former local official in the church, has had to face squarely this question. His answer has been, "look at my record on civil

---

108. This is a lay priesthood with two main divisions, Aaronic and Melchizedek. Only Melchizedek priesthood members can participate in the "ordinances performed" in the temple, marriage, and work for the dead. Not all members can "enter the Temple." They must qualify especially for the privilege and receive a "recommend" from their bishop and stake president. For this each member is interviewed by these functionaries. Non-members cannot "enter the Temple" in any event. Negroes may become members of the church, and Negro Mormon families have resided in Utah for many years.

107. This effort by the John Birch Society should not be construed as an index of its strength. Actually, the associations representing property owners, particularly real estate, behind-the-scenes actually opposed the proposition. In a sample, 79 percent of the property owners opposed urban renewal, as it was called, and 77 percent of renters and all other non-property holders opposed it.

109. Armand L. Mauss, "Mormonism and the Negro," *Dialogue*, II (Winter, 1967), 38.

110. Letter from Hugh B. Brown to the writer, dated September 5, 1967.

rights." Elected three times governor of Michigan, a state with a heavy Negro population especially in Detroit, Romney's record on the question apparently has been satisfactory to critical politicians and Negro pressure group representatives. The impact of national trends on Utah eventually will bring a full slate of enlightened public policies on civil rights and social legislation.

In 1967, the state legislature passed two of the three civil rights measures which comprised "the package deal" in this field. It is anticipated that it will pass the third, "open housing," in the 1969 session, again due to pressure from the national capitol. Republican Sherman Lloyd, a conservative from Salt Lake City, voted for the national legislation on this subject.

As in other states (even in Oregon which has had a full slate of civil rights acts on its statutes for some time now), *de facto* compliance with law will not follow immediately *de jure* rulings. This fact is realized by the Negroes everywhere and in the years to come this will constitute their major complaint.

Utah is a "different state" in more ways than one. It is not precisely politically minded, as is New Mexico, or Arizona. It expects favorable treatment from Congress and the federal government, but at the same time declines to send congressional delegations to Washington favorable to the Administration. Some key reclamation projects have been delayed or have developed very slowly because of the failure of the state to secure the necessary allotments even after the appropriations have been made by the Congress. Although Republicans like Governor Clyde, Senator Watkins, and Congressman Dawson have done a great deal to secure funds for resource development in the state, there is always something lacking—chiefly, perhaps, the all-out support of the dominant economic interests of the state for the projects. Republican congressmen, no matter how moderate and enlightened in politics and economics, cannot refuse to listen to the interests of those who finance their campaigns. There is a disposition, although it does not show through too clearly at times, for Senator Bennett and Representative Lloyd to let some enlightenment show through a cautious conservative exterior on social questions affecting the people. Especially is this true in the development of the state's resources. Their recalcitrance at times appears to be a holding action, not designed to thwart eventual development of a good state and federal relationship. Representative Burton in the First District has openly revealed this enlightenment. The state has gradually turned from all-out opposition to the philosophy of the New Deal in the press and in the pressure group circles of the dominant interests to a more moderate political position on economic and social questions. This ideological struggle has been won by the moderates in the Republican party; it exists today.[111] It is exemplified by Michigan's George Romney, New York's Nelson Rockefeller, and Oregon's Mark Hatfield. President David O. McKay of the Mormon church and his counselors, Hugh B. Brown and Nathan Tanner, have been in harmony with this development within the state and the Republican party and have aided and abetted it.

Actually, it has been this development toward liberalism which has both helped and hurt the Democratic party. Moderation of the old-line Republican conservative position has taken the wind out of the sails of the strong liberal elements in the Democratic party. Whenever, as for example in 1958 and 1964, the Democratic party has demonstrated some moderation of its extreme liberal stance, it has had the support of influential business and church leaders and coincidentally it has won at the polls.

111. For the development of this thesis see Gerald Edwin Hansen, "The Conservative Movement in Utah After World War II" (Ph.D. dissertation, University of Missouri, 1962).

WASHINGTON STATE:

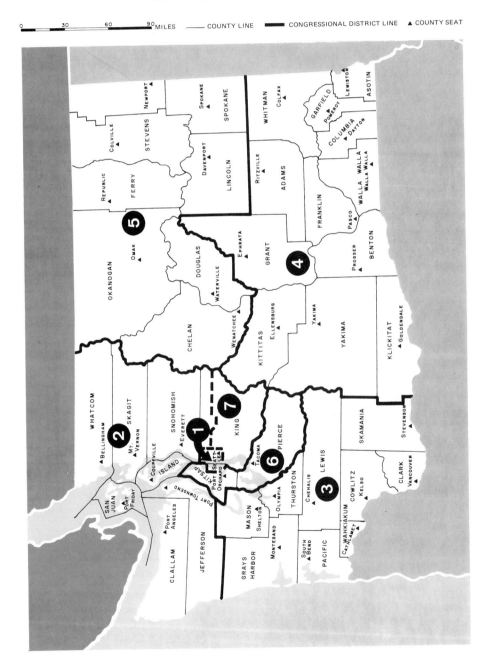

Hugh A. Bone

Free Style Politics

Washington, admitted as the forty-second state, has been characterized by fresh and breezy politics. The young English newspaperman, Rudyard Kipling, after a visit to Tacoma, was moved to write, "They are all mad here, all mad." Another writer called it "a region producing eccentric politics." James A. Farley's comment about "the forty-seven states and the soviet of Washington" is still not forgotten. The state's history has been punctuated by a general strike in Seattle in 1919 and a vigorous pensioners' movement.[1] In the Depression of the thirties the jobless organized the Unemployed Citizens' League of Seattle, which, under the guidance of erratic, left-wing leadership, played a powerful role in politics, almost winning control of the Democratic party and frightening businessmen and property owners. Communist influences were undoubtedly felt in many organizations.

These incidents characterized the lusty-gusty flavor of Washington's politics. Yet the state's past political life has differed only in detail from the bread and circuses so often staged by political bosses in the East, demagogues in the South, and frontier politicians in many western areas. Today Washington is far more staid, mature and serious, for politicians are faced with finding vast new sums for schools, welfare, institutions; attracting new business; solving traffic congestion; combatting water pollution; and meeting a host of other problems. Harry Bridges is no longer an important power in the state and there are no popular leaders to kindle enthusiasm for radical causes either of the political right or left.

But a heritage of the older ebullience and freshness of politics remains. From the early days to the present, populism (the state went for Bryan and elected a Populist governor in 1896) and "progressivism" are major currents. The state rather quickly adopted many of the major policies of the Progressive movement including direct legislation, direct primary, recall, woman suffrage, and economic reform. It was the only western state to support Theodore Roosevelt and the Bull Moose movement in 1912. The Progressives fielded a full slate of candidates for Congress and state offices, elected two congressmen-at-large and several state legislators. Robert M. LaFollette ran second to Calvin Coolidge in 1924 but far ahead of John W. Davis. Although large numbers of minor parties have offered candidates for governor and numerous other offices since 1912, only the Progressives were of electoral significance.

During the last generation the most successful politicians have possessed the image of progressivism. When Republican Senator Miles Poindexter (1910-22), a leading Progressive insurgent, suddenly swung to the right and joined the red-baiters in the twenties, he lost his bid for re-election. Arthur B. Langlie, elected

1. On the strike see Robert L. Friedheim, *The Seattle General Strike* (Seattle: University of Washington Press, 1964).

governor in 1940, 1948, and 1952, and Daniel J. Evans in 1964, resembled the Rockefeller, Scranton, and Hatfield approaches with strong appeal to independents; both incurred enmity from extreme right-wing Republicans. Democratic senators C. C. Dill, Homer T. Bone, Warren G. Magnuson, and Henry M. Jackson all built reputations as "liberal-progressive" lawmakers.

There is, however, a deep-seated conservative undercurrent in the state's politics and a vociferous, articulate far right which attracts particular attention in the Spokane area but is found throughout the state. After World War II the state legislative un-American Activities committee (Canwell Committee) conducted investigations into education causing several resignations. Many employers put up large sums of money in an unsuccessful attempt to secure adoption of a "right to work" initiative. But middle-of-the-road to left-of-center attitudes and programs have prevailed. Generous support is given to schools and for welfare, but is becoming increasingly difficult in the face of a regressive tax structure. Voters and public officials are carefully scrutinizing the cost of public programs.

GEOGRAPHY AND POPULATION

Next to Hawaii, Washington is the smallest of the western states in area (67,000 square miles) but is exceeded in population only by California. It entered the Union in 1889 with a population of 240,000 and had grown to 2,853,214 by 1960; 3.6 percent were nonwhite.[2] The Washington State Census Board estimated 3,120,000 inhabitants as of April 1966. The Board projects a "medium" forecast of 3,386,000 in 1970 and 4,086,000 in 1980.[3] During the decade from 1940 to 1950 the state saw its most rapid increase—three times as great as the national rate. From 1950 to 1960 the rate became more moderate (19.9 percent compared to 37 percent the previous decade). Since 1960 the rate appears to be declining to 10 percent or lower. Population expansion has been based about one-third on natural increase and two-thirds on immigration.

Many areas of the state are virtually uninhabited, while in others there are densities of thousands per square mile.[4] Topography, climate, natural resources, rainfall, rivers, Puget Sound, and the Pacific Ocean have had much influence on the distribution, as have cultural factors such as irrigation, transportation, location of dams, educational institutions, and military installations. Natural topography is undoubtedly the major reason for the pattern of population distribution.

2. In contrast, 8.4 percent of Seattle's population was nonwhite. For an analysis of the minority groups in this city see Calvin F. Schmid and Wayne W. McVey, Jr., *Growth and Distribution of Minority Races in Seattle, Washington*, published by the Seattle Public Schools, 1964. Many characteristics of the state's nonwhite population are found in Calvin F. Schmid and Charles H. Nobbs, "Socio-Economic Differentials Among Nonwhite Races in the State of Washington," *Demography*, 2 (1965), 549-66.

3. The Washington State Census Board's publications contain a storehouse of information on population trends and forecasts from 1870 to 1985 broken down according to age, sex, economic areas, counties and other groupings. See especially Calvin F. Schmid and V. A. Miller, *Population Trends and Educational Change in the State of Washington* (1960); Schmid, *et al.*, *Population Forecasts State of Washington 1965-1986* (Olympia, 1966); and Schmid's *Population Trends Cities and Towns State of Washington 1900 to 1965* (Seattle, 1965).

4. A somewhat fuller treatment of population characteristics and distribution is found in Daniel M. Ogden, Jr., and Hugh A. Bone, *Washington Politics* (New York: New York University Press, 1960), Chapter 2. The volume is useful for numerous aspects of the state's politics.

The most significant feature is the Cascade mountain range which runs north-south; approximately two-thirds of the land area lies to the east, characterized by plateaus, deserts, coulees, little rainfall, and considerably more extreme temperatures than west of the range. Western Washington has many contours, lakes, mild temperatures and rainfall from very heavy on the coast to 30 inches or less in some interior valleys. Since 1900 the population ratio has been maintained at about one-third to the east, and two-thirds to the west.

More than half of the state's population is in the southern Puget Sound trough, from Everett on the north to Olympia on the south, including Seattle and Tacoma.[5] Two other sizable metropolitan areas are found in western Washington, Vancouver across the Columbia River from Portland, Oregon, and Bellingham near the Canadian border. Eastern Washington has three important population centers—Spokane, the state's second largest city; Yakima; and the Tri-City area (Kennewick, Pasco and Richland) on the Columbia River. Unlike Chicago or New York, Seattle contains only about one-fifth of the state's population so that cleavages do not run to a "big city" vs. "outstate" most of the time. On occasions an "east-west" struggle develops, but state legislative politics is not so simply explained in these terms.

Over half of the native-born immigrants come from the North Central states; 36 percent are from Minnesota, the Dakotas, Iowa, Missouri, Kansas, and Nebraska. New England and the South have contributed relatively few emigrants. Negroes numbered 48,700 in 1960 with over half living in the city of Seattle.

In 1960, 6 percent of the population was foreign born. Immigrants from Canada ranked first in numerical importance followed in order by those from Norway, Sweden, England, Germany, and Finland. Asiatics constitute about 1 percent of the foreign stock but only about 7,000 of them were foreign born. These figures suggest that nationalistic politics characteristic of many states is of little importance in Washington and politicians find it unnecessary to address strong appeals for the vote of ethnic blocs. Canadians assimilate rapidly and are dispersed so there is no political mileage to be gained in directing attention to them. Surprisingly however, until 1966 voters repeatedly refused to repeal a constitutional restriction against ownership of land by aliens.

Reliable statistics on religious affiliation are rarely available and the canvass made by the National Churches of Christ in the U.S.A. in 1956 has not been updated.[6] This survey found that over half of the people of the state claim no church membership. The segment reporting showed 61.6 percent Protestant, 37 percent Roman Catholic and 1.4 percent Jewish. The Mormons, who have significant membership in Utah and to a lesser extent in Idaho and Oregon, had less than 3 percent in Washington. Christian Scientists have considerable but undetermined following in the state and are believed important in the active opposition to fluoridation proposals in many cities.

The predominantly Protestant composition has minimized the religious issue in politics. The blanket primary has made it next to impossible to prepare a

5. This includes the counties of Snohomish, King, Kitsap, Pierce and Thurston. The U.S. Census classed Washington as 68.1 percent urban in 1960. This compares with 62.2 in Oregon and 86.4 in California.

6. Washington's statistics are covered in "Churches and Church Membership in the United States," Series B, No. 8. The Catholic Directory listed the state's Catholic population in 1960 as 345,331 or about 13 percent of the total population.

"balanced ticket" even if party leaders were wont to do so. Publicly no appeals are made to the Catholic vote and such appeals would be resented. Privately an undertone of religion has entered into campaign discussions and into party organizational matters. One reason is that large numbers of Catholics have successfully sought public office, generally on the Democratic ticket. Sensitivity was particularly acute in 1960 but has diminished considerably since that time.

RESOURCES

The state is richly endowed. The Columbia River and its tributaries provide about one-third of the nation's physical water-power potential and Washington shares generously in this resource. Early in the century the economy was essentially an agricultural and extractive one resting primarily on land, timber, mineral resources, and fishing. Mining has become less important over the years: the state's mineral production in 1964 was $77 million. Fishing has been hurt with serious competition but the state ranks fourth as a producer of canned fish and by-products. Commercial and sports fishermen have their quarrels, and the industry has found itself at loggerheads with hydroelectric power interests. Balancing these interests has been an important job for the state's politicians.

Basic economic data are shown in Table I. In 1966 agricultural employment averaged 79,500 and nonagricultural 1,123,000. Per capita income in 1966 was

TABLE I

WASHINGTON ECONOMIC DATA, 1966

Source of Income	Millions of Dollars	% Total
Manufacturing Payrolls		
Food Products	$ 175.1	9.2
Forest Products	477.1	25.0
Aerospace	675.3	35.3
Other	583.2	30.5
TOTAL	$1,910.7	100.0
Value of Farm Products		
Field Crops	335.4	40.9
Livestock and Dairy	292.5	35.6
Fruits and Berries	124.0	15.1
Vegetables	43.5	5.3
Specialty	25.1	3.1
TOTAL	$ 820.5	100.0

Source: Adapted from Summary of Pacific Northwest Industries Annual Review, published by Seattle First National Bank, May, 1967.

$3,125 and total personal income was almost $10 billion. Foreign trade is important with imports and exports combined exceeding $1.5 billion per year. Aero-
space and aircraft are basic industries, and, because of their dependence upon federal as well as commercial contracts, fluctuate in employment and income.

Agricultural employment, while oscillating less violently, has been in a slow
decline, but farm products remain a significant part of the state's economic life.
There are four distinct farm areas. Wheat, the leading crop, is centered in the
southeast. The rich, irrigated areas of central Washington are noted for fruit and
the state leads the nation in the production of apples. A third area is the irrigated
Columbia Basin which grows diversified crops. Finally the logged off areas and
valleys west of the Cascade Mountains provide prosperous dairy farming and ber-
ry crops.

The federal government owns 29.4 percent of the land in Washington which
is less than in any other western state except Hawaii. But the national government's profound impact on the state's economic life is omnipresent. In the fiscal
year 1964 Washington ranked third (behind Connecticut and Alaska) on a per
capita basis of Department of Defense prime contract awards. Over $1 billion in
contracts placed the state sixth in over-all dollars received and Washington has
twice as many military installations as the average state. The Puget Sound shipyards and federally owned Hanford Atomic Power Works at Richland (though
now segmenting work and facilities to non-governmental nucleonics industries)
depend heavily on federal contracts.

There are large federal investments in the fifteen huge multipurpose dams on
the Columbia and Snake rivers. These, with many publicly and privately owned
hydroelectric power facilities, give the state the cheapest electric power in the
nation and have attracted industries (e.g., aluminum) into the region. The execu-
tion of a treaty with Canada in 1964 provided for three storage dams in British
Columbia to firm up the capability of downstream hydroelectric projects on the
Columbia River in the United States. It is apparent if one adds together federal
land-holdings in parks and forests, military installations and contracts, reclamation projects and many other enterprises, that much of the state's prosperity—or
lack of it—is in the hands of the national government.

EDUCATIONAL POLITICS

In 1967 there were two state universities and three colleges, twelve private
institutions and twenty-two public community colleges with more of the last
mentioned in the process of being built or authorized. About 58 percent were
attending the public institutions, 20 percent in the private institutions and 22
percent in the junior colleges. College enrollment figures are mushrooming and
rapidly becoming out of date. In 1946, 46,959 were attending college. This rose
to 60,950 in 1959 and to 115,254 in 1965. A figure of 145,000 is projected for
1970 and close to 180,000 for 1975. The Washington resident has reasonably
good access to regular, extension, or part-time higher education at a reasonable
cost. About 30 percent of the college-age population were actually attending college in the mid-sixties, a sharp contrast to 1950 when 15.6 percent were in attendance. Higher education remains the third largest item in the state's general fund
budget and its proportion in relation to public education is on the increase.

In the proportion of public school pupils attending school daily (92.7 percent) Washington is tied for second place in the nation and is second only to Utah

in proportion of the state's adults who have finished high school.[7] The state ranks ninth in average salary of instructional staff. The influence of this high educational level on the state's politics cannot be measured objectively. The press often compliments the voters for their discrimination in verdicts on ballot propositions. Although impressionistic, a review over the years of the propositions accepted and rejected indicates a high level of discernment among large numbers of voters. There is a large reservoir of trained manpower and per capita income ranks the state fourth highest in the West. A study of Republican precinct committeemen in 1951 found that 53 percent had attended college,[8] a percentage undoubtedly substantially increased in subsequent years. A very large number of the state's elected officeholders are likewise products of higher education.

Public education is in the center of the stage of state legislative politics since it constitutes the largest single item in the general fund budget, $762,815,000 in a total budget of $1,687,500,000 for the biennium 1965-67. The Washington Education Association has an effective lobbying staff and claims membership of about 92 percent of the state's teachers. Significantly, a teacher belonging to WEA must also have membership in his local education affiliate and in the National Education Association. There is also a small but active Washington Federation of Teachers. Parent-teacher associations and school administrators are also well organized and as a part of what is popularly called the "school lobby" roll up their big guns for local referenda on excess levies for the public schools. Much of the legislative battle centers in reconciling the financial requests for education coming from the governor, the state superintendent and the various educational groups.

The state superintendent of public instruction is popularly elected on a non-partisan ballot and the teacher groups often play a prominent part in the organizing and financing of the campaign of the candidate favored by them. In 1966, the Washington Education Association incorporated a political arm christened PULSE (Political Unity of Leaders in State Education) with the formally declared purpose of stimulating teacher political activity and "to enlist support of interested lay citizens in promoting desirable legislation affecting students in Washington state, and to assist in the recruitment and selection of qualified candidates for public office supportive of good, sound school legislation." It is raising money to assist state and national legislative candidates in the 1968 election.

NEWS MEDIA AND PUBLIC OPINION

The Seattle area is served by six television channels, one of which (Channel 9) is an excellent educational station bringing many programs of cultural, civic, and national interest throughout the Puget Sound region. All candidates for state office, the state legislature, and the Congress, living in the region, were given free prime time in the evening hours for a speech in the 1964 and 1966 campaigns. A number of Channel 9's programs are taped and appear on the four local Ultra High Frequency educational stations elsewhere, and in the daytime on commercial stations. A rather large number of sets in central Washington have UHF converters

7. For comprehensive educational data see *Research and Education*, Volume 8, No. 7 (April 1965) published by the Washington Education Association and *Ranking of the States 1967* published by the National Education Association, Washington, D.C.

8. Hugh A. Bone, *Grass Roots Party Leadership* (Seattle: Bureau of Governmental Research and Services, University of Washington, 1952). When a much smaller but fairly wide sample of 69 Republican precinct committeemen was studied in 1960, it was found that 66 percent had attended college.

and it is estimated that from 60 to 70 percent of all sets in the state can receive programs directly from Channel 9, or microwaved from it, or by tape. Only two states claim greater educational television coverage than Washington. The larger cities are reasonably well served by commercial networks; but because of mountainous terrain and deeply cut river valleys, a number of small cities and outlying areas have good reception on only one or two radio stations during daytime hours and limited television reception day or night. Competition is keen among sponsors for these limited facilities and public affairs often come off second best.

As elsewhere in the nation, the number of newspapers in Washington is declining but circulation continues to gain. There are 23 daily newspapers and only Seattle and Spokane have two dailies. There are about 150 weekly newspapers which carry mostly local news and frequently little of public affairs, so that citizens must rely on the importation of one of the dailies for wider coverage. The *Seattle Post-Intelligencer*, a Hearst publication which carries many *New York Times* features, and Spokane's *Spokesman-Review*, both morning papers, receive wide distribution in smaller communities and provide the main source of press information on state and national affairs. The Portland *Oregonian* and *Seattle Times* are also widely distributed.

The Seattle newspapers are generally moderate Republican in orientation, but from time to time endorse Democrats for public office. The *Spokesman-Review* speaks for arch conservatism and gave staunch support to Goldwater. The *Argus*, a weekly published in Seattle, reaches an elitist group of opinion leaders and has many well-written and sharply critical columns on state and municipal political problems. A new liberal monthly, *Seattle Magazine*, was started in 1964 and has published a number of feature articles on the state's politics and political personalities.

There are fewer than a dozen political columnists in the state; but reporting of state government in the press, and on television and radio, is quite good during legislative sessions and the citizen has reasonable opportunity to become informed about problems before the legislature. Between sessions state government affairs do not receive very consistent attention and coverage is likely to be limited to the spectacular.

Newspaper owners and editors appear to have more influence on legislators through personal contacts than through editorial pages. Fewer than half of the papers consistently endorse candidates. Most are probably Republican in sympathy, yet the news editors generally treat the opposition fairly. The large independent vote has led the press to play down partisanship and to refrain from alienating independents and Democrats.

NOMINATIONS AND ELECTIONS

Washington uses the unique "blanket" primary, a system profoundly affecting the state's politics. Every voter may participate without disclosing his party identity and is permitted to vote for any candidate seeking nomination, regardless of party. The office-block type of ballot used permits a voter to support Democratic candidates for certain offices and Republicans for other offices.

Washington adopted a closed primary law in 1909. In time sentiment developed to give voters the same degree of independence in the primaries as they appeared to exercise in the general election. Senator Homer T. Bone was one of the more influential advocates of this view and helped proponents with legal problems in the blanket primary measure. To the Washington State Grange goes major credit for putting the proposal through the legislature.[9]

Motivations for the Grange's energetic campaign for the wide-open primary have never been publicly recorded. Former officials recall that Depression times hit most farmers, leading them to demand better roads, cheaper power and other beneficial programs. They realized that their party identification under the closed primary could easily be discovered and that if they were known to support one party and the opposite party won the public offices, it might hamper their success. Grange newspapers featured many letters favoring a system which would permit voters to "vote for the man" for each office irrespective of party.

The Grange began its educational work in 1931 and by 1934 tried to initiate a statute but failed to get enough signatures to place the measure on the ballot. However, it secured enough signers to present it to the legislature in 1935. The constitution provides that an initiative submitted to the legislature must be voted upon without amendment and that an adverse vote refers the measure to the people at the next election. The initiative passed the House by a huge majority and the Senate by a much closer margin.

The initiative had attracted widespread attention before it was submitted to the legislature and obtained much newspaper, labor union, and civic group support. Rumors that the closed primary might be repealed and the old convention system restored, aided the blanket primary movement. Party leaders generally opposed it and filed a referendum petitition which failed to obtain the necessary signatures. The new law's constitutionality was challenged on almost every conceivable ground—that it contained more than one subject, abridged the right of assembly, interfered with freedom of elections, destroyed party integrity, permitted double voting, and so on. But the state Supreme Court sustained constitutionality on every point.[10]

The blanket primary arrangement invited expectations of a high voter turnout and of raiding, hypotheses which have not been fully borne out. Since a voter need not disclose party preference, large primary participation would seem to be encouraged. Further, with eight statewide positions to be filled there is certain to be a contest somewhere which will bring out voters. It is unusual for even one of the eight positions to go uncontested, at least for the out-party. Voter turnout was very high in the early years. From a participation of over 60 percent of the registered voters in the earlier primaries a fall-off came during World War II and the vote never reached earlier levels (Figure 1). It has remained more or less constant and since 1950 has averaged around 42 percent of the registered voters in mid-term contests and 55 percent in presidential election years when the state executive officers are up for election. In contrast, the presidential-statewide general elections generally draw over 80 percent, placing the state in the top fifteen in the nation. With a long ballot a fall-off of vote is expected and Table V, below, bears out that the drop-out rate is larger in primaries than in the general election. Participation in the Washington primary, while disappointingly low to its supporters, compares favorably with that in a great many other non-southern states. The state's experience underlines that easy voter access to the primary in itself does not mean significantly higher participation; other variables obviously must be considered.

9. On the earlier years of the primary see Claudius O. Johnson, "The Washington Blanket Primary," *Pacific Northwest Quarterly*, 33 (January 1942), 27-29, and "Washington's Blanket Primary Reviewed," *ibid.*, 48 (October 1957), 113-19.

10. *Anderson v. Millikin*, 186 Wash. 602 (2d sec.) 295 (1936).

A persistent allegation against all types of open primaries, and particularly against the blanket primary, is that it invites raiding. In a few cases there has been indication of considerable cross-voting, but opponents of the Washington system have admitted that there is no evidence of extensive raiding.[11]

In all but 15 out of 64 statewide executive partisan primary elections through 1964 the candidate polling a majority of the votes in the general election also polled a party vote majority of 50 percent or more in his primary. All 15 who won the general election without having won 50 percent of the primary vote faced contests in their own primary with an expected dilution of their vote, but most of the votes for their opponents in their own primary went to them in the general election and not to the opposition party. Candidates, including incumbents, try to mount a big vote in the primary in the belief that it results in a very significant psychological boost and assists in enticing both campaign funds and party workers for the general election. Party chairmen, even where an incumbent faces inconsequential challenges in his own primary while the opposition primary is hotly contested, urge their faithful to support the incumbent and eschew cross-overs to the opposite party.[12] To make a weak showing in the primary is to lose prestige;

FIGURE 1

PARTICIPATION IN PRIMARY AND GENERAL ELECTIONS 1944-1964

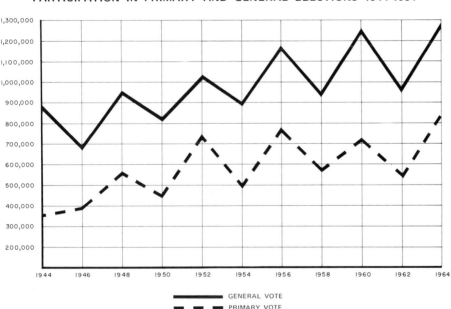

GENERAL VOTE

PRIMARY VOTE

11. On raiding as well as other aspects of the primary, see Ogden and Bone, *op. cit.*, Chapter 4 and Ogden's "The Blanket Primary and Party Regularity in Washington," *Pacific Northwest Quarterly*, 33 (January 1948), 33-38, and "Washington's Popular Primary," *Research Studies of the State College of Washington*, 19 (September 1951), 139-61.

12. In 1950 there was a "classic" primary of rather typical political behavior of both party leaders and voters. Senator Warren G. Magnuson was unopposed for renomination while the Republicans featured a lively contest with two weak and three strong contenders. Sharp political tactics dictated that Democrats infiltrate the Republican primary to pick a weak candidate, thereby assuring Magnuson's re-election. But voters chose the seemingly strongest Republican candidate, and the Senator's supporters turned out in droves to give him a total vote of only 33,000 less than the combined vote of all five Republicans; Magnuson won re-election by 56,000 votes.

so the blanket primary encourages candidates to seek support from all groups and to avoid strongly partisan appeals.

Although sample interviews have not been made, statistics suggest the hypothesis that very large numbers of voters view the results of the primary as indicative of the outcome in the general election, resulting in little change in voter opinion between the primary which is held in mid-September and the November election.[13] It is rare for a mass vote to enter one primary, then move to the oppo-

TABLE II

PERCENTAGE OF VOTE CAST IN
PRIMARY AND GENERAL ELECTION FOR STATEWIDE OFFICES

| Office | 1960 Primary | | General Election Winner |
	D	R	
Governor	42.1	57.9	50.3 (D)
Lieutenant Governor	59.5	40.5	63.8 (D)
Secretary of State	54.7	45.3	53.3 (D)
Treasurer	65.2◊	34.8◊	62.1 (D)
State Auditor	68.5	31.5◊	64.3 (D)
Attorney General	100.0◊		66.1 (D)
Public Lands Commissioner	64.3◊	35.7◊	69.0 (D)
Insurance Commissioner	65.8	34.2	58.9 (D)

| Office | 1964 Primary | | General Election Winner |
	D	R	
Governor	35.5	64.5	55.7 (R)
Lieutenant Governor	56.9	43.1	55.8 (D)
Secretary of State	52.1	47.9	54.4 (R)
Treasurer	62.8	37.2◊	57.1 (D)
State Auditor	57.1	42.9	59.1 (D)
Attorney General	65.0◊	35.0◊	68.1 (D)
Public Lands Commissioner	63.8◊	36.2◊	66.0 (D)
Insurance Commissioner	55.5	44.5	60.7 (D)

Note: Primary figures refer to total percentage of vote polled by all candidates entered for respective office.
◊Only one candidate on party's ballot.

13. A law passed by the 1965 legislature moved up the primary slightly to the third Tuesday in September.

site party in the general election. There has been more of this in gubernatorial contests than those for other offices.[14]

The blanket primary appears as a rational system of nomination to the majority of Washington's citizens, including segments of the press and many civic groups, and consistent with a political bias for personality politics. It keeps open the channels to public office and facilitates ascent to power of those who have built up strength outside party organizations. A considerable number of state legislators favor the device in the belief that they could not have attained public office without it. It has aided persons who were active in the Young Democrats and Young Republicans to get nominated through the efforts of their fellow members. It helps factions within the party to secure a nomination provided some help comes from outside the party's adherents. In this sense both liberals and conservatives are able to tap resources outside the liberals and conservatives of their own party. It is a reasonable assumption that the primary makes it possible to attain high public office without first serving in the state legislature. Since 1936 fewer than one-third of those elected to Congress or to state executive offices served an apprenticeship in the state Assembly. Many persons also secure nomination without long years of yeoman's service in party organization but by attaining a reputation and visibility in athletics, or in civic, fraternal or other activities. Although not susceptible to measurement, it is a reasonably safe assumption that the primary has heightened factionalism in the state legislature because so many lack feelings of strong party allegiance.

Washington law specifically prohibits nomination by convention "of any candidate to be voted for at any primary election." Measures are introduced in every session of the legislature (1) to permit a pre-primary convention for purposes of giving or withholding endorsement and (2) to reduce the blanket features by going over to an open primary ballot where one could vote only in one's party's primary in a given election. Most party leaders and a goodly number of legislators favor one or both of these changes, but fear the wrath of many voters and groups if they pressed these measures through the legislature. Prospects for a return to a closed primary seem remote.[15]

Mavericks and insurgents have often beat the preferences of the regular organization and enjoyed long tenure in office. The system alone, however, is not the only factor. Neutrality on the part of party officials is a rather deeply entrenched practice and sharp resentment is expressed when county or state chairmen express support for one person over another in a contested primary. Chairmen have actually been forced out of office on some occasions when they have

14. One of the few examples was in 1960 (Table II) when Governor Albert D. Rosellini lagged very seriously behind in the primary but picked up 8 percent to win the general election. But in 1964 he fell so far behind in the primary that even with another 8 percent gain he was decisively defeated in November. In that same election the Democratic secretary of state lost 8 percent between the primary and the general election and with it his bid for another term. Both of these instances were exceptional and involved long-time incumbents whose popularity had diminished.

15. In 1950 a statewide poll found 85 percent preferred the blanket to either the open or closed primary, with Democrats and Republicans about equally pleased with it. A poll in Seattle in 1964 found that 63 percent were unable to describe the primary, but 70 percent of the total respondents wished no change—a case of supporting the status quo when unaware of the implications either of it or of change. The polls found that the higher one's education, the more likely he was to support the primary and, not surprisingly, split-ticket voters favor it more than straight-ticket voters.

violated this norm. Precinct committeemen are much less restricted and do support favorites—but assistance is more often circumspect than overt.

The tradition of neutrality in the primary on the part of party officials and the system's openness make slate-making difficult. A balanced ticket is not easy to make in a closed primary—and is virtually impossible in a wide-open one. Statewide tickets in Washington are often very lopsided in terms of geography, section, religion, and faction; central and eastern Washington often receive few nominations. One state Democratic ticket a few years ago fielded an all-Catholic slate. There was no "plot" on the part of Catholics to dominate the slate but a number of fortuitous circumstances favored Catholics seeking the nominations.

Slate-making or slate-influencing by party officials is not, however, nonexistent.[16] When positions appear to be going begging or no one announces intention to challenge a popular incumbent, local party chairmen frequently try to find candidates. Chairmen expect to be consulted by an aspirant before he files in the primaries for a state legislative or county office, but it is not unusual for hopefuls to ignore this even though it may lead to bad feeling. Where an incumbent is unopposed or virtually unopposed in the primary, as is frequently the case with U.S. representatives and senators, the regular organization generally campaigns openly for him during the primary. Organization leaders will often aid a candidate informally and undercover by recommending strategy and persons suitable for campaign work.

Notwithstanding the openness of the primary, incumbents have continued to be at a great advantage.[17] Part of this is undoubtedly due to a willingness of voters to split tickets to support popular incumbents, irrespective of party label, both in the primary and in the general election.

Although there has been some sentiment for the presidential primary, the state retains the convention system for choosing delegates to the national conventions. Nearly all party leaders support this arrangement even though the state parties have undergone bitter battles such as the Taft-Eisenhower fight in 1952. Unhappily no record has been kept over the years except for a 1952 convention study, but long-time observers regard it as fairly characteristic of how the system operates.[18]

Delegates to the national convention are chosen in congressional district and state conventions by means of a stairway of precinct caucuses and county conven-

16. The legislature in 1965 passed several laws designed to facilitate partisanship, which slightly restricted insurgents and independents. Where two or more state legislative representatives are to be chosen from the same district, each office is to be selected by position. An incumbent maverick, therefore, could be challenged directly by a more loyal partisan and would not need to run, in effect, against two or three incumbents. To protect a partisan incumbent or challenger somewhat from a write-in campaign by outsiders, especially in the primary, the law henceforth requires that no stickers or labels may be used in lieu of writing the name, and that a voter must include the name of the political party as well as that of the candidate. Persons nominated as write-in candidates must pay a filing fee within five days after the official canvass of the primary if their names are to appear on the official general election ballot.

17. In a rare move in 1966 the Seattle area Democratic executive board refused to endorse 3 state legislative incumbents and 16 others who entered the Democratic primary while approving 71 other persons who sought nominations. Persons receiving endorsement, according to the board, were those whose records were "in agreement with the party platform" and who upheld "party responsibility."

18. See Paul T. David, Malcolm Moos, and Ralph M. Goldman (eds.), *Presidential Nominating Politics in 1952: The West* (Baltimore: Johns Hopkins Press, 1954), pp. 160-84.

tions. At the precinct caucuses polls are often taken on preferences for presidential nominees and items for the platforms. In some large counties the precinct meetings name delegates to state legislative district conventions, which in turn choose delegates to the state convention. The county convention is composed of each precinct committeeman: it elects and instructs (at times) the delegates to the state convention. Therefore, a presidential hopeful's managers concentrate on electing as many of their sympathizers to precinct offices as possible, and on prevailing upon the county chairmen to fill vacancies with their men. Goldwater enthusiasts volunteered their services to fill precinct positions in 1963 and by early 1964 had become dominant in the state and congressional district conventions. Twenty-two of the twenty-four delegates chosen to the national convention were either committed to or leaning toward Goldwater. According to the Goldwater managers, this was accomplished with a "bargain basement" expenditure of only $35,000.

Several traditions govern the selection and behavior of the national convention delegations; one of these is that the delegation shall go uninstructed. On the Republican side this dates back to 1920 when the delegation, instructed for Miles Poindexter, virtually became the laughing-stock of the convention because of its tenacity. Reaction was so strong to instruction that, except for endorsing an incumbent president for renomination, little effort has been made to pledge the group to a specific aspirant. In 1960, however, the pro-Nixon people, certain that the Vice President would receive the nomination, decided to strengthen his hand and their own position by getting the Republican state convention to instruct the delegates to vote for him. Goldwater supporters might have been able to do the same in 1964 but realized that there were many non-Goldwater delegates in the state convention and decided not to press the matter; most national convention delegates were for Goldwater anyway.

Democratic delegations in recent years have been rather badly split and highly individualistic in their behavior at national conventions. The 1960 delegation was rife with factionalism and Kennedy supporters caucused separately. The delegation's vote (instead of Wyoming's) could have pushed Kennedy over the top had it been unified. But Stevenson and Johnson supporters would not give in.

Several customs are evident in the choice of delegates. Republicans feel that the more permanent officeholders should not be delegates since they are usually able to attend the convention on their own. This is slightly less true for the Democrats. The latter have frequently assigned two half-votes to the Young Democrats and accorded convention seats to the state chairman and vice-chairman and to the national committeeman and committeewoman (even before this rule was adopted by the Democratic National Convention). The comparable Republican party officeholders have had no similar assurance, but the state chairman was a delegate in 1964. Both parties follow the unwritten practice that the delegate positions should be "passed around" and that, except for most unusual reasons, the same person should not be chosen as delegate to consecutive conventions. In 1952 over three-fourths of the delegates of both parties were attending their first national convention. Many were quite young and inexperienced—a characteristic of delegates to subsequent conventions as well. There are comparatively good opportunities to become a delegate if one is willing to work for it.

Washington has not been an important state in national convention roll calls because its voting strength is not large (24 votes in the Republican and 47 in the Democratic convention in 1968). Alphabetically it is near the end of roll calls and very seldom has had opportunity for a dramatic "yield" or "switch" which might put over a candidate. On only a few occasions has either party's delegation placed a favorite son in nomination. At the same time the state's role on platform committees, credentials, and other activities has probably been as important if not more so than that of states of comparable size.

The state's electoral practices are not strikingly different from those of other western states where vast spaces must be conquered to reach voters. From the northeast corner of the state to the southwest on the Pacific Ocean is close to 500 miles with many sparsely-settled communities in the arid central and eastern part and in and around the great mountain ranges. Statewide campaigning is, therefore, a formidable task necessitating considerable reliance on travel by auto to out-of-the-way places, and billboard advertising.

In the heavily populated Puget Sound area television is widely employed by congressional and statewide candidates. Candidates with a Seattle constituency buy sign space on the outside of the city's transit buses and there is much competition to get one's name on the "traveling billboards." Doorbell ringing is widely used as are mailings, passing out literature at bus stops, and riding the circuit of district party clubs. In one congressional contest a candidate's organization visited 40,000 homes with literature and a potholder. His opposition put out 200,000 facsimiles of a tabloid with a case for their nominee.[19] Both sides resorted to the very common practice of making thousands of telephone calls.

A most conspicuous feature of campaigning is decentralization of management and operation. With eight statewide partisan offices and one nonpartisan position to be filled in addition to the federal positions, it becomes difficult to find the manpower necessary to conduct an effective campaign. Yet many candidates build their own organizations, raise their own funds, and conduct their campaigns separately from the rest of the ticket. In the urban areas, the county organizations commonly give major attention to state legislative and county commissioner positions. The state committee is especially concerned with the office of governor and the citizens' groups and Young Republicans and Democrats are often preoccupied with the presidential contest. The more active members of political clubs and sometimes the clubs themselves are of much aid to candidates. Congressional candidates are forced to fend for themselves with some financial help from the national party committees and moral support from the local organization. The split-ticket voting behavior leads candidates to place little reliance on coattail riding, and conversely, to avoid too close association with others on the party's ticket who may be a "drag" to them. Although state and county chairmen go through the ritual of exhorting party workers and voters to vote a straight ticket, this is not emphasized in campaign operations.

Public relations and advertising men are playing an increasing role in statewide campaigns but their influence within a candidate's organization appears less than in California. They are seldom used for state legislative races. Since much emphasis is placed upon "voting for the man," it is not unusual for the candidate's party affiliation to be played down. Prior to 1960, campaign literature often carried no reference to party, but a law became effective that year requiring it to

19. See William J. Gore and Robert L. Peabody, "The Functions of a Political Campaign," *Western Political Quarterly*, XI (March 1958), 55-70. Another case study illustrative of techniques in a Seattle campaign by a candidate for a state legislature is by Willard H. Leavel, "The Election of Wes Uhlman," in Richard T. Frost (ed.), *Cases in State and Local Government* (Englewood Cliffs: Prentice-Hall, 1961), pp. 79-84.

carry a party designation. Nevertheless, campaigning remains highly individualistic and personal, and political advertising, whether prepared by a public relations
firm or by the candidate, reflects this fact. The law provides for a voters' pamphlet
containing information on both candidates and propositions. Until 1966 the pamphlet contained material only on questions appearing on the ballot. The 1966
edition, which for the first time featured pictures and statements of legislative
candidates, was particularly attractive and probably was more widely read than
usual.

There have been only a few campaigns where scurrilous campaign materials
have been used. Two instances where the Communist issue was raised resulted in
court suits. In one case the complainant received some damages in an out-of-court
settlement. In the other, the celebrated Goldmark case, substantial damages were
awarded but later set aside when the judge ruled that malice was not established.[20] Right-wing groups nonetheless continue to make an issue of a candidate's membership in the American Civil Liberties Union or the Americans for
Democratic Action.

Fund-raising is a perennial and serious problem. Campaigns are increasing in
cost and Washington's long ballot means that large numbers of candidates must
seek money for their operations. Although party organizations supply financial
assistance it is rather minimal and supplemental for most candidates. The Republican united finance drive has resulted in a better integration and centralization of
finance than the Democratic organization has, but decentralized fiscal management is the general order of the day. The major portion of funds must be raised
independently by the candidates, their friends, and party clubs and auxiliaries.
Political dinners, as in most states, constitute an important source of revenue.
Candidates employ independent committees to raise money on their own from
individual party members, political jobholders, and interest groups. Education,
business, and labor are among the biggest contributors but many other interests
donate.

Campaign finance remains a dark continent in the state's politics because
there is no law requiring state and local nominees to file statements of contributions and expenditures in general elections. Accounting is required in the primary,
but many ignore this provision with impunity since there is no enforcing agency.
Fragmentary figures on direct primary expenditures find their way into the press
but always bring charges that the opposition is guilty of gross underestimation. In
1964 Governor Rosellini reported pre-primary expenditures of $72,000, while
the successful Republican Daniel J. Evans recorded $135,000. Republicans
charged that Rosellini would spend about $600,000 between the primary and
general election to about $100,000 for their man. The charges are typical ones.
The more knowledgeable newsmen now regard a statewide campaign for governor
as costing close to a half-million dollars, with U.S. Senate races somewhat less, and
$100,000 for the Seattle mayoralty contest. It is likely that a few state legislative
contests have approximated $12,000, but usually much less is spent. County com-
mittees try to give small amounts to each legislative nominee but the candidate
must look elsewhere for most of his funds, which are often depleted in the pri-

20. John Goldmark, an incumbent state legislator, was the object of a smear campaign
by ultra-right wing journalists. See the *Seattle Times*, October 7, 8, 9 and 10, 1962, and
Hugh A. Bone, "The 1962 Election in Washington," *Western Political Quarterly*, XVI (June
1963), 468-69.

mary contest. There is little question that many aspirants for public office are "priced out of the market."

Civic leaders, many newspapers, and some legislators repeatedly call for laws governing campaign finance in general elections. But too many incumbents profit from the present sub rosa arrangements and are fearful of changes which laws might bring. A former floor leader collected campaign money and doled it out to certain lawmakers thus providing himself with a potential lever of control. This action was attacked by others as inviting "conflict of interest" but no legislation was passed to curb it or other similar practices. Most lobbyists are, privately at least, opposed to stringent laws governing disclosure of campaign contributions.

PARTY ORGANIZATION

Washington has an element of political paradox. Much of its politics is played outside the responsible two-party model. Machine politics in the conventional sense has never flourished in its larger cities. Yet both parties are well established, and active competition in elections exists at the state, congressional district, and county levels. By almost any criteria the state party system would be among the top dozen having the greatest degree of interparty competition.[21]

Three factors have significant impact on the operation of the state's political parties. First, the direct primary minimizes the control of party leaders over recruitment of persons for public office. Second, a new personnel system which went into effect in 1961 reduced patronage available to the parties.[22] However, exemptions still give the governor a number of appointments useful in his political role. Covered employees are not permitted to hold any political party office or participate in the management of a partisan political campaign. But they may campaign for constitutional amendments and other ballot propositions and for nonpartisan offices. They also have the usual exemptions from solicitation for political donations on state property and freedom from "any compulsory assessment or voluntary contribution." Prior to this act an incumbent governor was in an advantageous position to build what the opposition invariably called a "political machine" for his re-election or to assist his heir designate. There remain a great many boards and commissioners offering opportunities for nonpaying "prestige" jobs, positions of small compensation, and some full-time appointments. It is estimated that a governor has a total patronage resource of some 150 positions useful to his party and his own political future.

Third, as elsewhere in much of the West, nonpartisan primaries and elections are used to select judges, school officials, and municipal officers. The party ballot is retained for county offices, giving the county committees an important psychological base if nothing else. County commissioners have considerable patronage and party chairmen try to keep in close contact with them. County commission-

21. Richard E. Dawson and James A. Robinson rank the state as tied for ninth with Connecticut in interparty competition. See their "Inter-Party Competition, Economic Variables, and Welfare Politics in the American States," *Journal of Politics*, 25 (May 1963), 265-89. In this respect the state exemplifies several hypotheses such as the linking together of high interparty competition with urbanization, high median income and extensive public welfare programs.

22. Provisions and analysis of the law are provided by Paul L. Beckett in "Operation Self-Help: Washington State's New Merit System Law," *Public Personnel Review*, 24 (January 1963), 52-59.

ers are often active in local party decision-making. Municipal officers are another matter; a broad civil service system in cities has virtually eliminated party patronage. Mayors, city councilmen, and other nonpartisan officeholders by tradition would be unlikely to give jobs on the basis of party even if such patronage were available.

It is often said that nonpartisan municipal elections are an illusion because the party organizations in reality are backing and running candidates. This is true in some instances but in others it is not the case. In many communities open activity by a party on behalf of a candidate would be resented, if not harmful, and the parties must be very circumspect about providing financial or electoral assistance. County chairmen are seldom willing to devote their limited resources to nonpartisan campaigns. Rarely does a party leader publicly endorse a candidate for a nonpartisan office although party clubs on occasion do so. City nonpartisan politics and partisan county and state politics are not only separated by different times for their elections, but psychologically as well. In only a few conspicuous instances have apprenticeships in one area of politics been used to cross over to the other. Only on infrequent occasions does a municipal office provide a stepping-stone to a partisan office. There are many true nonpartisan-type elected officials who are content with their lot, eschew all party connections and affairs, and are elected and re-elected by both Republicans and Democrats who in many instances are unaware of the candidate's party faith. The nonpartisan system has reduced, to some extent, the potential talent available for recruitment for party office.

Party organization is decentralized and diffused. In addition to the informal leadership, there are three more or less formal types of organization. First is the hierarchy of committees provided for by law; second is the convention hierarchy; and third are the numberless clubs and auxiliary groups constituted on various bases such as political geography, sex, and age. Those in the last-mentioned category vary from highly casual to well-organized associations, from the nondescript Evergreen Club to the Chelan County Republican Women's Club and the various campus associations. These groups are usually outside the party hierarchy but may be chartered by it. Their purposes are diverse and include social, educational, fund-raising, and campaign activities, candidate endorsement, and recruitment of party members. In general, they seek to provide an opportunity for fulfilling the democratic ethos of "participation by all."

A comprehensive set of laws on primaries and committees established the structure of the party organization.[23] A political party is defined as one which gained more than 10 percent of the votes for one of its candidates in the election. This percentage obliges a party to nominate its candidates at the primary. An organization not entitled to participate in a primary may nominate by convention. A "convention" for this purpose is defined as an organized assemblage of at least 25 registered voters representing a political party, organization, or principle. Those participating in a minor-party nominating convention may not vote in the primaries.

A precinct committeeman in each party is chosen at the general election of even-numbered years for a two-year term; the committeemen form the county central committee. They meet shortly after the election to organize (required by law) and select a chairman and vice-chairman "who must be of opposite sexes"

23. Revised Code of Washington, Title 29, Chaps. 29:18, 29:21, 29:24, and 29:42. The Secretary of State, State of Washington, *General Election Laws*, 1965 edition, brings together cognate laws to that date.

and a state committeeman and committeewoman. Where vacancies exist a county chairman may appoint the precinct official, but no appointments may be made between the general election and the organization meeting. County committees have the important function of recommending candidates for premature vacancies in public office.

By placing only one man and one woman from each county on the state central committee a "rotten borough" system of representation is imposed. Eastern Washington with over half of the counties has 40 of the 78 committeemen, or a constitutional majority. A balancing factor is the selection of an executive committee on the basis of two from each congressional district giving western Washington ten of the fourteen members. The executive bodies meet several times a year to take care of interim business and are useful for endorsing and approving certain programs for the full committee. They have no coercive powers but handle matters of organization, fund-raising, press relations, recruiting members, and publicity for the state party.

State chairmen and vice-chairmen need not be members of the committee and commonly are selected from outside the membership. Customarily the two come from opposite sides of the state to give "balance." State chairmen run to no particular type or occupation. Recent chairmen included several attorneys and businessmen, a Weyerhauser public relations man, a one-time school teacher, a public official, and a leader in the Grange. Turnover in the chairmanship has been high with few serving more than four years. Both state chairmen are salaried and full time with a year-round headquarters and staff. The state central committees publish sizable papers known as the *Democratic Digest* and the *Republican Report*.

The governor and the two U.S. senators take much interest in the state chairman because of his role in statewide campaigns, fund-raising, and attempted management of factions. Both chairmen generally live in Olympia during the legislative sessions and confer with legislative leaders over the "party program." The chairman of the party controlling the governorship is usually close to the governor and serves as his aide in diverse political matters. All recent governors have in fact been leaders of their parties and have taken a vigorous interest in party affairs.

Local organizations vary widely. Most counties have no intermediate positions between the chairman and the precinct committeeman but a few of the populous ones have a state legislative district organization. In some urban counties the county commissioner districts are used as subdivisions for party organizations. In several counties only a small fraction of the precinct positions are filled and the chairmen are phlegmatic and only sporadically active, but the county chairman willing to give time to the organization wields influence. County leaders jealously guard their domain, and state and national officials must carefully refrain from giving the impression that they are circumventing the local authorities. Often there is no serious competition for the county chairmanships. These positions tend to be held by persons in the higher status occupations. In the last decade over 50 percent of the chairmen in both parties have come from business-managerial positions, with farmers and lawyers tied for second place. A woman has held the Democratic King County (Greater Seattle Democratic) chairmanship since 1962, probably the largest county organization in the nation to be headed by one of her sex.

When Daniel J. Evans became governor in 1965 his party was badly split between the ultra-conservatives and the moderates, with the governor representative of the latter wing. Goldwater people had infiltrated much of the Young Reublican organization and many county committees. Evans's people lost the battle to elect their own chairmen in two of the state's largest counties, King and Spokane, but won in several others.[24] It became the task of the new state chairman, C. Montgomery Johnson, who was a leader in the Evans campaign organization, to combat the conservative forces and to try to rally support for the rather liberal legislative program of the governor. Evans's supporters, however, controlled the great majority of the Republican legislative party and remarkable cohesion was shown on important roll calls in the 1965 and 1967 sessions. In contrast, when new county organization elections were held at the end of 1966 the Evans forces lost further ground and it seems unlikely that they can contest the 1968 delegation to the Republican National Convention. The Republican National Committeewoman elected in 1964, Mrs. Frances Cooper, continues her ultrarightist criticism of the Evans wing of the party, and the right-moderate split among the organization activists is a serious one.

The loss of the governorship in 1964, factionalism within the Democratic legislative party, and concern that Republicans might gain strength in 1966 because of redistricting, led the state chairman to create a 27-member Democratic Council in May 1965. The council consisted of the party's two U.S. senators and five congressmen, six elected state officials, four state senators and four state representatives, and six from the state central committee. At once speculation arose as to whether the group would attempt to become a party mouthpiece and make policy announcements on the pattern of Democratic National Chairman Paul Butler's Democratic Advisory Council during the Eisenhower Presidency. The chairman, Frank Keller, was more modest in initial statements indicating that he expected the leadership group to concern itself with preparing for the 1966 campaign and with the problem of party finance which has plagued many Democratic state legislators. The council was the first of its kind in recent party history and was used little. Keller resigned in 1967 and his successor, Robert R. Kull, did not convene the council. Factionalism is strongly personal, centering around potential candidates and those unhappy with the Johnson Vietnam policy.

An important function, performed by the biennial county and state conventions, is the resolution of ideological differences in the drafting of the parties' platforms. Here factionalism often manifests itself—liberals vs. conservatives; youth vs. senior leaders; labor vs. capital; and in the state convention, east vs. west. Quite specific policy pronouncements are often included in the platforms and party leaders appear to see a role for parties in policy-making. But, comparable to the national level, party leaders of the in-party are forced to recognize the governor as the policy leader, and the out-party sees policy proclaimed by diverse legislative leaders. Governor Evans has led the Republican legislative party toward a more urban orientation and championed constitutional reform. However, the majority of Republican legislators remain more conservative on revision and other matters than the Democrats.

PRESSURE GROUPS

It is often hypothesized that where parties are weak, pressure groups are likely to be strong. Although not necessarily proof of this, interest groups are enor-

---

24. Articles on Republican factionalism are found in the *Seattle Times*, April 8 and May 26, 1965. For an account of factionalism in 1967 see Hugh A. Bone, "The 1966 Election in Washington," *Western Political Quarterly*, XX (June 1967, Part 2), 607-9.

mously important in Washington's political life and appear to many as more significant in the state's political system than the parties. The loose character of the direct primary and the party system invite activities by private groups in the nominating, electoral and legislative processes. The geography and resources of the state make "functional" politics imperative. State and local groups with a constant or sporadic interest in public policy number in the hundreds. There is no lobby registration law, but a lobbyist, in order to have access to the floor of the house, must present a card issued only when he registers his organizational connection. The list is not published but at times has been examined.[25]

In addition to the powerful education lobby, agriculture, business and labor are well organized and influential. Over the years the Washington State Grange has earned the reputation of representing the farmers since the farm bureaus and Farmer's Union have made only a little headway. In contrast to the National Grange, it has generally supported "liberal" causes including public power and government work projects. Until overridden by initiative the Grange kept out legislative authorization for daylight time, reapportionment, and colored oleomargarine.

Timber, aircraft, trades, transportation, commercial fishing, banking, and other business associations often send their own representatives to the legislature although the Association of Washington Industries serves as the general spokesman for the business community. Business and aircraft in particular have much latent power. They are more a negative than a positive force, better able to defeat proposals detrimental to them than to obtain law.

Several business organizations have "practical politics" classes for their executives, and business is very active in electoral as well as legislative politics. The Business-Industry Political Action Committee which was active in many states in 1964 was, however, of little importance in Washington. The Boeing Company operates a number of eleven-week government courses which are open to all of its employees and their families. To encourage political participation the company gives leaves of absence without pay to employees elected to full-time public office. Those serving in the biennial state legislative session are given leave without pay or receive full pay during the session and repay it later. In 1964 some 46 Boeing employees ran in the partisan primary and general election; five were elected. About two-thirds ran under the Republican label. Boeing employees enjoy considerable success in being elected to nonpartisan city councils, boards of education and other local offices. As many as 150 are in office at a given time in the Greater Seattle area. Provision for time off can be made for persons involved in campaigns or serving as election officials.

A larger percent of non-agricultural workers are unionized in Washington than in any other state. Reliable figures are unavailable but there is little question that the state's percentage of those belonging to labor unions is at least double the national average. The unions are powerful in the state's politics and have succeeded in obtaining favorable welfare, social security, and workmen's compensation

---

25. One of the few publications of an incomplete list of over 100 lobbyists and their employers appeared in the *Argus*, March 26, 1965, p. 2. So far as can be determined a full list has never been published. Lobbyists on the *Argus* list showed these numbers by categories–54 business and finance, 15 governmental (municipal and like corporations), 14 labor, 12 professional, and 5 each agricultural and miscellaneous. This list included the best known lobbyists and constitutes a rough distribution of representatives of the various interests.

legislation. Several union executives and numerous active members have run for the state legislature and several have been elected. The unions are generally friendly to the Democratic party, have endorsed a large number of its candidates and assisted them with campaign finance; but they have not infiltrated the party as in Michigan. In a given election as many as 20 percent of the Republican candidates for the state legislature have been endorsed by the Teamsters or other unions, a factor keeping Democrats aware that union endorsement can not be taken for granted. The AFL-CIO and COPE are somewhat more inclined to be Democratic but they have supported Republicans. The steelworkers and labor councils utilize educational programs to familiarize their local leaders with public issues, policy goals, and the operation of government.

Almost since statehood the public power movement has been a contentious issue. Municipal ownership began in Tacoma in 1893 and spread rapidly. In the 1920's the Grange sponsored the creation of county-wide municipal corporations called public utility districts (PUD's) to serve rural dwellers. The twenty-nine PUD's speak through the Washington Public Utility Districts' Association in Seattle, the Columbia River Development League of Wenatchee and the Northwest Public Power Association. Opposition to public power is led by the Washington Water Power Company of Spokane and the Pacific Power and Light Company of Portland. Private power has numerous allies in "development" groups. Public power goals are supported by numerous groups because of a desire for comprehensive development of the Columbia River.

Recreational objectives have provided a politics in themselves. The Washington State Sportsmen's Council looks out for the interests of fishermen and hunters of game. Local councils exist in most cities. Small but energetic "wilderness" and "mountaineers" societies attempt to protect primitive hiking areas from the onslaught of motorists, civilization, and loggers. Metropolitan Seattle boasts the largest number of boats per capita in the world, and producers of pleasure craft protect their buyers. Conflicts between the recreational groups are not unusual, while commercial fishers have often found themselves opposed to the strongly organized·sportsmen.

The professions are well organized to conduct their public relations and carry their cases to government. Bar groups make endorsements in judicial elections and medical practitioners commonly form *ad hoc* campaign groups. The legal profession is especially well represented within the state legislature, boasting 19 of the 49 senators and 15 of the 99 representatives in the 1965 session. The Association of Washington Cities, the County Commissioners' Association, and many other government officials' groups meet, adopt resolutions, urge action and send lobbyists to Olympia. As observed earlier, the education forces are regarded as the most effective of all groups, and the president of the Washington Education Association is a member of the lower house.

Beer is a sizable export and the breweries as well as the liquor interests are well organized. Retail liquor is a monopoly of the state. The anti-liquor forces are capably led by lobbyists for the Alcoholic Problems Association. The group can quickly mobilize the ministers and church groups and rain telegrams and letters on legislators in a rather fearsome fashion. As a result, the liquor forces have been unable to ease the strict closing laws, nor have they been able to prevent liquor and wine from receiving very high taxation. After the voters repealed a blue law by initiative in 1966, the state changed regulations to permit the sale of liquor for eight hours on Sunday.

Lobbyists are commonly divided into three groups. First are the officers and full-time lobbyists who work year-round for their groups and during the legislative session generally live in Olympia. From thirty to forty "professional" lobbyists can be placed in this category and for the most part represent the larger occupational interests. A second group is composed of many lawyers who are retained on a fee basis to represent and look after varied interests particularly during the session. Charges are often made that a number of legislator-lawyers are on retainers to work from within the legislature for special interests. Although these charges have not been proved, the fact is that numerous lawyers in the legislature serve clients between sessions who have or are likely to have legislative interests. Finally there are many sporadic lobbyists who are active during a session promoting individual or group goals varying from the abolition of capital punishment to particular curriculum interests for the public schools and changes in election laws. The League of Women Voters, the parent-teacher associations, and private individuals without visible organizational connections exemplify the "amateur lobbyists."

Lobbyists enjoy many advantages.[26] There is a marble corridor (known as Ulcer Gulch) running from the House to the Senate equipped with telephones, chairs, vending machines and a switchboard which is the center of a paging service for lobbyists. The corridor teems with lobbyists, facilitates communication, and affords opportunities to buttonhole legislators. This Third House, as it is called, has its own organization with dues of $10 per session. It holds a weekly luncheon or breakfast meeting to generate good feeling and cooperation, and the occasion is helpful in promoting alliances. Governor Rosellini officially entertained the Third House and it has gained much public recognition.[27] Legislators rely heavily on lobbyists for information and printed materials; and one organization distributes a widely used bill status report.

LEGISLATIVE POLITICS

Lawmaking in Washington has expanded beyond the sixty-day biennial legislative session. The regular session is invariably closely followed by an extra one, usually confining itself to completing work on the tax and appropriation bills. No action has been taken to amend the constitution to provide for an annual session. A twenty-seven-member Legislative Council and several interim committees conduct research and investigations helpful to the legislature. The Ford State Legislative Internship Program has provided the legislature with a number of graduate and law students for short terms but both houses remain greatly understaffed. Excessive turnover in membership also limits effectiveness to some extent. In 1967, fifty-one of the ninety-nine members of the House were in their first or second session; only six of the forty-nine senators had comparable lack of experience. About one-fourth of the representatives and half of the senators had four or

26. For an intimate portrait of Washington lobbyists and their techniques see Rillmond Schear, "How To Win Friends and Influence Lawmakers," *Seattle Magazine*, March 1966, pp. 16-23.

27. Legislators, however, appear to deal only with a comparatively few lobbyists catering to certain interests. A survey of 20 legislators (conducted in 1965 by a University of Washington graduate seminar) surprisingly found that they could not identify a rather large number of lobbyists.

more sessions of experience.[28] Experienced representatives frequently seek election to the Senate; over a third of the senators in 1965 had served in the House.

The turnover in membership reflects itself in a spectacular way in legislative organization. Legislative rules authorize the speaker of the House and the president of the Senate (lieutenant governor) to appoint all standing committees. In the Senate, however, a committee on committees is very important in the selection, although when the lieutenant governor is of the majority he is likely to participate in the process. The speaker considers seniority as merely one factor in appointing a chairman—and often not a very important one. Geography, occupation, ability, and personal compatibility and friendships are important. A number of persons become chairmen in their first or second terms. In the House, speakerships and floor leaderships have had a rather heavy turnover contributing in turn to changes in committee chairmanships. The Senate leadership is somewhat more stable due in part to the election of only half of the body every two years.

Members of the legislature report their ages and occupations in the *Legislative Manual*. Several designate more than one occupation, making it difficult to analyze vocational backgrounds. The Senate in 1967 had a very heavy predominance of lawyers (36 percent) and businessmen (27 percent) with the remainder scattered from "retired" to engineers. The House was composed of 29 percent from business and only 19 percent from the law; 12 percent were farmers or ranchers. Labor had only two senators and four members in the House. There were nine educators in the lower chamber, but none in the Senate. Although there was only one woman in the Senate, there were seven in the House. There was a rather large number of young persons in the House; twenty-seven were under forty, and the median age was forty-two. Only six senators were under forty, and seven over sixty. Although perhaps without much significance, about half of the representatives and two-thirds of the senators were born in Washington.

Multifactionalism is a major characteristic of the legislative parties. There are constellations of groups in both parties with coalitions affecting legislative organization in recent sessions; bitter fights generally occur over leadership positions. Democrats have seen their majorities on important roll calls frequently dissipated. In 1963 the House was governed by a coalition of seven Democrats and forty-nine Republicans with the latter receiving seventeen of twenty-one chairmanships.[29] The Cascade mountain range offers a psychological basis for an "east-west" conflict, but it seems not to have any consistent effect on voting. Effort is made to get sponsorship or support of bills from both sides of the mountains. Up to 1965 the section east of the Cascades commonly received around one-third of the chairmanships.[30] City-county factions are often in conflict over tax measures and allocations of gas taxes. Since the big cities are to some extent in competition with

28. For a detailed account on the characteristics of lawmakers see Paul Beckett and Celeste Sunderland, "Washington State's Lawmakers: Some Personnel Factors in the Washington Legislature," *Western Political Quarterly*, X (March 1957), 180-202. See also Donald R. Farmer, "Profile of the Washington Legislature 1959-63," in the same journal, XVII (supp. September 1964), 90-91.

29. On the coalition see the writer's "The 1962 Election in Washington," pp. 469-70.

30. A sharp deviation—not explained by the leadership—occurred in 1965 when only 23 percent of the House and 17 percent of the Senate chairmanships went to legislators east of the Cascades. Under a new reapportionment the 1967 representation from the east was reduced by three in the House and two in the Senate so that section will probably receive fewer leadership positions than it did prior to 1965.

each other they often do not act in concert against the "cow" counties. Factions frequently have a strongly personal basis of friendships and political ambition.

Undoubtedly the wide-open system of recruitment and the blanket primary contribute to legislative factionalism. The party leadership exercises relatively little control over nominations. Many persons capturing the primary and the general election feel no strong obligation toward the party, seeing themselves as self-starters and/or group representatives. In some cases a safe district really means that it is safe for the candidate rather than for the party. Over-all, the splintering of leadership encourages pressure politics but it has also kept any one group from completely dominating legislative policy formation.

Despite weaknesses in party organization and an obvious multifactionalism, the party tie serves as an integrating force. Near the end of the session there are usually sharp party divisions over forms of taxation, appropriations, and welfare. When these matters are before the chambers for action, the parties hold one or more caucuses every day. Although members are not formally bound by caucus decisions, there is pressure to go along with them. Most legislators admit that the caucus influences lawmakers where there is no special commitment to their constituencies. The respective party caucuses also have the highly important function of choosing the membership of both the Legislative Council and the interim committees.

The hypothesis has been advanced that legislative representation of the minority party lags behind the growth of its share of the gubernatorial vote. This proposition is often but not invariably true in Washington (see Figure 2 and Table III). The fact that only half of the Senate is chosen at each gubernatorial election

FIGURE 2

PERCENT OF DEMOCRATIC SEATS IN LEGISLATURE AND DEMOCRATIC VOTE FOR GOVERNOR 1940-1964

tends to distort the picture. What is most apparent in the graph is the very sharp swing in the percentage of seats in the legislature compared with the percentage of votes cast for governor.

Although the state constitution calls for legislative reapportionment every five years, the legislature complied only in 1901, 1957, and 1965. Twice the initiative was used to accomplish reapportionment, but the legislature substantially amended the plan adopted in 1956. In 1963 the federal district court declared it unconstitutional because of sharp inequities and ordered the legislature to make reapportionment the first item of business in 1965. It took forty-seven days to bring about agreement between the Republican governor[31] and the Democratic majorities. The 1965 redistricting act brought each member's constituency within roughly 15 percent of the "ideal." Most districts were nearer the 15 percent deviation than the ideal and the court grudgingly accepted the act only until the next

TABLE III
PARTY COMPOSITION OF STATE LEGISLATURE
1939 - 1965

Year	Senate		House of Representatives	
	Democrats	Republicans	Democrats	Republicans
1939	40	6	73	26
1941	37	9	68	31
1943	27	19	57	42
1945	32	14	63	36
1947	23	23	28	71
1949	19	27	67	32
1951	25	21	54	45
1953	21	25	41	58
1955	22	24	50	49
1957	31	15	56	43
1959	35	14	66	33
1961	36	13	59	40
1963	32	17	51	48
1965	32	17	60	39
1967	29	20	44	55

31. The governor's item veto is a powerful weapon in legislative politics and Governor Evans made skillful use of it in disapproving two reapportionment bills and threatening to continue to use the veto until he got a measure palatable to the Republican minority.

census. All but seven of the old districts were outside the 15 percent range and thus had to have people added or subtracted; in the end only four of the forty-nine districts (senators and representatives are elected from the same district) remained the same under both the 1957 and the 1965 acts. No fewer than five of the Senate seats and fifteen of the House seats were moved from one part of the state to another.

The political effects of the new law will not be fully known until after the 1968 elections, but the designers of the measure and the press tend to agree that the following is likely and was borne out in part in the 1966 election. In two-thirds of the seats little change is expected in party strength. In the House both parties are expected to strengthen themselves materially in each of sixteen districts. Republicans will do better in the Senate with a major shift to them likely in three districts and picking up strength in two others. No major shift to the Democrats seems likely but the party will strengthen itself in ten districts. The three seats sacrificed to the Republicans, according to many observers, were held by Democrats hostile to the Democratic leadership. Concisely, the redistricting was the result of negotiations between the governor, a united Republican party in both houses, and a majority of Senate Democrats including the leadership. The House Democratic leadership boycotted the negotiations, and the act was passed through the House over their opposition. They were bitter at many Senate Democrats for a "sell-out" and believe the Republicans were the beneficiaries of redistricting in the House. The Republicans undoubtedly won several seats in the House in 1966 because of more favorable districting. Newspapermen were almost unanimous in their view that, considering that the Republicans were substantially in the minority, they fared much better than expected.

In a special session of the legislature in the spring of 1965 the Democrats succeeded in revising the congressional districts with a plan which had general approval of the state's congressional delegation. Because Governor Evans seemed certain to veto the measure, the legislature bypassed him by placing it on the ballot as a referendum in 1966. The voters adopted it by a 52 percent majority, and it will become effective in 1968.

The heart of legislative politics is the budget, and the great tax and appropriation battles are at the state level. Three factors dominate. First, the state shares generously with local government the taxes it collects. It ranks near the top in per capita state taxation with a concomitantly low rate of local taxation compared with other states.

Second, there is a stiff restriction on taxing powers. A graduated income tax has been ruled unconstitutional and the electorate has refused constitutional authority for the tax. Property taxation is limited to 40 mills on half of the assessed evaluation. Property taxes may be raised beyond this point only by a three-fifths majority based on 40 percent of the total votes cast in the last election. School forces must constantly fight for an additional levy, often at special elections, and apathy occasionally defeats such proposals. Rates of taxation, moreover, are left to county assessors with many inequities between counties. The 4.5 percent sales tax covers almost everything except personal services and is the basic source of state revenue. It is denounced as "regressive," but in the face of the limitations on revenue from income and property the legislature continues to increase sales tax rates, and heavily taxes alcoholic beverages, tobacco, and certain other items. The tax structure is badly in need of overhauling and the state's merchants bordering Idaho and Oregon complain of loss of business to those states.

A third characteristic of fiscal politics is the large number of special, self-sustaining funds of hundreds of millions of dollars over which the governor has no significant control. The fact that seven state officers including lands and insurance commissioners are popularly elected likewise reduces some of the governor's control. Although their budgets go through the governor's office their friends can and often do get legislative support beyond the governor's recommendations.

Washington's free-style, open political society gives nearly all citizens who wish it an opportunity to influence the course of many public policies. Since its availability in 1914 the initiative process has been an important decision-maker both statewide (Table IV) and locally. Only about one-fourth of the measures filed have fulfilled the necessary requirements to be placed on the ballot.[32] The same holds true for referenda demanded by the voters. There are, therefore, many more "starts" than finishes, suggesting that persons and groups are well aware of the availability of direct legislation but cannot garner the requisite number of signatures of registered voters. Eight percent of the number voting for governor in the preceding election is required for initiatives, or about 100,000 in 1966. Twenty-five initiatives appeared from 1946 through 1966 or about the same rate as in

TABLE IV

DATA ON INITIATIVES AND REFERENDA

1914 - 1966

Type of Proposition	Number Filed	Number of times on ballot	Number Passed	Number Failed
Direct Initiatives (presented to voters)	234	60	29	31
Indirect Initiatives (presented to legislature)	30	7	5	2
Petition Referenda	34	28	25◊	3
Referenda by Legislature	16	16	11	5
TOTAL	314	111	70	41

◊"Passed" indicates that the sponsor of the referendum was successful in attempting to prevent the measure from becoming effective law.

the preceding years. After higher frequency of use during the first decade 1914 to 1924, the rate has remained relatively constant. The close to 50 percent success in the use of the initiative does not adequately reflect its significance. Voters enacted legislation dealing with nonpartisan school elections, old age pensions, World War II veterans' bonuses, liquor by the drink, sale of colored oleomargarine, fishing regulations, legislative reapportionment, daylight saving time, civil service extensions, recreation facilities, public power, and the repeal of Sunday blue laws.

32. A very brief and often inadequate summary of the content of ballot measures was published by the secretary of state in 1966 under the title "History of State Initiative and Referendum Measures 1966 Edition."

Between 1948 and 1952 a sizable portion of the state's welfare program was directly initiated.

Washington and California are the only states providing for both direct and indirect initiative procedures. Only seven indirect initiatives, however, have been presented to the Washington legislature, three in the last twenty years. The blanket primary, which has had so much impact on the state's political life, was the result of an indirect initiative. Of the seven, two were passed by the legislature in original form; two lost out entirely; two were passed at the ensuing election and another became law but was later invalidated by a petition referendum. In view of the availability of the other form of direct legislation, the indirect procedure is of questionable utility. If voters wish a measure passed, an initiative directly to the people is more efficient. If the people are dissatisfied with the legislature's action, the referendum provides a means of censure if not veto.

Referendum may be at the behest of either the electorate or the legislature. In the former case, 4 percent of the voters (about 50,000) in the preceding gubernatorial election must sign a petition to have a law which has been passed by the legislature placed on the ballot. Referenda are much fewer than initiatives and petition referenda are more common than legislative ones (Table IV). About 90 percent of the measures on which a referendum was forced have gone down to defeat, suggesting that the device is used only when the legislature is not in tune with powerful voting coalitions and passes a measure which is anathema to them. Particularly notable in recent cases where the electorate slapped down the legislature were measures providing for inheritance taxes on life insurance proceeds, disability compensation for certain employees, and liberalizing gambling laws.

During the elections from 1946 through 1966 the legislature itself referred ten measures to the electorate, or 62 percent of the total in the state's history. Nearly all of them sought ratification for bond issues to cover indebtedness for schools and state institutions. Voters sustained the legislature for about 85 percent of the bonded indebtedness. As expected, the legislature was criticized for abdicating its responsibility for raising school moneys by "passing the buck" to the voters. The legislative referendum has been used at times by the legislature to avoid an anticipated veto, most recently in the case of the 1965 redistricting bill. The action was challenged by friends of the governor. In an historic decision in September 1966, the state Supreme Court ruled (8 to 1) that a referred bill need not go to the governor for his signature.

It is true that many, if not most, initiatives and petition referenda get on the ballot through the financial and door-to-door efforts of large private interest groups. The state's new personnel law was prepared and sponsored by the Washington Federation of State Employees (AFL-CIO) and approved by the voters in 1960.[33] The cost of the petition-circulating campaign alone was about $47,500 defrayed mainly by means of a special 25-cent monthly assessment on WFSE members. The "voluntary unionism" measure was twice placed on the ballot by conservative business interests and locked the biggest names in commerce, industry, and labor in sharp combat. The contests were notable for fantastically large amounts of campaign literature, newspaper advertising, and costly television and radio programs. Since expenditures for ballot propositions go unreported there is

33. For this campaign and its background see Beckett, *op. cit.* This initiative provides an illustration of how legislative inaction especially in the House was out of touch with the public's interest in a new policy. There was no organized opposition to the initiative and it carried by an affirmative vote of 56.25 percent.

no way of knowing how much was spent, but both sides expended huge sums. One united labor group admitted spending $450,000 to defeat the proposition. Veteran observers are certain that more than $1 million was spent by the contenders. This should not obscure the fact that there have been a number of cases, including a reapportionment initiative sponsored by the League of Women Voters, where groups without large financial resources were able to put a proposition on the ballot and rely on the good judgment of voters to support it with a minimum expenditure for publicity. A voters' handbook listing all propositions with arguments for and against each is mailed at public expense to every registered voter. This gives only minimal exposure to a measure but every interested voter is at least reached; and communications media during campaigns urge people to read the booklet, and tell listeners where additional free copies may be obtained.

In the last twenty years there has been a noticeable increase in the use of direct legislation by more conservative factions. A seemingly sound hypothesis is that the "outs" in terms of successful access to the legislature are more likely to use direct legislation than the "ins" who are able to move the legislature to action or inaction by a capacity to bottle up legislation. In recent years the conservatives have frequently been on the outside; in earlier days the reverse was often the case with direct legislation a tool of the more liberal factions and groups.

VOTING HABITS

An analysis of voting behavior yields interesting, though not necessarily surprising observations. On about one-third of the ballot propositions a sectional note is evident, suggesting that direct legislation is used on occasion to enhance or protect a sectional interest. The rural county electorate votes out of fear of urban domination and loss of power in the legislature. It has tended to oppose the following measures which also include some constitutional amendments—redistricting, daylight time, relaxation of residence requirements for voting, increasing the number of signatures on initiative and referendum petitions, pension plans, governmental reorganization, extension of civil service, permitting land ownership by aliens, and a dam construction and water diversion initiative which was of particular benefit to Puget Sound and central Washington counties. (The vote on this last issue was far less rural-urban than geographic.) Two "right-to-work" measures were overwhelmingly defeated though several small rural counties voted for them.

Voter turnout or, conversely, "fall-off," often shows striking variation from measure to measure and from county to county. The average percent drop-off rate in the last two decades on welfare measures was 16.6; on governmental organization and bond measures about 20; on liquor, 10; daylight time, 11; and on the two right to work initiatives, only 12 and 5 percent. The last of these, which appeared on the ballot as Initiative 202 in 1958, was voted on by a total of 936,000 persons compared to 886,000 who cast ballots for U.S. senator. This was the only time in the state's history when more votes were cast for a measure than for the office leading the ticket.[34]

Little in-depth research into voting behavior on propositions in Washington has been conducted and almost none of it has been published. Reviewing aggregate electoral results on measures, however, leads one to conclude that voting be-

34. A fuller account appears in the writer's "The 1958 Election in Washington," *Western Political Quarterly*, XII (March 1959), 358-61.

havior is fairly rational and that large numbers of voters see the possible consequences to themselves and their community in the enactment of a measure. They
may not calculate the costs, risks, and benefits of a proposed policy, but they
appear to know something about its intent—whether it be redistricting or easing
liquor and gambling laws. Voters at times appear to have picked and chosen between propositions very carefully and with discrimination. Education interests
have learned that majorities will not automatically support excess levies or extend
bonded indebtedness for schools and have, both at the state and local levels,
turned down propositions when they were unconvinced of the need or regarded
the costs as too great. Locally fluoridation has, with only one or two exceptions,
been consistently defeated as it has elsewhere in the nation. This, like the dog-
leash and open-housing referenda, generated much emotion, but on a majority of
measures debate has been relatively free from demagoguery and extreme statements. It would be difficult to prove, but city councils and the state legislatures
appear to take some comfort from the fact that they can "pass the buck" to the
voters on fiscal and certain other "hot" issues.

Washington voters make no declaration of party choice when registering,
and few estimates of party membership have been made. A series of polls, most of
them unpublished, substantiates the widely held impression that the state is predominantly Democratic with a large percentage uncommitted. A Washington
Public Opinion Laboratory sample poll in 1950 found 45 percent favoring the
Democrats, 31 percent independent or favoring a minor party, and 24 percent
Republican. Some subsequent polls conducted confidentially for party managers
have found as many as 40 percent self-styled independents. No poll has found as
many as 50 percent willing to classify themselves as Democrats. A select sample in
Seattle in October 1964 showed the following percentages: 35.2 Independent;
32.2 Democratic; 28.6 Republican; 2.3 refused to answer; 1.7 reported other parties or didn't know. In terms of voting in recent years the poorest Republican
showing against a popular Democrat has not fallen below 28 percent which would
appear to be the basic hard-core vote. Conversely, no Democrat for a statewide
office has fallen below 43 percent. The impression that western Washington is
basically Democratic and central and eastern Washington Republican is an over-
simplification. Democrats frequently capture 40 to 50 percent of the state legislative district vote in the latter area though a high proportion of Republican representation has come from that part of the state.

An analysis of aggregate election results warrants several generalizations (see
Tables II and V). The voter frequently separates his state and national politics,
tends to favor incumbents irrespective of party labels, and votes name familiarity
and personality. Split-ticket voting is widespread and not limited to a few areas;
on the other hand, pockets of strong one-party attachment are likewise found all
over the state.

Gubernatorial and presidential elections are held the same years but candidates for state offices cannot depend upon "presidential coattails." Except for
1944 and 1952 during the last generation, presidents and governors of rival parties
were elected. While Eisenhower won the state in 1956 by 97,000 votes, the Democratic gubernatorial candidate, Albert D. Rosellini, won the governorship by a
comfortable margin of 109,000. In 1960 Nixon carried the state and Rosellini was
re-elected. Although the Republican presidential nominee won, the Democrats
swept all statewide offices, in many cases by enormous pluralities. Clearly Republican candidates for state offices benefited little if any from Eisenhower and Nix-

on. In a dramatic reversal, Johnson's plurality in 1964 was 309,000 while Republican candidate Daniel J. Evans retired Rosellini by 148,000. In the same election Senator Henry M. Jackson, Democrat, won by a record plurality of 538,000 (72 percent of the popular vote) while the Republican candidate for secretary of state took his opponent by 106,000. Cross-voting also appears in state legislative politics. Of the fourteen legislatures since 1940 only six have seen control of both houses by the party of the governor. In 1949, 1955, and 1967, the two houses were controlled by opposite parties.

TABLE V
FALLOFF VOTE IN PRIMARY AND GENERAL ELECTIONS
1956 - 1964◇

Office	1956		1960		1964	
	Primary	General	Primary	General	Primary	General
Governor	2.0	3.4	3.2	4.1	2.9	2.0
Lieutenant Governor	10.2	8.9	10.3	9.7	9.7	6.7
Secretary of State	12.0	9.4	9.3	9.5	11.1	6.9
Treasurer	17.1	11.5	15.1	13.4	13.4	9.0
Attorney General	13.7	10.9	□	13.4	14.3	9.1
Auditor	16.6	10.8	11.5	11.4	17.8	11.2
Lands Commissioner	12.6	11.1	16.9	13.4	14.9	10.1
Insurance Commissioner	18.8	13.1	11.7	14.8	21.1	13.0
Superintendent of Public Instruction (nonpartisan)	10.3	13.4	17.8	35.4	20.0	□

◇Falloff means percent of voters who cast ballots but did not vote on a particular position.
□No contest.

Though it may horrify advocates of party responsibility and those who regard a primary as exclusively a party election, huge numbers of voters see the primary as the most effective method of getting the "best people" nominated on both tickets. A 1950 poll asked respondents if they voted for the candidates of one party or more than one party in both elections; 78 percent said they split their tickets in the primary, and 73 percent reported doing so in the general election. At the same time there is obviously a hard-core party vote which participates in the party's primary. Even with the weakest of candidates and in the absence of a contest, Republican vote in the primary for every office almost never falls below 33 percent of the total polled by both parties.

The remarkable deviation from straight-ticket voting suggests a closely related pattern of voting behavior—the importance of name familiarity and personality. Out of over a million votes for each state office pluralities for particular candidates show fantastic variations. In 1964 the Democratic incumbent attorney general had a plurality of 421,000 in contrast to 139,000 for the Democratic incumbent lieutenant governor. A cross-over of 570,000 votes between the office of governor and attorney general took place. A "jungle-ballot" consisting of federal offices, nine statewide officials, two county commissioners, at least one judge, state legislative candidates, and many propositions, presents itself in presidential years. It is helpful to a candidate to have a name which has been connected with a prominent family, civic affairs, or sports attainment.

Incumbents have enjoyed enormous advantage at almost every level except the governorship. Only four incumbents for the U.S. Senate have been defeated since the Seventeenth Amendment, and in 101 House contests involving incumbents from 1932 through 1962 only eight went down to defeat. In 1964, however, prognosticators were flabbergasted when three very long-time Republican incumbents were defeated. A fourth, who had won in a strongly Democratic district in 1962, also lost out; but this was expected. A Democratic state auditor served from 1932 until he voluntarily retired in 1964. Several other incumbents in such offices as insurance commissioner, lieutenant governor and secretary of state have held office from twenty to thirty years.[35] Voters appear to see these offices as careers in themselves and ignore party labels. Incumbents have generally viewed the offices similarly and rarely have regarded them as steppingstones to the governorship or to Congress.

In a word, many candidates are highly successful with a brand of personal politics which draws strength from independent voters and weak partisans from the opposition party. Campaign speeches are usually lacking in strong partisanship, and an effort is made to elicit votes on the basis of retaining an incumbent because he is the most experienced and the "best man." Personal politics is undoubtedly important elsewhere but it is doubtful if one could find another state where more careers are based on it.

An exception to incumbency politics is the office of governor, where competition has always been very keen. Although there is no constitutional limitation on the terms in office, no one person has been elected for three consecutive terms. In the seventeen elections since 1900 the Republicans have captured the office nine times, the Democrats eight times. In about half of the elections the winner has received less than 55 percent of the two-party vote and, with only one exception, no party has held the governorship more than two consecutive terms. Voter perception of this office is obviously quite different than that for other offices.[36]

35. The state uses the office block ballot in the primary but a party column ballot in the general election. Though state law makes it impossible to vote a straight ticket in a single operation, all of a party's candidates are on the same line so that a voter can easily support every candidate of a party by pulling all levers straight across the machine.

36. Although there is no apparent special career line or ladder which successful candidates for governor follow, the electorate has expected its governors to have had experience in elective public office. The first governor was the only one never to have held an elective office. He had, nevertheless, been territorial governor by appointment, a major factor in his later election. Six of the fifteen governors had been mayors and three had served on city councils. Five had been members of the state legislature, of whom two were floor leaders. Several had been active in political parties and one served as a state chairman. Two lieutenant governors, three prosecuting attorneys, and one U.S. senator all became governors.

As might be expected, these men come from the higher socio-economic brackets. Only three of the state's chief executives were without some higher education. Eight came from

King County which includes Seattle had a population of 1,050,000 in 1966, or about one-third of the state's inhabitants. It is crucial in statewide elections, following the adage that as the county goes so goes the state. From 1936 through 1964 in the 24 contests for president, governor, and secretary of state, only two candidates winning a statewide majority failed to carry King County. In nonpartisan elections for superintendent of public instruction and judges of the Supreme Court, winning in King County usually means victory in the state. Both parties have reasonably effective county organization with a permanent staff. There is always lively competition between the parties, and many candidates for state positions reside in the area.

No comprehensive analysis of partisan voting habits of the ethnic or religious groupings has been undertaken. Party leaders find the large Scandinavian vote highly independent but a Scandinavian background appears to be a real asset to a candidate. Oriental population is small and its vote is inconsequential except in very close elections. Filipinos appear to be overwhelmingly Democratic; the Chinese- and Japanese-American vote is more widely distributed and independent. As elsewhere in the nation, the Catholic vote appears to be predominantly Democratic and many Catholics are active in the party and seek office under its banner. Democratic politicians, however, have learned that Catholic voters cannot be invariably counted upon as "reliable" and indeed have often been quite independent.

The small Negro population is unable to influence the outcome of a state election except in very close contests. The largest concentration is to be found in the Thirty-seventh District in Seattle. For several years the district has elected one Negro member to the state House of Representatives. The district is strongly Democratic and electoral results point to a strong Negro preference for the Democratic party.

Two additional voting habits are of interest. One of these is the fairly large "fall-off" of votes for state offices (Table V). A sharp drop takes place with the offices of lieutenant governor and secretary of state and a still further decline for the remaining offices. Over the years the vote fall-off for superintendent of public instruction has sometimes doubled that for the lowest of the other state offices.[37] The fall-off might be attributed to the absence of opportunity to vote a straight ticket with a single operation. This simple shot system was in effect until 1948 and after its abandonment there was only a perceptible increase in the drop-out rate. The voting arrangement for a straight ticket seems not to be a major variable and one must look to other factors. Lack of interest in and visibility of the lesser state offices plus their occupancy by established incumbents probably leads many to ignore marking the ballot for them. Many incumbents do not face popular challengers who dramatize the importance of the office, especially among the sporadic voters who turn out to vote only for president, governor, or a heated ballot proposition.

the legal profession, four from business, two from farming, and one each from banking, pharmacy and engineering. (A few claimed two occupations.) Except for some value in a Scandinavian name, ethnic and religious background have played a small part in the nomination and election of governors. Geography seems to be of some importance; only four of the seventeen persons who have held the office have come from east of the Cascades. The native son factor is unimportant, only three having been born in the state.

37. For a comparison of vote fall-off in other states see Hugh A. Bone, *American Politics and the Party System* (New York: McGraw-Hill, 1965), pp. 526-27.

Another characteristic, needing much further study, is the higher turnout of registered voters in the rural and small town areas than in the cities.[38] The difference is somewhat less pronounced in general elections than in primaries. This is paradoxical because the urban county organizations are more vigorous than the rural ones and, though they make no endorsements in primaries, are active in urging registration and trying to get out the vote. Mobility may be greater in the cities at election time coupled with a failure to take advantage of the liberal absentee vote laws. However, very large numbers of absentee ballots are cast and local contests are often decided by them. The Grange has always stressed the importance of voting, a factor important in the open primary which had original Grange sponsorship. Though not verified by study, it is possible that proportionately more rural voters have established patterns of voting in the primary than is the case in the cities. Some election officials believe that the roster of registered voters is kept more up to date in some smaller counties which, if true, would give them a higher percentage of turnout than counties carrying obsolete names. However, in terms of actual turnout on election day there is frequently a larger fall-off in votes for propositions and lesser offices in urban than in rural counties.

IMPACT OF NATIONAL POLITICS AND TRENDS

Depending upon what are cited as criteria, a case might be made to show that Washington does or does not follow national trends. From 1953 to 1965 (1961 excepted) the state was represented in the House of Representatives by six Republicans and one Democrat, a period when Democrats dominated all but one Congress. Yet in 1964 the state followed the Democratic trend and only two of the six Republicans were re-elected. The voters again departed from the national trend in 1966, and returned the four freshman Democrats, who rode in on the Johnson landslide, by larger margins than in 1964. As observed earlier, voters since 1940 have preferred a governor and president of opposite parties in five out of seven elections, and other statewide officers are frequently not of the same party as the president. Despite these striking exceptions general voting has fluctuated cyclically: the national trend was Republican in state legislative and congressional composition prior to 1932, and Progressive candidates fared reasonably well from 1912 to 1920. Presidential trends have also been followed. After supporting Bryan in 1896 the state failed only in 1912 and 1960 to give its vote to the winning side. Further, the vote has very often approximated the national average.

The hypothesis that where a party is traditionally weak on the congressional level, the President will run ahead, and where the party is entrenched on the congressional level, congressional candidates will lead the President, is neither sustained nor entirely disproven by Washington's experience. Eisenhower, who ran very well in the state, led only two of the six successful Republican incumbents in 1952, and in 1956 his percentage exceeded three. The Democratic congressman-at-large ran ahead of Eisenhower both times; Kennedy ran ahead of five Democratic congressional candidates and behind two. Johnson exceeded by more than 10 percent the total vote percentage for Democratic congressional candidates and ran ahead of all but one of them. There is no such thing as an entrenched party at the congressional level; rather it is the candidate who is entrenched. Although the

38. For a discussion of this point as applied to the primaries see Bone, "The 1962 Election in Washington," pp. 472-73.

voters tend to follow preponderant national opinion and presidential candidates, the latter's coattails only seldom can be depended upon to sweep in their party's candidates for Congress.

Great national issues appear in Washington campaigns, particularly farm policy, expenditures for civil and military projects, the tariff, public power, medicare, social security and federal aid to education. General civil rights legislation is approved but has not elicited the interest among the mass of voters that it has in many other states. In 1964 local propositions providing for "open housing" in Seattle and Tacoma stirred emotions and were overwhelmingly defeated. A statewide bill, endorsed by the Republican governor, passed the House by a large margin but was sidetracked in the Senate. In general, national issues play no great part in city, county, or state elections. With the state's economy strongly dependent upon federal appropriations a major preoccupation of the congressional delegation, irrespective of party, is to keep a generous flow of federal contracts and money coming to the state. War cries of "socialism" and "federal interference" appear in letters to the editor, conservative newspapers, and from the mouths of some politicians; but Republicans are likely to give as much support as the Democrats to federal spending programs for the military, and for "internal improvements."

Washington is a long way from the nation's capital and from Europe, but its sea and airports serve as a gateway to the Orient and its politicians give much attention to Far Eastern politics and foreign policy. Senators Jackson and Magnuson deliver many speeches both within and outside the state on aspects of foreign trade and policy and civic interest in such matters remains high. For example, in a depth interview on the importance of seven issues during the 1956 presidential campaign, defense and foreign policy ran far ahead of jobs and income, farm policy, the vice presidency, Eisenhower's health, and desegregation.[39]

The Washington delegation, though small, has had considerable influence in both houses of Congress thanks to seniority and cooperation.[40] They have acted in closest concert on public works and other projects of much benefit to the state. Until several House Republicans were defeated in 1964, the state had considerable seniority including the ranking minority member on the Merchant Marine Committee. Even after the change all members had committee assignments of singular value to the state. The state was one of three in the 89th Congress to hold two Senate committee chairmanships. Magnuson is in his fourth term and Jackson is in his third, and between the two much influence is exerted on the Aeronautical and Space Science, Appropriations, Commerce, Interior and Insular Affairs, Armed Services, and Government Operations committees—which pays off in federal contracts.

39. On a 1-7 rating from little to no importance, with 6, 7 indicating very important, the following percentages of respondents gave ratings of 6 or 7: to defense policy 62, foreign policy 53, jobs and income 48, farm policy 40, vice presidency 40, desegregation 34, and Eisenhower's health 32. See Marilyn E. McCurtain, "An Investigation of the Voter's Decision Process and His Political Behavior" (Ph.D. dissertation, University of Washington, 1965), p. 111.

40. On the behavior and techniques of the delegation see John H. Kessel, "The Washington Congressional Delegation," *Midwest Journal of Political Science*, 8 (February 1964), 1-21.

WYOMING:

0   30   60   90 MILES   ——— COUNTY LINE   ▰▰▰ CONGRESSIONAL DISTRICT LINE   ▲ COUNTY SEAT

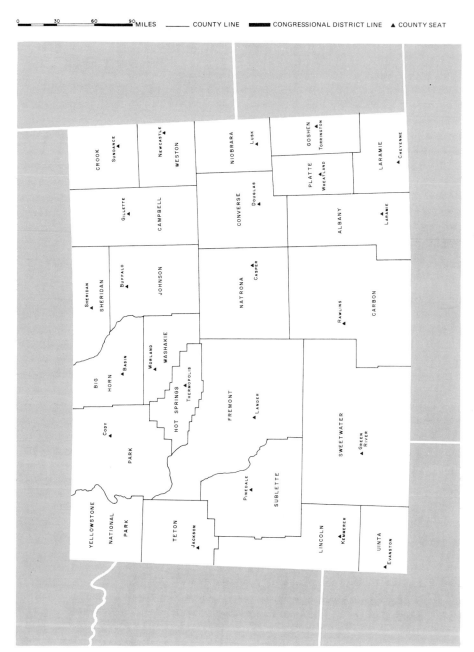

CROOK   SUNDANCE ▲   NEWCASTLE ▲   WESTON   NIOBRARA   LUSK ▲   GOSHEN   TORRINGTON ▲   LARAMIE   CHEYENNE ▲

GILLETTE ▲   CAMPBELL   CONVERSE   DOUGLAS ▲   PLATTE   WHEATLAND ▲   ALBANY   LARAMIE ▲

SHERIDAN ▲   SHERIDAN   BUFFALO ▲   JOHNSON   NATRONA   CASPER ▲   RAWLINS ▲   CARBON

BIG   HORN   BASIN ▲   WORLAND ▲   WASHAKIE   THERMOPOLIS ▲   HOT SPRINGS   FREMONT   LANDER ▲   SWEETWATER   GREEN RIVER ▲

CODY ▲   PARK   PINEDALE ▲   SUBLETTE

YELLOWSTONE   NATIONAL   PARK   TETON   JACKSON ▲   LINCOLN   KEMMERER ▲   UINTA   EVANSTON ▲

Ralph M. Wade

The Frontier State

To many people Wyoming is symbolic of the old West, a land of sagebrush, antelope, wild horses, and cowboys. This image, in the minds of some who have never visited the area, may have been created by the symbol of the bucking bronco on the state's automobile license plates. Although much of this imagery may still be true, the region has undergone great transformation since the days when hardy emigrants trekked wearily from the old East to the land of the Golden West. Few of these early visitors tarried long in the territory but those who did built the foundation for the present-day "Equality State."

Ranching and mining absorbed the energies of the early residents and the same activities are still important today. Mining, in the early days characterized by the pick and pan, is today highly mechanized. Ranching, too, has progressed from the day when the early settler built up his herd by rustling or purchase of foundation stock from the drovers of the Southwest. The rancher today is often lord of all he surveys and this frequently includes thousands of acres. He no longer depends on the grace of God and nature to bring his herds through an unfavorable winter for he safeguards his enterprise with hay and commercial feeds.

Combatting the hazards of nature and building an empire in a rigorous environment has tended to create a democratic pattern of thinking by Wyoming dwellers. A man is accepted for what he does and not because of his social status. His importance as an individual is emphasized.

While livestock raising is still a significant aspect of agriculture, both dry and irrigated farming is important in many parts of the state. The most significant extractive or mining activity of today is concerned with petroleum. Oil was discovered in the Salt Creek area in 1888 but extensive exploration and development did not occur until several decades later. Coal, of which the state has an abundance, provided the energy units for railroad locomotives until recently when diesel fuel from the state's vast petroleum resources was substituted.

With the beginning of federal aid for highway construction came trucking. Automotive transportation now enables the formerly isolated community to receive an abundance of goods and supplies previously unavailable. Good roads have also contributed greatly to tourism, another important economic activity in the state. Yellowstone National Park, established in 1872, together with Grand Teton National Park of a later period have been tourist lodestones. Big game hunting and the dude ranch facilities have also attracted many to the state.

The military posts which were established in territorial days to protect the immigrant and early settler from the Indians have largely disappeared. The Cheyenne area, however, continues to have a significant establishment. Through the years it has been transformed from a cavalry post to a missile base with subinstallations in two neighboring states.[1]

Wyoming's economy has shown continuous although slow growth. It has never sustained the severe shocks of more highly industrialized areas. Oil, beef, and tourism combined to form the basic elements of its stable economy. The various interest groups supporting these economic activities constitute the controlling factor in state politics.

Often candidates for public office, whether Democrats or Republicans, will exhibit little difference in political philosophy. This has resulted in a tendency to vote for the man rather than the party. The character of economic growth has fostered conservatism in both business and politics which has infiltrated both of the major political parties. Sparse population, great distances between ranches, and the absence of great metropolitan centers have encouraged self-reliance, a component of individualism. While Wyoming may in general be characterized as a Republican state, the voters have usually elected some candidates of the opposite party to high state and national office.

Still another characteristic of the state's politics is its geographic political pattern. In the northern two-thirds of the state, except under unusual conditions, voters support the Republican party while those in the southern tier of counties generally support the Democrats. Basically, again economic factors control, for the northern area is largely devoted to ranching and small business activity, while in the southern third railroading, coal mining, and oil refining with their attendant unionized labor, predominate. The outcome of a given political party campaign will frequently depend on how Casper, with its oil industry, located in the south central part of the state, goes.

The political philosophy of both parties tends to be right-of-center on major state and national issues. Since the days of the Populist movement in the 1890's and the Progressive party in the second and third decades of the twentieth century, no third party has been a real threat to the two major ones.[2] Candidates for political office generally enunciate their own platforms which may or may not emphasize the issues of the party under whose banner they seek voter support. Political party affiliation in fact is often played down.

GEOGRAPHY AND RESOURCES

Wyoming, carved out of one-time possessions of the French, Spanish, English, and Mexicans, was made an organized territory of the United States on July 15, 1868, and achieved statehood in 1890. Its rectangular territory ranks ninth among the fifty states in size, with a gross area of 97,914 square miles. The state may be divided roughly into four major basins, a great plains region, and scattered mountain areas. The basins are the Wyoming, located in the southwestern part, the Laramie in the south central, the Big Horn in the north central, and the Wind River in the northwest central section. The great plains area includes approximately the eastern third of the state.[3]

1. The post is currently the F. E. Warren Missile Base.

2. From 1957 to 1964 there was an attempt made to establish the Benjamin Franklin party as a third political party in Wyoming. Its major objective was to promote scientists for public office. Wayne Bud Kinney, Laramie, was its national chairman and its principal supporter in the state.

3. Herman H. Trachsel and Ralph M. Wade, *The Government and Administration of Wyoming* (New York: Crowell, 1953), pp. 1-10, 214.

Wyoming has more large rivers than any of its neighbors in the arid or semi-arid western region, with headwaters of four major drainage basins in the United States. Although these streams produce an annual runoff of almost twenty million acre feet, the state is currently using only about 20 percent of it. It is estimated that about four million acre feet are available for expansion of irrigation and industry, potential support for many times the present individual and industrial demands. In the early days much water was used by miners, but currently its use is devoted almost entirely to agricultural and domestic purposes. Approximately two million acres are now irrigated and an additional one million could be furnished sufficient water for their needs.[4]

The average elevation of cities in Wyoming is about one mile. Altitudes vary from a low of 3,125 feet above sea level near the northeast corner to the 13,785 feet of Gannett Peak in the west central part.

The United States Weather Bureau places the state in the so-called "comfort zone" and as such it is rated as one of the ideal spots of the nation where one can live comfortably. The rating is based upon a compilation of normal annual temperatures combined with mean relative humidity.[5] The normal monthly average temperature is 45.1 degrees Fahrenheit and the normal average precipitation is 14.1 inches as recorded in Casper. This city also had an average of 68 percent of possible sunshine days which compares favorably with many major cities in the United States.

Nearly half of Wyoming's land is still owned by the federal government. One seventh of the state is in natural forests. Commercial harvesting of yields from them does not equal the annual growth: consequently the forests are actually increasing.

Of the land devoted to agricultural purposes less than 4 percent is being cropped, the rest being used for livestock grazing. Between 70 and 80 percent of the agricultural income is derived from livestock and its by-products. The state ranks second in wool production and twenty-fifth in number of beef cattle.[6] It ranks among the top ten in the production of spring wheat, sugar beets, and dry beans. There were in 1959 some 9,744 farms and ranches with an average acreage of 3,715 and a per unit value of approximately $79,447. Over half of them marketed products over $10,000 in value per year.[7]

The oil and natural gas industry has been and is today the largest employer and income producer in Wyoming. Crude oil and natural gas are produced in twenty-one of the twenty-three counties. Proven reserves are at an all-time high. There are no proration laws such as are found in some states and thus exploration is encouraged for the cost may be recovered much faster. Success in wildcatting has consequently been higher. Wyoming does not levy an ad valorem tax on production. Approximately two-thirds of the crude oil is shipped out of the state for refining although there are a number of refineries within its borders.

The Green River basin in southwestern Wyoming has within the last few years become exceedingly active in oil and gas exploration. Very recently produc-

4. Floyd A. Bishop, Wyoming State Engineer, letter, December 13, 1965.

5. Hubert J. Soher, *Wyoming: Its Economy, Its Future, Its Resources* (Portland: Pacific Power and Light Co., 1961), pp. 4-5.

6. O. Henry Engendorff, Wyoming Commissioner of Agriculture, letter, December 23, 1965.

7. *Statistical Abstract of the United States*, p. 612. Source: Department of Commerce, Bureau of Census, *U.S. Census of Agriculture*, 1959, Vol. II. This is the most recent one for the state.

tive discoveries have been made in the Powder River area and the southeast portion of the Wind River basin as well as in the Big Horn basin and Campbell County.

The state ranks first in the nation in coal reserves, estimated to be 121 billion tons. The area underlain by known or probably coal-bearing strata totals over forty thousand square miles or over 41 percent of the entire state. While the coal industry has been affected by technological developments in recent years it now appears to be on the verge of recovery for new uses are being found for this resource. Much coal is currently being used in steam plants to generate electric power.

During 1963 iron ore output in Wyoming was 110 percent larger than in the preceding year.[8] The United States Steel Corporation has a new ore processing plant in operation at Atlantic City in the western part of the state while the Colorado Fuel and Iron Corporation has one in operation at Sunrise in the southeastern part.[9] Large deposits of trona, bentonite, oil shale, uranium, and other secondary minerals give promise of future mining and industrial expansion. The estimated total mineral production decreased 1 percent in value in 1965 from that of 1964 for a total of $501.0 million. This was because the value of uranium production declined some ten million dollars from the preceding year.[10] According to preliminary figures released by the Bureau of Mines the value of Wyoming's mineral production reached an all-time high of $530.8 million in 1967.[11] The state ranked thirteenth in the nation in value of minerals produced.

Resources and economics are inevitably intertwined as are politics and economics. Certainly a great many political programs have an economic origin. Wyoming's economic history begins with the trappers and traders in the early nineteenth century. They were the forerunners of the great western trek. During the 1840's thousands of people crossed Wyoming on the Oregon, Mormon, and Overland trails. Only a few visionary and hardy individuals who saw a future in cattle and sheep raising took up land and stayed in the territory.

Transportation was a problem for these early residents and it was only partially solved by the coming of the railroads. The latter's arrival provided employment for thousands of men and also created a demand for energy units. Wyoming's vast coal reserves were the answer to this demand.

Approximately 70 percent of all revenue arising from agricultural activity in the state is accounted for by cattle and sheep. In 1963-64 there was much concern over the continuation of record-breaking importation of red meat from foreign countries, particularly in view of falling prices for domestic meat. This matter became a political issue in the 1964 election campaign. United States Senator Gale McGee attempted to show that it was the supermarkets that were controlling the prices paid to the rancher and the farmer for their products. The issue has recently become less important because of the higher prices paid for beef.

During 1963 some 65,000 acres of land in Wyoming were planted in sugar beets which yielded an all-time high record crop of over a million tons valued at

8. Soher, *op. cit.*, pp. 1-36.

9. U.S. Department of the Interior, Bureau of Mines, *Mineral Industry Survey*, January 4, 1965.

10. U.S. Department of the Interior, Bureau of Mines, *Mineral Industrial Survey, Preliminary Annual Figures*, January 3, 1966. Iron ore production increased 4 percent in quantity and 11 percent in value in 1965 over 1964.

11. U.S. Department of the Interior, Bureau of Mines, *Mineral Production in Wyoming in 1967, Preliminary Annual Figures*, January 2, 1968.

$17,000,000. The average yield was 17 tons per acre with a value of $261.54. The failure of Congress to authorize an increase of acreage for sugar beet production has been condemned by both political parties.

As previously mentioned it is in the area of energy units that Wyoming abounds. To date, petroleum has been extracted from the earth in liquid form, but it is estimated that the shale oil reserve, much of which lies in the Green River area of southwestern Wyoming, is over ten billion barrels. Coal is being used primarily to generate electric power. In addition, extensive experiments are going on to provide many by-products. It is being converted to coke to be used in steel furnaces and in some instances powdered and liquefied to be transported in pipelines to places where it can be used more economically.

Uranium production in dollar value ($28,218,000) reached an all-time high in 1961. Recently, because of the federal government's cutback in stockpiling, this phase of mining and processing has gone into an economic slump. Trona production, new in Wyoming mining history, is booming and the future outlook is bright. Several large corporations are now exploiting this resource which is used in detergent production.

Industry is also beginning to utilize natural gas to produce fertilizers. A new complex capable of producing 50,000 tons of anhydrous ammonia and ammonium nitrate annually was recently constructed in the Cheyenne area.[12]

Two other industries are and will be of continuing economic significance: lumbering and tourism. Currently there is considerable waste in the lumbering industry because of the failure to harvest the trees as fast as they become mature. One suggested remedy, not yet exploited, is to provide a market for pulpwood. Cost of transportation has delayed this development.

Tourism is proving to be one of the most valuable basic industries of the state. It is estimated that visitors spent 120 million dollars in 1963 and that such expenditures will continue to increase rapidly in the years to come. The tourist's dollars are usually new dollars in the community and they have a multiplier effect. The two national parks, Yellowstone and Teton, and the twelve national forests in Wyoming, as well as the excellent hunting and fishing available, provide irresistible attractions to those from areas having less favorable recreational facilities.[13]

Federal aid in 1963 accounted for 49 percent of the state's total general revenue. General revenue includes all state revenue exclusive of receipts from liquor wholesaling and from insurance trusts. This amounted to $175.91 per capita based upon an estimated state population of 337,000. Highways received the lion's share, some 63.2 percent; welfare got 5.3 percent; education 2.9, and employment security 2 percent. The rest went to natural resources, health and hospitals, and airports.[14]

Under the Federal Royalties Act of 1920 the federal government returns 37.5 percent of the royalties it receives from mineral production on federal lands located within the state. Over twelve million dollars or 23 plus percent of the federal grants to Wyoming came initially from this source. The distribution to the state of funds received by the federal government from mineral production has

12. Public Administration Services, University of Wyoming, *Wyoming Public Affairs*, December 1964, pp. 1-2. The Wycon Chemical expanded its operation by adding a $3 million urea plant, completed in 1966. *Mineral Industrial Survey*, Department of the Interior, January 3, 1966.

13. *Wyoming Public Affairs*, December 1964, pp. 3-5.

14. U.S. Department of Commerce, Bureau of Census, *Compendium of State Government Finances in 1963*, pp. 10, 14-15.

been a bone of contention and a political issue in Wyoming for some time. It is estimated that of the approximately $800 million which the United States government collected in receipts under the Mineral Leasing Act from all states from 1920 to 1959 approximately 40 percent came from Wyoming.[15] Its congressional delegation contends, on the basis of title to offshore oil resources being given to the seacoast states, that Wyoming should get all or at least a greater percentage of the royalties from federal lands with mineral resources within the state. The members of the state legislature have also expressed this opinion in memorials addressed to the Congress.

Wyoming's total value in retail trade increased from $415,828,000 in 1958 to $484,586,000 in 1963, some 16 percent, while the value of its wholesale trade expanded from $211 million to $248 million. In each area the volume is small in comparison with that of larger, more industrialized states but it does indicate a firm steady growth in the economy.[16]

On the basis of broad occupational grouping, about 41 percent of the employed persons in the state are white-collar workers; 46 percent fall in the blue-collar class; the remainder are classified as farm workers. The average annual income per family is $5,880 which is second highest in the Rocky Mountain region and exceeds the average for the United States by $220.00.[17]

Manufacturing in the state is currently limited to food canning, lumber and wood products, refining of petroleum, by-products from coal, quarrying of stone, processing of iron ore and trona and the making of commercial fertilizer. The greatest weakness in the state's economy is to be found in its lack of processing facilities for its many resources. Many of its mineral and agricultural products are sent elsewhere for processing, which curtails the labor market within the state.

The extent and rate of industrialization of the state in recent years was a matter of political controversy in the 1966 election campaign. Republican leaders claimed that during Governor Hansen's tenure the economy had been enriched by some $225 million in new and expanded industrial investment.[18] Democrats, on the other hand, deplored the record, pointing out that Wyoming had not kept pace in industrial growth with other Rocky Mountain states. According to one gubernatorial candidate, the problem could be solved by creating a more favorable tax structure as it effects oil, gas and other mineral extractors to encourage them to keep their processing and payrolls in the state.[19] Governor Stan Hathaway in a press conference at the end of his first year in office said, "Economic development of Wyoming is my number one goal. The fundamental problem in this state is that the economic base is not diverse enough."[20]

Wyoming is truly a frontier state with extensive, rich and varied natural resources, as yet largely underdeveloped. With its sparse population it is a fertile area for future economic expansion.

15. State of Wyoming, *Biennial Report of the State Auditor*, June 30, 1964, Schedule 7A. Soher, *op. cit.*, pp. 1-2.

16. U.S. Department of Commerce, Bureau of the Census, *1963 Census of Business, Retail Trade in Wyoming; Wholesale Trade in Wyoming*.

17. *1960 Census of Population, Vol. I*, "Characteristics of the Population, Part 1, U.S. Summary," U.S. Department of Commerce, Bureau of the Census, Figure S60, S64.

18. *Time* Magazine, "Wyoming Change on the Range," February 11, 1966.

19. *KTWO*, "The State of the State." Casper, Wyoming, February 5, 1966.

20. The *Laramie Sunday Boomerang*, December 31, 1967.

POPULATION

Many residents of Wyoming are happy about its sparse population. They have had and continue to want so-called elbow room. The state is the second lowest in population in the Union—330,066 according to the 1960 federal census. From 1940 to 1960 the population increased by 79,324 which was a gain of 31.6 percent over that of the 1940 census. In the past decade the increase was 39,537 or 13.6 percent. The rate of increase has been lower in recent years than that of many other western states.

On the basis of an area which has 8,000 or more inhabitants within its boundaries being considered urban, some twelve Wyoming counties would be so classified. If, however, such classification is made on the basis of more than 50 percent of the people living in an incorporated municipality of 2,500, then some thirteen counties would be urban. Not all of them would be the same as under the first classification. Nine counties lost a total of 9,802 inhabitants between 1950 and 1960. Natrona was the fastest growing county in the 1950's, increasing from 31,437 to 49,623 or 57.8 percent; Fremont was second with 33.6 percent. Niobrara had the greatest percentage loss (20.2) but Sweetwater lost the greatest number of people (4,097), primarily due to the closing of coal mines in this area.

Although twelve counties were classified as urban rather than rural according to the 1960 census, only eight contained one or more cities with a population over 5,000. Wyoming law classifies any incorporated area with less than 4,000 people as a town; all those with a greater population are first class cities. The 1960 census listed nineteen of the state's incorporated municipalities as urban areas. In 1940 Wyoming had eight cities between 2,500 and 10,000, and they contained 12.7 percent of the state's population. By 1960 their number had increased to fourteen and they had gained 33,591 persons. This accounted for over 42.3 percent of the increase in the state's population during the twenty-year period. In 1940 there were only four cities in the state with over 10,000. By 1960 there were five and their population had almost doubled. Casper and Cheyenne, each in the over 10,000 bracket in 1940, accounted for 52 percent of the growth by 1960. Casper increased by 64.4 percent from 1950 to 1960 (23,673—38,930). Rock Springs had the greatest loss (.044 percent) among the major cities of the state.[21]

Wyoming's population has shown an increasing tendency toward concentration. The percentage of persons living in cities of 10,000 and over rose from 24.5 in 1940 to 32.2 in 1950 to 36.9 in 1960. Those living in places of 1,000 and over in 1940 rose from 50 percent to 65 percent in 1960. The state as a whole was 56.8 percent urban in 1960 in comparison with 49.8 in 1950 and 29.6 in 1910.

The latest and most reliable estimates of the state's population, July 1, 1967, indicated a loss of some 15,000 from the 1960 figure of 330,066. This may be accounted for by the completion of much construction work in the intercontinental ballistic missile complex about Cheyenne and the realignment and removal of administrative personnel to other states by petroleum producing companies.[22] Future estimates, however, indicate that the state will have a 7 percent population increase between 1965 and 1975 and a 30 percent gain by 1985.[23]

21. *1960 Census of Population, Vol. I*, "Characteristics of the Population, Part 52, Wyoming," Table 8, U.S. Department of Commerce, Bureau of the Census.

22. *Current Population Reports*, "Population Estimates," Series P-25, No. 375, July 1, 1967, U.S. Department of Commerce.

23. *Ibid.*, Series P-25, No. 380, November 24, 1967.

Over 90 percent of the people are native-born whites, half of whom were born in one of the other 49 states. The remainder is composed of a small percentage of Indians (4,020) who are rural dwellers; Orientals (706) who are mostly urban; Negroes (2,183), nearly 50 percent of whom live in cities of 10,000 or over; and foreign-born whites. Several cities in the state have sizable communities of persons of Mexican or Spanish extraction. This is particularly true of Cheyenne, Laramie, and Rawlins. Rock Springs, the state's fifth largest city, has the greatest percentage of foreign-born whites of any of the state's large municipalities. The greatest percentage of foreign stock came originally from the United Kingdom. Many British were engaged in the livestock business in Wyoming during its territorial days, and a number of their descendants are today prominent ranchers in the northern part of the state. Shoshone and Arapahoe Indians on the Wind River Reservation have had some effect upon the economic, social, and political aspects of the Lander-Riverton area. There has been an actual decrease in the percentage of non-whites in the state since 1950.[24]

Slightly over 41 percent of the state's population in 1960 were war veterans in comparison with 38.8 percent for the United States as a whole. While this group has not usually exerted pressure on the lawmakers, it has been able to keep in effect veterans' preference in taxation. Candidates for political office invariably list service for their country as one of the qualifications. Because of the Korean and Vietnam conflicts it is reasonable to expect that the 1970 census will show a larger percentage of the population to be veterans.

EDUCATIONAL POLITICS

Providing the youth of Wyoming with all of the educational advantages they are capable of using is a problem similar to that existing in other states with vast areas and sparse populations. In the past these factors led to the establishment of many school districts with low pupil-teacher ratios and poor financial support. As the state developed some districts achieved a very favorable tax base while others were poverty-stricken. This led the legislature to provide by law for a foundation program of state-aid for each classroom. For years almost every town, regardless of size, also had a local high school. The trend in recent years has been toward consolidation and elimination of the one-room rural school and the small, poorly equipped and staffed high school. Currently in the larger cities of the state there are the problems of shortages of classrooms; inadequate salaries; lack of facilities for vocational training; and pupil dropouts. Throughout all school systems is the absence of a satisfactory retirement system for teachers.[25]

Wyoming is more fortunate than many states in regard to higher education. Its one four-year institution established during territorial days at Laramie has the admiration and support of both political parties and the general citizenry. There is not the bartering and lobbying for financial support among a number of competing collegiate institutions so common in many of the states. The University does, however, play a major role in the state financing for its operation has called for from 25 to 28 percent of the state's general fund expenditures each biennium or about 10 percent of the total state expenditures.[26]

24. *1960 Census of Population, Vol. I,* "Characteristics of the Population, Part 1, U.S. Summary," Figures S42, S43, U.S. Department of Commerce, Bureau of the Census.
25. *Retirement of State Employees and Teachers, Wyo. S. 1957,* Sec. 9-284 to Sec. 9-340.
26. *Executive Budget 1965-1967,* State of Wyoming. (This biennium 15 percent.)

In recent years junior (community) colleges have been established in five of Wyoming's major communities. These are supported by local funds augmented by some state appropriations. In 1965 the legislature allotted to the five which existed at that time $1,245,000. With the establishment of a sixth at Riverton in Fremont County and voter rejection of one proposed for Cheyenne, the Executive Budget of 1966-67 called for the expenditure of $1,645,000.[27]

Higher education is respected and eagerly sought by residents of the state. Candidates for public office stress their educational attainment particularly if it was achieved in a Wyoming institution. There is no serious anti-intellectualism in the state, and both high school and college enrollments are increasing.

Education at the elementary and secondary levels has caused the greatest concern in recent years. To study this problem Governor Clifford Hansen in 1964 appointed a committee of the state's leading citizens. They came from all walks of life, from large communities as well as small, from wealthy as well as poor districts, and from the several geographic areas in the state. Their mission was to bring to the people and to the members of the legislature a full knowledge of prevailing educational conditions and problems and to provide recommendations for the improvement of Wyoming public school education in the areas of finance, organization, educational progress, and special problems.[28]

This committee, after extensive study and consultation, recommended that special high school districts be abandoned; a new reorganization law be passed with suggested criteria for organizing districts; and that the office of county superintendent be abolished thus making the superintendent of a reorganized district the responsible administrator.

The legislature did not enact into law all recommendations of the committee. It did, however, accept the Governor's recommendation for proposing a constitutional amendment requiring each county of the state to levy a 12 mill tax on the assessed valuation of property for the support and maintenance of the public schools of the county.[29] This amendment was ratified by the voters in the 1966 general election. The Wyoming Educational Association opposed some of the recommendations.

The legislature did authorize and direct that all statutes relating to schools and education be revised and compiled.[30] It also raised the assessed valuation requirement and pupil-high-school registration requirement for the establishment of a junior college.[31]

One of the notable accomplishments of the 1965 legislature was the repeal of the existing law prohibiting the acceptance of many types of federal aid for education.[32] For many years the dominant political party had opposed federal aid in this area. Governor Hansen, although a Republican, recommended in his message to the legislature that it take such action.[33] Many Democrats had long

27. *Session Laws of Wyoming, 1965*, Chap. 63; Executive Budget, 1967-69, State of Wyoming, p. 1.

28. *Summary of Recommendations*, Governor's Committee on Education, September 1964.

29. *Original Senate Joint Resolution, No. 10*, March 1, 1965. This became Constitutional Amendment No. 5.

30. *Wyoming Statutes, 1957* (Pocket Supplement), Sec. 8-10.8.

31. *Ibid.*, Sec. 21-446.

32. *Session Laws of Wyoming, 1965*, Chap. 44, Sec. 1-4.

33. Clifford P. Hansen, Governor, *Message to the Legislature, 1965*, p. 8.

favored repeal and from time to time had not only included a plank in their platform to this effect but had also introduced bills to repeal existing prohibitive legislation, all to no avail until 1965.

The state expenditure pattern for education has changed radically since 1947. As a result of the School Foundation Program enacted in 1950 to support a minimum level of education throughout the state, expenditures have increased almost sevenfold, from $12.93 per capita to $87.90 in 1963. The percentage of Wyoming's total general expenditures increased from 20.6 percent in 1947 to 26.5 percent in 1963.[34]

The overwhelming approval by the electorate of proposed Constitutional Amendment No. 5 in November 1966 made it incumbent upon the legislature to improve the financing of public education. Governor Hathaway in his 1967 budget message recommended an increase in the state's foundation program per school classroom per year to $8,000. The Wyoming Educational Association lobbied for $8,500 but the final outcome was $8,200. Efforts by educational pressure groups in 1967 to secure a special legislative session to have the foundation amount raised were unsuccessful.[35]

The level of formal education received by residents of Wyoming is high. The median attained in 1960 by those 25 years old and over was 12.1 years of formal schooling compared with 12 years in the Rocky Mountain region and 10 plus years for the United States as a whole.

In Wyoming less than 5 percent of the population 25 years of age or over are classed as illiterate. Illiteracy is defined as existing when a person has completed less than five years of elementary schooling. For the United States as a whole the figure is 8.4 percent. Six percent of the state's population have four or more years of college education.[36]

NEWS MEDIA AND PUBLIC OPINION

Early in the political campaign of 1964 most of the state's papers supported the political party that they had backed traditionally. The majority, as in the past at this stage of the campaign, supported Senator Goldwater for President. As time passed, however, a number swung their allegiance to President Johnson or took a neutral stand. This was particularly evident with the McCraken chain of newspapers.[37] Those papers that had been Democratic in editorial policy in the past remained loyal to the party.

Both of Denver's daily papers, the *Post* and the *Rocky Mountain News*, have wide circulation in Wyoming, particularly in the southern and eastern parts. The *News* remained a supporter of Goldwater or at least of the Republican party until the end of the campaign but with waning interest as time passed. The *Post*, which prides itself on being independent, supported President Johnson's candidacy and beyond that divided its allegiance among the candidates within Colorado. It did not editorialize on Wyoming state candidates. The *Deseret News* from Salt Lake

34. *Compendium of State Government Finances, 1947-1963*, U.S. Department of Commerce, Bureau of Census.

35. *Session Laws of Wyoming, 1967*, Chap. 161.

36. *1960 Census of Population, Vol. I*, "Characteristics of the Population, Part 1, U.S. Summary," Figure S49.

37. The chain includes the *Cheyenne Eagle; Cheyenne Tribune; Laramie Daily Boomerang; Rock Springs Rocket; Rawlins Daily Times* and the *Northern Wyoming Daily News* at Worland.

City has substantial circulation in the western part of the state and in general, supported the Republican party's candidates for office.[38] Montana's *Billings Gazette*, with wide circulation in the Big Horn basin, gave mild support to the national candidates of the Republican party.

During the 1964 campaign Wyoming had thirty-one weekly and ten daily newspapers. Of the former only five could be considered as having an editorial policy strongly supporting the Democratic party, and one other giving the party moderate support. Three of the weeklies gave the Republican party strong support, twelve others were Republican party-oriented, and the remaining ten were either independent or had no editorial policy. Four of the state's leading daily newspapers strongly supported the Republican party but again particularly candidates for national offices. Two others called themselves independent but favored the Republicans. Three supported the Democrats but only one of these editorialized, while the last one claimed party independence, but its news stories had Democratic overtones.[39] Both the Democrats and the Republicans published official party organs that had wide circulation during the campaign.[40] Each tended to give unity and coherence to its party's effort.

Radio and television stations did play a significant part in the campaign, but most of them simply broadcast speeches of or for party candidates without taking an editorial stand in support of the candidates or the parties. In some instances Wyoming candidates made speeches using KSL-TV of Salt Lake City and the Intermountain Radio Network from a Wyoming station as vehicles of communication to reach their constituents.

Radio facilities were used in connection with sports broadcasts by candidates of both parties. Athletic contests in Wyoming attract a wide group of radio listeners and such spots are greatly desired and were widely used by United States senatorial candidates McGee and Wold as well as by Roncalio and Harrison, candidates for the House of Representatives.

Some twenty-nine radio stations in Wyoming were active politically during the 1964 campaign. Twelve of them broadcast programs produced by leading spokesmen of the radical right. This is not to imply that all these stations would editorially support such opinions, but probably in the interest of their listening public or to augment their programs—and perhaps their income—were obliged to do so.[41]

Although Wyoming has only two television stations at present, viewing programs are received from a number of stations located in other states of the Rocky Mountain area. Virtually all candidates regardless of the level of the office sought made wide use of this medium. It was the most effective of any used but also the most expensive, thus a contributing factor in making the 1964 campaign, in the judgment of many, Wyoming's most costly. As indicated earlier, most of the mass media adhered to their previous positions of party support, but there was a show

---

38. The editors of these three out-of-state papers each stated by personal letter that his paper's editorial policy was nonpartisan. The *Billings Gazette* admittedly supported the Republican candidate, Babcock, for governor.

39. Party support and editorial policy were determined by a review of the editions and by consultation with staff members of the Journalism Department, University of Wyoming.

40. The *Democratic Spokesman* and the *Wyoming GOP Trunkline*.

41. A number of radio and television stations, and newspapers are supplied by the Wyoming Travel Commission, Cheyenne. Programs of the radical right broadcast by the Wyoming stations were secured from the producers themselves.

of weakness by Republican party supporters as the campaign wore on.

A unique publicity device used by each party's United States senatorial candidate and by the Democratic candidate for the U.S. House of Representatives was the airplane with streamers attached urging the support of a candidate. This type of publicity was extensively used to inform crowds attending athletic contests and other large gatherings. The telephone was also used, particularly on election day, by county and city party committees urging their partisan registered voters to get to the polls and offering transportation and baby-sitting assistance if it was needed.

Still another method of appeal to public opinion during the campaign was a series of debates between Clifford Hansen and Teno Roncalio, Republican and Democratic candidates respectively for the U.S. Senate. Candidates for the U.S. House of Representatives failed to meet in formal debate, each accusing the other of evasion. Both Republican candidates were elected.

NOMINATIONS AND ELECTIONS

Wyoming was the first state in the Union to extend suffrage to women on an equal basis with men. A policy of equality without discrimination to any person or group has been generally followed. For this reason Wyoming has been designated "the Equality State." Although there is a constitutional provision prohibiting anyone from voting who cannot read the constitution, no testing of applicants is practiced. In 1962 there was a veiled threat, alleged to come from the state central committee of the Republican party, that voters would be challenged in questionable cases and the test applied, but apparently the rumor was unfounded.

In 1961 the legislature undertook a general revision of the state's election laws but ended with only minor changes in party convention dates and procedures.[42] Young Democrats and Young Republicans were authorized delegates at their respective party state conventions. The use of voting machines in lieu of paper ballots was provided for, the cost of the equipment being borne by the individual counties. Consideration was given to a recommendation that no one could become a candidate in a state primary without prior party convention approval. It was the opinion of those sponsoring the change that convention approval would prevent candidates with little popular support from getting nominated and thus strengthen the party in the general election. This was rejected largely because of the basic democratic philosophy which prevails in the state. Any eligible voter may become a candidate in the state's closed primary system by filing a certificate stating that he is a registered member of the party and by paying the required small fee. Depending upon whether a local, state, or national office is sought the place of filing and amount paid (which is always only nominal) varies. Those nominated by their party in the primary or those who run as independents contest for the designated office in the following regular election.

Undoubtedly more money was spent in the 1964 election than in any previous one,[43] but no one contested or filed a complaint alleging violation of the state's Corrupt Practices Act.[44] This requires each candidate and each district, county, and state chairman of a political committee to file within twenty days after any primary and general election sworn statements of their campaign re-

42. *Wyoming Statutes, 1957*, Chap. 6.1, Sec. 22-118.1 to Sec. 22-118.188.
43. Based upon records filed in the office of the secretary of state in Cheyenne.
44. *Wyoming Statutes, 1957*, Chap. 18, Secs. 22-346 to 22-361; 22-354.

ceipts and expenditures with the county clerk or the secretary of state, depending upon the level of the office sought. While there are legal limitations on candidate expenditures, there are none on the amount spent by party organizations.

A significant development in recent years has been the maintenance of a more organized and active state political party central committee office in the interval between general elections. At least one of the state's major political parties generally employs a part- or full-time secretary. Each party makes much use of its state chairman to speak to local groups throughout the state and to blast in press releases the opposite party on its record and policies.

Other election law changes in 1961 required that each party file a copy of its convention's rules of procedure with the secretary of state. Such rules must be followed until changed by formal convention action and then they would not become operative until again filed with the prescribed state official.

No changes have been made in the state's merit system since 1957 when the legislature established the Wyoming Personnel Commission.[45] Prior to that time and continuing to the present, the state has had the Wyoming Merit Council operating under what is known as the Merit Rule.[46] In order to secure federal funds for health, welfare, and employment security as provided by the Social Security Act of 1935 each state had to select its personnel for these agencies on a merit basis. Accordingly, a council of three members, to be appointed by the governor from nominees proposed by these agencies, was created. The Council drafts the rules for its administration and also appoints an executive director called the supervisor. His duties include the preparation, administration, and scoring of examinations, the preparation, custody and maintenance of registers, the certification for appointment, and such other duties as the Council may prescribe. Even under the Merit Rule many positions in these various agencies are, however, exempt from its application.

All other appointive positions in state agencies and institutions, except the State University which is independent, come under the supervision of the Wyoming Personnel Commission. While this agency requires that certain standards and qualifications must be met, political affiliation and party activity are dominant factors considered when appointments are made. State law requires that the membership of a number of boards and commissions must be bipartisan. When appointments are made to them by the governor of members from other than his own party, he is very likely to select a "good Indian," one who is a luke-warm member of the opposition party and one whose political philosophy is most like his own.

Sometimes a governor in making an appointment, as was the case with Governor Hansen in 1965, will mistakenly violate the law by appointing more than the legal number of his own party to a given agency. While the general practice over the years has been to appoint well-qualified people to office, the merit principle of selecting only those best qualified for the job regardless of party affiliation has been and is being violated.

PRESSURE GROUPS

Because political party organization in Wyoming has been weak, party platforms have not been important. Candidates could not be disciplined for going

45. *Ibid.*, Art. 1, Secs. 9-277 to 9-283.
46. *Ibid.*, Art. 2, Sec. 35-24.

their own way, which was often that of a dominant pressure group. Because of the very nature of the economy in territorial days and early statehood, the Wyoming Stock Grower's Association in a sense was the state government.[47] This Association with its social club in the state's capital city and its annual state convention practically formulated the legislative program. About its only opposition in the early history of the state came from the sheepmen, but both groups were interested in furthering the livestock industry.

As the state's economy became multifunctional other groups arose to pressure for their interests. Among the significant economic, professional, and social groups exerting political influence at the present time—other than those previously mentioned—are the following: For agriculture, there is the American Farm Bureau Federation, the Grange, and the Farmers Union. Of these three, the Bureau is by far the most influential. Among its members are most of the large ranchers of the state and thus it has cross-membership with the Stock Growers' and Wool Growers' Associations. Politically its membership is largely Republican. At times it aligns itself with business interests, as was the case in 1963 when it was for "right-to-work" legislation. The Grange at one time seemed destined to embrace most of the small farmers in the irrigated areas of the state, but in comparison with other agricultural groups its influence is insignificant. The Farmers Union is not strong as a state group but when combined, as it is in organization with Colorado members, it influences national policies in the region.

For labor the AFL-CIO and the Railroad Brotherhoods have been influential. Each of these groups has largely embraced Democrats in its membership. In the 1963, 1965, and 1967 legislative sessions the Democrats opposed "right-to-work" legislation.

The oil and gas interests, working through the Rocky Mountain Oil and Gas Association, have been very successful in keeping legislation which they opposed from being passed. This group's well-organized lobby has prevented a severance tax from being levied on petroleum and natural gas.

Educational pressure groups include the Wyoming Educational Association, the Wyoming School Boards Association, the Parent-Teacher Association, the University of Wyoming, and the Community College Commission. While these groups are very active, they sometimes work at cross purposes. In 1963 disagreement among them on tax sources worked to the advantage of the County Officers Association and the Farm Bureau Federation which opposed any increase in taxes.[48]

The University and the junior colleges have not, in the past three legislative sessions, been opposed in their requests for revenues by either political party except as to the amount, and in all cases they have been relatively successful with their budgetary demands. This group has secured state funds to supplement those raised locally, thus changing an earlier policy of no state support for junior colleges.

Transportation interests have been represented in the state by the Union Pacific Railroad and the Truckers Association. The interests of these two groups are often in conflict, but in recent years the latter organization seems to have been the more successful, for no really burdensome tax has been levied on trucking activities.

47. Henry Peterson, "Wyoming: A Cattle Kingdom," in Thomas C. Donnelly (ed.), *Rocky Mountain Politics* (Albuquerque: University of New Mexico Press, 1940), p. 118.

48. Ralph M. Wade, "Legislative Politics in Wyoming," *Western Political Quarterly*, XVII (Supplement to September 1964), 92-93.

Among the other organized interest groups active from time to time must be mentioned the Wyoming Association of Municipalities, the Retail Merchants Association, the Wyoming Liquor Dealers, the League of Women Voters, the American Legion, and the Veterans of Foreign Wars. During the 1963 legislative session the Wyoming Association of Municipalities was unsuccessful in getting more financial aid, but in the 1965 session and again in 1967 a portion of the increased sales tax and certain other revenues were made available to towns and cities.[49]

Programs sponsored by the League of Women Voters have been general in character. It was largely due to this organization's efforts that women were declared eligible to serve on juries in 1949.[50] During the 1965 session this group lobbied unsuccessfully for municipal home rule.

Of lesser consequences but sometimes with effectiveness such groups as the Wyoming Ministerial Association and the Issac Walton League have accomplished their objectives. The former has been active in opposing pari mutuel betting. The Wyoming Taxpayers Association has been active in keeping its members informed on proposed legislation in which they should be interested and lobbying against new taxes which would be detrimental to the membership.

At one time legislation existed to bring lobbying activities of pressure groups under control by requiring that any association actively engaged in the business of sponsoring and formulating legislation file in the office of the State Examiner a budget covering its expenditures, the salaries paid its employees, a list of its membership, the contributions or membership fees paid by each member, and a complete itemized list of all the association's expenditures. The 1947 legislature repealed the law.[51] Many legislators contend that no regulation of pressure groups is desirable since they assist the lawmakers with information—although it may be biased.

Groups operating in Wyoming do not differ significantly from similar groups in other states. In the last three regular sessions and in an intervening special session of the legislature those groups particularly active have been the Wyoming Association of Municipalities, the AFL-CIO, the Farm Bureau Federation, and the Wyoming Education Association.

LEGISLATIVE POLITICS

In two of Wyoming's past legislative sessions there was diversity of partisan political control in the executive and legislative branches. In 1963 the Republicans controlled both branches of the state government, but two years later Republican Governor Clifford Hansen was confronted with a legislature in which the Democrats dominated the lower chamber while the Republicans controlled the upper. President Johnson's landslide in the state was unable to give his party control of the Senate because only half of the senators are elected biennially. But in 1967 the Republicans captured all the major offices and both chambers of the legislature.

Party lines, however, usually have not been significant in legislative decision-making because the members are predominantly ranchers and businessmen

49. *Session Laws of Wyoming, 1967*, Chap. 210; 245.

50. *Session Laws of Wyoming, 1949*, Chap. 61, Sec. 12-101; *State v. Yazzie*, 67 Wyo. 256, 218 Pac. (2d) 482.

51. *Wyoming Compiled Statutes, 1945*, Sec. 20-816; *Session Laws of the State of Wyoming, 1947*, Chap. 42, Sec. 20-815, par. 6.

with conservative orientation. Although a number of lawyers are also elected to the legislature, they are usually directly or indirectly involved in the same kinds of occupations.

Issues confronting the past four sessions of the legislature have been largely the same in character. In order of their importance they are as follows: legislative reapportionment, adequate finances for municipalities and schools, revision of labor laws including "right-to-work," medical care for the aged, pari mutuel betting, and trading stamps.

Because the legislature did not reapportion itself when it met in 1961, an attempt was made to force such action through the state courts. The state Supreme Court to which the case finally went in early January of 1963 held that the question was now moot and that the legislature, soon to meet, should be given an opportunity to carry out its constitutional duty.[52]

TABLE I

PARTY COMPOSITION OF WYOMING STATE LEGISLATURES,

1961-1967

Year	Senate		House	
	Republicans	Democrats	Republicans	Democrats
1961	17	10	35	21
1963	16	11	37	19
1965	13	12	27	34
1967	18	12	34	27

Source: *Wyoming Official Directory, 1961*, pp. 36-37; 1963, pp. 44-45; 1965, pp. 46-47; 1967, pp. 57-59.

In the 1963 session six apportionment bills were introduced, one of which finally passed.[53] It provided for an increase of five representatives and two senators to be assigned to the most populous counties; but the total membership of the Senate was reduced to twenty-five while that of the House was raised to sixty-one. It was the first reapportionment law enacted since 1933, but it left the law-making body substantially in the control of the rural voters of the state. This act was soon challenged in the courts on the basis that the apportionment of the Senate resulted in invidious discrimination.[54] As a consequence, Governor Hansen called a special session of the legislature in the summer of 1964 specifically for the purpose of having a constitutional amendment proposed to remove the requirement that each county have at least one senator and one representative. The legislators did not agree upon any constructive proposal and the session adjourned without accomplishment. Each political party blamed the other for obstructionist tactics. Again during the 1965 session the legislators were unable to agree upon any reapportionment plan which would meet the requirement of "one man one

52. *State ex rel. Whitehead v. Gage*, 377 Pac. (2d) 299 (1962).
53. *Session Laws of Wyoming, 1963*, Chap. 22.
54. *Schaefer et al. v. Thomson*, 247 (1964) D. Wyo., 240 F. Supp.

vote" laid down by the United States Supreme Court, so the issue still remained unresolved.[55]

The United States District Court on October 8, 1965, filed a decree reapportioning the state Senate and declaring that all senators must be elected in 1966.[56] The apportionment of the House of Representatives made by the 1963 legislature to become effective for the 1965 session was held to be satisfactory. No longer was each county entitled to at least one senator. Converse was combined with Niobrara, Johnson with Campbell, and Hot Springs with Fremont. Lincoln County was split, the northern part being united with Sublette and Teton, while the southern part was districted with Uinta. Weston was joined with Crook County in still another district. The splitting of Lincoln County set a precedent for dividing the counties in any future reapportionment. See state map.

Criticism of the Court's decree was both favorable and unfavorable. Some contended that the lawmakers could not complain because they could not agree among themselves on a reapportionment plan. The state's Attorney General said that the new districts should have been subdistricted rather than allowing all senators to be elected at large thus permitting the urban voters to elect all senators from a city. Leaders of both major parties termed the new apportionment order an equitable and fair solution to a difficult problem.[57] The door seemed to be left open for the legislature to establish subdistricts in the future and thus give the voter a better opportunity to know the senatorial candidates and also prevent possible complete urban control. A later development in the controversy was the refusal of the United States Supreme Court to review an appeal, by a group of Laramie County residents, from the three-judge U.S. District Court's apportionment plan set forth in its decree on October 8, 1965, on the basis that their county should be subdistricted.[58] The issue again arose when Governor Hathaway urged the legislature in 1967 to provide more equitable representation. The several plans for subdistricting proposed by the majority party were, however, successfully opposed by the Democrats who described them as examples of pure political gerrymandering.[59]

After unsuccessful attempts by the Wyoming Association of Municipalities to secure more financial aid for cities and towns, in both the 1961 and 1963 sessions, an increase in the state's general sales tax was urged with some success in 1965. Governor Hansen had proposed an increase of one cent in this tax in his State of the State address, the income from which was to be placed in the general fund.[60] A final compromise measure in the state legislature resulted in a one-half cent increase for the state; while counties and/or municipalities, by popular vote or ordinance respectively, were permitted to raise one-half cent more for their own use.[61] The state's share would provide additional funds for public school financing.

55. *Reynolds v. Sims*, 377 U.S. 533 (1963). See also *Baker v. Carr*, 369 U.S. 186 (1962).

56. *United States District Court*, District of Wyoming, Decree, October 8, 1965.

57. "Reaction to Order Runs Hot and Cold," *Laramie Daily Boomerang*, October 9, 1965, p. 15.

58. *Wyoming Eagle*. "Apportionment Appeal Declined by Court," March 1, 1966.

59. Stanley K. Hathaway, Governor, *Message to the 39th Legislative Assembly*, January 1967, p. 4.

60. Clifford P. Hansen, Governor, *Message to the 38th Legislative Assembly*, January 13, 1965, p. 17.

61. *Session Laws of Wyoming, 1965*, Chap. 118.

Perhaps the hottest issue in the 1963 and 1965 legislative sessions was "right-to-work." In 1963 when the final vote was to be taken on the measure the galleries were packed with laborites. Fear of disorder prompted the governor to use National Guardsmen as extra police but no violence occurred, even though the bill was passed.

Between sessions organized labor campaigned for repeal of the statute and the Democratic party platform contained a plank favoring such action. When the party won control of the House in 1965, its leadership threatened to hold up certain Republican-sponsored measures if the Senate did not go along with repeal of "right-to-work." In the final days of the session a House bill for repeal failed to pass by one vote in the Senate. The result was largely due to some half-hearted Democratic support in that chamber. In 1967 labor leaders were again thwarted in their attempt to have the statute repealed.

In 1963, legislation implementing the Kerr-Mills Bill was enacted, but medical care for the aged failed to get top billing in 1965. Medical care for the indigent was further improved by the 1967 legislature.[62]

A pari mutuel wagering bill was passed in the 1961 session supported by both the Retail Merchants Association and the Wyoming Association of Municipalities, but it was vetoed by acting-Governor Gage to whom the bill came after the legislature adjourned. In 1963 similar legislation was urged on the basis that gambling would be a tourist attraction, stimulate attendance at county fairs and municipal celebrations, and provide additional revenues for distressed municipalities: it did not fare as well as its counterpart in 1961. Gambling legislation received a similar reception in 1965. However, in 1967 a pari mutuel bill to permit horse racing and betting on a county optional basis was passed.

In the three legislative sessions prior to 1965 the question of the use of trading stamps had usurped a considerable amount of the legislators' time. In 1959 their use by merchants had been barred.[63] Even though several stamp companies spent considerable money lobbying for repeal of the law during the intervening years between sessions, the law still remains on the statute books. Currently stamps are being issued by a number of retail establishments but they are redeemable only for cash within the state.

Governor Hansen, in his message to the legislature, urged the repeal of the twenty-year-old law prohibiting the state from accepting federal funds for education.[64] The Democrats in their platform had urged such legislation. The law was repealed despite the opposition of some of the state's right-wing members in both parties.[65] The new act contained a statement to the effect that acceptance of federal funds was not to be interpreted as surrender of local control of the schools.

The legislative session of forty calendar days every two years is one of the shortest held by any state. From time to time in recent years the legislature has provided for interim committees or research committees, the exact terminology having gone through several changes, to facilitate its work. In 1963 no funds were appropriated for such a group, and the 1965 legislature continued the policy. The reason seemed to be that the interim group was thought to be usurping the power

62. *Ibid.*, 1963, Chap. 78.

63. *Session Laws of Wyoming, 1959*, Chap. 84.

64. Clifford P. Hansen, Governor, *Message to the 38th Legislative Assembly*, January 13, 1965, pp. 7-9.

65. *Session Laws of Wyoming, 1965*, Chap. 44.

of the legislature. However, in 1967 the Interim Ways and Means Committee was given an appropriation.[66]

In the past there has been no concerted effort for general constitutional revision, although one candidate for governor in the 1966 primary laid the blame for many of Wyoming's ills on its "horse and buggy" constitution. He did not get his party's nomination. Governor Hathaway in his first message to the 1967 legislature advocated several changes in its date and duration. More recently political leaders of the state including the governor have proposed streamlining the state's administrative structure for greater efficiency and economy.[67]

During the past twenty years twenty-nine constitutional amendments proposed by the state legislature have appeared on the ballot for voter ratification. Of the eighteen ratified, eight have involved tax levies, public indebtedness, or procedures for financing public improvements. The majority of the others provided for some change in the structure of the state's governmental organization.

The generally conservative character of Wyoming's citizenry has precluded the possibility of such democratic devices as recall, initiative, and referendum, but the Democratic platform in 1964 called for a constitutional change to permit legislative initiative. It met with no success in the session. While Wyoming has the usual state constitutional provision for impeachment, no use has ever been made of it; and, as for recall, it is only provided for in cities operating under the commission form of city government.

Until 1931 there was no budget bureau, so all planning for the state as a whole had to be done by the governor, his secretary, and some advisers he saw fit to call to his assistance. Now the budget bureau consists of an assistant budget officer and some clerical personnel. The governor is responsible for the executive budget.[68] Before the budget is presented to the legislature, where it is considered by a joint standing committee in charge of appropriation measures, there is considerable maneuvering behind the scenes by the several spending agencies. The State University, one of the largest spenders, usually does some effective spade work. Its president has at times in the past visited every county in the state prior to a legislative session where he has explained the institution's requests to members of the legislature and to prominent citizens of the areas. To a lesser degree a similar procedure is followed by leaders of other groups whose financial needs are great. Another maneuver frequently resorted to by spending agencies and interest groups in order to win public support is the submission of news stories to the press, explaining their need for additional revenues.

VOTING HABITS AND PARTY AFFILIATION

Politics, like beef and oil, is the subject of daily conversation in Wyoming, but strong attachment to a given party exists only on the surface. When the time comes to put the "X" on the ballot, voters have exhibited a great degree of independence. They often vote for the man regardless of his party, especially when electing a member to Congress. When it comes to county or state legislative positions, predominance in party registration in the county will usually foretell the

66. *Ibid.*, 1967, Chap. 110.

67. See Stanley K. Hathaway, Governor, *Message to the 39th Legislative Assembly*, January 1967, pp. 12-13.

68. *Wyoming Statutes, 1957*, Sec. 9-504 to Sec. 9-524.

results. In Laramie County, the state's most populous, the voters usually send Democrats to the state legislature and support the same party's candidates for Congress while electing Republicans to county offices.

Although the political philosophy of the Equality State voter must be characterized as conservative, he is not always consistent. The record indicates he has elected to Congress men with such diverse political leanings as Robertson and O'Mahoney or Milward Simpson and Gale McGee or William H. Harrison and Teno Roncalio. There is a pattern of Republican success in filling high state offices, but this does not hold true for congressional seats. In fact there seems to be a rather popular belief that the state should have both a Republican and a Democrat in the United States Senate.

Although Wyoming is relatively free of minority ethnic groups, to the extent that they are present their voting habits tend to conform with those observed in other states. The precincts with predominant Spanish-American voters support the Democratic party and the same is true in precincts which are populated largely by Negroes. It is significant that those counties where minority groups are prevalent habitually go Democratic in national elections.[69] The Indian vote in Fremont County in 1964 also emphasized the independent and protest voting by an ethnic group.[70]

Religion plays no important part in state politics. Both Catholics and Protestants have been elected to high national and state office and a candidate's religion has not been an issue in any campaign. Members of the Church of Jesus Christ of Latter-day Saints (Mormons) are numerous in western Wyoming, but they appar-

TABLE II

PARTY AFFILIATION OF SUCCESSFUL CANDIDATES
FOR THE NATIONAL OFFICES AND THE FIVE-STATE
ADMINISTRATIVE ELECTIVE OFFICES, 1956-66

Year	Pres.	U.S. Sen.	U.S. Rep.	Gov.	Sec. of State	State Audit.	State Treas.	State Supt. Pub. Instr.
1956	R		R					
1958		D	R	D	D	R	R	D
1960	R	R	R					
1962		R	R	R	R	R	R	R
1964	D	D	D					
1966		R	R	R	R	R	R	R

Source: *Wyoming Official Directory and Election Returns*, 1957-56; 1961-60; 1963-62; 1965-64; 1967-66.

69. William E. Duke *et al.*, *A Study and Comparison of the Political Participation of the Spanish-American in Laramie, Wyoming*, pp. 1-55. This was a research project sponsored by the Rocky Mountain Center for Education in Politics, 1964. Maurice S. Shier, *A Comparative Analysis of the Political Participation and Political Attitudes of Members of Minority Groups in Two Wyoming Cities* (Master's thesis, University of Wyoming, 1964).

70. *Wyoming Official Directory and Election Returns*, 1965-64; 1967-66; et al.

ently have never voted as a bloc in state elections. There is no strictly Jewish community in the state and according to the records no one of this faith has ever been elected to an important state political office. In recent elections some candidates have boasted of being native sons, born and educated in the state, a qualification, if such it be, not available to many in the state's early history.

Although Wyoming was one of the first states to grant the franchise to women, not many have been elected to high office. An exception has been in the office of state superintendent of public instruction. One woman, Nellie Tayloe Ross, served as governor from January 5, 1925, to January 3, 1927. Currently two women hold statewide elective administrative offices, secretary of state and state treasurer. There were also three women, one senator and two representatives, in the 1967 legislature.

Wyoming elects state and county officials on off years from presidential elections. Exceptions occur at times because of vacancies in a given office. Because of the closed type of primary, there is no opportunity for splitting votes and only by thorough prior planning could party raiding be accomplished. There is no evidence to substantiate that such a practice has been carried on.

In general elections there has been much "ballot scratching." This was particularly evident in the 1964 election, for counties with high Republican registration in the primary voted for President Johnson and also for the Democratic candidates for the United States Senate and House in the November election.

TABLE III

PRIMARY ELECTION VOTE 1954-1966◊

Year	Republican	Democratic
1954	42,612	31,996
1956	34,321	28,395
1958	34,675	33,687
1960	37,724	47,091
1962	50,354	32,916
1964	41,821	42,499
1966	47,466	37,183

◊These votes are the ones cast for candidates for U.S. House of Representatives. They do not in every case present a true picture of those registered because if only one candidate is contesting for his party a large vote may not turn out. No records are available relative to the total number of registered voters and their party affiliation.

In the past there has been a larger number of voters registered as Republicans than as Democrats. This is borne out by the number voting in the primary elections. Republican party registrants have always been most numerous in rural agricultural counties. The party needs to develop greater appeal for city dwellers if it looks to future success as the state becomes more urban.

IMPACT OF NATIONAL POLITICS AND TRENDS

Since statehood in 1890 Wyoming voters have, in presidential elections, gone with the nation sixteen out of nineteen times. The three exceptions occurred in 1896[71] when the electoral vote was for Bryan rather than McKinley; in 1944 when it was for Dewey instead of Franklin D. Roosevelt; and in 1960 when it went for Nixon rather than Kennedy.

Beginning in 1932 the Democratic candidate for President of the United States has received the state's electoral vote five times. In 1944 only 48.8 percent of the popular vote was Democratic, but in 1948 Harry Truman received 52.2 percent. Not again until 1964 did the voters of the state favor a Democratic candidate for this high office. Table IV indicates which political party held the U.S. Presidency and the governorship of Wyoming at the same time.

The 1964 presidential election in Wyoming represented a sharp reversal in recent voting trends. Since 1936 the Republican party had steadily increased its strength in presidential elections with only minor setbacks. Franklin D. Roosevelt in that year carried all twenty-three counties. In 1940 the Democratic nominee carried twelve, in 1944 eight, in 1948 ten, in 1952 and 1956 only one, but in 1960 three counties. In 1964 President Johnson carried fourteen counties and his state-wide percentage of the popular vote (56.6) was exceeded only by Franklin D. Roosevelt's in 1932 and 1936.[72]

Johnson's popular vote represents an increase of 11.6 percent over that cast for Kennedy in 1960. Johnson's gain over Kennedy (in every single county in the state) ranged from 3.6 percent in Johnson County, a Republican party stronghold, to 17.7 percent in Albany County.

The past four presidential elections have pointed up a correlation between population and Democratic party strength. Fremont County, now the third most populous in the state, has become increasingly Democratic in its vote. In 1952 it ranked seventeenth among twenty-three counties in terms of the percentage of its vote going to the Democratic party; in 1956, fourteenth; in 1960, tenth; and in 1964, eighth. This gain in Democratic strength corresponds to the fairly rapid population increase brought about by expanding industry.

Regardless of how the residents of Wyoming affiliate themselves with one political party or the other, they can be proud of their voting participation. The number of potential voters in 1964 was 195,000. The actual vote in the presidential election that year was 142,716 or 73.2 percent. Four years earlier it was 63.2 percent of the potential voters. Only five other states surpassed Wyoming in 1964. Among them was Utah which topped the nation with 76.9 percent of its potential.[73]

It is not possible to point out the political significance of the 1964 general election in Wyoming without referring to the one held in 1962. For the first time in over 28 years every major administrative office on the state level as well as the vacancies in the state's congressional offices were filled with Republican candidates. This party also gained control of both houses of the state legislature. A Democratic governor and a U.S. senator were ousted by the voting. This over-

71. The vote for Bryan in 1896 was a combination Democratic and Populist party vote, as indicated by the *World Almanac and Encyclopedia 1901*, p. 486.

72. *Wyoming Official Directory and Election Returns*, 1935 to 1965 editions.

73. *U.S. Census Bureau*, "Estimate of Potential Vote in 1964 Elections," September 8, 1964.

whelming defeat shocked the Democrats out of their apathy. The Republicans that year had very effective state and local organization under the leadership of their state chairman. Shortly after the election, however, he resigned to start building a base for his own candidacy for U.S. senator in 1964. The change in the chairmanship together with a feeling of party security because of the 1962 success did not augur well for the party two years later.

TABLE IV
PARTY OF PRESIDENT AND GOVERNOR

Year	President and Party	State Presidential Vote	Governor and Party
1892	Harrison (R)	Same	◇Barber (R) Osborn (D)
1896	McKinley (R)	Bryan (D)	Richards, W. (R)
1900	McKinley (R)	Same	Richards, D. (R)
1904	Roosevelt, T. (R)	Same	◇Chatterton (R)
1908	Taft (R)	Same	Brooks (R)
1912	Wilson (D)	Same	Carey, J. (D)
1916	Wilson (D)	Same	Kendrick (D) ◇Houx (D)
1920	Harding (R)	Same	Carey, R. D. (R)
1924	Coolidge (R)	Same	Ross, W. (D) ◇Lucas (R)
1928	Hoover (R)	Same	Ross, N. T. (D)
1932	Roosevelt (D)	Same	Emerson (R) ◇Clark (R)
1936	Roosevelt (D)	Same	Miller (D)
1940	Roosevelt (D)	Same	Smith (R)
1944	Roosevelt (D)	Dewey (R)	Hunt (D)
1948	Truman (D)	Same	Hunt (D) ◇Crane (R)
1952	Eisenhower (R)	Same	Barrett (R) ◇Rogers (R)
1956	Eisenhower (R)	Same	Simpson (R)
1960	Kennedy (D)	Nixon (R)	Hickey (D) ◇Gage (D)
1964	Johnson (D)	Same	Hansen (R) Hathaway (R)

◇Elected secretary of state but due to the death or resignation of the governor were elevated to acting governor. *Encyclopedia Americana*, Vol. 29, p. 585.

The Democrats, on the other hand, had developed some rather significant issues due to the Republican domination of the 37th state legislature. The majority party in that body was responsible for passing a "right-to-work" law over bitter opposition of organized labor and the Democratic minority in both chambers. Still another issue favoring the Democrats arose out of the legislature's failure to provide needed revenue for state municipalities. School supporters were also incensed because the lawmakers had not seen fit to repeal legislation which prohibited the state from accepting federal funds which required state matching. With these issues in their arsenal the Democratic party was able to launch a substantial offensive against the opposite party on state matters alone.

At the Republican state convention delegates to the party's national convention were pledged to support Barry Goldwater for President. The Democratic delegates for their party's national convention were uninstructed.

All seemed serene on the surface in the period immediately following the primary elections. However, after the national party conventions which nominated Goldwater and Miller for the Republicans and Johnson and Humphrey for the Democrats, the "no holds barred" final stage of the campaign was set.

As the campaign progressed what was apparently at first strong general Republican voter support for Goldwater faded away. His own irrational statements about the use of nuclear weapons, social security, and segregation were pounced upon by the Democrats and used to create for him an image of irresponsibility in international affairs, disregard for the needs of senior citizens, and opposition to minority groups. Goldwater's denials and claims of misinterpretation of his utterances were unable to dispel the image. The Democrats, on the constructive side, hammered away on the themes of peace, prosperity, and equal rights for the underprivileged. This, together with a much improved party organization over that in 1962 on both the state and local levels, began to have telling effect.

Opinion polls in the state early in October indicated that Johnson's popularity was much greater than Goldwater's and that the Democratic candidates for lesser offices were being carried along on the rising swell. There was also an indication that there would be much "free wheeling" by the voters in which they would cross party lines at the polls. William Henry Harrison, Republican candidate for re-election to the U.S. House of Representatives, a poor campaigner but a good vote-getter, remained in Washington, D.C., until Congress adjourned, leaving it up to his wife to "carry the ball" for him at home. Although she is a good campaigner, her efforts were not enough to overcome the effects of the whirlwind campaign of his opponent, Teno Roncalio, who piloted his own airplane to visit almost every hamlet in the state.

The Republican candidate for the U.S. Senate, John Wold, attacked his opponent, incumbent Gale McGee, for not truly representing his state in Washington and also for being irresponsible in national fiscal matters. He also criticized the administration's policy on foreign red-meat imports which he said was ruining Wyoming's cattlemen.

As November 2 neared, the only candidacy in doubt insofar as presidential and congressional vacancies were concerned was that of Teno Roncalio. Harrison's name and past vote-getting record seemed to assure his success. However, when the votes were counted, Johnson had won over Goldwater by an 18,720 majority, McGee over Wold by 11,300, and Roncalio over Harrison by the narrow margin of 2,211.

The Democratic victory among other things pointed up the effect of urbanization in the state. For example, Harrison carried eighteen counties to Roncalio's five, and yet these five urban counties gave him a slight edge over his opponent. Johnson carried fourteen counties, Goldwater nine, McGee ten, including all the urban ones except Natrona, Wold's home county, which gave the latter a slightly favorable margin. Wold carried the other thirteen.[74]

Issues, candidates, and organization were factors that led to a Democratic victory in Wyoming in 1964. Johnson's popularity did have a "coattail" effect that certainly carried some Democrats into office who would not otherwise have been elected.

In 1966 Wyoming voters returned to their usual pattern of voting. On the basis of votes cast for U.S. representative only four counties went Democratic. In the voting for United States senator Teno Roncalio, incumbent representative making a bid for the Senate against Cliff Hansen, the incumbent governor, won in five counties. Three counties gave a majority vote to Ernest Wilkerson, Democratic candidate for governor who opposed Stan Hathaway, Republican.[75] The Vietnam War, failure of some of the "Great Society" programs, and domestic violence were factors in the decline of Democratic party strength.

74. *Wyoming Official 1965 Directory and 1964 Election Returns*, p. 62.
75. *Ibid.*, 1967-66, p. 74.

Frank H. Jonas

WESTERN POLITICS

Growth has characterized the West as a whole, and each state individually, particularly since the end of World War II. As a concomitant of population growth and industrial expansion, the area has become urbanized. And this urbanization has characterized the West during the past decade. Since 1930, the West has increased measurably in both population and area. In that year, with an area of 865,017 square miles–larger than the ten states of the South–the eight Rocky Mountain states had a population of only 3,701,789, slightly more than that of North Carolina. Thirty years later, the population in these eight states had almost doubled. When the three coastal states are added, together with Alaska (1958) and Hawaii (1959), the total is 28,053,104 or 15.2 percent of the population of the entire country. The next six years witnessed even more spectacular gains. By April 1, 1966, the eight intermountain states had increased by another 50 percent, while the other five had gained 80 percent. Population of the thirteen states then came to 38,508,000 or 19.6 percent of the nation's people. The area they inhabit now totals 1,780,664 square miles, one-third of which was added when Alaska achieved statehood, but their distribution varies widely, from Alaska's 0.3 persons per square mile to California's 110.3.[1]

Nationally, from 1960 to 1966 the population has increased by 9.3 percent. For more than a century the West has outstripped other regions, but there has been considerable variation in the rate for each state. Eight have grown more rapidly than either the region or the nation (Alaska, Arizona, California, Colorado, Hawaii, Nevada, Oregon, and Utah), while five (Idaho, Montana, New Mexico, Washington, and Wyoming) lagged behind.

The major part of the increase took place in California which added 3.1 million people by births and migration from 1960 to 1966. This figure represented more than two-thirds of the population gain in the West as a whole, and is more than double the number gained by New York (1.4 million), its closest rival. Shifts in the ranking of states with respect to the total resident population since 1960 generally have not been very drastic. California replaced New York as the state with the largest population, and Hawaii came up from forty-fourth to forty-first. California and New York account for 20 percent of the nation's total population. California, Nevada, Arizona, and Alaska (along with Florida, Maryland, and Delaware) are the fastest growing in the nation. Nevada grew more than 50 percent, a rate twice as high as that of its nearest contender, Arizona, which increased by

---

1. In 1960 the Mountain states totaled 6,804,929, an increase of 83.8 percent over 1930. Adding the West Coast's 20,094,535 and the 824,440 people of Alaska and Hawaii, the total is 27,723,903. In 1966, the Mountain states totaled 13,701,000, and the five others, 24,807,000.

about 23 percent during the period. Of the states outside the West, only Florida's population gain of 19 percent was substantially above the national average.

The predominant movements in the regional redistribution of population through interstate migration during 1960-66 continued to be westward, but the average annual rate of increase of the western states has been considerably below that of the 1950's. Arizona and California were particularly affected. California gained net in-migration at the average annual rate of 15 percent per 1,000 during the 1960's compared with an average annual gain of 24 per 1,000 in the 1950's. Arizona dropped from 32 per 1,000 in the 1950's to 12 per 1,000 in the 1960's. Only Nevada's rate continued to be strong in the early 1960's with an average gain of 48 per 1,000 compared with slightly more than 39 during the previous decade, making her the fastest growing state. The rate, however, has slowed since 1963.

In terms of absolute numbers, the West as a whole gained 1.8 million persons through net migration from April 1960 to July 1966. The South gained about 806,000 and the northeastern states about 446,000. Only the North Central States had an estimated net out-migration for the period. Ten states added more than 100,000 net migrants during the period, led by California with 1.6 million, and Florida with 570,000. A striking change in trend is evident during this period. Between the years 1963 and 1966 the rate of in-migration is slower than during the earlier part of the decade. Nevada, for example, which was growing close to 10 percent per year in 1960-63 declined to about 3 percent in 1963-66, the dropoff being mainly in net in-migration. Arizona, the second most rapidly growing state, declined from 5 to less than 2 percent per year.

Reduction in population growth through natural increase was also more striking in 1963-66. Nationally, the average annual rate was 1.4 percent in the early part of the decade, whereas it was only 1.1 percent in the latter period.

The population of the United States as a whole, on the basis of the most recently published projections, would increase by about 50 to 80 million by 1985. In terms of absolute growth, California is projected to outstrip by far all other states, with an estimated increase of from 10 to 14 million persons.

The bulk of the nation's population growth continued to be registered in its metropolitan areas. Three areas in southern California, three in Texas, and two in Florida were among the dozen highest ranking large metropolitan areas that passed the one million mark between 1960 and 1965, bringing to 26 the number of areas in that class. Los Angeles replaced Chicago as the second largest. The metropolitan population over-all increased about twice as rapidly as the non-metropolitan between 1960 and 1965, and the proportion of the population living in such areas (now more than three out of five) continued its upward trend. Compared with the previous decade, however, there appears to be some slowing down of metropolitan growth, from 2.3 to 1.9 percent in the first half of the current decade. The contrast between the heavy gains in the outlying parts of the areas and the modest increases or decreases in the central cities has become some-what less marked, suggesting that the trend termed the "flight to the suburbs," which characterized the past two decades, may be losing some of its impetus.

The nation's farm population, by contrast, continued to drop, while the nonfarm population increased by 10 percent. The 12 million persons now living on farms represent only about 6 percent of the total population. In 1960, the farm population numbered 15.6 million, nearly 9 percent of the total. The 1930 census classified the population in the Rocky Mountain states as approximately 40 percent urban and 60 percent rural. In 1960 there were 74 cities with populations of 10,000 or more in the intermountain area. In addition, California had 167, Washington 24, and Oregon 14. Alaska and Hawaii had 2 and 6, respectively. Albuquerque, Phoenix, Tucson, and other intermountain cities have reached over 200,000.

In Washington, Oregon, California, Arizona, Nevada, Utah, Colorado, and Hawaii, over 50 percent of each state's population is found in Standard Metropolitan Statistical Areas[2] or in from one to three counties. In Colorado, Arizona, and Hawaii, over 50 percent is concentrated in and about one city (Denver, Phoenix, and Honolulu). In Arizona, California, Nevada, Utah, and Colorado, over 40 percent resides in a single county: the percentage for Washington is 38.8 in King County (Seattle), for Oregon, 30 percent in Multnomah County (Portland). The two metropolitan areas in Montana contain only 23 percent of the state's people. Since 1960 Idaho has acquired one SMA, Boise, with 14.2 percent of the state's population. Wyoming and Alaska have a few small cities, but no large single concentration comparable to those found in other western states.[3]

Hypothetically it may be advanced that, instead of the usual notion that metropolitan areas have become more Democratic and that the rural areas have remained predominantly Republican, the voting in urban areas may actually have become more Republican or at least more conservative and the rural areas more Democratic and more liberal. Conservative and liberal views appear indiscriminately in both urban and rural areas.

The people of the West have been and are far from homogeneous—the native Indians, Spanish soldiers and settlers, French-Canadian voyageurs, pioneer settlers from other states, Chinese, Japanese, immigrants from Europe, late-comers from Canada and Mexico and millions more from all the more easterly sections of the country. No effort has been made here to generalize about these people or to place them into distinct ethnic, occupational, religious, or income groups for the entire region. More recently probably the principal immigrant has been the Negro.

The rate of increase of the Negro population has varied widely; the West shows the greatest gains, and the South the smallest. Whereas the Negro population for the country as a whole is estimated to have increased by approximately 11 percent, it has shown little change in the South, and by contrast, has increased by 24 percent in the Northeast, 23 percent in the North Central region, and 59 percent in the West. These changes represent an extension of trends observed during the 1950's. At the beginning of that decade only one-third of the Negroes lived outside the South: now that proportion is approaching one-half.

So far the West has escaped violent racial disturbances with one exception, the Watts area in Los Angeles. Negroes have marched in protest in some cities but without the incidents which characterize the riots in other parts of the country. No state has a Negro population sufficiently large to be influential at the polls, and as long as this and other groups are allowed the same voting privileges accorded all citizens there can hardly be a reason for protest movements because of polit-

2. The area definition of an SMA in the West is usually a single county in which the city, from which the area takes its name, is located. For Denver, however, the area includes five counties. For Salt Lake City, it includes two counties.

3. Estimated figures for cities were not available later than 1960. However, the trends which were reflected in the 1960 figures would be projected in any current figures from 1965 to 1968. The great increases in population have taken place in metropolitan areas. Therefore, the percentage of population in the cities and metropolitan areas in 1967 corresponds roughly to the shifts in population due to net in-migration and shifts from rural to urban areas.

TABLE I

STATE AND STANDARD METROPOLITAN STATISTICAL AREAS
1967 POPULATION

State◇ and SMS Area□	Total	% of State
Alaska △	267,000	100.0
Arizona	1,575,000	100.0
Phoenix	818,000	51.9
Tucson	307,000	19.5
California	18,403,000	100.0
Anaheim-Santa Ana & Garden Grove	1,107,000	6.0
Bakersfield	319,000	1.7
Fresno	403,000	2.2
Los Angeles-Long Beach	6,765,000	36.7
Oxnard-Ventura	318,000	1.7
Sacramento	737,000	4.0
Salinas-Monterey	222,000	1.2
San Bernardino-Riverside-Ontario	1,026,000	5.6
San Diego	1,136,000	6.2
San Francisco-Oakland	2,918,000	15.9
San Jose	885,000	4.9
Santa Barbara	243,000	1.3
Stockton	273,000	1.4
Vallejo-Napa	239,000	1.3
Colorado	1,949,000	100.0
Denver	1,073,000	55.1
Pueblo	119,000	6.1
Colorado Springs	176,000	9.1
Hawaii	710,000	100.0
Honolulu	571,000	80.4
Idaho	693,000	100.0
Boise City	99,000	14.3
Montana	703,000	100.0
Billings	84,000	11.9
Great Falls	82,000	11.7
Nevada	434,000	100.0
Las Vegas	232,000	53.4
Reno	113,000	26.4
New Mexico	1,014,000	100.0
Albuquerque	288,000	28.4

TABLE I   (CON'T.)

State◇ and SMS Area□	Total	% of State
Oregon	1,938,000	100.0
Eugene	194,000	10.1
Portland	897,000	46.3
Salem	172,000	8.9
Utah	994,000	100.0
Ogden	120,000	12.1
Provo-Orem	118,000	11.9
Salt Lake City	523,000	52.6
Washington	2,973,000	100.0
Seattle-Everett	1,179,000	39.4
Spokane	267,000	9.0
Tacoma	343,000	11.5
Wyoming △	330,000	100.0

◇U.S. Bureau of the Census, *Current Population Reports*, Series P-25, No. 362, "Illustrative Projections of the Population of States 1970-85" (Washington: Government Printing Office, 1967), p. 4.

□*Ibid.*, Series P-25, No. 371, "Estimates of the Population of Standard Metropolitan Statistical Areas: July 1, 1965" (Washington: Government Printing Office, 1967), pp. 14-31.

△No Standard Metropolitan Statistical Area.

ical discrimination. Nor can there be much valid protest on grounds of civil rights. Most western states have enacted legislation in response to nearly all that the Negroes have demanded for the protection of their rights, with the exception of "open housing."

The plight of the farmers, the abandonment of small family farms, the elimination of small herds of cattle and small interests in sheep, the industrialization and rationalization of larger land-holdings and large agricultural enterprises could account for rural areas becoming more "liberal" or perhaps Democratic, at least at the grass-roots level. Prosperity, found chiefly in industrial urban and highly concentrated metropolitan areas, could have a greater effect on voting behavior and election results than traditional party allegiance or sectional and group interests. The dramatic emergence in the nation of the disadvantaged Negro and his plight, and both the sympathy for him and the antipathy developed because of his demands which infringe on property rights will certainly affect voting behavior in 1968. The injection into the campaign of the Vietnam War may also upset voting patterns. It is doubtful if these two issues will have the same effect on voting behavior as they may have in other regions in the nation.

POLITICAL BEHAVIOR

Probably the most salient characteristic of the voter in the West is his independence. This does not mean, however, that he is inactive or unconcerned, for he stands high in performance in the various types of political activity. If six types are considered—talking to others, wearing a button, giving money, joining political clubs, attending political meetings, working for the party—and evaluated by regions—Northeast, Midwest, Far West and South—the South stands lowest in all except the last two. In these two types the West stands low with only 1.7 percent of the respondents in the survey recording that they worked for a party.[4] On the other hand, western states on the average have stood high in the other types of political activity. This analysis assumes that voters are independent if they are not very active in working for a party but are active in other ways and vote in great numbers. Western voters average far higher in turnout for presidential elections than do those of the nation as a whole.

TABLE II

TURNOUT IN PRESIDENTIAL ELECTIONS◇

State	1956	1960	1964
Utah	75.2	80.1	76.9
Idaho	77.6	80.7	75.8
Wyoming	67.8	74.0	73.2
Washington	70.8	72.3	71.5
Montana	71.0	71.4	69.8
Oregon	68.2	72.3	69.6
Colorado	67.6	71.4	68.1
California	63.8	67.4	64.7
New Mexico	59.6	62.1	63.8
Nevada	59.6	61.2	55.5
Hawaii		51.3	52.5
Arizona	50.8	54.5	54.7
Alaska		45.5	47.3
U.S. AVERAGE	62.0	63.8	69.3

◇Vote as a percentage of the civilian population of voting age.

The attachment of the western voter is clearly to personalities rather than to a political party. Generally it can be said that seldom does he wear a "party yoke." In the past, however, this independence has been more prevalent in local and state than in national elections. Politically minded states such as Montana and New Mexico will frequently elect a congressional delegation of the Administration party and a governor of the opposite party, while splitting on a state slate. In any event, instead of listing election results to support the contention of the inde-

4. See Herbert Jacob and Kenneth W. Vines (eds.), *Politics in the American States* (Boston: Little, Brown, 1967), p. 35.

pendent voter in the West, one can with credence accept Hugh A. Bone's chapter title in this volume for the western states as a whole, "free style" politics. Any one of the individual states could have been entitled the "independent state."

In 1956, only three states gave the Eisenhower-Nixon ticket a higher percentage of votes than in 1952, but only Utah elected its entire Republican slate for state and national office. New Mexico elected a Republican governor and Arizona a Republican congressman. In 1958, however, while Utah was electing all Democrats to high office, Arizona, with a preponderant Democratic registration, returned two Republicans (Senator Barry Goldwater and Congressman John J. Rhodes) to Washington and captured the governorship from the Democrats.

Candidates can also become independent of party organization. In 1958 Mark Hatfield almost completely bypassed Oregon's Republican party and won the governorship, as he did in 1966 when he won his election for United States senator. In 1962 Senator Wayne B. Morse, who was elected to the United States Senate as a Republican, stood as a Democratic candidate and won. Morse, a great individual performer, is known for waging his political campaigns independently of party. In 1958 the two-term incumbent Nevada governor, Charles Russell, tried the same method, that of bypassing the Republican party, and failed, although he did bracket his name with that of movie star and Lieutenant Governor Rex Bell, the only Republican to win against the Democratic tide in that state. These opposite results in the two states, Nevada and Oregon, where similar techniques were used perhaps can be explained by the political personalities and the campaign methods of the two candidates, and by local conditions.[5]

In Utah J. Bracken Lee has developed his own campaign organizations. The Republican party and conservative members of the Democratic party helped him to become governor in 1948. Thereafter he ignored party and constructed a chain of personal supporters throughout the state. In 1956, having attacked publicly the Eisenhower Administration and alienated the Republican party, he was defeated in the primary when he sought a third term. Twice more he ran for state and national office and was defeated; but he has been elected mayor of Salt Lake City three times.

In 1962 Representative Joseph M. Montoya (D-New Mexico), standing for re-election on his liberal record and views and supporting the Kennedy Administration, barely slipped through to victory. But Nevada's Representative Walter S. Baring (D) scored higher for re-election than Senator Alan Bible (D) who received the highest vote for senator in Nevada's political history. Both Bible and Baring waged personal and independent campaigns. Indeed, it can be said that Baring was read out of the Democratic party for stating views on social legislation and public policy contrary to the statements in the Democratic platforms.

In this same election year, 1962, the Republican party in both California and Hawaii collapsed and was left in a shambles at the end of the campaign. While no Republican nominee won in Hawaii, United States Senator Thomas Kuchel retained his seat in California. It cannot be said that he had the active support of the Republican party. Considered a moderate in politics, he has organized his own campaigns. Senator Ed Johnson in Colorado could tell the voters that they did not have to vote for a party, and still personally be successful at the polls. But three United States senators, incumbents Barrett in Wyoming, Watkins in Utah, and

5. See Don Driggs, "The 1958 Elections in Nevada," *Western Political Quarterly*, XII (March 1959), 319; and John M. Swarthout, "The 1958 Elections in Oregon," *ibid.*, pp. 333-40.

Malone in Nevada, all of whom had been successful at the polls in 1946 (Barrett was elected to the House, the other two to the Senate) when conditions and not personalities prevailed, could not weather the storms in 1958; they had not become popular political personalities.

In Utah in 1964, all three defeated Republican nominees waged personal campaigns independently of the party, just as did their three successful counterparts in the Democratic party. Two years earlier Senator Bennett's well-organized and well-directed representatives had knocked on individual doors, in spite of the fact that party district officers and workers were doing the same thing. Each group worked independently of the other.

Candidates and nominees can no longer depend on the political party to work for them, let alone win for them at the polls. This is substantially true in the majority, if not all, of the western states. Political parties in California, although torn asunder by intra-party conflicts, do still play a considerable role in political campaigns on behalf of candidates, but even in this state no candidate dares rely solely on his party if he expects to be elected.

To account for the independence of both candidates and voters in the West, one must look closely at the nominating systems. All thirteen states use the primary. Of the basic types, eight use the closed, and five the open primary. Washington uses a variant of the latter, the "blanket" primary, a system not found in any other state. The blanket primary incorporates the features of the open primary, which does not require the voter to disclose his party identity, and allows him, in addition, a free choice to vote for any candidate seeking nomination, regardless of party. As a result, the Washington voter does more ticket-splitting, perhaps, than do his counterparts in the region.

California has been distinctive in the past for its experience in cross-filing. The practice was curtailed in 1954 and the double nominations practically disappeared. It was finally abolished in 1959, the 1960 election being the first in modern times to be held without it. This action could be construed as a curtailment of the independence of the candidate and the voter. Also, in California, delegates to the national conventions are elected on a statewide basis as a group, a feature found elsewhere only in South Dakota. Although only the names of national candidates to whom the state is pledged appear on the ballot, the voter receives a list of the delegates' names with his sample ballot. Cross-voting is not permitted in the presidential preferential primary.

Alaska's system is distinctive in that it elects only one state officer. A vote for the gubernatorial candidate is simultaneously a vote for the secretary of state on the same ticket. Alaska uses the party column ballot. The voter can mark only one column.

Ten states use the direct primary where a candidate's name is placed directly on the ballot. Three states, Colorado, Utah, and New Mexico, have pre-primary party nominating conventions. Colorado's is a pre-primary endorsing convention. In New Mexico candidates' names may be placed on the primary ballot even if they are not chosen at the convention.[6] In Utah no more than two names for each office from each party emerge from the convention vote and are placed on the primary ballot. This insures that the nominee will be the majority candidate of his party. The convention vote—county and state conventions and the district mass

6. New Mexico tried this system in 1952 but soon abandoned it. It introduced the system again in 1963, but a year later the Republicans were circulating petitions and organizing a campaign to repeal it. This time the repeal effort was not successful.

meetings where the delegates to the convention are chosen—is by secret ballot, the unique feature of Utah's system.

Pre-primary endorsing conventions generally are not popular. An attempt was made by the Republicans in 1962, in Multnomah County, Oregon, to secure county party endorsements for candidates. There were as high as thirteen candidates for an office and the number for most offices was five or six. So much anguish was produced among the supporters of the candidates who were not endorsed and there was so much danger that the non-endorsed candidates would turn on the party during the elections or at least drag their feet that the method was soon abandoned.

TABLE III
PRIMARY ELECTIONS FOR STATE OFFICERS

State	Primary date	Runoff	No. ballots received
Alaska	August 9	None	All ballots
Arizona	September 13	None	1
California	June 7	None	1
Colorado	September 13	None	1
Hawaii	October 1	None	1
Idaho	August 2	None	1
Montana	August 16	None	1
Nevada	September 6	None	1
New Mexico	May 3	None	1
Oregon	May 24	None	1
Utah	September 13	None	All ballots
Washington	September 13	None	Blanket (all on one)
Wyoming	August 16	None	1

In Colorado, if a candidate receives 20 percent of the delegate vote in the assembly (pre-primary convention), he advances to the primary list. Colorado permits a party candidate to get on the primary ballot by petition, but not on the general election ballot. Both Colorado and Utah allow independent candidates to come on the general election ballot by petition. In comparison with the direct primary, the nominating system in these two states has neither appreciably increased party responsibility nor produced party leadership, nor has the open primary in other states completely discouraged party leadership.

At a time when 44 out of 50 states in the nation had the closed primary, 5 of the open primary states were in the West, indicating, perhaps somewhat remotely, that there was a positive correlation between the independence of the voter and the nominating system, the direct primary (all thirteen states) and the open primary (five states).

The direct primary has also been instrumental in destroying the dependence of a candidate on the political party. The primary has given an advantage to the sophist in politics, the glib and able speaker, who can sell himself and his personality to the electorate. Television has tended to be instrumental in achieving the same result. There are some persons who believe that the greatest innovation in recent years in political campaigning was the so-called "great debate," which occurred on television between the 1960 presidential nominees. This debate proved little or nothing about the administrative ability of either candidate. It merely demonstrated who had the more popular personality in a very superficial sense. A quiet person, a good organizer, a shrewd manipulator in human relations, knowledgeable in foreign affairs, might make a far better president or governor than the good looking, glib speaker with ready answers at his tongue's tip. Indeed, men with brilliant ideas and facile expression of them are often the worst administrators of the details of a pragmatic program.

Western elections give very little credence to the hypothesis that ticket-splitting in the West can be correlated positively with the independence of the voter and candidate. The prevalence of ticket-splitting in the 1966 election certainly indicated a weakening of traditional party ties and emphasized the fact that voters tend to vote for and elect attractive candidates at all levels.

Republican congressional districts have been more likely to split between congressional and gubernatorial candidates. Ticket-splitting took place in five western states in 1966 in which a senator and a governor of opposing parties were elected. The percentages of voters who split their tickets in this manner were as follows: Idaho, 14; New Mexico, 4.8; Colorado, 4.0; Oregon, 3.5; and Wyoming, 2.5. These splits indicate that the voters felt sufficiently independent to vote for personalities rather than parties. What happened in Utah in 1964 might be indicative of what happened in other western states. A very popular Republican congressman, Laurence Burton, in the First District, was elected by almost the same margin as three successful Democratic candidates for governor, congressman (Second District), and United States senator. In the same election a Democrat, not wanted by the Democratic organization, and without its support, won over a popular incumbent Republican attorney general.

Although California and Arizona have closed primaries and predominantly Democratic registrations with ratios as high as three to two, these states have elected Republican governors, senators, and state legislators during the past decade. And although Republican incumbents in major elective offices in California could not overcome the Democratic tide in 1958 and their own internal party dissensions, all their candidates failing at the polls, in Arizona the Republicans were highly successful.

Elections from 1958 to the present in the West have been topsy-turvy, to say the least. The Democrats won in 1958; the Republicans in 1960 and 1962, by narrow margins, leaving a substantial number of national and state offices, and majorities in some cases in one or both houses of state legislatures in Democratic hands. In 1964, the Democrats swept the West with President Lyndon Johnson, but it was principally the death of President John Kennedy which was responsible for this result. Trends seem to be meaningless when a president is assassinated.

All in all, politics in the West as a whole is decidedly "free-style"; it is often flamboyant. But the free, open spaces, the pervading bright sunshine, and the clear, distinct outline of the mountains against a deep blue sky drifted with thick velvety white clouds, have not evoked a particularly free, open, and frank spirit in political campaigns. Once, perhaps, elections in the West were characterized by the direct and bitter campaigns for the office of sheriff as portrayed on television, but in recent years the familiar subtle techniques in American politics generally have increased in quantity and intensity. The 1950 and 1954 campaigns in California and Utah, and the more recent campaigns in Arizona, California, Oregon, and Washington, have become increasingly scurrilous. In Arizona in 1958, Senator Barry Goldwater rode hard with three other horsemen, fear, doubt, and anger.

TABLE IV

TRENDS IN PARTY STRENGTH

IN 13 WESTERN STATES SINCE 1956◊

Year	Governor		U.S. Senate		U.S. House		State Senate			State House		
	D	R	D	R	D	R	D	R	Tied	D	R	Tied
1956	4	7	14	8	26	31	6	3	2	7	4	
1958	7	6	19	7	33	26	9	4		13	0	
1960	6	7	18	8	33	26	9	4		10	3	
1962	5	8	17	9	42	27	8	5		6	6	1
1964	7	6	17	9	47	22	9	3	1	11	2	
1966	2	11	16	10	37	32	7	6		4	9	
TOTAL	31	45	101	51	218	164	48	25	3	51	24	1

◊As measured by control of major offices and legislative bodies. Both Alaska and Hawaii figure in the totals beginning with 1958.

In the same year, the religious issue in Washington, California, and Oregon rose to new heights, due to an increased number of Roman Catholics in active politics, the parochial school question, and in Oregon, the fact that Mark Hatfield, in the middle of the gubernatorial campaign, married a Catholic who almost immediately became a Protestant. Observers in Wyoming, Montana, Hawaii, and New Mexico, states with substantial Catholic populations and prominent Catholics in public office, contend that religious bigotry has not been evident in their states, except in the 1960 presidential election. This election, due to Kennedy's Catholicism, heightened and sharpened the religious issue in all western states, especially in such typically Protestant areas as eastern New Mexico and Oregon. Religion does not seem to have been a factor or a variable in any western state election since 1960. Neither has it appeared that scurrilous or "mean" campaigns have been as prevalent as they were in the decade of the fifties. This aspect of political campaigning, really hard-hitting and then degenerating into the genuinely dirty, was most evident from 1950 to 1954 and then again in 1960-62.

Except in California, in the West as a whole the public relations man has not taken over completely in politics. However, the increased, but more discriminating use of television by candidates, especially when they themselves appear, has brought the expert, usually on the public relations firm staff, into politics on a greater scale in every western state. Personal contacts still play a heavy role in political campaigning, and the printed page is still an effective means of mass communication. The hazards for the candidate and the expense of using television have caused politicians to use it more cautiously and in some places as sparingly as possible.

The vote for governor in the thirteen western states from 1930 to 1958 illustrates the demarcation between one- and two-party states. The figures for Alaska, Arizona, Nevada, and Washington would suggest that these are Democratic states; California reveals a strong Republican tendency; the rest are two-party states. Actually, the Democrats have remained in the saddle in four of the five principal categories of elective office, U.S. senator, U.S. representative, state senator, and state representative. Although the Republicans have won 45 of 76 governorships, the Democrats have taken 101 of 151 Senate and 218 of 382 House seats. The Democrats have had majorities in 48 of 75 state senates and 51 of 75 houses of representatives or assemblies.

The trend in Arizona, New Mexico, Oregon, and California of electing candidates to major office from a single party was finally broken in 1950, although in Oregon the trend, begun in 1930, of electing Democratic candidates in that historically Republican state, has continued to the present time. Today New Mexico and Arizona, states with a two-to-one Democratic registration, have Republican governors. From 1950 to 1960 in both these states the Republicans elected three of the five governors. One Democratic governor in each state has been elected since 1960 only to be replaced by a Republican.

California and Arizona have high Democratic registrations. Originally, the great influx of people into California during New Deal days would have tended to bring a traditionally Republican state around to the Democratic lists. This happened to some extent. Since 1938 California has had one liberal Democratic governor (Culbert Olson, 1939-43), two liberal Republican ones (Earl Warren, 1943-53 and Goodwin Knight, 1953-59), one conservative Democrat (Edmund G. "Pat" Brown, 1959-67), and one conservative Republican (Ronald Reagan), but it was not until 1958 that both houses of the legislature came under the majority control of the Democrats. In that year, for the first time since 1889, the Democrats made a grand slam of state politics, winning six out of seven statewide elective offices, a majority of the congressional seats, a United States senatorship, and even the entire five-man State Board of Equalization as a bonus.

Arizona, on the other hand, has become more Republican. Its population which came originally from Democratic southern states, has come recently from Republican ranks in the north. In reality, it has become a two-party state—and although its legislatures have remained nominally Democratic, the voting has been conservative.

Briefly, the patterns of voting in Arizona, California, New Mexico, and recently in Alaska, would indicate that these are two-party states. Republicans have served as governors in Nevada and Montana, states that have consistently elected Democrats to Congress.

These have been but a few of the political vagaries in the western states. The foregoing chapters have attempted to account for these tendencies and the many variables found in the separate state elections. Usually the western states have "gone with the nation," but in 1960 ten of them cast their electoral votes for the losing Republican nominee, Richard M. Nixon. In addition, four of the five states with gubernatorial contests elected Republicans, but the congressional elections were not so favorable to the GOP. The Democrats captured four of the seven senatorial seats at issue but wound up with five. In Wyoming, incumbent Democratic Governor J. J. Hickey assumed the seat won by Keith Thomson, who died before he could take office.

In the 1960 congressional elections, local conditions and political personalities were undoubtedly the prevailing factors regardless of national ideologies, issues, and party voting trends. In many cases, these elections followed traditional voting patterns.

TABLE V

REPUBLICAN PERCENTAGES OF TWO-PARTY STATEWIDE VOTE FOR U.S. HOUSE OF REPRESENTATIVES

State	1956	1958	1960	1962	1964	1966
Alaska		42.5	53.2	45.5	48.5	51.3
Arizona	47.6	49.8	52.4	51.4	49.9	56.1
California	47.6	40.0	46.1	48.1	47.1	53.2
Colorado	47.2	41.8	48.2	52.7	41.8	46.8
Hawaii		31.4◊	25.6	32.2	37.3	31.6
Idaho	53.6	48.0	45.2	47.1	50.6	60.2
Montana	44.4	35.3	49.1	52.0	50.7	54.5
Nevada	45.8	33.1	42.5	28.3	36.7	32.4
New Mexico	46.9	37.4	41.5	41.6	43.4	46.8
Oregon	47.1	43.1	48.9	45.7	39.8	52.6
Utah	58.9	50.8	49.5	52.8	47.1	63.1
Washington	55.0	53.3	57.7	61.7	48.8	48.7
Wyoming	58.2	53.6	52.3	61.4	49.2	52.7

◊Hawaii special election, 1959.

The effect of the religious "issue" in the 1960 campaign cannot be discounted entirely. Washington re-elected its Catholic governor, Albert Rosellini, a Democrat, but gave its electoral vote to Nixon. Alaska, a state which had been earmarked as the last surviving single-party area (Democratic) in the West, also gave its vote to Nixon. Oregon, which gave Senator Maurine Neuberger, a liberal Democrat, a 37,000 vote margin, chose Nixon over Kennedy. However, for the 1960 results, one may advance an hypothesis that reasons in addition to Kennedy's Catholicism may account for Nixon's acceptance in the West.

Many states in the West, notably Washington and Alaska, depend heavily on federal subsidies to defense industries and federal spending to support military installations. Kennedy's statement that he would deploy federal defense payrolls in areas of greatest unemployment could have been enough to frighten many western states into Nixon's camp.

Early in the campaign, it was evident that neither presidential nominee was really popular for reasons other than his personality, a situation which resulted in a strong protest vote in both parties. The West had reason to vote against Kennedy on the grounds of his fourteen-year record in Congress. It was charged that he had sponsored no major legislation; his record of attendance at roll-calls was very poor, as was his attendance at committee meetings.[7] Since westerners generally conceive of their congressional representatives as errand boys in Washington who ought at all times to keep their noses to the legislative grindstone, the charge of absenteeism is an effective technique.

Most significant for the West, especially for the intermountain area, was the revelation that Kennedy had directly or indirectly (by pairing his vote) voted against the Colorado River Basin development program, especially the key to the whole system, the proposed Echo Park Dam, which was lost in Congress. This branded him as a representative of industrial New England and financial New York.

Nixon, on the other hand, had the unenviable political position of being duty-bound to reflect the policies of the Administration and of the personally popular President, while at the same time creating his "new" image of a politically reincarnated individual who, in the White House, would show a stronger hand in both domestic and international affairs than had his predecessor. But he was from the West. Moreover, his public relations counsel performed admirably in modifying the unfavorable "Tricky Dick" image created by his extremely vicious cam-

TABLE VI
NATIONWIDE REPUBLICAN GAINS, 1964 - 1966

Office	1964		1966		Republican Gain
	R	D	R	D	
U.S. Senator	32	68	36	64	+ 4
U.S. Representative	140	295	187	248	+ 47
Governor	17	33	25	25	+ 8
State Legislator	2,520	5,071	3,023	4,337	+503

7. The Republican "Truth Squad," made up of Senator Wallace F. Bennett from Utah, Senator Roman L. Hruska from Nebraska, and Under-Secretary of Commerce Philip A. Ray, pointed out that not a single piece of major legislation bore his name; that he had missed 331 roll-call votes out of 1,189 from 1953 to 1960, excluding those when he was ill; and that although he expressed vital concern for America's position in international affairs, he had not attended a single meeting in 1960 as chairman of the Afro-Asian Subcommittee of the Senate Foreign Relations Committee, nor as a member of either the Senate's Disarmament Subcommittee, or the Subcommittee on Automation and Energy Resources.

paigns against Jerry Voorhis in 1946 when he won his first seat in Congress and against Mrs. Helen Gahagan Douglas in 1950 when he won his senatorial seat. The incident of his $18,000 private "kitty" in 1952 also did little to make him acceptable to westerners who knew him at close range. Yet during his years in the vice presidency he had appeared to conduct himself with restraint and dignity: his 1960 campaign reflected this same pattern.

Kennedy won Nevada, Hawaii, and New Mexico by close margins. The others he lost—even Montana and Wyoming which have substantial Catholic populations and several prominent Catholic laymen in major state and high national offices.

In 1964, Lyndon B. Johnson swept the nation. In the West he lost only Arizona, his opponent's home state. His announced determination not to run in 1968 was a blow to political seers, who found themselves suddenly in a position of having to re-evaluate a situation which had seemed simplicity itself. One must review, then, the results of the 1966 election campaigns in the West for their significance as preludes to the 1968 elections, especially the presidential election.[8]

TABLE VII
THE VOTE FOR SENATOR IN THIRTEEN WESTERN STATES, 1966

State	R	D	Other	Total	Plurality	% D	% R
Alaska	15,961	49,289		65,250	33,328 D	75.5	24.5
Arizona	No Election						
California	No Election						
Colorado	368,307	266,198		634,505	102,109 R	42.0	58.0
Hawaii	No Election						
Idaho	139,819	112,637	NONE	252,456	27,182 R	44.6	55.4
Montana	121,697	138,166		259,863	16,469 D	53.2	46.8
Nevada	No Election						
New Mexico	120,988	137,205		258,193	16,217 D	53.1	46.9
Oregon	354,391	330,374		684,765	24,017 R	48.2	51.8
Utah	No Election						
Washington	No Election						
Wyoming	63,548	59,141		122,689	4,407 R	48.2	51.8
TOTAL	1,184,711	1,093,010		2,277,721	91,701 R	47.8	52.2

8. The details of the 1962 and 1964 elections have been enumerated and placed in perspective in two series of articles in the *Western Political Quarterly*. This academic journal can be cited favorably for its publishing a section every two years since 1948 on the elections in the West. This journal is available in most of the larger libraries of the land.

Following national trends, great numbers of voters in the thirteen western states voted the Republican ticket. While close, the results were not up to landslide proportions, except in a few states, but they did produce gains in political control for Republicans in all but one of the thirteen states. In this shift of control, the Republicans re-established the trend which had been interrupted in 1964. In view of this trend, one would have predicted that the Democrats should not have won in 1964. Despite the Democratic debacle two years later, a majority of western voters still are Democrats.

TABLE VIII

THE VOTE FOR REPRESENTATIVE IN CONGRESS
IN THIRTEEN WESTERN STATES, 1966

State	R	D	Other	Total	Plurality
Alaska	33,630	31,951		65,581	1,679 R
Arizona	204,478	159,945		364,423	44,533 R
California	3,336,943	2,937,862		6,274,805	399,081 R
Colorado	298,472	339,750	2,263	640,485	41,278 D
Hawaii	129,754	280,990		410,744	151,236 D
Idaho	149,434	98,794		248,228	50,640 R
Montana	140,940	117,431		258,371	23,509 R
Nevada	41,383	86,467		127,850	45,084 D
New Mexico	234,977	267,041		502,018	32,064 D
Oregon	349,902	314,881		664,783	35,021 R
Utah	196,996	114,983		311,979	82,013 R
Washington	449,765	474,021	15,655	939,441	24,256 D
Wyoming	62,984	56,442		119,426	6,542 R
TOTAL	5,629,658	5,280,558	17,918	10,928,134	349,100 R

Senator Mark Hatfield's win in Oregon accounted for the gain of one Senate seat registered by the Republicans in the West in 1966. Elsewhere, with the exception of Wyoming where the incumbent retired, incumbent senators irrespective of party were re-elected. In Montana, where the popular Republican governor ran against the incumbent senator, the latter's success was quite unexpected.

In contests for the United States House of Representatives, Republicans made a net gain of 10 seats compared to their total gain in the nation of 47. These gains occurred in eight of the thirteen western states. However, the Democrats still have an advantage of 5 seats for the West as a whole. The totals show 37 Democrats and 32 Republicans holding House seats in 1968.

Republican gains in gubernatorial races were more impressive. They won nine of the offices at stake, a net gain of five. Presently, only two of thirteen states have Democratic governors, Hawaii and Utah. Utah's governor, Calvin Rampton, is the only Democrat in the state capable of victory at the polls in 1968. Incumbent Democrat John Burns won re-election in Hawaii by an uncomfortably narrow margin.

TABLE IX
THE VOTE FOR GOVERNOR IN THIRTEEN WESTERN STATES, 1966

State	R	D	Other	Total	Plurality	% DEMOCRATIC 1966	Previous
Alaska	33,145	32,065		65,210	1,080 (R)	49.2	52.3◊
Arizona	203,438	174,904		378,342	28,534 (R)	46.2	53.2□
California	3,742,913	2,749,174	11,358	6,503,445	993,739 (R)	42.3	51.9◊
Colorado	356,730	287,132		643,862	69,598 (R)	44.6	42.9◊
Hawaii	104,324	108,840		213,164	4,516 (D)	51.1	58.3◊
Idaho	104,586	93,744	54,261	252,591	10,842 (R)	47.3	45.4◊
Montana	No Election						
Nevada	71,807	65,870		137,677	5,937 (R)	47.8	66.8◊
New Mexico	134,625	125,587		260,212	9,038 (R)	48.3	60.2□
Oregon	337,346	305,008		642,354	32,338 (R)	47.5	43.4◊
Utah	No Election						
Washington	No Election						
Wyoming	65,624	55,249		120,873	10,375 (R)	45.7	45.5◊
TOTAL	5,154,538	3,997,573	65,619	9,217,730	1,156,965 (R)	43.3	50.3

◊Last gubernatorial election in 1962.
□Last gubernatorial election in 1964.

Perhaps the most controversial issue common to all western legislative bodies has been reapportionment. Due to the insistence of the federal courts the issue now is dead. As of January 1, 1966, all thirteen western states either had apportioned according to a population plan or had adopted plans to be used in the next elections.

Of considerable interest in the contests for legislative seats is the fact that reapportionment did not appear to have had an appreciable effect on the outcome. That all the legislatures, with the exception of Oregon's and possibly Utah's, were affected in some measure is beyond doubt. Yet the trends in the results for legislative seats reflected or duplicated the pattern of Republican success in other contests. Republicans gained control of three state senates (Alaska, Arizona, and Utah) and now control six in all. Alaska's Senate since statehood had been Democratic; Arizona has had a predominantly Democratic registration; and Utah's Senate since 1932 has been more often Democratic than Republican. Republicans experienced a cumulative gain of 62 senate seats in the West. They now control 51 percent of all seats.

TABLE X

COMPOSITE SHIFT IN CONTROL OF SEATS IN LEGISLATURES
OF THIRTEEN WESTERN STATES, 1965 - 1967

Upper Chambers						Lower Chambers					
Party	1965	%	1967	%	Change	Party	1965	%	1967	%	Change
D	265	62	215	49	-50	D	543	60.9	391	45.1	-152
R	162	38	224	51	+62◇	R	349	39.1	477	54.9	+128◇

◇Gains and losses are not equal because of adjustments in size resulting from reapportionment.

TABLE XI

POLITICAL COMPOSITION OF STATE LEGISLATURES
IN THIRTEEN WESTERN STATES, 1967

State	Upper House		Lower House	
	R	D	R	D
Alaska	14	6	25	15
Arizona	16	14	33	27
California	19	21	38	42
Colorado	20	15	38	27
Hawaii	10	15	12	39
Idaho	22	13	38	32
Montana	25	30	64	40
Nevada	9	11	19	21
New Mexico	17	25	25	45
Oregon	11	19	38	22
Utah	23	5	59	10
Washington	20	29	55	44
Wyoming	18	12	33	27
TOTAL	224	215	477	391

Republicans gained even more impressively in lower chambers, adding seven to the two they already controlled, with a new gain of 128 House seats: they now control 54.9 percent of the seats. The seven lower chambers captured by Republicans in 1966 were those in Alaska, Arizona, Colorado, Montana, Utah, Washington, and Wyoming. Democrats continue to control both houses of legislatures in California, Hawaii, Nevada, and New Mexico. Party control of the legislatures of Montana, Oregon, and Washington is divided, with Democrats in command of the upper chambers in each of the three states and Republicans in control of the lower chambers. Three states in which Democrats control both houses—California, Nevada, and New Mexico—have Republican governors. On the other hand, the Democratic governor of Utah must deal with a legislature in which both houses are Republican-controlled.[9]

The legislatures of the western states are as diverse as the states themselves. They range in efficiency from bodies apparently meant to represent a nineteenth century constituency to the ultramodern and effective twentieth century bodies found in Alaska, Hawaii, and California. Members come from all walks of life. Occupational data clearly indicate, however, that legislators come from occupations that lend themselves to flexible work responsibilities. In most states a legislator's responsibility is only part time and his compensation is meagre. Legislative

TABLE XII
COMPENSATION FOR STATE LEGISLATORS, 1965

State	Annual Pay and per diem allowances 1964-1965	Controlled by Constitution or Statute	Per Capita Expenditure per year on entire Legislative operation 1961-62
California	$7,425	Const.	$ .23
Alaska	5,248	Statute	1.57
Hawaii	4,385	Const. & Statute	.08
Oregon	4,200	Const.	.20
Colorado	3,200	Statute	.17
Arizona	2,718	Statute	.36
Washington	2,400	Const.	.09
Nevada	1,950	Statute	.67
Montana	1,500	Statute	.06
Idaho	1,050	Const.	.07
Utah	650	Const.	.10
Wyoming	640	Statute	.02
New Mexico	600	Const. & Statute	.16

9. Thomas Payne, "The 1966 Election in the West," *Western Political Quarterly*, XX (June 1967, Part 2), 519-20.

salaries range from an annual high in California of $7,425 to $600 in New Mexico. Only four of the thirteen western states have "professionalized" legislatures so that a member can give his full time and attention to his legislative duties. Such occupational groupings as businessmen, lawyers, and farmers predominate in western legislatures because their work schedules may be flexible. Another factor which contributes to overrepresentation of certain occupational groups is the extent of public contact incidental to each occupation. Here again businessmen,

TABLE XIII

WOMEN IN STATE LEGISLATURES: THE WEST, 1967

Alaska			**Utah**			
Senate	R	1	Senate	R	1	
	D	0		D	0	
House	R	0	House	R	0	
	D	0		D	3	
Arizona			**Nevada**			
Senate	R	1	Senate	R	0	
	D	0		D	1	
House	R	1		?◇	1	
	D	2	House	R	0	
				D	4	
Oregon			**Hawaii**			
Senate	R	0	Senate	R	1	
	D	0		D	0	
House	R	4	House	R	0	
	D	3		D	1	
Montana			**Washington**			
Senate	R	2	Senate	R	0	
	D	0		D	1	
House	R	1	House	R	5	
	D	2		D	4	
Wyoming			**Colorado**			
Senate	R	1	Senate	R	1	
	D	1		D	0	
House	R	1	House	R	2	
	D	1		D	1	
New Mexico			**Idaho**			
Senate	R	0	Senate	R	1	
	D	1		D	0	
House	R	0	House	R	2	
	D	0		D	2	
California						
Senate	R	0				
	D	0				
House	R	0				
	D	3				

◇Party unknown.

such as insurance agents and farm implement dealers and lawyers predominate. In short, the typical legislator's background arms him with social respectability, extensive contacts, and time.

The low pay scale through the West produces other legislative problems—a rapid turnover of legislators and a large proportion of inexperienced lawmakers. It also attracts certain kinds of legislators who fill the more permanent positions. These are usually the financially independent interest group members, or the retired lobbyists. It is evident that in most of the thirteen western states many legislators do not stand for re-election because the financial sacrifice is too great to allow them to continue in service.

The number of women in the West who are in public office, including the national Congress, has not been impressive. Women in this area are more apt to be in the state legislatures, but not by great numbers, and in state offices. In Arizona the state auditor and secretary of state are women. In Wyoming, the secretary of state, and in Colorado, Idaho, and Wyoming, the state treasurers are women. They are more numerous in appointive state offices, especially on boards. In Congress, out of a total of twelve women, four are from the West. Three, one each from Hawaii, Oregon and Washington, are Democrats; the fourth, also from Washington, is a Republican. Although the total number of women in Congress has decreased in recent years, the number elected to state legislatures has increased.

TABLE XIV
WOMEN IN STATE OFFICES: THE WEST, 1966

State	Number	State	Number
Alaska	3	Nevada	5
Arizona	7	New Mexico	1
California	4	Oregon	7
Colorado	7	Utah	5
Hawaii	2	Washington	10
Idaho	6	Wyoming	5
Montana	5		

Negro candidates were more successful in winning elections in the nation to a variety of political offices in 1966 than at any other time since Reconstruction. Studies revealed that there were 154 Negroes in 27 state legislatures. In 1960 there were only 30 state representatives and 6 senators. In the West there was a total of 10 divided as follows: California 5, Colorado 2, Nevada 1, Arizona 1, and Washington 1. Arizona's Negro member was the first to be elected in the state's history.

Lobbying and pressure-group activities can be found in varying degrees throughout the West. These are usually accomplished in one or both of the following ways: overlapping membership in the legislature and the interest groups, and lobbying activities before the legislature. Lobbyists represent many diverse

TABLE XV

NEGRO MEMBERSHIP IN STATE LEGISLATURES:
THE WEST, 1967

| State | In House or Assembly | | | In Senate | | | % Negro Population |
	Total Members	Negro Members	%	Total Members	Negro Members	%	
California	80	5	6.2	40	2	5.0	5.6
Colorado	65	2	3.0	35	1	2.8	2.3
Nevada	37	1	2.7				4.7
Arizona	50	1	2.0				7.1
Washington	99	1	1.0				1.7

TABLE XVI

REGULATIONS GOVERNING LOBBYING

State	Improper activities prohibited	Registration required	Expenditure report required	Contingent payment prohibited	Fine	Imprisonment
Alaska		yes	yes	yes	$200-1000	1 yr.
Arizona	yes					1-10 yr.
California		yes	yes	yes	$5000	0-1 yr.
Colorado		yes				
Hawaii						
Idaho	yes				$0-200	0-6 mo.
Montana		yes		yes	$0-200	0-6 mo.
Nevada	yes					2-10 yr.
New Mexico						
Oregon	yes				$50-500	0-1 yr.
Utah	yes				$500-10,000	0-5 yr.
Washington		yes				
Wyoming						

interests through the West. Labor, commodity organizations from salmon to liquor, mining, cattle, agriculture, education, and increasingly, religious organizations are but a few of the pressure groups.

Lobbying laws and regulations throughout the western states are quite diverse in their scope and effect. They vary from no regulation at all to various
forms of registration and severe fines and imprisonment. Generally, most lobbying regulations are patterned after federal legislation requiring such information
from lobbyists as identification of groups they represent, amount of compensation, and, a recent development among states in general, payment of fees for registration. A notable exception is Washington which regulates lobbyists by means of
a House Rule. Most lobbying regulations seek to eliminate felonious bribery,
blackmail, and intimidation per se. However, there appears to be little enforcement of the law and little attempt to publicize it. The lobbyist's stock in trade is
still free meals and libations, and a goodly measure of socializing coupled with
promises of campaign contributions.

In the West, only California has been known for a large number of referenda
and amendments on the ballot each election. However, in 1966, Utah was the first
with eight (all defeated), and California and Colorado with five each were tied for
second place. In California three were defeated and two passed; in Colorado, three
were passed and two defeated. Alaska passed six major bond proposals. Hawaii
passed a proposal for a constitutional convention (a similar proposal was defeated
in Utah), and Nevada, the second state to have only one proposition on the ballot,
repealed its poll tax by this method. Montana and New Mexico each passed two
proposals. Idaho passed three propositions and defeated one, and Washington
passed one and defeated three, one of these its Sunday blue law legislation. In
Wyoming, one proposition failed but three were passed, among these the abolish-
ment of the decennial state census. Utah has never repealed the requirement that
it conduct a decennial census in the years ending in five. The state has never observed this part of the constitution.

Requirements for voting and other laws for electoral behavior in the thirteen
states may be found in Table XVII.

Lockard assumes that "two-party competition results in a more salutary political atmosphere."[10] He argues that in interpreting the whole political picture it
would be inadequate to restrict one's view to elections, campaigning, and intra- or
interparty maneuvering on the hustings. The necessary broader perspective includes a scrutiny of the legislative process. Legislative politics has been merely
touched upon in the preceding chapters. Yet on the whole, one may conclude that
the West is a salutary two-party area. Arizona, New Mexico, Oregon, and California have relinquished their one-party positions, and even Alaska may do so as party organizations develop in the nation's "last frontier."

Many of the hypotheses which have been suggested throughout this volume
will be tested in the November 1968 elections. It is always difficult to predict the
outcome of any political campaign, particularly in the West, characterized as it is
by the independence of the voters. In the middle of this election year Nixon appears on the political stage as the leading Republican contender. Only Nelson
Rockefeller would seem to stand in his way as a shoo-in for the Republican presi-

10. See Duane Lockard, *New England State Politics* (Princeton University Press, 1959),
p. 6, for a comparative commentary on this basis between the New England and Southern
states. See also Table II, Party Tendencies of the Western States, 1930-58, in *Western Politics*,
Frank H. Jonas (ed.) (Salt Lake City: University of Utah Press, 1961), p. 13.

TABLE XVII

ELECTION LAWS

State	Residence in state under 1 year	No literacy test	Permanent registration	General civilian absentee registration permitted	Precinct registration	Registration closes within 1 month of election	Civilian absentee vote	Mere absence a ground for absentee vote	Absentee ballot application by mail	Polls open 12 hours or longer	Presidential voting by new residents	Presidential voting by former residents
Idaho	•	•	•	•	•	•	•	•	•	•	•	
Utah		•	•	•	•	•	•	•	•	•		
Wyoming			○	•	•	•	•	•	•	•		•
Washington			•		•	•	•	•	•	•	•	
Oregon	•		•	•	•	•	•	•	•	•	•	•
Colorado		•	•		○	•	•	•	•	•	•	•
Montana		•	•	•	•	•		•	•	○		
California		•			•			•	•	•	•	•
New Mexico		•	•	•	•	•						
Nevada	•	•	•		•	•			•		○	
Arizona			•	•			•	•	•	•	•	•
Hawaii			•	•	•	•	•	•	•			
Alaska		•	No registration				•			•		

●Statewide ○Some

dential nomination. Nixon's election as President would appear to be almost as certain as his nomination.

The 1960 presidential election was spectacular in breaking the tradition that a Catholic had never been a successful contender for the presidency. The 1964 election was spectacular in the wake of the assassination of President John F. Kennedy. The 1968 presidential election promised to be equally spectacular with an unprecedented withdrawal from the race of the White House incumbent, President Lyndon Johnson, the return to the hustings of Republican Nelson Rockefeller, and the entry of three energetic Democratic contenders to the lists—Senator Robert F. Kennedy, who bore the charismatic appeal of the Kennedy clan, Vice President Hubert Humphrey, and an almost unknown senator, Eugene McCarthy, who gathered momentum rapidly. Added to these factors were the unprecedented civil disturbances in American cities, the brutal assassination of the Negro leader, Dr. Martin Luther King, and the unrest caused by the prolongation of the

Vietnam War. The event which further shocked the public, and put a damper upon the entire campaign, was the tragic and wanton assassination of Senator Robert F. Kennedy on the very eve of victory, as he won the significant presidential primary in California. It is now doubtful if the two old warhorses, Humphrey and Nixon, can kick up enough fuss to arouse the national electorate to feverish heights, should they win out over their respective opponents in the national presidential nominating conventions.

Neal A. Maxwell

THE WEST ON CAPITOL HILL

It is difficult to assess the significance of the changes occurring in the profile of the West in Congress. Where once powerful western senators could shout "silver!" and cause tremblings in the Treasury, today western solons have had to settle for the elimination of silver in American coins except for 40 percent silver content in half dollars. Where once mining interests provided a common political flag in which most western senators and congressmen could happily wrap themselves, mining interests have lost some significant battles in the sixties to conservation-recreation interests, and western solons from urbanized constituencies have only casual interest in mining. Where once Senator Carl Hayden (D-Arizona) was one of a band of western political patriarchs who provided the United States Senate with much of its color as well as with some of its decisions, he is now the only survivor of that band, and will retire at the end of 1968. Seniority-encrusted Hayden has been a kind of regional redwood who has defied time and the caprice of the ballot box; where some western solons have elbowed their way briefly into senatorial history, Hayden is history.

Yet the western phalanx in Washington may simply be passing a phase line, not ending an era. Hayden himself sees "no change in the legislative objectives of senators and congressmen from the western states since I became a member of Congress in 1912."[1] The roles reflective of regionalism continue to be acted out, but with a newer cast—perhaps less dogmatic, but still careful to manage their small western publics well.

Western solons have provided the Republican party with its last two presidential candidates, Richard M. Nixon, an alumnus of both House and Senate, and former Senator Barry Goldwater; the West with its only vice president ever, Nixon; and the present Senate with its president pro tempore, Hayden;[2] its majority leader, Mike Mansfield (D-Montana); its minority whip, Thomas H. Kuchel (R-California), who was defeated in the 1968 California primary in his bid for re-election; its only movie star, George Murphy (R-California); and one of its few genuine mavericks, Wayne Morse (D-Oregon). The West also supplies Congress with four of its women lawmakers: Representatives Edith Green (D-Oregon), Patsy T.

Note: A special word of thanks is due L. Ralph Mecham, a valued observer, Frederick L. Scott of the Library of Congress for much of the data used, and the *Congressional Quarterly* for its useful blend of highlights and detail, for those of us who have reluctantly given up regular reading of the *Congressional Record*.

1. Letter to the author dated June 21, 1965.

2. Two other westerners have served, though many years ago, as president pro tempore, Kay Pittman of Nevada and William H. King of Utah, the latter for but two months in a special session after his defeat in the Utah elections and before a new Congress convened. No westerner has ever been speaker of the House.

Mink (D-Hawaii), Catherine May (R-Washington), and Julia B. Hansen (D-Washington); and with its legislators of Oriental or Polynesian extraction.

After the 1970 census, California will provide the House with its largest state bloc of congressmen.

Western solons still worry most about water, only now instead of programs of an intra-state or regional nature, they also have fixed solemn senatorial sights on the water in the arctic, northwestern reaches of this continent.

Thus the symbols of change are present, but they seem neither profound nor routine. Western solons are not deliberately careless in managing ancient western shibboleths or symbols; the political genuflections are made, but there is a noticeable generational difference in the emotion which accompanies regional rituals. What we see, therefore, is clearly neither a requiem for a region nor a resurgent regionalism, but change. How the western solons deal with change in terms of their future cohesion will be significant, additionally, in view of the South's "Appomattox" as a racist bloc.[3] The long-range effects this may have on southern lawmakers—who have long formed the Senate's most powerful regional bloc—will be very significant.

What follows is a fresh look at the political and party profile, the placement, the potency, the voting patterns of western solons and the issues that activate this group on Capitol Hill in the nineteen sixties. Only a book masquerading as a chapter could examine much more than the top of the iceberg. A series of floor votes often produces the legislative "moment of truth" well before final passage; the intricacies of "pairing" for votes yield fascinating tales; and the real gut decisions are often hammered out in conference committees, etc., but the profile sketched herein is too large to permit much detail or subtle shading.

PARTY STRENGTH

The profile of party strength in Congress is very revealing so far as the West is concerned (see Chart 1). In the years 1939 to 1968, Democrats have controlled the Senate in thirteen congresses out of fifteen. However, western Republican senators, during this same period, were even weaker—in terms of their regional strength—than their party in the Senate. Only once, in the Congress which convened in 1951, did western Republicans outnumber western Democrats in the upper chamber. In fact, the number of western seats held by Republicans during this period has been below the general GOP ratio in the Senate in ten of the fifteen congresses. Even when Republicans controlled the Senate in 1947, western Republican senators were still outnumbered by western Democratic senators. In 1959 and 1961 when Democrats had a two-to-one Senate-wide ratio, western Democratic senators outnumbered their GOP counterparts by more than three-to-one.

The pattern of party strength is significantly different in the House. In the period 1939-65 Democrats also controlled the House thirteen out of fifteen times, but western Republican congressmen have outnumbered western Democrats in six of the fifteen congresses from 1939 through 1968. In four of these congresses, western Republican representatives outnumbered western Democrats even though the Democrats controlled the House. In 1953, western Republicans

---

3. A judgment of the South's situation advanced in an editorial in *Life Magazine*, May 21, 1965. Westerners are less likely to make "Kamikaze" stands on vital issues than are their southern brethren. Tariffs, water, and silver make political adrenalin flow in the western body politic but not as the race issue does in the South.

outnumbered western Democrats in the House by a two-to-one margin even though the over-all GOP margin of control was only a modest eight seats.

House Democrats from the thirteen western states have achieved a two-to-one margin over their Republican counterparts only twice during the years 1939 to 1968. Western Democratic senators, on the other hand, have enjoyed a two-to-one ratio (or even better) over GOP western senators in 1939, 1941, 1943, 1945, 1959, 1961, 1963, 1965, and 1967—more than half the time!

CHART 1
PARTY COMPLEXION OF THE SENATE 1939-1965

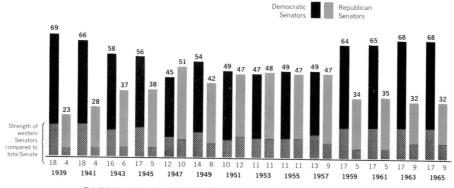

PARTY COMPLEXION OF THE HOUSE 1939-1965

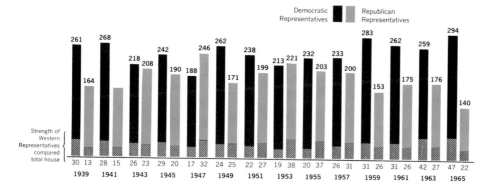

The possible explanations for this difference include: a rural conservatism in the West which can prevail in congressional elections but not in statewide Senate contests; geographical districting which has favored conservatives; the general failure of Republican senators or senatorial candidates in the West to convince their constituents of their record of service or their capacity to serve the region. Of course, the staggered Senate terms, the Eisenhower years (1952 and 1956) which helped western Republican congressmen considerably more than their Republican counterparts elsewhere, are all variables which must be allowed for.

PARTY LOYALTY

The *Congressional Quarterly* has identified, validated, and followed the existence of the conservative[4] coalition of southern Democrats and some Republi-

---

4. *Congressional Quarterly Almanac* and *Weekly Reports* are the sources for much of the data in the chapter, unless otherwise noted. Rather than providing profuse footnote references, readers may refer to the *Congressional Quarterly* for the month or year noted.

cans in Congress. In 1963, western Democrats in the House supported this conservative coalition 14 percent of the time on key votes; western Republicans, 74 percent. In 1964 the coalition got western Democratic support in the House 13 percent of the time, and Republican support 74 percent of the time. It is important to note, however, that where the South could count on some western help on cloture, etc., and the western conservatives could count on some southern help on fiscal matters, this is changing now and may mean that the coalition is losing its significance.

In the Senate in 1963, the coalition got western Democratic support 20 percent of the time—the highest of any region except the South—and western Republican support 71 percent of the time; in 1964 support ratios in the Senate were almost identical. Hayden supported the coalition more than any western Democrat in the Senate, and Nevada's Baring the most of any western Democrat in the House. Fong and Inouye of Hawaii opposed the coalition most often of any westerners in the Senate, and Olsen of Montana had the highest opposition (100 percent) in the House.

Actually, western senators appear to form three groups which interact with some fluidity: the western liberals, Frank E. Moss (D-Utah), Gale W. McGee (D-Wyoming), Joseph M. Montoya (D-New Mexico), Ernest Gruening (D-Alaska), Clinton P. Anderson (D-New Mexico), Daniel K. Inouye (D-Hawaii), Frank Church (D-Idaho), Henry M. Jackson (D-Washington), Warren G. Magnuson (D-Washington), Lee Metcalf (D-Montana), E. L. Bartlett (D-Alaska), and Wayne Morse (D-Oregon); western moderates, Alan Bible (D-Nevada), Howard W. Cannon (D-Nevada), Carl Hayden (D-Arizona), Gordon Allott (R-Colorado), Thomas H. Kuchel (R-California), Mike Mansfield (D-Montana), and Hiram L. Fong (R-Hawaii); western conservatives, Wallace F. Bennett (R-Utah), Peter H. Dominick (R-Colorado), Paul J. Fannin (R-Arizona), George Murphy (R-California), and Len B. Jordan (R-Idaho). New senators, Clifford P. Hansen (R-Wyoming) and Mark O. Hatfield (R-Oregon) do not provide us with a lengthy enough sample although Hatfield will probably be a moderate and Hansen a conservative.

Ranked among those senators who voted more than 70 percent of the time as the Americans for Democratic Action would like them to vote were: Neuberger, Metcalf, Moss, Church, Jackson, Mansfield, Morse, Magnuson, McGee, Inouye, Bartlett, Montoya[5] and Kuchel. A similar pattern appears in terms of the AFL-CIO's Committee on Political Education approval: Montoya, Mansfield, Metcalf, Moss, Inouye, Bartlett, Magnuson, Morse, Church, McGee, Anderson, Neuberger, Hayden, and Gruening.

Those who voted more than 70 percent of the time as the Americans for Constitutional Action would approve of were: Jordan, Bennett, Dominick, and Allott. A.C.A.'s disapproval was most clear, percentagewise, in the cases of Inouye, Metcalf, McGee, Bartlett, Jackson, Mansfield, Moss and Morse.[6]

The lines are not rigid, however, Morse, Magnuson, and Mansfield have broken with western liberals from time to time. Mansfield's role as majority leader probably requires him to be somewhat more "regular" than would otherwise be the case.

Senate Democrats from the West opposed the Kennedy Administration 14 percent of the time on key votes in 1962, 12 percent in 1963, and the Johnson Administration 17 percent in 1964, showing the larger measure of personal inde-

5. Based on his voting record in the House.
6. *CQWR*, October 23, 1964, pp. 2542, 2543.

pendence and/or political security of western solons in the upper chamber. Western Republicans in the House opposed the Democratic Administration 49 percent
of the time in 1962, 57 percent of the time in 1963, and 52 percent of the time in
1964.

The parties in the Senate generally appear to be less inclined to seek or less
able to enforce party discipline than in the House, yet party regularity among
western senators has probably risen in recent years which would tend to diminish
regionalism.

SENIORITY AND PLACEMENT IN THE HOUSE

The Senate is the natural impact area for western legislators. With eight of
the thirteen western states having two or less representatives and little chance for
dramatic representation change in most of these eight states, and given the risks of
a two-party region, few western congressmen are apt to be highly impactful individuals in terms of placement or seniority in the power structure of the House (see
Chart 2).

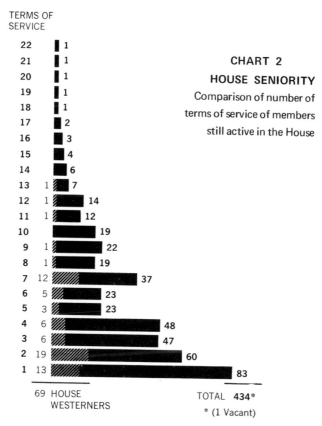

TERMS OF
SERVICE

22		1
21		1
20		1
19		1
18		1
17		2
16		3
15		4
14		6
13	1	7
12	1	14
11	1	12
10		19
9	1	22
8	1	19
7	12	37
6	5	23
5	3	23
4	6	48
3	6	47
2	19	60
1	13	83

69 HOUSE
WESTERNERS

CHART 2

HOUSE SENIORITY

Comparison of number of
terms of service of members
still active in the House

TOTAL **434***

* (1 Vacant)

Of the sixty-nine western congressmen, thirty-eight, or 55 percent, represent
California. After the 1970 census, California should pass the New York delegation
in total size and increase its dominance of the delegation from the West. Such
seniority as it has in the House, the West now gets largely through Californians.

One can count down twenty-three names on the House seniority list before
encountering a westerner, Cecil R. King (D-California). Only three more westerners, Chet Holifield (D-California), George P. Miller (D-California), and Wayne

Aspinall (D-Colorado) appear among the first seventy-three representatives. Presently, in a Democratic House, westerners chair two committees, Interior and Science and Astronautics. Westerners hold second-ranking spots on Education and Labor, Government Operations, and Ways and Means. One must count down thirty names on a GOP House seniority list before reaching the eight western Republicans who share with several colleagues rank sixteen. Of these eight, six are Californians, one is from Washington, and one from Arizona.

Should the Republicans control the House, westerners would probably chair the Merchant Marine and Fisheries Committee through the person of William S. Mailliard (R-California), the Rules Committee with H. Allen Smith (R-California), and the House Administration Committee through Glenard P. Lipscomb (R-California). Republicans, under these conditions, would also have second- and third-ranking seats on the Interior, Foreign Affairs, Merchant Marine and Fisheries, Ways and Means, Interstate and Foreign Commerce, Agriculture, Public Works, Rules, and the Un-American Activities committees. Additionally, fifth- and sixth-ranking spots would go to Republican westerners on both the Armed Services and Appropriations committees. Of course, given the myriad of subcommittees, one would no doubt see westerners in some subcommittee chairs under Republican leadership as they now are under a Democratic regime.[7]

Thus, given the present placement on committees, each party would have two chairmanships (under the Democrats, Interior and Science and Astronautics; under the Republicans, Merchant Marine and Fisheries and House Administration). So far as rank relevant to the traditional needs of the West, generally, is concerned, this power placement favors the Democrats, for both the obvious reasons as well as the likelihood that Republican control of Interior could mean a chairmanship for Representative John P. Saylor (R-Pennsylvania) who has opposed certain western reclamation projects and insisted, or tried to, that western projects meet reclamation law and criteria.

Relevant rank, placement, and seniority which provide leverage on committees crucial to the West are very important. Aside from chairmanships, the GOP has eighteen westerners among the first six ranking spots on House committees as against twelve for the Democrats, a far different party picture than prevails in the Senate.

Depth in committee placement is as crucial as relevant rank. Since depth is, in part, simply a function of numbers, Democrats now have more depth on House committees. Were Republicans to control the House, presumably many of the western Democrats now on certain committees would be replaced with Republicans from the West—but not in all cases. Not re-electing congressmen who have acquired high rank in committee positions can be expensive for any region regardless of party.

States pay a price for being two-party states—a fact southern leaders must now begin to face in terms of their own Senate and House power placement.

Allowing for the present ratio of Democrats and Republicans in the House, the following generalizations about depth appear to be justified: the Interior Committee is virtually western territory with nine Democrats and eight Republicans—seventeen westerners—presently serving on it; on Appropriations and Public Works, the general House ratio of party representation prevails; Democrats have a beyond-ratio edge in Education and Labor (a natural reflection, perhaps, of party

7. Conscious of its political significance, western solons in the House often list their subcommittee memberships on their stationery.

interest), Foreign Affairs, Judiciary, Government Operations, Post Office and Civil Service, Science and Astronautics, and Veterans Affairs. Republicans have a beyond-ratio edge on Banking and Currency, Merchant Marine and Fisheries, and Ways and Means.

Another way in which the West can increase its impact in the House is for its congressmen to have multiple committee assignments. Of the sixty-nine western representatives, slightly less than half have two or more committee assignments; the general pattern in the House is one in which slightly over one-half of the members have additional committee assignments.

Distribution of western manpower in the House committees (see Chart 3) reflects regionalism to a great extent. As of 1966 westerners held 16 percent of all House seats and the following percentages of seats on House committees: Agriculture 14 percent, Appropriations 14 percent, Armed Services 16 percent, Banking and Currency 12 percent, District of Columbia .04 percent, Education and Labor 19 percent, Foreign Affairs 11 percent, Government Operations 9 percent, House Administration 4 percent, Interior 44 percent, Interstate and Foreign Commerce 10 percent, Judiciary 8 percent, Merchant Marine and Fisheries 15 percent, Post Office and Civil Service 12 percent, Public Works 18 percent, Rules 13 percent, Science and Astronautics 13 percent, Un-American Activities 22 percent, Veterans Affairs 20 percent, and Ways and Means 16 percent.

CHART 3
WESTERNERS SERVING ON HOUSE STANDING COMMITTEES
(Westerners hold 95 seats on committees)

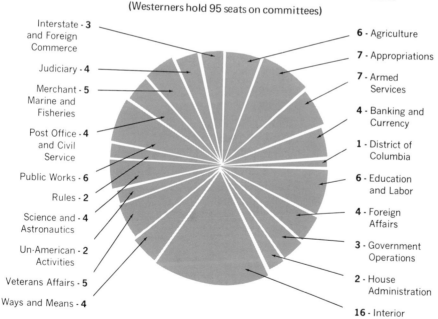

Interstate - 3 and Foreign Commerce
Judiciary - 4
Merchant - 5 Marine and Fisheries
Post Office - 4 and Civil Service
Public Works - 6
Rules - 2
Science and - 4 Astronautics
Un-American - 2 Activities
Veterans Affairs - 5
Ways and Means - 4

6 - Agriculture
7 - Appropriations
7 - Armed Services
4 - Banking and Currency
1 - District of Columbia
6 - Education and Labor
4 - Foreign Affairs
3 - Government Operations
2 - House Administration
16 - Interior

Placement on committees can confer regional advantages which the name of the committee does not suggest. For instance, former Congressman Compton I. White, Jr. (D-Idaho), no doubt found his seat on the House Banking and Currency Committee a vantage point from which to try to influence governmental monetary policies as they affect silver mining in his state, such as in the 1965 controversy over coinage policy; George P. Miller (D-California), through his chairmanship of Science and Astronautics, is well situated in connection with space industry and defense-related interests which are so vital to California. California receives nearly one-quarter of all the nation's prime military contracts.

Assignments can also be conducive to legislative lobbies, giving congressmen influence of an individual nature, such as John E. Moss's (D-California) "watchdog" role on Government Operations in connection with discouraging censorship by executive departments and agencies.

SENIORITY AND PLACEMENT IN THE SENATE

In the Senate, where the West holds 26 percent of all seats, western senators held as of 1966 the following percentages of committee seats (see Charts 4 and 5): Aeronautical and Space Sciences 31 percent, Agriculture .06 percent, Appropriations 30 percent, Armed Services 18 percent, Banking and Currency 14 percent, Commerce 33 percent, District of Columbia 28 percent, Finance 12 percent, Foreign Relations 16 percent, Government Operations 36 percent, Interior 81 percent, Judiciary .06 percent, Labor and Public Welfare 25 percent, Post Office and Civil Service 25 percent, Public Works 41 percent, and Rules 22 percent.

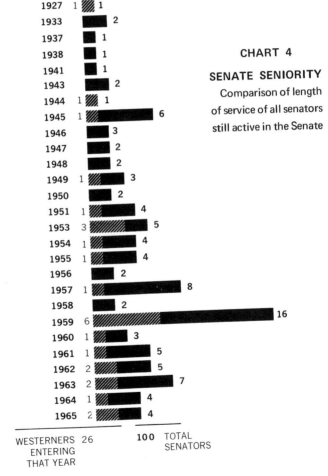

CHART 4

SENATE SENIORITY
Comparison of length
of service of all senators
still active in the Senate

WESTERNERS 26   100 TOTAL
ENTERING   SENATORS
THAT YEAR

Service on a committee like the District of Columbia is often a matter of serving a tour of duty or individual dedication; there is not much political mileage

CHART 5
WESTERNERS SERVING ON SENATE STANDING COMMITTEES
(Westerners hold 67 seats on committees)

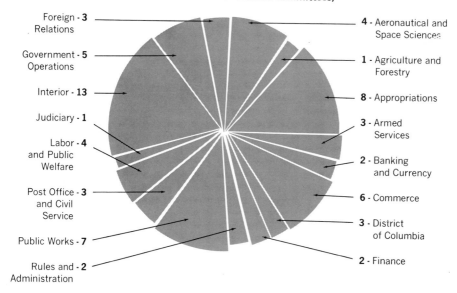

Foreign - **3** Relations

Government - **5** Operations

Interior - **13**

Judiciary - **1**

Labor - **4** and Public Welfare

Post Office - **3** and Civil Service

Public Works - **7**

Rules and - **2** Administration

4 - Aeronautical and Space Sciences

1 - Agriculture and Forestry

8 - Appropriations

3 - Armed Services

2 - Banking and Currency

6 - Commerce

3 - District of Columbia

2 - Finance

"back home" in the West for this kind of service. As indicated earlier, the names of committees can be misleading in terms of regional considerations. Traditional western concerns like freight rates and tariffs would, for instance, be acted out, in part, in the Commerce and Finance committees, respectively.

In the predecessor-volume of this book, *Western Politics* (1961), the author called attention to the paucity of western senators on the Senate Agriculture Committee. Senator Allen J. Ellender, chairman of that Committee and a member of it for twenty-nine years, notes[8] that when he came to Congress, the Agriculture Committee, along with the Appropriations Committee, was a real political prize and that it took "quite a lot of political maneuvering" for him to get on the Agriculture Committee. When Congress convened in 1965, Ellender had no request from any senator for a seat on his Committee and finally had to fill the vacancies "by drafting two senators." Ellender does not see this disinterest as a reflection of regionalism, but as a consequence of the postwar complexities of agriculture which have made work on the Committee "most frustrating" and "aggravating" rather than "glamorous." Significantly, former Secretary of Agriculture Clinton Anderson has left this Committee.

Even though it is a two-party region, the West chairs five out of sixteen Senate committees in the 90th Congress: Aeronautical and Space Sciences, Appropriations, Commerce, District of Columbia, and Interior. If the GOP were to control the Senate—not probable until at least 1970—given today's rankings, the West could chair Banking and Currency, and Interior.

Under present Democratic control, the West has men in second- or third-ranking spots on the following committees: Aeronautical and Space Sciences, District of Columbia, Finance, Foreign Relations, Government Operations, Interior, Labor and Public Welfare, and Rules. Under Republican direction, the West would hold second- or third-ranking spots on the District of Columbia, Finance,

8. Letter to the author dated June 15, 1965.

Interior, Judiciary, Labor and Public Welfare, Post Office and Civil Service, and Public Works Committees. It must be said, however, that while regional depth on a Senate committee like Interior[9] is in line with party ratios, the situation on the powerful Appropriations Committee favors the Democrats not only in terms of depth—a function of numbers, alterable in an election—but in placement. As in the case of the House, a network of subcommittees provides some western senators with only moderate seniority with significant chances to be influential.

THE 1964 CONGRESSIONAL ELECTIONS

In the House races in the thirteen western states in 1964, the Democrats captured nine GOP seats, and the GOP captured four Democratic seats. In nineteen of their present forty-seven seats, the Democrats strengthened their percentage hold but lost ground to the GOP in fifteen cases. The Republicans increased their hold in six instances, but were gained on by the Democrats in twelve of their twenty-two seats. In terms of "consensus" seats (those in which the winning candidate receives over 70 percent of the vote), the Democrats had eight in the 1964 elections, the GOP none.

The 1964 election was one in which there were several potent variables: the presidential race, regional or local issues, and the image-incumbency-service to the district factors. In a survey by the author of over fifty congressmen and candidates to be such, the following generalizations emerged:

a.   Winners said "No" by a four-to-one margin when asked if the presidential race "completely overshadowed" the importance of regional or local issues. Seven winners hedged by saying the presidential was "important" but did not "overshadow" regional or local issues completely. The losing candidates divided about evenly on the question. The "pull" of Lyndon B. Johnson and/or the "drag" by Barry Goldwater was seen as "tipping the scales" in several races, according to the losers. Yet both Democrat and Republican losers report running ahead of their presidential ticket. Thirteen losing Republican congressional candidates said the presidential race was a major factor in their defeat; nine of these men said it was *the* major factor in their loss.

b.   The "image" projected by the candidates, including the incumbency factor, was seen by winners as more impactful than local or regional issues by a three-to-one margin. Losers also saw image as more important than issues by a slight margin. "Image" may be a derivative of how the candidate is perceived as managing these particular issues or needs.

c.   Regional or local issues identified were varied but almost always were related to the congressman's role of advocate for the district with the federal government.

d.   All but five of the fifty indicated genuine or "complete disagreement" between themselves and their opponents on the campaign issues, though these differences often occurred around conservatism versus liberalism rather than local issues.

e.   Most saw their position on the issues as reflective of the prevailing public opinion in their districts, although several who lost to veteran incumbents conceded that the voters' views must more nearly match the incumbents' than their own.

f.   In rank-ordering the three major factors that affected the outcome of their congressional races, the winners noted first, by a very wide margin, factors related to "incumbency and

9.   Since several western Democrats have received campaign funds from eastern labor organizations, they may be less dependent on traditional western economic power groups than were their predecessors and, therefore, may become more "free" politically and yet not become politically careless about traditional constituent groups. The "nationalizing" of financing campaigns tends to reduce regionalism.

image"; second, the quality and vigor of their campaign or their opponent's tactical failures, etc.; third, factors related to the presidential race; and fourth, their party's "natural" strength in their district. Losers, most of whom were Republicans, ranked the presidential race as first, and second, their travails in a "hostile" district, third, their opponent's advantages growing out of his incumbency, and fourth, lack of money which prevented their getting wider exposure to the electorate. The "emotionalization" of the presidential race resulted, in several congressional races, in a large voter turnout which unseated Republicans who had been able to win previously in Democratic districts because of Democratic voter apathy.

An effective incumbent who has relevant rank with which to affect affirmatively the federal projects which meet his district's needs is a blend of the factors which make for re-electability. An example is Congressman Aspinall who in 1964 was returned to the House with a resounding victory. He reports that "careful emphasis" was placed on "the value of my chairmanship of the House Interior and Insular Affairs Committee to the people of the District and the State." Aspinall's opponent "could take no exception" to the resource development that had occurred in the past nor to the need for continued development; this left the opponent, in a sense, issueless.

Yet freshman Congressman Brock Adams of Washington's 7th District reported that certain local issues related to water and electrical power were important, but "they did not, however, overshadow the material issues of medicare, anti-poverty, civil rights, etc."

Issues in the interior West often vary sharply from those on the Pacific Coast or in urbanizing areas, and newcomers trying to defeat an incumbent in an urbanized constituency reported real difficulty in communicating with voters.

THE COMING CONGRESSIONAL ELECTIONS

In the 1966 congressional elections, the GOP gained ten western House seats: one each in Alaska, Arizona, Colorado, Idaho, Oregon, Utah, and Wyoming, and three in California. The western Republicans netted one seat in the Senate (Oregon).

The rip tide in 1966 had its own sources of momentum—some of which may still exist, but the 1968 elections will be too entangled with public reactions to the prospects of peace in Vietnam and the scrambled presidential picture to do any wise forecasting. The 1966 elections did show the strength of the western Democrats in the U.S. Senate.

In 1968, nine western senators will stand for re-election; three of the seats are now occupied by Republicans and six by Democrats. The Republicans may gain two or three of these seats.

Of course, with increasing population, the West will come to have not alone increasing legislative leverage, but leverage connected with presidential politics—especially will this be true of California. The President, as Clinton Rossiter has observed in his book, *The American Presidency*, is our "chief legislator." Therefore, presidential politics may reflect additional regionalism as the executive preempts legislative terrain as a result of the decline of Congress.

RELIGION

Though religious affiliations seldom play a visibly causal role in legislative behavior, some interesting regional differences appear among western congressmen and senators when compared with their colleagues from other regions. As of

1966, whereas Protestants outnumber non-Protestants by a four-to-one margin in all of Congress, Protestants among western solons outnumber non-Protestants by more than eleven-to-one. Other striking differences in the West are: solons who are affiliated with the Church of Jesus Christ of Latter-day Saints (LDS or Mormon) are the fourth largest group among the thirteen religious groups with which western legislators claim affiliation;[10] Roman Catholic legislators who comprise the most sizable single group in the national legislature rank but fifth within the western region; no western legislators claim the Jewish faith; and there are significantly fewer solons who claim Baptist affiliation among westerners than is generally the case in Congress.

VOTING PATTERNS

Voting by western lawmakers on a number of key issues in the sixties is worth examining.[11] In the 1964 action on Civil Rights, westerners in the House voted 57 to 9 for final passage while the entire House voted 290 to 130 for the bill. When the Senate version was voted on later, westerners supported the bill 58 to 8. In the Senate, when in June 1964 senators voted 71 to 29 for the first time in history to cut off debate in a civil rights filibuster, only six western senators cast "no" votes: Hayden, Goldwater, Bible, Mechem,[12] Bennett, and Simpson. On final passage, only two western senators cast votes against the Civil Rights Act of 1964, Goldwater and Mechem.

On an allied issue, Edward M. Kennedy's (D-Massachusetts) amendment prohibiting the collection of a poll tax as a condition of registration or voting, which the Johnson Administration opposed because of constitutional concerns about congressional and/or state prerogatives in this field, the following twelve western senators cast "no" votes: Hayden, Fannin, Murphy, Allott, Dominick, Jordan, Mansfield, Bible, Anderson, Montoya, Bennett, and Simpson. Most of these were supporters of the Civil Rights Bill in 1964 but either shared the Administration's concern about constitutionality or questioned the political wisdom of overloading the Voting Rights Bill. When the Voting Rights Bill passed the Senate in May of 1965 by a 77 to 19 margin, no western senators voted against the measure.

The controversial proposal by the late President Kennedy in 1962 to create a Department of Urban Affairs resulted in a congressional expression of disapproval which had the legal effect of blocking presidential action. When the House acted, 27 western congressmen voted to support Kennedy's plan and 28 voted for a resolution of disapproval; the resolution passed the House 264 to 150. In the Senate, 15 western senators voted in support of a new department and 11 to disapprove of the plan. Significantly, Democrats Hayden, Anderson, Bible, and Cannon were among the westerners who then disapproved of the proposal, or, perhaps, the way

10. The numerical growth of the LDS Church is indicated by the fact that in the 89th Congress, there are as many legislators from California who claim LDS affiliation as there are from Utah. In the summer of 1965 the First Presidency of the LDS Church came out against the repeal of Section 14b of the Taft-Hartley Act and so wrote all eleven LDS legislators in Congress. Five of these men replied that they could not accept the view of the First Presidency "as binding upon us." Salt Lake *Tribune*, July 13, 1965.

11. *Congressional Quarterly Almanac* or *Weekly Reports* are the bases for these data on voting and their indices for the year or month indicated may be referred to.

12. Defeated by Montoya in the 1964 elections in New Mexico.

it was handled. In 1965 this proposal was approved with strong support by western Democrats in the House and Senate.

In the international area, western lawmakers were predominantly supportive of Democratic administrations' recommendations. For instance, in a 1962 vote to expand the size of the Peace Corps from 920 to 10,000 which the House supported 317 to 70, only nine western congressmen joined the opposition. Seven of these were California Republicans. Regarding the giving in 1962 of congressional authority for the United States to purchase United Nations bonds, which won House approval 257 to 134, "no" votes, in the quantity indicated, came from Arizona (1), California (11), Colorado (1), Montana (1), Nevada (1), Oregon (1), Washington (4), and Wyoming (1). When the same issue was before the Senate in 1962, only three western senators opposed the financial plan: Goldwater, Jordan, and Magnuson.

On the sale of wheat to the Soviet Union, which, in 1963, passed the Senate 52 to 32, six western senators voted in opposition: Goldwater, Fong, Jordan, Mechem, Morse, and Jackson. The Limited Nuclear Test Ban Treaty passed the Senate 80 to 19. "No" votes were cast by Goldwater, Jordan, Mechem, Bennett, and Simpson.

Western regionalism clearly clashed with international considerations in 1964 when efforts were made to impose import quotas on meat. President Johnson opposed these efforts and the Senate, in April of 1964, rejected the quota proposal 46 to 44. Ten of the 26 western senators supported the Administration's stand on the matter, perhaps, in part, because New Zealand and Australia had meanwhile announced voluntary limitations on exports of beef. The limits announced were higher than acceptable to many senators from meat-producing states, however. All of the western votes cast in support of the President were cast by Democrats.

A mild meat import quota bill was passed later in 1964 by Congress. In the Senate, final passage was by a 72 to 15 margin. No western senators cast "no" votes. A drop in the income of U.S. meat producers, although imports reportedly accounted for only 11 percent of the American market, may have altered senatorial sentiment, and even though the Johnson Administration continued its opposition to such quotas, the pressures were less than in April. When the House voted on the milder conference version of this meat import quota bill, 27 western representatives cast votes against the bill out of a total of 149 "no" votes in the House. Twenty-three of these "no" votes were from California. No congressmen from nine of the thirteen western states voted against the bill establishing import quotas.

In 1962 an effort was made to restore the "peril point" procedure which would require the President to explain to Congress if he chose to lower tariffs below the point where the Tariff Commission predicted damage to domestic producers. Former Senator Prescott Bush (R-Connecticut) offered the amendment which failed 38 to 40. Seven western senators supported Bush: Bennett, Bible, Church, Fong, Goldwater, Jordan, and Kuchel. "Peril point" was once a powerful political shibboleth for western senators.

In votes on what might be called "Great Society" legislation, westerners usually followed party lines in both chambers. The Senate vote on the Poverty Bill in the summer of 1964 resulted in a 61 to 34 passage. Opposition votes were cast by Goldwater, Allott, Jordan, Mechem, Bennett, and Simpson.

In the fall of 1964, the Senate voted on Medicare; it passed the Senate easily with the following western senators opposing the bill: Goldwater, Allott, Dominick, Fong, Jordan, Mechem, Bennett, and Simpson.[13] In successful House action early in 1965 only 15 "no" votes were cast by westerners. In July 1965 action on Medicare, following the bill's death in Conference Committee two years earlier, the following senators from the West voted against final passage: Allott, Bennett, Dominick, Fannin, Jordan, Murphy, and Simpson.

A "gut" issue for both parties was the repeal of Section 14(b) of the Taft-Hartley Act—the so-called "right-to-work." The House voted 221 to 203 for repeal in July 1965. The western vote was along party lines with the exception of four Democratic "defectors": Aspinall of Colorado, Edith Green of Oregon, Baring of Nevada, and Morris Udall of Arizona.

Mass transit legislation passed the Senate in 1963 by a 52 to 41 vote. Goldwater, Allott, Fong, Jordan, Mechem, McGee, and Simpson, so far as the Administration was concerned, were in this instance the "abominable no men."

Senate voting in 1963 on Volunteers in Service to America, the domestic Peace Corps, was very close; the bill passed by a scant 47 to 44 margin. In this instance, the western Democrats who actually voted were solid in their support, and thereby gave Johnson a narrow victory. Seven GOP senators from the West voted against the legislation.

In 1963 the bill on federal aid to higher education brought voting opposition in the Senate from only five western Republicans. In 1965 when the Senate approved federal aid to elementary and secondary schools by a vote of 73 to 18, six western Republicans opposed this measure.[14]

In a 1965 summer vote in the House on federal rent subsidies for low income families a motion was made to recommit the bill and delete the subsidies; it failed 202 to 208. Western solons followed party lines with the exception of California's Lionel Van Deerlin, Colorado's Frank E. Evans and Roy H. McVicker, Idaho's Compton I. White, Jr., Nevada's Walter S. Baring, New Mexico's Thomas G. Morris, and Washington's Thomas S. Foley, all Democrats who opposed the rental supplements. When voting is this close on key measures, Democratic "defections" become very significant. Some western Democrats dissent from portions of the "Great Society" legislation. This dissent will probably outcrop from time to time in both House and Senate; inland constituencies, especially, do not always share the "felt need" of other segments of America for certain of these measures. These western reservations, as they were reinforced by the 1966 elections, formed a barometric reading of real significance for the Johnson Administration.

In a significant vote in 1964 to bar the federal courts from any role in the reapportionment of state legislatures which passed the House 218 to 175, western "no" votes were distributed in this manner: Alaska (1), California (21; all but two of these were from populous Los Angeles County), Colorado (1), Hawaii (2), Idaho (1), Montana (1), Oregon (4), and Washington (1). The Senate vote on the Dirksen proposal for a constitutional amendment allowing for factors other than population in apportioning one chamber of state legislatures was 59 to 39. Western solons voting against the proposal were: Inouye, Anderson, Montoya, Morse,

13. Kuchel's frequent departure from his GOP colleagues' stand is probably not only a function of his personal philosophy, but of the different political climate in California.

14. As was suggested in Frank H. Jonas (ed.) *Western Politics* (Salt Lake City, University of Utah Press, 1961), p. 361, the youthful population profile in the West, among other factors, made support for federal aid to education predictable.

Neuberger, Jackson, Magnuson, and Meger. The other eighteen western senators voted with Dirksen.

Western congressmen have been supportive of the controversial House Un-American Activities Committee. In 1963 only 20 House votes were cast against the proposed expenditures for H.U.A.C.; seven of these were western votes, including four California Democrats. In a similar vote in 1965, eight of the 29 dissenting votes came from westerners—seven from California and one from Oregon. This means that roughly 90 percent of western congressmen support H.U.A.C. or at least do not wish to go on record as opposing the funding of that committee.

In the voting on the Communications Satellite Act of 1962 only eleven senators voted against the plan involving private ownership. Four of the eleven dissenters were westerners: E. L. Bartlett (D-Alaska), Morse, Neuberger, and Moss. Significantly, Jackson, Warren G. Magnuson (D-Washington), Hayden, and Mansfield supported the successful Administration-backed plan.

One sample vote in the annual game of poker the Senate plays with the House on appropriations for the Department of Interior is adequate. In June 1962 Dirksen and other senators made an effort to cut appropriations for Interior back to the level previously approved by the House; about $54 million was at issue. The Senate rejected this effort by a vote of 60 to 26. Only three western senators, including Goldwater, supported the effort to cut.

A controversial proposal of long standing has been the Burns Creek project in Idaho. The public-versus-private-power issue was clearly drawn in this instance. In House voting in 1962 to recommit the bill containing Burns Creek with instructions to delete this particular project, "no" votes were cast by 25 western representatives, "yes" votes by 18. The California congressional delegation's vote on this issue was strictly down party lines.

Voting on the Bennett amendment in 1964 to extend foreign sugar quotas and to increase domestic quotas slightly for the same period resulted in Senate approval. Only four western senators opposed the amendment and two of these were from Hawaii, since only mainland cane sugar was included in the quota increase. The other two negative votes were by Bartlett of Alaska and Anderson.

The Dominick amendment in 1963 to permit present mining and leasing laws to continue in connection with wilderness legislation was opposed by nine western senators: Engle, Kuchel, Daniel K. Inouye (D-Hawaii), Church, Morse, Neuberger, Moss, Jackson, and McGee. On the repeal of the Silver Purchase Act in 1963 many of these same senators voted "yes"; noteworthy was Church's vote against repeal in view of his state's important silver mines.

Western congressmen voted against repeal by a three-to-two margin in the House vote. The recurring battle over this Act used to be a more simple fight between silver users and silver producers, but as noted later in the chapter, the issue is much more complex now.

The extension of the Mexican farm labor program was rejected by the House, 174 to 158; 34 western congressmen voted for extension and 25 against. Area and cultural interests are visible in such a vote; both of Hawaii's representatives voted "no" on extension as did Alaska's lone representative. Californians voted 19 to 13 for extension.

Wilderness legislation which has had rough going previously in the Senate passed in 1963 in the form of the National Wilderness Preservation System by a 73 to 12 vote after several critical amendments had failed. On the final passage only four westerners voted "no": Hayden, Goldwater, Dominick, and Jordan.

FEDERAL GRANTS

One of the best indices to regionalism is the pattern formed by federal grants to states. According to the *Congressional Quarterly*, in 1963 twelve of thirteen western states received federal grants from various programs in excess of revenue paid to the federal government—a benefit-to-burden formula; only California fell below the break-even point and thus gave more than it received. Thirty-four of fifty states received more from the federal government than they paid, while western states finished impressively high in the benefit-to-burden rankings: Alaska was first, Wyoming second, Montana sixth, New Mexico eighth, Idaho ninth, and Utah twelfth.

In this same 1963 survey, western states received the largest and next largest dollar amounts for grants involving these programs: Alaska, highways and education; Arizona, highways and public assistance;[15] California, public assistance and highways; Colorado, public assistance and highways; Hawaii, education and national guard; Idaho, highways and public assistance; Montana, highways and agricultural conservation; Nevada, highways and education; New Mexico, highways and public assistance; Oregon, highways and conservation practices; Utah, highways and public assistance; Washington, highways and public assistance; and Wyoming, highways and conservation practices. It is noteworthy that in all but one western state, Hawaii, federal grants for highways programs are a major source of federal aid; the distances in the West make this understandable. It was the Hayden-Cartwright Act of 1934 that was the forerunner of massive federal aid for highways. Hayden maintains simply that "owing to the area or distances between centers of population, the West was in greater need for quicker ways of transportation of persons and things than any other part of the nation. . . ."

As federal grant programs increase, the establishing of distribution formulas will become more crucial; these formulas are usually the result of the interaction of legislators and executive officials. The formulas may or may not reflect regionalism, and the formulas may benefit a region but not meet the peculiar needs of a state. For instance, in Utah the per-taxpayer effort made for revenue devoted to education is among the highest in the nation, but this effort is offset by a high birthrate, the paucity of parochial schools, and persistence in staying in school longer, which result in a low per-pupil outcome in state expenditures. Thus the federal allocations under any formula which relies, in part, on per-pupil expenditures will produce results which do not reward Utah's per-taxpayer effort. This is not to quarrel with the formula but to note the complexity of allocation problems and their uneven outcome. Federal funds as a share of current expenditures in elementary and secondary schools find the South as the chief beneficiary. See map No. 1. Obviously, maps drawn to reflect other federal programs would see western states as swollen rather than shrunken in relation to other regions.

With the major share of the national budget going to defense purposes it is to be expected that the western states would receive substantial monies through military prime contracts. According to the *Congressional Quarterly*, the thirteen western states in fiscal 1961 received prime contracts amounting to over $7 billion; this was about one-third of the national total of $22 billion. Of the West's share, the eight Mountain states received $1.2 billion, the three Pacific Coast states, $5.9 billion and Hawaii-Alaska, $119 million. Actually, California in fiscal

---

15. Public assistance grants involve old age benefits, dependent children allowances, disability allowances, aid for the blind, etc.

THE STATES AS THEY REFLECT THE FEDERAL SHARE OF
CURRENT EXPENDITURES IN ELEMENTARY AND SECONDARY SCHOOLS

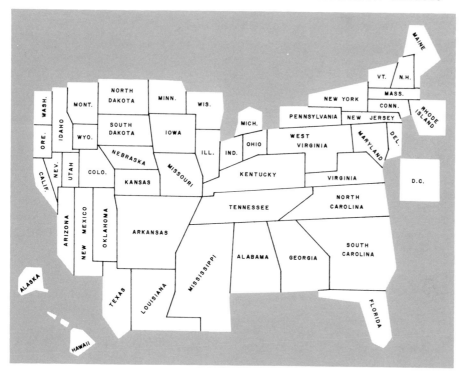

1961 received military prime contracts totaling $5.2 billion, 24 percent of the entire national total. In fiscal 1964, the western states again received contracts from the military amounting to over $7 billion with similar ratios in the region; California accounted for $5.1 billion of the prime contracts, 21 percent of the national total. Washington and Colorado finished second and third among western states but were very far behind California.[16] The pattern of distribution for sub-contracts is crucial, however. Utah, for instance, gets most of its federal money from military contracts on a sub-contract basis.

PUBLIC LANDS

As a "have not" region, both in political self-concept and by objective measurements, westerners justify extra federal funds, in part, by citing the unusually high portion of land owned by the federal government in all of the western states. The percent of land owned by the federal government in the thirteen western states is as follows:

Alaska	99.8%	Hawaii	5.6	Oregon	51.8
Arizona	44.7	Idaho	64.6	Utah	68.3
California	44.5	Montana	29.6	Washington	29.4
Colorado	35.9	Nevada	85.4	Wyoming	48.2
		New Mexico	34.9		

16. *CQWR*, October 2, 1964, 2320.

This involves federal ownership of more than 726 million acres of western land! Admittedly much of it is desert, but it is, nevertheless, the equivalent of the entire combined acreage of Alabama, Arkansas, Florida, Georgia, Illinois, Iowa, Kansas, Michigan, Minnesota, Nebraska, New York, Ohio, Pennsylvania, Texas, Virginia, West Virginia, and Wisconsin! Omitting Alaska, the amount of land owned by the federal government in the western states still equals all the combined acreage in the states of Florida, Illinois, Iowa, Kansas, Michigan, Nebraska, New York, Ohio, Pennsylvania, and Louisiana. It is obvious that how and for what purposes these federal lands are managed is a major political concern to western solons.[17]

WATER

Water continues to be the *leitmotiv* of western politics, and with the population explosion the rest of America is beginning to feel concern regarding the adequacy of the water supply for culinary and industrial use; estimates range from indications that all available water will be in use somewhere by 1975 to 2,000 A.D.

In the West, this concern with water is historical. The regionalism of the West in Congress clearly reflects a preoccupation with water in terms of placement on committees, speeches given, bills introduced, etc. Even western penetration of presidential cabinets reflects to some extent the crucial role of water in the West.

In a June 1965 meeting, western governors formed the Western States Water Council as an important effort to work cooperatively on a regional program embracing all western rivers and water sources. Cooperation in the western states has often been achieved within a basin or area such as the northwest or the Upper Colorado Basin, but now development needs require regional cooperation, especially if arid western states seek trans-basin diversion programs which depend on wet western states or if area trade-offs of water rights are to depend on the success of de-salinization programs. To be sure, the role of the federal government will be crucial, and the less populous western states are understandably concerned that decisions affecting water in the West are now allowed to turn solely on the mercurial presidential politics which would naturally favor California. The new Council gives each state one vote and the same annual assessment. The Council may prove a boon to large-scale water development or it could become a symbol of the futility of trying to plan cooperatively and creatively on a regional basis around such a critical resource as water.

Western memories include the fact that water has sold for a dollar a barrel at a time when the same amount of oil brought only ten cents. With such long memories westerners know that quarreling over the water in the Colorado River is not a final answer, since demands for water are so large. International cooperation will be required, involving Canada, Mexico, and the United States. One proposal, the North American Water Alliance, envisions a $100 billion, forty-year program of diversion from the northwest portion of the continent through Canada, the United States, and Mexico; this would be history's largest reclamation pro-

17. Oil shale reserves in Colorado, Utah, and Wyoming are estimated to contain 2.6 trillion tons of recoverable oil. The total known or proved reserves of crude petroleum in 1963 was 31 billion barrels. Three-fourths of this shale is under federal land. How it should be developed—private enterprise versus public means—will be a major political decision in this decade.

ject.[18] Other benefits of such a vast program as N.A.W.P.A. would include the restoration of the Great Lakes to their normal level, the generation of 70 million kilowatts of new power, one-third the present generating capacity of the United States, and 110 million acre-feet of water annually. Regardless of the viability of this proposal, western senators on the Interior Committee are busy exploring all possible long-range sources of water for the thirsty West.

The allocation of appropriations for reclamation for fiscal years 1958-65 is a clear indication of how much of an investment—political and economic—western states have in the Bureau of Reclamation as it works with water management problems. See Table I. This tabulation reflects not only where the rivers are, but also where the solons sit and their relevant rank on committees. The number of "shared" projects which involve more than one state is also shown, a reflection of the degree of senatorial reciprocity required. Even non-arid Hawaii received over $4 million during this eight-year period. California received allocations of well over one-half billion dollars for projects wholly within California. One can

TABLE I
ALLOCATION OF RECLAMATION APPROPRIATION ACTS
1958 - 1965

State	Amount	State	Amount
Alaska		**Nevada**	
wholly	$ 6,192,839	wholly	1,171,526
		partly	62,843,164
Arizona			
wholly	82,961,290	**New Mexico**	
partly◊	319,759,650	wholly	30,103,290
		partly	69,841,823
California			
wholly	527,275,010	**Oregon**	
partly	75,306,492	wholly	48,269,583
		partly	6,749,751
Colorado			
wholly	148,901,858	**Utah**	
partly	67,087,526	wholly	97,706,240
		partly	93,098,620
Hawaii			
wholly□	4,505,100	**Washington**	
		wholly	122,142,010
Idaho		partly	1,473,570
wholly	9,298,847		
partly	25,104,431	**Wyoming**	
		wholly	72,656,203
Montana		partly	61,754,552
wholly	69,561,019		
partly	81,814,923		

◊Amounts "partly" within a state are duplicated for each participating state.
□1963 and 1964.

18. According to Frank C. Porter, Washington *Post* writer, Salt Lake *Tribune*, March 21, 1965.

see why western senators play the annual "poker game" with the House over the level of Department of Interior appropriations. The chart also indicates that Arizona received allocations of over $400 million for the same period for projects wholly or partly within Arizona—an allocation that reflects not only how arid Arizona is, but the Hayden factor.[19] The Reclamation Act of 1902 began to be "westernized" first with the construction of the Salt River Project in Arizona. Aspinall's state finishes third in terms of expenditure benefits flowing from reclamation allocations. The *Denver Post* on October 4, 1964, called for Aspinall's re-election in 1964, noting his key chairmanship of the House Interior Committee and how ". . . a man's state and his region profit . . ." when he achieves such an important position.

RECREATION AND CONSERVATION

Using appropriations for recreation and conservation programs as indices of regional outcome during the period 1958 through 1964, the thirteen western states, according to the Legislative Reference Service, have received in excess of two and one-half times as much federal money as the eleven southern states. Granting the West is a larger area with much public land and less past development and hence might naturally receive more money, it is still obvious where western solons have been spending some of their time and their realization that the West will probably become America's playground, in a leisure-bent culture; tourism, unlike mining, is an apparently inexhaustible economic resource.

Using appropriations of the Department of Agriculture and Interior, the Army Corps of Engineers, and the Tennessee Valley Authority, western states received over $7.1 billion for recreation and conservation from 1958 through 1964. The eleven southern states, during the same period, received $2.7 billion.

It is highly significant that allocations to western states for conservation and recreation exceeded those to the same states for reclamation purposes, even though the latter covered an additional year's allocations. Both California and Oregon exceeded by three times the most benefited southern state, Kentucky, in terms of federal appropriations for conservation and recreation programs. Oregon has also received much federal money over the years for flood control.

Noting the concern of western solons in regard to the development of natural resources,[20] it is significant that federal expenditures in all states for this purpose as a percentage of the national budget have risen from 2.3 percent in 1955 to 3.0 percent in 1965, which represents in raw dollars an increase of over $1.5 billion. Of the total anticipated expenditure in 1965 for development of natural resources, $3 billion, a significant share, will be expended in western states. Natural resources as used here include expenditures for agricultural land and water resources, forest resources, mineral resources, fish and wildlife resources, recreational resources, and general resource surveys and administration. These are obviously core programs for western states. The most significant increase from 1955 through 1965 by category is recreation where expenditures rose about four times.

19. The current dispute between Arizona and upper Basin states over the starting of the Central Arizona Project relates to concern over the adequacy of water in the Colorado. Arizonans have felt the need to get the project underway while Hayden's help is available lest it never be brought to fruition.

20. Senator Moss has advocated replacing the Department of the Interior with a new Department of Natural Resources which would combine a number of programs which are now somewhat dispersed through the executive structure.

Expenditures for forest resources nearly tripled during the same period. Allocations for land and water resources are by far the most significant items, dollar-wise: $1.8 billion in 1965 alone.

SILVER

Silver, like water, is somewhat symbolic of the American West. What is happening to silver currently deserves at least cursory mention, though the issues involved are both very simple and complex. There is a production shortage of silver; in 1964 only three ounces were produced in the free world for every four ounces used. This is a result of growing industrial demands, of an American society with a striking dependence on vending machines, and, incidentally, but curiously, the growing number of coin collectors, and hoarders, etc. The federal government's depression-designed program of silver purchasing has been a rigid factor in stabilizing silver prices, but under pressures of the market-place, etc., the Silver Purchase program was repealed in 1963. Since then the shortage of silver has driven prices up and required the government to change its policy on silver content in coins. The vending machine industry feared the money it would spend in adjusting machines to accept non-silver coins, but the government feared high prices that might tempt people to melt down silver coins if prices continue to rise.

Most western senators and congressmen from states with silver mines resisted the removal of silver content from dimes and quarters and the reduction of silver content in half-dollars from 90 percent to 40 percent. Senator Moss's amendment to retain 40 percent silver content in dimes and quarters was offered in July 1965, and failed by 34 to 57. Only two western senators voted against the amendment: Bennett and Fong. Bennett was helping to steer the Administration's bill along which retained 40 percent silver in half-dollars, the West's "half-a-loaf." Events appear to have vindicated Bennett's position on this issue. The House Banking and Currency Committee's proposal sought complete elimination of silver from all coins, but the House concurred in the Senate version. Meanwhile, some silver mines in the West may reopen, but often silver mines are a part of a mining complex; other metals would need to become profitable as well as silver if many mines were to be opened. The shortage of silver might have to double to open many mines. Idaho, Utah, Montana, and Arizona have supplied 85 percent of America's output of silver; Idaho leads in production by a wide margin and two-thirds of its silver mines are quite "pure." In any event, there have been enough prophecies of various kinds in the Senate to insure a continued congressional dialogue on this matter in which westerners can be expected to take a lively part.

The relative importance of various minerals within each state may be seen from Table II. The over-all economic significance of mining in western states varies as does the order of value of the minerals produced. The western states, in 1954, produced minerals valued at amounts shown in the table with minerals ranked according to the dollar value of production.

SPEECHES AND SPONSORSHIP OF LEGISLATION

Political preoccupations can also be a reflection of regionalism. One of the devices that may be used with some validity as an index to regional and other factors that influence the activities in the United States Senate of western senators is to note the subject matter of the bills they introduce and the topics of their speeches or remarks on the floor of the Senate. Usually, senators are moved to floor action—other than voting—only when they feel they have good reason, personal or political, to become involved.

TABLE II
VALUE OF MINERALS PRODUCED
IN WESTERN STATES IN 1954

State	Value in Million $	Minerals
Arizona	$ 252	copper, cement, zinc
California	1,400	petroleum, natural-gas liquids, natural gas
Colorado	256	petroleum, molybdenum, coal
Idaho	69	lead, silver, zinc
Montana	126	copper, petroleum, zinc
Nevada	89	copper, tungsten, manganese ore
New Mexico	373	petroleum, potassium salts, copper
Oregon	32	sand-gravel, stone, cement
Utah	255	copper, coal, iron ore
Washington	53	cement, sand-gravel, stone
Wyoming	281	petroleum, coal, clays

For the purpose of this survey, ten senators were selected who were serving during the period 1957-59 and who now serve in the Senate. The *Congressional Record* index was used as a guide to the subjects concerning which these men introduced bills and made remarks. Five periods of time were selected: the entire Eighty-fifth Congress, First Session (January 3, 1957, to August 30, 1957); the entire Eighty-fifth Congress, Second Session (January 7, 1958, to August 24, 1958); the Eighty-sixth Congress from January 7, 1959, to January 23, 1959; the Eighty-sixth Congress from March 23, 1959, to April 10, 1959; and the Eighty-sixth Congress from August 3, 1959, to August 14, 1959.

A few caveats are appropriate. First, the introduction of a bill or remarks on the Senate floor may reflect not only regional factors, but a personal legislative hobby of a senator, or a request from important constituents; or, very often, the action is the result of committee assignments—the latter is a major determinant.

The categories used were: *Admission* of new states; *Agriculture; Appropriations; Atomic Energy; Civil Rights; Defense; Fiscal* matters, including taxes, interest rates, inflation, banking, bonds, and national debt; *Fishing and Maritime; Foreign Policy*, including foreign aid and matters related to other countries; *Health, Education and Welfare*, including unemployment problems, social security, pensions, retirement matters, and education; *Housing*, including federal community facilities programs; *Indian Affairs; Justice*, including claims, patents, code revisions and appointment of judges; *Labor* matters, including corruption in unions (then a popular topic); *Miscellaneous*, including activity ranging from serious comments, political barbs, speeches and bills on land conveyances, the need for a "Cowboy Hall of Fame" to a jukebox bill; *Natural Resources*, including all matters dealing with water, reclamation, forests, parks, flood control, mining, minerals, and public power; *Post Office* matters; the *Presidency*, including comments on disability, succession, and the conduct of the President; the *Senate*, including rules, reports, cloture (which might actually reflect a civil rights problem), recognition of visitors to the chamber and housekeeping matters; *Small Business; Tariffs and Imports; Television*, including boosters, etc.; *Transportation*, including airlanes, airport aid, highways, railroads, and freight rates; and finally, *Veterans* affairs.

The direct and peculiar interests of various states cropped out all the way through the index: Bible's interest in tax reductions for cabarets, Magnuson's interest in the eradication of the dogfish shark, Kuchel's concern over sonic blasts from military aircraft, Hayden's interest in a U.S.S. "Arizona" Memorial, and Morse's concern over taxes on logtrucks. Personal legislative hobbies account for involvements, too. Morse's persistence with his "formula" on land conveyances, Mansfield's urging of a Joint Committee on Central Intelligence, Anderson's expressions on nuclear power development, and Bennett's concern over inflation were examples.

Setting aside the Miscellaneous category because of its catch-all nature,[21] the balance of the categories appeared to be reasonably reflective of the interests which occupied the senators. Rank-ordered, without the Miscellaneous category, the first five major interests of each of the senators are shown in Table III. It is noteworthy that with over one-half of the senators Natural Resources was the dominant single category of interest and that it was among the first five categories of interest of every senator. When one considers that many times remarks on Appropriations also actually involved the Natural Resource category, the total involvement of these western senators with this particular regional interest is even more impressive.

REGIONAL ORGANIZATIONS

Three regional organizations have been formed by western solons which are reflective of regionalism: The Conference of Western Senators, the Conference of Western Democrats, and the Western Regional Republican Conference. The first group was formed in 1949,[22] the second in 1959 involving only Democratic senators, and the third in 1965. None of these groups appears to be active regularly. The Conference of Western Senators is probably dead except on paper. Although it met in June 1965 to discuss the Administration's silver coinage bill in the first meeting in several years, the Conference of Western Democrats is moribund.[23]

21. If the Miscellaneous category were included it would have ranked *first* in the lists of Bennett, Bible, Jackson, Kuchel, Magnuson, and Morse. In all cases, it would have been among the first five, a fact which shows the tremendous variety of matters which interest senators or with which they must take time.

22. See Frank H. Jonas (ed.) *Western Politics* (Salt Lake City, University of Utah Press, 1961) for details.

23. Senator Moss notes in a letter to the author dated June 18, 1965, that the two Senate groups "only stir when specific problems arise."

TABLE III
MAJOR INTERESTS OF WESTERN SENATORS

Interest	%◇	Interest	%◇
Allott		**Jackson**	
1. Natural Resources	21.0	1. Natural Resources	17.6
2. Labor	13.3	2. Admission of new states	14.0
3. Agriculture	8.5	3. Defense	10.0
4. Health, Education, Welfare	9.3	4. Appropriations	3.5
5. Civil Rights	8.0	5. Civil Rights	2.7
Anderson		**Kuchel**	
1. Natural Resources	25.0	1. Natural Resources	18.5
2. Atomic Energy	18.6	2. Transportation	11.4
3. Appropriations	7.5	3. Civil Rights	5.9
4. Foreign Policy	7.5	4. Admission of new states	5.0
5. Agriculture	7.4	5. Foreign Policy	4.6
Bennett		**Magnuson**	
1. Fiscal	26.8	1. Fishing and Maritime	22.0
2. Health, Education, Welfare	8.2	2. Appropriations	11.6
3. Housing	7.2	3. Transportation	8.2
4. Natural Resources	7.2	4. Natural Resources	7.2
5. Agriculture	4.0	5. Fiscal	3.4
Bible		**Mansfield**	
1. Natural Resources	25.0	1. Foreign Policy	20.3
2. Appropriations	8.5	2. Natural Resources	12.2
3. Transportation	4.2	3. Appropriations	9.0
4. Fiscal	3.5	4. Senate	7.3
5. Agriculture	3.5	5. Agriculture	4.5
Hayden		**Morse**	
1. Appropriations	66.4	1. Foreign Policy	15.3
2. Agriculture	5.6	2. Natural Resources	13.2
3. Natural Resources	5.0	3. Labor	6.6
4. Senate	3.1	4. Senate	4.9
5. Post Office	1.9	5. Fiscal	4.9

◇Percent of speeches made and of bills introduced dealing primarily with the subject listed.

The House group is active only sporadically; one recent activity of the Western Regional Republican Conference was to challenge Secretary of Labor, W. Willard Wirtz, and President Johnson regarding their authority "to fix wages for agricultural work" as it affected the importation of supplemental farm labor.

It appears that when a party is out of power, such regional groups meet some occasional strategy needs, but generally the existing machinery of the Senate and the House appear adequate most of the time.

THE SOLONS SPEAK

In responding to a survey by the author, western solons made several observations. They indicated that the most important congressional activities or legislation so far as the West was concerned, since 1958, listed in descending order of importance, were: increased water development, the Wilderness Act,[24] the Land and Water Conservation Fund Act,[25] and the establishment of the Land Law Review Commission.[26] Understandably, a Hawaiian senator believed the Hawaii Statehood Act of 1959 was the most important legislation, and Senator Dominick named the Frying-Pan–Arkansas Project Authorization Act, which involves his state. But consistent consensus formed around land and water development.

As to the increase or decrease of influence on the part of western solons, those responding were split. Some saw an increase for the West as a result of sheer numbers, or know-how, or greater political solidarity. Increased appropriations for reclamation and the passage of the Beef Import Quota Bill were cited as examples of increased western legislative leverage. Several other solons, however, saw little basic change in western influence, since influence is tied to seniority which is tied to re-electability in a two-party West.

Regarding the most persistent political or economic problems that must be worked on or resolved in Washington, western solons—by a wide margin—listed most often the problems that are related to water; next came federal land management policies, including the vexing resolution of competing possibilities for use such as mining,[27] grazing, recreation, reclamation, etc.; and third, obtaining federal or private capital to develop the West's resources. Specialized state problems were such as Nevada's legalized gambling and Hawaii's distance from the mainland as it relates to special shipping, transportation problems.

Chief regional rallying points according to the lawmakers were reclamation, resource development, mining, including silver purchase and coinage, and conservation. Recreation appeared to be an increasing tie that binds westerners as it relates to tourism.

These same solons, when asked to look ahead to assess future problems in the West, were nearly unanimous in noting that the future would mirror past concerns, but with perhaps greater attention being given to technological solutions, such as interstate coal slurries and mine-mouth production of electric power, both of which could make it possible for the inland West to become, in the words of Senator McGee, an "energy supplier for the West Coast," and, specifically, for Wyoming to become the "Pennsylvania of the West."[28]

24. The Act, according to Congressman Aspinall, ". . . keeps designated wilderness areas for operation under the mining and mineral leasing laws for a limited period of time, provides for maximum possible multiple use not incompatible with wilderness preservation as well as possible other uses if needed in the national interest. . . ." Aspinall believes the cause of "multiple use" has been more successfully advanced in recent legislation except when national parks were involved and where, Aspinall asserts, it (multiple use) has "never been an acceptable basis" for legislation. Letter to the author dated June 22, 1965.

25. The Act included what has been called a "Parks for America" program featuring user fees which will facilitate the acquisition of additional land for parks. Of a dozen new parks for which land would be sought, five are in western states.

26. The Commission is composed of nineteen members: twelve from House and Senate Interior Committees, and six Presidential appointees from outside the federal government. Aspinall was chosen as chairman. Pennsylvania's Representative Saylor urged the choosing of some easterners on the Commission's twenty-five member advisory committee because easterners ". . . also have a great stake in these western lands." *Deseret News*, July 14, 1965.

27. Though mining has lost some of its political punch, its dollar significance to the West has increased from 1955 to 1963 by over $800 million in terms of annual production in the thirteen western states. In comparing 1955 to 1963, only Nevada showed a decrease and Alaska, Hawaii, and Wyoming more than doubled the dollar-value of mining production.

28. Accompanying a letter to the author dated June 27, 1965.

Significantly, a Hawaiian senator may have looked furthest downstream, not only for his state but all of the West, in noting the possibility of and need for greater trade with Asia. Several believe, with Representative Aspinall, that the West will face its most challenging problems as a consequence of the "westward tilt" of the nation's population weight. The "tilt" is significant. Between 1965 and 1975, population in the thirteen western states will rise an estimated nine million, making the region by far the fastest growing in the United States, though, of course, all western states will not share equally in this growth.

As to the matter of voting with party, western solons responding to the survey said overwhelmingly that westerners voted with their party except on regional issues. In addition to independence of party on regional issues, several noted some independence on matters involving foreign policy.

FOREIGN RELATIONS

It is quite true that such senatorial dialogues and dissent as there have been over Vietnam (until dissent became widespread) have been dominated by or significantly participated in by several western senators. The Vietnam controversy both before and after involvement of American fighting men found Senators Mansfield, Morse, Church, and Gruening warning, with varying kinds of jeremiads, of the dangers of increased American commitment in a war that, according to Gruening, is essentially a "civil war, a war in which we have no business, which could draw into its vortex the major world powers."[29] Gruening, however, supported the Johnson policy of involvement in the Dominican Republic crisis and noted that non-intervention by the United States in Latin affairs could be a reality only when "an adequate collective system of security is available." Gruening also observed that the collective system was geared to traditional aggression and had not been able to cope with the problems of subversion. Gruening, once the managing editor of *The Nation*, defended Johnson against charges of reviving "gunboat diplomacy" on the grounds that Johnson acted not out of economic interest, but to protect American lives and to prevent "a Castro-Communist takeover."

Mansfield, long a thoughtful observer of Latin America and the Far East, though the Senate's majority leader and, therefore, the bearer of special leadership responsibilities in promoting support for the foreign policies of Johnson, has certainly had an impact as he has called attention to long-range factors and consequences with which American foreign policy must deal. For instance, in a 1962 speech, Mansfield noted that both American commercial and cultural contacts with Southeast Asia were limited, and that our security interests in that area "are still limited." Yet he noted that our "minimum involvement" policy apparently was changing and saw as a critical decision the matter of whether or not this change would become a permanent part of American policy which might involve us in a conflict of "indefinite depth and duration, dependent largely on our forces for its prosecution." Mansfield questioned the justification of a policy of deep involvement "on the basis of any enduring interests of the people of the United States in Southeast Asia." Reluctant to have the United States shoulder the "vague responsibility" for the internal evolution of the nations of Southeast Asia, Mansfield noted the American relinquishment in the Philippines of a responsibility "we had no intention of assuming elsewhere." Mansfield has similar reserva-

29. Only two senators voted against the now controversial 1964 Vietnam Resolution which supported the Johnson Administration: Gruening and Morse, both westerners.

tions about U.S. involvement in the Congo, regarding it as "most unfortunate if we were to be drawn into the internecine warfare of the Congolese."

No isolationist, though from a state which years ago gave to the Senate Burton K. Wheeler, Mansfield writes[30] that all Americans lost "the comfort of distance," and this loss has been felt and realized by the citizens of his own state as well as all others.

Senator Church has indicated on a number of occasions his concern with the fact that America has moved in the span of thirty years from "an excess of isolationism" into "an excess of interventionism." Concerns such as those expressed by Church, no doubt, are part of America's effort to focus on its proper world role.

It would be impossible to assess the influence on American foreign policy of men like Mansfield when it is hard even for the Administration to stay abreast of events, let alone influence them greatly. The point, therefore, is not the degree of influence, which may be more than is now realized, but that several westerners are activists in this crucial area, and that as some "moments of truth" were reached in foreign crises the senatorial voices heard were very often those of westerners.

THE EXECUTIVE

Penetration into the executive power structure is another index of regional strength and interests. The West has had little quantitative impact on presidential cabinets. According to the Legislative Reference Service, as of 1966, only nineteen westerners have ever been so honored, and six of the thirteen western states have never provided a member of the cabinet: Alaska, Hawaii, Idaho, Montana, Nevada, and Wyoming.

Yet the pattern that emerges in the few cabinet positions held is highly indicative of regionalism: of the nineteen westerners appointed, seven served as Secretary of the Interior, three served as Secretary of Agriculture. Westerners have filled each of the following cabinet posts twice: Attorney General, Secretary of Commerce, Secretary of the Navy, and Postmaster General. One Secretary of Labor has been a westerner as has one Secretary of War.

Only one westerner is serving in the cabinet in 1968; former Congressman Stewart L. Udall of Arizona, Secretary of the Interior. Of the nineteen westerners in presidential cabinets, California has furnished eight and Colorado four. Only two westerners, Douglas McKay, Secretary of the Interior, and Ezra Taft Benson, Secretary of Agriculture, served in the Eisenhower cabinets. Four from the West served in Truman cabinets: Charles F. Brannan, Oscar L. Chapman, Clinton P. Anderson, now senior senator from New Mexico, and Lewis B. Schwellenbach. Only one westerner served Franklin D. Roosevelt—Utah's George Dern, Secretary of War; this was before World War II. As western population increases, its share of cabinet seats will probably rise, too.

Western representation on federal alphabet agencies has been frequent though probably not more than what would be a fair share. In this century, according to the Legislative Reference Service of the Library of Congress in a sample of ten commissions, sixty westerners have served as commissioners: six on the Atomic Energy Commission, three on the Civil Aeronautics Board, four on the Federal Communications Commission, ten on the Federal Power Commission, four on the Federal Trade Commission, eleven on the Interstate Commerce Com-

30. Letter to the author dated June 17, 1965.

mission, six on the National Labor Relations Board, seven on the Securities and Exchange Commission, five on the Tariff Commission, and four on the U.S. Civil Service Commission. A reflection of the northwest's interest in power and the continuing controversy over private versus public power is the fact that of the thirteen Washingtonians who have served as commissioners, four have served on the Federal Power Commission. Freight rates and the dependency of the West on transportation account for the strong quantitative showing of western membership on the Interstate and Foreign Commerce Commission.

Once again, it has been California that has supplied the most manpower with nineteen commissioners; Washington is next with thirteen; Utah is third with six. Nine westerners were serving on the ten commissions surveyed, but five of these individuals had terms which expired during 1966.

Of course, the subtleties of policy-making often mean that less status-ful federal positions may actually be more important to a state or region. An appointment of an individual like Idahoan John A. Carver, Jr., as Undersecretary of the Interior is very important to the West. With the abundant coal reserves in the Mountain West an appointment like that of Frank C. Memmott as Director of the Bureau of Mines could give westerners an advocate for additional federal support for coal research, which has had neither the attention nor the subsidy given by the federal government to nuclear fuel. It must also be noted, however, that even if an appointee were a militant regional advocate, in some federal agencies there is little role for regionalism to play and such appointments are simply political rewards or an effort to tap the talent of the appointee.

There can be little doubt that an individual legislator is often most impactful as a result of his interaction with an official in an executive department or agency. Thus the chance for a legislator to "team up" with a "sympatico" in the executive makes certain federal appointments of more than passing interest to western legislators.

SUMMARY

In summation, it might be useful to note that legislators have several roles: first, as advocates for their district; second, as national legislators; and, perhaps, third, as suggested by writer David S. Broder, as teachers of their people.[31] As a group, westerners do especially well in the first role and just as well as their colleagues in the other two. Since Congress does not really make its own agenda any more, true congressional creativity is rare; yet, in this respect, western solons often exercise influence of a quasi-creative nature though it is usually related to new proposals for parks, reclamation projects, etc., either in tandem with the executive or in prodding the executive. As a check on irresponsibility in the executive, especially as it might adversely affect their constituents, congressmen do fairly well; the West probably does even better on Capitol Hill in terms of regional requirements.

One particular paradox remains. Men like McGee feel that "large parts of the West have been relatively by-passed by our great postwar boom" and that programs must be developed for those areas; yet California is almost the nation's

31. The first role is one for which congressmen need not apologize. The assumptions of the nation's founders, as reflected in the *Tenth Federalist*, and elsewhere, indicate regionalism was not only expected but counted on to provide the pluralism that could check factions, moderate and reconcile them. Broder's article appeared on page 7455 of the May 8, 1963, *Congressional Record*.

growing tip in more ways than just urbanization and population and, therefore, is apt to feel first and deeply, both politically and economically, developments that only later affect the country. This paradox and other variables suggest there are really *two Wests*: the traditional West and the urbanizing, big-city West. It might also be said that there are two "Californias" which heightens the complexity of the situation.

This paradox and its possible resolution hold the key to much of the West's political future. If western cooperation holds sway in the midst of stress, then California can be a "big brother" on Capitol Hill so far as the less populous western states are concerned. If cooperation ebbs as a consequence of a lack of shared needs, shared philosophy, or good will as between California and inland western states, then California could be—even unintentionally—a regional "bully," both economically and politically, and constitute a threat to its other western "brethren" on Capitol Hill.

It is perhaps this kind of duality in developmental prospects in the West that Senator Richard B. Russell (D-Georgia) notes.[32] Reflecting, to be sure, his hope for some western identification with the South as it seeks to check the influence of populous states as they wear down southern power and prerogatives around race issues, but also his hope for pluralism and legitimate regionalism, Russell hopes ". . . the less populous states of the West will realize that their only means of retaining an effective voice in our federal government is through the maintenance of our constitutional system . . . our scheme of divided government . . . [without which] the smaller states of the West, South, and every other part of the country may as well resign themselves to becoming geographical entities. All power would then be exercised by a monolithic, centralized government in Washington that would be responsive to every whim of the large, urbanized centers of population."

This hope is not likely to be shared by a majority of western solons because of their differing views of federalism, because they represent areas that are too busy becoming "urbanized centers" and/or because they have not generally feared big, centralized government but have, instead, used it to enrich their region.

Yet if the "two Wests" concept is valid and events force a cleavage, the face of the West on Capitol Hill will be twain. If not, inland states will try to see to its logical conclusion the politics of emulation and follow in the economic footsteps of California.

Finally, any analysis of the West in Congress must note that, in general, in recent years there has been a breaking up of congressional "blocs" such as the "farm bloc," the "Southern Bloc," etc. The truly local issue which is "felt" by constituents will still be "felt" by their legislators and acted on, but the "breaking up" does suggest an increasing political homogeneity in which regionalism is reduced to localism. Issues will be increasingly internationalized, nationalized, and decision-making centralized, and then not only will the age of legislative giants be over, but solons will seldom know the "dignity of causality" except within the confines of localism.

32. Letter to the author dated January 25, 1965.

SELECTED BIBLIOGRAPHY

THE WEST

CARTER, HARVEY L. *The Far West in American History.* Washington: Service Center for Teachers of History, 1960.

COOLEY, RICHARD A. *Politics and Conservation.* New York: Harper & Row, 1963.

COTTAM, WALTER P. *Our Renewable Wild Lands — A Challenge.* Salt Lake City: University of Utah Press, 1961.

CRAMPTON, C. GREGORY. *Standing Up Country.* New York: Knopf, 1964.

DONNELLY, THOMAS C. (ed.). *Rocky Mountain Politics.* Albuquerque: University of New Mexico Press, 1940.

FARB, PETER. *Face of North America.* New York: Harper & Row, 1963.

HALPER, HARRIETT J., and I. M. LABOVITZ. *Federal Revenues and Expenditures in the Several States.* Washington: Library of Congress, Legislative Reference Service, July 24, 1968.

HAWGOOD, JOHN A. *America's Western Frontiers.* New York: Knopf, 1967.

HAWKES, H. BOWMAN. *The Paradoxes of the Conservation Movement.* Salt Lake City: Extension Division, University of Utah, 1960.

HIBBARD, BENJAMIN H. *A History of the Public Land Policies.* Madison: University of Wisconsin Press, 1965.

HOLLON, W. EUGENE. *The Great American Desert.* New York: Oxford University Press, 1966.

HOWARD, ROBERT W. *This Is the West.* New York: Rand McNally, 1957.

JENSEN, MERRILL. *Regionalism in America.* Madison: University of Wisconsin Press, 1951, 1965.

JONAS, FRANK H. (ed.). *Bibliography on Western Politics.* Salt Lake City: Institute of Government, University of Utah, December 1958.

————. "The Spirit of Contemporary Politics in the American West," *Western Political Quarterly,* XVIII (September 1965), 5-20.

———— (ed.). *Western Politics.* Salt Lake City: University of Utah Press, 1961.

KRAENZEL, CARL FREDERICK. *The Great Plains in Transition*. Norman: University of Oklahoma Press, 1955.

LANE, EDGAR. "The Western Stance in Congress: Notes Toward a Sectional Theory." Prepared for presentation before the Western Political Science Association, San Diego, March 22, 1963.

MANN, DEAN E. *The Politics of Water in Arizona*. Tucson: University of Arizona Press, 1963.

MARWELL, GERALD. "Party, Region, and the Dimensions of Conflict in the House of Representatives, 1949-1954," *American Political Science Review*, LXI (June 1967), 380-99.

MAUGHAN, JAY (ed.). *The Book of the American West*. New York: Julian Messner, Inc., 1963.

MAXWELL, NEAL A. "The Conference of Western Senators," *Western Political Quarterly*, X (December 1957), 902-10.

————. *Regionalism in the United States Senate: The West*. Institute of Government Research Monograph No. 5, July 1961.

————. "The Sagebrush Senators," *Frontier*, March 1963, pp. 7-9.

MAYHEW, DAVID R. "The Parties and the West," in *Party Loyalty Among Congressmen*. Cambridge: Harvard University Press, 1966.

McBRIDE, CONRAD. "Federal State Relations in the Development of the Water Resources of the Colorado River Basin." Unpublished Ph.D. dissertation, University of California at Los Angeles, 1962.

MORGAN, NEIL. *Westward Tilt: The American West Today*. New York: Random House, 1961.

MOSS, FRANK E. *The Water Crisis*. New York: Praeger, 1967.

New Horizons for Resources Research: Issues and Methodology. Boulder: University of Colorado Press, 1964.

POMEROY, EARL. *In Search of the Golden West*. New York: Knopf, 1957.

————. *The Pacific Slope*. New York: Knopf, 1965.

————. "What Remains of the West," *Utah Historical Quarterly*, 35 (Winter 1967), 37-55.

REINHARDT, RICHARD. *Out West on the Overland Train*. Palo Alto: The American West Publishing Co., 1967.

WEBB, WALTER PRESCOTT. *The Great Plains*. New York: Grosset & Dunlap, 1931.

Western Political Quarterly (published by the Institute of Government, University of Utah, Salt Lake City, Utah). See especially:

"The 1948 Elections in the Eleven Western States," II (March 1949), 89-90. Boyd A. Martin and Jack E. Holmes.

"The 1950 Elections in the West," IV (March 1951), 67-96. Joseph P. Harris.

"Western Politics and the 1952 Elections," VI (March 1953), 93-110. Hugh A. Bone.

"The 1954 Elections in the Eleven Western States," VII (December 1954), 589. M. R. Merrill.

"Western Politics and the 1956 Elections," X (March 1957), 80-95. Frank H. Jonas.

"Western Politics and the 1958 Elections," XII (March 1959, Part 2), 241-56. Frank H. Jonas.

"The Political West in 1960," XIV (March 1961, Part 2), 289-99. Totton J. Anderson.

"The 1962 Elections in the West," XVI (June 1963, Part 2), 375-85. Frank H. Jonas.

"The 1964 Elections in the West," XVIII (June 1965, Part 2), 431-38. Ross R. Rice.

"The 1966 Elections in the West," XX (June 1967, Part 2), 517-619. Thomas R. Payne.

ALASKA

"Alaska Builds on Her Constitution," *National Civic Review*, July 1959.

BARTHOLOMEW, P. C. "Constitution of the State of Alaska," *Southwest Social Science Quarterly*, XL (June 1959), 40-53.

BEBOUT, JOHN. "Charter for the Last Frontier," *National Municipal Review,* April 1956.

BROOKS, PAUL. "The Plot to Drown Alaska," *Atlantic Monthly*, 215 (May 1965), 53-59.

Constitutional Studies. Prepared on Behalf of the Alaska Statehood Committee for the Alaska Constitutional Convention by Public Administration Service. 3 vols. Juneau, 1955.

COOLEY, RICHARD A. *Politics and Conservation.* New York: Harper & Row, 1963.

CRAIN, MELVIN. "Governance for Alaska: Some Aspects of Representation." Unpublished Ph.D. dissertation, University of Southern California, 1957.

DAVID, PAUL T., MALCOLM MOSS, and RALPH M. GOLDMAN (eds.). "Alaska," in *Presidential Nominating Politics in 1952: The West.* Baltimore: Johns Hopkins Press, 1954.

DRUCKER, PHILIP. *The Native Brotherhoods: Modern Intertribal Organizations on the Pacific Coast.* Bureau of American Ethnology, Bulletin 100. Washington: Government Printing Office, 1958.

EAKIN, TERRY C. "Who Makes Our Laws: The Alaska Scene." Unpublished manuscript presented to the Alaska Science Conference, Anchorage, Alaska, August 1963.

GRAVES, W. BROOKE. "Establishing Local Government in Alaska." (A statement prepared for and at the request of the Alaska Legislative Council.) Unpublished manuscript, University of Alaska Library, 1960.

GRUENING, ERNEST. *The State of Alaska.* New York: Random House, 1954.

MILLER, ORLANDO. "The Frontier in Alaska and the Matanuska Colony." Unpublished Ph.D. dissertation, Columbia University, 1966.

MOBERG, DONALD W. "The 1958 Election in Alaska," *Western Political Quarterly*, XII (March 1959), 257-65.

National Resources Committee. *Alaska — Its Resources and Development.* Washington: Government Printing Office, 1938.

NICHOLS, JEANNETTE P. *Alaska: A History of Its Administration, Exploitation and Industrial Development During Its First Half Century Under the Rule of the United States.* Cleveland: Clark, 1924.

ORDWAY, SAMUEL H. (Survey Director). *Alaska Program Appraisal.* New York: The Conservation Foundation, 1952.

RAY, CHARLES K. *A Program of Education for Alaska Natives.* College, Alaska: University of Alaska, 1959.

ROGERS, GEORGE W. *Alaska in Transition: The Southeast Region.* Baltimore: Johns Hopkins Press, 1960.

ROGERS, GEORGE W. *The Future of Alaska: Economic Consequences of Statehood.* Baltimore: Johns Hopkins Press, 1962.

ROGERS, GEORGE W., and RICHARD A. COOLEY. *Alaska's Population and Economy: Regional Growth, Development and Future Outlook.* 2 vols. Report to Division of State Planning, Office of the Governor. Juneau, 1962.

SLOTNICK, HERMAN E. "The 1960 Election in Alaska," *Western Political Quarterly*, XIV (March 1961), 300-304.

_____. "The 1962 Election in Alaska," *Western Political Quarterly*, XVI (June 1963), 386-89.

_____. "The 1964 Election in Alaska," *Western Political Quarterly*, XVIII (June 1965, Part 2), 439-42.

_____. "The 1966 Election in Alaska," *Western Political Quarterly*, XX (June 1967, Part 2), 524-28.

SPICER, GEORGE W. *The Constitutional Status and Government of Alaska.* Baltimore: Johns Hopkins Press, 1927.

STONE, KIRK H. "Alaskan Problems and Potentials," *Journal of Geography*, L (May 1951), 177-88.

_____. "Populating Alaska: The United States Phase," *Geographical Review*, XLII (July 1952), 384-404.

SWAP, C. RALPH. "The Capital Relocation Issue in Alaska," *Western Political Quarterly*, XVII (June 1964), 213-34.

ARIZONA

"Arizona Voters Accept Legislative Inequality," *National Civic Review,* January 1963.

BARNEY, DAVID R. "Arizona and Public Utility Control: A Problem in Constitutional Law and Politics." Unpublished Master's thesis, Arizona State University, 1962.

BELL, JACK. *Mr. Conservative: Barry Goldwater.* Garden City: Doubleday, 1962.

BINGHAM, DAVID A. *Arizona's New "Third": A Look at Congressional Reapportionment.* Tucson: Bureau of Business and Public Research, University of Arizona, 1963.

————. *Legislative Apportionment: The Arizona Experience.* Tucson: Bureau of Business and Public Research, University of Arizona, 1962.

FANNIN, PAUL. *The Office of Governor in Arizona.* Tempe: Bureau of Government Research, Arizona State University, 1964.

GOODALL, LEONARD E. "Charter Candidates Win Again in Phoenix," *National Civic Review*, January 1964.

Griffenhagen Report. *General State Organization.* Supplement to the Senate Journal, 19th Arizona Legislature, 1949.

HARRISON, CHARLES B. "The Development of the Arizona Labor Movement." Unpublished Master's thesis, Arizona State College, 1954.

HOROWITZ, WAYNE S. "A Survey of Arizona Occupational Boards and Agencies." Unpublished Master's thesis, Arizona State University, 1963.

JOYNER, CONRAD. "The 1962 Election in Arizona," *Western Political Quarterly*, XVI (June 1963), 390-95.

KELSO, PAUL. "Arizona Legislature Ends Long Controversial Session," *National Civic Review*, June 1964.

KOPKIND, ANDREW. "Modern Times in Phoenix, a City at the Mercy of Its Myths," *New Republic*, November 6, 1965.

"Lost Coattails," *Time*, September 21, 1962.

"Mac v. Mo," *Time*, April 28, 1961.

MANN, DEAN E. *The Politics of Water in Arizona.* Tucson: University of Arizona Press, 1963.

MASON, BRUCE B. *A Guide for Arizona Voters — 1962.* Tempe: Bureau of Government Research, Arizona State University, 1962.

————. *A Model Constitution for Arizona.* Tempe: Bureau of Government Research, Arizona State University, 1962.

————. *Turnover, Tenure, and Occupation in the Arizona Legislature.* Tempe: Bureau of Government Research, Arizona State University, 1962.

MASON, BRUCE B., and HEINZ R. HINK. *Constitutional Government in Arizona.* Tempe: Bureau of Government Research, Arizona State University, 1963 and 1965.

————. *Revision of the Arizona Constitution: A Commentary.* Tempe: Bureau of Government Research, Arizona State University, 1961.

MCDOWELL, EDWIN. *Barry Goldwater: Portrait of an Arizonian.* Chicago: Regnery, 1964.

MEYER, LOUIS S. "Federal Aid and Its Impact on the State of Arizona." Unpublished Master's thesis, Arizona State University, 1962.

————. *Federal Aid to Education — Its Impact on Arizona.* Tempe: Bureau of Government Research, Arizona State University, 1962.

_____. "Federal Grants-in-Aid and States' Rights in Arizona." Unpublished Ph.D. dissertation, University of Arizona, 1964.

MOREY, ROY D. "Politics and Legislation: The Office of Governor in Arizona." Unpublished Ph.D. dissertation, University of Arizona, 1964.

"Phoenix Infrequent," *Economist*, November 3, 1962.

RICE, ROSS R. *Extremist Politics: An Arizona Recall Election.* New Brunswick, New Jersey: The Eagleton Institute, Rutgers, The State University, 1964.

_____. "The 1966 Election in Arizona," *Western Political Quarterly*, XX (June 1967, Part 2), 529-34.

RIGGS, ROBERT E. *Arizona State Personnel Policies.* Tucson: Bureau of Business and Public Research, University of Arizona, 1962.

_____. *The District Five Primary — A Case Study in Practical Politics.* Tucson: Bureau of Business and Public Research, University of Arizona, 1963.

SHADEGG, STEPHEN. *Barry Goldwater: Freedom Is His Flight Plan.* New York: Fleet, 1962.

_____. *How To Win an Election.* New York: Taplinger, 1964.

_____. *What Happened to Goldwater?* New York: Holt, 1965.

SMITH, DEAN, and ROB WOOD. *Barry Goldwater: The Biography of a Conservative.* New York: Avon, 1961.

Tributes to Honorable Carl Hayden, Senator from Arizona. 87th Congress, 2d Session, February 19, 1962. Washington: Government Printing Office, 1962.

"Udalls of Arizona," *New Republic*, February 27, 1961.

VICHULES, LEO D. *Maricopa County Party Leaders.* Tempe: Bureau of Government Research, Arizona State University, 1963.

WHITE, JOHN P. "The 1964 Election in Arizona," *Western Political Quarterly*, XVIII (June 1965), 443-50.

WHITE, JOHN P., and NORMAN C. THOMAS. *Michigan's "80-20" Plan and Its Possible Application to Arizona and Other States.* Tempe: Bureau of Government Research, Arizona State University, 1964.

CALIFORNIA

ALLEN, DON A. (ed.). *Legislative Sourcebook.* Sacramento: State Printing Office, 1965.

ANDERSON, TOTTON J. "Bibliography on California Politics," in Frank H. Jonas (ed.), *Bibliography on Western Politics.* Supplement to *Western Political Quarterly*, XI (December 1958), 23-51. Salt Lake City: Institute of Government, University of Utah.

_____. "The 1956 Election in California," *Western Political Quarterly*, X (March 1957), 102-16.

———. "The 1958 Election in California," *Western Political Quarterly*, XII (March 1959, Part 2), 276-300.

ANDERSON, TOTTON J., and EUGENE C. LEE. "The 1962 Election in California," *Western Political Quarterly*, XVI (June 1963), 396-420.

———. "The 1964 Elections in California," *Western Political Quarterly*, XVIII (June 1965, Part 2), 451-74.

———. "The 1966 Elections in California," *Western Political Quarterly*, XX (June 1967, Part 2), 535-54.

ASHLEY, THOMAS J. (ed.). The Dickenson Series in California Government, 1967-68. A paperback series on the various aspects of state government. Belmont, California: Dickenson Publishing Co., 1968.

BAKER, GORDON E., and BERNARD TEITELBAUM. "An End to Cross-Filing," *National Civic Review*, XLVII (June 1959), 286-91.

———. "The California Senate: Sectional Conflict and *Vox Populi*," in Malcolm E. Jewell (ed.), *The Politics of Reapportionment*. New York: Atherton, 1962.

BARCLAY, THOMAS S. "The 1954 Election in California," *Western Political Quarterly*, VII (December 1954), 597-604.

BEAN, LOUIS H. *Forecasting the California Election*. Washington: Public Affairs Institute, 1958.

BEAN, WALTON. *Boss Ruef's San Francisco*. Berkeley: University of California Press, 1952.

BEEK, JOSEPH A. *The California Legislature*. Sacramento: State Printing Office, 1965.

BOLLENS, JOHN C., and STANLEY SCOTT. *Local Government in California*. Berkeley: University of California Press, 1951.

BRAZIL, BURTON R. "The 1950 Elections in California," *Western Political Quarterly*, IV (March 1951), 67-71.

BUCHANAN, WILLIAM. *Legislative Partisanship: The Deviant Case of California*. Berkeley: University of California Press, 1963.

BUCHANAN, WILLIAM, and Others. "The Legislator as Specialist," *Western Political Quarterly*, XIII (September 1960), 636-52.

BUNZEL, JOHN H., and EUGENE C. LEE. *The California Democratic Delegation of 1960*. Inter-University Case Program Series: Number 67. University, Alabama: University of Alabama Press, 1962.

BURKE, ROBERT E. *Olson's New Deal for California*. Berkeley: University of California Press, 1953.

California, Assembly Interim Committee on Elections and Reapportionment. *Political Party Organizations*. Sacramento: State Printing Office, 1963.

———. *Report*. The final report on the 1961 reapportionment. Sacramento: State Printing Office, 1961.

California, Assembly Committee on Legislative Representation. *Report*. Sacramento: State Printing Office, 1961, 1963.

California, Department of Finance. *California State Government.* Sacramento: State Printing Office, 1958.

California, Economic Development Agency. *California Statistical Abstract.* Sacramento: State Printing Office, 1964.

CARNEY, FRANCIS M. *The Rise of Democratic Clubs in California.* New York: Holt, Rinehart and Winston, 1958.

CHINN, RONALD E. "Democratic Party Politics in California, 1920-1956." Unpublished Ph.D. dissertation, University of California, Berkeley, 1958.

CLAYTON, JAMES L. "Defense Spending: Key to California's Growth," *Western Political Quarterly*, XV (June 1962), 280-93.

CLELAND, ROBERT W., and GLENN S. DUMKE. *From Wilderness to Empire* (rev. ed.). New York: Knopf, 1959.

CLONER, ALEXANDER, and RICHARD W. GABLE. "The California Legislator and the Problem of Compensation," *Western Political Quarterly*, XII (September 1959), 712-26.

COSTANTINI, EDMOND. "Intra-Party Attitude Conflict: Democratic Party Leadership in California," *Western Political Quarterly*, XVI (December 1963), 956-72.

CRESAP, DEAN R. *Party Politics in the Golden State.* Los Angeles: Haynes Foundation, 1954.

CROUCH, WINSTON W. "California's Constitution and Future Government of Metropolitan Areas," *BGR Observer*, July 1960, pp. 1-4. Published by the Bureau of Governmental Research, University of California at Los Angeles.

CROUCH, WINSTON W., and BEATRICE DINERMAN. *Southern California Metropolis.* Berkeley: University of California Press, 1963.

CROUCH, WINSTON W., DEAN E. McHENRY, JOHN C. BOLLENS, and STANLEY SCOTT. *California Government and Politics* (3rd ed.). Englewood Cliffs: Prentice-Hall, 1964.

DVORIN, EUGENE P., and ARTHUR J. MISNER (eds.). *California Politics and Policies.* Palo Alto: Addison-Wesley Publishing Co., 1966.

ENGELBERT, ERNEST A. "Legislative Reorganization in California," *State Government,* XXXVI (Winter 1963), 58-64.

ENGELBERT, ERNEST A., and JOHN G. GUNNELL. *State Constitutional Revision in California.* Los Angeles: Bureau of Governmental Research, University of California, 1961.

EULAU, HEINZ. "Bases of Authority in Legislative Bodies: A Comparative Analysis," *Administrative Science Quarterly,* VIII (December 1962), 309-21.

EULAU, HEINZ, and DAVID KAFF. "Occupational Mobility and Political Career," *Western Political Quarterly*, XV (September 1962), 507-21.

EULAU, HEINZ, J. C. WAHLKE, L. C. FERGUSON, and W. BUCHANAN. "American State Legislators' Role Orientations Toward Pressure Groups," *Journal of Politics*, XXII (May 1960), 203-27.

EULAU, HEINZ, and Others. "Career Perspectives of American State Legislators," in Dwaine Marvick (ed.), *Political Decision-makers*. Glencoe: Free Press, 1961.

————. "The Political Socialization of American State Legislators," *Midwest Journal of Political Science*, III (September 1962), 507-21.

FARRELLY, DAVID, and IVAN HINDERAKER. *The Politics of California: A Book of Readings*. New York: Ronald Press, 1951.

FINDLEY, JAMES C. "Cross-Filing and the Progressive Movement in California Politics," *Western Political Quarterly*, XII (September 1959), 699-711.

GREENFIELD, MARGARET. "New Bases for Legislative Seats," *Public Affairs Report*, I (April 1960), 1-4. Published by the Institute of Governmental Studies, University of California, Berkeley.

GREENFIELD, MARGARET, PAMELA FORD, and DONALD R. EMERY. *Legislative Reapportionment: California in Perspective*. Berkeley: Bureau of Public Administration, University of California, 1959.

Governor's Commission on Metropolitan Area Problems. *Metropolitan California*. Sacramento: State Printing Office, 1961.

HARRIS, JOSEPH P. *California Politics* (3rd ed.). Stanford: Stanford University Press, 1961.

HILL, GLADWIN. *Dancing Bear*. Cleveland: World Book Publishing Co., 1968.

HINDERAKER, IVAN. "The 1952 Elections in California," *Western Political Quarterly*, VI (March 1953), 102-7.

HYINK, BERNARD L. "The California Legislature Looks at the State Constitution," *Western Political Quarterly*, XV (March 1962), 157-69.

HYINK, BERNARD L., SEYOM BROWN, and ERNEST W. THACKER. *Politics and Government in California*. New York: Crowell, 1963.

KELLY, STANLEY, JR. *Professional Public Relations and Political Power*. Baltimore: Johns Hopkins Press, 1956. (Discussion of Whitaker and Baxter, pp. 39-66.)

LANE, EDGAR. *Lobbying and the Law*. Berkeley: University of California Press, 1960.

LAPHAM, LLOYD (compiler). *California Blue Book*. Sacramento: State Printing Office, 1963.

LEE, EUGENE C. (ed.). *The California Governmental Process*. Boston: Little, Brown and Co., 1966.

————. *California Votes: 1928-1960* (with 1962 supplement). Berkeley: Institute of Governmental Studies, University of California, 1963.

————. "Senate Reapportionment — A Problem of Balance," *Public Affairs Report*, I (August 1960), 1-5. Published by the Institute of Governmental Studies, University of California, Berkeley.

————. *The Politics of Nonpartisanship*. Berkeley: University of California Press, 1960.

_____. "The Sixties, the Stork and the Golden State," *Public Affairs Report*, I (February 1960), 1-4. Published by the Institute of Governmental Studies, University of California, Berkeley.

_____. "The Three Arenas of Two-Party Politics: The California Election of 1962," *Public Affairs Report*, IV (February 1963), 1-4. Published by the Institute of Governmental Studies, University of California, Berkeley.

LEE, EUGENE C., and WILLIAM BUCHANAN. "The 1960 Election in California," *Western Political Quarterly*, XIV (March 1961), 309-26.

MAYO, CHARLES G. "The 1961 Mayoralty Election in Los Angeles: The Political Party in a Non-partisan Election." Unpublished Ph.D. dissertation, University of Southern California, 1963.

MORLAN, ROBERT L. *Analysis of the Measures on the California Ballot, November 4, 1958.* Los Angeles: Haynes Foundation, 1958.

MOWRY, GEORGE E. *The California Progressives.* Berkeley: University of California Press, 1951.

OHNIMUS, ARTHUR A. *California State Government: Its Tasks and Organization.* Stanford: The American Assembly and Stanford University, 1956.

_____. *The Legislature of California.* Sacramento: State Printing Office, 1963.

_____ (ed.). *The Legislature of California.* Sacramento, California: State Printing Office, 1966.

PANIER, R. A., PAUL JACOBS, and PHILIP SELZNICK. *Old Age and Political Behavior.* Berkeley: University of California Press, 1959.

PITCHELL, ROBERT J. "Reapportionment as a Control of Voting in California," *Western Political Quarterly*, XII (March 1961), 214-35.

_____. "The Electoral System and Voting Behavior: The Case of California's Cross-Filing," *Western Political Quarterly*, XII (June 1959), 459-84.

_____. "Twentieth Century California Voting Behavior." Unpublished Ph.D. dissertation, University of California, Berkeley, 1955.

POLAND, ORVILLE F. "Public Employment in California," *Public Affairs Report*, IV (December 1963), 1-4. Published by the Institute of Governmental Studies, University of California, Berkeley.

RADABAUGH, J. S. "Tendencies of California Direct Legislation," *Southwestern Social Science Quarterly*, XLII (June 1961), 66-78.

ROSS, IRWIN. "The Supersalesmen of California Politics: Whitaker and Baxter," in Reo M. Christenson and Robert O. McWilliams (eds.), *Voice of the People: Readings in Public Opinion and Propaganda.* New York: McGraw-Hill, 1962.

ROWE, LEONARD C. "Political Campaign Funds in California." Unpublished Ph.D. dissertation, University of California, Berkeley, 1957.

_____. *Preprimary Endorsements in California Politics.* Berkeley: Bureau of Public Administration, University of California, 1961.

ROWE, LEONARD C., and WILLIAM BUCHANAN. "Campaign Funds in California: What the Records Reveal," *California Historical Society Quarterly*, XLI (September 1962), 195-210.

SCOTT, STANLEY (ed.). *Metropolitan Area Problems*. Berkeley: Bureau of Public Administration, University of California, 1960.

TITUS, CHARLES H., and CHARLES R. NIXON. "The 1948 Elections in California," *Western Political Quarterly*, II (March 1949), 97-102.

TURNER, HENRY A., and JOHN A. VIEG. *The Government and Politics of California* (2nd ed.). New York: McGraw-Hill, 1964.

UNRUH, JESSE M. "Scientific Inputs to Legislative Decision Making," *Western Political Quarterly*, XVII (September 1964), 53-60.

VIEG, JOHN A. "A New Design for California Politics," *Western Political Quarterly*, XIII (September 1960), 692-701.

VIEG, JOHN A., and Others. *California Local Finance*. Stanford: Stanford University Press, 1959.

WARSHAW, STEVEN. "California: The Union Shop and the Amendment Game," *Reporter*, XIX (October 30, 1958), 14-16.

WAY, H. FRANK. "California: 'Brutal Butchery of the Two-Party System'?" in Malcolm E. Jewell (ed.), *The Politics of Reapportionment*. New York: Atherton, 1962.

WILSON, JAMES Q. *The Amateur Democrat: Club Politics in Three Cities*. Chicago: University of Chicago Press, 1962.

Specialized libraries containing materials of interest to students of California government and politics:
California State Library, Sacramento
Institute of Government and Public Affairs, University of California, Los Angeles
Library of the Institute of Governmental Studies, University of California, Berkeley.

Journals and magazines regularly publishing articles on California politics:
Frontier, published in Los Angeles
Public Affairs Report, published by the Institute of Governmental Studies, University of California, Berkeley
The Liberal Democrat, published in Berkeley.

COLORADO

BARDWELL, GEORGE E., and HARRY SELIGSON. *Organized Labor and Political Action in Colorado: 1900-1960*. Denver: University of Denver, 1959.

BRIDGE, FRANKLIN N. *Metro Denver: Mile High Government*. Boulder: University of Colorado Publications, 1963.

BROWN, ROY E. "Colorful Colorado: State of Varied Industries," in Thomas C. Donnelly (ed.), *Rocky Mountain Politics*. Albuquerque: University of New Mexico Press, 1940.

Bureau of Business Research. *Manufacturing: Colorado Basic Data Report No. 5.* Boulder: University of Colorado Publications, 1958.

Colorado Legislative Council:
> *Colorado Criminal Code.* Denver, 1962.
> *Colorado Property Assessment Methods.* Denver, 1958.
> *Financing Government in Colorado.* Denver, 1959.
> *Financing Public Schools in Colorado.* Denver, 1964.
> *Index of Laws Relating to State Government.* Denver, 1955.
> *Judicial Administration in Colorado.* Denver, 1960.
> *Legislator's Handbook.* Denver, 1964.
> *Migratory Labor in Colorado.* Denver, 1962.
> *Review of Various Fee-supported Activities in Colorado.* Denver, 1962.
> *Revision of Colorado General Election Laws.* Denver, 1962.
> *Tax Exempt Property in Colorado.* Denver, 1964.
> *Water Problems in Colorado.* Denver, 1964.

Colorado Planning Commission. *Colorado Yearbook, 1959-1961.* Denver, 1962.

_____. *Colorado Yearbook, 1962-1964.* Denver, 1965.

DAVID, PAUL T., MALCOLM MOOS, and RALPH M. GOLDMAN (eds.). *Presidential Nominating Politics in 1952: The West* (Colorado chapter by Curtis Martin). Baltimore: Johns Hopkins Press, 1954.

DUNBAR, LAIRD, and LEO RIETHMAYER. *Administrative Reorganization in Colorado.* Boulder: University of Colorado Publications, 1954.

FRITZ, PERCY S. *Colorado: The Centennial State.* New York: Prentice-Hall, 1941.

GOMEZ, RUDOLPH. "Legislative Voting Behavior in Colorado," *Western Political Quarterly*, XVII (September 1964), 70-72.

_____. *Urban and Rural Voting Behavior in the Colorado General Assembly.* Unpublished Ph.D. dissertation, University of Colorado, 1963.

GOODYKOONTZ, COLIN B. *The Papers of Edward P. Costigan Relating to the Progressive Movement in Colorado, 1902-1917.* Denver: World Press, 1941.

Governor's Local Affairs Study Commission. *Interim Reports on Local Government.* Denver, 1965.

_____. *Metropolitan Problems.* Denver, 1965.

HAFEN, LEROY R. (ed.). *Colorado and Its People.* Denver: Old West, 1948.

HENSEL, DONALD. "A History of the Colorado Constitution in the 19th Century." Unpublished Ph.D. dissertation, University of Colorado, 1957.

HUNTER, E. M. "We Gave 'em Fits in Colorado," *Saturday Evening Post*, January 27, 1951.

IRWIN, WILLIAM P. "Colorado: A Matter of Balance," *The Politics of Reapportionment*, Malcolm E. Jewell (ed.). New York: Atherton Press, 1962.

League of Women Voters of Colorado. *Cooperation or Confusion? Local Government in Colorado.* 2 parts. Denver, April 1960, July 1962.

————. *Representative Government in Colorado.* Denver, September 1961.

————. *This Is Colorado Springs and El Paso County.* Colorado Springs, 1964.

McBRIDE, CONRAD L. "The 1966 Election in Colorado," *Western Political Quarterly,* XX (June 1967, Part 2), 555-62.

McKEAN, DAYTON D. "The 1954 Election in Colorado," *Western Political Quarterly,* VII (December 1954), 604-6.

MARTIN, CURTIS. "Bibliography on Colorado Politics," in Frank H. Jonas (ed.), *Bibliography on Western Politics.* Supplement to *Western Political Quarterly,* XI (December 1958), 51-54. Salt Lake City: Institute of Government, University of Utah.

————. *Colorado Politics.* Denver: Big Mountain Press, 1960.

————. "Political Behavior in Colorado," *Colorado Quarterly,* Summer 1957.

————. "The 1950 Elections in Colorado," *Western Political Quarterly,* IV (March 1951), 72-75.

————. "The 1952 Elections in Colorado," *Western Political Quarterly,* VI (March 1953), 108-10.

————. "The 1956 Election in Colorado," *Western Political Quarterly,* X (March 1957), 117-21.

————. "The 1958 Election in Colorado," *Western Political Quarterly,* XII (March 1959, Part 2), 301-8.

————. "The 1960 Election in Colorado," *Western Political Quarterly,* XIV (March 1961), 327-30.

MARTIN, CURTIS, and RUDOLPH GOMEZ. *Colorado Government and Politics.* Boulder: Pruett Press, 1964.

STUMPF, HARRY P. (ed.). *The Colorado Cattlemen's Association.* A Study Undertaken in Conjunction with the Rocky Mountain Center for Education in Politics. Fort Collins, 1964.

WELTY, RICHARD C. "The Greenback Party in Colorado," *Colorado Magazine,* October 1951.

HAWAII

BLOEDE, V. CARL. *Hawaii Legislative Manual* (2nd ed.). Legislative Reference Bureau Report No. 2, 1962. Honolulu: University of Hawaii Press, 1962.

CHAMBERS, HENRY E. *Constitutional History of Hawaii.* Johns Hopkins University Studies in Historical and Political Science, Fourteenth Series. Baltimore: Johns Hopkins Press, 1896.

CHUTE, CHARLTON F. "The Honolulu Metropolitan Area: A Challenge to Traditional Thinking," *Public Administration Review,* XVIII (Winter 1958), 7.

DAVID, PAUL T., MALCOLM MOOS, and RALPH M. GOLDMAN (eds.). "Hawaii," in *Presidential Nominating Politics in 1952: The West.* Baltimore: Johns Hopkins Press, 1954.

DIGMAN, JOHN M., and DANIEL W. TUTTLE. "Statistical Analysis of Oahu's 1954 General Election," *Proceedings of the Hawaiian Academy of Science,* XXXI (1956).

FUCHS, LAWRENCE H. *Hawaii Pono.* New York: Harcourt, Brace and World, 1961.

GEORGE, WILLIAM H., and PAUL S. BACHMAN. *The Government of Hawaii* (rev. ed.). Honolulu: University of Hawaii Press, 1940.

GRAVES, W. BROOKE. "Centralization of Government in Hawaii," Legislative Reference Service, Library of Congress, 1962.

"Hawaii: Sugar-coated Fort," *Fortune,* XXII (August 1940).

HOBBS, JEAN. *Hawaii: A Pageant of the Soil.* Stanford: Stanford University Press, 1935.

HORWITZ, R., and N. MELLER. *Land and Politics in Hawaii* (3rd rev.). Honolulu: University of Hawaii Press, 1966.

JONES, STEPHEN B. "Geography and Politics in the Hawaiian Islands," *Geographical Review,* XXVIII (April 1938), 193.

KAMINS, ROBERT M. *The Tax System of Hawaii.* Honolulu: University of Hawaii Press, 1952.

KOSAKI, RICHARD. *Home Rule in Hawaii.* Legislative Reference Bureau Report No. 2, 1954. Honolulu: University of Hawaii Press, 1954.

KUYKENDALL, RALPH S. *The Hawaiian Kingdom, 1778-1854.* Honolulu: University of Hawaii Press, 1938.

_____. *The Hawaiian Kingdom, 1854-1874.* Honolulu: University of Hawaii Press, 1953.

KUYKENDALL, RALPH S., and A. GROVE DAY. *Hawaii: A History.* New York: Prentice-Hall, 1948.

LAU, KENNETH K. *Reapportionment of the Territorial Legislature.* Legislative Reference Bureau Report No. 2, 1958. Honolulu: University of Hawaii Press, 1958.

League of Women Voters of Honolulu. *In Honolulu Hale — They Appoint.* Honolulu, 1952.

_____. *In Honolulu Hale — We Elect* (rev. ed.). Honolulu, 1954.

LIND, ANDREW W. *An Island Community.* Chicago: University of Chicago Press, 1938.

_____. "Hawaii at the Polls," *Asia,* XXXVI (October 1936), 643.

_____. "Voting in Hawaii," *Social Process in Hawaii,* I (1935), 2.

MELLER, NORMAN. "Administrative Reorganization in Hawaii," *Western Political Quarterly,* XV (September 1962), 45.

_____. "Centralization in Hawaii: Retrospect and Prospect," *American Political Science Review,* LII (March 1958), 98.

————. "The Legislative Party Profile in Hawaii," *Western Political Quarterly*, XVII (September 1964, supplement), 72.

————. "Missionaries to Hawaii: Shapers of the Islands' Government," *Western Political Quarterly*, XI (December 1958), 788.

MORGAN, THEODORE. *Hawaii, A Century of Economic Change.* Cambridge: Harvard University Press, 1948.

OGURA, SHIKU I. *County Government in Hawaii.* Hilo: Hawaii News Print Shop, 1935.

Plan of Organization (rev. ed.). Honolulu: Management Services Division, State Department of Budget and Finance, 1965.

PORTEUS, STANLEY D. *A Century of Social Thinking in Hawaii.* Palo Alto: Pacific Books, 1962.

ROBERTS, HAROLD S. "Reapportionment and the Revision and Amending Procedures of the Hawaii State Constitution," Program in Political Parties, Department of Political Science, University of Hawaii, 1966.

ROWLAND, DONALD. "Orientals and the Suffrage in Hawaii," *Pacific History Review*, XII (March 1943), 11.

SCHUMAN, FREDRICK L. "Aloha: Racial Relations in the 50th State," *North American Review*, I (Summer 1964), 44.

State and Local Government Relationships in the State of Hawaii. Chicago: Public Administration Service, 1962.

STEVENS, SYLVESTER K. *American Expansion in Hawaii, 1842-1898.* Harrisburg: Archives Publishing Company of Pennsylvania, 1945.

TANSILL, WILLIAM R. *Hawaii and Statehood.* Public Affairs Bulletin No. 63, Legislative Reference Service. Washington: Library of Congress, 1948.

TATE, MERZE. *The United States and the Hawaiian Kingdom.* New Haven: Yale University Press. 1965.

TUTTLE, DANIEL W., JR. (compiler). "The Hawaiian Democratic and Republican Party Platforms, 1952-1964," Program in Political Parties, Department of Political Science, University of Hawaii, 1964.

————. "The 1960 Election in Hawaii," *Western Political Quarterly*, XIV (March 1961), 331-38.

————. "The 1962 Election in Hawaii," *Western Political Quarterly*, XVI (June 1963), 426.

————. "The 1964 Election in Hawaii," *Western Political Quarterly*, XVIII (June 1965), 481.

———— (compiler). "Papers on Hawaiian Politics, 1952-62," Program in Political Parties, Department of Political Science, University of Hawaii, 1964.

————. "A Statistical Anatomy of Hawaii's 1964 General Election Vote Count," Program in Political Parties, Department of Political Science, University of Hawaii, 1965.

U.S. Department of Commerce, Bureau of Census. *Census of Governments, 1962.* VII, No. 11, *Government in Hawaii.* Washington: Government Printing Office, 1964.

U.S. Department of Justice. *Law Enforcement in the Territory of Hawaii.* Senate Doc. No. 78. 72d Cong., 1st sess., 1932.

U.S. Senate. *The Report of the Hawaiian Commission.* Senate Doc. No. 16. 55th Cong., 3d sess., 1898.

"When Coconuts Dropped on the G.O.P." *Reporter,* XIII (December 1, 1955).

YAMAMOTO, GEORGE K. "Political Participation Among the Orientals in Hawaii," *Sociology and Social Research,* XLIII (May-June 1959).

IDAHO

BORNING, BERNARD C., and BOYD A. MARTIN. "Idaho," in *The States in the Pacific Northwest.* Seattle: Regional Sponsoring Committee of the Pacific Northwest Assembly, 1957.

DUNCOMBE, HERBERT SYDNEY. "The 1964 Election in Idaho," *Western Political Quarterly,* XVIII (June 1965), 486-90.

DUNCOMBE, HERBERT SYDNEY, CLINTON E. GRIMES, and ROBERT ROSS HALL. *Idaho Election Statistics 1966.* Moscow: University of Idaho Bureau of Public Affairs Research, 1967.

DUNCOMBE, HERBERT SYDNEY, and BOYD A. MARTIN. "The 1966 Election in Idaho," *Western Political Quarterly,* XX (June 1967), 568-75.

DUNCOMBE, HERBERT SYDNEY, and KATHERINE D. PELL. *Idaho Election Statistics 1960-1964.* Moscow: University of Idaho Bureau of Public Affairs Research, 1966.

HARMSWORTH, HARRY C. *Population Trends in Idaho 1950-1960.* Moscow: University of Idaho Department of Social Sciences, 1964.

LEWIS, WILLIAM O. "The 1962 Election in Idaho," *Western Political Quarterly,* XVI (June 1963), 432-38.

LUJAN, HERMAN D. L. "Voting Behavior in Idaho, 1950-1962: A Study of Party Predisposition at the Precinct Level." Unpublished Ph.D. dissertation, University of Idaho, 1964.

MARTIN, BOYD A. "Idaho: The Sectional State," in Frank H. Jonas (ed.), *Western Politics.* Salt Lake City: University of Utah Press, 1961.

NYBROTEN, NORMAN. *Idaho Statistical Abstract.* Moscow: University of Idaho Bureau of Business and Economic Research, 1966.

RUSCO, ELMER R. *Voting Behavior in Idaho.* Reno: University of Nevada Bureau of Governmental Research, 1966.

ZUBERBUHLER, JUDITH MANVILLE. "The 1966 Campaign and Re-election of U.S. Senator Len B. Jordan: A Case Study." Unpublished Master's thesis, University of Idaho, 1967.

MONTANA

ABBOTT, NEWTON CARL. "Montana: Political Enigma of the Northern Rockies," in Thomas C. Donnelly (ed.), *Rocky Mountain Politics*. Albuquerque: University of New Mexico Press, 1940.

BROWDER, W. GORDON. "The Center of Population in Montana," *Montana Business Review*, February 1959.

BROWDER, W. GORDON, and HAROLD J. HOFLICH. *Population and Income in Montana*. Missoula: Bureau of Business and Economic Research, Montana State University, 1953.

DEFORTH, SHIRLEY JEAN. "The Montana Press and Governor Joseph M. Dixon, 1920-1922." Unpublished Master's thesis, Montana State University, 1959.

Directory Newspapers and Periodicals 1965. Philadelphia: N. W. Ayer & Son, 1965.

Election Laws of the State of Montana 1956 and 1960 Supplement. Helena: Secretary of State, 1956 and 1959.

GLASSCOCK, CARL B. *The War of the Copper Kings*. New York: Grosset & Dunlap, 1935.

HOWARD, JOSEPH K. *Montana: High, Wide and Handsome* (rev. ed.). New Haven: Yale University Press, 1959.

————. "The Decline and Fall of Burton K. Wheeler," *Harper's Magazine*, CXCIV (March 1947), 226-36.

KELLY, JOSEPH P. "Senator Wheeler's 1946 Democratic Primary Loss." Unpublished Master's thesis, Montana State University, 1959.

The Montana Almanac. Missoula: Montana State University Press, 1958.

PAYNE, THOMAS. "Bibliography on Montana Politics," in Frank H. Jonas (ed.), *Bibliography on Western Politics*. Supplement to *Western Political Quarterly*, XI (December 1958), 65-72. Salt Lake City: Institute of Government, University of Utah.

————. "The 1956 Election in Montana," *Western Political Quarterly*, X (March 1957), 127-31.

————. "The 1958 Election in Montana," *Western Political Quarterly*, XII (March 1959), 313-16.

————. "The 1960 Election in Montana," *Western Political Quarterly*, XIV (March 1961), 343-46.

————. "The 1962 Election in Montana," *Western Political Quarterly*, XVI (June 1963), 439-42.

————. "The 1964 Election in Montana," *Western Political Quarterly*, XVIII (June 1965, Part 2), 491-94.

————. "The 1966 Election in Montana," *Western Political Quarterly*, XX (June 1967, Part 2), 576-80.

Public Schools of Montana: A Report to Montana Taxation-Education Com-

mission. Division of Surveys and Field Services, George Peabody College for Teachers, 1958.

RENNE, ROLAND R. *The Government and Administration of Montana.* New York: Crowell, 1958.

RUETTEN, RICHARD F., "Anaconda Journalism: The End of An Era," *Journalism Quarterly*, Winter 1960, pp. 3-12, 104.

Superintendent of Public Instruction, State of Montana. *Biennial Report,* December 1, 1958.

TOOLE, K. ROSS. *History of Montana.* 3 vols. New York: Lewis, 1957.

_____. *Montana: An Uncommon Land.* Norman: University of Oklahoma Press, 1959.

TOOLE, K. ROSS, and J. W. SMURR. *Historical Essays on Montana and the Northwest.* Helena: Western Press, 1957.

U.S. Department of Commerce, Bureau of the Census. *Census of Population: 1960, I, Characteristics of the Population*, Part 28, "Montana." Washington: Government Printing Office, 1963.

_____. *Census of Population: 1960, I, Characteristics of the Population,* Part 1, "United States Summary." Washington: Government Printing Office, 1964.

WALDRON, ELLIS. *Montana Politics Since 1864: An Atlas of Elections.* Missoula: Montana State University Press, 1958.

WHEELER, BURTON K., *Yankee from the West.* Garden City: Doubleday, 1962.

NEVADA

Bureau of Governmental Research. *Nevada Votes: Selected Election Statistics, 1910-1964.* Data Series Report No. 2. Reno: University of Nevada Press, 1965.

_____. *Voter's Handbook.* Reno: University of Nevada Press, 1966, 1968.

BUSHNELL, ELEANORE. *The Nevada Constitution: Origin and Growth.* Reno: University of Nevada Press, 1965; rev. ed., 1968.

_____. "The 1964 Election in Nevada," *Western Political Quarterly*, XVII (June 1965), 495-98.

_____. "The 1966 Election in Nevada," *Western Political Quarterly*, XX (June 1967), 581-85.

DRIGGS, DON W. *The Constitution of the State of Nevada, a Commentary.* Reno: University of Nevada Press, Nevada Studies in History and Political Science, No. 1, 1961.

ELLIOTT, RUSSELL R. *Nevada's Twentieth Century Mining Boom.* Reno: University of Nevada Press, 1966.

_____. *Radical Labor in the Nevada Mining Booms, 1900-1920.* Reno: University of Nevada Press, Nevada Studies in History and Political Science, No. 2, 1961.

ELLIOTT, RUSSELL R., and HELEN J. POULTON. *Writings on Nevada: A Selected Bibliography*. Reno: University of Nevada Press, Nevada Studies in History and Political Science, No. 5, 1963.

FOLKES, JOHN GREGG. *Nevada's Newspapers: A Bibliography*. Reno: University of Nevada Press, Nevada Studies in History and Political Science, No. 6, 1964.

HULSE, JAMES W. *The Nevada Adventure: A History*. Reno: University of Nevada Press, 1965.

JAFFE, ERWIN A., and STANLEY A. PEARL. "The 1962 Election in Nevada," *Western Political Quarterly*, XVI (June 1963), 443-47.

KOONTZ, JOHN (Secretary of State). *Political History of Nevada*. Carson City: State Printer, 1965.

Legislative Counsel Bureau. *A Study of General Fund Revenues of the State of Nevada*, 1966 ("Lybrand Report").

Nevada Highways and Parks. Special Centennial Issue. Carson City: Department of Highways, 1964.

PETERSEN, WILLIAM, and LIONEL S. LEWIS. *Nevada's Changing Population*. Reno: Bureau of Business and Economic Research, University of Nevada, 1963.

POULTON, HELEN J. *Nevada State Agencies: From Territory Through Statehood*. Reno: University of Nevada Press, Bibliographical Series, No. 5, 1964.

RUSCO, ELMER R. *Minority Groups in Nevada*. Reno: Bureau of Governmental Research, University of Nevada, 1966.

————. *Voting Behavior in Nevada*. Reno: University of Nevada Press, 1966.

SHEPPERSON, WILBUR S. *Retreat to Nevada*. Reno: University of Nevada Press, 1966.

ZUBROW, R. A., R. L. DECKER and E. H. PLANK. *Financing State and Local Government in Nevada*. Carson City: Nevada Legislative Counsel Bureau, Report No. 44, 1960.

NEW MEXICO

BLUMENFELD, ARTHUR A. *New Mexico's Population Since 1910*. Business Information Series No. 40. Albuquerque: Bureau of Business Research, University of New Mexico, November 1962.

————. *Some Aspects of Municipal Finance in New Mexico*. Albuquerque: Bureau of Business Research, University of New Mexico, 1959.

BOROFF, DAVID. "A New Yorker's Report on New Mexico," *Harper's*, CCXXX (February 1965), 72-78.

CLINE, DOROTHY I. "New Mexico Makes Changes in Pre-primary Convention Law," *National Municipal Review*, XL (September 1951), 423.

————. "New Mexico Retains Primary," *National Municipal Review*, XXXIX (May 1950), 233-36.

————. *Proposed Constitutional Amendments in New Mexico — 1964.* Albuquerque: Division of Government Research, University of New Mexico, 1964.

CLINE, DOROTHY I., and JOEL V. BARRETT. "Concepts and Planning in the Use and Conservation of Natural Resources," *New Mexico Business*, XVII (December 1964), 1-10.

CLINE, DOROTHY I., and T. PHILLIP WOLF. "Albuquerque: The End of a Reform Era," in Leonard Goodall (ed.), *Urban Politics in the Southwest.* Tempe: Institute of Public Administration, Arizona State University, 1967.

EDGEL, RALPH L. *Estimates of the 1964 Population of New Mexico Counties.* Business Information Series No. 43. Albuquerque: Bureau of Business Research, University of New Mexico, September 1964.

EDGEL, RALPH L., and ELDON G. MARR. *Estimates of the 1966 Population of New Mexico Counties.* Business Information Series No. 45. Albuquerque: Bureau of Business Research, University of New Mexico, January 1967.

ENARSON, HAROLD L. "Profile of the University of New Mexico," *New Mexico Business*, XVIII (February 1965), 1-13.

FILE, LUCIEN B. "Labor Unions in New Mexico's Nonferrous-Metals Mining Industry," *New Mexico Business*, XVII (October 1964), 1-14.

FOLMAR, RICHARD H. *Legislative Apportionment in New Mexico, 1844-1966.* Santa Fe: New Mexico Legislative Council Service, 1966.

GONZALES, NANCIE L. *The Spanish Americans of New Mexico: A Distinctive Heritage.* Los Angeles: Mexican American Project, Graduate School of Business Administration, University of California, 1967.

HARVEY, JAMES C. *Reapportionment of the New Mexico Legislature, 1910-1966.* Silver City: Publication of the Humanities Department, Western New Mexico University. Vol. 1, Issue 1, 1966.

HILL, A. SPENCER. "The 1964 Elections in New Mexico," *Western Political Quarterly*, XVIII (June 1965, Part 2), 499-501.

HOLMES, JACK E. "Party, Legislature and Governor in the Politics of New Mexico, 1911-1963." Unpublished Ph.D. dissertation, University of Chicago, 1964.

————. *Politics in New Mexico.* Albuquerque: University of New Mexico Press, 1967.

————. *Science Town in the Politics of New Mexico.* Albuquerque: Division of Government Research, University of New Mexico, 1967.

IRION, FREDERICK C. *Apportionment of the New Mexico Legislature — 1850 to June, 1964.* Mimeographed manuscript by author, 1964.

————. "Bibliography on New Mexico Politics," in Frank H. Jonas (ed.), *Bibliography on Western Politics.* Supplement to *Western Political Quarterly*, XI (December 1958), 77-109. Salt Lake City: Institute of Government, University of Utah.

————. *Reapportionment and Redistricting in New Mexico, October-*

November, 1963. Albuquerque: Division of Government Research, University of New Mexico, 1963.

————. *Selected and Annotated Bibliography on Politics in New Mexico* (4th ed.). Santa Fe: Legislative Council Service, 1959 (mimeographed).

KNOWLTON, CLARK S. "Land-Grant Problems Among the State's Spanish-Americans," *New Mexico Business,* XX (June 1967), 1-13.

LAHART, EDWARD. "The Early Career of Dennis Chavez." Unpublished Master's thesis, University of New Mexico, 1959.

LANDMANN, ROBERT S. *New Mexico State Hospital.* Albuquerque: Division of Government Research, University of New Mexico, 1965.

MANLY, PHILIP T. *District Court Financing in New Mexico.* Santa Fe: State Judicial System Study Committee, 1964.

————. *Private Law Practice by District Attorneys in New Mexico.* Santa Fe: State Judicial System Study Committee, 1962.

————. *Survey of the Judicial System in New Mexico.* Santa Fe: State Judicial System Study Committee, 1965.

"New Mexico: An Appraisal," *New Mexico Quarterly,* XXXVII (Winter 1957-58), entire issue.

New Mexico, Constitutional Revision Commission. *Annual Report.* Santa Fe, 1963-67.

————, County of Santa Fe. *Judges Memorandum* (Civil Action No. 33237), August 27, 1963.

————, Department of Finance and Administration, State Budget Division. *Budget News,* I (August 1965).

————, Director of the Administrative Office of the Courts (Lowell C. Green). *Annual Report, 1964, 1965.* Santa Fe, 1964, 1965.

————, Legislative Council Service. *Biennial Report, 1951-1965.* Santa Fe, 1951-65.

————, Legislative Council Service. *The 1965 Reapportionment Acts.* Santa Fe, 1965.

————, Secretary of State. *New Mexico Bluebook, 1965-66.* Santa Fe, 1965.

————, State Judicial System Study Committee. *The Courts of New Mexico.* Santa Fe, 1961.

————, State Planning Office. *A Design for Development Decisions.* Santa Fe, 1962.

Progress Report: Mexican-American Study Project. Los Angeles: Division of Research, Graduate School of Business Administration, University of California. Nos. 1-10 (January 1965-September 1967).

RICHARDS, ALLAN R. *Some Aspects of Higher Education: Arizona, Colorado, and New Mexico.* Albuquerque: Division of Government Research, University of New Mexico, 1961.

RIDER, DONALD C. *Municipal Development in New Mexico*. Albuquerque: Division of Government Research, University of New Mexico, 1964.

SCOTT, WAYNE E. "Spanish Land-Grant Problems Were Here Before the Anglos," *New Mexico Business*, XX (July 1967), 1-9.

"The State's Economy in 1964," *New Mexico Business*, XVIII (March 1965), entire issue.

U.S. Department of Commerce, Bureau of the Census. *Census of Governments, 1962*, VII, No. 31, *Government of New Mexico*. Washington: Government Printing Office, 1964.

U.S. Governmental Affairs Institute, Commission on Intergovernmental Relations. *A Survey Report on the Impact of Federal Grants-in-Aid on the Structure and Functions of State and Local Government*. Section on "New Mexico" by Dorothy I. Cline and Charles Judah. Washington: Government Printing Office, 1955.

WILEY, TOM. *Public School Education in New Mexico*. Albuquerque: Division of Government Research, University of New Mexico, 1965.

WINTERS, GLENN R. "The New Mexico Judicial Selection Campaign — A Case History," *Journal of the American Judicature Society*, XXXV (April 1952), 166-76.

WOLF, T. PHILLIP. "The 1964 Elections in New Mexico." Paper read at the Southwest Social Science Association Meeting, Dallas, Texas, April 17, 1965.

————. "The 1966 Elections in New Mexico," *Western Political Quarterly*, XX (June 1967, Part 2), 586-92.

————. "Urbanization in New Mexico: With Emphasis on Electoral Patterns," in Clyde J. Wingfield (ed.), *Urbanization in the Southwest: A Symposium*. El Paso: Public Affairs Series, No. 1, University of Texas at El Paso, 1968.

OREGON

BAKER, GORDON E. "Reapportionment by Initiative in Oregon," *Western Political Quarterly*, XIII (June 1960), 508-19.

BALMER, DONALD G. "Intraparty Relations in Oregon," *Western Political Quarterly*, XI (September 1958), 710-11.

————. "The 1962 Election in Oregon," *Western Political Quarterly*, XVI (June 1963), 453-59.

————. "The 1964 Election in Oregon," *Western Political Quarterly*, XVIII (June 1965, Part 2), 502-8.

————. "The 1966 Election in Oregon," *Western Political Quarterly*, XX (June 1967, Part 2), 593-601.

CROSS, T. "1958 Hatfield Campaign in Oregon," *Western Political Quarterly*, XII (June 1959), 568-71.

GOLDSCHMIDT, MAURE. "The 1952 Elections in Oregon," *Western Political Quarterly*, VI (March 1953), 123-26.

HAGGARD, MARKO L. "A Voter Response Study of Selected Democratic Precincts in Multnomah County, General Election, 1958." Portland: Parties and Politics Class, Portland State College, 1960 (mimeographed).

HAGGARD, MARKO L., and K. GERVAIS. "An Explorative Study on the Correlation Between Party Registration and the Vote on the Revenue Measures, Primary Election, 1960 — Multnomah County." Portland: Portland State College Political Research Bureau, 1960 (mimeographed).

SELIGMAN, L. G. "Political Recruitment and Party Structure: A Case Study," *American Political Science Review*, LV (March 1961), 77-86.

————. "Prefatory Study of Leadership Selection in Oregon," *Western Political Quarterly*, XII (March 1959), 153-67.

SELIGMAN, L. G., and MARTHA SWANSON. "Bibliography on Oregon Politics," in Frank H. Jonas (ed.), *Bibliography on Western Politics*. Supplement to *Western Political Quarterly*, XI (December 1958), 110-32. Salt Lake City: Institute of Government, University of Utah.

SWARTHOUT, JOHN M. "The 1954 Election in Oregon," *Western Political Quarterly*, VII (December 1954), 620-25.

————. "The 1956 Election in Oregon," *Western Political Quarterly*, X (March 1957), 142-50.

————. "The 1958 Election in Oregon," *Western Political Quarterly*, XII (March 1959), 328-44.

————. "The 1960 Election in Oregon," *Western Political Quarterly*, XIV (March 1961), 355-64.

SCHUMACHER, WALDO. "The 1948 Election in Oregon," *Western Political Quarterly*, II (March 1949), 121-23.

UTAH

An Economic Study of the Proposed Canyonlands National Park and Related Recreation Resources. Salt Lake City: Bureau of Economic and Business Research, University of Utah, 1962.

ARRINGTON, LEONARD J. *Beet Sugar in the West*. Seattle: University of Washington Press, 1966.

————. *From Wilderness to Empire*. Salt Lake City: Institute of American Studies, University of Utah, 1961.

ARRINGTON, LEONARD J., and GARY B. HANSEN. *The Richest Hole on Earth: A History of the Bingham Copper Mine*. Logan: Utah State University Press, 1963.

ARRINGTON, LEONARD J., and GEORGE JENSEN. *The Defense Industry of Utah*. Logan: Utah State University Press, 1965.

BITTON, DAVIS. "The B. H. Roberts Case of 1898-1900," *Utah Historical Quarterly*, XIV (1957).

BLANCHARD, ROBERT, *et al. Presidential Elections, 1948-1960*. Research Monograph No. 4, pp. 42-52. Salt Lake City: Institute of Government, University of Utah, 1961.

BRADLEY, RULON L. "The Use of Mass Media in the 1960 Election." Unpublished Ph.D. dissertation, University of Utah, 1962.

CLAYTON, JAMES L. "An Unhallowed Gathering: The Impact of Defense Spending on Utah's Population Growth, 1940-1964," *Utah Historical Quarterly*, 34 (Summer 1966), 227-42.

DAVIES, J. KENNETH. "The Mormon Church and the Union Security Issue." Utah Academy of Sciences, Arts and Letters, *Proceedings*, 38 (1960-61), 117-18.

EVANS, JOHN C. *Utah School Crisis, 1963.* Salt Lake City: Utah Education Association, 1963.

GILCHRIST, DONALD B. "An Examination of the Problems of L.D.S. Church Influence in Utah Politics, 1890-1916." Unpublished Master's thesis, University of Utah, 1965.

GORDON, OAKLEY J., et al. *Personnel Management in Utah State Government.* Research Monograph No. 6. Salt Lake City: Institute of Government, University of Utah, 1962.

GROW, STEWART L. "The 1962 Election in Utah," *Western Political Quarterly*, XVI (June 1963), 460-66.

HADDOCK, D. R., et al. *Election Law Reform in Utah.* Salt Lake City: Hinckley Institute of Politics, University of Utah, 1967.

HAINSWORTH, BRAD E. "Reapportionment in Utah, 1954-1965." Unpublished Master's thesis, University of Utah, 1966.

HANSEN, GERALD E. "The Conservative Movement in Utah After World War II." Unpublished Ph.D. dissertation, University of Missouri, 1962.

HANSEN, KLAUS J. *Quest for Empire: The Political Kingdom of God and the Council of Fifty in Mormon History.* East Lansing: Michigan State University Press, 1967.

JACK, RONALD C. "Political Participation in Utah Before the Formation of Political Parties, 1847-1869." Unpublished Master's thesis, University of Utah, 1967.

JONAS, FRANK H. (ed.). *Western Politics.* Salt Lake City: University of Utah Press, 1961.

————. "The Mormon Church and Political Dynamiting in the 1950 Election in Utah." Utah Academy of Sciences, Arts and Letters, *Proceedings*, 40, Part I (1963), 94-110.

————. "The Role and Responsibility of the Teacher in Politics," *Utah Educational Review*, January-February 1964, pp. 94-95.

————. "Teachers as Politicians," *Utah Educational Review*, November-December 1964, pp. 8-9 ff.

————. "The 1964 Election in Utah," *Western Political Quarterly*, XVIII (June 1965), 509-13.

————. *The Story of a Political Hoax.* Salt Lake City: Institute of Government, University of Utah, 1966.

————. "Mormons and Politics," in Charles Press and Oliver P. Williams (eds.), *Democracy in the Fifty States*. Chicago: Rand-McNally & Co., 1966.

————. "The 1952 Elections in Utah." Utah Academy of Sciences, Arts and Letters, *Proceedings*, 45 (1968).

————. "President Lyndon Johnson, the Mormon Church and the 1964 Political Campaign." Utah Academy of Sciences, Arts and Letters, *Proceedings*, 44, Part I (1967), 67-90.

JONES, GARTH N. "Integration of Political Ethos and Local Government Systems: The Utah Experience with Council-Manager Government," *Human Organization*, XXIII (Fall 1964), 210-23.

JULANDER, RODNEY O. "The Composition and Voting Record of the Utah State Legislature, 1957-63," *Western Political Quarterly*, XVII (September 1964, Supplement), 88-90.

LARSEN, KENT SHELDON. "The Life of Thomas Kearns." Unpublished Master's thesis, University of Utah, 1964.

Mineral and Water Resources of Utah. Report of the United States Geological Survey. Washington: Government Printing Office, 1964.

MOSS, FRANK E. *The Water Crisis*. New York: Praeger, 1967.

NELSON, ELROY, and OSMOND L. HARLINE. *Utah's Changing Economic Patterns*. Salt Lake City: University of Utah Press, 1964.

ROBERTS, B. H. *Comprehensive History of the Church of Jesus Christ of Latter-day Saints*. Vols. 5 and 6 (citation Bitton and Cummings), Smoot case, Vol. 6; accommodation at turn of the century, Vols. 5 and 6.

RUSSELL, GEORGE B. *J. Bracken Lee: The Taxpayer's Champion*. New York: Robert Speller and Sons, 1961.

SHIPPS, JAN. "Utah Comes of Age Politically: A Study of the State's Politics in the Early Years of the 20th Century," *Utah Historical Quarterly*, 35 (1967), 91-111.

SNOW, R. J. "The American Party in Utah: A Study of Political Party Struggles During the Early Years of Statehood." Unpublished Master's thesis, University of Utah, 1964.

State and Local Government in Utah. Salt Lake City: Utah Foundation, 1962.

Statistical Review of Government of Utah. Salt Lake City: Utah Foundation, 1968.

State of Utah:
  A Supplemental Report to the Report of the Commission on the Organization of the Executive Branch of the Government. Thirty-sixth Legislature, Salt Lake City, 1966.
  Constitution of the State of Utah, as Amended. Secretary of State, Salt Lake City, 1967.
  Governor Calvin L. Rampton's Conference on Education. Salt Lake City: Office of the Governor, 1965.

Interim Report by Utah's School Study Committee to the Honorable George Dewey Clyde, Governor of the State of Utah, May 1964.

Laws of Utah, 1961, 1963, 1965, 1967. Kaysville, Utah: Inland Printing Co.

Report of the Commission on the Organization of the Executive Branch of the Government. Thirty-sixth Legislature, January 1966.

General Election Laws, State of Utah. Secretary of State, Salt Lake City, 1968.

TURNER, WALLACE. *The Mormon Establishment.* Boston: Houghton-Mifflin, 1966.

Utah: A State-wide Study of School Conditions. National Commission on Professional Rights and Responsibilities of the National Education Association of the United States. Washington, D.C., March 1964.

Utah Almanac. Utah Republican State Central Committee, 1966.

"Utah's Economic Prospects," *Utah Outlook.* Salt Lake City: Walker Bank and Trust Co., January 1968.

WASHINGTON

AVERY, MARY W. *History and Government of the State of Washington.* Seattle: University of Washington Press, 1961.

BECKETT, PAUL L. "Operation Self-Help: Washington State's New Mint System Law," *Public Personnel Review*, January 1963, pp. 52-59.

CALDWELL, WALLACE F. "Campaigning in a Weak Party State: Some Political Campaigns in Washington." Unpublished Master's thesis, University of Washington, 1959.

COLLINS, RICHARD C. "Legislative Apportionment in Washington," *Western Political Quarterly*, XVII (September 1964, Supplement), 137-38.

CROW, JOHN E. "Lawyers and Politics: A Behavioral Analysis." Unpublished Ph.D. dissertation, University of Washington, 1965.

FARMER, DONALD R. "Profile of the Washington Legislature 1959-63," *Western Political Quarterly*, XVII (September 1964, Supplement), 90-91.

FLINT, DAVID P. "The Supreme Court of Washington: A Quantitative Analysis of Judicial Behavior, 1958-1962." Unpublished Master's thesis, Washington State University, 1963.

FRIEDHEIM, ROBERT L. *The Seattle General Strike.* Seattle: University of Washington Press, 1964.

GORTON, SLADE. "New Methods Urged," *National Civic Review*, April 1964, pp. 176-81.

GOTTFRIED, ALEX. "Political Slander in Election Campaigns," *Western Political Quarterly*, XVI (September 1963, Supplement), 19-20.

————. "Political Attitudes and Behavior of a University Faculty," *ibid.*, XIV (September 1965, Supplement), 43-45.

ITTNER, RUTH, and RICHARD A. FEHNEL. *Washington Municipal Data Book.*

Seattle: Bureau of Governmental Research and Services, University of Washington, 1964.

KESSEL, JOHN H. "The Washington Congressional Delegation," *Midwest Journal of Political Science*, VIII (February 1964), 1-21.

_____. "Cognitive Dimensions and Political Activity," *Public Opinion Quarterly*, XXIX (Fall 1965), 377-89.

LEAVEL, WILLARD H. "The Election of Wes Uhlman," in Richard T. Frost (ed.), *Cases in State and Local Government*. Englewood Cliffs: Prentice-Hall, 1961.

MCCURTAIN, MARILYN M. "An Investigation of the Voter's Decision Process and His Political Behavior." Unpublished Ph.D. dissertation, University of Washington, 1965.

MITCHELL, STEPHEN R. *Washington County Officials: A Political Profile*. Pullman: Division of Governmental Studies and Services, Washington State University, 1966.

OGDEN, DANIEL M., JR. "Relations Between Pressure Groups and Political Parties in the State of Washington," *Western Political Quarterly*, XI (September 1958), 711-13.

OGDEN, DANIEL M., JR., and HUGH A. BONE. *Washington Politics*. New York: New York University Press, 1960.

SCHEAR, RILLMOND. "How to Win Friends and Influence Lawmakers," *Seattle Magazine*, March 1965.

SCHULMAN, ROBERT H. "Maggie A-Go-Go," *Seattle Magazine*, July 1965, pp. 36-44.

Secretary of State, Washington. *History of State Initiative and Referendum Measures* (Olympia: 1964 ed.).

SHIPMAN, GEORGE A. "The Columbia River Basin," *Western Political Quarterly*, XV (September 1962, Supplement), 34-36.

_____. "A Projection of Washington's Financial Needs," *Washington Law Review*, XXXIX (January 1965), 976-99.

SIMMONS, ROBERT. "The Washington State Plural Executive: An Initial Effort in Interaction Analysis," *Western Political Quarterly*, XVII (June 1965), 368-81.

VAN ASSELT, KARL A. "The House of Representatives Coalition in the 1963 Washington State Legislature." Unpublished Master's thesis, Washington State University, n.d.

WARREN, ROBERT. "Metropolitan Decision-Making: A Report on the Seattle Area Study," *Western Political Quarterly*, XIV (September 1961, Supplement), 39-41.

WYOMING

BEALL, CHARLES P. "Wyoming: The Equality State," in Frank H. Jonas (ed.), *Western Politics*. Salt Lake City: University of Utah Press, 1961.

————. "The 1962 Elections in Wyoming," *Western Political Quarterly*, XVI (June 1963), 477-82.

CLOUGH, WILSON O. *A History of the University of Wyoming, 1887-1937.* Laramie: Laramie Printing Co., 1937.

DAVID, PAUL T., MALCOLM MOOS, and RALPH M. GOODMAN (eds.). *Presidential Nominating Politics in 1952.* Baltimore: Johns Hopkins Press, 1954.

Democratic Spokesman. Democratic State Central Committee of Wyoming, 1964, 1965, 1966.

Directory, Newspapers and Periodicals. Philadelphia: N. W. Ayer and Sons, 1965.

DONNELLY, THOMAS C. (ed.). *Rocky Mountain Politics.* Albuquerque: University of New Mexico Press, 1940.

DOWNING, CHARLES O. *Wyoming Legislative Procedure and Other Facts About Wyoming Government.* Torrington, Wyoming: Telegram Press, 1924.

DUKE, WILLIAM E., and Others. "A Study and Comparison of the Political Participation of the Spanish American in Laramie, Wyoming." Unpublished paper, 1965.

GARST, DORIS S. *The Story of Wyoming and Its Constitution and Government.* Douglas, Wyoming: Douglas Enterprise Co., 1938.

GRIFFENHAGEN AND ASSOCIATES. *State of Wyoming, Report Made to the Special Legislative Committee on Organization and Revenue.* Vol. 1, Cheyenne: Wyoming Labor Journal Printers and Binders, 1933; Vol. 2, Casper: Prairie Publishing Co., 1933.

GUNTHER, JOHN. *Inside U.S.A.* New York: Harper, 1947.

HENDERSON, HARRY B., SR. "Governors of the State of Wyoming," *Annals of Wyoming*, Vol. 12, No. 1 (January 1940).

HINCKLEY, JOHN T. "The 1952 Election in Wyoming," *Western Political Quarterly*, VI (March 1953), 135-38.

————. "The 1964 Elections in Wyoming," *Western Political Quarterly*, XVIII (June 1965, Part 2), 523-26.

JONES, MRS. RAYMOND R. *Look at Wyoming Government, 1958.* Laramie: League of Women Voters of Wyoming, 1958.

LARSON, T. ALFRED. *Wyoming's War Years, 1941-1945.* Laramie: University of Wyoming Press, 1954.

————. *History of Wyoming.* Lincoln: University of Nebraska Press, 1965.

McGOWEN, JOHN D. *The Development of Political Institutions on the Public Domain.* Laramie: University of Wyoming Press, 1947.

PETERSON, HENRY J. *The Constitutional Convention of Wyoming.* Laramie: University of Wyoming Press, 1940.

RICHARD, JOHN B. *Government and Politics of Wyoming.* Dubuque, Iowa: William C. Brown Co., 1966.

Session Laws of Wyoming, 1947, 1949, 1959, 1963, 1965.

SHANAHAN, JOHN R. *The State Highway Department of Wyoming.* Cheyenne: Pioneer Printing Co., 1950.

SHIER, MAURICE S. "A Comparative Analysis of the Political Participation and Political Attitudes of Members of Minority Groups in Two Wyoming Cities." Unpublished Master's thesis, University of Wyoming, 1964.

SOHER, HUBERT J. *Wyoming: Its Economy, Its Future, Its Resources.* Portland: Pacific Power and Light Co., 1961.

State of Wyoming. *Governor Hansen's Message to the 38th Legislative Assembly*, 1965.

————. *Biennial Report of the State Auditor*, June 1964.

————. *Summary of Recommendations*, Governor's Committee on Education, September 1964.

————. *Executive Budget*, 1965-67.

THOMPSON, JOHN T., and ROBERT J. FAIR. "Patterns of Wyoming State Finance: A Comparative View," *Wyoming Trade Winds*, No. 37 (June 1965).

TRACHSEL, HERMAN H. "The 1954 Election in Wyoming," *Western Political Quarterly*, VII (December 1954), 632.

————. "1956 Election in Wyoming," *Western Political Quarterly*, X (March 1957), 166.

————. "The 1958 Election in Wyoming," *Western Political Quarterly*, XII (March 1959), 363.

————. "The 1960 Election in Wyoming," *Western Political Quarterly*, XIV (March 1961), 383.

TRACHSEL, HERMAN H., and RALPH M. WADE. *The Government and Administration of Wyoming.* New York: Crowell, 1953.

TUTTLE, DANIEL W., JR. "The 1948 Election in Wyoming," *Western Political Quarterly*, II (March 1949).

————. "Legislative Personnel in Wyoming, 1949," *University of Wyoming Publications*, Vol. 15, No. 6 (1949).

U.S. Department of Commerce, Bureau of Census. *Statistical Abstract of the United States*, II, "U.S. Census of Agriculture." Washington: Government Printing Office, 1959.

————. *Compendium of State Government Finances*, 1963.

————. *1963 Census of Business, Retail Trade in Wyoming; Wholesale Trade in Wyoming*, 1963.

————. *1960 Census of Population*, I, Part 52.

————. *Current Population Reports*, "Population Estimates, Series P-25," August 27, 1965.

————. *1960 Census of Population* I, Part 1, "Characteristics of Population."

————. *Estimate of Potential Vote in 1964 Elections*, September 8, 1964.

U. S. Department of the Interior, Bureau of Mines. *Mineral Survey*, January 4, 1965.

United States District Court Reports. *Schaefer et al. v. Thomson et al.*, D. Wyo. 240 F. Suppl. 247 (1964).

————. *District Court of Wyoming Decree*, October 8, 1965.

United States Supreme Court Reports. *Reynolds v. Sims*, 377 U.S. 533 (1963).

————. *Baker v. Carr*, 369 U.S. 186 (1962).

WADE, RALPH M. "Legislative Politics in Wyoming," *Western Political Quarterly*, XII (September 1964, Supplement), 92.

————. "Legislature Faces Critical Issues," *The Wyoming Alumnews*, XII (January-February 1965).

————. "Legislative Apportionment in Wyoming," in *Compendium on Legislative Apportionment* (2nd ed.). National Municipal League, January 1962.

————. "Development of the Administrative Process in Wyoming," *Wyoming Law Journal*, XVI (Spring 1962).

————. "Political and Judicial Aspects of Wyoming Legislative Apportionment," *Wyoming Public Affairs*, I (August 1963).

————. "Presidential Nominating Procedures in Wyoming," in *Presidential Nominating Procedures in 1964 — A State by State Report*, National Municipal League, February 1965.

————. "The 1950 Elections in Wyoming," *Western Political Quarterly*, IV (March 1951), 95-96.

Wyoming Compiled Statutes 1945. Indianapolis: Bobbs-Merrill, 1946.

Wyoming G.O.P. Trunkline. Republican State Central Committee of Wyoming, 1964, 1965, 1966.

Wyoming Official Directory. Published biennially by the Secretary of State of Wyoming (1935 to 1965 incl.).

Wyoming Public Affairs. Public Administration Service, University of Wyoming, I (December 1964).

Wyoming Statutes, 1957.

Wyoming Supreme Court. Wyo., 377 Pac. (2d) 299 (1963); 67 Wyo. 256 (1950); Wyo., 218 Pac. (2d) 482 (1950).

CONTRIBUTORS

TOTTON J. ANDERSON is a former chairman of the Department of Political Science and presently Associate Dean, College of Letters, Arts and Sciences, University of Southern California. He received his A.B. (1930) and M.A. degrees from the University of California (Berkeley) and his Ph.D. from the University of Southern California. He was a teaching fellow at the University of California in 1932-33 and registrar and dean at Ventura College, 1935-47. During World War II he served in the U.S. Army Air Corps in the European Theater of Operations. He was separated in the rank of Lieutenant Colonel; in 1954 he was promoted to Colonel, U.S. Air Force Reserve, and served as an Intelligence Staff Officer, USAFR. In the last several years he has served as president of the Western Political Science Association; as National Associate Director of the Citizenship Clearing House, New York; and as Director of the Southern California-Arizona Citizenship Clearing House, 1959-63. He has also served as a member on the Board of Trustees of the Coro Foundation, San Francisco and Los Angeles, on the Executive Committee of the California Legislative Intern Program, Sacramento, on the Executive Committee of the California State Constitution Revision Commission, on the Mayor's Advisory Commission on Community Development (Los Angeles), and on the Reserve Officer Advisement Board to the Commandant, Air ROTC, Air University, Alabama. He is co-author of *Problems of Democratic Society; Readings and Study Outlines* (1941), *Introduction to Political Science* (1967), and *Bibliography on Western Politics* (1958). He has contributed to *Collier's Encyclopedia*, the *Western Political Quarterly*, *The Annals of the American Academy of Political and Social Science*, the *World Affairs Interpreter*, the *Social Science Review* (Los Angeles), and the University of Southern California *Law Review*.

HUGH A. BONE, professor of political science and chairman of the Department of Political Science at the University of Washington, received the B.A. from North Central College in 1931, the M.A. from the University of Wisconsin in 1935, and the Ph.D. from Northwestern University in 1937. He has served on the staff of the University of Maryland (1937-42) and of Queens College (1942-48). Since 1948 he has been at the University of Washington. He was a research associate of the New York State Legislative Committee on Industrial and Labor Conditions (1944-48), a Ford fellow (1954-55), president of the Pacific Northwest Political Science Association (1960), and has served as director of Washington State Northern Idaho Center for Education in Politics since 1953. In 1961 he was elected president of the Western Political Science Association. Professor Bone has contributed to the *National Municipal Review*, *Annals of the American Academy of Political and Social Science*, the *American Political Science Review*, the *Western Political Quarterly*, the *Public Administration Review*, *Law and Contemporary*

Problems: Parliamentary Affairs, and *Washington Politics* (with Don Ogden). His publications include the following books and monographs: *Smear Politics* (1941); contributor to *Public Men* (1946); *Grass Roots Party Leadership* (1952); *Presidential Politics in 1952: The West* (1954); *Party Committees and National Politics* (1958); and a textbook on political parties, *American Politics and Party System* (1965).

ELEANORE BUSHNELL is professor of political science and chairman of the Department of Political Science at the University of Nevada. She received the A.B. from the University of Washington in 1935, and the Ph.D. from the University of California (Berkeley) in 1952. She has served on the faculty at the University of Washington and San Francisco State College; since 1956 she has been at the University of Nevada. In 1964 she became a member of the Board of Editors of the *Western Political Quarterly*, and in the following year a member of the Executive Council of the Western Political Science Association; she was on the Board of Councilors of the Northern California Political Science Association, 1965-67. Professor Bushnell is an associate director of the Desert Research Institute of the University of Nevada. She has presented research papers at the American Political Science Association Convention (1966), and the Western Political Science Association Convention (1964, -65, -66). Her publications include the 1964 and the 1966 Nevada election articles in the *Western Political Quarterly* and various summaries of papers in "Proceedings" of that journal. Her book, *The Nevada Constitution: Origin and Growth* (1965, rev. ed., 1968), contains the first analysis of Nevada's constitutional convention.

KENNETH ROBERT GERVAIS, assistant professor of political science since 1965 at Portland State College, did his undergraduate work at this college before receiving his doctorate in government in 1968 at the Claremont Graduate School and University Center. His major interest has been urban studies. His dissertation was entitled, "The Portland Police Offices." In 1965, he served as lecturer in government at California State College at Los Angeles. His practical experience in politics includes activity in recruiting candidates and conducting, in 1954, the campaign for mayor and councilman in the city of Coos Bay, Oregon; serving as precinct committeeman on the Multnomah County Democratic Central Committee, 1960-62; and as delegate to the Multnomah County and Oregon State Democratic Platform Convention, 1962. He organized and conducted the voter turnout for five precincts in southern California in 1964. He served for eight years in the active Naval Reserve in North Bend and Portland, Oregon, at times as an instructor of electronics theory.

RUDOLPH GOMEZ, assistant professor of political science at Colorado College in Colorado Springs, was born and reared in Wyoming. He received his B.S. degree from Utah State University, his M.A. from Stanford and his Ph.D. from the University of Colorado. He is a veteran of the Korean War, a former Woodrow Wilson Fellow, and has been on the faculty of Colorado College since the fall of 1962. He is the co-author of *Colorado Politics and Government*, and has published several articles on legislative behavior in Colorado.

FRANK H. JONAS, professor of political science at the University of Utah, received the B.S. and M.A. degrees from the University of Utah, and the Ph.D. from the University of Washington. He also holds certificates of achievement from the

University of Berlin and the Hochschule fuer Politik in Germany (1931). After holding teaching and research fellowships at the University of Washington, he served subsequently on the staffs of the following universities: Idaho State, Southern California, New Mexico, Utah State, and, in summer sessions, Illinois and Vanderbilt. He held the Chester W. Nimitz Chair of Social and Political Philosophy at the Naval War College in Newport, Rhode Island (1960-61). From 1943 to 1945 he served in the U.S. Army Signal Corps; he spent 1951-53 in Germany as a Press Scrutiny Officer, Cultural Exchange Officer and Information Specialist in HICOG, United States Department of State; and in 1958 he was a guest exchange professor of the Federal Republic of Germany. Professor Jonas was a member of Utah's first Legislative Council (1947-49); chairman of the Veterans' Council, Utah State Department of Veterans' Affairs (1948-51); and a consultant in personnel administration at Hill Air Force Base, USAF, Ogden, Utah (1951). He has served as president of the Western Political Science Association (1964-65) and of the University of Utah Education Association (1965-67). He has been a member of the UEA Political Action Committee (1964) and the Salt Lake County Planning Council (1963), and is now on the Salt Lake County Welfare Board. Beginning his writings in local politics with "Utah: Sagebrush Democracy," in *Rocky Mountain Politics* (1940), he has produced over fifty articles on local and regional politics and has edited and contributed to *Western Politics* (1961) as well as the following monographs: *Western Politics and the 1956 Elections, Bibliography on Western Politics, Western Politics and the 1958 Elections, Western Politics and the 1962 Elections.* His most recent monograph is *The Story of a Political Hoax*.

BOYD A. MARTIN, professor of political science and dean of the College of Letters and Science at the University of Idaho, was born and reared in the state and received his B.A. degree from its University in 1936. He received his M.A. and Ph.D. degrees from Stanford University, where he has returned three times to teach. He served as head of Idaho's Department of Social Science from 1947 to 1955, when he was named dean. From 1947 to 1958 he was chairman of the Borah Foundation Committee for the Outlawry of War, and is now a member of the Commission to study the Organization of Peace, a research affiliate of the American Association for United Nations. He is a consultant to the Idaho Municipal League. He has also served as president of the Western Political Science Association, as a member of the Executive Council of the American Political Science Association, and as president of the Pacific Northwest Political Science Association. He has contributed articles to the *American Political Science Review*, the *American Scholar*, the publications of the *American Assembly*, and the *Western Political Quarterly* as well as being on its editorial board. He is author of the *Direct Primary in Idaho*, and has served as a state editor for the *National Municipal Review*. He also helped prepare *A Survey Report on the Impact of Federal Grants-in-Aid on the Structure and Function of State and Local Government.*

NEAL A. MAXWELL, executive vice president and assistant professor of political science at the University of Utah, graduated in political science from the University of Utah in 1952 with honors. He received his M.A. in 1961 from the same institution. From 1952 to 1954 he served as an analyst with the Central Intelligence Agency and from 1954 through 1956 he was legislative assistant to Utah's Senator Wallace F. Bennett. Mr. Maxwell joined the University of Utah staff in 1956 as assistant director of Public Relations. Vice President Maxwell makes time for a variety of community services: general campaign manager for the United

Fund, trustee of the Utah Educational Television Foundation, member of the Advisory Board of the Utah Museum of Natural History, vice president of the Utah Symphony Board, and regional editor for the National Educational Television Network. He moderates a weekly television program called "Tell Me." In 1967 he received "The Liberty Bell Award" from the Utah State Bar. He has published articles in the *Western Political Quarterly*, *The Nation*, the *Journalism Educator*, *Great Issues Concerning Freedom*, the *Western Humanities Review, Frontier*, and the *Deseret News*, and has written a monograph, "Regionalism in the United States Senate: The West."

NORMAN MELLER is professor of political science at the University of Hawaii. He spent his undergraduate days on the Berkeley campus of the University of California and received an LL.B. degree from Hastings College of Law. After being admitted to the California bar, he obtained the M.A. and Ph.D. degrees from the University of Chicago. While a Japanese language officer in the Navy during World War II, he became associated with the Legislative Reference Bureau of the University of Hawaii and returned to the Islands in 1947 as its head. Previously he had extensive service as a deputy legislative counsel for the State of California. For the period 1955-58, he was chairman of the Political Science Department of the University of Hawaii, and he again served in that capacity in 1964-65, after being a Senior Specialist at the East-West Center. He has been a visiting faculty member in mainland institutions and has acted as research director of numerous governmental studies in Hawaii. Currently, his research interests lie in the developing legislative process in the Pacific Basin. He has conducted extensive field research in Fiji, Guam, the Trust Territory of the Pacific Islands, and the Samoas. His articles on government and administration in Hawaii and the islands of the Pacific are well known to readers of the *Western Political Quarterly* (on whose editorial board he has served), the *American Political Science Review*, *Asian Survey*, the *National Municipal Review, State Government*, and *Sociology and Social Research*.

THOMAS PAYNE, professor of political science at the University of Montana, was born in Fulton, Missouri, where he graduated from Westminster College in 1941. After serving in the Army Air Force (1942-46), he was discharged as a First Lieutenant and entered the University of Chicago from which he received his Ph.D. in 1951. He was instructor in political science at the University of Tennessee from 1948 to 1950. He has been a member of the University of Montana faculty since 1951. From 1958 to 1964 he served as a member of the Board of Trustees of the Missoula Elementary School District, and was chairman of the Board from 1962 to 1964. He has contributed articles to the *Western Political Quarterly* and other professional journals, and a chapter to *Presidential Nominating Politics*; and he is co-author of *Service and Security: Municipal Retirement in Tennessee*. He has also contributed to such regional studies in government and politics as the *Bibliography on Western Politics* and *The States in the Pacific Northwest*. He has served as a member of the Board of Editors of the *Western Political Quarterly*, and was president of the Pacific Northwest Political Science Association, 1964-65. He was chairman of the Department of Political Science at the University of Montana from 1959 to 1966.

ROSS R. RICE, professor of political science at Arizona State University, was born in Shenandoah, Iowa, received his undergraduate education at Creighton University and the State College of Iowa, and his M.A. and Ph.D. degrees from the

University of Chicago. Following three years of military service in World War II, he doubled as research assistant and secretary to Professor Charles E. Merriam while pursuing graduate study at Chicago. He has been on the faculty at Arizona State University since 1950, was chairman of the Department of Political Science from 1959-62, and was elected to serve as chairman of the university faculty, 1965-66. He served as visiting professor at the University of California, Santa Barbara, in 1962-63, and on the Summer faculty at Western State College of Colorado. From 1958-61 he was a city councilman in Tempe, and in 1961-62 he served as mayor. He has been a member of the executive committee of the League of Arizona Cities and Towns, a member of the Arizona Academy, and a party precinct committeeman. In 1963 he was awarded the alumni citation for community service by the Alumni Association of the University of Chicago. He has served two terms on the executive council of the Western Political Science Association. Besides his contributions to professional journals, he is the author of *Extremist Politics*, and edited the symposium on the 1964 elections in the West, published in the *Western Political Quarterly*, on whose board of editors he is now serving.

HERMAN E. SLOTNICK, professor and head of the Department of History at the University of Alaska, was born in Salt Lake City, Utah. He received his B.A. degree at the University of Idaho in 1939 and his Ph.D. at the University of Washington. His doctoral dissertation was entitled, "The French Academy and the Third Republic, 1897-1914." He taught at Humboldt State College, Arcata, California, and at Central Washington State College. He is now director of the NDEA History Institute at the University of Alaska. He has been editor of the *Science Conference Reports*, Alaska Division, American Association for the Advancement of Science, 1954, 1955, and 1956, and Field Representative and Examiner for the U.S. Civil Service Commission, 1941-48 (exclusive of war years). He has contributed to the *Western Political Quarterly* and is at present a member of the Board of Editors of that journal. He served in the United States Army from 1943 to 1946.

HARRY P. STUMPF is assistant professor of political science at the University of New Mexico. He received the A.B. from the University of Colorado in 1954, the A.M. from George Washington University in 1958, and the Ph.D. from Northwestern University in 1964. He has served on the faculty at Colorado State University and since 1964 has been at the University of New Mexico. He was an affiliate director for the Rocky Mountain Center for Education in Politics and is past vice president and program chairman of the Southwest Political Science Association. He has been a panelist at Western, Midwestern, Southwestern and American Political Science Association meetings. His articles have appeared in the *Journal of Public Law* and the *Western Political Quarterly*, and he is author of the New Mexico chapter in the forthcoming book, *Reapportionment—Prelude and Aftermath, the Western States*. Professor Stumpf is currently on leave from the University of New Mexico in order to direct a research project on the impact of OEO legal services programs in the Bay Area of California.

JOHN M. SWARTHOUT, professor of political science at Portland State College, was born in Jacksonville, Illinois. He was awarded his B.A. degree, *cum laude*, at the University of Southern California in 1934, his M.A. in 1937, and his Ph.D. in 1942. His teaching career includes four years in California high schools and a year as an instructor at New Mexico State College. Enlisting in the Army Air Corps, he was commissioned in 1934, and left the service in 1946. In that year he went to Oregon State College, serving as department head from 1947 until 1958, when he accepted his present position, subsequently becoming dean of faculty. In 1953-54 he was a Ford fellow engaged in independent research in political theory at Stanford University and in 1957-58 was associate director of the Citizenship Clearing House with offices in New York City. His publications include three textbooks on American government and politics. He has held the presidency of the Western Political Science Association (1953-54), of the Pacific Northwest Political Science Association (1957-58), of the Oregon Federation of the American Association of University Professors (1956-57), and of the World Affairs Council of Oregon (1959-60). He has served also on a number of committees and commissions for the state of Oregon, including the Oregon "Little Hoover Commission" (1951-53) and the Governor's Committee on Administrative Reorganization (1959-60). His television experience has been very extensive; he is now permanent panelist on "Let's Face It," KOIN-TV, Portland. In 1967 he was elected president of the Portland chapter of the American Society for Public Administration. In September 1967, he stepped down as dean and resumed his full time position as professor of political science.

DANIEL W. TUTTLE, JR., was associate professor of government at the University of Hawaii and political columnist for the Honolulu *Advertiser* when he accepted in 1966 the position of Executive Secretary of the Hawaii Education Association. After graduation from Illinois College he received his M.A. from the University of Minnesota, then taught at the University of Wyoming. He joined the staff of the University of Hawaii in 1950 where he was at first associated part-time with the Legislative Reference Bureau as well as with the Department of Government. In 1952, he was a visiting faculty member at Stephens College. His several specialized studies for the Legislative Reference Bureau have been followed by studies on Hawaiian political topics as a consultant. He has contributed articles to the *Public Administration Review*, the *Western Political Quarterly*, *Proceedings of the Hawaiian Academy of Science,* the *Illinois College Alumni Quarterly*, and to several University of Wyoming publications. He also contributed materials to *Presidential Nominating Politics* in 1952 and to *The Politics of National Party Conventions.*

RALPH M. WADE is acting chairman of the Political Science Department, University of Wyoming. He received his B.A. degree from the University of South Dakota and his M.A. and Ph.D. degrees from the State University of Iowa. He also has an LL.B. degree awarded following his studies in law at Stanford University, the University of Utah and the University of Wyoming. He taught at Northern State Teachers College (Aberdeen, South Dakota), the University of South Dakota, and Indiana State Teachers College before going to the University of Wyoming in 1948. During World War II he served with the Third U.S. Army in the E.T.O. as an Infantry Colonel, and at the end of hostilities as a War Crimes investigator for the Nuremberg Trials. Professor Wade has served on the Executive Council of the Western Political Science Association, as director of the Rocky Mountain Center for Education in Politics, and as Commander of a Wyoming Logistical Command unit in the U.S. Army Reserve. He is co-author of a textbook, *The Government and Administration of Wyoming* (1953); author of *Natural Resources* and *The State Legislature* for the American Assembly (1957); and has contributed articles to a number of professional and other journals among which are the *Western Political Quarterly*, the *Wyoming Law Journal*, the *National Municipal Review*, and *Wyoming Public Affairs*.

T. PHILLIP WOLF did his undergraduate work at the University of Wichita. He received his M.A. and Ph.D. from Stanford University, and has been teaching at the University of New Mexico since 1963. His research interests are parties and elections, public opinion, British politics, and research methods. He has published articles in the *Western Political Quarterly* and the *Rocky Mountain Social Science Journal*. He is a contributor to: Leonard Goodall, ed., *Urban Politics in the Southwest* and Clyde Wingfield, ed., *Urbanization in the Southwest*. He is a past president of the New Mexico chapter of the American Society for Public Administration and serves as a consultant to NBC News for its biennial election coverage.

INDEX

economy of, 3-6
federal aid to, 7
political implications of, 3-5, 18-23
water resources of, 7-18
West on Capitol Hill, 468-97
Western Energy Supply and Transmission Program, 14, 16-18; *see also* Water
Western Politics, 442-67
Wyoming, 416-41; *see also* The West on Capitol Hill, Western Politics, and The Western Scene, *passim*
Young Democrats, 57, 134
Young Republicans, 57, 134

NAME INDEX

Adams, Brock, 479
Allen, Kay, 365
Allott, Gordon, 136, 146, 148, 472, 480, 481, 482, 492
Amsden, Forrest, 308
Anderson, Clinton P., 277, 472, 480, 482, 483, 491, 492, 495
Anderson, D. G. "Andy," 167
Anderson, LeRoy H., 228
Anderson, Totton J., 531
Angell, Homer, 311
Aronson, Hugo, 207, 218, 219, 228
Ashurst, Henry Fountain, 55
Aspinall, Frank, 137
Aspinall, Wayne, 17, 70, 137, 147, 150, 474, 479, 482, 493
Astor, John Jacob, 181
Atwood, Bob, 30

Babcock, Tim, 214, 218, 228, 427
Baggen, E. I., 36
Baker, Bobby, 242
Bamberger, Ernest, 330
Bamberger, Simon, 330
Baring, Walter, 243, 245, 251, 252, 255-56, 449, 472, 482
Barlocker, William, 350
Barrett, Frank A., 449, 450
Bartlett, E. L. "Bob," 33, 472, 483
Battin, James F., 228
Baus, Herbert M., 91
Baxter, Leone, 91
Beatty, Orren, 6
Bell, Rex, 249, 250, 449
Bennett, Wallace F., 10, 360, 370, 374, 376, 379, 450, 472, 480, 481, 482, 483, 489, 491, 492
Benson, Ezra Taft, 335, 336, 341, 376, 495
Benson, Reed, 335, 336
Beppu, Tadao, 167
Bible, Alan, 243, 256, 449, 472, 480, 481, 491, 492

Blaisdell, Neal S., 167
Blood, Henry H., 333
Boddy, Manchester, 90
Bolack, Tom, 278, 279
Bone, Homer T., 382, 387
Bone, Hugh A., 531
Bonner, John W., 228
Borah, William E., 193, 194, 197, 199
Bosone, Reva Beck, 362
Bouton, Clark, 127
Bradley, Donald, 100
Brannan, Charles F., 495
Brewster, Sheldon, 366
Bridges, Harry, 381
Brontzman, Don, 136, 147
Brophy, Frank Cullen, 59, 67
Brown, Edmund G. "Pat," 74, 81, 83, 86, 90, 92, 97, 98, 99, 104, 106, 107, 110, 114, 117, 454

Brown, George, 137
Brown, Hugh B., 350, 378
Bryan, William Jennings, 197, 373, 381, 415
Burnett, Peter H., 74
Burns, Hugh, 101, 107
Burns, John A., 163, 166, 167, 179, 459
Burroughs, John, 279
Burton, Laurence, 339, 358, 370, 452
Bush, Prescott, 481
Bushnell, Eleanore, 532
Butler, Paul, 399

Campbell, Jack M., 6, 279
Cannon, Frank, 330
Cannon, Howard W., 237, 240, 242, 243, 251-52, 254, 256, 472, 480
Cargo, David F., 269, 278-79
Carlson, Grace, 362
Carpenter, F. R., 138
Carroll, John, 134, 151
Carter, Anderson, 278
Carver, John A., 496
Caughey, John W., 2
Chaffee, Douglas C., 224
Chamberlain, George, 301
Chandler, Howard, 82
Chapman, Oscar L., 495
Chavez, Dennis, 275, 277
Chavez, Fabian, 292
Cheadle, E. K., 227
Christopher, George, 90, 100
Church, Frank, 19, 199, 350, 472, 481, 483, 494, 495
Clark, J. Reuben, 331, 376
Clark, William A., 181, 204
Clyde, George Dewey, 334, 340, 346-48, 350, 354, 359, 360, 379
Colton, Don B., 331, 333
Conrad, Charles J., 107